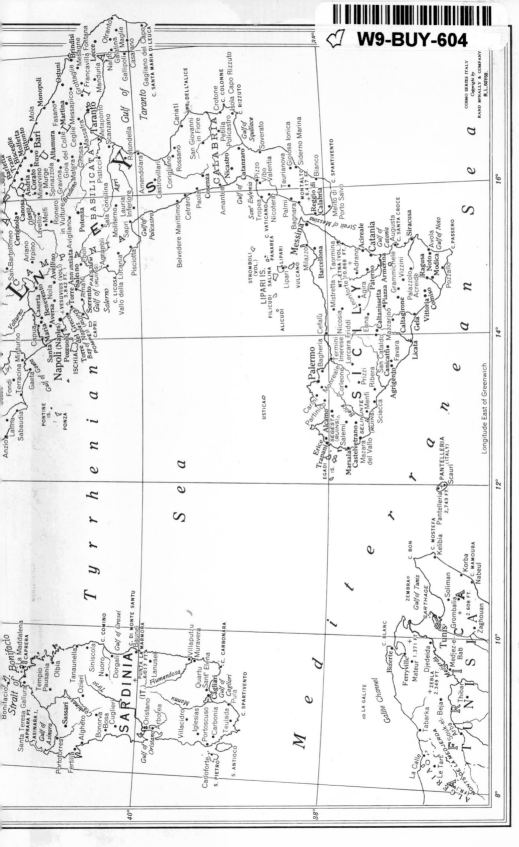

COSMO SERIES ITALY
Copyright by
RAND McNALLY & COMPANY
R.L.60Y68.

CORNELL INTERNATIONAL INDUSTRIAL
AND LABOR RELATIONS REPORTS—*NO. 5*

PUBLISHED BY

New York State School of Industrial and Labor Relations
A Unit of the State University of New York
at Cornell University

Labor Unions and National Politics in Italian Industrial Plants,
    by Maurice F. Neufeld.   160 pp. $2.00, paper

American Labor and the International Labor Movement, 1940 to 1953,
    by John P. Windmuller.   260 pp. $3.00, paper

Jobs and Workers in India,
    by Oscar A. Ornati.   236 pp. $3.00, paper

Contemporary Collective Bargaining in Seven Countries,
    Adolf Sturmthal, Editor.   392 pp. $4.50, cloth

Italy: School for Awakening Countries,
    by Maurice F. Neufeld.   600 pp. $9.00, cloth

ITALY:

School for Awakening Countries

*The Italian Labor Movement in Its Political,
Social, and Economic Setting from 1800 to 1960*

MAURICE F. NEUFELD

*Professor of
Industrial and Labor Relations
Cornell University*

NEW YORK STATE SCHOOL
OF
INDUSTRIAL AND LABOR RELATIONS
CORNELL UNIVERSITY, ITHACA, NEW YORK

1961

Copyright © 1961 by Maurice F. Neufeld

Library of Congress Catalog Card Number: 60–63276

PRINTED IN THE UNITED STATES OF AMERICA
BY CAYUGA PRESS, INC., ITHACA, NEW YORK

Contents

CONTENTS

Preface

ITALY first drew my admiration thirty years ago. George C. Sellery, spirited scholar and masterful Dean of the College of Letters and Science at the University of Wisconsin, stirred both mind and imagination as he guided his fortunate students through the life and thought of the Middle Ages, Renaissance, and Reformation. He united, incomparably, the gifts of artist and teacher. He made of me the vassal of his learning and wisdom; the liege, too, of his beloved Italy.

Italy first claimed my affection during World War II. For almost three years, I served as executive officer to Colonel Charles Poletti, the brilliant Allied military governor in the regions of Sicily, Campania, Lazio-Umbria, and Lombardy. Thousands of Italians from every field of endeavor passed through A.M.G. headquarters. I came to cherish their astonishing range of talk, talent, and temperament.

Italy first evoked the beginnings of understanding when I lived there continuously from 1955 to 1957. To be sure, in 1952 I had retraced the course of war, up from Palermo, while surveying the historical development of grievance committees and investigating their contemporary role in Italian industrial plants. Nevertheless, not until my longer stay, three years later, did more intensive research and more intimate knowledge of Italian character buttress admiration and affection with insight.

Experience of Italy over three decades and the interest of fond friends prodded this book into existence. Philip Taft of Brown University, Theresa Wolfson of Brooklyn College, and M. Gardner Clark of Cornell repeatedly lamented the dearth of information in English about the evolution of the Italian labor movement. To supply this need, I determined to record and appraise the drift of historical events, the growth of union institutions, and the ideological struggle for the loyalty of workers against the turbulent rush of political, social, and economic developments from 1800 to the present time. The plan of study thus departed widely from the hallowed procedure employed by almost all Italian writers on the subject. They have treated labor history as a mere phase of the Marxist movement, a procedure which tended to confuse the strengths and weaknesses of union life with those of the Socialist Party and other radical groups.

Both Professors Taft and Clark read the manuscript with time-consuming care and commented with the most useful kind of precision. The valuable advice and suggestions of Professor Leonard Adams, Director of Research and Publications at the School of Industrial and Labor Relations, like the help and encouragement of Professor Robert Ferguson, who replaced him temporarily, provided an atmosphere of interest and appreciation so important to authors. The generosity of Professor Mario Levi of the University of Milan, while serving as Visiting Professor of Ancient History at Cornell, placed me deeply in his debt. He read the entire manuscript with searching attention, offered excellent counsel, and pointed out errors of fact or interpretation.

During the period of research and the early stages of preparing the manuscript, Mrs. Maxine Henry, my secretary then, turned out reams of tables and narrative with cheerful speed and proficiency. Later, my present secretary, Mrs. Joyce Wright, took on the formidable assignment of completing the major portion of the work. She managed to survive this ordeal, only to move on to a more tedious one: the reading, correction, and rechecking of galleys and page proofs. She accomplished these tasks with constant patience, unostentatious diligence, gratifying interest, and marked intelligence.

Miss Frances Eagan represents to me the ideal editor. She discharged with distinction the countless editorial duties involved in guiding this long manuscript through the press. I am grateful not only for her thoughtfulness, critical faculties, knowledge, and skill, but also for her intellectual congeniality. She and I both drank at the same "wells of English undefiled." Our agreement reaches down even to commas, the subjunctive mood, and capitalization. Yet more, she kept me sane during our black trial by proofreading, both galley and page.

Mrs. Rita Zimmerman designed the cover. It owes its handsome guise to her artist's eye and enthusiasm. I wish also to acknowledge help received from David Singer, John Popular, Andrew Thomson, Phyllis Van Etten, Ila Gardner, and Catherine Howard. The index, so unusual in its detail, owes its excellence to one whose modesty must preclude proper acknowledgment.

Hinda, my wife, met with forbearance and ever-ready mind and shoulder her husband's five-year immersion in research, composition, and publication. She faced these added duties with intelligence, concern, and perception. She remains, as always, devoted to the reading of books. On the writing of books, she feels strong reservations.

MAURICE F. NEUFELD

Ithaca, New York
December 1960

I

Italy:

School for Awakening Countries

FOR almost two millennia of human history, Italy led Western man in creating the most towering monuments of European civilization. Over the centuries, in dazzling displays of tireless genius, the incomparable peninsula bred Imperial Rome, the Medieval Church, the revived town life of the late Middle Ages with its pioneering ventures in commerce and banking, and then the opulent trade of the Renaissance which nourished art, science, literature, and, not the least of its attainments, double-entry bookkeeping. Later, the Atlantic gradually eclipsed the fabled Mediterranean as England fought for control over the lands and sea-lanes of world commerce and as France, Spain, and Austria reduced Italy to political chaos. The creative spirit of that land subsided into dominated somnolence. Thrusts of economic change began to stir Italy again during the latter part of the eighteenth century, and the resurgence of patriotism during the first half of the nineteenth century joined the peninsula's finest spirits in the twin aspirations of the *Risorgimento* for independence and national unity. But decades after industrialization had transformed the productive systems of England, Belgium, France, and Germany, Italians continued to live predominantly by agriculture. Their economic apathy, picturesque poverty, costumed feudal arrangements, and peasant good nature — when draped with the bedimming gauze of past glories — metamorphosed the country into a vast museum. Tourists invaded Italy. They escaped with Elizabeth and Robert Browning from the harsh winters, crowded cities, and dark Satanic mills of their homelands to wander in

1

the sun among romantic ruins, to crane their necks in the imposing *duomi,* to roam in galleries stuffed with history, and to watch choral armies deployed to the sound of music upon the stages of baroque opera houses. Since these transients regarded contemporary Italy as a quaint backwater of the modern world, they ignored its current life.

Most professional scholars, whether foreign or native, also failed to come to serious grips with the Italy of their own time. Although they studied minutely the *Risorgimento* as yet another manifestation of Liberalism Triumphant, they would not deign to explore, underfoot, the debris of Italy's retardation. They left that task to occasional legislative investigations which Parliament respectfully shelved when completed, or to the rising generation of intellectuals outside the institutes and universities. Those young men brought moral indignation or the wrath of Marxian analysis to their inquiries. They prepared Italy for the rigidities of leftist politics, but failed to unearth and methodize the details of the country's economic and social plight. So it went until the triumph of fascism when national pride and colonial adventures blocked serious public consideration of Italy's true condition. Only since the end of World War II, when old as well as new nations emerged from age-long feudal and colonial imprisonment, has Italy's continual struggle for economic fulfillment over the course of 160 years arrested attention and converted Italy from a museum into a school for awakening countries.

During those sixteen decades, Italy experienced almost every variety of economic, social, and political adversity, including totalitarian dictatorship, which has lately assailed countries in Africa, Asia, Latin America, and Eastern Europe as they turned for salvation to nationalism, scientific agriculture, and mechanized industrial life. Like them, Italy endured centuries of domestic misrule or anarchy, followed by generations of humiliating foreign domination. Its exploited peasant population lived just at the verge of survival. Italy also found freedom almost exclusively through the sacrificial energy of educated leaders from the nobility and the professions. They represented but the smallest fraction of the population since dire poverty, illiteracy, and ignorance shut out the masses from active engagement in the nationalist struggle. In Italy, too, radical doctrines from abroad served, at first, only as heady left-wing expressions of nationalist hopes. But soon their universal mission emerged. By generating simple panaceas to banish all evils of the day along with foreign rule, they impelled their few but zealous disciples to separate themselves from the larger patriotic movement. These imported visions of revolutionary social justice, despite their vagueness and irrelevance to Italian time and circumstance, gathered special force when

2

independence did not, of itself, miraculously create immediate heaven on earth.

Indeed, the conservative statesmen who succeeded Count Camillo Benso di Cavour, the Piedmontese architect of Italian unity, proved unsuited by temperament for the political task of governing Italy once Cavour created the constitutional monarchy and died. They resembled the American federalists in character, philosophy, and training. From 1861 until 1876, they exerted control with firm, sound, and disinterested patriotism. Wholly committed by moral conviction to the principle of the balanced budget, they performed their bounden duty even when threatened by certain popular revolt. But their personal and fiscal rectitude could neither reconcile the country's narrow regional loyalties and interests, nor avoid the enduring social damage of bitter economic conflicts, nor offset the absence of a large and responsible middle class whose cohesive and mediatory influence might have advanced community harmony and welfare.

In 1876, the highly restricted electorate shifted its allegiance to less principled leaders of the so-called Left, a conglomeration of disgruntled voters in all provinces and all classes. To them now passed the responsibility for maintaining national institutions and preserving the unity of the peninsula, so hastily joined together and so artificially centralized at Rome. (Today, substitute, at pleasure, for Rome: New Delhi, Karachi, Jakarta, Accra, Baghdad, or Beirut.) Three Prime Ministers, who enjoyed long periods of service from the fall of the Right until 1922, successively devised, improved, and perfected a form of guided democracy. The shrewd and complex system of political deals, favors, accommodation, bribery, electoral corruption, and violence at the polls changed clashing parliamentary groups with paltry sense of country or democracy into workable legislative majorities. Termed *trasformismo* because it persuaded enough members of the opposition to support the equivalent of a dominant party, thus transforming political rivalries into partnerships, that benign dictatorship assured relatively steady rule to a nation which lacked most elements of stability.

Meanwhile, Italy's labor movement also anticipated qualities, inclinations, attitudes, and developments which have characterized the evolution of unions in many awakening countries of the contemporary world. When the first Italian Parliament proclaimed the united Kingdom in 1861, the handicraft system of production by artisans for limited markets still prevailed. Only the lightest touch of industrialization had disturbed the antiquated agricultural economy of the country, and then in but three areas of the North: Lombardy, Piedmont, and Liguria. There, the primitive factory system engaged a small peasant labor force. Ancient oppression branded it with illiteracy, ignorance, physical and mental isolation, resignation to social subordination, and dependence upon outside leaders. Whether these workers toiled in fetid country mills or sought employment in degrading urban shops, they turned deaf faces to appeals for organization and concerted action. Instead, like their kinsmen who still tended the fields, they gave way periodically to blind fury without warning and without specific, attainable purpose. Once the foredoomed protests spent themselves, the rebels reverted to abased submission until intolerable suffering goaded them once again into disordered and hopeless revolt.

Then, in the 1870's and 1880's, anarchist and socialist doctrines replaced Mazzini's nationalist-socialistic-republican-international preachments in the affection of the people. They managed to hypnotize the masses long before Italy's economic development had advanced far enough to summon up permanent unions as natural countervailing forces of constructive opposition to the exactions of mechanized factory life or commercial agriculture. Thus, labor's revolutionary political zeal antedated the nation's industrial revolution. It fortified the natural volatility, indiscipline, and simple-minded hankering after grand schemes of Italy's peasant workers. By exploiting their weaknesses and not their virtues, it prevented them from acquiring that sense of responsibility which willingly supports the regular payment of union dues and the building of modest societies which could, in due course, expand outward from the individual plant to commune, province, and nation. Unfortunately for the future of the Italian labor movement, the several varieties of Marxism and syndicalism conditioned their adherents to believe implicitly radical promises of quick salvation and to seek the Kingdom of Earth through the complete destruction of the old order.

At the turn of the century, Italy experienced its long-delayed industrial upsurge. The boom, fated for deceleration by encumbrances thrown up by the country's economic structure and policies, could spare no breathing time and required, ideally, fresh sacrifices by the nation's already heavily burdened workers. But at this crucial period of growth from 1896 to 1908, revolutionary syndicalism — a persistent undercurrent and, at times, the main force within the ranks of Italian labor — fostered general strikes of almost purely symbolic import. These agitations, which plagued the nation until the very eve of the country's entry into World War I, quickened the other forces of retardation present in the economy. They secured no benefits for the demonstrators, only repressive measures by public authorities and employers.

4

The general strikes also hid fatal defects in the seemingly vigorous labor movement. The propensity of Italian workers to street-and-plaza turmoil, when manipulated by left-wing leaders and paraded as militancy and radical conviction, lent an impression of strength and effective organization to the factious union groups which affiliated in 1906 with Italy's first enduring trade union center, the General Confederation of Labor (C.G.L.). In truth, although the moderate socialist leadership of the highly centralized Confederation spoke for the Italian masses, it did not represent them. The C.G.L. and its two principal types of constituent bodies — the national craft and industrial unions, known as category federations, and the local chambers of labor, which like American city centrals gathered in all confederal adherents within commune or province — failed to escape from devastating internal controversy over political creeds despite repeated protestations of organizational neutrality. Nor could they ever command stable dues-paying members, strike funds adequate to even modest calls for aid, and extensive collective bargaining contracts.

The category federations appealed to the more conservative elements within the labor movement and tried to achieve day-to-day economic gains. They should have formed the backbone of the C.G.L. if that body hoped eventually to serve the industrial welfare of its members, but they remained largely unorganized, small, and ineffective. Collective bargaining rarely reached beyond provincial boundaries, and even then in only limited areas of the North, among scattered trades and industries. The provincial chambers of labor unfortunately fulfilled their purposes best in those very areas where many category federations had not established local branches. By their heterogeneous and inclusive nature, they appealed to the unity of the working class and drew its particular loyalty. Their geographical proximity to the people aided them even more in dominating the union scene. More often than not under the sway of radical regional leaders, the chambers served as ideal centers for revolutionary political activity.

Since the Italian labor movement before 1914 lacked strong category unions and since its administrative arrangements under the C.G.L. encouraged political agitation instead, it could not wrest noteworthy improvements of wages, hours, and working conditions from employers for its members through the device of collective bargaining. Later, during the vast social upheaval which followed upon the Armistice of 1918, revolutionary forces overwhelmed the moderate influences within both the Socialist Party and the Confederation. Anarchy convulsed the peninsula as workers occupied factory after factory under the inspiration of the Bolshevik example in Russia. Within two years, the Black Shirts brought an end to left-wing intransigence. The independent labor movement, at the peak of membership but now divided by political strife into four confederations, collapsed into silence under truncheon blows and heavy doses of castor oil.

When its aged master, Giovanni Giolitti, returned as Prime Minister for the fifth time in 1920, *trasformismo* had already lost its power of endowing the State with the will to preserve civic order during Italy's most momentous crisis as a nation. Benito Mussolini supplied the substitute for benevolent autocracy: fascist totalitarianism. After twenty years, that experiment in enforced social harmony also crumbled, but only under the pressure of foreign intervention. The revived free labor movement after World War II skirted formal political rift for three difficult years and then split asunder as before. Financially impoverished, poorly organized, deficient in supporting strength among the category federations, and impotent in collective bargaining, the present labor movement like its predecessor has also invested its meager fortunes in political gambles. This policy, although futile, grew out of desperation and necessity rather than realistic hopes.

Since 1945, Italy, like younger countries pledged to freedom, has lived on the borrowed time of financial aid from the United States and international agencies succored by American funds. Against these thick dollar ramparts, all the impeditive forces of Italy's past have hammered mercilessly and with increasing effect to sound joint challenges: Can Italy, or any nation limited in native resources and traditions of self-rule, but rich in social hatreds and unrest, meet the economic needs of its people fast enough to uphold and extend the institutions of democracy? Can strong and free labor unions arise and endure save under conditions of exceptional economic, social, and political good fortune? The Italian past would seem to indicate a prophetic answer: No.

II

The Pull of History: 1800 to 1860

The Realm of Politics

THE Italian *Risorgimento*, a vibrant era of political and cultural resurgence, dates from the middle of the eighteenth century when it was
essentially literary in spirit. However, the first six decades after 1800
hold the crowning years of this movement. Not until then did the struggle for national independence and unity establish its intellectual basis,
muster its adherents, grow intense, and finally triumph in the realm of
politics, if not in the moral sphere.

Italy's choicest sons gave themselves with generosity to the succession of new ideas, the valiant opposition to censorship, the patriotic
insurrections, the fervid martyrdoms, the daring personal exploits, the
invasions, the wars for freedom. But reflection indicates that these beliefs and deeds form a pattern common to most past and present nationalist movements for independence. What distinguishes the *Risorgimento* is the startling emergence of a tiny northwestern state, whose
ruling family and aristocracy preferred to speak French rather than
Italian, as the dominant liberating force of the entire country. First,
Piedmont engineered the miracle of freeing the other Italian states from
foreign domination.[1] Of even greater wonder, it then convinced those
states to merge themselves, after exultant and freely conducted plebiscites, with the House of Savoy to become the Piedmont-dominated Kingdom of Italy. Despite dateless local loyalties and newly rising republican
sympathies, a centralized monarchy rather than a federation of regional
states was maneuvered into being. This singular feat, which would
trouble the destiny of Italy in future years, was largely the accomplish-

ment of one man, Count Camillo Benso di Cavour (1810–1861), Italy's most versatile modern statesman. His skill looms supernatural when the recalcitrant raw materials from which he created a nation are contemplated.

Between 400 and 1800 A.D., Italy was never an administrative unity. Yet, throughout these centuries, the concept of Italy as a nation had never completely died. Medieval poets, with Dante crowning their visions, had dreamed of a great union of states centering in Rome. Later writers like Petrarch, Machiavelli, Foscolo, and Alfieri created an incandescent national literature which kept this aspiration glowing in the hearts of cultivated Italians who formed an all-too-narrow minority of the largely illiterate population. In the end, war, and not these aspirations, intervened as the decisive force. Like the unforeseen aftergrowth of foreign conquest and rule in Asia and Africa which flowered into independence after World War II, the invasion and occupation of Italy by Napoleon's troops during the last years of the eighteenth century released age-old hopes from their long imprisonment within the treasure house of books and pushed them out into the disordered realm of the possible: politics.

Napoleon commanded Italy through three great groupings of states, rather than through one central government. Nevertheless, this experience aroused in Italians of many persuasions a taste for a united nation. Of more lasting importance, Napoleon introduced the liberal laws and institutions of France into the retrograde economic, social, and governmental structure of the Italian states. Feudal rights and privileges were abolished in Piedmont and Sardinia in 1797; in Naples, Lombardy, and Venetia in 1806; in Tuscany in 1808; in the Papal States in 1809; and in the Kingdom of the Two Sicilies in 1810. These reforms met with little difficulty in North Italy and in Tuscany where the burdensome, antiquated obligations of feudalism had all but vanished. In contrast, Napoleon's officials encountered 1,395 clearly distinguished feudal rights and privileges in Naples and in Sicily. Since concessions were made to the nobility if positive title could be proved, the main characteristics of land ownership and custom-bound agrarian operations in these regions were not fundamentally disturbed.[2]

The Treaty of Vienna in 1815 and the formation of the Holy Alliance smothered these freshening changes and the longings they satisfied. The old régimes of the Italian states were restored under the domination of Austria. The only significant territorial adjustments involved the annexation of the moldering Venetian Republic by Austria and of the resentful Genoese Republic by Piedmont. The nine post-Napoleonic states were dedicated to ecclesiastical obscurantism, as the Jesuits again returned to positions of influence, and to political orthodoxy, ranging from unrelieved despotism in the South to candid reaction in the Duchy of Modena. Maffeo Pantaleoni has formulated these nuances in the practice of autocracy among the three leading states: "There can be no doubt that the Austrian government was *technically* and *morally* superior to that of the Papal States; the latter, in turn, greatly excelled the Bourbon government in morality, mildness, and relative enlightenment."[3] The tiny House of Savoy, destined to be the forerunner of liberalism in Italy, was not at this time less autocratic than the other governments of the peninsula. As Cecil Sprigge points out, Piedmont was just less efficiently and willfully oppressive.[4]

The severity of the restoration of 1815 dashed the hopes of Italian patriots, intensified the full meaning of the enlightened laws and administration enjoyed under French rule, aroused bitterness, evoked the desire to liberate Italy from foreign domination, and finally quickened the impulse toward national unity for the entire peninsula and the islands. Secret societies dedicated to "noble" action came into being, spreading from Naples to the other Italian states. The most famous were the Carbonari. The principles they espoused were broadly Christian and humanitarian. Their political concepts were republican. Their ritual was masonic.

Between 1820 and 1848, when the Italian War of Independence began, numerous revolts broke out. In Naples, during July 1820, the Carbonari in the army, encouraged by the success of the revolution in Spain, instigated an uprising. The ensuing revolutionary government was overthrown, however, by the Austrian army in March 1821. At the same time that the Neapolitan rebellion was suppressed by foreign arms, the Carbonari instigated an uprising in Piedmont. A liberal constitution, similar to that of Spain, was secured. But, in April, the new government in Piedmont collapsed under the combined attacks of the House of Savoy and the Austrians. Ten years later, in February 1831, insurrections, inspired by the July revolution in Paris, took place in Parma and Modena. Widespread revolts also flared up in the Papal States. These insurrections were also beaten down with the aid of Austrian troops. Later in the same year, fresh revolts shook the Papal States. Once more the authority of the Church was restored by Austria on January 18, 1832.

The failure of sporadic uprisings, engineered by free-wheeling secret societies, impressed Giuseppe Mazzini (1805–1872), once a member of the Carbonari and a citizen of the former Genoese Republic. He felt no sentiments of loyalty to Piedmont or the semi-French House of Savoy.

He saw the need of a coordinated drive for freedom, careful group preparation through effective propaganda, and close attention to organizational details, thus pioneering in the techniques of modern liberation politics, advertising, and public relations. Such revolutionary efficiency actually ran counter to Mazzini's own virtuous but impulsive temperament. Still, he dreamed that the movement he espoused, once it applied these methods to his program of pure but violent idealism, could summon up a united Italy under a republican form of government. His vision of the future stretched beyond Italy to Europe. He hoped that as the nations there achieved freedom they would join in a confederation dominated by a spirit of Christian brotherhood.

In March 1831, Mazzini launched a new revolutionary society, "Young Italy." He directed his propaganda from Marseilles, where he lived in exile after his imprisonment in Italy, a year earlier, for insurrectionary activities. Mazzini planned a general uprising in Italy for June 1832, but before it could eventuate, the governmental authorities of Piedmont uncovered the plot. Arrests followed and the scheme collapsed. Despite the obvious competence of the authorities in Piedmont, the Mazzinians instigated another uprising for February 1834. This conspiracy also ended in failure. Thus far, the followers of Mazzini, despite the lip service paid to meticulous preparation and closely linked endeavors, had been no more successful than the Carbonari in staging successful revolutions. At this point, Mazzini, instead of concentrating his efforts on Italy, was moved by failure to extend his activities. He organized the "Young Europe" movement. From London, where he resided after 1837, he kept in touch with "Young Italy," "Young Germany," "Young Poland," and similar groups. Abortive rebellions followed one another with the monotony of disappointment and the blood of new martyrs.

Meanwhile, two important books appeared. In 1843, Vincenzo Gioberti (1801–1852) published *On the Moral and Civil Primacy of the Italians*. Ordained a priest in 1825, he had suffered exile between 1833 and 1848 in Paris and Brussels because of his liberal ideas, but returned to Italy in 1848 when he became deputy, senator, and finally Prime Minister of Piedmont. Count Cesare Balbo (1789–1853), who served as Premier of Piedmont's first constitutional cabinet in 1848, had published *On the Hopes of Italy* in 1844. These two landmarks in the history of the *Risorgimento* expressed the doctrine of moderate Italian liberals, especially those in North Italy, who were opposed to Mazzini. In their view, Mazzini's republicanism was radical to the extreme, since they distrusted universal suffrage. His methods were even worse, obviously insurrectionary and futile. These moderates agreed that some type of unification for the Italian peninsula had to be sought and that constitutional reform was necessary. They disagreed, however, on the type of future government for a united Italy. The Neo-Guelphs, led by Gioberti, advocated a union of Italian states under the presidency of the Pope. Balbo and his followers were primarily concerned with the ousting of Austria from Italy, peaceably if that could be arranged. They saw every reason why, with Austria out of the way, the consequent unification of the peninsula should come to pass under the leadership of the Piedmont dynasty.

When, in July 1847, Austrian troops occupied Ferrara, exercising a right granted by the Treaty of Vienna, indignation ran strong among liberals throughout Italy and helped to foster even greater anti-Austrian feelings. In October 1847, Charles Albert (1798–1849, king 1831–1849) of Piedmont, although himself conservative, succumbed to liberal pressures and allowed the criminal code to be revised. He also softened the rigors of the censorship and consented to rendering more tolerable the law on public meetings. In January 1848, the year when revolution swept throughout Europe, Sicily was roused to rebellion. The outbreaks in Sicily stimulated Neapolitan liberals to revolt. When Pope Pius IX (1792–1878, pope 1846–1878), who, at first, in contrast to his predecessor, was democratic in his political philosophy, refused to allow Austrian troops to cross his territory, Ferdinand II (1810–1859, king 1830–1859) of Naples was forced to grant a liberal constitution modelled on the French Charter of 1830. On February 17, 1848, the Grand Duke of Tuscany was also required to concede a constitution. Pius IX instituted similar reforms in the Papal States, including a constitution and the establishment of an elective council of deputies. However, veto powers were reserved to the Pope and the College of Cardinals. The event of most lasting and widespread significance occurred on March 4, 1848. Charles Albert promulgated a constitution for Piedmont, the famous *Statuto,* which later formed the basis for the organic law of all Italy.

The Italian War of Independence swept through the peninsula in 1848 and 1849. It was touched off by the insurrection of the people of Milan against foreign rule. During the famous Five Days of 1848, March 18 through 22, the people erected barricades in the streets and fought the Austrian troops. The revolution in Vienna, which had given courage to the Milanese, also gave heart to the Venetians who proclaimed a republic on March 22. On that same day, Charles Albert of Piedmont declared war on Austria in response to an appeal from the Milanese.

During the Italian War of Independence, the second great figure of the *Risorgimento,* Giuseppe Garibaldi (1807–1882), emerged. He was handsome, romantic, dashing, courageous, and dedicated. He symbolized

11

the transformation, through action, of the concept of Italian unity into reality. His mission contrasted to Mazzini's role of implanting the idea of unity in the minds of Italians. Garibaldi, a Piedmontese, had fallen under the influence of Mazzini very early in his career and, because of an unsuccessful republican plot, for which he was condemned to death in 1834, fled to South America. There, he gained invaluable firsthand experience for his later Italian exploits in the art of irregular warfare. When revolution convulsed Europe in 1848, Garibaldi returned to the continent. Although he remained a convinced republican and still followed the leadership of Mazzini, he did not hestitate to ally himself with Charles Albert of Piedmont to liberate Lombardy from Austria. Mazzini himself, despite his unaltered republican convictions, also sought out that northern capital when Milan fell to the monarchial forces of liberation.

After the defeat of Charles Albert by Austria in 1849, Garibaldi found his way to Rome where he fought for Mazzini's short-lived Roman Republic against the French forces which had come to the aid of Pope Pius IX. During the brief interval between victory and ultimate defeat, Mazzini served as one of the triumvirate of the Roman Republic. With the fall of the Republic, Mazzini resumed his life of agitation from abroad. Garibaldi fled to the United States after he was refused asylum by Victor Emmanuel II (1820–1878, king, Piedmont 1849–1861, Italy 1861–1878), who had succeeded his father when Charles Albert went into exile following his defeat by Austria. The physical separation of these two leaders symbolized the growing divergence of their ideas. Since the popular veneration of both Mazzini and Garibaldi was intense, their differences were fated to spread rapidly among varied elements of the Italian population, including those craftsmen, not as yet large in number, who had succeeded in forming organizations of their own. Thus early did political controversy over commanding issues appropriate the energies of Italian workers.

After 1848, Piedmont, alone among the Italian states, retained its liberal constitution, the noteworthy *Statuto*. The political leadership sought and eventually gained by Piedmont belonged rightfully to the only liberal state in Italy. Soon, Piedmont began to outstrip even Lombardy economically because of momentous commercial, industrial, financial, and agricultural developments. Count Camillo Cavour must be credited with this transformation. He was an admirer of French and, especially, English liberal ideas. He was convinced that economic reforms in Piedmont had to buttress political changes and improvements. This design was vital to his dream of elevating his sovereign, Victor

Emmanuel II, to the kingship of a united Italy. To this end, Piedmont had to assume the leadership in the movement for Italian independence. Cavour's energy, foresight, and accomplishments demonstrated concretely that enlightened governmental policies, political sagacity, diplomatic arrangements, and shrewd alliances of war could achieve more than patriotic slogans, abortive insurrections, and uncompromising purity of ideals. He brought an obscure kingdom, defeated in war and heavily in debt, into league with the great powers of Europe. In the Crimean War, he allied Piedmont with England and France. He concluded a free-trade treaty with England, never hestitating over possible internal economic dislocations. In 1859, with consummate skill and acumen, he persuaded Napoleon III to attack Austria. For the banishment of Austria from North Italy, he lost Nice and Savoy to France, but gained a kingdom for his monarch.

Already by 1851, when Garibaldi returned to Italy, Cavour's policies and the course of events had persuaded Garibaldi to renounce Mazzini's immutable principles: Italy must be a republic; it should achieve its independence from foreign rule through its own heroic efforts; it must reject liberation through the arms of Piedmont, abetted by alliances with countries beyond the Alps. Garibaldi, henceforth, supported Cavour and acknowledged publicly that the monarchy should be the basis of Italian unity. His appeal to the people won over many of Mazzini's republican followers for the monarchist cause. He also took part in Piedmont's war of 1859 against Austria.

Meanwhile, Mazzini had organized unsuccessful uprisings in Milan in 1853 and an abortive expedition to Southern Italy in 1857. He returned to London in 1858 and was condemned to death in Italy in absentia. Nevertheless, he entered Italy secretly from time to time.

In May 1860, with the blessing of King Victor Emmanuel II, Garibaldi started from Genoa on the most magnificent exploit of his life. With his famous Thousand volunteers, called the Red Shirts, he landed in Sicily. The entire Island, which had meanwhile rebelled against King Francis II (1836–1894, king 1859–1861), welcomed Garibaldi and his gallant Red Shirts with enthusiasm. Once Sicily was united to Italy, Garibaldi crossed the Straits and won Naples and Southern Italy for the Kingdom. Mazzini wished to declare Southern Italy a republic, but Garibaldi remained faithful to his promise to Victor Emmanuel. This was an act of great self-abnegation. The people of Naples had acclaimed Garibaldi as their ruler. But after meeting with Victor Emmanuel in a small town near Naples, Garibaldi presented his conquests to the sovereign. Only a portion of the Papal States, policed by troops of the French Empire, and Venice, still held by Austria, now remained outside the new Italy.

In March 1860, the people of Parma, Modena, Romagna, and Tuscany had approved, through plebiscites, annexation to Piedmont. In October, Naples and Sicily also voted in favor of union with the North. The next month, similar popular approval was voted in the Marches and in Umbria. With the union of 20,000,000 Italians to Piedmont, Cavour and his followers had alienated the cherished feelings of both the conservative Catholic powers of Europe and the radical republicans of Italy. Cavour was therefore determined not to run the risk of interference with his program. He immediately proceeded to furnish the new Italian State with ready-made institutions, leaving no basic questions open to unsettling political debate. The 1848 *Statuto* of Piedmont became the Constitution of united Italy. Almost as though a wand had been waved, Italy received a Parliament of British inspiration: the Chamber of Deputies was elected by men of property, while the Senate was appointed by the King. Overnight, Cavour's inflexible economic policy of free trade, likewise of English origin, was imposed upon all of Italy, including the more backward, almost wholly agricultural South. On the other hand, French influence dictated the new type of uniform local administration: the rigidly centralized prefectural system devised by Napoleon. These arrangements not only violated Italy's strong localist traditions, but also subordinated southern interests to northern policies. To add disillusion to dismay, most of the people who had voted in the holiday-like plebiscites of unity learned that they were barred from suffrage under the national Constitution. Only 418,696, or 1.9% of a population of almost 22,000,000, possessed the qualifications for the right to vote. During the approaching period from 1860 to 1890, the problems created by Cavour's triumph would have to be solved politically. Unfortunately, they were politically insoluble.[5]

Social Realities

The stirring political events in Italy from 1800 to 1860 arrest attention and engender admiration because they highlight the ideal elements of historical drama which the peoples emerging into nationhood after World War II re-enacted: the pathos of fellow men divided and subjugated, the battle of liberty against autocracy, dashing patriotism, fervent pace, and dedicated personalities of strong attraction. Unhappily, the noble enthusiasms of the *Risorgimento* tend to obscure the important truth that the struggle for freedom and the creation of a unified state engaged, then as now, the minds and energies of a narrow segment of the entire population. These devoted men were drawn largely from the intellectual and professional classes and from the liberal elements of the aristocracy. It could not have been otherwise, for Italian society suffered from a crippling, immobilizing malady: illiteracy.

Not until 1861, when the Kingdom came into being, could Italy ascertain the extent of illiteracy on a national scale through an official agency employing standard definitions and procedures. According to data provided by the first census, illiteracy afflicted 75% of the population 5 years of age and above in 1861: 68% of the men and 81% of the women. Among regions, the ratios of illiteracy increased from north to south: Piedmont, Liguria, and Lombardy, 54%; Tuscany, 74%; Emilia-Romagna, 78%; the Marches, 83%; the Neapolitan provinces, 86%; Sicily, 89%; and Sardinia, 90%. Almost a century later, in 1950, among the more important independent and developing countries of the world, Egypt, Sudan, Libya, Tunisia, Morocco, Jordan, Syria, Iran, Iraq, Saudi-Arabia, Afghanistan, Pakistan, India, Vietnam, Laos, and Indonesia, showed illiteracy rates for population over 15 years of age comparable to Italian proportions ninety years before.[6]

Of children between the ages of 5 and 12 in Italy, over 82% were illiterate. During 1861–1862, out of every 100 children in the nation between the ages of 6 and 12, only 37 were enrolled in elementary schools.[7] Education was more widespread in North and Central Italy. In 1861–1862, Piedmont claimed almost a third of the private and public elementary schools (8,467 out of 28,524) and almost a third of all elementary school pupils (361,970 out of 1,008,674). It is safe to assume that Piedmont's educational superiority among the Italian states had also prevailed for some years before 1861–1862. In Lombardy and Veneto, the Austrian government had established universal and compulsory education. Yet enforcement, even in Lombardy, one of the most advanced and prosperous of all Italian regions, was more than lax. In 1846, 25% of the boys of school age in the provinces of Milan and Cremona were untutored. In Lodi and Crema, this proportion rose to a third, while in Mantua and Pavia, 50% remained outside of classes.[8]

Illiteracy alone was malignant enough to retard the potential growth of Italy as a democratic industrial state and to distort the future development of an effective labor movement. Unfortunately, illiteracy accompanied other equally devastating social evils. The overwhelming mass of Italians were agricultural and remained fixed in feudal immobility. Peasants lived and died where they were born. The center of their existence was the village and it was impossible for them to know about life elsewhere. Their isolation and ignorance were vividly portrayed by

15

Sir John Bowring in his *Report on the Statistics of Tuscany, Lucca, the Pontifical and the Lombardo-Venetian States.* It should be remembered that John Bowring was describing conditions during the 1830's in North and Central Italy. They were mercifully superior to those in Southern Italy and the Islands. He wrote:

> But there is a point of view, it seems to me, which has not excited sufficient attention; this is the universal *isolation* of the peasantry, which is a necessary condition of the mezzeria system. Where there is no association there must be much ignorance. Every peasant's family in Tuscany stands as it were alone; this is indeed a great security for the public tranquillity; but it is tranquillity purchased at a fearful price—at the price of a stationary and backward civilization. I do not perceive how education can break down the barriers which surround every contadino family. I had occasion more than once to see four generations inhabiting the same cottage; but the last had not added a particle of knowledge to the ignorance of the first: the same gross superstitions; the same prejudices against books; the same unwillingness to introduce any species of improvement in husbandry; the same reference to ancestral usages. In innumerable cases families have occupied the same farms for hundreds of years, without adding a farthing to their wealth, or a fragment to their knowledge . . . . But, after all, *can* the system be changed? Certainly not by direct or violent legislation, nor by individual efforts, which have failed again and again, because they have struggled against the *vis inertiae* of generations. Yet if experiments were made in the new lands, where the mezzeria has not yet been introduced (though it *is* gradually introducing itself into the Maremme); if the more improved systems of husbandry gave to the proprietors of land higher rents, and to the labourers higher gains, the influence of example and the calculations of self-interest might alter the existing state of things. The period, however, must be remote.[9]

Illiteracy, isolation, ignorance, superstition, and hostility to innovation bred not only a persistent provincialism of spirit, but of language as well. The ensuing babel increased the plight of the artisan and peasant by diminishing their prospect of self-improvement through association. Hundreds of different dialects were spoken on the Italian peninsula. Only a highly placed, cultivated, restricted minority formed a cohesive group, bound together by the language of Dante, travel, and friendship. On the other hand, the various dialects employed by craftsmen and peasants within a region, and often within a single province, were scarcely intelligible elsewhere and sounded hardly akin to the language spoken by the cultivated upper classes. As distances increased, the language barrier between North Italy and Central and Southern Italy grew formidable for the bulk of the people. Thus, the most natural bond of association among men — speech — had degenerated into the kind of hindrance made familiar to the world of the 1950's and 1960's by large Asian countries like India, as well as by the small tribal states of Africa.

As a consequence of these social ills, most Italians were isolated politically from the momentous events which culminated in national emancipation. Those who embraced Mazzini's doctrines of freedom, unity, and republicanism, or Cavour's liberal formula for the triumph of Piedmont and the monarchy, were recruited from the limited ranks of professional men, intellectuals, radical elements of the aristocracy, and the more skilled and educated artisans. Nor did those who actually fought in the campaigns of battle spring from the great mass of the people. Garibaldi, in his *Autobiography*, returns frequently to a theme which troubled him, the peasants. He recalls the triumph of his Thousand, "glorious in their motley array, just as they came from their offices and workshops, at the trumpet-call of duty—in the student's coat and hat, or the more modest garb of the mason, the carpenter, or the smith." In a footnote, Garibaldi confesses sadly: "From my heart I wish I could have added 'of the peasant,' but I will not distort the truth. This stalwart and laborious class belongs to the priests, who make it their business to keep it in ignorance. I do not know a single instance of one of its members being seen among the volunteers. They serve in the army, but only when forced to do so; and form the most effectual tools of despotism and priestcraft."[10] Clearly, a nation established itself without the participation of most of its inhabitants.

Italy, then, was conferred upon the Italian masses without any personal cost to them. They had been rendered incapable of understanding the forces loose in their land, or of participating in the events which these forces summoned up. Of this tragedy, Luigi Dal Pane has said: "Sad condition of Italy! She was condemned to initiate her *Risorgimento* without the contribution of the multitudes; to base it upon the heroism of the few and the general interest of Europe. She was destined to have a liberty which the common people did not really feel as their own, a liberty written into the laws, but empty of that social content which constitutes its only secure basis."[11]

This popular willingness, before unification, to accept supinely both good and evil from above, provided a ready-made, pivotal role for the professional man of the future who would brandish a political and social cause, promising newer, better worlds to the helpless, the ignorant, and the illiterate in return for their support. This symbiotic pattern had actually come into small view even before 1860 when, here and there, peasants and craftsmen were organized into associations to safeguard their interests. Educated persons outside the working class nurtured these groups during their formative stages. After a few of the societies managed to survive, they still continued under the guidance and control of their sponsors. Thus, there was foreshadowed, quite early, the decisive influence upon future labor unions of educated men who were neither artisans nor peasants.

The illiteracy and ignorance which the first half of the nineteenth century bequeathed to the new Italian State also insured popular dependence in the world of politics. As noted before, once the provisions of the *Statuto* with regard to suffrage were duplicated in the national Constitution, fewer than 500,000 persons had the literacy and property qualifications which made them eligible to vote. Therefore, the early trade unionists had to depend upon middle-class parliamentarians for safeguarding the welfare of workers. Disenfranchisement also forced the fledgling labor movement into agitation for compulsory elementary school education, suffrage, and other social reforms instead of concentrating on economic aims. Here, too, their demands could be satisfied only through importuning middle-class politicians and relying upon their good will.

It should be recalled that in the United States universal manhood suffrage, except for negro slaves and Indians, had been wrested from the conservative classes of the most important states by 1825. Free, tax-supported, universal elementary school education had been won from the state legislatures by the end of the 1830's. Consequently, these two political issues, which sapped the energies of most European labor movements until almost the end of the nineteenth century, had been removed from the agenda of demands by American labor soon after the first beginnings of city-wide union movements. As a result, at no time in their history, were American unionists dependent upon outsiders for guiding their organizational affairs, nor were they ever forced into long political struggles for the right to vote. In countries like Italy, this acrimonious fight came to embitter the disenfranchised against existing parties and the classes they represented. It enhanced, by contrast, the virtues of the rising radical parties which workers without a vote could think of as their own.

During the late nineteenth and early twentieth centuries, as the character of modern Italian unions took form, demonstrations of protest, particularly among agricultural workers, all too often ended in violence. This feature of the labor movement was not new; its lineage was ancient and its recurrence persistent. "Through the centuries, the southern peasants have borne their lot with patience. Only very occasionally, when the measure of their sufferings has seemed to pass all human bearing, have they risen in desperate, inarticulate protest. Then for a few days or years their fury has known no limits as they have burned and murdered with the blind pent-up anger of centuries."[12] Nor had Central and North Italy escaped these periodic eruptions over the long years. As late as 1848, the Five Days of Milan struck like "an abrupt and sudden leap from apparent inertia and political immaturity to heroic and self-directed action. . . ."[13]

Undoubtedly, many ills of varied intensity generated these mass explosions during the centuries before national liberation and in the following decades when unions were first organized. Nevertheless, the frustration of workers cut off by illiteracy, ignorance, and disenfranchisement from manifesting their just demands through normal political channels cannot be underestimated. If economic misery of almost universal proportions and debasing social stagnation closely attend the stifling of political expression, then periodic violence may be counted upon as almost inevitable. When an atmosphere of religious authoritarianism hovers over the orthodoxies which support these evils, then countervailing doctrines of universal, apocalyptic solutions to economic and social distress find it possible to enjoy easy acceptance. Inured to dependence, Italian workers would receive such revelations from above as in the natural order of affairs. Of more tragic consequence, they would also learn to assimilate the notion that their welfare as well must be controlled from on high in their name.

The Economic Reality

Economic conditions in Italy during the first six decades of the nineteenth century now demand attention. They can be viewed in proper perspective only by recalling the stages of the industrial revolution reached elsewhere in Europe. Advance was most marked in England where industrialization had begun before 1750. In Belgium and France, this development came later, while Germany held behind France for some forty years. Not until the Franco-German War of 1870 did the German Reich begin to forge ahead rapidly. Sweden, Austria, Hungary, and Italy then joined the trend in Europe. Of the principal countries of the continent, only Russia, which appeared on the industrial scene around 1890, tarried behind Italy.

Before 1860, the overwhelming majority of Italian workers were peasants and agricultural laborers. It has been estimated that in 1850, 62.4% of the total population was attached to the land.[14] These people toiled in the fields all their lives and depended wholly upon the land.

19

They knew only abject poverty and were ignorant of the uses of a cash economy. They themselves supplied almost all of their own extremely limited needs. They were their own bakers, coopers, shoemakers, spinners, weavers, and tailors. Barter was the prevailing method of exchange.[15] They employed traditional agricultural methods and received little encouragement toward improvements either from the landowners or from the governments in power. To add to their misery, rainfall was inadequate, plagues of insects bit into the meager fruit of their efforts, and the quality of the soil was poor.

Within the stark boundaries of peasant life, the depths of privation varied from state to state. Lombardy, the most prosperous region of the entire peninsula measured by Italy's impoverished standards, still supported its dense population mainly from the soil. This task was accomplished with increasing difficulty, for Lombardy lagged far behind Western Europe in adopting improved agricultural practices. Conditions of peasant life worsened south of the Po valley. In Tuscany, they congealed into the harsh immobility which Sir John Bowring described. Peasants in the Papal States suffered worse want than those in Tuscany. But agrarian misery reached the nadir for all of Italy in the Kingdom of the Two Sicilies with its capital at Naples.

If Italy were almost wholly agricultural, and rudely so, even as late as 1860, governmental deficiencies and restrictions in the decades before unification impoverished the economy even more. Political demarcations, guild restrictions, tariffs, discriminatory taxes, tolls and imposts, proliferation of monetary and measuring systems, lack of communications, impassable or nonexistent roads, absence of credit facilities, hazards of trade, and brigandage placed a blight upon all remaining forms of enterprise by freezing initiative. The market was reduced to the locality, often not extending beyond the confines of the commune. Only local rulers and foreign sovereigns prospered. Whether governments were native or alien, they were primarily concerned with securing maximum revenues through taxes on trade, industry, and banking, as well as agriculture. In fact, the decline of Italy from the high economic position it had enjoyed during the Middle Ages and the Renaissance can be explained by these feudal regulations and devices as well as by the westward shift of the centers of trade and finance. Unfortunately, these vestiges of economic feudalism persisted on into nineteenth-century Italy.

For a few years after the conquest of Italy by Napoleon in 1797, it had seemed likely that these antiquated political and economic institutions would be reformed or abolished. However, after the fall of Napoleon, the seven states of Italy again imposed the same handicaps upon themselves. They were once more isolated from each other by absurdly high tariffs. Piedmont, after the Restoration, adopted protective tariffs which averaged from 80% to 150%. The Po River, the only large river in Italy, could not serve as a highway of water transportation. Between its mouth and Pavia, five customs lines, embracing 80 different stations, brought the progress of goods to a halt. Products destined for Milan, if they were to earn a profit, could travel up the Po only to a certain juncture. They were diverted at this point to the little river, Mincio, and then borne overland to dodge the trade barriers. Yet, even with the aid of smugglers and of corrupt customs officials, commerce was thwarted, for the most part, from reaching outside markets. Moreover, within the confines of a single state, trade was not free. In the course of 50 to 100 miles, goods of all kinds might have to pass through six barriers. Disregarding "foreign" commerce, internal trade was hampered not only by burdensome restrictions, inherited from the past, but also by the poverty of the peasants, the only remaining buyers of goods as long as trading outside the boundaries of a state remained unprofitable. If any life finally managed to remain in the pursuit of trade, brigands hunted it down. Well documented was the sorrowing and pessimistic judgment of Melchiorre Gioja that the history of commerce was simply "the history of the efforts made by nations to bring about their own ruin."[16]

Trade and commerce, then, were feeble and shackled. Lombardy, the natural gateway between Italy and the rest of Europe, could show a spirit of enterprise only slightly livelier than those of the other states, for the merchants even there had not as yet become modern entrepreneurs.[17] If inertia gripped trade and commerce, it should be recalled that agriculture, still the dominant economic activity everywhere on the peninsula, endured more crippling rigidities imposed by custom. Lombardy, the leading state, could not as yet "expect an agricultural revolution . . . comparable with that which took place in England during the eighteenth century. . . ." [18] Obviously, it would have been futile to hope for agrarian reform anywhere else in Italy. But agriculture and commerce at least existed. The third basic element in a modern economy, manufacturing industries, hardly achieved true beginnings as late as 1850.

Why was large-scale factory production introduced with greater effort and so much later in Italy than elsewhere in Western Europe? Despite learned, plausible, and conventionally repeated explanations, perplexities continue for two reasons. The economic history of Italy during the nineteenth century has been neglected by scholars in comparison with their notable and numerous studies of the Middle Ages and the Renaissance. In addition, when contemporary sources are available for study, they have the exasperating habit of assuming that the familiar needs no description, leaving research on the verge of knowledge, but deprived of understanding.

With mesmerizing regularity, the slow progress of the Italian industrial revolution is explained by emphasizing the failure to mechanize factory production in Piedmont, Lombardy, Venetia, and Tuscany where there seemed to be a favorable economic climate for change. After this kind of tautological generalization, there usually follows a listing of other contributory causes: the lack of resources, above all, coal, iron, an adaptable and disciplined work force, and organizational and technical skills; the modest amount of available capital; the oppressive or badly devised systems of tariffs and taxation; the absence of political unification, and therefore, of a national market; the prevalence of an essentially retrograde agricultural structure; the narrow and backward mentality of the population; the want of audacious enterpreneurs with imagination and vision; the failure to establish economic and technical contacts beyond the Alps and across the seas; and the deficiency and slowness of communications, especially the poverty of the highway and railroad systems.

Indeed, the retardation of railway construction is startling. In 1841, there were 20 kilometers (a kilometer is nearly ⅝ of a mile) of railroad tracks in all of Italy, largely represented by the Naples-Portici line completed in 1839 to satisfy the progressive aspirations of a feudal prince. These 20 kilometers should be compared with 1,349 kilometers for England in 1841, 435 kilometers for France, 335 for Belgium, 580 for Germany, and 144 for Austria. At the time of unification, in 1861, Piedmont claimed 803 kilometers of railroads, the highest total among the Italian states. This supremacy had been won between 1849 and 1859 under the guidance and prodding of Cavour. After Piedmont came Veneto with 298 kilometers, followed by Tuscany with 256. The vast Papal States attained the midpoint on this list, while Lombardy with 202 kilometers and the Kingdom of the Two Sicilies with 98 kilometers occupied the last two places. In 1861, when all Italy was endowed with only 2,773 kilometers of railroad track, England possessed seven times, France nearly five times, and Germany almost six times this kilometrage.[19]

The uneven distribution and meagerness of the Italian railway structure were not balanced by an adequate system of transportation by state, provincial, and communal roads. In 1830, it required 36 hours to travel from Milan to Venice and 11 days to reach Milan from Messina in Sicily. Goods were transported with scandalous languor, necessitating 40 or 50 days to cover 200 miles in good weather. The absence of diligences between important centers like Milan and Florence and Rome and Naples

22

was publicly lamented in 1835. In 1861, the Kingdom inherited only 86,000 kilometers of badly maintained roads, ill adapted to traffic. Of this total, 71,000 kilometers were located in Central and North Italy (excluding Veneto and Rome).

If land transportation plagued the economy, water transportation offered no alternative. In 1861, all Italian ports, with the exception of Genoa and Leghorn, were in a condition of abandon. Communications suffered equal retardation. As late as 1862, only 3.29 letters per inhabitant were mailed in Italy, while in England seven times that number were posted. Using the same criterion to compare the citizen of Piedmont and Sicily, the proportion reached 7 to 1. The first electrical telegraph system was erected in 1847 between Pisa and Leghorn. In 1849, Piedmont was still using an aerial telegraph. Not until 1850 was an electrical telegraph mentioned in connection with Lombardy, and not until the next year for Piedmont. In 1852, electrical telegraphs were installed in Veneto, Parma, and the Naples region, while the Papal States followed in 1853 and Sicily not until 1857.[20]

Such were the deficiencies, in the usual scholarly view, of material resources, human skills, available capital, financial arrangements, technical capacity, governmental policies, and social organization which hindered the development of Italy's economic life during the years from 1800 to 1860. Antonio Fossati, the economic historian, agrees that they undoubtedly delayed a movement toward industrialization, already foreshadowed in exceptional regions since the second half of the eighteenth century. However, these explanations, convincing as they seem, leave fundamental questions unanswered: During the period from 1800 to 1860, which had the larger weight, capital or labor? Did the capital employed in industry, or did the wages employed there, grow at a faster rate? What was the rhythm of production with reference to the increase of capital in various types of industrial enterprises? What was the average productivity per worker and the cost of labor per unit of product at a given date? Thus far, as Fossati explains, these questions have remained largely unanswered for Italy because of the absence of basic data.[21] (In truth, they cannot be satisfactorily answered for most countries, and for the same reason.)

Fossati is fashionably preoccupied with rather sophisticated economic relationships which have not as yet been clearly articulated for want of adequate knowledge. His scholarly distress, however, must not obscure the plain circumstances of the moment: answers to much less difficult questions are still cut off either by the total lack of data, or by deficiencies in available statistical information. What was the total industrial labor force of Italy and of its several states at given intervals during the period from 1800 to 1860? How many workers were engaged in various industries and in different operations within these industries? Of these workers, how many pursued their tasks in centralized plants or factories in the modern sense of the words? How many were artisans, rather than factory workers? How many were peasants engaged in cottage production during the winter months? How many country folk merely plied their skills at home for their own consumption, but were counted in the census as part of the industrial population? Quite apart from problems of definition and distinction, suspicion often arises, with regard to certain figures, that the entrepreneurs questioned might have exercised an understandable pride in exaggerating the size of their labor force.

Statistical obstacles of this simple variety have impeded the accumulation of fundamental knowledge without which the history of Italian labor becomes a chronicle of agitations, radical heroics, and heresies. Indeed, students of the union movement in Italy have neglected, almost without exception, the most elementary aspects of economic development and their influence upon the growth of workers' organizations. Yet this relationship brings meaning to events and makes their interpretation possible. Labor unions with economic and political goals, permanently based at their sites of work, cannot arise until a money economy of some strength exists, the market for handicraft goods widens, or true factory production begins. Only then do men and women become associated, in numbers beyond the family group, at their place of labor; then, too, communication among workers employed in different shops and plants becomes possible as production becomes geographically concentrated. These are the elementary economic and social prerequisites for union organization. They do not obtain so long as goods are made by peasants for home consumption and barter, or while cottage industries are still the predominant mode of production. When town and city artisans come together in small but slowly expanding handicraft shops, and especially when true factory organization triumphs, unions first appear and learn to persist.

The most exhaustive treatments of industrial development from 1800 to 1860 are the studies of Roberto Tremelloni, *Storia dell'industria italiana contemporanea dalla fine del settecento all'unità italiana* (*History of Contemporary Italian Industry from the End of the Eighteenth Century to Italian Unity*) and Kent Roberts Greenfield, *Economics and Liberalism in the Risorgimento: A Study of Nationalism in Lombardy, 1814–1848.* Both scholars have mined stubborn materials from abundant sources of heterogeneous character and grade of accessibility. They have given these refractory data perhaps the only rational shape they will ever achieve, thereby affording us a clearer insight into Italy's economic evolution throughout the period under consideration.

During the earliest years of the nineteenth century, the textile industry (as contrasted to family handicraft work for home use or barter) was the most organized manufacturing activity in Italy, largely confined to the North. Despite operational advance, the use of power-driven machinery was negligible.[22] Figures for textile production in the Napoleonic Kingdom of Italy[23] have been unearthed for 1806. Given the unique and paramount position of textiles in the incipient and still extremely limited manufacturing hierarchy, these statistics may be taken, with reservations, as a reflection of the extent of industrial enterprise at this time. Of the 6,500,000 total population, 222,000 workers, or 3.4%, were engaged in various forms of textile production. The woolen industry occupied 38.3% of all textile workers, while silk spinning and silk weaving engaged 20.3% and 11.2%. Weavers of hemp, linen, and cotton comprised 30.2%. The number of spinners of hemp, linen, and cotton was undetermined. The defects of the data were two, primarily: peasant cottage workers were counted as factory employees and many declarations were false.[24] Thus, the percentage of true factory workers in the most advanced industry of the Kingdom was probably even smaller than 3.4% of the total population. If it were possible to estimate a comparable percentage for the entire peninsula at this time, the proportion would have been much smaller still, since the Kingdom of Italy did not include the backward South and the Islands.

For estimates concerning the rough distribution of Italy's labor force in 1830, Tremelloni was driven to employ sources of English origin: Charles Babbage's study, *On the Economy of Machinery and Manufactures*, which, in turn, relied upon Richard Jones' work, *An Essay on the Distribution of Wealth, and on the Sources of Taxation*. Jones had concluded that for every 100 persons in Italy engaged in the cultivation of the soil in 1830, there were 31 who pursued nonagricultural occupations. In contrast, for every 100 persons laboring in agriculture in England, France, and Bengal, there were 200, 50, and 25 individuals who derived their livelihood from nonagricultural work, trades, or professions. Thus, by 1830, from the point of view of economic growth and industrial evolution, Italy had not yet reached a level much above that of Bengal. Unfortunately, this condition persisted into the future. Tremelloni found that at the time of unification, three decades later, the proportion between the agricultural and nonagricultural population of Italy had remained the same as in 1830: 3 to 1.[25]

More detailed occupational data are on hand for 1850. Italy's active population for that year has been calculated at 12,100,000 out of a total population of 24,861,000. Of the entire work force, 62.4% were classified as agricultural workers and peasants; 16.5% as artisans; 15.3% as property owners; and 5.8% as sailors, soldiers, and beggars. The percentage distribution of Italy's 1,991,000 so-called artisans among the states for which statistics were cited showed: the Papal States, 35%; Lombardy, 34.3%; the Kingdom of the Two Sicilies, 17.1%; and Piedmont, 13.6%. In the Papal States with 3,100,000 inhabitants, artisans comprised 22.5% of the population; in Lombardy with 2,900,000 people, 23.6%; in Piedmont with 4,400,000 persons, 6.1%; and in the Kingdom of the Two Sicilies with the largest aggregate of population, 9,300,000, only 3.7%, despite the very loose application of the term "artisan."[26]

These statistics and additional sources of information would seem to indicate that the mid-twentieth century pattern of widely diverse states of economic development among Italy's regions had already established itself before unification. For this reason, the level of economic development in the most important areas of the peninsula between 1800 and 1860 will be described. Details about specific kinds of production have been summarized and collated in Appendix E of this study.

The Kingdom of the Two Sicilies. As late as 1850 the most primitive economic arrangements prevailed in the Kingdom of the Two Sicilies, a state which occupied a third of Italy's geographic area and contained 40% of its population.[27] The potential market was logically vast, but actually empty of customers. Land was almost the sole source of income, but ownership was so concentrated that small proprietors were virtually unknown. In Sicily, where the feudal triangle of power remained untouched, the clergy, the crown, and the nobles divided the land among themselves. In consequence, nearly the entire working population of the Kingdom were landless agricultural laborers. The heavy pressure of people upon the soil could be surmised by the eye alone. Each year this imbalance grew worse, deranged by agricultural practices more barbarous than the tools employed in cultivating the soil. A contemporary writer observed: ". . . one never meets a peasant, and rarely an artisan, who knows how to read and write." [28]

Everywhere, roads were as primitive as the people, or did not exist at all. Sicily's expenditures for public works remained those of four or five centuries earlier. In some localities on the Island, when peasants went to the fields of their work, they remained away from their families for the entire season because the absence of bridges so prolonged short distances.

26

Limited construction of new roads for the Kingdom began in 1838, but it was concentrated around Naples and undertaken more for reasons of state than for civic improvement or convenience. Navigation, though an ancient tradition in South Italy, could not cope with inadequate craft, decrepit harbors, unsafe and marshy coasts, pirates, and smugglers. To be sure, life in the larger cities was less troglodytic than the struggles for existence on the land, particularly in Naples, whose population had increased to 450,000 by mid-century. But there, too, most of the population lived in wretched hovels, brutalized by deep poverty, the disdain of the local nobility, and the neglect of government.

The economy, perforce, functioned on the classic, precapitalistic level: immobile subsistence. Here was a medieval system of production which, imposed by the feudal guilds, survived into the nineteenth century, constricting commerce, production, earnings, consumption, and all of the ramifying relationships among them. Indeed, not until 1831 were guild regulations abolished in the Kingdom. Without doubt, changes were occurring between 1830 and 1860, but progress, in the exploitive terms of the industrial revolution, lingered. When, by 1839, the hours of labor reached 12 to 14 hours a day in England and Belgium, they rarely reached 8 or 9 hours in Naples. Exportation of raw silk, long debarred, was finally allowed. Commerce within the Kingdom between Sicily and the mainland, previously enjoined, was unshackled, but only in 1845 were prohibitive duties somewhat lightened. But these reforms, more often motivated by the snobbery of the monarch who wished to appear modern than by inner conviction, came too late and accomplished too little. The difference between the prices of articles manufactured locally and those of imported goods remained so great that, despite periodically raised equalizing duties, home industries could not withstand foreign competition.

The Papal States. The judgment of scholars is unanimous that economic conditions in the Papal States before 1860 were backward in the extreme. If nature had not endowed the Tyrrhenian areas with rich pasture lands (albeit malarial) and the Emilia region with fertile soil (shockingly husbanded), the Papal dominions might have shared with the Kingdom of the Two Sicilies equal distinction for maintaining the most stagnant economy on the peninsula. However, because of these natural blessings, the Papal States ranked merely second worst.

Agricultural activities were basic, for navigation and fishing on the Adriatic were of minimal consequence, while handicraft work gained but the most modest proportions. Commerce depended upon the internal yield of agriculture and the wide range of goods which had to be introduced from the outside. The lack of roads, schools, credit, banking facilities, and capital placed obstacles in the way of trade and turned it into an irregular operation. Umbria, the Marches, and Romagna exported wool, skins, cheese, and unprocessed agricultural products, but their preponderance over imports for these areas was regularly annulled by the commercial deficit piled up by Lazio, with the Eternal City as its center. The Prussian representative at Rome, writing in 1837, described the countermeasures taken: "To enrich the treasury, the right of importation has been successively raised with the result that revenues have fallen and smuggling increased." Seventeen years later, Monsignor Felice Peraldi characterized the state of finances as deranged and disastrous. Possibly concerned about the harshness of his judgment, he observed that "it would be deceitful or stupid to dissemble what public documents or budgets reveal."

Available sources mention no manufacturing activity, not even, as Tremelloni puts it, "the industrial darkness before the dawn." There is one exception, the production of paper, which stands alone in the entrepreneurial skill devoted to the seventy plants of record during this period. Otherwise, artisan shops, small in number and in size, dominated the scene. They were all still frozen at the handicraft stage. Machinery was still rare. In Rome, more opulent than other areas of the sprawling Papal States, the basis of economic life was religion. The artisan shops devoted their energies to the creation of gold and silver objects, statuary, tapestries, mosaics, painting and incision of hard stone, souvenirs, and religious books. Humbler products, few in number, also received passing mention: tanneries conducted on a semihousehold basis, primitive weaving mills, soap plants, and the usual oil presses.

No summary can be more telling than Monsignor Peraldi's comment that there was no example in the history of misfortunes in the Papal States when disastrous political and economic conditions "assumed such extensive proportions as in the fourth, fifth, and sixth decades of the present century."[29]

The Duchies of Parma and Piacenza, of Reggio and Modena, and of Lucca. Modest local enterprises throve in these small duchies primarily because of the tariff belts which surrounded them and lent encouragement to provincial markets. However, so fragile were manufacturing activities in these areas that during the years from 1853 to 1857, when the duchies were bound to Austria in tariff alliance, the products of Lombardy rapidly submerged the industrial products of Parma and Modena.[30]

Tuscany. By the end of the eighteenth century, Tuscany had already established the reputation for being the most advanced of the Italian states in the public management of its economy. The crafts and trades were freed from guild impediments; tariffs were lowered; restrictions upon commerce were suppressed. Later, Tuscany, alone among the Italian states, escaped damage by the economic policies of the Restoration. Under the influence of economic liberalism, agriculture and commerce flourished, while prices of consumer goods were lower than elsewhere in Italy. From 1844 to 1860, because of its interest in commerce, Tuscany equalled Piedmont's record in railroad construction. Leghorn grew as a port. In 1850, seventy-three Tuscan limited-liability joint stock companies had three times the capital possessed by all such companies in Piedmont. Industry, however, achieved only modest dimensions.

Lombardy. Kent Roberts Greenfield described the economy of Lombardy between 1814 and 1848 in these terms: "Agriculture overshadowed all other forms of economic activity in Lombardy during the first half of the nineteenth century. It created the conservative atmosphere which the whole economic community breathed; it was the chief source of wealth; and it employed most of the available resources of capital. Stefano Jacini estimated that the total sum invested in agriculture was more than six times that invested in commerce and industry combined."[31] Jacini, the leading agricultural economist of his time, also reckoned that in 1855 Lombardy's "agriculture occupied three-fifths of the population, and that one-half of the population were peasant tillers of the soil."[32] Nevertheless, Lombardy was universally acknowledged as the richest and most progressive region among the Italian states. Prosperous and advanced it was when compared with the other communities of Italy, but its economy was backward indeed when contrasted with the transformative industrial changes which were tearing Western Europe to its foundations. This irony — Lombardy poor when facing the Alps and rich when turned toward Naples — projects into high relief the poverty and retrogression of the other Italian states.

Greenfield, moreover, found no evidence that the tenor of agricultural life in Lombardy had suffered drastic change between 1814 and the middle of the century. Inherent in this stagnant system was the plight of the agricultural laborer of the Plain, who, it should be remembered, led a paradisiacal existence compared with his peasant brother in the South: "It was a problem that was beginning to trouble the public-spirited observers of the first half of the nineteenth century, for it created a submerged mass that was potentially restless but what was worse from the

point of view of progress and patriotism, normally inert." Luigi Torelli
called them "slaves of the glebe." "On this population," he wrote, "there
is no hope to be founded, since it lacks any motive of excitement. . . ."[33]

Commerce in Lombardy depended upon agriculture and shared its
conservatism. To be sure, the silk trade expanded at a lively rate, spinning the illusion that Lombardy, and particularly Milan, had warmed and
quickened to the commercial pace of Europe. But silk remained the telling
exception if it were conveniently forgotten that a large proportion of the
commerce in silk was directed by Swiss-Germans and men from Geneva
and Lyons. In most transactions, Lombardy's merchants moved with
caution. They took exception to mere suggestions of change, quite apart
from interference, in the traditional business habits they observed. They
refused to be either cajoled or driven into fresh spheres of action. They
managed to drag their custom-shod feet when the Austrian government
itself goaded them on to find new markets. "If the modern spirit of enterprise had here and there produced a stir in the economic life of Lombardy, it had made little difference in the attitude of the mercantile class.
They remained passive in a changing world."[34]

As might be expected, during the first six decades of the nineteenth
century, Lombardy also failed to advance industrially at a rate comparable to that of England, Belgium, France, Switzerland, and parts of
Germany and Austria. A few industries, to be discussed later, just touched
upon the early techniques of modern production, but many enterprises
designated as factories were, in reality, command centers for the distribution of work to the cottages of peasants. Handicraft labor still prevailed
and the contemporary manufacturer was primarily concerned with coordinating the widening circle of cottages to which he was farming out
his work.[35]

Human, economic, technical, and governmental impediments combined
to keep Lombardy industrially backward. To be sure, its population was
active, industrious, tenacious, practical, and serious. Moreover, in 1839,
Carlo Cattaneo estimated that Lombardy had a population of industrial
age (men from 20 to 60 years old) larger, relatively, than that of all the
other European countries.[36] Nor was this possible supply of labor restricted
by guild regulations,[37] as in Germany. Unfortunately, it was firmly agricultural in body and in spirit, rooted to the soil and to tradition. Lombardy,
at first glance, had economic advantages as well: unlike other parts of
Italy, there were unexploited reserves of industrial metals. But here again,
as in the instance of the labor supply, this resource proved futile. Fuel was
precious: wood stocks were vanishing, while Lombardy had never been
blessed with coal deposits. As a result, the iron industry failed to develop

and steam engines, which had to be imported, remained too costly for extensive adoption and operation. Consequently, in 1839, the steam engines in Lombardy could be counted on the fingers of two hands.[38] Exigency also dogged the technical skills available in Lombardy. The educational system was neither geared to impart vocational skills, nor did the potential supply of labor show eagerness to learn them. Thus, Lombardy, as well as the other states of Italy, came to be dependent upon other European countries not only for venture capital and the spirit of enterprise but for managerial and technical skills as well. What these human, economic, and technical factors left undone in thwarting even modest industrial progress, governmental policy accomplished. The manufacturers of Lombardy possessed no attractive markets. They were called upon to function in a Europe divided by high tariffs, hemmed in, at the same time, by Austria's own constrictive system. Within the free market of Austria itself, they either had to compete against long-established rivals in Bohemia and Lower Austria, or turn to Lombardy-Venetia as a market. But there, the largest portion of potential customers were peasants with simple needs which they themselves supplied.

By 1860, an inventory of Lombardy's industrial economy might have been prefaced by the declaration that handicraft production at the wholesale stage was still dominant, although certain tendencies augured a higher degree of organization. The central workshops of the textile industries — the command centers — represented a yet undeveloped form of capitalistic enterprise, more concerned with commercial advantages than manufacturing and technical ascendancy. The manufacture of woolen and linen yarns and coarse cloth remained either stationary or was declining. Mining and metallurgy also failed to advance. In contrast, and expanding rapidly, was the production of raw silk, silk yarn, spun cotton, and ordinary grades of silk and cotton cloth. In these areas of manufacture, to which the infant machine-building industry must be added, the true power-driven factory was appearing. Since this initial development took place in industries new to Lombardy — cotton spinning not connected with local agriculture, silk twisting which was entirely new, linen spinning which was closely associated with the mechanical spinning of cotton, and metal products which depended upon the freshly emerging industrial life of the region — it can be thought with some justice that Lombardy's generally retarded industrial life can be attributed, in part, to the rigidities imposed by the traditional and conservative habits of a society oriented toward agriculture.[39]

The character of industrial enterprise in Lombardy during the first half of the nineteenth century has thus far been prefigured: overwhelmingly handicraft, with feeble beginnings of factory production in a few branches of textile production. The magnitude of these operations must now be determined by industrial category since their evolving patterns shape the origin and nature of unions. To that end, this study has examined the industrial statistics assembled by Kent Roberts Greenfield for the years from 1814 to 1848, supplemented and expanded with the evidence garnered by Roberto Tremelloni, by industry, number of plants, number of employees, occupation, and stage of development. The resulting data, presented in detail in Appendix E of this volume, are sparse and not comparable in most cases from year to year, but they nonetheless manage to point up the handicraft nature of production during this period.[40]

Available evidence about "industry" as a whole indicates that the small handicraft shop dominated the productive scene generally between 1800 and 1860. In 1833, of 203 establishments recorded at Milan, only 13 employed more than 100 workers, while 59 plants employed between 10 and 25 persons. No data on size were provided for the remaining 131 shops so that it is impossible to tell how many engaged between 25 and 100 workers and how many employed less than 10 workers. These figures can be supplemented by statistics for Brescia which revealed 18,000 enterprises in 1837, each employing an average of 3.5 persons.[41]

Although almost one-third of the population of Lombardy was classified as attached to "industry" in 1840, it is fairly clear that much of this employment took place on a seasonal or part-time basis, supplementing major work in agriculture. Greenfield notes that Lombardy, with 2,524,000 inhabitants, was credited with an "industrial" labor force of 800,000. He hastens to add that "industrial" cannot be interpreted in the modern sense of the word, for "a large proportion of those who were thus employed were also tilling the soil."[42] Tremelloni offers an additional difficulty in interpreting the occupational terminology encountered in contemporary sources: the interchangeable use of "industrial workers" and "artisans" or "craftsmen." He records that the artisan population was estimated at 683,000 in 1850, but warns that the number of artisans seems unduly large and that the figure must have included those employed in "industry."[43]

Turning now to individual segments of industry, it would be well to ask: What stage had the textile industry, that universal harbinger of the industrial revolution, achieved in Lombardy, Italy's most economically advanced region, by 1860? The answer is plain. Silk and cotton spinning arrived, in solid part, at factory production. All other branches of the industry remained at the handicraft level, with production either wholly directed to home consumption, or partly to domestic use and partly to occasional outside sale, or to a combination of family use and regular sales (as a result of steady off-season work) to the owners or agents of "command centers."

The mining and metal-mechanical industries, a second barometer of industrial evolution, received little stimulus in Lombardy. On the contrary, discouragements loomed large: no coal, little wood, modest metal resources mined by primitive methods, imperfect furnaces, and indifference to new technical knowledge and improvements. To turn discouragement into despair, high tariffs excluded English and Swedish iron, while Austria promoted the use of its Istrian and Carinthian iron, better in quality and cheaper in price than Lombard iron. Iron production fared no better than iron mining. At the close of the era under review, no plants producing steel of fine quality had as yet taken hold. Perhaps the metallurgical industry might have logically veered toward the second stages of production. In other countries, expanding railroads were providing a splendid market of this kind. However, the railroads of Lombardy could furnish no such viable demand: 45 kilometers of track in 1848 and 221 kilometers eleven years later. Forced to confine itself to the traditional fabrication of metals, the industry formed its nucleus in the customary products of the small smithy or forge: wire, nails, simple agricultural implements, and domestic utensils. Even skilled operations like the ancient arms industry of Brescia did not prosper. Like the fabrication of other metal products, the machinery industry also froze at the handicraft-artisan stage of small and medium-sized operations.

The nonferrous metal-working industries were more fragmented and more securely locked within the grip of handicraft labor than the metal-mechanical trades. The remaining industries of Lombardy were small and traditional: dairy products, skins and leather, dyeing, jewelry, textile printing, silk hats, combs, buttons, paper, bottles, tiles, panes, bricks, and candles. Neither the production nor refining of sugar on an industrial basis had as yet proved successful. But three additional industries served to distinguish Lombardy from other states: the wholesale production of felt hats, furniture, and carriages.

Thus, at the time of unification, Lombardy's industrial balance sheet read: handicraft manufacture of traditional goods; mining and metallurgy of some importance, but failing; spinning and coarse weaving of wool and linen, either stationary or declining; expansion of raw silk production, silk spinning of an industrial nature, cotton spinning at the factory level, and handicraft weaving of ordinary silk and cotton cloth; finally, the faint beginnings of a modern metal-mechanical industry. So stood the achievement of the paragon of all Italian regions, pre-eminent among them until Cavour remade his beloved Piedmont.

Piedmont. Before 1848, Piedmont was less advanced industrially than Lombardy, nor did its economic and social environment betray encouraging signs of potential development. The only influential class consisted of "a restricted Turin aristocracy, more inclined toward the sword than the toga. . . ." Cavour observed that, if one wanted to live at peace in Piedmont, it was necessary to think only of agriculture. His compatriots felt a firm repugnance toward industry which they considered an ally of liberalism. Meanwhile, keen observers detected the gradual rise of an active, thrifty, and sagaciously educated middle class. Simultaneously, after 1830, King Charles Albert, no convinced liberal, nevertheless began to direct government policy toward economic goals more consonant with the needs of the State, including modest tariff reforms. The government interested itself in the wine and silk industries and conducted an investigation of manufactures in 1836. Six years later, alongside Piedmont's famous Academy of Science, rose the Agraria. This institution was liberal in spirit and concerned itself with industrial as well as agricultural progress. In 1844, the foundations were laid at Genoa for a discount bank; in 1847 a similar institution appeared in Turin, destined to be the nucleus of the National Bank which later became the Bank of Italy.[44]

After 1848, Piedmont began to outstrip Lombardy in economic importance. This miracle now remains to be described since it served to buttress the political ambitions of the Kingdom of Sardinia. By the time that Piedmont claimed leadership in freeing the Italian states from foreign domination and uniting them under its own aegis, the Kingdom had already aligned itself with Western Europe in four important ways: foreign trade, international loans used to develop the economic resources of the region, the gradual but impressive mechanization of its industries, and its modern financial institutions. Such economic assets were lacking in other parts of Italy, not excepting Lombardy itself. Given the modest dimensions of economic development even in Lombardy, the accomplishments of Piedmont are indeed impressive. They must be credited to Count Cavour.

This greatest of modern Italian statesmen had made several fortunes speculating and trading in grain, silk, securities, and foreign exchange. His role in founding the Bank of Turin was a leading one, as was his influence in encouraging the earliest royal concession to a private company for building a railroad line in Piedmont. Cavour first entered the government's service as Minister of Marine, Commerce, and Agriculture in 1850. Until then, the Piedmont government had taken only short steps to promote industry, to lower the grain duty, and to abolish differential navigation charges. But Cavour worked extremely fast. Within a month after his assumption of office, he had negotiated a new trade treaty with France. This treaty was followed shortly by other treaties with Belgium, England, Switzerland, Holland, Norway, the German Zollverein, and even Austria, its potential enemy. Cavour became Minister of Finance in 1851 and Prime Minister in 1852.

Between 1850 and 1855, exports increased by 50% and imports trebled. Cavour was not satisfied merely with free trade. He also wished to stimulate the internal economy of Piedmont through the abolition of municipal taxes on bread, the elimination of the last remaining feudal dues, the fostering of joint stock companies, the promotion of agricultural credit, the encouragement of education, the reformation of the postal system, and the complete administrative overhauling of the navy. It was he who removed the naval arsenal from Genoa to LaSpezia to permit the enlargement and the complete re-equipment of Genoa as a first-class port. He secured the services of two French engineers for supervising the construction of the Turin-Savigliano railroad. He was also responsible for the granting of government concessions to French engineers and entrepreneurs for developing railroads, gas companies, banking and insurance companies, mines, and even agricultural enterprises.[45]

Cavour showed great acumen in financing these variegated enterprises. On the eve of 1848, the public debt of the Kingdom of Sardinia amounted to 135,000,000 lire.[46] Between 1848 and 1860, new government securities, with a face value of almost 1,200,000,000 lire, yielded to the Sardinian treasury approximately 950,000,000 lire. More than half of these funds came from France. To the 500,000,000 lire invested by Frenchmen in the *public* securities mentioned, a like amount must be added to measure French investments in *private* enterprises in the Sardinian Kingdom. This latter amount, in turn, represented about one-half of the newly created capital employed in industry, foreign commerce, transportation, banking, insurance, and public utilities, or in almost every economic activity except agriculture, handicrafts, and retail trade.

By 1860, when the political ascendency of Piedmont was universally recognized, its economic and financial supremacy among the regions of Italy was also secured. In that year, in all of Italy there were 281 *società anonime* (limited-liability joint stock companies) and 96 *accomandite* (limited partnerships with shares) with a combined capital of roughly 1,350,000,000 lire. More than two-thirds of these companies and partnerships were in Piedmont. Of great significance, from the point of view of Cavour's foreign policy and economic activities, the majority of these companies and partnerships, both in Piedmont and elsewhere in Italy, were the result of French initiative and were formed with the assistance of French capital. The Victor Emmanuel railway, the largest single private enterprise in the Sardinian Kingdom, alone employed some 90,000,000 francs in French capital. The banking and insurance industries in Italy used almost exclusively foreign capital, mainly French. French capital was also employed in silk, cotton, mining, metallurgy, and public utilities.[47] It is not to be marvelled, then, that Cavour was able to convince Napoleon III to declare war on Austria in 1859 to the greater glory of the House of Savoy!

Social Attitudes, National Income, and Diversity of Demand. The predominance of foreign credit as well as managerial skill in Italian economic enterprises reflected feudal attitudes among the wealthier classes of Italy which persisted long after the leadership of Piedmont had achieved national liberation and unity. These rich remnants of the past looked down upon commercial and industrial endeavors, criticized their risks, and, at the same time, cut off funds desperately needed for economic development by their timidity, lack of initiative, and ignorance of worthwhile investment opportunities. The years after 1860 wrought light changes in these prejudices, but as Alessandro Rossi remarked even then, "our wealthy classes certainly give industry the respect due it, and that means a great deal; but they do not as yet give the credit due it; and that means a great deal more."[48] Fundamental to these antiquated economic and financial notions were the social postures which engendered them. Before and after 1860 in Italy, the business man or industrialist, once he realized substantial profits, hastened to withdraw his funds in order to invest them in lands and buildings, so immune to risks, so real, so socially approved. Cavour, in commenting upon this fixation, concluded: "This was, I believe, one of the principal reasons for the slow progress of industry among us."[49]

Before turning to review the forms, tasks, and limits assumed by workingmen's organizations in responding to the cramped economic arrangements which prevailed during the first six decades of the nineteenth century, two substantial questions remain to be considered: What size of income did Italy's backward agriculture, constricted commerce, and stunted industry provide? What economic elements, other than those already suggested, might help to explain this country's uncertain and awkward groping toward industrialization?

Trustworthy statistics concerning the national income before 1860 are not available. For that year, however, the national income has been estimated as not more than 6,250 million lire, or about 1,900 billion lire in today's currency. The income for each inhabitant came to 223 lire annually, or about 70,000 lire in today's currency. The lowness of the national income for 1860 is marked when contrasted with that of the United Kingdom in the same year, or even to comparable data for France and Germany, countries which were far behind England in industrial progress. These figures should also be contrasted with those of Italy itself in 1955, when the national income was estimated at 11,600 billion lire, or more than 240,000 lire annually for each inhabitant. The income today for each inhabitant of Italy is therefore more than three times that of a century ago.[50]

Italy's poverty and feeble industrial growth before 1860 were enmeshed with the country's inability to mechanize its economy. According to Antonio Fossati, this failure continued as long as the most important condition for the application of machinery was absent: uniformity of demand. In Italy, where, despite the nineteenth century, a medieval agricultural economy prevailed and production consisted largely of perishable goods, the rate at which machinery could be introduced was bound to be more gradual than in countries no longer predominantly agrarian and traditional in their habits and tastes.

In explaining the nature of textile manufacturing, the most important Italian industry before 1860, Fossati maintains that individual tastes, the desire for variations in style, the search for refinements of fabrication, especially where the work was the product of feminine and delicate labor, made it inevitable that variety of demand would remain alive for decades to come. Yet, the possibility of uniform demand could alone supply the major stimulus for increasing use of machine products. Such mechanization could occur most readily in those fields of Italian production where primary materials, like iron and steel, became a part of the finished product: machinery, tools, railroad rolling stock, industrial sheds, and ships. In short, standardization of demand understandably arose first in the new metal-mechanical industries where personal and traditional tastes counted least simply because most of the products were new to the industrial revolution. By contrast, in the more customary crafts, the space devoted to true factory operations was greatly restricted: silk, cotton, and woolen textiles, especially fabrics; activities allied to clothing; the confectionery industry; printing, even though highly developed; the ceramics field; tanning; and leather goods. (As if conforming to Fossati's hypothesis, these fields are still largely dominated by small and medium-sized enterprises in Italy today for the very reason that wide and disordered variations of demand still exist.) Accordingly, before and even after 1860, textile production, particularly silk and wool, did not lend itself to specialization. Integration in the textile industry therefore sought vertical rather than horizontal development. As a result, silk and wool workers labored traditionally under conditions of exploitation. As prices shifted up or down, more attention was paid to immediate speculative and commercial results than to technical problems of productivity.

Standardization of tastes and demand constitutes one of the triumphs of modern industry, according to Fossati, for industry alone imposes or directs uniformity, watches over it, and determines tastes. Although there were no signs of this kind of true industrial revolution in Italy before 1860, strangely enough production increased. Ironically, too, this trend developed in the face of increasing unit costs and of production limited to those principal types of goods desired not only locally, but abroad as well. The industries concerned used a labor force of both men and women who were not highly specialized. Thus, notwithstanding the competition of countries better equipped industrially, despite progressive decreases in the tariff, and under the handicap of the most modest degree of mechanization, textile production in Piedmont and Lombardy rose as a result of continuing foreign and domestic demand.[51]

Workingmen's Associations

Between 1800 and 1860, the various Italian states could count no true unions, as currently defined, among their economic and social institutions; least of all, could they claim a labor movement. Associations of artisans, when they took form at all, and then only with caution and official permission, assumed the benevolent character of mutual aid societies. Rinaldo Rigola (1868–1954), after seeking diligently for clues of militant unionism (leghe di resistenza) among the documentary relics of these decades, designated the era as "prehistorical," in the sense, it must be assumed, of "primitive," for he based his judgment upon historical materials. The summary exploration of industrial development, just completed in these pages, has served to reinforce the aptness of his meaning, if not of his terminology. Production — gauged by unit size, the employment of machinery, the application of motive power, and total volume of output — had reached but a primitive level of performance. In the absence of a factory system, the peasant reigned in miserable supremacy as Italy's most representative worker both in field and cottage.

This time without industry and without unions nevertheless deserves the closest attention. A setting may lack the cynosural jewel and compel the eye all the more, for at last its design comes into relief. In truth, the kinds of cultural, economic, social, political, and intellectual forces which simultaneously energize and weaken labor unions today surrounded Italian workers during the *Risorgimento*, even if they touched few of them directly. These eventual constants in the history of Italian labor, already evident before 1860, are six: (1) Most workers lived at the lowest level of bare subsistence. (2) Violent demonstrations and insurrections, politically inspired but rarely organized, ended in repression, abject defeat, and severe punishment. The few recorded strikes shared this same spontaneity, ineptitude, and rout. (3) A sense of concern for urban and rural workers spread among some members of the wealthier classes. Whether the urge toward social obligation took on conservative or radical life, it necessarily stooped to help. This spirit of noblesse oblige permeated, although unconsciously, the rhetorical thoughts and melodramatic deeds of the economic and social radicals who spoke and published in the name of the downtrodden with that unique fervor which thrives on self-appointment. Thus early, the unorganized workers and peasants acquired a new dependence: already humble before master, shop boss, and landlord, they were driven by diffidence and illiteracy to look up to their friends at revolutionary court for the articulate expression of their group identity, needs, and aspirations. (4) More conservative thinkers expressed the spirit of noblesse oblige precisely, making it clear that the more fortunate should assume civic responsibilities in order to preserve the integrity of the social system they prized. (5) Closely related to this conservative outlook, the doctrine and practice of cooperation among classes, moderate in nature and often religious in origin, gained acceptance among the more highly skilled and better-paid artisans in establishing their first organizations. (6) In contrast, two or three groups of superior and well-remunerated craftsmen began to make demands upon their employers, and a few producer and consumer cooperatives grew out of established workingmen's organizations. Feeble as they were, they represented faintly the dominant lines in the pattern of Italy's future labor movement.

Conditions of Work, Hours, and Wages. In the earliest days of factory production, shops rarely began as places specifically built for manufacturing activities. Most often, stable-like structures, after quick conversion from completely unrelated uses, served as work areas for the motley collection of hands from the countryside. The resulting mills were low, dark, and badly ventilated. Not until the middle of the century did entrepreneurs erect factories designed for a definite purpose. Even then, the innovation involved only a limited number of fuller-scaled industries, like cotton spinning. Meanwhile, the deficiencies of factory construction and the irrational internal arrangements spawned by makeshift buildings compounded the physical discomforts suffered by workers. Ironically, their own homes, especially in rural areas, were wretched enough, and, to add filth to misery, they were callous to the most elementary standards of personal hygiene. To their own unhealthful habits the overcrowded factory contributed smoke, dust, river dampness, mediocre lighting, heat in the summer, and intense cold in the winter.

Factory operations began at the break of dawn and lasted until sunset, not out of consideration to labor, but because artificial illumination was as yet insufficiently developed to permit the prolongation of hours. Thus, during the spring and summer, workers remained in the factory about 15 hours a day. This régimen was interrupted by two hours set aside for rest and meals. Food was far from plentiful and consisted mostly of vegetables. Admittedly, as far as the better part of the total work force was concerned, the schedule of long hours prevailed only during the limited number of months when plants operated at daylight intensity. Nonetheless, as long as the very active period lasted, the entire run of workers, including children, could enjoy at most five or six hours of sleep. Often the considerable walking distance between factory and home intruded upon the little free time these workers managed to garner after their exhausting day in the shops. Contrast established the prevalence of these harsh practices: sources available for 1840 regarded the schedule followed in a wool factory at Treviso, 11 hours of work during the summer and 9 during the winter, as uncommonly short. Yet these conditions in Italy compared favorably with those in England: the average workday there consumed 16 hours before Parliament limited them to 14.

These early Italian factory workers, inured to hard agricultural labor and to long auxiliary hours of handicraft toil in their own farm cottages, seemed more resigned than irritated at the new sacrifices imposed upon them by the heavy demands of the mill. This resignation deepened as they confronted insufficient sleep, the plant owner's unlimited power over living or starving, and the crude severity of supervisors. Granted, the discipline of family and rural life at that time possessed features hardly less uncouth and immoderate; to be sure, the distress of the laboring population *before* the industrial revolution has been muted by anguished outcries against satanic mills in once green and pleasant lands; undoubtedly, the slow introduction of power and machinery into the body of Italian production imposed the demands and tempo of factory life more gradually upon workers in Italy than elsewhere. Still, the transition to factory discipline brought daily suffering to millhands, especially to the large group of women and children who bore the major shock of the industrial revolution in Italy. Their docility pleased employers to the point of open praise.[52]

Employers throughout the nineteenth century also lauded the sobriety and diligence of shop workers in general, although they waxed less enthusiastic about the pliability of the men in their plants. Complaints abounded that they came reluctantly, or not at all, to work on Monday. Of more serious consequence, when former craftsmen and artisans were recruited from villages of the countryside for jobs in town factories, restlessness entered as well. Although quick to learn and fast in performing their tasks, they could not easily renounce their former habits. Like their brothers in England earlier and later in Germany, they remained prone to interrupt their work at the first hint of weariness, to rebel against fixed hours of labor, and to grow disquiet under the monotonous execution of a single operation. As a result, they very rarely remained for long in the same factory. Their mobility was constantly lamented by employers. To call a halt to roaming, factory owners eventually came to require the presentation of a workbook (*libretto di scorta*) by job applicants. This document was designed to discourage workers from quitting jobs solely because of whim or because of debt to employers. Before this practice took hold, some industrialists had been in the habit of requiring a certificate of good conduct from the parish priest of the person to be hired.

Once employed, what did workers earn? Factory wage data for the first half of the nineteenth century pertain only to particular plants or to certain regions. The figures are far from reliable since their origin reaches back to a time when the gathering of statistics did not proceed under rigorous standards of precision and comparability. Even more serious limitations apply to agricultural wage data. The heroic attempts to glean statistical order from these original compilations and to elaborate its meaning are not well known. Two names deserve particular attention: Luigi Bodio, who drudged tirelessly for the General Office of Statistics (Direzione Generale della Statistica) and succeeded in imposing system and sense upon available information; and Pietro Rota, who refined the data and sought their significance for the years from 1847 to 1874.[53]

Sufficient evidence supports the belief that factory wages (which still concerned a very small percentage of Italian workers) reached higher levels during the first half of the nineteenth century than agricultural wages, although those earnings also improved noticeably. Moreover, industrial work resulted in greater income than an equal amount of effort expended at rural handicraft labor.[54]

The level of daily wages is extremely difficult to establish since it varied with the seasons: high when agricultural labor was needed and low during the winter. Locality differentials also occurred, not only varying markedly from city to countryside, as already noted, but also from region to region. Yet, of more importance than the determination of daily nominal wages, which, despite complications, have been measured approximately and are thought to have changed very little during the first half of the nineteenth century, is the estimation of an annual wage. The task bristles with obstacles. The imperfect organization of production resulted in extreme seasonality of work and in very high and low points of industrial activity. As a result, prosperous periods of relatively high wages were succeeded, recurrently and at brief intervals, by times when wages sank so low that they seem completely insufficient to the minimum needs of workers. Worse yet, once full production resumed, wages often lagged far behind their former levels.

The meaning of available statistics is further obfuscated because economists have found it next to impossible to estimate real wages during the years from 1800 to 1860. For want of better evidence, they tend to accept the judgment of Giuseppe Sacchi, expressed in 1845, that wage rates paid in Lombardy could maintain working families decently, and, in a majority of cases, even generously. He also thought them superior to French wage rates of that era. Agreement with Sacchi begins with the proposition that, except for work stoppages like those at Genoa and Milan in 1848 which took place for strictly local reasons, no important demonstrations or strikes, as far as can be determined, insisted upon wage increases. To explain this phenomenon, economists have been led to believe that economic forces did not yet influence wages directly. Tariff protection for manufactured goods was still high; competition was minimal in the secure internal market; the manufacturer could suspend his operations whenever he chose to do so; and wages still constituted only a complementary proportion of the total family income still derived primarily from the land. Moreover, some scholars find evidence to support the notion that real wages probably increased from 1818 to 1849 since world prices fell 45% and nominal wages in Italy remained steady. Unfortunately, this happy persuasion is somewhat dispelled by the contention of other students that international price fluctuations counted for little within Italy's almost closed economy.[55]

Left largely with a series of guesses, it would be well at this point to present specific available bits of evidence, by region, about nominal daily wages of both agricultural and nonagricultural workers, annual wages in these categories, and, where possible, estimated expenditures for basic family needs.

In Piedmont, the average wage of men in workshops has been calculated as 1.35 lire a day. Women and children earned .50 and .40 lira a day there. Weavers and warpers drew .75 lira. Those who regulated the thread were better paid, at rates varying from 2.30 to 3.50 lire. Laborers received from 1 lira to 1.25 lire. Wages of bricklayers varied from 1.80 to 2.25 lire a day, while those for laborers and apprentices in the building trades ranged, in one source of data, from 1.10 to 1.50 lire, while, in another source, it shifted from .60 to .80 lira. If the average earnings of a *skilled* city worker may be said to have fluctuated between 1.80 and 2.30 lire a day, it should be remembered that minimum, indispensible expenditures for an urban working-class family amounted to 1.20 lire daily, or about 438 lire annually. Moreover, before 1860, holidays came more frequently than today. Therefore, the difference between earnings and essential disbursements, except for the most skilled workers, approached zero or fell below that dividing line between bare necessity and destitution.

In the rural areas of Piedmont near Vercelli, farm laborers with steady employment earned from 90 to 100 lire a year and also received moderate quantities of rye, sorghum, rice, and beans. They obtained the use of a house and garden plot, raised chickens, and could glean from the fields. Their lot seemed more than tolerable. But casual laborers of the same vicinity worked under appalling conditions of deadly hours, instability of employment, and perpetual debt. Their wages declined as low as .50 lira a day and shot up as high as 1.45 lire. Average annual earnings were calculated at 346 lire, while the estimate of essential expenditures amounted to 317 lire for the year. This left the casual agricultural laborer with a total annual surplus of 29 lire.

Rota has supplied limited data on average daily minimum and maximum wage levels for Lombardy in 1847 and 1859. His statistics cover casual workers, marble quarrying, and four branches of textile production: linen, cotton, silk, and wool. Average daily textile wages in 1847 extended from a minimum of 1 lira to a maximum of 1.60 lire. By 1859, this spread ranged from 1.45 lire to 1.70 lire.

What standard of living did these wages afford the average worker in Lombardy's textile industry, the most advanced manufacturing activity in all Italy? The laboring population depended upon farinaceous food-stuffs for the major part of its diet and enjoyed meat but rarely. In terms of prices for Milan (1836–1860), bread cost .40 lira a kilogram (2.2 pounds), while wheat retailed at .284 lira a kilogram. (Beef sold for 1 lira a kilogram.) If, as estimated, a family of four annually consumed about 510 kilograms of wheat in the form of pasta and bread, then the average Lombard textile worker in 1847 had to labor 90 full days if he earned maximum wages, and 145 full days if he drew only minimum wages, merely to satisfy the most basic nutritional requirements of his family. By 1859, the comparable number of working days needed to purchase these minimal quantities of wheat had fallen to 85 and 100, reflecting the slight improvement in maximum wages and the marked improvement in minimum wages.

Wages in Central Italy varied from 1.50 to 2.20 lire per day for workers like blacksmiths, day laborers, bricklayers, and carpenters, indicating a daily average of 1.85 lire. Wheat cost 25.50 lire a hectoliter (approximate-ly 165 pounds), or about .34 lira a kilogram. A craftsman earning this average daily wage of 1.85 lire — only slightly higher than the maximum pay of Lombardy's textile factory workers — would have had to devote 94 full days of labor to provide just the basic family requirements of bread and pasta. In the Abruzzi, bordering the Adriatic, a shepherd re-ceived 28 ducati annually (the ducato equalled 4.25 lire), or 119 lire, in addition to bread, oil, salt, and a few skins to cover himself. An ag-ricultural day laborer rarely earned more than .85 lira a day. At this rate, he would have had to assure himself about 204 full days of work to satisfy the minimal staple food needs of his family, measured in terms of wheat.

In the Kingdom of Naples, the level of wages stood high only for skilled craftsmen (1.70 to 1.80 lire). Many of them had been brought from the North to perform tasks then beyond the capabilities of southern workers. According to N.F. Faraglia, who was describing conditions in the Kingdom of Naples, during the period from 1815 to 1860, "wages and salaries, while tending to increase in Europe, have come to dimin-ish among us." He commented that monthly wages of a large number of workers amounted to only 4 (17 lire), 5 (21.25 lire), or 6 (25.50 lire) ducati. He also noted that from 1840 to 1850, in Naples, the highest daily wage of a blacksmith, a carpenter, or a bricklayer was 1.70 lire. It seemed to Faraglia that this compensation might not have equalled the wage enjoyed by arsenal workers in 1636. In 1834, the annual rent at Naples for one room and a kitchen came to 40 ducati (170 lire), equal to 100 full days of work by a skilled craftsman.

Demonstrations, Insurrections, and Strikes. The first strikes recorded by Alfonso Leonetti occurred in North Italy among textile workers during the commercial crisis in the textile industry of 1788 and 1789. In the Province of Como alone, the protest, which reflected fears of prolonged unemployment, affected more than 200 establishments. Hundreds of workers demanded raises in salary and a reduction in hours of work.[56]

Like romanticists seeking the amorous line of verse and skimming the rest, Italian labor historians, who generally tend to follow the Marxian persuasion, must find evidence of militancy among working men and women during the early decades of the nineteenth century. Bowing to this compulsion, they have recorded rather curious strikes and demonstrations. A strike broke out in January of 1817 among the poor lodgers in the Pious House of Industry in Milan and bakeries were attacked. In the same year, the butcher boys of Rome quit their jobs to obtain better working conditions. They possessed, even then, that dramatic verve so sharp among their descendants today. Vaguely cognizant of history and in imitation of their illustrious ancestors, the plebeians of ancient Rome, the butcher boys retired to Monte Pincio with the curious idea that by planting themselves there they would be able to enforce their demands. For the sake of straight record keeping, it should be noted that their forebears had sought the Aventine Hill. With less flare, in the same year typographical workers at Rome refused to render further service as long as they lacked a guaranteed monthly wage. For some years after 1817, labor disturbances, if they occurred, failed to leave durable traces. Then, in 1831, the grain reapers of the Roman countryside achieved notoriety by leaving their scythes in protest against the bad quality of bread and low wages. They undertook a march on Rome to present a petition of grievances to the Pope. However, they were arrested while en route by the Pontifical Police.

These years, although relatively innocent of strikes, lived intimately with political uprisings. The Carbonari societies, already mentioned as pioneers in the political drive for national liberation, had attempted unrehearsed insurrections in Naples and Piedmont in 1821, in Naples again in 1828, in the Papal States in 1829, and in Romagna in 1831. Botched, they all ended in failure. After the eclipse of the Carbonari, the followers of Mazzini in Romagna attempted an insurrection of their own at Bologna in 1843. This uprising ended in relentless suppression, followed by a long series of trials, severe sentences, and seven executions. Nothing daunted, an insurrection erupted at Rimini two years later.

During the next year, 1846, rebellion stirred against the high cost of living in Lombardy, notably in Milan, a city of 160,000 inhabitants. The grain merchants, because of the European crisis, preferred to export their wares to Switzerland or Germany where they derived large profits. As a result, the price of flour increased in Italy, while the cost of bread rose .5 lira a kilogram in Milan. Throughout the countryside, as well as in the cities, crowds assaulted bakeries and grain wagons. They also demonstrated against the grain merchants.

From 1848 to 1860, in Italy as in Europe, revolutions and counter-revolutions alternated, with violence the constant companion of both. On January 3, 1848, conflict flared up between the people and the police at Milan in the wake of a smokers' strike initiated to embarrass the Austrian government financially as well as to protest against its authority. Little more than a week later, Palermo revolted on January 12 and the insurrection triumphed on February 4. A socialist of the Saint-Simon variety, Pasquale Calvi (1794–1867), became the Prime Minister of the provisional government. The February revolution in France and the rebellion in Vienna of March 13 touched off uprisings throughout Italy. On March 17, Venice took arms and proclaimed a republic under Daniele Manin (1804–1857). A new upheaval agitated Milan, beginning on March 18 and known as the Five Days, an event already mentioned in this account. This famous uprising merits elaboration at this point because, for the first time in the unhappy chronicling of Italian patriotic revolts, uncontested evidence appears that workers played an illustrious and principal role. During the course of the insurrection, a total of 480 people died. Of the 426 men who lost their lives, 300 were workers, 81 belonged to the middle classes, and 45 were aristocrats. Of the 54 women who perished, 30 belonged to the working class, 5 to the middle classes, 2 to the aristocracy, while 17 had no classification. Of those wounded, statistics are available only for those who were hospitalized: 733 workers, 141 members of the middle classes, 65 aristocrats, and 26 women without classification.[57] After the Five Days of Milan, barricades fortified the streets of Naples; there, the people held out against Ferdinand II's troops until May 15 when the revolution crumbled. Meanwhile, the spirit of radicalism grew bolder in Rome itself; by the middle of November, insurrection ruled the city; by early February 1849, a constituent assembly proclaimed the Roman Republic. Despite the universal radical fervor and idealism, the end of August saw all revolutionary movements overwhelmed, starved out, and suppressed.

For two whole years, 1848 and 1849, as in earlier and later periods of critical change, all of Italy seemed to have taken to the roads, streets, and piazzas. Inevitably, workers and peasants must have surged in revolt along with aristocratic and middle-class liberals and radicals. These insurrections accorded political freedom priority over all other claims, no matter how urgent. But if organizations dedicated wholly to the welfare of workers, as distinct from the rest of the community, were ever to entrench themselves in Italy, economic, social, and political demands of particular urgency for labor alone would have to take clear precedence over the more general reforms sought by revolutionaries of the privileged upper classes. Not unexpectedly, Italy did move toward this requirement in 1848. As in many other countries during the sharp turns of historical fortune contrived by the modern Fates a century later, economic strikes and demonstrations merged in the piazzas with political discontent.

In February 1848, Florentines demonstrated against a measure which would have obliged advance payment of eight months' rent. On the walls of Florence signs read: "Death to the Rich." In March, the porters and printers in Florence went on strike. In April, clothing workers, organized in military fashion, maneuvered in the streets of Milan demanding better working conditions. At Rome, the unemployed gathered in the piazzas to cry: "Bread and Work." Genoese printers also struck and then the clothing workers (perhaps the first instance in Italy when the employees of an entire industry withdrew their labor at the same time) and the waterfront porters followed their example. The printers of Naples went on strike in April, too. During May, the printers in Turin struck twice, while the shoe workers and clothing workers threatened to strike if their grievances were not satisfied. In Milan, printers demonstrated in front of the headquarters of the provisional government. At Empoli and Lucca, a strike of coachmen took place. Later, the porters at Bologna quit work. In the midst of all these disturbances of ephemeral importance at best, the first true unions, the leagues of resistance (to be discussed later), took root.

Even after the crushing of the uprisings of 1848 and 1849, first by military force and then by the trial and imprisonment or execution of radical leaders, the spirit of political as well as economic rebellion refused to play safe during the next decade. Popular demonstrations took place in Rome on February 1, 1851 in remembrance of the Roman Republic of 1849. In April, the Milanese again attempted to embarrass the Austrian government financially by organizing a smokers' strike. Similar financial strikes spread from Milan to Vicenza, Modena, and Rome. In July, the Bourbon police at Palermo arrested 84 bakers who refused to work unless they received better wages. They had made these demands while commemorating the revolutionary years of 1848 and 1849. The year 1853 witnessed a new revolutionary attempt by the ever-resilient Mazzini at Milan and a fresh failure on February 6. In Piedmont, as well as in the Papal States, the high cost of living, especially reflected in the price of bread, provoked uprisings.

In 1857, Carlo Pisacane (1818–1857), a Neapolitan nobleman whose ideas will soon be discussed, lost his life near Sanza, south of Naples, at the rifle-end of a squad of local police. He and fellow conspirators from Genoa had disembarked at Sapri, hoping to march triumphantly to Naples, where, they were certain, workers had thrown up barricades in revolt against the throne. Instead, their arrival had been anticipated by the well-informed Bourbon police and they were soon sighted by the monarch's soldiers. Pisacane barely escaped the first massacre, but met his doom a few days later. His futile death symbolizes for this entire period the inconsequence of noble acts and lofty gestures. They filled Italian hearts with strong emotion, whether or not they succeeded in bringing freedom and relief to those marked off for deliverance by self-designated saviors. Magnanimous spirits like Pisacane could never harbor the least suspicion that bungled rebellion might actually deepen the misery of the wretched poor they felt obliged to liberate.

Economic and Social Radicalism. The utopian and socialistic thought propounded by a variety of Italian thinkers during the first half of the nineteenth century probably assured the triumph of Marxism among workers and peasants after 1880 by transforming strong notions into familiar bromides through repetition in sundry forms, decade upon decade. Before 1860, few artisans and fewer peasants had been stirred by radical views to precipitate action. Moreover, these doctrines, often closely allied with freemasonry, might have run even less clamorously than they did had not political unrest and surgent nationalism seized the peninsula from the time of Napoleon's triumphs. Thus, Italian nationalism during the *Risorgimento*, like its twentieth-century counterparts, lent to radical thought an infectious strength far beyond its normal powers of penetration.

The economic naïveté betrayed by most patriots of the *Risorgimento* had been preceded by a notable period of intellectual ferment in the eighteenth century. Italian economists, rebelling against feudal rigidities, had engaged in enough challenging speculation to draw the later esteem of Karl Marx, who promptly and Germanically, divided them into the Neapolitan and the Lombard schools. The first group claimed Antonio Genovesi (1712–1769) whose *Lectures in Commerce* (1765), the first comprehensive work on economics produced in Italy, stressed human wants as the basis of economic theory; Ferdinando Galiani (1728–1787) who largely innovated modern theory of value and the historical approach to economics, while opposing the dogmatism of both the mercantilists and the physiocrats; and Gaetano Filangieri (1752–1788) who espoused, in six volumes of his unfinished *Science of Legislation*, the cooperation of social classes — a system founded upon the pre-eminent position of agriculture and maintained through education. The school of Lombardy claimed Pietro Verri (1728–1797) who not only concerned himself with tax systems, monetary theory, and greater freedom for internal trade, but with the concept of economic equilibrium as well; and Cesare Beccaria (1738–1794), the renowned criminologist who also analyzed population problems and anticipated the wage and labor theories of Adam Smith (1723–1790). The importance of agrarian reform was not overlooked by some of these figures who urged the breaking up of large estates for distribution among the greatest possible number of peasants. These men reasoned radically for their day, but their sophisticated approach to intricate economic phenomena disappeared as a process of thought when the economic extremists of the following generation promised new worlds in speech or print at little or no economic cost. This was not to be the sole instance in modern times that excessive patriotic enthusiasm and the life of agitation would insure the failure of historic memory and honest common sense. There would also be, in the fullness of time, Africa, Asia Minor, and the entire gorgeous East.

The agitational doctrines of the Carbonari societies and the socialistic ideas of Claude Saint-Simon (1760–1825) dominated the decade from 1820 to 1830. As noted earlier, the patriotic Carbonari sprang up during the period of the Napoleonic domination of Naples out of the freemasonry of that city. (Freemasons, by subscribing to the traditions of the French Revolution, not only partook naturally in Carbonari activities, but allegedly continued to dominate Italian political life, the press, the armed forces, and even the Socialist Party during the nineteenth and early twentieth centuries.) After the fall of Napoleon, the ranks of the Carbonari filled with a host of malcontents. Although extremely diverse in their political doctrines, they united in their hatred of tyranny, obscurantism, and social inequality. One of the catechism-like tenets of the Carbonari read: "Private property is a crime against the rights of human beings." In Sicily, an association of Carbonari, the "Ultra," was reputed to have exerted influence upon the workers of Palermo. In Apulia, in Southern Italy, a branch of the Carbonari called the "Decided Ones," headed by a priest, believed in economic equality and the immediate partition of all lands among the peasants.

The social and political philosophy of Saint-Simon added to the generous confusion of ideas and ideals. At this time, Italian refugees in London and Paris steeped themselves in his teachings. Two chief centers for the dissemination of his doctrines appeared in Italy, one at Florence and the other at Pisa. From the center at Florence, which received Saint-Simon's writings by way of the port of Leghorn, literature was disseminated to the Riviera and Central Italy. Under the inspiration of Saint-Simon's theories, a secret society, the "Sons of Young Italy," took root in Calabria. Luigi Settembrini (1813–1877), the ardent liberal who conspired against the Neapolitan Bourbons and spent many years in prison, came to be regarded as its most illustrious member. This group of egalitarians felt itself united in spirit with the celebrated Tommaso Campanella (1568–1639), a native of Stilo in Calabria who composed the *City of the Sun* where he developed his socialist views.

The next two decades, 1830 to 1850, pullulated a wide assortment of associations. Reports in the police archives of Lombardy and Venetia revealed that in 1838 a secret society was formed in the Kingdom of Sardinia dedicated to the destruction of religion and property. Police records in the Papal States for 1843 mentioned an organization called the "Avengers of the People." In 1844, another police document discussed the spread of a communist organization into many parts of Italy; its membership allegedly came from among the common people with whom the bourgeois revolutionaries sought to form a close alliance. Almost all Italian police files before 1848 contained frequent references to secret meetings of workers, revolutionaries, and communists — all mentioned as a single species endowed with the same characteristics. Not surprisingly, therefore, the police of the Grand Duke of Tuscany in 1846 pretended to have discovered a secret communist conspiracy, the "Society of Progressive Italians." According to the police reports, the widespread organization proposed to persuade the entire peninsula to accept the leadership of Piedmont's Charles Albert. To their consternation, the police discovered that its members talked of equality and the division of wealth during their meetings instead of devoting themselves to independence and national unity. The police added that the chapter at Ponte a Serchio (Pisa) had adopted as its particular hymn one which resembled the *Song of the Equals* by Darthé. The society is now thought to have been, perhaps, a band of patriots who believed in the principles of Babeuf who held that a small conspiratorial minority could effect large revolutionary changes throughout society.

Two events of intellectual importance to the radical movement occurred in 1847. In Paris, Andrea Luigi Mazzini (1814–1852), not to be confused with the more famous Giuseppe, published *Italy in Its Relation* to *Liberty and Modern Civilization*. On June 14 of that same year, *L'Alba* (*Dawn*), destined to become the leading socialistic journal of politics in Italy, appeared in Florence. Just as *L'Alba* anticipated the imminent birth of a lively, articulate, and prolific radical and labor press, so Mazzini led the way in expounding unadorned socialist and communist doctrine. Acutely aware that political freedom could not live in an impossible economic and social vacuum, purified of the worker and peasant, Mazzini opposed Gioberti's doctrines and challenged as visionary the designs of Giuseppe Mazzini and his followers to transform mankind through republican politics, with Italy in the forefront. He reasoned, quite correctly, that republican idealism flowed from unselfish sacrifice of personal happiness. Precisely because it bubbled from a fountainhead of altruism, it had not stirred, nor could it ever stir, the destitute masses out of their lethargy. Instead, they had to be lured into action and self-organization by specific goals attuned to their immediate, worldly interests. He wrote:

> Italy has never been a revolutionary country in the English or French sense. . . . I have always thought that the Italian people could not become a revolutionary people as long as the revolution had an exclusively political aim; it must have a social aim as well, and a large one. It is for this reason that I am induced to believe that the doctrines of the socialists and the communists are perhaps the only doctrines which can nurture effectively the revolutionary germs among all those people of Italy who have become incapable of progressing, incapable of raising themselves up, incapable of regenerating themselves by means of ideas and interests which do not touch the material and social existence of each one of them.[58]

L'Alba launched the persistent Italian tradition of a radical press, directed by middle-class intellectuals who spoke in the name of all workers. The journal, extensively read and circulated, represented the extreme left-wing of political and social opposition. In a letter to *L'Alba*, where he announced that the *Rhine Gazette* would again be published, Marx wrote: "This newspaper will follow, in our North, the same principles that *L'Alba* represents in Italy." The revolutionary years of 1848 and 1849 produced other newspapers. In Turin, the *Giornale degli Operai* (*Workers' Journal*) appeared. Milan claimed at least four radical newspapers: *L'Operaio* (*The Worker*), *La Politica per il Populo* (*Politics for the People*), *L'Operaio Galantuomo* (*The Worker of Integrity*), and *Il Lombardo* (*The Lombard*). In Bologna, *Il Povero* (*The Poor One*) was founded to defend "socialism as the basis for new democratic government." To the South, in Naples, the newspaper, *Mondo Vecchio e Mondo Nuovo* (*Old World and New World*) published articles on socialism. Three Genoese publications appeared, successively, in 1851,

1852, and 1853: *Il Povero, Il Lavoro* (*Labor*), and *L'Associazione e Lavoro* (*Association and Labor*). Later, in 1854, the weekly *La Ragione* (*Reason*), openly socialist, came from the presses in Turin.

The various governments which had been formed during the popular uprising of 1848 and 1849 reflected the radical dogmas then current. The government at Milan approved a municipal public works program in order to help unemployed weavers. In Venice, Manin is said to have practiced a benevolent socialism by making the rich pay in behalf of the people. With symbolic flair, following French example, Manin invited a tailor to form part of his government. He suggested that this worker become the Minister of Arts and Crafts. In Rome, after the creation of a Ministry of Public Beneficence was proposed, the Pope accused its sponsor of favoring and promoting socialism. In Naples, "Work Houses," modelled on the Phalanxes of Fourier, were envisaged. The cry went round in Sicily to sell the large estates and ecclesiastical properties as the first step in creating a new democracy based on small land holdings. Popular agitation for the cutting up of great estates also grew in Lombardy and in Venetia.

Meanwhile, Italian exiles were returning from France; they brought to the regions where they lived socialist ideas and the spirit of French reform. They spread their ideas in Lombardy as well as in Southern Italy, particularly in Calabria. These propagandists found a public waiting for them in the Popular Circles of the time. Some of the most famous were located in Florence. In June 1848, Alexander Herzen (1812–1870), the famous Russian revolutionary, toured Italy. In a frequently quoted appraisal which did more credit to his heart than his mind, he found that the Italian peasant resembled his Russian brother: they were both exceptions to the rule which prevailed in other countries, for centuries of oppression had failed to brutalize them or disfigure their proud and noble faces.[59]

Carlo Pisacane, who was again in exile, finished writing his four volumes of *Historical, Political, and Military Essays on Italy* in 1855. The third essay was socialist in sentiment and called for a study of revolution. These essays were not printed until 1858–1860, after the death of Pisacane. Just before his departure for Sapri, he had drawn up a political testament. According to this document, the great question of the hour, national liberation, stood inseparable from the social question. Therefore, he framed his famous binomial: "Liberty for the Country and Socialism." Until Pisacane equated national deliverance with socialism, and then socialism with peasant rebellion, little attention had been paid to the peasant as a pivotal economic and social force. As early as 1753, the Academy of the Georgofili was founded in Florence. It was the first institution in Italy to dedicate itself solely to the social and economic aspects of agrarian problems. Hence, the group often found itself in difficulties with the Tuscan government. The Florentine Academy was little emulated in the rest of Italy. Not until 1842 did Piedmont establish the Agraria, modelled directly upon the Georgofili. Until mid-century, so neglected were the social and economic features of agricultural life that historians find it noteworthy enough to mention that in 1846, *L'Ausonio* (*The Italian*), a monthly magazine published by Italian refugees in Paris before it shifted to Naples in 1848, sponsored an article in its second volume on the lot of the peasants of Lower Lombardy. After the failure of Mazzini's attempt at insurrection in Milan on February 6, 1853, a schism first divided and then dissolved the National Italian Committee in London. Those who opposed Mazzini favored a direct appeal to the material interests of the peasants and agitated for an agrarian revolution on the French model of 1789. Four years before Pisacane's scant works were published, Count Stefano Jacini (1827–1891), whose name was to be inseparably linked with the famous government-sponsored agrarian inquiry of the 1870's and 1880's, unveiled to the Italian public the shameful conditions under which the miserable agricultural day laborers of the Po Valley toiled in the rice fields and harvested wheat.

In view of the limited accurate knowledge concerning agriculture and the peasant in his day, Pisacane's insight was all the more startling. So was his versatility. He ran off to England with another man's young wife. While in London, he arrived at Karl Marx's leading ideas independently since he was familiar with the coming master's writings only in small part. This aristocratic forerunner of Italian socialism concerned himself in unique fashion with the potential role of the peasant in the cause of Italy's freedom. Pisacane held that emancipation could not be achieved, either in spirit or in fact, through the diplomatic maneuvers of politicians, the mystic republicanism of Mazzini and his liberal disciples, or the well-publicized exploits of Garibaldi. Instead, he maintained that only a national insurrection by Italy's numerous peasantry would have the inherent force to create true and lasting liberty. However, ignorant and diffident peasants could never be fired by the ideal of political freedom. Yet, they did have the capacity, under guidance, to recognize their closest enemy, the landowner. Once convinced that the landlord could be overthrown, the peasant would liberate Italy by freeing himself. The ruling dynasties throughout the peninsula would then necessarily crumble. In short, Pisacane's perceptions emphasized class hatred, the increasing misery of the poor, the growing prosperity of the rich, impatience with liberal reform, and economic discontent as the dynamic elements in social change. Pisacane's ideas are rehearsed here neither because they came from Italy's first modern socialist, nor because they constitute a more realistic, "scientific," or successful recipe for revolution than the slogans shouted by the ebullient liberals and radicals at odds with Pisacane. Obviously, given the nature of Pisacane's death, his ideas on rebellion had no salvation value, even to himself. They became prized by others years after his death when Marxian doctrines grew attractive to Italians. Yet they are relevant at this particular point of discussion because they reveal a special concern for Italy's numerous, retarded, apathetic, and neglected peasants as a potential source of progress. Without them, no labor movement could truly represent the workers of Italy, late or soon.[60]

The Institutions of Conservatism. By the beginning of the eighteenth century, most medieval guilds had already lost many of their former political, military, legal, and economic attributes. They survived largely on the strength of tradition. Their members satisfied themselves with spiritual and charitable good deeds. With ceremonial self-importance, they honored dead members and celebrated the birthdays of their patron saints. As early as the seventeenth century, the so-called pious unions (*unioni pie*) in both Italy and France, organized according to crafts and trades and encouraged by the ecclesiastical authorities, seem to have existed alongside the older guilds. They gave aid to old, sick, and unemployed members.

Authorities differ from book to monograph and from treatise to essay on the venerability, nature, and accomplishments of various "universities," "communities," "companies," and "unions," pious or otherwise, whose names, charters, or institutions have survived to tweak our curiosity. Sufficient to the needs of this history will be a brief review of the more ancient societies, for they illustrate poignantly both the persistent human need for organizations dedicated to mutual assistance and the ability of some of these institutions to endure across the centuries despite wars and revolutions.

The Pious Union of Tailors and Tailoresses of Jesus dated its beginnings from 1628. In that same year, master coachmakers and saddlers in Turin organized themselves into the Company of S. Eligio; they took the name of the Pious Union of Master Coach Blacksmiths in 1783. In Turin, too, the following groups claimed existence from the time indicated: The University of Woodworkers (*minusieri*) which later became the Mutual Association of Master Carpenters, Cabinetmakers, and Coachmakers, 1636; the Community of Master Blacksmiths (*serraglieri*) which later became the Mutual Aid Society of Blacksmiths, 1689; the Pious Union of Journeymen Shoemakers, 1700; the Pious Union of Journeymen Blacksmiths which later became the Society for Mutual Aid, Instruction, and Placement of Journeymen Blacksmiths, 1717. The Pious Union of Hatters was also organized at Turin in 1736. The group aided sick members and those who were unable to work because of old age or chronic disabilities. It also furnished modest funds to comrades who found it necessary to travel in search of work; it made grants, as well, to travelling hatters who found themselves in Turin, strangers and unemployed. In 1737, the hosiery workers of Turin established a common fund for mutual aid. The origin of the Pious Union of Printers in Turin is said to date from the early years of the eighteenth century. Records also attest to a meeting of four members of the organization in 1738 at the monastery of the Augustinian Fathers where they elected Saint Augustine as their patron and, taking a solemn vow in the name of their confreres, obligated themselves to assist each other with fraternal charity. They not only provided help to sick members, but also supported members who had paid dues for fifteen years and could no longer work because of old age or serious disabilities. Either in 1744 or 1748, a Society of Coachmen and Grooms came to light. The Society of Black Capes and the Society of Liveried Servants, both pious unions, started up at Modena in 1757. The foundation of the Pious Typographical Institute in Lombardy took place in 1804.

The closing years of the eighteenth century witnessed additional expressions of concern by conservatives for workmen, entirely outside the sphere of pious unions. They command attention as foretokens of a coming age of prolific but inadequate social welfare activities, rather than as ideas and developments of intrinsic importance at the time. In trying to deal with unemployment, various governmental authorities already granted direct aid to the unemployed, reopened shut-down plants as community projects, instituted public works programs, provided credit to afflicted factories, forbade the firing of workers, and granted special protection and privileges to industries as a way of tiding them over the crisis. Then, in 1788, the Academy of Sciences of Turin set out to study means that might be adopted to sustain unemployed workers in the unstable silk industry when they were reduced to indigence through no fault of their own. The inquiry elicited 68 replies. Some of the proposals limited themselves to immediate remedies, but others looked toward fundamental reforms whereby assistance, hitherto regarded as pure charity or beneficence, would give way to social insurance. Forward-looking plans called for the establishment of a fund to be filled and replenished either by the sole contributions of workmen, or by the joint contributions of both employers and employees. These suggestions never materialized because the revolutionary movement erupted in Piedmont during the last years of the century. However, the preoccupation of a few of the larger Italian cities with workers' housing did result in the building of such dwellings at Turin in 1781. The master builders of the city first undertook this task. When they failed to raise the necessary capital, they turned the execution of the plans over to an order of priests, which, after receiving special concessions from the royal authorities for obtaining money, preferred to rent the best accommodations to tenants who were not workers. At this point, government officials intervened and themselves administered the project, basing rentals on the cost of construction, subsidies apart.[61]

Around 1815, a philosophy of "philanthropism" began to attain prominence among the more liberal members of the wealthier middle classes. The doctrine espoused the principle that men with wealth had to assume responsibility for the less fortunate. Adherents placed their faith upon social moderation.

Perhaps the savings bank movement, which began in Lombardy, spread to Piedmont, and eventually found its way to other centers of North and Central Italy, best illustrates the practical application of philanthropism. On the initiative of the Austrian government, the Savings Bank of the Lombard Provinces (*cassa di risparmio*) was founded in 1823. The policy of the directors provided that the bank would invest one part of its funds in government bonds, make another part available as loans to benevolent institutions, and loan the remainder to landed proprietors. The sponsors did not intend the bank as a commercial venture, but rather as an institution of charity. However, as early as 1829, suspicion arose that those benefitting most from its activities were the small capitalists, merchants, landowners, public employees, and domestic servants — not the poor. Day laborers and artisans had acquired neither sufficient foresight nor high enough earnings to achieve savings and hence deposits in the bank. Those elements which gained from the bank's services were undoubtedly attracted by the 4% interest rate. To preclude this possibility, the rate was lowered to 3% in 1830. By 1836, the maximum limit for a single account was reduced from 300 to 75 lire since the lowered interest rate had not produced the desired effects. By 1840, publicists in Lombardy called for a printed list of depositors, similar to that already disclosed in Bologna, because of the continuing rumor that large depositors still persisted. Despite these difficulties, the movement continued to grow. In 1846, Lombardy-Venetia claimed 22 of the 83 savings banks in Italy.

Neither the philosophy nor program of moderation went unchallenged. An anonymous pamphlet of 1847 denounced philanthropism and warned the people against the rich and their flunkies who preached moderation. The pamphlet ended with a "Declaration of the Rights of Man," the very one delivered by Robespierre to the Jacobin Club. In Tuscany, during the same year, Guerrazzi, railed against philanthropism and the new "Tartuffes." He was already organizing the artisans of Leghorn along craft lines.

The forces of moderation were nothing daunted; in fact, radical excesses stiffened their resolution. In 1846, Massimo D'Azeglio (1798–1866) published a brochure *On Recent Events in Romagna*. In this short work, he blamed the revolutionary movement for the Mazzini-inspired insurrection at Rimini the year before. He proposed, as a substitute for violence, a program of reformist nature. This short but important work inspired the formation of the Moderate Party as the chief opposition to the Action Party of Mazzini and Garibaldi.

Nor did radical criticism deter Count Cavour. In January 1859, he spoke in behalf of legislation calling for the creation of a Fund for Old-Age Annuities. He declared that wherever "savings banks and mutual aid associations exist, an old-age annuity fund must complete the welfare system which does not have as its basis the charity of the more fortunate, or as its instrument their donations, but is based upon insurance and is nourished by savings."[62]

Class Collaboration. Irony never long absents itself from human affairs. The philosophy and practice of class collaboration, not unrelated to the conservative spirit of reform, found its most brilliant, if not most lasting, expression among radicals. The Union of Italian Workers, a section of Mazzini's "Young Italy" formed in 1831, furnished the first example of the philosophy of associationism proposed by Mazzini. His mystique of the social bond between workers and employers, never clear at any point in his career, achieved its greatest influence after 1860. A fuller discussion of Mazzini's alternative to the Marxian doctrine of class warfare will therefore be postponed.

The spirit of class collaboration possessed the mutual aid societies. They had sprung up on their own and without benefit of Mazzini's influence during the first half of the nineteenth century. Before describing the purpose and development of these associations — the most numerous and characteristic organizations of workers before 1880 — it is necessary to explore the right of association in the Italian states. Prior to national unity, obviously no uniform legislation existed which could perform the function of France's Le Chapelier law of June 17, 1791. This edict prohibited the de facto revival of guilds, which had theoretically been abolished with the adoption of the Constitution, among citizens of the same craft, trade, or profession. The Le Chapelier law reflected the legal doctrine then prevalent that society recognized only individual and national interests in the field of economic activity. It held any action or compact, which tended to favor a group of persons, economically inimical to the right of work and therefore justifiably subject to prohibition.

While discussing the abolition of the guilds, two observations must be made: (1) Even at the height of their powers, considerable distances separated the aims enunciated by the guilds and the goals they achieved. To draw conclusions from their regulations is invalid; it is also necessary to test the enforcement of these rules. There is no other procedure for determining whether or not they constituted a restraint upon trade and commerce. (2) The strength of the guilds, especially during the seventeenth and eighteenth centuries, when they were in marked decline, has been exaggerated by the advocates of laissez faire. But exaggeration must not be taken for truth. Until the eighteenth century, open criticism of the guilds came infrequently. However, the eighteenth century gave voice to systematic and persistent criticisms. While the reformation of the guilds in Italy began as limitations upon certain kinds of behavior and involved relatively minor questions of detail, later the changes became organic and radical, influencing the very essence of the guilds as institutions. As laissez faire doctrines took shape, guild criticism eventually acquired theoretical prestige. Cesare Beccaria, the famous criminologist and economist already singled out, observed that the guilds, like all other things, hardly ever prospered when they exercised monopolistic control.

Although the guilds during the eighteenth century thus suffered from assaults upon their day-to-day operations as well as upon their intellectual foundations, changes in their character and force varied from state to state. In the Kingdom of the Two Sicilies, the economist, G. M. Galanti, although most acute in his observations concerning the obstacles which impeded the development of agriculture, had no concern about the guilds. The almost exclusively rural nature of the Kingdom, the absence of true cities, and the essentially agricultural nature of most town and village centers very likely explain his lack of interest. Moreover, the guilds in the Kingdom accentuated, more than anywhere else and at the expense of professional functions, their religious activities and their mutual assistance programs. No great need to suppress them ever arose;

they disappeared without bother after a series of acts which culminated in Ferdinand I's (1751–1825, king 1816–1825) final decree of October 23, 1821. In the Kingdom of Sardinia, the guilds were not legally abolished until 1844. But it is well to recall that Piedmont, even in the eighteenth century, possessed a strong constitution and a fairly efficient government. The Crown did not hesitate to temper or root out abuses whenever they occurred. In dominating the guilds effectively, the State rendered their monopolistic character less offensive. The Senate of Venice, as early as 1719, had listened attentively to proposals to open certain guilds to wider membership. The courts there, as well as writers and economists, helped the process along. One of the principal Venetian economists, Giammaria Ortes, elaborated a theory based on the principle of complete freedom of work. Florence abolished many powers of the guilds in 1770. Although the legislation did not signify their complete suppression, other laws dealing with freedom of commerce made devastating inroads into the monopolistic regulations of the guilds. Lombardy stripped the powers of the guilds without ceremony by a series of partial measures effected from 1773 to 1787. In the Papal States, Pius VII gradually weakened the guilds through a group of solemn acts promulgated during the first decade of the nineteenth century. Beginning with food supplies and fats, the Pope's guild reforms dovetailed with other laws establishing freedom of internal commerce. Meanwhile, the Napoleonic régime in Italy imposed upon all regions subject to its powers the principle of complete freedom of work as incorporated into the complex of Napoleonic legislation and in conformance with the property concepts found in the civil code. In brief, between the second half of the eighteenth century and the early years of the nineteenth century, the powers of the guilds declined toward infirmity. Later attempts in certain states during the Restoration to revive them failed.

Without question, the suppression of the guilds blessed subsequent economic development. Whether their destruction had wholly benign effects upon workers as well is open to serious doubt. The guilds did protect the rights of their own immediate members. Among them were many independent artisans. As the enfeebled guilds degenerated as instruments of defense, these artisans stood exposed before the unfamiliar attacks brought on by freer competition. The guilds had also exercised welfare and insurance functions. With their disappearance, a social fissure emerged into the open and was filled in the course of time by the organization of mutual aid societies.[63]

The passing of the guilds also left the entire issue of the right of association unclarified. In Piedmont, as has been noted, the guilds were abolished by royal decree in 1844. The Constitution of 1848, the famous *Statuto,* guaranteed the "liberty to unite peacefully and without arms. . . ." No distinctions could be drawn from this phraseology between trade, craft, or professional organizations — groups with present-day labor union characteristics — and those societies with strictly fraternal and benevolent purposes. Theoretical doubts vanished with the removal of Articles 483 to 486 from the penal code. These clauses had proscribed any religious, literary, or political association constituted without the permission of competent authorities. From that time on, jurists and politicians deduced that Italian public law — after 1860, the Constitution of Piedmont became the Constitution of Italy — recognized implicitly the right of association. Yet, in actual practice, the principle was not this readily identified. Both before and after unification, large and arbitrary powers remained in the hands of local governmental authorities who often felt free to dissolve associations at their whim. When, on May 29, 1864, the Italian Parliament approved legislation which suppressed all societies, companies, fellowships, unions, associations, assemblies, groups, and other similar privileged trade, craft, and professional guilds of workers located in the Kingdom under whatsoever denomination, the death of the guilds in Italy received the courtesy of national burial. Unfortunately, the right of association by labor groups remained vague and uncertain.[64]

Mutual aid societies began to form in earnest during the early part of the nineteenth century; by and large, they did not take on class-conscious character. As voluntary organizations, they admitted persons engaged in trades or professions, including masters and employers. Most of the societies welcomed craftsmen of all callings, not unlike the mixed assemblies of the Knights of Labor in the United States after the Civil War. This practice grew out of expediency. Except in the most important industrial centers, no other form of organization would have been feasible. Indeed, only in the larger cities were examples found of societies limited to one craft or trade. Organization of societies occurred among printers, hatters, coachmen, hairdressers, weavers in silk, gold, and silver, and bookbinders. Doctors, surgeons, and master shoemakers also formed themselves into mutual aid societies. These Italian groups took life from the same motive which quickened similar institutions in the United States, Western Europe, and England: the "ancient and most laudable custom for divers artists . . . to meet and form themselves into societies for the sole purpose of assisting each other in cases of sickness, old age, and other infirmities, and for the burial of their dead."[65]

It is difficult to establish with any high degree of exactitude the precise time when mutual aid societies first came into existence. Before 1860, sources of information are both sparse and unofficial; they cannot pretend to present full coverage. After 1860, the data offered by both official and private agencies for earlier years vary considerably not only among themselves but even within the figures published from time to time by a single agency. Moreover, in any given year, the time of origin of only those societies still existing in that particular year is tabulated. Thus, societies which had fallen away before the time of survey would not be included in the statistics concerning the decade of origin. This limitation holds true for the figures revealed in the following table.[66]

Mutual Aid Societies in Existence on December 31, 1904 According to the Period of Their Foundation.

Period of Foundation	Total Number of Societies
Before 1500	5*
1500–1599	3
1600–1699	8
1700–1799	10
1800–1849	38
1850–1859	174

* (1) Agricultural Worker Society, Rivara, Torino province, 1379; (2) Society of Carpenters and Blacksmiths, Faenza, Ravenna province, 1410; (3) Veneto Mutual Aid Society of Calkers of the Royal Arsenal of Venice, 1454; (4) Calkers of the Port of Genoa, 1456; (5) Society of Shoemakers and Allied Trades, Faenza, 1474. The next oldest society, that of the Goldsmith and Silversmith Masters of Rome, dates from 1509.

In order to indicate the distribution of mutual aid societies according to geographical regions, as well as by date of origin, a different source of information had to be used. The total figures in the table on page 62 vary from those in the above table, but they are useful because of the insight they provide regarding the leadership of North Italy.

Before 1850, the Kingdom of Sardinia could lay claim to 35% of the mutual aid societies. Surprisingly, at first glance, the Kingdom contained 69% of all societies extant between 1850 and 1860. Many Italian economists and historians tend to be legalistic in their thinking. They have sought to ascribe the predominance of Piedmontese societies to the right of association theoretically guaranteed by the liberal Constitution of 1848. Others of a more political bent of mind tread firmer ground. They maintain that official government policy encouraged the societies and showed open sympathy for them, especially after the rise of Cavour to power. He adopted this device as a means of improving the economic welfare of the members of mutual aid societies and so wed them to the existing political and social structure. He saw their prosperous growth as insurance against subversive ideas.

Classification of Mutual Aid Societies
According to Region and Time of Origin.

Region	Before 1850	1850–1860
Peidmont	17	98
Liguria	—	9
Lombardy	4	27
Veneto	9	7
Emilia	7	6
The Marches	1	1
Umbria	1	—
Tuscany	4	6
Lazio	2	—
Abruzzi e Molise	1	—
Campania	—	2
Puglie	—	—
Basilicata	—	—
Calabria	—	—
Sicily	2	—
Sardinia	—	2
	48	158

Certainly this view prevailed in Lombardy among forward-looking public figures. They agreed that the working population needed some form of self-organized protection. The already functioning mutual aid societies engendered most discussion and received widest support. Gottardo Calvi, one of the editors of *Rivista Europea,* proposed that the annual meetings of the Congress of Italian Scientists stimulate and regulate this movement by drafting a model constitution for the societies. The magazine opened its pages to discussion and called for information about all mutual aid societies in Italy and abroad. Some members of the Congress of Italian Scientists opposed Calvi's idea. They took alarm at the endorsement of mutual aid societies since by this act they would interfere with the principles of laissez faire and so hamper the expansion of industry. Nonetheless, the Lucca congress of 1843 appointed a committee to investigate the recommendation, with Calvi at its head. Throughout the year, Calvi searched vigorously for material through the pages of his magazine and championed the cause of mutual aid societies with enthusiasm. He presented a report to the Milan conference of 1844 entitled, *Societies of Mutual Aid Existing in Italy, Report to the Sixth Scientific Congress, by G. Calvi.*[67] Advocates of the mutual aid societies most carefully emphasized their hostility to the French *compagnonnages* — secret societies of bachelor craftsmen which linked the medieval guilds and modern unions, then in bad repute because of the disorders caused by them in France — and to the guilds. They insisted that they favored mutual aid societies as an act of conservatism, justice to labor, and precaution against impairment of the social system. Moreover, such encouragement to labor had to be viewed as a measure of charity and a fulfillment of a debt of honor to the struggling poor. In this spirit, the friends of labor even proposed that wealthy patrons be appointed to supervise the use of mutual aid society funds. As Greenfield remarked, those who favored the societies would have opposed strenuously the free organization of labor with purposes other than mutual aid.[68]

Responding to the natural play of events, mutual aid societies sought to federate on a city-wide basis and later to establish a national confederation of mutual aid societies. On the morrow of the revolutionary events of 1848, a General Association of Workers formed at Turin. Article 2 of its constitution read: "The society has as its purpose brotherhood and mutual aid among workers themselves; it tends to promote education, morality, and welfare, and in so doing, to cooperate effectively for the public good."[69] A General Association of Mutual Aid Societies raised its banner in Milan during the same year, following the city's liberation. It disbanded when the Austrians retook Milan and was not reconstituted until January 1, 1860.

The first attempt to federate existing mutual aid societies on a wider scale originated in October 1850. Not until 1853, however, did Stefano Boldrini, a lawyer from Vigevano, and his brother Vincenzo, succeed in establishing annual congresses on a formal basis. Representatives of some 30 societies from the Piedmont region attended the first convention, held at Asti on October 17–19. The assembly was concerned primarily with questions of social welfare and mutual assistance. During the following six years, other regional conventions took place at Alessandria (October 1854), Genoa (November 23–25, 1855), Vigevano (1856), Voghera (September 1857), Vercelli (October 2–4, 1858), and Novi (October 1859) in Piedmont, where the overwhelming majority of societies flourished.[70]

Emerging Cooperatives and Unions. In the wake of the revolutionary zeal of 1848, associations were formed in Italy to establish workshops owned in common by their members. Worker-stockholders organized other plants. The Industrial Mechanical Social Factory of Working Blacksmiths in Turin was a typical example of this variation. The Social Printing House (Stamperia Sociale), encouraged by the publisher, Pomba, seemed to take on the characteristics of a producer cooperative. However, Ugo Rabbeno and Salvatore Fenicia, the two leading authorities on cooperation during this early period, consider the Society of Artistic Glassware (Società Artistica Vetraria) the first true producer cooperative of importance. On Christmas night of 1856, Giuseppe Cesio took the lead in bringing together 84 artisans of this ancient craft in Altare. They proposed to better their lot, greatly threatened by economic depression and the aftermath of the cholera epidemic, through the formation of a cooperative association. The ritual which elaborated this declaration of purpose suggested the revival of the medieval tradition of this region of Liguria where, around the year 1000, there sprang up the famous guild of Altare which survived until its suppression by King Carlo Felice (1765–1831, king 1821–1831) on June 6, 1823. Although Fenicia states that the Altare venture remained alone among producer cooperatives until 1874, Rabbeno cites the Printing House of Compositors (Stamperia dei Compositori Tipografici), founded in 1859 in Turin, as the second oldest producer cooperative.

Both Fenicia and Rabbeno place little emphasis on those consumer cooperatives which grew up prior to 1860 since they were not endowed with the principles of the Rochdale pioneers. Nor do they accord true cooperative designation to those committees and stores of foresight (*comitati e maggazini di previdenza*) which mutual aid societies, municipalities, or middle-class subscription funds organized to sell necessities at low prices, thus forcing the regular merchants to reduce their prices. Nonetheless, the distinction of creating the first consumer cooperative on record must go to the Workers Society of Pinerolo in Piedmont which, organized in 1849, set up its own store of foresight in that same year. Since cooperative ventures, like mutual aid societies, drew official encouragement in Piedmont, the societies fathered pioneering cooperative groups in Castellamonte, Savigliano, Venaria Reale, Caselle Torinese, Ciriè, Villarbasse, and Fossano. All authorities concede that the consumer cooperative sponsored by the General Association of Workers in Turin in 1853 achieved particular fame. Forty founding members provided the modest capital by purchasing redeemable shares valued at one lira each. They opened their first store on October 4, offering limited quantities of spaghetti, flour, rice, and wine for sale. Out of this four-string start grew the later hegemonic Turin Cooperative Alliance. There is record of two consumer cooperatives coming into existence during 1854: one in Alessandria and another established by railroad workers of Piedmont. This early alliance of workers associations and mutual aid societies with the cooperative movement established from the very start the two-sides-of-one-coin feature of working-class activity in Italy. It presaged the strong fraternal bonds which later made inseparable the destinies of cooperatives and unions. This single instance of persistent characteristics illustrates the constancy of special attributes throughout the history of the Italian labor movement.[71]

On May 7, 1848, the primitive period of Italian labor reached a turning point. Forty Turinese printers, all workers, founded the Society of Printing Compositors under the leadership of Vincenzo Steffenone. Just before this pioneering event, they had reached agreement with their employers on hours and wages: a weekly minimum wage of 16 lire based on a 40-hour week. The first aim of the society, which also accounts for its coming into being, centered in the members' determination to protect the provisions of the agreement against possible future impairment by the employers. The society also proposed to advance progress in the graphic arts and to provide financial help to members who were unemployed or chronically ill. The Turin printers, by limiting their adherents to workers alone and by adding economic self-interest to the mutual aid society formula of furthering professional progress and group benevolence, anticipated by a generation the prevailing nature of Italian unionism.

Little is known about the association of women workers sponsored at Turin in 1852 by the General Association of Workers. In the same year, the Genoese printers followed the example of their Turinese brothers and founded a society with a similar purpose. The following year, 1853, saw the birth of the General Consociation of Workers in Liguria which, in time, became the Genoese Confederation of Labor. The textile workers of Croce Mosso (Biella) joined together in a mutual aid society ten years later. The authorities banned the group more than once since it persisted in acting like the later leagues of resistance, stirring up demonstrations and promoting strikes.

Rinaldo Rigola believed that freedom of association in Piedmont stimulated the flowering of mutual aid societies and the cooperatives they cherished. The assertion fails to recognize the more positive state policy of encouragement and is weakened thereby. The two elements combined possess sufficient logic not only to explain the flourishing of benevolent and cooperative activities among Piedmont's workers, but also to make clear why the printers of Turin and Genoa founded unions with economic goals, under the *Statuto* and Cavour's eye, while their peers in Milan under the Austrians did not. However, these factors do not explain why printers, rather than silk throwers or longshoremen, were the first to arrive at a common understanding with their employers about hours and wages.

Rigola afforded insight here. He stressed two prerequisites for organizations like those of the printers: (1) Workers must earn a wage not so meager that they can barely sustain themselves. Otherwise, neither independence of spirit based upon savings nor ability to spare money for dues can develop. (2) They must also possess a modest fund of education. The working class of Piedmont itself — even after the right of association had been granted — lacked these two requirements in overwhelming part. This universal circumstance for all Italian regions necessarily restricted the growth of mutual aid societies, cooperatives, and unions to a very limited circle of craftsmen in shops and highly skilled workers in the still rare factories of town and countryside.[72] Thus, as late as 1860, Italian labor organizations resembled those in the more advanced parts of Western Europe, England, and the United States many years earlier when friendly and benevolent societies among artisans preceded the more militant phases of union development. Italy also followed a pattern common to Western Europe and England when budding cooperatives aligned themselves with mutual aid societies. Even the pioneering society of printers in Turin with its concern for both economic improvement and welfare-insurance benefits had at least one counterpart at a comparable stage of development in the United States. The Philadelphia Typographical Society, organized in 1802 — one of the earliest American labor organizations which endured for awhile — made successful wage demands of its employers and also provided payments to the sick and funeral aid to families of deceased members.[73]

FOOTNOTES — CHAPTER II

[1] In the literature of the *Risorgimento,* Piedmont is often referred to as the Kingdom of Sardinia. This interchange of terminology took place after that then desolate, malarial island was added to Piedmont's miniature realm by an award of the European powers in 1720.

[2] Witt Bowden, Michael Karpovich, and Abbott Payson Usher, *An Economic History of Europe since 1750,* p. 266.

[3] Quoted in Roberto Tremelloni, *Storia dell'industria italiana contemporanea dalla fine del settecento all'unità italiana,* p. 180, footnote 2.

[4] Cecil Sprigge, *The Development of Modern Italy,* p. 24.

[5] H. Stuart Hughes, *The United States and Italy,* Chapter 3, "The Legacy of History"; Istituto Centrale di Statistica, *Sommario di statistiche storiche italiane 1861–1955,* p. 105.

[6] Appendix A, Table 7 of this study; UNESCO, *Monographs on Fundamental Education — XI,* "World Illiteracy at Mid-Century," pp. 38–41. See also Alfonso Leonetti, *Mouvements ouvriers et socialistes (chronologie et bibliographie): L'Italie (des origines à 1922),* p. 35; *Annuario statistico italiano 1886,* "Introduzione," p. lxii; Humbert L. Gualtieri, *The Labor Movement in Italy,* pp. 10–11; Nello Rosselli, *Mazzini e Bakounine: 12 anni di movimento operaio in Italia (1860–1872),* pp. 20–23.

[7] *Annuario statistico italiano 1886,* p. 957. In 1861–1862, 1,008,674 children were enrolled in private and public elementary schools.

[8] Rosselli, cited above, p. 22; Kent Roberts Greenfield, *Economics and Liberalism in the Risorgimento*, p. 37.

[9] *Commons Papers*, 1839, Vol. XVI, p. 460 (Cd. 165, p. 40).

[10] Giuseppe Garibaldi, *Autobiography of Giuseppe Garibaldi*, Vol. II, p. 147.

[11] Luigi Dal Pane, *Storia del lavoro in Italia dagli inizi del secolo xviii al 1815*, p. 380, translation of passage by M. F. Neufeld; Rosselli, cited above, p. 38.

[12] Hughes, cited above, p. 41.

[13] Greenfield, cited above, *Introduction*, p. xi.

[14] Tremelloni, cited above, pp. 112–113.

[15] The same, p. 123, footnote 1.

[16] Clive Day, *Economic Development in Europe*, p. 613; Tremelloni, cited above, pp. 9–10, 151, and 156; Greenfield, cited above, pp. 84–90.

[17] Greenfield, cited above, p. 94.

[18] The same, p. 36.

[19] Rondo E. Cameron, "French Finance and Italian Unity: the Cavourian Decade," *American Historical Review*, Vol. LXII, No. 3 (April 1957), pp. 552–553; Alfonso Leonetti, cited above, p. 37; Tremelloni, cited above, pp. 166–167.

[20] Tremelloni, cited above, pp. 163–164; p. 168, footnotes 3 and 4.

[21] Antonio Fossati, *Lavoro e produzione in Italia*, pp. 88–91.

[22] Even as late as 1839, the number of steam engines in Lombardy could be counted on the fingers of two hands. See Tremelloni, cited above, p. 174.

[23] The Napoleonic Kingdom of Italy included North Italy, except Piedmont and Liguria, which belonged to France proper; also, the Adriatic coast down to the borders of the Kingdom of Naples. Tuscany and the region of Rome were also part of France.

[24] Tremelloni, cited above, p. 69.

[25] Tremelloni, cited above, pp. 114–115, footnote 2. The book by Babbage was published in London by Charles Knight in 1832, while the Italian edition was published in Florence in 1834. The book by Jones was published in London by J. Murray in 1831.

[26] Tremelloni, pp. 112–113. Tremelloni's work-force data for 1850 are based upon estimates made by Cesare Correnti and Pietro Maestri in their *Annuario* of 1853. No figures concerning the number of artisans in Tuscany, Veneto, or the Duchies of Parma and Modena were supplied by them. The population figures ascribed to the various states by Tremelloni refer to the year 1858. The total population estimate for 1858 is taken from *Annuario statistico italiano 1911*, p. 4.

[27] The picture of economic stagnation which follows is based primarily upon the account in Tremelloni, cited above, especially pp. 220–228; also Clive Day, cited above, pp. 612–614, 617–618. Tremelloni presents statistics concerning industrial development on pp. 228–245.

[28] Luigi Bianchini, as quoted by Tremelloni, cited above, p. 221; translation of passage by M. F. Neufeld.

[29] The quotations in this section are derived from Tremelloni, cited above, p. 251; translation of passages by M. F. Neufeld.

[30] Tremelloni, cited above, pp. 253–254.

[31] Greenfield, cited above, p. 59.

[32] The same, p. 1.

[33] The same, p. 31.

[34] The same, pp. 93–94; Tremelloni, cited above, p. 137, footnote 2.

[35] Tremelloni, cited above, pp. 72–73.

[36] The same, p. 181, footnote 1.

[37] "The guilds had been abolished in 1787, and the efforts of the employers to obtain a renewal of some of the discarded legal disciplines during the Napoleonic era had fallen to the ground." Greenfield, cited above, p. 138, footnotes 78 and 79,

where it is stated that Eugène Tarlé places the abolition of the guilds later, during the Napoleonic régime.

38 Greenfield, cited above, p. 174, footnote 22.

39 The same, pp. 108–109, 127, 130–131, and 149–150.

40 The same, pp. 95–152; Tremelloni, cited above, pp. 179–206.

41 Tremelloni, cited above, p. 182, footnote 2.

42 Greenfield, cited above, p. 95, footnote 1.

43 Tremelloni, cited above, p. 113.

44 The same, pp. 206–210; passage translated by M. F. Neufeld.

45 Cameron, cited above, pp. 556–558. The results of these efforts with regard to the building of railroads in Piedmont are shown by the calculations reported by Ferdinando Milone, L'Italia nell'economia delle sue regioni, p. 75. Between 1839 and 1860, the average annual increase in railroad trackage, as measured in meters per square kilometer of area, was 1,122 for Piedmont as against 365 for the rest of Italy.

46 According to Cameron, in the article cited above, the gold lira was equal to the gold franc and was worth about 20 cents in pre-1914 gold dollars. No accurate way of measuring the lira's value in terms of present-day currencies exists, but it can be said that the purchasing power of the gold lira or franc in 1850 was roughly the same as that of the United States dollar in 1950.

47 Cameron, cited above, p. 568. See also, Tremelloni, cited above, p. 136, footnote 1. Tremelloni states that during the Napoleonic period there were only 2 anonime in Piedmont. By 1864, half of all the capital of commercial anonime in Italy was ascribed by Correnti and Maestri in the Annuario of that year to the ex-Kingdom of Sardinia. Toward 1860, the 281 Italian anonime had an estimated capital of 1,149,000,000 lire, while the 96 accomandite might have had a capital of 203,000,-000 lire. In Lombardy, in 1845, 21 anonime were cited as functioning in Milan with a capital of 70,000,000 Austrian lire, three-quarters of which was invested in transport enterprises.

48 Tremelloni, cited above, p. 128, footnote 4; passage translated by M. F. Neufeld.

49 The same, p. 128, footnote 3; passage translated by M. F. Neufeld.

50 Roberto Tremelloni, Storia recente dell'industria italiana, pp. 7–9.

51 Fossati, cited above, pp. 91–92.

52 Rosselli, cited above, pp. 23–24; Tremelloni, Storia dell'industria italiana contemporanea . . . , pp. 141–144.

53 For the work of Bodio, see Annali di statistica, Serie I, Vol. VI, 1875; for the study by Rota, see "Contribuzione per una statistica delle mercedi," in Annali di statistica, Serie IIIa, Vol. XIV, 1885. For wage data concerning the second half of the nineteenth century, and, therefore, the decade from 1850 to 1860, see A. Geisser and E. Magrini, "Contribuzione alla storia e statistica dei salari industriali in Italia nella seconda metà del secolo XIX," in La Riforma Sociale, 1904, p. 852.

54 Tremelloni, cited above, p. 138.

55 This review of the limitations of available wage data, as well as the statistics cited in the following discussion, are based, after considerable ordering of ideas and facts, upon Fossati, cited above, pp. 135–139; Rosselli, cited above, pp. 24–26 (for chief sources of data, see p. 25, footnote 1); and Tremelloni, cited above, pp. 138–146.

56 The facts, upon which the analysis pursued in the remainder of this chapter rests, have been gleaned from Dal Pane, cited above, pp. 253–267; Fossati, cited above, pp. 121–135; Gualtieri, cited above, pp. 6–47; Leonetti, cited above, pp. 15–38; and Rinaldo Rigola, Storia del movimento operaio italiano, pp. 9–44.

57 These figures are found in Leonetti, cited above, footnote 1, pp. 27–28. The statistics concerning the wounded, upon analysis, offer difficulties. Leonetti states that 1,005 persons were hospitalized, but his classified list of wounded cites figures which add up to only 965.

[58] Dal Pane, cited above, p. 379; passage translated by M. F. Neufeld.

[59] Roberto Michels, *Storia critica del movimento socialista italiano dagli inizi fino al 1911*, p. 60.

[60] The same, pp. 7–9. Richard Hostetter, *The Italian Socialist Movement — I: Origins (1860–1882)*, pp. 17–26. For bibliographical details on Pisacane's life and writings, see Hostetter, cited above, p. 18, footnotes 30–33.

[61] Dal Pane, cited above, pp. 359–363; Oscar Spinelli, *La mutualità in Italia e all'estero*, pp. 30–32.

[62] Rigola, cited above, p. 43.

[63] Dal Pane, cited above, pp. 224–235.

[64] Not until 1926 did Italy have a specific law concerning the right of association. The law of April 15, 1886, No. 3818, formally recognized the right of association of groups like the mutual aid societies when they requested the privilege of organization as benevolent associations (*l'erezione in corpo morale*). See Rigola, cited above, pp. 23–24; Antonio Toldo, *Il sindacalismo in Italia*, p. 4.

[65] Preamble to "Rules of the Friendly Society of Ironmoulders," Manchester, 1809, quoted in Sidney and Beatrice Webb, *Industrial Democracy*, p. 112.

[66] *Annuario statistico italiano 1905–1907*, p. 789, Table II, C. For source of the second table on mutual aid societies, see Fossati, cited above, p. 134.

[67] *Rivista Europea*, n.s., 1844, II, Pt. 2, pp. 710–723.

[68] Fossati, cited above, pp. 134–135; Greenfield, cited above, pp. 145–146.

[69] Leonetti, cited above, p. 29; passage translated by M. F. Neufeld.

[70] For summaries of the congress proceedings, see Rosselli, cited above, p. 33, footnote 1; Gastone Manacorda, *Il movimento operaio italiano attraverso i suoi congressi*, pp. 27–42; Hostetter, cited above, pp. 27–37.

[71] Salvatore Fenicia, *La cooperazione in Piemonte*, pp. 2, 237–256; Fossati, cited above, pp. 82, 135, 296; Ugo Rabbeno, *La cooperazione in Italia*, pp. 9–11, 105–106; Rosselli, cited above, pp. 31–35.

[72] Rigola, cited above, pp. 24–25.

[73] Ethelbert Stewart, "A Documentary History of the Early Organizations of Printers," *Bulletin of the Bureau of Labor*, Document 61, November 1905, p. 942.

Italian Governments and Prime Ministers, 1860 - 1960[*]

1860 January — 1861 June
Count Camillo Benso di Cavour

1861 June — 1862 March
Baron Bettino Ricasoli (First Ministry)

1862 March — 1862 December
Urbano Rattazzi (First Ministry)

1862 December — 1863 March
Luigi Farini

1863 March — 1864 September
Marco Minghetti (First Ministry)

1864 September — 1866 June
General Alfonso La Marmora

1866 June — 1867 April
Baron Bettino Ricasoli (Second Ministry)

1867 April — 1867 October
Urbano Rattazzi (Second Ministry)

1867 October — 1869 December
Luigi Federico Menabrea

1869 December — 1873 July
Giovanni Lanza

1873 July — 1876 March
Marco Minghetti (Second Ministry)

1876 March — 1878 March
Agostino Depretis (First Ministry)

1878 March — 1878 December
Benedetto Cairoli (First Ministry)

1878 December — 1879 July
Agostino Depretis (Second Ministry)

1879 July — 1881 May
Benedetto Cairoli (Second Ministry)

1881 May — 1887 July
Agostino Depretis (Third Ministry)

1887 July — 1891 February
Francesco Crispi (First Ministry)

1891 February — 1892 May
Marquis Antonio Di Rudinì (First Ministry)

1892 May — 1893 December
Giovanni Giolitti (First Ministry)

1893 December — 1896 March
Francesco Crispi (Second Ministry)

1896 March — 1898 June
Marquis Antonio Di Rudinì (Second Ministry)

1898 June — 1900 June
General Luigi Pelloux

1900 June — 1901 February
Giuseppe Saracco

1901 February — 1903 October
Giuseppe Zanardelli

1903 October — 1905 March
Giovanni Giolitti (Second Ministry)

1905 March 16 — 1905 March 28
Tommaso Tittoni
1905 March — 1906 February
Alessandro Fortis
1906 February — 1906 May
Baron Sidney Sonnino (First
Ministry)
1906 May — 1909 December
Giovanni Giolitti (Third Ministry)
1909 December — 1910 March
Baron Sidney Sonnino (Second
Ministry)
1910 March — 1911 March
Luigi Luzzatti
1911 March — 1914 March
Giovanni Giolitti (Fourth Ministry)
1914 March — 1916 June
Antonio Salandra
1916 June — 1917 October
Paolo Boselli
1917 October — 1919 June
Vittorio Orlando
1919 June — 1920 June
Francesco Nitti
1920 June — 1921 June
Giovanni Giolitti (Fifth Ministry)
1921 June — 1922 February
Ivanoe Bonomi
1922 February — 1922 October
Luigi Facta

1922 October — 1943 July
Benito Mussolini
1943 July — 1944 June
Marshal Pietro Badoglio
1944 June — 1945 June
Ivanoe Bonomi
1945 June — 1945 December
Ferruccio Parri
1945 December — 1953 August
Alcide De Gasperi (Eight Cabinets)
1953 August — 1954 January
Giuseppe Pella
1954 January — 1954 February
Amintore Fanfani (First
Ministry)
1954 February — 1955 July
Mario Scelba
1955 July — 1957 May
Antonio Segni (First Ministry)
1957 May — 1958 July
Adone Zoli
1958 July — 1959 February
Amintore Fanfani (Second Ministry)
1959 February — 1960 March
Antonio Segni (Second Ministry)
1960 March — 1960 July
Fernando Tambroni
1960 July —
Amintore Fanfani (Third Ministry)

---

* The terminal date of each ministry coincides with the time the succeeding ministry took office, since the outgoing government served as caretaker from the day of its fall until the new government assumed power.

71

III

The Pull of History: 1860 to 1890

The Politics of Disenchantment and Accommodation

IN 1870, King Victor Emmanuel II addressed the opening of Parliament and displayed once more his abiding good sense. As succinct historian of the immediate past and prophet of the approaching future, he cautioned: "Now the prose must follow the poetry."[1]

After 1870, as though heeding royal command, prosy humdrum possessed the political life of the country. So fatefully toward Marxism and fascism flowed the tedium of governmental responsibility as ministries confronted Italy, the reality, instead of Italy, the rhetorical dream, that its course must be measured with the interest usually accorded to more brilliant passages. Under the influence of its matter-of-fact rhythm, Italian governments of both the Right and the so-called Left ground out momentous economic and fiscal policies. When the turn of these screws pressed the people too harshly, political leaders pulled their own and the country's attention away from domestic cares by focussing national endeavors upon adventures overseas. The burdened workers and peasants, along with young middle-class intellectuals, grew restless and alienated. They started a search, still in progress, for the makings of a better society by espousing revolutionary doctrines utterly distant in origin, spirit, and purity of motive from parliamentary and bureaucratic opportunism.

Toward 1890, at the very time when Italian unions were just moving toward national organization, the politics of accommodation had thoroughly disenchanted the laboring classes. Now, only the various guises of socialism — that mixture of Old Testament fervor, economic self-interest, Christian justice, and historic inevitability — held out for them

72

the twin promise of realizing their mundane needs at the same time that they released their ideals from the dull bondage of Italian political life to soar once again. Mazzini had warned that the monarchical men of diplomatic alliances and busy affairs would betray the *Risorgimento*. And so it came to pass that socialism shone forth like "the sun of the future" (the 1871 phrase which Garibaldi, who really had no clear understanding of socialism, applied to the First International in his celebrated letter to Giorgio Pallavicini) to the growing Far Left at the end of the century.[2]

The extravagances of Italian character had responded with enthusiasm to the lofty ideals of the *Risorgimento*. For ten years between 1860 and 1870, this romantic and generous spirit could still thrive by partaking in a just cause: the political demand for the union of Venetia and Rome to Italy. Only differences concerning proper timing and methods divided the liberals of the Right, who were Cavour's political heirs, and the leaders of the Party of Action, who were once republican disciples of Mazzini and Garibaldi, but now accommodated themselves to the monarchy. Legitimists and clericalists execrated the liberals as destroyers of Church and Throne. On the Left, the Party of Action looked upon liberal caution with regard to the liberation of Venetia and Rome as cowardice. Although the Party of Action had forsworn an Italian Republic, it nevertheless remained faithful to the noble vision of the complete Italian State and kept fresh the old impatience to act at once, impulsively.

In the end, the moderate policies of the government prevailed and the rounding out of Italy's territory proceeded by diplomatic alliance, war, and accession, as earlier in 1859 and 1860, rather than by the exploits of patriots and republicans. In May 1866, Italy, encouraged by Napoleon III of France, concluded an offensive and defensive alliance with Bismarck: in the event of war between Prussia and Austria, Italy pledged to come to the aid of Prussia within three months. Venetia loomed as the reward. In July 1866, after Italian defeat on land, but before future naval humiliation near Lissa, Austria ceded Venetia to France. Subjected to the same painful procedure set in 1859, when Austria turned Lombardy over to France for gracious transfer to the Kingdom of Sardinia, Italy received Venetia at the hands of Napoleon III.

Rome now remained to heat the conscience of the Left. Garibaldi, who had tried to force the capture of Rome in 1862, only to be wounded, defeated, and taken prisoner by royal troops on August 29 after a skirmish at Aspromonte, often referred to as a battle, again gathered volunteers. He invaded papal territory in December 1866. He not only suffered defeat, but also double capture, yet managed to escape in September 1867. Garibaldi planned an insurrection in Rome for October;

it failed. He received some solace, however, by defeating the papal forces. Next, the papal troops, with French support, defeated Garibaldi in November at Mentana, captured him, and sent him to Caprera, the island he had purchased north of Sardinia. From that day until 1870, the Roman question divided France and Italy and prevented natural alliance between them: Napoleon III's fealty to the Pope overpowered the demands of Realpolitik itself. In August 1870, on the eve of the Franco-German war, the dénouement cleared into sight. French troops left Rome. Toward the end of September, the Italians profitted from the defeat of France at Sedan. They bombarded Rome and breached the Eternal City at the Porta Pia. Following a plebiscite, Italy annexed Rome on October 2, 1870. The Eternal City became the capital of the Kingdom of Italy, incarnating the fondest of all patriot dreams. Never before in history had Italy enjoyed so extensive a political realm under an independent government — not even in the most imperial days of the Roman Empire or in the time of the Ostrogoths.

Certainly the Venetian and the Roman questions had perturbed the minds of parliamentary leaders and patriots during the decade from 1860 to 1870. But the processes of government had not halted while awaiting the final political solution. On the contrary, the *Statuto* now needed to serve the entire Kingdom, but the constitutional framework of a tiny state could not effectively stretch itself over the long extent of Italy until the King's ministers contrived new nationwide institutions and administrative arrangements. While enthusiasm had run strongest for union with the Kingdom of Sardinia, Cavour seized with furious energy the occasion to impress upon the whole peninsula the governmental routine of Piedmont's centralized bureaucracy. His decision must be judged both shrewd and wise if that particular moment in Italy's historic destiny is understood as it was by Cavour: a unique instant of altogether exceptional opportunity offered to Italians by the gods, perhaps only that once, after sorrowful centuries of division and conflict among the rival states.

His successors, the liberals, dared not slow the pace he urged and set. Nor could they invite the falling apart of the Kingdom by granting home rule here and exerting strong supervision there, for such discrimination would surely have bred resentment. Necessity therefore urged them to erect a top-heavy system of centralized Roman control which thickened with usage and persisted with the obduracy of vested interest. It also spread beyond government and became the form of organization adopted by both public and private institutions, regardless of economic, social, and political outlook or commitment. Italian character apparently requires a greater than normal concealment of weakness at the base by an impressive superstructure, no matter how flimsy or makeshift. Within, somehow or other, adjustments will take place here and there, suitable agreements will be reached, and advantages will be taken of circumstances.

After Cavour's death in 1861, the liberals had to forge a royal army out of the diverse fighting forces of the Italian states, including Garibaldi's heroes, despite jealousies, rivalries, and pride of region. Paralleling the achievement of Alexander Hamilton in the wake of the American Revolution, Italian financial experts consolidated the public debt of the Italian states and also devised a unified system of taxation. These feats were accomplished between 1862 and 1865. The codes of 1865 established legislative unity, while the laws of 1867 dealt with ecclesiastical property. In November 1859, Victor Emmanuel II promulgated the Lex Casati, the mother decree on public elementary education. Acts dealing with charity, public health, and welfare were also adopted. To shape a truly unified government out of geographical entities joined only by decree required the creation, training, and deployment of a national civil service. Moreover, these men, mostly recruited from northern regions, had to be transformed into Italian officials by weaning their loyalties away from the governments of their origin.

These legislative and administrative tasks of state moved forward from day to day despite politics, war, and even brigandage. Bands of plunderers always accompany wars, revolutions, and extreme political change as though legitimized violence gives courage to revenge, reaction, and lawlessness. After 1860, banditry in the South sullied Italy's name and made it synonymous with maraud, for Italy was the last of civilized countries in Europe to suffer this plague. The Bourbons shared in Italy's shame. They did not accept the loss of their kingdom with resignation. From Rome, while still under the sway of the Pope, the King and Queen of Naples encouraged plundering bands of legitimists, adventurers, destitute peasants, unemployed soldiers, deserters, and professional brigands to impede and embarrass the new abhorrent government. Cecil J. S. Sprigge has vividly described Italy's plight which foreshadowed the travail of twentieth century newborn countries like Indonesia where, as late as April 1960, thousands of rebels still held out against the central government at Jakarta from the mountain fastnesses of central and northern Sumatra:

> Small armies of a thousand men apiece lurked in the mountains near the Ionian Sea. Against these the new State had to wage a veritable internal war, shooting hundreds of them, destroying their villages, and imprisoning the priests and friars who befriended them. In parts of northern Italy, also, the new State had to affirm its au-

75

thority against a double opposition of loyalists attached to the old régime, and of Italian patriots impatient of Piedmontese ways.[3]

Of all the governmental changes, consolidations, and reforms hammered out between 1860 and 1870, the extension of Piedmont's communal and provincial laws of 1859 to the length and breadth of the peninsula concerns us most. Benedetto Croce (1866–1954) has reminded us that these enactments followed the model of France, "or rather of Belgium, which is known to be derived historically from Dutch institutions; it divided the country into provinces, not always according to historical and geographical principles, all being directly under the control of the central government." The radical shift to tight central control in the affairs of state — some 69 prefects appointed by the Minister of the Interior shared the rule of Italy with other Roman forces through the power of favors and patronage — necessarily induced other Italian institutions, including the future labor movement, to swerve also in the same direction.

As early as 1861, Marco Minghetti (1818–1886) proposed the creation of six independent districts. Nothing came of this plan, nor of Count Stefano Jacini's cogent admonitions. The more the argument ran that the regions of Italy were too diverse to be administered from the same grab bag in Rome, the more grew the fear that regional autonomy in the backward South and the Islands would surely lead to renewed chaos and fresh disunity. Despite Lombard complaints against Piedmont rule, most conservatives throughout the country thanked God that they had survived the *Risorgimento* and Mazzini's insurrectionary notions with their property intact and law and order preserved. They knew very well that the House of Savoy and its ministers had brought off this miracle. In gratitude, they were not disposed to question Piedmontese bureaucracy, centralization, and push; rather, they were welcomed.

Croce has interred the issue, as it was raised during the second half of the nineteenth century, under a load of common sense:

> Centralization itself could not be so vexatious, or so contrary to the temper and political practice of the people, if the attack on it remained theoretical and never took shape in definite and urgent demands for reform, whilst the words "decentralization" and "autonomy" recurred in the programmes of the various parties like a refrain, which was repeated without conviction, and to which no one attached any definite meaning.[4]

Analysis must probe beyond Croce's satisfied lucidity. The drive for central control did not work against the national grain; it soothed it. Italians enjoyed then and continue to cherish theatrical displays of outward authority, no matter how ineffective. While protesting volubly, they bask in the sweep of all-embracing decrees vainly commanded from on high. Perhaps this proclivity for concealing fundamental weakness and individualistic irresponsibility under the formal toga of authority — brandishing magisterial fasces all the while — betrays a never-ending nostalgia for the lost empire of antiquity. Even Gioberti and Mazzini, each in his own way, conceived of Rome as the leader of the world, but panoplied in moral magnificence. Certainly the veneration of Roman law and the habit of mind which confounds mere legal enactment and reasoning with the practical solution of problems reflect that yearning.

After 1870, as Venetia and Rome settled into the family circle, external excitement ran down and an atmosphere of almost pure prose dominated the public life of Italy. The zeal for administrative brass tacks, so characteristic of the Piedmontese bureaucracy in the last decade of the *Risorgimento,* matured into a passion for administrative tidiness once the boundaries of the country had been rounded off. Its most fervent embrace was reserved for the balanced budget. No respectable statesman in Europe at this time questioned the sanctity of this first principle of state finance. So estimable were Italy's liberals of the Right that "the whole Italian people took upon themselves greater burdens than perhaps any nation has ever borne, and became the most heavily taxed people in Europe." Croce regarded both the government and the people as heroic. The implication is false. The historian and philosopher admitted that the people "grumbled and gave way to acts of impatience and outbursts of weariness and discouragement. . . ." He saw them as bowing to inevitable sacrifice for their country, thus at last winning the battle. Croce knew very well that the Mazzinian and Garibaldian Left was the first to profit from a fiscal policy balanced in favor of solvency at the expense of misery and discontent among the poor. He also knew that Marxian socialism ultimately won this same battle. But an abiding faith in liberalism and its practitioners tugged too hard at his judgment.[5]

Liberal-conservative leaders of Italy were indeed a remarkable group of politicians. Like the American federalists, they were wealthy landholders and professional men. Again, like the federalists, they impress us, across the years, by their integrity of character, scrupulous honesty, and dedication to public service. These qualities led to an aristocratic vision of life and duty; they stressed the wisdom of maintaining a strict distance from the hurly-burly and desires of the marketplace. They counselled a rigorous tax structure based upon firm budgetary principles wedded to the concepts of free trade.

The wars of liberation had been fought with money as well as ardor.

After every war, and especially after wars interlaced with ideals, expectations pile up as high as the public debt. Italians after 1860 looked for vast improvements in their lives as compensation for the benefits previously withheld by the evil greed of foreign and feudal masters. The new government, intent upon knitting the country together as a national and therefore military unit, proposed to extend public works, especially those which would improve communications, throughout the Kingdom. Among these, railroad construction took priority. But this ambitious program demanded large expenditures. The fiscal policy immediately pounced upon by the government proved easy under the circumstances, but impoverished still more the lands of the South and embittered the Catholic Church for years. The second step, less easy, led to a balanced budget, but alienated the Italian people.

The leaders of Piedmont, even before unification, had been so enlightened that they did not hesitate to estrange the most potent moral forces in Italy, the Roman Catholic Church and God's vicar, the Pope. Religious congregations were closed and Church lands and treasure confiscated. This drastic policy was extended to the rest of Italy during the 1860's, outraging a proud religious empire which had already lost most of its territorial possessions when the Papal States were stripped from the Church. The new State also resorted to the sale of governmental property. A large proportion of this public wealth had been turned over by the new Kingdom to the local authorities in a grand gesture of economic munificence and political acumen. But the remaining state assets, packaged with Church lands, now crowded upon the open market at bargain-counter prices. These properties, most extensive in the former Kingdom of the Two Sicilies, were bought up eagerly by land speculators and wealthy peasants. To turn a quick lira, the new owners mined the forests and squandered other resources which had accumulated slowly over the years. According to Francesco Saverio Nitti (1868–1953), the sale of lands in the Kingdom of the Two Sicilies brought 500,000,000 lire into the coffers of the Italian State. However, the cost to later generations in the Mezzogiorno (the South) defies estimate. The denuding of public and Church lands distorted the distribution of water in neighboring areas and intensified still further the agricultural misery of the South.

Other elements in the government's fiscal program took equally drastic form. The state railroads of the former Kingdom of the Two Sicilies were sold off. The excise on salt was doubled and the sale of tobacco became a state monopoly. Taxes increased on land, manufactured articles, and income; the government imposed a new levy upon inheritance. The results were most disastrous for the impoverished South. The fiscal measures of the Bourbons, for all their backwardness in the view of liberals, had not pressed too heavily upon the peasants. Low taxation on articles of basic consumption balanced high duties on imports. The Kingdom of Italy reversed this policy and transformed South Italy from an area with one of the lowest tax rates in Europe into a region with one of the heaviest. Thus, Piedmont's statesmen of moral rectitude and fiscal probity simultaneously reduced the South to chronic discontent and incited the Church to chronic intransigence.

To be sure, the books of the State were well ordered and became more and more balanced. The regions of Italy before unification had produced a public revenue of 500,000,000 lire. This income fell far short of the necessary expenditures of the new Kingdom. By 1862, the annual deficit grew almost as large as the revenue itself: 450,000,000 lire. By 1866, the deficit amounted to more than 600,000,000 lire. The national debt of the former states had totaled a little less than 2,000,000,000 lire, whereas by 1871 the national debt of the Kingdom had risen to more than 8,000,000,000 lire.

The name of Quintino Sella (1826–1884), when he served as Minister of Finance, came to mean "economy to the bone." True, he reduced the rolls of civil servants and cut the salaries of ministers. But, in addition to imposing the taxes already cited, he also favored a tax on the milling of grain. This was the hated excise which Piedmont had abolished in the regions it liberated, thereby earning by this symbolic act the gratitude of the population. Sella pressed for his measure each year until he finally had his way in 1868. Heavy taxation of the people's bread and pasta at the same time that expenditures for military reform and armaments mounted did little to increase the government's popularity. Despite opposition from the diversified, ill-defined, but vociferous Left, the fiscal policy of Sella prevailed. Between 1870 and 1875, normal revenues increased by 234,000,000 lire; governmental expenditures increased by less than 40,000,000 lire. Finally, Marco Minghetti, the Prime Minister, announced in his financial statement of March 16, 1876 that the budget had been finally balanced.

Tariff changes exacerbated the sufferings imposed by the government's fiscal measures. The advent of unity swept aside the internal custom barriers between the various states. Then, the system of free trade between nations, as expounded and practiced by Piedmont, spread its theoretical blessings over the entire Kingdom as it took on the body of commercial treaties enacted between 1860 and 1870. Foreign competition engaged freely now with the agriculture of the South at a moment when it suffered heavier taxation than ever before. Industry there, never robust at best, suffered double assaults from which it never recovered. Local handicraft production found it impossible to compete with machine-made commodities from the North when they began to invade the Mezzogiorno by way of improved roads and extended railways. In time, when the price tags of foreign wares caused the goods of North Italy to vanish from the shelves, the handicraft economy of the South suffered even more, storing up fresh resentments.[6]

Discontent mounted in other parts of Italy as well. The followers of Mazzini and Garibaldi lost no opportunity to keep groups of the distressed population in ferment. In Romagna, where the republicanism of Mazzini survives to the present day, sedition smoldered. Based at first in Naples and Florence, the purveyors of anarchism began to operate throughout the country from their shabby furnished rooms in down-at-the-heel bystreets; they crowded upon the socialisms of the day and claimed excitedly their niche in the Panthéon of the Italian Far Left. Yet, for all their noise and pathetic insurrections, the anarchistic and socialistic radicals remained forlorn sects with more numerous followers among the police than among the public at large. Since the Far Left still formed at this time merely part of a numerous supporting cast on the fringes of the political scene, the protagonists of the effective Left must be honored with first attention. They sat in Parliament where they assailed the Right until the government toppled over just at the time when it had achieved its heart's desire: the balancing of the budget.

Already by 1874, suspicion emerged among those 500,000 literate Italians who possessed the vote that the prosperity of a small proportion of the total population had been wrung out of the feeble-enough customary security of the many. Despite assurances that freedom and time would bring flourishing adjustment, in the elections of that year the voters returned deputies to Parliament who supported the government by only a bare majority. Two years later, on March 18, 1876, the Minghetti cabinet fell after Tuscan deputies voted against the government. This event represented more than the shifting of power to a rhetorical Left which still milked the frustrated yearnings of the *Risorgimento* for all they were worth. The defeat of Cavour's followers cut short the possible development of even an imperfect system of two-party government. Henceforth, not even a coalition of parties would rule Italy. Instead, the politicians of the Left worked out a viable scheme of accommodation which obliterated party lines.

The so-called Left and the Cavourian liberals of the Right differed in traditions and personalities: their origins, social attitudes, general cast of ideas, and posture toward government. Yet both possessed this feature in common: neither constituted a clearly distinguishable national party. Before 1860, adequately financed national parties with well-organized followers in each region of the peninsula could not have evolved. Nor had events during the sixteen years since unification encouraged the creation of true national parties. Italy had united physically, but different needs and motives, varying from province to province, forced Italians into such diverse attitudes and resentments that they defied restraint for long within even a series of parties and certainly not within two strong established parties which alternated in power. In this inevitable failure to fashion a new national purpose strong enough to bend sectional interests to the welfare of the whole country, as in the sacrificial days of the *Risorgimento*, lies the key to the political system which took the place of parties: *trasformismo*. This term, which was used with opprobrium by political purists of the late nineteenth century, characterizes a technique by which governments stay in power through the acquisition of votes wherever they may be found. Votes are bought by the group in power through promises and patronage. Gradually, the distinction between parties tends to disappear as deputies are transformed from members of the so-called opposition into the backbone of the majority which often controls only a minority of its own party.

Who were the men who sat on the Left and devised *trasformismo* as the sole instrument for governing Italy in the years after 1876? They were neither united in principle nor in program. They were led, for the most part, by politicians from the South. Many of them had originally been ardent Mazzinians who had come to terms with the monarchy since they were privately convinced of what Francesco Crispi (1819–1901), Mazzini's most gifted disciple, publicly declared: "The Republic would divide us, the Monarchy unites us." They attracted to themselves the disgruntled and frustrated of all provinces and classes: those whom the fiscal policies of the Right had thrown into economic straits; those, especially in the South, who had been toppled from local positions of prestige and influence by the emissaries and civil servants of the national government; and even those unreconciled adherents of the lost Bourbon cause who could scarcely support the Right. Closer to the new dissatisfied middle classes than the liberals, this conglomerate Left committed itself, at least in revivalist moments of enthusiasm, to rectify the injustices perpetrated by the unfeeling Right, to aid the hard-beset South, and to restore some measure of autonomy to the regions. It also promised to deal firmly with the papacy and the priests, who, despite the Law of

81

Guarantees of May 13, 1871, which the Pope had rejected, continued to act out their firm belief: the Kingdom consorted with the forces of the Devil himself.

King Victor Emmanuel, although under no constitutional constraint to do so, took the stance of a British monarch during the crisis of 1876. He summoned a representative of the new majority despite the *Statuto's* silence about the necessity for constituting the ruling ministry from the parliamentary majority. Victor Emmanuel, however, did exercise his kingly prerogatives by not summoning the most obvious candidate, Francesco Crispi, but the mildest leader of the Left, Agostino Depretis (1813–1887) of Piedmont. After assuming office, Depretis went to the country where the Left won resounding majorities.

From 1876 to 1887, Depretis established the art of *trasformismo;* on his death, Francesco Crispi, who dominated politics until 1896, improved the system; finally, it reached an apogee of perfection under the guidance of its greatest master, Giovanni Giolitti (1842–1928), from 1901 to 1914. The record of the Left, whether written by Depretis or by Benedetto Cairoli (1825–1889), twice boosted into office when deputies grew impatient with Depretis' cautious tactics, was far from inspired. The budget remained fully balanced from 1876 until 1881, when income still exceeded rising expenditures by 53,000,000 lire. Meanwhile, the salt tax had been reduced and in 1880 the unpopular tax on the milling of grain had been entirely removed. But the nature of the Left and of the constituencies it courted made the maintenance of a rigidly balanced budget impossible. The Left was eventually pushed into deficit financing by necessary expenditures imposed by an expanding state trying to become a nation and by the mounting burden of political debts in the form of local public works and other log-rolling favors which required money or jobs. The financial wizard of the Left, Agostino Magliani (1825–1891), cultivated the art of financial expediency as assiduously as Depretis pursued the art of political accommodation. State revenues rose steadily each year and reached 1,449,000,000 lire in 1887–1888, but the deficit amounted to 253,000,000 lire. After 1888, increasingly large budgetary deficits once again became standard features of government. The policy of the Left spelled financial heresy, but it accompanied years of prosperity, especially after 1878; its program of improvements, though extravagant, undoubtedly benefitted the country both socially and economically.[7]

In all, there were three Depretis ministries until the Premier's death in 1887. He usually ruled without the consent of half the deputies of the Left. Five of their leaders — Francesco Crispi of Sicily, Benedetto Cairoli and Agostino Bertani (1812–1886) of Lombardy, Giuseppe

Zanardelli (1826–1903) of Brescia, and Giovanni Nicotera (1828–1894) of Calabria — each with his own regional followers, came to be known as the Pentarchy. But their opposition could not prevail, for each one cherished strong views on some issue which disqualified him for the type of leadership by which Depretis obtained a parliamentary majority. Italy as a nation continued along bewildered paths while Depretis, always competent and without illusions or enthusiasms, scored time and again by counting upon the placation of local ambitions and interests to wipe out party loyalties and distinctions. Parliament now fulfilled Count Jacini's prediction that bureaucratic centralization would transform the Chamber and the Senate into forums for concluding bargains between the King's ministers and local constituencies, thus preventing its development as the center for the molding of national policy.

Those Mazzinians who viewed the creation of Italy as the first step in the regeneration of Europe, and then of the entire world, lived to see Italy count as a cipher in international affairs. The cure for this lack of influence came, ironically, as a result of the severe jolt to the patriotic sentiments of the nation, as well as to the large-minded Mazzinian segment of public opinion itself, when the French Republic suddenly invaded Tunis in 1881. On May 20, 1882, Depretis answered the French by committing Italy to the Triple Alliance with Germany and Austria. He was omnipotent from 1881 onward and could outrage the old patriots with impunity even when he favored Austria, an old enemy, in whose empire the "unredeemed" territories of Trieste, Istria, and Trentino still pined for union with the mother country. Depretis went further. In 1885, Italian forces occupied Assab and Massawa on the Red Sea. With one gesture, the venerable Premier of flexibility had stripped the Mazzinian romantics of any remaining illusion that Italy would purify the world of imperialistic greed and compensated Italians at the same time for their humiliation in Tunis by France.

The Left managed to stage still another about-face which bore down heavily upon the immediate interests of labor and upon ultimate social stability and unrest. The needs of the budget had introduced customs reform as early as 1878. By reducing imports and raising duties, Italy offended France, for that country provided the largest amount of Italian imports. Then, in 1887, six years after the French coup in Tunis, Italy repudiated its commercial treaties with France. Afterward, France refused to conclude another agreement and both nations proceeded to levy special taxes on each other's goods. While the presses of France and Italy outdid themselves in virulence, foreign trade between the two neighbors halved. Fast upon Italy's now completely protected customs system, in just one year from 1887 to 1888, Italy's entire foreign trade, including exports as well as imports, shrank to a quarter of its former size.[8]

Through his control of Parliament, so universally deplored by those who sought his power, Depretis made good his promise to strengthen Italy's democratic structure although few in positions of influence had pressed him to do so. In 1882, he sponsored laws which extended the franchise by reducing the age limit for voting from 25 to 21 and lowering the tax requirement from 40 to 19 lire. Upon their enactment, the electorate increased from 621,896, or 2.2% of the entire population, in the May 1880 elections, to 2,017,829, or 6.9% of the total population, in the elections of October and November 1882. This widening of democracy, while hardly revolutionary, nevertheless represented social and political progress of a respectable order.

During the last years of Depretis' rule, the Italian Parliament moved feebly toward the institution of a system of protective labor legislation and social security. The law of July 8, 1883 established a national workmen's compensation fund on a voluntary basis in cooperation with a group of banks. It therefore remained virtually a dead letter upon the statute books until compulsory insurance came into existence, after bitter legislative wrangles, on March 17, 1898. The first law which sought to regulate the employment of women and children dated from February 11, 1886, although a mining law of 1865, never effectively enforced, already prohibited the employment of children under ten years of age in underground work. These mild acts, crippled by indifferent administration, proved as ineffectual as the education law of July 1877. In attempting to improve upon the pioneering Lex Casati of November 1859, it prescribed compulsory elementary school education for children between the ages of 6 and 9. Other legislative proposals, which failed of enactment, concerned emigration, old-age pensions (to invigorate the decrepit law of July 15, 1859, a task not achieved until July 17, 1898), the legal status of mutual aid societies, and the recognition of unions and the right to strike (the bill introduced in 1883 by the Marchese Antonio di San Giuliano (1852–1914) was defeated 121–117). These impotent enactments and legislative failures of an era inebriated by the liberal promises of theoretical laissez faire nevertheless measured the degree of rising pressure in the social air outside the chambers of Parliament. Although these laws and proposals lagged far behind the expectations of their sponsors and the needs of the people, they already foretold the day when the national legislature would be forced to abandon the sanctified principles of liberalism and busy itself with the details of social and economic amelioration, thus imposing upon a weak and divided Italian labor movement inevitable concern with politics in all its forms.

Upon the death of Depretis in July 1887, Francesco Crispi, the Minister of the Interior, became Premier for the first time. Crispi had been a member of Garibaldi's Red Shirts and virtual dictator of Sicily for a short time in 1860. As a reward for his patriotism, he bore Cavour's enmity; this barred him from responsible political employment. Only with difficulty did he manage election to the first Italian Parliament. Now, as Prime Minister, he represented the aspirations of the South. His considerable Sicilian vigor contrasted sharply with Depretis' gently ironic manner. Because of his passionately expressed convictions and his deeply felt sense of indispensability to Italy, Crispi gave the impression of being a man of destiny, more dedicated to policy than to political maneuverings and deals. But Crispi, for all his apparent differences from Depretis, resembled him in the most fundamental and telling way: by 1887, at the age of 67, Crispi no longer took seriously formal parliamentary groupings. During his régime, he did not hesitate to incur the displeasure of both the Right and the Left as long as he procured the votes necessary for his purposes at the moment. He rolled with time and circumstances. His need to possess political power alone dictated his tactics from day to day.

Crispi had been so Mazzinian in his bitter hostility to the Holy See that on the death of Pius IX in 1878 some of the Cardinals favored holding the election conclave abroad since Crispi was Minister of the Interior and responsible for relations with the Vatican. Despite past utterances and attitudes, Crispi prepared to make peace with the Pope a few weeks before Depretis' death when Crispi actually ran the government. The move was dictated by his desire to win for himself political acclaim and a secure place in modern Italian history by reconciling the government and the papacy.

The rift went back in time and spirit to the very beginnings of the *Risorgimento,* for the Church had opposed by word and force Italian nationalism, patriotism, and liberalism in all its manifestations from extreme Left to moderate Right. From the start of his reign, Leo XII (1760–1829, pope 1823–1829) sought to counter the revolutionary activities of the Carbonari with the creation of a secret Catholic propaganda society, the "Sanfedisti." Within three months of his election, Pius IX, the liberal Pope from whom so much was expected in the springtime of Italy's hopes, issued an encyclical against communism, *Qui pluribus,* on November 9, 1849. From then on, Pius IX's anger and intransigence increased with each new advance toward national unification. His encyclical of 1864, *Quanta cura*, condemned the religious neutrality of states, freedom of opinion and press, popular sovereignty, and the legal supremacy of the State over the Church. The now famous *Syllabus*, attached to the encyclical, listed the principal errors of the age. After 1870, Pius IX refused to recognize the Italian State. He brushed aside parliamentary guarantees of royal honors, spiritual and diplomatic freedom, and annual monetary compensation equivalent to the income he had formerly received from his territories. He dramatized himself as "the prisoner of the Vatican." He excommunicated the founders of the Kingdom and encouraged the secession of Catholics from the political life of the Italian State.

The policy of Catholic withdrawal from political life antedated the establishment of the Kingdom. Devout defenders of the Church who disagreed with Cavour's lay and ecclesiastical policies formed a center of resistance in Turin. Their views found principal expression in the daily newspaper, *L'Armonia della Religione con la Civiltà*, (*The Harmony of Religion and Civilization*), edited from 1848 to 1863 by Don Giacomo Margotti (1823–1887), the most outspoken advocate of political abstention. In 1857, he hurled the cry which convinced Catholics for decades: "Neither elected, nor electors" (*Nè eletti, nè elettori*). After 1863, Margotti continued to defend the Church and its view of the Italian State through the more moderate *L'Unità Cattolica* (*Catholic Unity*). Pius IX is reported to have said to Margotti in 1868: "One should not go to the polls" (*"Non si vada alle urne"*). By formal decree of February 29, 1868, the Holy Penitentiary sanctioned the injunction: "Neither elected, nor electors." Then, on October 11, 1874, Pius IX reaffirmed this prohibition in a papal audience where he used the phrase, *Non expedit*. The Church considered it inexpedient for Catholics to vote in the elections of the Italian State. To sensitive ears, the Pope's words were fraught with Biblical compulsion: "All things are lawful for me, but all things are not expedient. . ." (I Corinthians, X, 23).

The hostility of the Holy Father had proved most salutary to the State, for the new government gained time to establish in fact its liberal ideals of civil society. The universities abolished their theological faculties and the schools removed their spiritual advisors. Charities underwent reform and Catholic schools had to endure state inspection. In 1877, parents of elementary school children were granted the option of requesting or refusing doctrinal instruction for their offspring. Civil marriage became mandatory and religious rites were dropped from oath-taking ceremonies.

Parliament accomplished these reforms by 1878, the year which witnessed the death of both Victor Emmanuel II and Pius IX, those symbols of irreconcilable Throne and Altar. It was now hoped that their successors, Humbert I (1844–1900, king 1878–1900) and Leo XIII (1810–1903, pope 1878–1903), might compose their differences. But the new Pope took on the public obduracy of Pius IX. In practice, however, even the Vatican realized that temporal power would never again revert to its hands, and matters of common concern like education and ecclesiastical appointments began to arrange themselves, as Italians express this kind of process, through unofficial intermediaries. Catholics began to vote in local elections and to accept local offices. At the time of the extension of suffrage in 1882, liberal Catholic circles were stirred by the thought that the Church might encourage limited participation in national elections. These expectations met with immediate disappointment. Four years later, on December 30, 1886, the Holy Office declared that the terms of the *Non expedit* implied a grave precept. Such were the circumstances between Church and State when Crispi sent out feelers of good will.

When his overtures were rebuffed, Crispi reverted to loud anticlericalism. He attempted to reduce the influence of the Church upon national education; he suspended the Mayor of Rome for congratulating the Pope on his jubilee day of ordination; and in 1889 he approved an anticlerical ceremony to commemorate the 300th anniversary of the burning of Giordano Bruno almost within sight of the Vatican grounds. But these attitudes were opportunistic and Crispi would have preferred an honorable peace.

Crispi's foreign policy upheld the Triple Alliance with more zeal than Depretis had shown and went much beyond Depretis in his hostility to France because of the occupation of Tunis. His anger, which Croce regarded as filled more with noise than evil, carried him into a senseless tariff war with France which demonstrated an indifference to economics equalled only by Mazzini and wrecked Italy's trade. France readily found alternate markets. As a convinced imperialist, Crispi strove to expand the foothold on the Red Sea which Depretis had secured. After initial setbacks, when Menelik (1844–1913) became King of Ethiopia with Italian support in May 1889, Crispi wrongly imagined that he had created an Italian protectorate there. Since Crispi served as his own Minister of the Interior, foreign and domestic policy took on extreme consistency. He eradicated patriotic Italian clubs dedicated to the redemption of Trieste as harshly as the Austrians exterminated them in Trieste itself. He lived in terror of imagined conspiracies: French seizure of Sicily, international freemasonry, republican separatists, aged survivors of the Cavourian

Right, and, undifferentiated in his mind, anarchists, socialists, and trade unionists. His gratuitous fuming against the Right caused them to join his enemies, the radicals, republicans, and socialists who had formed a pact against him. Together they withdrew support from him in 1891 and caused his temporary downfall.[9]

The displacement of Crispi as Premier from January 1891 to December 1893 coincided with the emergence of socialism as a political force at once serious, youthful, convinced, and dedicated. These fresh elements endowed Italian socialism with intense appeal as they simultaneously discredited the immediate past. For sixteen years between 1860 and 1876, men of idealistic temperament had still found it possible to believe that if only the Cavourian liberals were ousted, the aspirations of the *Risorgimento* would finally triumph. Instead, after the advent of Depretis to power, *trasformismo* presented the Left in a public spectacle of playing fast and loose with principles. Italians of serious mind and love of country watched with shame as the leadership of Parliament proclaimed to the nation and the world that the country of Mazzini and Garibaldi could not muster enough firmly held convictions to lead a decent political life. By contrast, socialism brimmed with virtues positive enough to hold idealists in a state of complete devotion. First, there was the open road of service to Italy's impoverished and restless millions. Second, the concept of political power as a by-product of the economic class struggle burst upon the rising generation as inspired intellectual revelation. After studious engrossment with dry constitutional and legal forms, they found the very theories of socialism throbbing with life. Third, the psychological and religious powers of socialism exerted that irresistible force described so wryly by Croce: "The human will never feels itself so free as when it is conscious of working in conformity with the will of God, or with the laws of necessity."[10] Yet for all their allure, these socialist virtues might not have compelled the Italian imagination after 1890 had they not also represented deliverance from an intolerable past to an incandescent future: honorable, just, and luminously clean of *trasformismo*.

The progress of Italian socialisms from 1860 to 1890 suffered pilgrim temptations, wandered into treacherous quicksands, and always lingered along byways far from the highroads of Italian political life. These socialist gospels, like all political and religious doctrines which reach for the well-springs of human energies and loyalties, bred dissent and factionalism ever more proliferating and rancorous. They struggled for nothing less than man's destined salvation. Fascinating and appropriate as the turns of socialist thought and experience might be for a history of Italian radicalism, only five of the doctrinal variations drew enough adherents to merit consideration in a work concerned with labor. Fastened to these creeds are the names of Mazzini, Garibaldi, Mikhail Bakunin (1814–1876), Benoît Malon (1841–1893), and Karl Marx (1818–1883).

A curious pastime, not to be indulged at this point, has centered on diligent inquiry by admirers and detractors of Mazzini into the purity of his socialism. Such exercises in distillation have been carried out by Gaetano Salvemini, Napoleone Colajanni, Eugenio Florian, Edoardo Bonaldi, Bolton King, Giuseppe Rensi, Francesco Saverio Merlino, and Humbert Gualtieri; the details can be examined at leisure in their works. Here, Mazzini's thought and influence may be approached more simply and with dispatch. In the course of his life, devoted as it was to the liberation and unification of Italy by political means, Mazzini wrote extensively, for almost fifty years, on a vast range of subjects and made innumerable appeals both to Italians and to humanity at large. Consequently, his collected works contain more than one vein of thought; they lend themselves easily to mining for particular elements sought by different prospectors; usually, they produce the desired nuggets. Therefore, it would be surprising indeed if outcroppings of socialism, so prevalent in the terrain of the nineteenth century, did not show in the Mazzinian deposits.

Having seen the defeat of his ideals by Piedmont, Mazzini tried, in his heartbreak, to arouse the workmen of Italy to his cause. This last rally during the final years of his life (1860–1872) carried the sounds of desperation rather more than of close conviction. But Mazzini's name was ringed with magic. His ideas, far from doctrinal purity or logical consistency, forced attention and popularized unorthodox economic theory and unorthodox means to achieve the ends he had in mind. As early as 1843, Mazzini had stated that a revolutionary movement must draw its main support from the working class. The precise meaning of this pronouncement is far from clear, since Mazzini abhorred Marxian ideas of class struggle. He advocated a positive alternative: associationism which presumed the collaboration of all classes in society. Mazzini's proclivity for moral and religious (Deist) education alchemized this notion into a vague utopia (for which he owed a laboratory fee to Saint-Simon) ruled by a mystical element of his own imagination called the People. His old-fashioned mentality now offended many intelligent Italians, but it nevertheless persevered to concoct the idea of an Inalienable National Fund. The scheme resembled the suggestion of Ferdinand Lassalle (1825–1864) that the State provide financial assistance to workers who wished to establish cooperatives. Admirers have discovered Mazzini's socialism in the proposed fund. Since Mazzini firmly believed that philanthropy could not abolish poverty, since he also recognized the futility of enjoining families with bare subsistence wages to save their centimes and raise their position in life thereby, and since Mazzini urged associations of workers to establish producer cooperatives with the aid of government, the deduction followed that his ultimate goal would have been a community of machinery and capital — socialism itself.

Mazzini's zeal after 1860 for organizing the support of workers must not be confused with union growth even when it resulted in the formation of labor groups. His exertions can only be represented as political endeavors. As Mazzini sought to spread republican doctrine among workers, his followers penetrated existing local groups, attempted to capture the annual congresses of the mutual aid societies, and established new bodies of workers, the artisan brotherhoods (*fratellanze artigiane*). The brotherhoods, arising largely in Tuscany, adopted a program with an eloquently Mazzinian purpose: "In the name of the Fatherland, of Humanity and of Progress, the Artisans of Italy, availing themselves of the liberties which the new times grant, join in brotherhood to cooperate for the intellectual, moral and material betterment of their class through education, mutual aid and credit."

Rinaldo Rigola devotes an entire chapter of his history to Mazzini's role in the Italian labor movement. His discussion is as detailed as it is uninformative. He never mentions the specific number of brotherhoods or their geographical distribution. He concedes that after the 1864 congress of mutual aid societies in Naples where the Pact of Brotherhood — the articles of faith of the Mazzinian movement — was ratified, the authority of the brotherhoods began to decline. At no point is he ever clear either about the exact magnitude of the forces they mustered before that date, or about the precise time of their apogee. Rigola also implies that republican victories in the battles over resolutions at the 1871 congress of the mutual aid societies (no meetings had been summoned for six years during the final struggle for national unification) secured no solid political advantages since the hostile forces of international socialism had already taken more strategic ground elsewhere. Rigola's failure to come to grips with the size and duration of the artisan brotherhoods encourages the suspicion that they enjoyed but a brief walk in the sun of Mazzini's last days on earth. Evasion thus became an act of piety. Indeed, he concludes his account of Mazzini with the reminder that Nello Rosselli, by patiently reconstructing the history of the artisan brotherhoods in his *Mazzini e Bakounine*, had demonstrated that "historians of the Italian labor movement all assigned too little importance to the movement inspired by Giuseppe Mazzini." Rigola then adds that the "observation is exact and the neglect of the historians with regard to the brotherhood movement can be explained only by the difficulties met when attempting to draw out of oblivion events concerning the humble working classes." Roberto Michels adds to the confusion by giving the appearance of exactitude. In a chronological chart of socialist events, he records the number of Mazzinian societies of workers as 453 in 1863, with a membership of 111,608. He made no attempt to note the source of these figures or to describe the character and distribution of the membership. One fact, however, stands clear of doubt: the Mazzinians abandoned all concern with the emancipation of labor after they walked out of the congress of Tuscan workmen's societies in 1877.[11]

By the end of 1871, Mazzini knew himself beaten. Seven years earlier, his innocent good will and generosity — hazardous endowments for success in politics — had sealed the fate of his own cause after Mikhail Bakunin arrived in Italy at the beginning of 1864. Through Mazzini who had met him in England, the Russian revolutionary presented himself to key figures of the parliamentary Far Left. Through Agostino Bertani, whom Bakunin had encountered in Geneva, he obtained permission to visit Garibaldi at Caprera. After carefully casing the centers of radicalism, Bakunin decided to settle in Florence. There, he maintained close communication with workers and freemasons. He particularly hoped to transform the masonic lodges into socialist and revolutionary cells. However, Bakunin succeeded in attracting disciples not from the class of workers and peasants, but from the ranks of idealists, adventurers, and professional radicals.

Meanwhile, a meeting took place in London on September 28, 1864. The deliberations of this assemblage, as yet inglorious and to fortune and to fame unknown, determined the immediate fate of Mazzini and the distant fate of the kingdoms and republics of the world. On that day, self-appointed spokesmen for the laboring poor made arrangements which eventuated in the formation of the International Workingmen's Association. Mazzini had been urged to participate in the discussions; since he sympathized with the idea of creating an international association of labor, he accepted the invitation but delegated two friends to represent him. The meeting elected a provisional committee to give substance to its objectives. A subcommittee of nine members charged with drafting a constitution welcomed, in the absence of Marx, the suggestion that the Brotherhood Pact of Mazzinian inspiration serve as a model for the task at hand. Marx, who attended a subsequent October meeting of the subcommittee, held his peace when he heard the proposed preamble. Privately, he later described it as childish, rambling, and confused — a potpourri of Mazzini's obscure ideas and French socialism. Publicly, at the time, Marx merely suggested that the wording be improved. As usual in circumstances of this kind, he was entrusted with the revision. He rewrote the preamble almost entirely. At a meeting in November, the version by Marx was approved. Friedrich Engels (1820–1895) predicted, less than a week after this coup, that the old patriot's "God and the People" would soon be interred by Italian workmen. So began the historical enmity between Mazzini and Marx.

Bakunin saw Marx in London later in November 1864. He had met Marx for the first time in Paris during his stay there between 1844 and 1847. Neither could abide the other, so antipathetic were they in temperament and philosophy. But for the moment Marx was ready to bear with Bakunin if the interests of the International Workingmen's Association in Italy could be served. Bakunin, in turn, found Marx less repellent than Mazzini. To hasten the destruction of Mazzini's influence, he accepted Marx's offer of collaboration. When he returned to Italy, Bakunin saw Mazzini in Genoa. Mazzini again gave Bakunin letters of introduction to help him in his supposed work of organizing for the International, a project still approved by Mazzini. As the year of 1864 drew to a close, Bakunin organized a secret alliance to fight Mazzini's leagues, alliances, and brotherhoods. Bakunin's opposing groups bore different names: Fraternity, Legionnaires of the Italian Social Revolution, and the Alliance of the Socialist Democracy. Meanwhile, the *Inaugural Address* of the International, as the preamble revised by Marx and the constitution came to be called, had been translated by the Italian Workingmen's Society of London and published on February 18, 1865 by *L'Unità Italiana,* the organ of the Mazzinians in Milan!

During the next two years, Bakunin extended his influence throughout Italy, especially at Naples. There, he created another organization known as the International Revolutionary Society. Openly, the group proclaimed that it sought to establish an Italian social democracy. Under the cover of private correspondence, Bakunin was more forthright. In writing to Alexander Herzen, the Russian revolutionary and friend of Mazzini and Garibaldi, Bakunin declared to his patron, like himself the son of a nobleman, that before Italians could be induced to embrace social democracy it was imperative to combat the unspeakable patriotic bourgeois rhetoric fed to them by Garibaldi and Mazzini. Shortly, his plans were interrupted. The uprising in Palermo between September 16 and September 23, 1866, known as the Seven-and-One-Half Days, elicited violent repression on the part of the governmental authorities.

From the moment in December 1865 when a bill was introduced into the Italian Parliament to levy a tax on the milling of grain until May 1868 when the bill was finally passed, controversy and demonstrations agitated the country. Just prior to the parliamentary elections in March 1867, Bakunin created at Naples another revolutionary organization, "Liberty and Justice." It was the first group set up by Bakunin to function openly. In August, it began to publish a weekly paper also called *Liberty and Justice*. Like Bakunin's other societies, this Neapolitan chapter also had a double purpose: to gather together adherents of the International who eventually could be induced to undermine Marx's influence, but who meanwhile would devote themselves to the more immediate task of destroying Mazzini's baneful prestige. Bakunin entered the March elections with fervor and rhetoric as windy as Mazzini's. *Liberty and Justice* cried out that the nation was passing through an economic, financial, and political crisis which had given rise to social unrest. The people demanded bread, work, liberty, and justice. Voters were urged to replace the old parties and the old flags by a completely new system. The mechanics for achieving this new order still remain unfathomable, for Liberty and Justice did not present a single candidate for election.

In 1868, Liberty and Justice officially became an Italian branch of the International by accepting the program of the London parent body. According to Gualtieri, its large membership consisted mostly of industrial workers concentrated in the steel, mechanical, and railroad trades. Each craft appointed its own representative to a federal commission which stood guard over general policy, coordinated working-class activities in Naples and surrounding towns, and corresponded with foreign branches as well as with the General Council in London. Although Gualtieri's account is innocent of membership statistics, he nevertheless finds it possible to characterize the Naples branch of the International as the largest, the most important, and therefore the center of activity in all of Italy. Later, other branches appeared along the coast south of Naples and in Sicily.[12]

For four years after the founding of the International in 1864, Bakunin worked ceaselessly to establish its supremacy in Italy. By September 1867, an open rupture alienated Bakunin and Mazzini. Against Mazzini's conviction that a holy war to liberate Europe as well as Italy must take precedence over peace, Bakunin held the anarchist views that only complete social revolution, not war, could abolish the tyranny of centralized states and their powerful armies. Thus, as long as states existed, wars would prevail rather than liberty. In dealing with Marx, Bakunin employed a different strategy. While protesting his friendship, he secretly fostered activities which were at complete variance with Marx's prin-

93

ciples. But Marx, like his political descendants today, was skilled at intrigue. Although aware of Bakunin's perfidy, Marx shrewdly calculated that Bakunin was the only man in Italy who could stand up against Mazzini. Despising Bakunin, Marx hated Mazzini, and so held his peace.

During these years, the annual parliaments of Europe's radicals met in those countries which extended hospitality to them, especially in Switzerland. At Berne, in September 1868, Bakunin and the Marxians came to ideological grips for the first time at the Second Congress of the Ligue de la Paix. Bakunin introduced a motion which took exception to a resolution earlier adopted at the Brussels meeting of the International. In the course of debate, he made his views plain: "I hate Communism, which is the denial of liberty, because by centralizing in the State all the social resources, the State would gain possession of all the property, with the result that individual talents would be hindered in their development. The organization of society should proceed upward through free association, not downward through an authority superior to the masses."[13] When a majority of the delegates rejected his motion, Bakunin left the League at the head of eighteen seceders. They held their own meeting and established still another association, the International Alliance of Socialist Democracy. The new Alliance immediately applied to the General Council of the International for recognition as a branch. Since Marx now began to express serious reservations about Bakunin, the General Council turned down the application. The Alliance then decided to dissolve and its branches were individually admitted to the International in July 1869.

All politicians have the instinct of gamblers; among radical politicians this inner faculty must be given widest berth. Bakunin's seeming passion for constantly fathering new organizations with resounding names (Mazzini's comparable proclivity should not be underestimated) sprang from the failure and not from the success of his undertakings. But hope and superstition stir easily in politicians; why not take the chance that another venture with a luckier name might finally triumph? Despite Bakunin's resurgent optimism, the Alliance could not have extended its hold much beyond the eighteen faithful adherents who walked out with him, else that stubborn anarchist would not have surrendered so easily to Marx. In the absence of credible evidence to the contrary, the entire incident casts doubts upon Bakunin's efficacy in Italy up to 1871 and upon the strength of his following. It also lends substance to the surmise that the verbal sallies of Bakunin's bands of zealots against Mazzini's forces had dented no more than the political skirmish lines of "poets and cranks" (as characterized by Leonida Bissolati (1857–1920), the moderate socialist of future years) unsupported by either workers or peasants. Marx's famous description of Bakunin's followers must be granted some weight since it probably reflected his considerable experience of radical groups, including his own. He derided them as declassed "lawyers without clients, doctors without knowledge or patients, billiard-playing students, commercial travellers, and various more or less unsavoury journalists of the gutter press."[14]

As so often before and afterward in Italian history, an outside event determined the outcome of the controversy between Bakunin and Mazzini. The National Guard and the radicals of Paris staged an uprising on March 18, 1871 and elected a municipal council of moderate republicans, radical republicans, disciples of Pierre Proudhon (1809–1865), adherents of Louis-Auguste Blanqui (1805–1881), and members of the International. The Commune did not possess enough unity of belief to advance a clear-cut program; the varieties of doctrine among the socialists alone prevented even them from espousing a group policy. Nonetheless, socialists everywhere basked in the fervor of Gallic insurrectionary courage and appropriated credit for the revolution. Although readily wiped out two months later, the Commune of Paris opened the passes of Italy to socialism. The International became the repository of the hopes of the people. Sensing this, Bakunin strengthened his position immensely by rushing at once to the verbal support of the Commune. Mazzini, instead, denounced the Commune.

Mazzini's insight could be chillingly precise at times. Just as he had foreseen, during the agitations and debate on the flour tax, that "while material reasons may create disturbances, they never engender revolutions," so, during the crisis created by the Paris Commune, he pinned down a persistent defect of Italian character, especially among young people: "The banner of insurrection fascinates us wherever and for whatever reason it is hoisted. Every bold undertaking strikes a responsive chord in the hearts of our youth not because it may, after careful consideration, reveal a truth hitherto unknown but because it is bold." Morally unable to truckle to popular delusions when they did not correspond to his own vision of truth, Mazzini went beyond denunciation of the Commune. In *La Roma del Popolo*, which he had first projected in late November 1870 and which published its first weekly issue on March 1, 1871, he attacked the International openly. His decision to fight both Commune and International brought political calamity. Andrea Costa (1851–1910) had absorbed Mazzinian republicanism at the University of Bologna through the lectures by Giosuè Carducci (1835–1907), the poet laureate of the *Risorgimento*. Costa had then carried his idealistic zeal with him to Parliament. Now, he turned to embrace Bakunin's violent brand of anarchistic socialism although in later life Costa came to advocate legal methods of reform. He has recorded the pain inflicted upon the new generation by Mazzini's seeming desertion of its cause:

> Mazzini's main fault was his alienation of our most ardent and generous youth which had been taught to appreciate the new ideas, his laying most of the blame for the crushing of France on materialistic theories, and his bitter denunciation of the fallen Commune. . . . In throwing ourselves into that movement we were impelled not so much by a conscious knowledge of our aims as by the desire of breaking away from a past which was oppressive and did not conform . . . to our ideal.[15]

The absurdities of Bakunin and the socialists who followed him must not blind a generation far-removed from the fierce loyalties of the decade from 1860 to 1870 to the deep sincerity, integrity, enthusiasm, courage, self-denial, and unusual qualities of intellect and heart possessed by these early socialists. Nor should their numerous, fatal, and often comic defects obscure the heroic qualities they displayed during the first ten years in the life of Italian socialism. In no other country in the world, with the exception of Russia, did the socialist movement endure such persistent and systematic persecution as in Italy. Socialist agitation of any kind usually ended in proscription, jail, or exile. In certain regions of Italy, where the uses of the dagger were traditional, men could become socialists only at the risk of their lives. Scores of socialists were treacherously murdered by their political enemies, especially by their republican adversaries.

For ten years following 1871, the Italian radical world belonged to Bakunin. He could count upon devoted men like Andrea Costa and Carlo Cafiero (1846–1892). At the age of 25, Cafiero, a member of an old, noble Apulian family, withdrew from his diplomatic post to devote himself to the study of the social sciences in Paris. From there he went to London where he came to know Marx well. Shortly afterward, his life as a socialist agitator began. In 1871, he sold his ancestral lands once he had inherited them. He realized a fortune from this transaction — 700,000 lire, a conspicuously large sum for that time and in a country like Italy — and turned it over entirely to Bakunin for the use of the Party. Cafiero himself led an exemplary life of poverty and ascetic personal virtue while inciting fellow-socialists to bloodshed and insurrection. He died mad. Another adherent, Errico Malatesta (1853–1932), who later became the leader of Italian anarchism, left his medical studies at Naples when his revolutionary activities landed him in jail. The International triumphed everywhere. No longer did Naples monopolize its energies. The Bakunin brand of socialists could now boast two dailies in Rome, one in Milan, and weeklies in Turin, Ravenna, Lodi, Bologna, Agrigento, and Catania. Even the nonsocialist press in Mantua, Alessandria, Rome, Parma, and Pavia could be counted on to support the International.

Garibaldi, born actor that he was, loved new roles and he hastened to assume the mantle of socialism. He lacked political sagacity and approached socialism through the foggy tunnel of noble sentiment, but these deficiencies merely encouraged him to lend the prestige of his name to the very events which were to destroy the influence of his cherished mentor, Mazzini. From the sheer habit of instinctively espousing all enthusiasms of the Far Left, Garibaldi sprang to the defense of the Paris Commune: in his view, it alone defended right and justice in the world. Consequently, he was flattered to become the honorary commander of the National Guard of the Commune. With flourish, he not only broke once again with Mazzini, but virtually delivered his devoted followers, who eagerly awaited his venerated opinions, into the camp of the International and Bakunin. To make his position symbolically clear beyond doubt, the aging military hero joined the Fascio Operaio (Workers Band) of Bologna in December 1871. He went on to support candidates with odd socialistic notions for seats in Parliament. Discussion circles, dedicated to socialism, took his name. He founded sections of the International in Catholic Rome itself. And so, this warm-hearted general, anxious in retirement for radical adulation and understandably weary of Mazzini's paternal condescension, took his niche among those notables of history who, past their prime but not past the need for staying in the public eye, gladly warranted the worth of new ideas about which they had vague knowledge and less understanding.[16]

Mazzini's death on March 10, 1872 enlivened Bakunin and freed him to turn up the heat under his simmering feud with Marx. As early as January 1872, the Turin section of the International had called for a congress of all sections in Italy. Next, the congress of the Fascio Operaio of Bologna, which met from March 17 to 19, approved of the initiative taken at Turin. The Bologna group represented an energetic segment of the Italian branch of the International for it had assumed leadership in organizing a regional Workers Federation which stretched across Emilia, Romagna, and the Marches as far as Ancona. The Federation had proclaimed its program tersely and vaguely: "Liberty with order; equality with law; fraternity with labor." Its publication, Fascio Operaio, was social-democratic in temper. This spirit manifested itself in the pronounced hostility

97

exhibited between the followers of Mazzini and the partisans of Bakunin at the Bologna congress. The bitterness assailed Romagna especially and the first International martyr fell at Lugo on May 2, 1872, presumably murdered by followers of Mazzini.

By the time that the nationwide congress of the Italian branch of the International assembled at Rimini in August 1872, the Bakuninites feared the harassment of the Mazzinians so little that they felt confident enough to assert their views against those of Marx. The twenty-five delegates elected Cafiero as president and Costa as secretary. They represented chapters located mostly in Central Italy and the South; in view of the later beginnings of moderate socialism in the more industrialized North, the failure of this region to send its share of delegates to Rimini should be stressed. The congress voted to establish its independence and to free itself from "the authoritarian doctrines professed by the General Council" in London. Nor did the delegates scruple, as dedicated internationalists, to introduce traces of national hostilities by referring to "authoritarian German communism, the negation of all the revolutionary sentiment of the Italian proletariat." They also proposed to call a conference in Switzerland in September of all factions from all countries which approved of the position taken by the congress of the Jura Federation of radicals which had met at Sonvilier in November 1871.

When the world congress of the International met at The Hague in September 1872, although Marx and his disciples made their views on the powers of the General Council prevail through parliamentary maneuvers, they were aware that the group under Bakunin showed obviously superior strength. Marx and his faction voted to remove the General Council for safekeeping to New York where faithful German socialists could be entrusted with the battered remnants of the already moribund organization. Charges preferred against Bakunin and his close associates resulted in recommendations for their expulsion from the tottering International. This act of purification released it from earthly bondage.

Bakunin's followers, who later came to be known as anarchists, met at Saint-Imier in Switzerland with some elements of the Jura Federation as soon as they had left The Hague. They founded the International Alliance of Socialist Democracy, taking the same name as the organization sired by Bakunin in Switzerland in 1868. They endorsed the independence of national federations and other affiliated groups; they called themselves federalists or antiauthoritarian collectivists. Once free of London and Marx, the Italian communicants of Bakunin should have enjoyed clear revolutionary sailing. But extreme radicalism, by the very intensity of its protest, is fated to provoke the elements; moreover, it most fulfills its destiny in stormy weather. The police authorities in Italy encountered no difficulties in deducing that the Bakuninites were now ready to bomb their way to a socialist millenium, for their master had made no secret of his philosophy: "The desire for destruction is at the same time a creative desire." Hence, only when the State, capitalism, and all of their institutions suffered annihilation by proletarian fire and sword could mankind enjoy liberty and happiness. Although Bakunin had devised no coherent system of thought and although the careful articulation of anarchist doctrine would not occur until Prince Peter Kropotkin (1842–1921) succeeded to world leadership of the movement, the police recognized in his consecration of the violent deed danger to the State. They countered the public threats of the anarchists with a most effective measure: Carlo Terzaghi who had founded *Il Proletario Italiano* in July 1871 in Turin. As their paid agent, he relayed to them the most reserved information entrusted to him by Garibaldi, Bakunin, and other prominent supporters of the federalists.

Because of police vigilance and interference, the second convention of the Italian International never took place in Mirandola as scheduled; when the meeting was shifted to Bologna, the police raided the session on March 16, 1873 and arrested some of the delegates, including Costa, Malatesta, and Cafiero. The police later ordered certain branches of the International to disband. Despite this evidence of governmental vigilance, on April 11 some fifty doughty delegates representing 153 branches met secretly in a factory near Bologna. This conclave pulled out all of the stops. It declared its principles to be atheistic, materialistic, anarchistic, and hostile to bourgeois political parties even when they claimed to be democratic or revolutionary. Moreover, political action received sanction only under the most special circumstances when it aided the principles proclaimed. The congress also discussed the best means to forge an alliance between city workers and peasants. Too, it undertook to study the organization of sections belonging to the International, including those federated on a craft or trade basis. As a result, the perennial confusion between political and labor movements now entered consequentially upon the Italian scene. After this fecund congress of declarations, the police instituted severe repressive measures. During the trial of arrested leaders, the International was declared a criminal organization. Although these prisoners were released after two months, other members of the International were seized in various parts of Italy.

By the end of 1873, after the December congress at Pisa, the International had to resort to secrecy. This provided no organizational hardship, for Bakunin's International Alliance of Socialist Democracy,

99

which Marx rejected in 1868 as a national affiliate, had so perfected the uses of secret internal groups that it immediately brings to mind the communist parties of the contemporary world. One hundred of the most trustworthy members of the Alliance formed the all-powerful International Brothers who served as the secret executive body with control over the entire organization, formulating its rules, principles, and programs. The National Brothers, also secret, were selected by the International Brothers on the basis of zeal, devotion, and control over the masses. Naturally, Bakunin, who railed against the authoritarianism of the London General Council and Marx, took on the mantle of supreme arbiter. With such experience behind them, the anarchists retreated underground in 1874 leaving self-implanted footprints. The newspapers ceased to mention the International, while the Italian Committee for Social Revolution began to attract attention through its public announcements that, although the International had gone into hiding, its secret activities would be devoted to conspiratorial measures leading to direct action.

By renouncing politics and legal methods of reform, the anarchists were brought face to face with the necessity of demonstrating that their principles could establish economic and social justice more effectively than those of Mazzini or Marx. At a meeting held in Switzerland, it was decreed that revolt would seethe throughout Italy during the summer of 1874. Before and after this synod, the hidden presses of the anarchists turned out manifestoes calling the people to revolt; they appeared on the walls of Rome and other cities. Then, during March and April 1874, preliminary disturbances occurred in Rome, Cremona, Brescia, Padua, Parma, Imola, and Faenza. In July, disorder filled the streets of Bologna, Florence, Pisa, Leghorn, Arezzo, Massa-Carrara, Rimini, Lucca, Forlì, and Prato. Seemingly Italy had returned by almost half a century to the decades of the Carbonari and their tactics of sudden assault upon the citadels of government.

The supreme uprising, R-Day, had been planned for the night between August 7 and 8, 1874. The leaders of the Committee for Social Revolution, including Bakunin, met secretly in Bologna at the end of July. Arms had already been purchased and only their distribution among the populace remained to be discussed. Although the police arrested Costa on August 5 at the railroad station, the others met intrepidly near Bologna to settle the question of arms and to fix the time of the march upon the city. The police, as usual, quelled the revolution rather easily since only 150 people, instead of the 2,000 expected, appeared to usher in the new day of liberation. Others, tramping in from Imola and elsewhere, either dispersed for home or took off to the mountains. Bakunin, costumed as a priest and bereft of his splendid beard which he had sacrificed to the exigencies of revolutionary escape, departed for Switzerland by train. Police measures also frustrated the grotesque plots of the internationalists in Florence, Leghorn, and Palermo. At Castel del Monte, a small village near Andria, Malatesta and only six confederates, rather than the several hundred comrades who had sworn to join him in liberating Apulia's peasants, battled eight *carabinieri* for several days before dispersing. Malatesta escaped to Naples in a wagonload of hay, but the police finally caught up with him at Pesaro.

Then followed a succession of trials in Rome, Florence, Trani, Perugia, Leghorn, and Massa-Carrara during the summer of 1875. Garibaldi himself demanded to be heard as a witness for the defense at Florence. The juries everywhere acquitted all but a handful of those accused, despite their obvious guilt as conspirators. These panels reflected the general run of public opinion throughout the country which condemned the economic and social misery upon which the pitiful attempts at insurrection throve in the absence of a true labor movement. The exonerations also exposed the wide gap between popular conscience and governmental will, a fault which had not closed almost a century later. On March 15, 1876, the chief trial against 79 revolutionaries opened at Bologna. Andrea Costa and his fellow prisoners, unlike their comrades the year before, readily admitted their membership in the International. Costa's heated eloquence appealed to Christianity, history, and the courtroom packed with middle-class citizens, their wives, and school children, who greeted Costa's fiery defense with expressions of loud approval. The jury, in rendering its decision of "Not Guilty" just after midnight on June 17, had not only felt the force of the acquittals of 1875, but had also responded to the formal shift in political opinion represented by the fall of the Right and the advent of the first ministry of the Left under Depretis on March 28, 1876. Meanwhile, in May 1876, a retrial of Rome's revolutionaries, ordered by the Court of Cassation, ended in the acquittal of all the defendants, including Malatesta. He claimed that they were freed, despite their avowed espousal of revolution and anarchistic collectivism, because the bourgeoisie still had no clear understanding of the true danger of socialism.

The split in the First International which made it impossible any longer for Italian socialists to see themselves as part of a united world movement, the complete failure of the heralded uprisings, the death of Bakunin at Berne on July 1, 1876, and the succession to world anarchist leadership of Kropotkin, who did not suffer from Bakunin's over-riding interest in Italy, insured the eventual decline of the movement in

101

that country. For the moment, however, not even the slap of defeat could startle Italian anarchists out of their hallucinations: they blithely plotted an uprising at San Lupo in the Matese mountains near Benevento to convert the peasants of the South to socialism. Malatesta and Cafiero took the lead, and again the police showed themselves fully informed concerning all phases of the revolution.

The details of this farcical venture rival the absurdities of an opéra bouffe. First, on April 3, 1877, an advanced scouting party consisting of Cafiero, Malatesta, and a blond girl with green eyes, together posing as an Englishman, his cousin, and his secretary, came to inspect the villa which had been rented for the Englishman's ailing wife. From this rustic retreat, they planned to direct the revolution. After unloading heavy boxes of insurrectionary supplies, they reconnoitered the surrounding knot of hills and then returned to Naples. On April 5, more antique rifles, 16 internationalists, and four *carabinieri* converged upon the villa. That night, two of the prowling police were wounded, one fatally, in an encounter with the revolutionaries. The police withdrew, but the insurgents realized that they would have to bring off the revolt faster than they had reckoned. Consequently, the plotters of San Lupo did not tarry for reinforcements. As they left the hamlet, they encountered, by sheer chance, 10 comrades who had escaped the police only because they missed their train in Rome. This doughty band of 26 rebels, armed with bombs and red flags, captured the tiny hamlets of Letino and Gallo on April 8. The liberators declared the King deposed, raised the scarlet banner of freedom, and distributed to the assembled villagers the arms and tax monies they had seized at the town hall. They made a bonfire of government records, but spared religious archives in deference to the common ideals of humanity. Meanwhile, the atheistic insurrectionists had converted the parish priests of each community; the clergymen joyously blessed the new Gospel. Accompanied by their frocked companions, the revolutionary band set out to liberate other communities. At a crucial point in their march toward earthly paradise, freezing rain dampened their powder to render them defenseless against the troops which already surrounded them. Worn, famished, and benumbed, the entire company of 26 conspirators surrendered. During their confinement in jail, they organized a branch of the International among the prisoners.

The government now retaliated for the San Lupo farce by a series of measures which sealed the doom of Bakuninism in Italy. It declared the organization illegal; it dissolved its sections and confiscated revolutionary newspapers; it arrested important as well as commonplace radicals in Bologna, Imola, Florence, Rome, and Naples. Costa fled into exile, while other key leaders languished in the jails of Naples and Benevento. At Santa Maria Capua Vetere, Cafiero and Malatesta awaited judgment. The trials of the San Lupo insurgents, including the two priests and a lost guide, who had strayed into the ranks of the Bakuninites as they tried to escape from the soldiers who surrounded them by retreating across Mount Casamara, dragged on until the summer of 1878. Cafiero and Malatesta, after their release in August, disappeared for some years from the Italian revolutionary scene.

The International disintegrated rapidly in a last hectic fever of senseless deeds. In February 1878, a Florentine worker threw a bomb into the midst of a parade organized to honor the memory of Victor Emmanuel II who had recently died. The police eventually freed him, due to the lack of evidence, but arrested four internationalists who disclaimed any connection with the outrage. On the strength of a ministerial decree of October 2, the police moved against the anarchists in Naples, Genoa, and Florence, where they also arrested Anna Kulishov (1857–1929) who had just arrived from Lugano at the end of September. On November 17, 1878, a young cook, wielding a knife, succeeded in slightly wounding King Humbert as the monarch's carriage carried him through the streets of Naples. The next day, an unknown assailant at Florence threw a bomb into a crowd of people who had assembled to watch the parade which celebrated Humbert's escape. The bomb killed four people and wounded ten more. Two days after the violence in Florence, another bomb fell among Pisans who were honoring the Queen's birthday. Immediate arrests in the Romagna virtually wiped out the International there.

In January 1879, the government secretly instructed prefects throughout the country to eradicate the International and to place its members under *ammonizione* (warning), a device the police usually applied only in the case of habitual offenders. Moreover, public opinion felt outraged at the bombings. Where those arraigned during the spring and summer of 1879 were found guilty of actual violence against persons, the juries handed down harsh sentences. However, in the purely political trials held in Forlì, Modena, Naples, Reggio Emilia, Genoa, Massa-Carrara, and Ancona, the courts declared that membership in the International was not in itself a crime. At the most celebrated political trial which opened on November 9, 1879 at Florence, Anna Kulishov and 13 other radicals stood accused of conspiracy against the internal security of the State. The government sought to support its case by citing presumed statements made by the defendants at a secret congress held in Pisa in April 1878, at a meeting in Florence during the fall of that year, or in correspondence intercepted during the summer of 1879 by the police. Although the jury arrived at a verdict of "Not Guilty" on January 5, 1880, the total impact of the prosecutions of 1879 assured the inglorious end of Bakunin's influence and the beginning of socialism in Italy. During the slow unwinding of the trials, "the authorities, the public, and what was more important the agitators themselves, began to see the distinctions between nihilism, anarchism, and socialism, words which had hitherto been used indiscriminately for an indiscriminate response of 'down with it' to any stimulus."[17]

The anarchists had not hesitated to set into motion the most fantastic schemes. Unwittingly, they underwrote the ultimate triumph of Marxian socialism so abhorred by them. Their wild belief in propaganda by sacred deed — one actual blow struck in the name of freedom exceeded volumes of theory in fundamental worth — stimulated their quixotic courage and single-minded devotion to explosive action. The gratuitous ruin to which these qualities led so alarmed even Italian radicals into second thoughts that Marxian socialism, by contrast, emerged as almost respectability itself. Marx and his followers disdained the mystique of violence, recognized the necessity of governmental institutions, maintained that the masses should be educated to partake in political elections where social rights were won, and emphasized the need to organize workers in the factories and on the land.

During the years when Bakunin's disciples enjoyed a monopoly of radical clamor and rebellion in Italy, the Marxian internationalists, although few in number, patiently held on to their convictions. Gradually, as the antics of the anarchists came to be understood as both dangerous and futile, the more moderate ideas of Marx and other schools of socialism started to receive wider circulation and acceptance. Finally, in 1892, the Italian Socialist Party took permanent form. But its intricate origins reach back into the decade between 1880 and 1890. They must be traced with tolerant care, for they include the first effort on Italian soil to free political organizations of workers from middle-class socialist domination. Once this attempt failed, the forces which were to link the Socialist Party and Italian labor unions could not be escaped.

Nicolo Lo Savio published *Il Proletario*, "a socialist economic journal for labor democracy," at Florence in 1865. Considered the first socialist publication to appear in Italy, *Il Proletario* emphasized economic problems and echoed Proudhon in abjuring political action. Two years later, Enrico Bignami (1847–1921) inaugurated the first Marxian periodical, *La Plebe*, at Lodi in Lombardy. In 1871, the year of the Paris Commune, *La Rivista Partenopea* printed a pioneering summary by Emilio Covelli of the first volume of Marx's *Das Kapital* which had appeared in German in 1867.

After the schism between the International and the Bakuninites in 1872, Bignami, the editor of *La Plebe,* remained faithful to the General Council. Engels wrote on November 2, 1872: "His paper is in our hands. But he must exercise caution as he is surrounded by autonomists." Engels had also asserted that Bignami alone in Italy sided with London, but he was mistaken to the extent that Osvaldo Gnocchi-Viani (1837–1917), the secretary of the Rome section of the International and the future founder of the chambers of labor in Italy, had also remained a Marxian.[18]

Meanwhile, curiosity concerning Marxism penetrated even among nonsocialists. At a meeting on September 8, 1873 of the Palermo Academy of Sciences, Letters and Arts, Giuseppe Di Menza, a member, presented a paper entitled: *Karl Marx and His Doctrines.* In the same year, Tullio Martello published his error-studded *Storia dell'Internazionale dalla sua origine al Congresso dell'Aja* (*History of the International from Its Origin to The Hague Congress*).

In 1874, Enrico Bignami, who had not yet reached the legal age for election as a deputy to Parliament, earned the historical distinction of becoming the first socialist to brave the Italian International's anarchist injunction against participation in politics and to present himself for that office when he decided to contest the seat for the district of Pescarolo Cremonese during the November elections. The government, it will be recalled, had ordered various sections of the Italian International dissolved and had arrested its leaders. Although he strongly opposed the Bakunin faction, Bignami's electoral platform neglected socialist demands and featured, instead, vigorous protests, on principle, against the action taken by the authorities. Falling victim to that irony which has always lent a humorous touch to Italian radicalism, Bignami found it necessary to conduct his electoral campaign from the privacy of a prison cell. The police provided him with these unlikely headquarters after the anarchists had attempted insurrections at Taranto and Molfetta, even though Bignami thoroughly disapproved of those ventures. Italian officials, then as now, like their counterparts elsewhere, apparently found it as easy as scholars to confound the contentions of various schools of radical thought.

Legalitarian socialism advanced another step when Benoît Malon fled his own country, France. A worker and a radical, he had been elected mayor of the district of Batignolles in the Paris Commune. After the fall of the Commune, Malon took refuge in Geneva where he founded *La Revanche.* When that publication was suppressed by the Swiss government in February 1872, he found his way to Italy where he lived at various times in Milan, Palermo, and Lugano. In 1874, together with Salvatore Ingegneros Napoletano, he started the newspaper, *Il Povero,* at Palermo. He could not remain in Sicily long, for the authorities demanded his departure despite the fact that he advocated moderate socialist views. In Milan, he exerted great influence upon Bignami who placed himself at Malon's disposition. In 1876, he was expelled from Milan and once again sought haven in Switzerland where he remained until the French amnesty of 1880. In France, along with Jules Guesde (1845–1922), Marx's most faithful Gallic disciple, Malon founded the Federation of the French Revolutionary Party in 1885. In that same year, he started the *Revue Socialiste* which he edited until his death. Soon, he differed from Guesde and founded an independent revisionist socialist party.

Malon, who wrote extensively and who impressed a wide variety of people as much by his goodness and gentle personality as by the strength of his arguments, called his socialism "integral." He maintained that religion, ethics, and esthetics were important factors in the solution of social problems. Since he did not think that socialism was as simple as the German socialists made it out to be, Malon deplored Marx's emphasis on materialism, economic interests, and class antagonisms. Malon presented socialism as a force at once spiritual and economic, seeking to reconcile all classes; it therefore required the cooperation of aristocrats, intellectuals, and the middle class, as well as labor. This foreigner, without standing among Italian workers and bereft of any claim upon them, strove against both Marx and Bakunin through press and platform to show the practical wisdom of those democratic reforms which the French and German socialist movements were already advocating: universal suffrage, freedom of speech and press, the right to form associations and to strike, protective labor legislation, and legal recognition for cooperatives and mutual benefit societies.

Malon's approach — mild, realistic, and just — represented the first attempt in Italy to counter both the Bakunin and Marxian brands of socialism with the socialism of reform and class alliance. His views appealed to those whose temperaments rejected the vision, essentially medieval, of employing force and hatred to destroy utterly the old world of evil by fire and brimstone as the prerequisite condition for building the new world of freedom and equality. But Malon's views, despite their enlightened quality, were not fated to prevail.

In 1875, those sections of the International which had remained faithful to Marx under the leadership of Bignami, Gnocchi-Viani, and others in Lombardy published a statement of principles which explained the socialist program and clarified the Marxian approach to revolution. During the same year, the Sicilian, Vito Cusumano, published a summary of *Das Kapital,* along with critical appraisals of the book which had appeared in England and Germany: *Le scuole economiche della Germania in rapporto alla questione sociale (The German Schools of Economic Thought in Relation to the Social Question).* Later, in February 1877, shortly before the April events of Benevento shook Italy, the Marxians assembled under the presidency of Bignami at Milan and listened with pleasure to a message from Engels in which he exalted the efficacy of the political struggle. They also heard Gnocchi-Viani openly approve of the participation of Italian socialists in elections, or, at least, in political agitation. This group, although still small, served a useful function in clarifying its own ideas concerning the proper uses of politics. Before 1882 when the franchise was extended, the question was academic in Italy, as in other European countries, with the exception of Lassalle's Germany and some Swiss cantons. As yet, the term, "Marxist," was not synonymous in Italy with "parliamentary socialist." Actually, Marxist theoreticians themselves had not defined their attitudes on this question with clarity, nor had Marx been overly tender toward parliamentarism or parliamentarians. He used the phrase, "parliamentary imbecility," which he defined as "a disease which infects its unfortunate victims with the conviction that the entire world, its history, and its future are governed and determined by the majority vote of the representative body." Despite the uncertainties of Italian Marxists, since Marx himself had never elevated his antiparliamentarian views into a theory, and despite the eight-year disappearance of socialist candidates for office after Bignami's pioneering run in 1874, the Bignami group of internationalists slowly arrived at an alternative to offer to those workers and intellectuals who had abandoned Mazzini's associationism, but had not yet broken away from the spell of Bakunin's infantile preachments of Armageddon.[19]

The brilliant Anna Kulishov, as noted before, made her first appearance in Italy in 1878. She possessed both emotional warmth and intellectual acumen. Rigola quotes a keen observer of men and affairs saying of her: "There is only one political figure of stature in Italy and that personage is a woman, and a Russian to boot." As mistress of Andrea Costa and mother of his child, as life-long companion of Filippo Turati (1857–1932) who became the future leader of the socialist right-wing, and as friend and advisor of other notable leaders, she guided three generations of Italian socialists. She had met Costa in Paris where he had taken refuge and stood trial with him there in 1877. The court condemned him to two years of imprisonment; the authorities expelled her from France. She eventually made her way to Italy and soon enough involved herself with the anarchists. Arrested in Florence and charged with conspiracy, she stood alone before the court, defending herself by pointing lucidly toward the futility of emotional extremism: "Socialism does not create armed bands, but it is ready to direct those that are thrown up naturally by social conditions."[20]

On August 3, 1879, *La Plebe* published Andrea Costa's open letter, "To My Friends in the Romagna," written on July 27 from Lugano where his legalitarian socialist friends feted him after his amnesty and release from prison. This declaration of principle changed Italian life more radically than the entire succession of bombings and insurrections executed earlier by Costa and his anarchist comrades. The letter not only marked a turning point in his life, for he had been converted to legalitarian socialism, but the entire movement in Italy also acquired a new orientation and character. Costa urged the formation of an Italian revolutionary socialist party which would continue the work begun by the International, but which would have the capacity to learn from experience and would renounce insurrectionary tactics and electoral abstention. His former comrades quickly associated the name of Costa with Judas, for only three years earlier at his trial in Bologna, Costa had said to the jurors: "We shall fight on until no stone built on stone will remain of present society."[21]

Italian radicalism continued to abound in irony. Since the Benevento fiasco in 1877, Carlo Cafiero had been imprisoned at Naples. In confinement, he wrote an abridgement of the first volume of *Das Kapital*, despite his conspicuous aversion toward Marxian socialism. Irony proliferated. Bignami, no political admirer of Cafiero, edited his summary. In this form, Marx's ideas received wider circulation than ever before, since Cafiero pitched his abridgement at a level of understanding comprehensible to the masses.

Andrea Costa returned to Milan in 1880 where he founded the *Rivista Internazionale del Socialismo*. In anticipation of a meeting of socialists at Milan in May, and in view of the March assembly of thirty Emilian socialist delegates at Bologna which Costa attended and where the creation of a socialist party had been proposed, Costa began to set forth his own program in the review he founded: freedom of the press, right of association, universal suffrage, reduction in the hours of work, limitation or abolition of child and female labor, regulation of factory working conditions, and the abolition of the milling tax and of all indirect taxes. Costa discussed his doctrine of evolution and his tactic of immediate legalitarian gains at the congress of the Italian International which met at Chiasso in Switzerland just over the border from Como on December 5 and 6, 1880. Cafiero presided over this stormy assembly where the old anarchistic and the new reformist tendencies came into open conflict. Despite Costa's pleas and Gnocchi-Viani's three-hour appeal in behalf of political action, the majority stood with Cafiero who adamantly rejected action at the polls in favor of armed revolt.

The minority moved ahead. On April 30, 1881, the first issue of *Avanti!* (*Forward!*), destined to become the official organ of the future Socialist Party, appeared as a weekly journal edited by Costa at Imola. The inspiration for its title and tone came from the famous publication of the German Socialist Party, *Vorwärts*.

The next year, 1882, Depretis widened the Italian franchise. Although the new electoral dispensation kept the rolls limited to little more than 2,000,000 male voters, comprising only 6.9% of the population, nevertheless the reform set into motion, for the first time in Italian history, the possibility of creating a party of workmen. Moreover, it shifted the balance of potential socialist power to its economically logical center. Even the lowered educational requirements of the Depretis law still excluded most workmen and peasants, especially in the South, from voting. As a result, the industrializing North, especially Milan, where workmen possessed relatively high literacy, became the principal center of socialist activity for the first time. Before 1882, socialism had developed and found greatest favor in the South, Central Italy, Romagna, and Emilia. Thus, the electoral law industrialized Italian socialism, hitherto agricultural and handicraft in character.

During the very year when Parliament extended suffrage, Giuseppe Croce, a glovemaker, and Costantino Lazzari (1857–1927), a printer, led the Italian Workers Party into existence. Lazzari received only an elementary school education. Nevertheless, through his own efforts he acquired considerable culture which deepened when he served as secretary to Agostino Bertani during the famous agricultural investigation of 1878. Later, Lazzari took to the highways as a travelling salesman, perhaps, thought Roberto Michels, to come into closer touch with the people. Eventually, he became the general secretary of the Socialist Party, one of the few leaders with a working-class background.[22]

Immediately after the electoral law was proclaimed, the Workmen's Circle of Milan formed a section made up wholly of urban labor with the avowed aim of forming a workers party. Overcoming the delaying tactics of those companions who were allied with the middle-class radical party, the victors lost no time in drawing up a manifesto addressed to the workers of the city and countryside on May 17, 1882. This manifesto marked the beginning of the first and last political organization of Italian workers which restricted its ranks solely to workers, chose its leaders, spokesmen, and editors from among its own members, and gravely and spiritedly rejected the offers of outside middle-class help and tutelage.

The program of the Workers Party distinguished between the activities it would pursue with regard to the State and those it would undertake with regard to capital. It felt justified in cooperating with other parties to force through social reforms since these were of a national and humanitarian nature and therefore could not be claimed as the exclusive domain of any one group of citizens. With regard to capital, however, the Party maintained that, since one part of the nation placed itself in opposition to another part, the Workers Party had the obligation to act on its own, without interference and without aid from middle-class groups.

The Party's demands upon the State included the right of association and of striking, universal manhood suffrage, home rule for cities, academic freedom, a single graduated tax based upon capital and income, and the abolition of government grants to religious orders. Its economic program, directed against capital, proposed the creation of "leagues of resistance" among all workers and their federation into a single organization; the sharing by labor of all profits derived from labor; the establishment of consumer, producer, and credit cooperatives; the formation of a placement service for unemployed workers to be administered by the Party; municipal housing for workers; and the award of all public works to labor associations formed for that purpose.

Although but recently organized, the Workers Party ran its own candidates independently of the socialists. One of them, Antonio Maffi (1845–1912), a type caster, was elected from Milan. When he reached Parliament, he immediately aligned himself with the republicans and gradually lost touch with those who helped to elect him. Of the eight socialists who contested seats, only Andrea Costa succeeded in becoming a deputy from Imola. Cafiero, the staunch Bakuninite, had come all the way from London, at the risk of arrest, to support Costa's candidacy along with Costa's principle of participation in parliamentary elections. Henceforth, the true believers among the anarchists were free to revile Cafiero along with Costa.

The socialist candidates, along with Antonio Maffi, had gathered up 49,154 votes, or about 4% of the total number cast. However, this substantial accomplishment during their first try for office should not be taken to mean that the entrance of the socialists into the political arena had been an easy step for them. They had to move with circumspection, for they dared not touch too harshly the sensibilities of their followers, so long nourished on the traditions of the Carbonari and Bakunin. With elaborate circumlocutions, they explained the benefits which would accrue to the working classes from the tactic of political participation. Just as Wilhelm Liebknecht (1826–1900) found it necessary in 1869 to explain the motives which impelled him to run for office some years back, so in 1882 Enrico Bignami thought it desirable to publish a pamphlet, *The Socialist Candidate,* in which he balanced curious justifications for becoming a deputy with revolutionary, abstentionist sentiments. In addition to these difficulties of an internal character, the socialists had to face in the election of 1882 candidates of the middle-class parties who, like their counterparts in France after the February 1848 revolution, divested themselves of their titles and tagged their names on the parliamentary election lists with humble occupations like farmer, mechanic, and worker. As for their attitude to the Workers Party, the socialists took a guarded but sympathetic stand. They knew that they were still too weak to fight the Party, but they hoped, in time, to absorb it. Costa, in *Avanti!,* saw clearly the relationship between the emergence of the Party and the industrial nature of Milan; he also was frank to admit that a purely working-class party could not as yet have been formed in his beloved Romagna.

After the elections of 1882, the Workers Party of Milan went into decline and its chapters disbanded. On the other hand, interest in socialism continued. Camillo Prampolini (1859–1930) of Emilia entered the socialist movement with the publication of an article in *Voce del Popolo* which he signed as "The Shirtless One." Nor did the intricacies of radical doctrine remain foreign to the Church itself. At Rome in 1882, a Jesuit priest, Valentino Staccanella published *Of Communism: a Critical, Philosophical and Political Inquiry.*

The next year, 1883, brought better fortune to the Workers Party. A group of wage earners organized the League of the Sons of Labor with the purpose of improving their economic condition. The League also established its own newspaper, *Fascio Operaio,* with a slogan on its masthead taken from Benoît Malon: "If Italian workers do not think of acting for themselves, they will never be emancipated." At a congress of the Sons of Labor held at Varese during 1883, the delegates reiterated their independence from middle-class tampering and proclaimed themselves the best judges of what ought to be done about working-class problems. Although this new group had its real center in Milan, branches

111

were also established in Bologna, Rome, and Naples. The character and influence of the Sons of Labor as a union will be explored more fully when the development of the labor movement between 1860 and 1890 is detailed later in this narrative. At this point, however, the Sons of Labor hold interest, principally, as a political force which resuscitated the Workers Party.

During the by-elections of 1884, two new socialists won seats as deputies, one from Borgo San Donnino and the other from Grosseto. The result of the Grosseto election was annulled, however, on the motion of Francesco Crispi. This meant that the number of socialists elected to Parliament, so far, was four. But only three were actually serving at Montecitorio; of these, Maffi had been lost to socialism by going over to the republicans. This left two socialists in Rome, but even these two had been elected with the aid of nonsocialist democratic votes.

On April 12, 1885, the Workers Party met in congress at Milan to perfect its program. Representatives of the Sons of Labor and other workers groups in Milan, Monza, Brescia, and Como attended this meeting; greetings arrived from socialist and labor groups in Forlì and Ravenna. The congress reaffirmed its exclusively proletarian character in article 7 of its program. Only those organizations of workers which concerned themselves with the social and economic improvement of the working class were eligible for membership. These acceptable bodies might be organized for mutual aid or in other ways, always provided that they were "constituted of pure and simple manual workers, of both sexes, from field as well as workshop, who were dependent for their wages upon proprietors, entrepreneurs, or capitalists." In other articles of the program, the Party declared itself opposed to governmental interference in labor matters and strongly favored "the necessary means of defense by workers against capitalist oppression: organization and the strike."[23] The executive arm of the Party, the Central Committee, reflected the convictions of the congress. It was made up solely of workers: a bronzist, a glovemaker, a printer, a lithographer, a mechanic, and an upholsterer. The delegates to this congress and their leaders would have found themselves quite at home, in many important respects, at the annual meeting of the Federation of Organized Trades and Labor Unions of the United States and Canada which assembled that year in Washington, D.C.

The Milan congress had expressed sympathy and solidarity with the agricultural strikes then in full swing in the province of Mantua and had collected money for the relief of the peasants. This action led the government to confiscate several issues of *Fascio Operaio*. Then, in July, seven leaders were brought to trial on the charge of inciting workers to strike and encouraging class hatred. The public prosecutor also charged the leaders with not being true workers and subverting the real ones. This accusation was indignantly rejected in a proud statement that it would be difficult to find a single spot on the skin of any of the indicted men which did not bear the scars of labor. Six of the accused received sentences of one month in jail; Giuseppe Croce, the managing editor of *Fascio Operaio*, drew a penalty of twenty days. During these prosecutions, the Party gained strength.

At the end of the same year, the Workers Party held another congress at Mantua from December 6 to 9. An Order of the Day recorded the adherence of the important Lombard Confederation of Labor to the Workers Party. Representatives from the Confederation, after examining the principles and system of organization of the Party, accepted the Party's constitution as the basis of union since they were convinced that only the coalition of all workers in all trades and crafts could bring about the emancipation of the proletariat. This alliance seemed of great moment. The Lombard Confederation, first created in 1881 under the auspices of the Workers Consulates of Milan and Como — organizations sponsored by left-wing members among the middle-class parliamentary radicals with the intention of winning the sympathies of the workers — numbered among its constituent bodies a substantial group of mutual aid societies. These societies had generally exhibited less militant tendencies than the newly forming leagues of resistance. The fusion of the Confederation and the Party therefore appeared to indicate a move toward the left among organized labor groups. Events were soon to prove this hope premature.

The dissemination of socialist doctrine and propaganda continued into the new year. On January 29, 1886, Camillo Prampolini published the inaugural number of *La Giustizia* (*Justice*) at Reggio Emilia, a newspaper fated to serve as a bastion of Italian reform socialism. For the first time, *Das Kapital* became available in its entirety as part of a series called "The Library of the Economist" which also offered in translation the works of Robert Owen (1771–1858) and of other socialists whose views differed from those of Marx. In March, *Fascio Operaio* published for the first time Filippo Turati's *Song of the Workers*, later called the *Hymn of the Workers*. Eight days later, the Donizetti chorus sang the *Song* during the dedication of the banner of the Mixed League of the Sons of Labor at Milan.

In April 1886, in preparation for the coming national elections, the Workers Party drew up a seventeen-point program. It ranged from the encouragement of labor unions, cooperatives, minimum-wage legislation, the eight-hour day, and equal pay for equal work, to the abolition of state monopolies, the legalization of divorce, home rule for cities, the adoption of universal suffrage, and the establishment of a bureau of labor statistics — a spate of proposals reminiscent of the wide-ranging reforms demanded by the Knights of Labor in the United States at this very time.

The electoral campaign of 1886 disclosed wide breaches within the ranks of both the workers and the middle class. Moreover, by engendering a bitter and violent battle between the Workers Party and the radical forces of the bourgeois parties, the electoral struggle forced the Workers Party to draw close to the socialists. First, the Workers Consulate of Milan, the mainstay of the Lombard Confederation representing fifty-one mutual aid societies, formed an electoral alliance with the middle-class parties of the Left. The rationale for this volte-face was put neatly: if a worker had the duty of participating in government along with other citizens, then the election of a proletarian ought not to assume the character of opposition to other social classes.

Depretis purposefully brought about the splits among the middle-class political forces. He regarded the socialists as heirs of the International and implacable enemies of the State. He viewed the Workers Party as more susceptible of cooperation with advanced sections of the bourgeoisie and the intellectuals of North Italy, especially of Milan. Therefore, he calculated that by expressing sympathy for the Workers Party he would not only weaken the new democratic and radical tendencies within the middle class, which fought his government, but might also garner the sympathy of those Milan voters who could not bring themselves to support the Workers Party, yet might possibly support a government democratic enough to encourage the Party with kind words. Once these words were uttered, the Workers Party was accused of shady dealings with Depretis by the radicals and republicans: the Party had been created by the government to undermine the democratic forces among the middle class; secret funds of the Ministry of the Interior subsidized the Party. Bereft of exaggeration, these rumors were finally reduced to the accusation that Costantino Lazzari accepted money from the government to conduct his campaign against the bourgeois candidates. Speakers in behalf of the Workers Party were greeted at meetings with cries of "Spy!" The quarrel burst into acute violence between Party members and the adherents of Felice Cavallotti (1842–1898), the leader of the radical democrats. The affair ended in arbitration by a jury of honor which decided in favor of the Workers Party.

The Lazzari case provided the first, if not the last, public notice in Italy of the acceptance by class-conscious workers and socialists of funds from presumably hostile middle-class conservative sources. This phenomenon has also occurred in the history of English and German socialism, nor is it absent from the contemporary scene in Italy among labor and socialist groups.

During the trying campaign, the Workers Party and the socialists came closer together. Although the Party backed Giuseppe Berretta, the working foreman of the streetcar station at Monza, many workers decided to back Gnocchi-Viani, the intellectual socialist, as well. In Milan, both groups conducted a joint campaign for their respective candidates. Although the Party elected no candidates of its own, it received a total of about 17,000 votes in the Lombardy and Emilia-Romagna regions, destined to become the supreme socialist centers of Italy. A socialist deputy was elected at both Borgo San Donnino and Mantua, while Andrea Costa was re-elected from Imola. The campaign results demonstrated that workers, even in Milan, did not as yet possess good enough candidates and clever enough propagandists to go it alone without the aid of the nonproletarian socialists.

The Depretis government, acting through the commissioner of police at Milan, moved quickly to dissolve the Italian Workers Party and suppressed *Fascio Operaio*. The decree of June 22, 1886 also ordered the dissolution of the Sons of Labor. The decree itself stated the grounds for such government action: "The Workers Party is engaged in organizing each trade and craft for the protection of the workers; it is also engaged in organizing resistance in the towns and countryside against capital and is working for the transfer of public lands in the communes to peasant families." The leaders of the Party and the editorial staff of the paper, after eighty days of "preventive detention" in jail, were brought before the Court of Assize where they received sentences ranging from two to eighteen months of imprisonment. Despite these repressive measures, at the beginning of October 1886, *Fascio Operaio* appeared once more, while the Sons of Labor re-formed their ranks and applied themselves busily to their former tasks.

Toward the end of 1886, the *Rivista Italiana del Socialismo* appeared under the auspices of Italy's leading socialists, including Filippo Turati, Gnocchi-Viani, and Leonida Bissolati of Lombardy; Andrea Costa and Camillo Prampolini of the Romagna-Emilia area; and Pio Schiapparelli and Gustavo Chiantore of Piedmont. Despite its short existence, the magazine served a useful purpose in attempting to bring about a meeting of minds among the various schools of Italian socialism.

The Workers Party, reconstituted after its dissolution, held a congress at Pavia in September 1887. Two currents manifested themselves there: the group which wished to maintain the Party as the domain of workers alone, excluding middle-class intellectuals, whether socialist or not; and the socialist faction headed by Costantino Lazzari, who, along with Filippo Turati, was an active member of the Socialist League of Milan. The Party met again in September 1888 at Bologna, but shortly thereafter, *Fascio Operaio* ceased publication.

The Workers Party, with its unshakable sense of mission and its strong conviction that membership should be limited to men who labored in shop or factory, had small chance of fulfilling its role on the Italian scene. Middle-class socialist intellectuals of all brands, whether or not sound in their views or sage in their actions, drew their eagerness to invade labor organizations from the fountainhead of theory itself. The ever forming and disbanding leagues and societies of workers were still too weak to resist their attention or refuse their assistance. Even in the industrial North, workers like Giuseppe Croce and Costantino Lazzari, sufficiently educated and gifted to assume leadership, were rare enough in Milan itself, the leading manufacturing center of the country. Gnocchi-Viani was convinced that, if the Workers Party "had not been dissolved by a stratagem on the part of the government, it would have brought about its own dismemberment and transformation, although not so easily and gracefully. The government's violent action hastened its change and strewed over the grave of the deceased the flowers of martyrdom."[24] Roberto Michels summed up the fate of the Party less flamboyantly: "The Workers Party died neither a violent nor a natural death. In a slow organic process lasting a decade, it became, almost inadvertently, a part of the Socialist Party."[25]

In 1888, Andrea Costa once more had to flee the country. Although a deputy in Parliament, he had been arrested during a demonstration calling for the redemption of Trent and Trieste. The Chamber of Deputies authorized the lifting of parliamentary immunity from him and he was condemned to three years in jail. During the same year, a group of socialists in Reggio Emilia dared to discuss in public the *Communist Manifesto*, not as yet translated into Italian. In 1889, the first translation of this classic Marxist work appeared in the appendix of *L'Eco del Popolo* (*The People's Echo*) of Cremona. It is thought that Leonida Bissolati was the author of this translation from the German text.

Up to 1889, the restrictive law of March 20, 1865 still applied to local elections. In that year, communal and provincial elections took place for the first time under the enlarged suffrage. In Milan, a working printer received 11,233 votes with the aid of the radical democrats and was elected to the city council. Filippo Turati, running as a candidate of the Socialist League of Milan, obtained a seat on the provincial council. At Imola, socialists, radicals, and republicans won resounding victories.

In 1889, the philosophy lectures of Antonio Labriola (1843–1904) at the University of Rome moved on from enthusiastic elucidation of positivism — the new learning inspired in Italy by the insights of Darwin and Herbert Spencer rather than Comte — to equally intense exegesis of orthodox Marxism. Labriola's conversion aroused the special attention which only the prestige enjoyed by a university professor on the continent could provoke. Indeed, his dedication to the strictest interpretation of Marx almost cost him his post. Although Labriola lacked originality himself, he influenced socialist thinking in the country profoundly, for his single-minded devotion to Marx as a powerful thinker made him a faithful exponent of Marx's ideas. The very limitations of his mentality and his lively style made him admirably suited to introduce Italians to a strict and rigid analysis of the "scientific" socialism of Marx. Labriola's most famous pupil, Benedetto Croce, who esteemed both his teacher and Marx, later took philosophic pains to prove that Marx's doctrines were considerably less than scientific. Unfortunately for Italy's future political welfare, too many socialists accepted Labriola's orthodox views of Marx, expressed in brisk and highly readable fashion, as gospel.[26]

The Italian delegation to the constituent congress of the Second International in Paris on July 14, 1889 reflected the divisions which still persisted among the socialists on the peninsula: Andrea Costa represented the legalitarians, Amilcare Cipriani (1844–1918) the anarchists, and Giuseppe Croce the all-but-defunct Workers Party. Representatives of these currents, together with the inevitable sprinkling of Mazzinians, Garibaldian revolutionaries, and other radical tag ends, consented to enter upon an uneasy alliance in 1892: the Italian Socialist Party. Despite the spectacular growth of socialism during the next three decades, the Party never achieved viable unity; inevitably, it fell prey to dissension and schism, opening the way to fascism. Clearly, that tragedy, which also destroyed the Italian labor movement, had already gathered dark momentum during the thirty tumultuous years after the proclamation of national unity in 1860. The parties of that era — whether conservative, radical-democratic-republican, anarchist, or socialist — all suffered from a common malaise: the continued frustration of the perceptive hope ex-

Chronology of Political Congresses of Italian Workers from 1853 to the Founding of the Italian Socialist Party in 1892.*

Year	Workers Societies (mostly of mutual benefit type, and, before 1860, all from Piedmont). National organization: Affiliated Italian Workers Societies.	Workers Societies of moderate orientation.	The International, Bakuninite. Later manifestation: Revolutionary Anarchist Socialist Party.	The International, North Italian Federation (Bignami group).	Revolutionary Socialist Party of Romagna, later of Italy.	Lombard Confederation of Labor.	Italian Workers Party.	Party of Italian Workers (name changed in 1895 to Italian Socialist Party).
1853	I Asti							
1854	II Alessandria							
1855	III Genoa							
1856	IV Vigevano							
1857	V Voghera							
1858	VI Vercelli							
1859	VII Novi							
1860	VIII Milan							
1861	IX Florence	Asti						
1862								
1863	X Parma							
1864	XI Naples							
1865–1870								
1871	XII Rome	Rome						
1872			I Rimini					
1873	XIII Rome		II Bologna					
1874								
1875	XIV Genoa	Bologna						
1876			III Florence	I Milan				
1877				II Milan				
1878			IV Pisa					
1879		Bologna						
1880	XV Genoa	Rome		III Chiasso				
1881					I Rimini			
1882					II Ravenna-Forli			
1883			Forli		III (I) Forli			
1884						I Milan II Como III Varese IV Milan V Brescia VI Mantua		
1885							I Milan II	
1886	XVI Florence				IV (II) Mantua			
1887								
1888	XVII Naples						III Pavia IV Bologna	
1889								
1890	XVIII Palermo				V (III) Ravenna		V Milan	
1891			Capolago					Milan
1892								Genoa

* This chart is a translation, with corrections and explanatory additions, of the chart which forms Appendix VI in Gastone Manacorda's *Il movimento operaio italiano attraverso i suoi congressi*, pp. 386–387.

pressed by Massimo D'Azeglio at the moment of liberation. That gifted son-in-law of Alessandro Manzoni (1785–1873) — D'Azeglio distinguished himself as statesman, warrior, painter, and novelist — who gave way in 1852 to Cavour as Piedmont's Prime Minister, declared: "We have made Italy; now we have to make the Italians." Hard to achieve as that partial task might have proved alone, in actuality both Italy and the Italians had to be created together — a truth which countries like tribal Ghana and Indonesia have had to discover anew at mid-twentieth century. The requirement meant a heroic outpouring of continuous energy already so recklessly squandered during the *Risorgimento,* and an unceasing struggle by dispassionate leaders against selfish regional interests, immemorially fixed in the very texture of life and avidly cultivated at the expense of the nation as a whole.

From 1860 onward, Italian politics, economics, and social development could never escape the need to assert their claims in the teeth of petty local power which endured longer and with more vigor on the peninsula and islands than elsewhere in Western Europe. The Marxists, even at the height of their fortunes after 1890, and certainly not before then, failed to propagandize themselves clear of this condition of Italian humanity; the other parties were equally unsuccessful in attempting to logroll nationhood into existence. The persistence of both socialists and nonsocialists in using the same bags of early devised tricks after 1890 as they had employed previously proved just as futile and more dangerous. Unfortunately, Italy did not suffer only from its famed *campanilismo* — the word admirably describes that breadth of local concern which extends just as far as the sound range of the town's church-steeple bells. Of calamitous consequence for the twentieth century, *campanilismo* preserved very near the surface of easy arousal age-old feelings of class antagonism. Along with history and geography, this narrow and bitter provincialism of the spirit rose to harry Italy, a country not yet a nation, before and after fascism.[27]

FOOTNOTES — CHAPTER III

[1] Benedetto Croce, *A History of Italy 1871–1915,* p. 2; W. Hilton-Young, *The Italian Left,* p. 6.

[2] Sprigge, cited above, p. 51; Croce, cited above, p. 38; Roberto Michels, *Le prolétariat et la bourgeoisie dans le mouvement socialiste italien particulièrement des origines à 1906,* p. 35.

[3] Sprigge, cited above, p. 42; see also, Denis Mack Smith, *Italy,* pp. 71–73.

[4] For the quotations from Croce, see Croce, cited above, pp. 43—45. Not even Croce could foresee the relatively near future: the 1948 Constitution provided for regional autonomy.

[5] The same, p. 47.

[6] The same, pp. 46–47, 53; Hughes, cited above, pp. 50–51; Sprigge, cited above, pp. 42, 50–51.

[7] Croce, cited above, pp. 48–49; Hughes, cited above, pp. 53–55; Sprigge, cited above, pp. 52–58.

[8] Sprigge, cited above, pp. 60–61.

[9] Croce, cited above, pp. 17–18, 31–33, 163–182; Hughes, cited above, pp. 51–52; Sprigge, cited above, pp. 62–65.

For the sources used concerning the breach between Church and State and the withdrawal of Catholics from public life, see especially, Croce, cited above, pp. 65–70; Arturo Carlo Jemolo, *Chiesa e stato in Italia negli ultimi cento anni,* Chapters 3 and 4; Luigi Sturzo, *Italy and Fascismo,* pp. 16–19, 94–95; and articles under "Margotti, Giacomo" and "Non Expedit" in the following reference works: *Catholic Encyclopedia,* Vol. IX, pp. 657–658 and Vol. XI, pp. 98–99; *Dizionario enciclopedico italiano,* Vol. VII, p. 403; *Enciclopedia cattolica,* Vol. VIII, pp. 74–75, 1930–1931; and *Enciclopedia italiana,* Vol. 24, pp. 907–908.

These sources are inconsistent, vague, or silent about the simplest facts concerning the origins or development of the Church's attitude toward participation in Italian political life. Margotti is generally credited with the origin of the cry, "*Nè eletti, nè elettori,*" but only Jemolo gives it time and place: Turin in 1857 (p. 351). The *Catholic Encyclopedia* casts doubt upon Margotti's actual origination of the phrase by describing him as the most influential expounder of the principle who convinced Catholics of its rightness, even "if he was not the author of the axiom . . . ." The *Catholic Encyclopedia* also states that the name of the newspaper, *Armonia,* was changed to *L'Unità Cattolica* at the wish of Pius IX on December 25, 1863. The *Dizionario enciclopedico italiano* reports simply that Margotti gave up the editorship of Turin's *Armonia* in 1863 to found *L'Unità Cattolica* in the same city. However, the *Enciclopedia cattolica* declares that he left the editorship of *Armonia* in 1863 at the express wish of Pius IX and later went to Florence where he founded and edited the more moderate *L'Unità Cattolica.*

With regard to the *Non expedit,* Croce is so loftily cryptic as to be completely uninformative. He merely summarizes by stating that "the Catholic Church kept the faithful from participating in elections or parliaments by means of the *Non expedit* of 1874 and the principle of 'neither electors nor elected' " (p. 68). However, Don Sturzo claims that the counsel of *Non expedit* was first enunciated "by a Roman Ecclesiastical Congregation in 1867 . . . " (p. 94). The *Catholic Encyclopedia* assigns this honor to the decree of February 29, 1868 by the Holy Penitentiary. The *Enciclopedia cattolica* gives the date of the decree of the Sacred Penitentiary as September 10, 1874. According to this same source, not until January 29, 1877 did Pius IX, in a *breve* to the Superior Council of Catholic Youth, rebuke those who urged Catholics to the polls. The *Catholic Encyclopedia* claims an earlier date for papal action in the matter: Pius IX approved the stand taken by the Holy

Penitentiary in 1868 in an audience on October 11, 1874 when he explained that the principal motive of the 1868 decree had been the fear that the oath taken by deputies might be interpreted as signifying approval of the spoilation of the Holy See. This papal audience seems to be the origin of the date usually tagged on to the *Non expedit.* Finally, while the *Catholic Encyclopedia* maintains that the Holy Office on December 30, 1886 declared that the *Non expedit* implied a grave precept, the *Enciclopedia cattolica* declares that on June 30, 1888 the Congregation of the Sacred Office issued a decree, approved by Leo XIII, which stated that the *Non expedit* included a real and true prohibition, thus making abstention a command. Don Sturzo declares: "Much later, and owing to anticlerical reprisals on the part of the Government of the time, the Holy See, in 1895, assumed direct responsibility for this policy, declaring that 'the *non expedit* signified a prohibition. . . .' " Don Sturzo is referring, without saying so, to a letter of Leo XIII to the Cardinal Secretary of State dated May 14, 1895. He merely fails to mention the earlier declaration of 1886 to which Leo XIII's letter of 1895 was meant to give emphasis. This emphasis was reinforced by the Congregation of Extraordinary Affairs on January 27, 1902 and by a declaration of Pius X, his *Motu proprio* of December 18, 1903, when the Pope forbade political activities to members of Christian Democracy.

Perhaps the inconsistencies cited do not, in fact, represent contradictions but different aspects across time of the Roman question since the Pope, Vatican officials, and the various Congregations could avail themselves of hundreds of occasions to make pronouncements on any one subject. Yet, it would be helpful if writers and scholars indicated which part of the elephant they thought they were feeling, and at what stage of his growth.

[10] Croce, cited above, p. 153.

[11] Rigola, cited above, pp. 47–62, both passages translated by M. F. Neufeld; Alfredo Gradilone, *Storia del sindacalismo,* III, "Italia," 1, pp. 125–154. Michels, *Storia critica . . .,* cited above, pp. 4–7, 419. For references to the Florence Congress of 1877, see Luigi Bulferetti, *Le ideologie socialistiche in Italia nell'età del positivismo evoluzionistico (1870–1892),* pp. 220–221. For the best account in English of Mazzini's relation to the Italian worker, see Hostetter, cited above, pp. 38–69, 122–163.

[12] Gualtieri, cited above, pp. 62–63; Hostetter, cited above, pp. 70–112.

[13] Gualtieri, cited above, p. 66.

[14] Hilton-Young, cited above, pp. 9–10; Hostetter, cited above, pp. 113–121.

[15] Gualtieri, cited above, pp. 72, 85–86 for the two Mazzini statements and p. 84 for the Costa statement. For a full account of the Mazzini-Bakunin controversy, see Nello Rosselli, *Mazzini e Bakounine: 12 anni di movimento operaio in Italia (1860–1872).* For a summary account of this controversy, see Michels, *Storia critica . . .,* cited above, pp. 10–33. For the fullest account in English of the controversy, see Hostetter, cited above, pp. 164–211.

[16] Michels, *Storia critica . . .,* cited above, pp. 33–39.

[17] Hilton-Young, cited above, p. 13. For details concerning the split between Bakunin and Marx and the subsequent activities of the Italian International, see Gualtieri, cited above, pp. 101–119; Gradilone, cited above, III, 1, pp. 155–226; Hostetter, cited above, pp. 212–408; Leonetti, cited above, pp. 41–57; Michels, *Storia critica . . .,* cited above, pp. 39–73; Rigola, cited above, pp. 63–73.

[18] Gualtieri, cited above, p. 104, footnote 12; Hostetter, cited above, pp. 270–273, 306–312; Leonetti, cited above, pp. 52–53.

[19] Michels, *Storia critica . . .,* cited above, pp. 78–79.

[20] For the first quotation translated by M. F. Neufeld, see Rigola, cited above, p. 107; for the second quotation, see Hilton-Young, cited above, p. 13.

121

[21] Rigola, cited above, p. 72. For the full text of Costa's open letter, see Manacorda, cited above, pp. 335–339.

[22] For the details of Costa's defection from anarchism and its demise in Italy, see Hostetter, cited above, pp. 409–431. For events of 1882, see Michels, *Storia critica* . . ., cited above, pp. 96–97.

[23] Michels, *Storia critica* . . ., cited above, pp. 93–94.

[24] Gualtieri, cited above, p. 158.

[25] Michels, *Storia critica* . . ., cited above, pp. 95–96.

[26] Croce, cited above, p. 161.

[27] For details concerning the growth of legalitarian socialism and the Workers Party, see Gradilone, cited above, III, 1, pp. 226–290; Gualtieri, cited above, pp. 119–126, 152–195; Leonetti, cited above, pp. 59–69; Michels, *Storia critica* . . ., cited above, pp. 73–97. For references to the writings of the Bakuninites and socialists mentioned in this chapter, consult the excellent name index in Bulferetti, cited above.

For the best treatment in English of general historical events for the entire period between 1860 and 1890, see Mack Smith, cited above, pp. 27–170.

IV

The Pull of History: 1860 to 1890

The Social and Economic Realities

SOCIAL and economic change in Italy during the critical period from 1860 to 1890, although severely limited, takes on the look of modest progress when viewed as a parade of index numbers. The low base year, hinging upon 1860, marks the time when illiteracy, disease, poverty, and disfranchisement spelled out the rule of life for most Italians. At the end of the steadily ascending curve, 1890 represents the point of universal departure when the process of factory production first managed to take hold in almost totally agrarian and alien surroundings. Italy's predicament during these three decades of transition resembled, like a startling ancestral image, the universal quandary which relentlessly confronted Indonesia, India, China, and the other awakening countries of Asia, Africa, and Latin America after World War II, regardless of their capitalist or communist predilections. This common and constant plight may be formulated simply: with only limited resources of capital, raw products, and manpower available for competing and insatiable demands by various segments of the economy, can a rate of social and material development be maintained which will satisfy the limitless expectations of people set suddenly free, but formerly long subjugated?

For thirty years after national independence had been achieved, this ever-sharpening dilemma forced the governments and ruling classes of Italy to live always at the very edge of political crisis. During the heroic days of the *Risorgimento*, most Italians had remained passive in the struggle for liberation. Nevertheless, the leaders of the movement, who possessed a pervading sense of mission, had taught them to anticipate universal plenty, as well as freedom, once the enemy were routed and

123

the people governed themselves. With the achievement of independence, the nation, ideally, had to heal the physical and financial ravages of war at the same time that it set aright ancient injustices and assured future prosperity. Unfortunately, programs of social and material reform could not proceed fast enough to slake desires politically aroused but economically impossible of fulfillment. The spectral gap between hopes engendered and possible achievements lay as a curse across Italy. The same incubus has oppressed the new countries of the mid-twentieth-century world. Like their nineteenth-century predecessor, they must either realize promises publicly shouted in the euphoria of patriotic zeal or reap unrest, rebellion, and constant changes in the governing hierarchy. Otherwise, dictatorship, whether open or concealed, must replace continual agitation and instability.

Italian workers and peasants wandered about aimlessly, without organization, during the preindustrial era between 1860 and 1890. Restive with poverty, powerless to realize a better life, and frustrated in their democratic aspirations, they so prized the voice in government still denied to them that they found it impossible to distinguish between political and economic goals. Although the entire sweep of modern Italian history has impressed itself upon the present character and philosophy of the Italian labor movement, nevertheless the three decades from 1860 to 1890 predetermined its contemporary nature most indelibly. In those fateful years — as social and economic realities kept pushing backward the day of Italy's quick deliverance from inequalities, injured feelings, and want — mounting misery and frustration alienated the Italian worker and peasant from his fellow countrymen who ate white bread instead of black. Under the guidance of aroused and educated leaders from outside their ranks (repeating the pattern of the *Risorgimento*), they learned to place themselves upon the barricades of class revolt and hatred, pledged to undo the system which tormented them. By 1890, when the beginnings of industrialization summoned up the possibility of ameliorating their lot, the socialism of Karl Marx, and not capitalism, shone forth to them like Garibaldi's sun of the future. This same mood of intransigent radicalism has emerged in the middle of the twentieth century as the dominant characteristic of the young labor movements of recently liberated countries as they have moved into that phase of their history which Italy traversed between 1860 and 1890.

What were the nature and specific dimensions of Italy's dilemma and how can they be ascertained? Beginning in 1860, perennial habits and conditions of life began to alter. These changes could be measured for the first time with some degree of accuracy, for nationhood imposed pride, while pride required that self-knowledge which periodic, country-wide censuses and parliamentary investigations could alone provide. They gathered up and summarized invaluable information with which it became possible to formulate the prevalence of illiteracy, the extent of primary education, the scope of participation in elections, the growth of communications, the state of the nation's health, the efficacy of public health facilities, and the character and magnitude of Italy's program of public works. These official sources also furnished important clues concerning the limits within which the country's economic expansion ranged: the extension of transportation facilities, changes in the proportionate importance of various segments of the labor force, the character of the national income, and the stirrings of industrialization. For all their aptness, these statistical manifestations of social and economic change — progress which remained pitifully inadequate to the needs of the age — cannot focus into clear view before three developments of commanding historical importance are first described: the findings of the disturbing agrarian investigation by Parliament published in fifteen volumes between 1881 and 1886, the transition of the Italian economy from Cavourian principles of free trade to almost complete tariff protection by 1887, and the widening of already perilous social and economic differences between North and South Italy.

The Social Realities. Even before official agencies developed the capacity to identify those forces which most revealed the true state of Italy's retrogressive social and economic arrangements, the most sensitive members of the educated middle classes had already addressed themselves to this task in discussion groups, political circles, and publishing ventures based upon serious investigation rather than heartfelt rhetoric. As early as 1878, the *Rassegna Settimanale* (*Weekly Review*) first appeared in Florence. Baron Sidney Sonnino (1847–1922), future foreign minister and Premier, and Leopoldo Franchetti (1847–1917), sociologist and deputy, who had both already merited limited but concerned attention through their pioneering findings about the sharecropping system of Tuscany and the administrative frame of poverty in the Neapolitan provinces, served as editors. It featured discussions of those social questions which most disturbed the rising generation in the hope of stimulating thorough study by which alone sound solutions could be found. The *Rassegna Settimanale*, which earned a high reputation, attracted to its editors enthusiastic young men like Giustino Fortunato (1848–1932), historian, reformer, and deputy, and Antonio Salandra (1853–1931), minister in future cabinets who became Premier in 1914.

In Benedetto Croce's view, this publication distinguished itself by promoting the calm discussion of socialism and the responsibility of the wealthier classes to the peasants and artisans. Through its emphasis upon the economic and social welfare of the working classes, it forced more consideration of these matters upon intellectuals than had ever before been accorded to them. Of more importance, it "did much to remove the instinctive tendency of the educated classes in Italy to 'shut their eyes' . . . ," a habit deplored in this phrase by Pasquale Villari (1826–1917), the conservative Neapolitan patriot, historian, and senator.[1]

The social findings of government investigators supplemented the less comprehensive but more vivid judgments offered by private studies. Grim columns of official statistics, marching on relentlessly year after year, forced eyes open and bore down upon nationalistic sensibilities with cumulative impact. Even the most conservative defenders of the status quo could not dismiss these facts as easily as they had ignored evidence of degradation descried by this or that unknown young writer and publicized in radical journals which had cropped up here and there. They could no longer argue their way clear of the appalling conditions of ignorance revealed among the Italian people.

In 1861, almost 17,000,000 people in the new nation, or 75% of the population five years of age and above, could neither read nor write.[2] (In 1950, almost a century later, as noted before, among the independent and developing countries of the world, Egypt, Sudan, Libya, Tunisia, Morocco, Jordan, Syria, Iran, Iraq, Saudi-Arabia, Afghanistan, Pakistan, India, Vietnam, Laos, and Indonesia showed illiteracy rates for population over 15 years of age comparable to Italian proportions in 1860.)[3] In 1871, Italian illiteracy stood at 69% of the population six years of age and above. By 1881, this proportion had fallen to 62%. Since the census due in 1891 never took place, it is necessary to rely upon statistics gathered from the marriage rolls for the incidence of illiteracy. They revealed that 51% of all registrants could neither read nor write in 1891, as compared with 67% in 1871 and 59% in 1881.[4]

The slow but persevering march against ignorance between 1860 and 1890 seems less resolute when trailed region by region. In Appendix A, Table 7 arrays the percentages of regional illiteracy among Italians six years of age and over. Clearly, the over-all descending rate of illiteracy did not reflect a uniform trend in which all parts of the nation shared evenly. As late as 1881, the South and the Islands still showed percentages of illiteracy for both men and women as high as 85%. In contrast, the educational superiority of Piedmont, Lombardy, and Liguria — destined to become the unique industrial triangle of the North as well as the most progressive area of the country — already stood out boldly with a rate of illiteracy as low as 32% for Piedmont in 1881.

Among children from 6 to 12 years of age, illiteracy fell from the shameful average of 82% in 1861 to the improved but still disturbing proportion of 64% in 1881 — a decline in twenty years of 18 percentage points.[5] This meager enough gain actually represented a determined effort by state officials to force compliance with the compulsory provisions of elementary school legislation under disheartening circumstances of abject poverty in the homes of pupils, lack of schools, and a disproportionate number of pupils with relation to available teachers. The Lex Casati, the organic law on primary education dating from November 13, 1859, required fathers of families to procure for their children from the ages of 6 to 12 at least three grades of elementary education (*corso elementare inferiore*). When, over the years, this mother statute proved ineffective, Parliament approved new legislation on July 15, 1877; its compulsory features took effect on October 15, 1877. Obligatory instruction covered only that part of the populace which lived within a radius of 2 kilometers of the communal school. Only illness, road difficulties, and absolute poverty excused parents from sending their children to school. The act also established standards of instruction based upon the proportion of teachers to pupils. During the academic year, 1883–1884, these norms officially obtained in 8,168 of Italy's 8,257 communes. Whenever parents or guardians did not provide an elementary course of instruction for their children, either in a private school or through family tuition, they were obliged to send them to the elementary schools of the communes. Children had to attend school from the ages of 6 to 9. The termination year could be prolonged to 10 if the pupil did not pass the final examination. The lower elementary course encompassed religious instruction, reading, writing, the rudiments of the Italian language, arithmetic, the metric system, physical education, and duties of man and citizen.[6]

During 1861–1862, of every 100 children in Italy between the ages of 6 and 12, only 37 were enrolled in private and public elementary schools. By 1871–1872, a little more than half of all children in this age group were so enrolled. Ten years later, the proportion had risen to 57%, representing an advance of 20 percentage points in a twenty-year period.[7] (Decades later, in 1958, despite the revolutionary impulses of two World Wars, only 25% of Italy's children attended school up to the age of 14.)[8]

Official reports on the expenditures of the national government provide ample evidence that the Italian State, hard pressed to meet manifold demands upon its restricted fiscal resources, acted niggardly toward edu-

127

cation and without wisdom. Between 1873 and the fiscal year 1889–1890, the cost of both education and fine arts rose from 1.9% of total national government expenditures to only 2.4%. Educational expenditures by the communes and provinces, especially the communes, attained a level slightly more worthy of the nation of Dante and the Renaissance. They grew from 8.3% of total communal and provincial costs in 1873 to 12.1% in 1889. Yet the addition of local outlays for education could offer small solace since their modest proportions dwarfed when confronted by the towering cost of building up and maintaining the army, navy, and merchant marine. These disbursements rose from 17.9% of the national budget in 1873 to 26.5% in 1889–1890. Just one year before, the comparable percentage had soared to 32%. The peacetime army now stood at 350,000 men. By 1885, the long peninsula counted as the third sea-power of the world.[9] Newly liberated in the Europe of that era, Italy justified these expenditures by reasoning like its counterparts a century later: huge investments in defense made the nation count for something in the world and served as prime insurance against foreign aggression. The danger seemed no less imminent to a young country in the 1870's and 1880's than in the 1950's.

Two observations may be drawn from this summary of Italy's endeavors to educate her largely illiterate citizens. By 1890, the task among school children remained little more than half done. This proportion held true for Central Italy and all but froze at a disturbingly higher level in South Italy and Sicily. Only in the North did illiteracy decline to percentages consistent with the pretentions of civilized existence. There, in Milan, educated artisans would pioneer in exercising the widened franchise of 1882 and would form the first organization of workingmen dedicated to the proposition that craftsmen should look after their own affairs without benefit of well-wishers from outside the pale of labor. This attempt at independence was the first and last ever launched in Italy. Inexperience, self-distrust, and a sense of inferiority — the fruits of popular ignorance — made the leadership of the Italian labor movement by educated, dedicated envoys of the middle classes both necessary and inevitable. Since these men seethed with indignation against the neglect of Italy's millions and saw in socialism the only solution consistent with scientific advances in the modern world, they turned their unschooled followers toward that goal and were rewarded by the kind of wholehearted enthusiasm of which only the ignorant are fully capable.

Italy's feeble support of education and firm endorsement of national defense, as measured in budgetary terms, gives rise to the second observation that new nations tend to follow similar patterns of governmental behavior, even when separated by almost a century on the historical scene. For reasons of national prestige and half-warranted, half-concocted fears of danger from neighboring states, Italy sacrificed the education of its people to large expenditures for more worldly purposes. This choice has been zealously repeated among new and poor nations today, nor has it lost favor in older, richer states. Unless governmental stability can be assured by firm and astute dictatorship, this choice, if long exercised, invites certain disaster by embedding distrust and even hatred of the governing classes in the hearts of the ignorant.

The slow dissemination of literacy among Italians from 1860 to 1890 affected the extent of suffrage itself since qualifications for the privilege of voting consisted of educational standards as well as minimum tax payments. When the old law of Piedmont, dating from March 1848, had been extended to liberated Italy in December 1860, only 418,696 citizens could become voters. This represented 1.9% of the total population. By 1870, there were still only 530,018 eligible voters, or 2% of the total population. Even under the laws of 1882, which widened the franchise, the eligibility lists contained the names of but 2,017,829 persons, or 6.9% of the total population. By 1890, this proportion of eligible voters to the entire population had risen only to 9%. Not for almost twenty-five years would this proportion rise from a maximum of less than 10% to 23.2%.[10] With these figures in mind, it becomes clear why the demand of Italian socialists for universal manhood suffrage became an integral part of the creed of labor unions. These percentages also help to explain the powerful attraction exerted upon Italian workers by political activity, so long denied them, and their adherence to the socialist cause which championed their right to vote.

During the first three critical decades in its changing life as a new country, Italy failed to provide with sufficiently encouraging vigor even three grades of elementary education to most of its voteless citizens. Of more serious consequence, it also neglected to supply rapidly enough a widening range of economic endeavors which steady industrialization, even if modest in scope, might have created. However, like many developing countries today — and India comes particularly to mind — Italy did manage to bring forth, much too fast for social stability, an intellectual proletariat. Unreconciled to human suffering, deprived by conviction as well as by the lack of opportunity from seeking normal channels for the exercise of their talents, these restive individuals turned against the kind of society which seemed to have betrayed them and most other Italians.

The growth of an intellectual proletariat dedicated to socialism can be traced indirectly from statistics regarding the proliferation of periodical literature and quite directly from contemporary wonder at the luxuriance, in a country as agrarian and backward as Italy, of a robust radical press. In 1836, only 185 periodicals circulated in the territory which later comprised the Kingdom of Italy, or an average of one periodical for every 118,785 inhabitants. By 1864, with 450 periodicals available, the average number of people to each publication had been reduced to 55,-593. By 1885, the number of periodicals had increased to 1,459, or one periodical for every 20,356 Italians. The regions of Rome, Tuscany, Piedmont, Lombardy, Liguria, and Emilia, not surprisingly, sponsored the highest number of periodicals in relation to their population in 1885. Not unconnected with the flourishing of a numerous periodical press was the concomitant development of the postal system. It grew from a total of 1,632 post offices throughout the country in 1861 to 4,437 in 1890. In twenty years, from 1862 to 1882, the number of letters, postcards, newspapers, and packages mailed had multiplied by over 300%. To effect this transformation, the State increased its investments in post-office and telegraph facilities from 27,011,900 lire in 1873 to 50,824,046 lire in 1889–1890.[11]

Among those who marvelled at the prosperity of the periodical press, and especially at the profusion of radical newspapers, John Rae spotted clearly enough the origin of the phenomenon, but failed to guess its full meaning. In the few observations he made about Italy in his book, *Contemporary Socialism*, he connected the abundance of socialist newspapers with the existence of an intellectual proletariat which had to live by its pen. Roberto Michels corrected Rae's impression by observing that Italy's intellectual proletariat certainly dedicated itself to the local socialist press, but far from receiving compensation for its work, it often had to contribute its own meager substance to keep the newspaper out of bankruptcy.[12]

The role of the central government as the sponsor of public works programs — the building of railroads, a task which the State had to assume, must be excepted — appears across the years as neither statistically impressive nor socially well conceived. In 1873, the national government spent 4.5% of its total expenditures on public works. By 1889–1890, this proportion fell to 3.9% of the entire budget. Communal and provincial expenditures for public works attained a higher magnitude, but failed to increase markedly with time: 27% of total local governmental costs in 1873 and 30% in 1889.[13]

The public character of Italian cities changed monumentally during these years. Although it is true that in one decade between 1870 and

1880, 50,000 new houses became part of the Roman landscape, the transformation of a small papal town into the capital of Italy was brought off not by these private activities, but by the grandiose ventures of the national government. Costly public edifices rose up in Rome, among them Giuseppe Sacconi's (1854–1905) monstrosity in whitest glaring marble which blocks the Campidoglio from view and dares to dwarf by its giant dimensions and immeasurable tastelessness Michelangelo's classic architectural wonder of the Renaissance. So the generation after Cavour, Mazzini, and Garibaldi honored the King in whose name independence and unity had been won. Memorial structures and government buildings of dignity also arose in Lombardy, Veneto, and Piedmont. Florence, when it played the capital city of Italy before the Pope lost Rome, and afterward as well, received a fortune to restore its former beauty and add conveniences to its allure. Palermo changed, while Turin grew from a French provincial town into a modern commercial and industrial city. In 1888, when Gladstone revisited Naples, instead of finding the festering community of unrelieved slums which had driven him earlier to castigate the Bourbons, he discovered to his delight streetcars, a fresh and adequate water supply, new streets, salutary construction in the meanest and filthiest sections of the city, and a decreasing incidence of typhoid and other infectious diseases.

Meanwhile, as the cities of Italy restored, replaced, or extended their façades at large expense to all levels of government without substantially reducing the squalor of their tenements, desperation mounted in the forgotten rural areas. To assuage the agony of the countryside, those in authority suggested a program of public works vast enough to require more than the available planning talents of their own generation and all the construction and engineering skills of the generation fated to come after them. Despite pitifully small funds, improvements began in the Po Valley and in the areas around Ferrara and Ravenna. Attempts at similar measures proved less effective in the South. When enacted, the laws of 1877 envisioned a sound policy of reforestation, but ended in failure.[14]

The annual outlays of the national government for public health purposes were both negligible and erratic. In 1873, they amounted to 0.1% of all expenditures, rose to 0.3% in 1884–1885, only to decline to 0.05% in 1889–1890. Public health costs in the communes, which contributed much more heavily than the provinces, included certain police expenditures for the years under scrutiny. The public health outlays for both communes and provinces rose from 7.4% of all communal and provincial costs in 1873 to 11% in 1889. In contrast, the death toll in Italy was never miserly during these decades. In 1884, out of every 100,000 inhabitants, 88 died of typhoid fever, 249 of tuberculosis and pulmonary consumption, 268 of enteritis and diarrhea, and 479 of bronchitis and pneumonia. Cholera, a disease transmitted by polluted food and water supplies, visited Italy in eighteen different years between 1835 and 1885. As late as 1884, 124 of every 100,000 persons still died of this dreaded disease which attacked 858 communes, a blessed improvement over 1867 when 128,075 people in 2,143 communes perished in the cholera epidemic of that year.[15]

Emigration, which would affect the economic and social stability of Italy most profoundly after 1890 (872,598 Italians left their country in 1913), had nevertheless increased from 134,865 persons in 1869 to 290,-736 persons by 1888. As contrasted with the pattern of the later period, when the largest proportion of emigrants came from South Italy and Sicily, this earlier emigration drew its strength mostly from Liguria, Piedmont, Lombardy, Veneto, and certain communes around Naples. Emigration was scarce indeed from Emilia, Tuscany, and Umbria. Few came from the Marches; even in the Naples area, most of the emigrants originated in the provinces of Salerno, Campobasso, Cosenza, and Basilicata. Emigration from Sicily was as yet negligible and no emigrants ventured forth from Sardinia.[16]

The number of emigrants of working age who were classified as workers and craftsmen, in contrast to those grouped as agricultural labor, was unexpectedly high. In 1876, when a total of 100,993 persons of working age emigrated from Italy, only 20,970 were agriculturists, while 70,223 were classified as workers or craftsmen. (The remaining emigrants of working age pursued other nonagricultural professions, claimed no profession, or did not indicate their profession.) In 1881, the proportion of agricultural workers to the total number of emigrants increased, but workers and craftsmen still predominated: of a total of 123,656 emigrants, 54,590 were agriculturists, while 60,051 were workers or craftsmen. Only in 1891 did the agricultural classification exceed that of workers and craftsmen: of a total of 241,487 emigrants of working age, 122,156 were agricultural, while only 101,826 were workers or craftsmen. (This predominance of agricultural emigrants over workers and craftsmen did not hold true, however, for any of the succeeding censuses from 1901 to 1951.) From 1860 to 1890, therefore, and in heavier measure later on, Italy exported, free of cost, assets in which the nation had invested heavily: adults of working age. Moreover, the figures just cited for workers and craftsmen would seem to indicate broadly that Italy, foreshadowing the later experience of countries like Puerto Rico in the

1950's, lost the kind of adult worker it could least afford to spare as it stood on the threshold of its industrialization.[17]

The Economics of Mythology. Italy's men of affairs, both inside and outside of government, could not have deciphered the portents of gathering social change even had they taken the occasion, now and again, to notice them. Such skill, as yet rare in Italy, completely eluded the comfortable reach of politicians and businessmen since it required the widest possible diffusion of knowledge about society. Until the turn of the century, the key to understanding still lingered in seldom read monographs, census reports, and articles of the radical press. Even the educated classes grew aware of social change only when the tinkling of statistical warnings amplified into the thunder of social disturbance. But their innocence of social realities contrasted chastely with the keen attention they directed toward economic life and with the knowledge of that vast subject they were ready to display in public. Their enthusiasm, however, suffered from only one defect: complete error.

Almost until the death of Depretis in 1887, intelligent Italians viewed their economy through the prisms of poetry and history rather than through the microscope of precise observation. They argued persuasively that their beloved country could never aspire to industrial eminence, for Nature had capriciously skipped over Italy on her way northward to endow France, Germany, Belgium, and England with generous iron and coal deposits. But these men were also quick to insist that the uneven distribution of the primary requirements of modern industrial life blessed Italy twice over. Had not Nature, instead, made of Italy an agricultural paradise? Would not this happy turn of fate bar from Italy's green and pleasant land (unlike Albion's) all those material and moral poisons which factory smokestacks engendered?

The governing classes well knew from their youthful Latin studies that North Africa and Sicily had been the breadbasket of ancient Rome. They also remembered that Sicily had been impoverished by rapacious administrators like Cataline, so eloquently excoriated by Cicero, and later by ruthless Moorish, Norman, and Bourbon exploitation. They were convinced, now that pitiless foreign rulers no longer held sway anywhere on the peninsula, that Italy's fertile soil and equable climate would produce economic felicity. This state of prosperity could be easily achieved once a humane and efficient government taught the ignorant and neglected peasant the right way to cultivate his land. Italian poets, anticipating the splendid exploits of Madison Avenue, kept alive in Italian hearts a picture of the Italian countryside drawn more from the scenes of Virgil's *Georgics* and *Eclogues* than from the drab and hungry rural life around them. If a minority of hard-headed skeptics dismissed as too roseate these visions of thriving peasants and national happiness, the outbreak of the Crimean War in 1854 and of the American Civil War seven years later turned the economic mythologists into lire-and-centimes realists.

First, Russian wheat and then American grain were cut off, in turn, from the Italian import markets. These vicissitudes of battle forced Italy to depend upon her own fields to fill her breadbaskets and her pasta pots. The pastures of Apulia in Southern Italy, long given to the nurture of flocks, were ploughed to wheat. The venerable Apulian system of agriculture, resting almost entirely upon the needs of home consumption, suffered revolutionary change in order to meet the demands of the Italian market. Then the wars ended. Foreign wheat again entered Italian ports, particularly when price wars among ocean freight lines of competing countries made it possible for foreign grain to undersell wheat grown in Italy. But, once again, events beyond the Alps distorted the truth about Italian agriculture and concealed its weakness. Disease had devastated the vineyards of France. Italian producers of wine found that they could make increasingly large profits from the export of blending wines to their northern neighbor. Vineyards multiplied throughout Italy, but especially in Apulia.

These changes in Italian agriculture were linked to nothing more reliable than temporary shifts in world commerce and represented no permanent advance. Despite increases in the importation of agricultural implements and fertilizers, no true progress had occurred in the application of new methods or in the intensity of production. Such growth of output as the peasants managed to achieve by following their old habits of work was slight indeed as compared with that in the rest of the world. Moreover, through all these years, the basic pattern of land tenure remained essentially what it had been on the eve of Italian unification. Then, the overwhelming majority of peasants possessed no land and lived on the edge of hunger. Of those cited as owners (and it must be stressed again that only a small minority of all peasants could be counted among them), 3,275,000 persons owned only from .01 to 1 hectare (2.471 acres), while 250,000 persons owned more than 8 hectares. The following distribution prevailed in the intervening gradations: 1 to 2 hectares, 614,000 owners; 2 to 4 hectares, 450,000 owners; and 4 to 8 hectares, 342,000 owners.[18] It is possible to understand quite readily how shifts in world commerce favorable to Italian agriculture might have convinced those prone to self-deception that the short periods of relative calm among the peasants represented a deep and abiding transformation. However, it is more difficult to understand why the statistics on land tenure, long available to the leaders of the nation, did not begin to clarify for them the reasons for the recurrence of unrest and rebellion in the countryside, the allure there of violent anarchism, and the eventual triumph of rural socialism which created in Italy the largest agricultural unions to be found anywhere in the world.

The first public attack against the myth of Italy's natural agricultural wealth took place in Parliament in June 1872. Agostino Bertani, a deputy, proposed a systematic agrarian inquiry. In trying to justify his project, he vividly described the damage which peasants in their misery might inflict upon the social order. He placed on official record the frightful conditions of life suffered by the cultivators of the fertile soil of North Italy; he termed their destitution a state of wretchedness equalled only by the lot of Sicilian peasants who worked the poorest land in all of Italy. Bertani went on to appraise the quality of bread which the peasants of Lodi in Lombardy ate when they had bread to eat. In Lodi, the center of agricultural wealth, out of a population of 20,000 inhabitants, 12,000 subsisted on public charity. Without this aid, they could not have provided for their most basic needs. He taunted his fellow deputies by this exclamation: "Black bread, then, for the workers of the countryside, poverty in the centers of the greatest agricultural prosperity! Now it is possible to distinguish even in Italy the races of men: the race of white bread and the race of black bread."[19] Despite Bertani's facts and eloquence, Parliament rejected his proposal. Not until 1876 did Parliament authorize the agrarian investigation. Count Stefano Jacini, who served as president of the commission and prepared the summary report, based his findings upon detailed studies of each region of Italy. In all, the commission published 15 volumes in 24 parts between 1881 and 1886.

During the years before the government saw fit to intervene, private studies had disclosed the most shameful misery. Privation among the peasants of the province of Mantua in North Italy grew so unbearable that hundreds of families emigrated to Brazil. Others fell victim to the diseases of poverty and hunger: pellagra, a malady of malnutrition characterized by skin lesions, violent intestinal disturbances, and nervous disorders, kept available insane asylums of the area crowded. Achille Sacchi noted in a famous monograph: "For us the terrain has gradually grown larger and larger. We found under pellagra a deep poverty, and under the medical question, a vast social question."

The social question, in turn, had deep economic roots. Under the pressure of new taxes and antiquated methods of cultivating the soil, small farms fell into the orbit of the developing system of large-scale centralized agriculture. Between 1874 and 1879 alone, the courts ordered 4,700 dispossessions. As a result, former small landowners joined the already crowded ranks of the agricultural proletariat to offer their labor for sale. But the increasing scale of production required fewer farm hands. In Mantua at this time, one laborer was needed for every 60 acres of a large farm. By contrast, one hand was required for every 30 acres on a medium-sized farm and for every 15 acres on a small farm. Unemployment inexorably resulted and affected more than half of the farm population. No longer could the peasants count on a fixed or constant wage. Moreover, specialized farming, such as the cultivation of rice and fodder, forced the concentrated employment of large numbers of peasants intermittently without the possibility of any continuity of work. Ironically enough, neither the enlarged areas of cultivation nor the cutting of labor costs resulted in technical progress or increased productivity. On the contrary, new marketing conditions and the greed of proprietors for immediate gains produced a system of land rentals for brief periods of time. The speculative exploiters of the soil soon exhausted it in their quest for maximum profits. So it came to pass that both land and people suffered: chronic unemployment and poverty for the abused peasants and decreased productivity for the abused fields.[20]

The final report of Count Jacini, who had rendered distinguished service as an agricultural expert in his native Lombardy long before he had been elected to Parliament, shocked the nation. Wherever the official investigators had turned their attention — North Italy, the Central provinces, or the backward South and Sicily — the myth of Italy as a potential rural paradise crashed against demonstrable fact and fell into diabolical splinters. Italians, perhaps somewhat more than most people, tend to move from one mood of extreme intensity to another. They reacted to the Jacini findings by embracing with enthusiastic conviction the doctrine of Italy's agricultural poverty which now replaced their former faith in Italy's agricultural wealth. As noted earlier, the answer to agricultural poverty came in the form of a vast program of public works. Quite apart from the demands it would have made upon technical skills which were wanting, the ambitious scheme ignored the irreducible nationalistic requirements of the already hard-pushed central budget which assigned priority to the construction of railways and to the reorganization and improvement of the army, navy, and merchant marine. If the inquiry inspired no spectacular reforms as alternatives to rural poverty, it did result in strengthening, modestly, the study of agriculture, especially at the schools established at Portici and Milan. Other centers of instruction and research encouraged advanced work in vine culture, the making of wine and cheese, pomology, horticulture, and animal husbandry. Experimental farms joined this scientific advance, and an institute of forestry was founded at Vallombrosa. But the chief benefit derived from the Jacini inquiry took less tangible form: once the report fixed the proportions of Italy's agricultural poverty in clear terms, and once the government and people recognized the findings as true, their implications never grew hazy. The countryside of Jacini's concern kept them clear, for it soon seethed with revolutionary fervor.[21]

The Industrial Lag. The myths of any generation have the habit of slowly destroying each other in favor of new myths. As we have already noted, so long as Italy believed in a prosperous agricultural destiny, the conviction remained fixed that the country might safely relegate industry to a secondary role in its economy. Under the guidance of this myth, the nation diligently tended its fields. It also assiduously fostered free trade and dexterously balanced its budget under the banner of two other economic fantasies not unrelated to the first. Together, these notions, although futile, did not wholly lack wisdom about human society. Many Italians, like Gandhi after them, wished to spare their own land the worst excesses of the industrial revolution in rampage elsewhere. Since they thought of themselves as practical men, these visionaries pointed out that Italy could never compete effectively with other industrial nations since the country lacked coal, the primary source of motor power which had raised England to industrial pre-eminence. Inevitably, then, when the agrarian inquiry robbed the Italian economic imagination of an agricultural utopia thriving in its freedom from dependence upon industry, a fresh myth ascended into doctrine: the natural total poverty of Italy.

This belief undoubtedly influenced the psychology of both public and private thinking about economic matters. Once the basic premise passed as truth, unassailable logic led to black conclusions. Italy lacked not only coal but iron as well. Since industrial hope had to depart from a nation without these resources, Italy's natural poverty counseled sage industrial resignation. Obviously, such hopelessness helped to choke off constructive thinking about alternative possibilities. This failure of economic imagination (not confined to the peninsula during these times) made the way of industrialization in Italy steeper and dictated a pace slower than they need have been had more open views prevailed. Yet it must be conceded that Italian entrepreneurs, bankers, and governmental authorities gathered up ample reason for pessimism when they looked back from 1890 to view their country's economic progress since 1860.

Alexander Gerschenkron has pointed out in his authoritative work on Italy that all available evidence — the use of technologically advanced equipment in production, requisite managerial and labor skills, relative productivity in key industries, the proportion of the total labor force engaged in industrial pursuits, or the density of the railroad system — demonstrates that the Italian economy remained very backward up to 1890, markedly when compared with that of England, and noticeably even when measured against the awakening economies of other European states. The calculations of Maffeo Pantaleoni provided startling additional corroboration of this conclusion: "the private *per capita* wealth of the richest and most advanced areas in North Italy in the second half of the eighties was still very much below one half of the contemporaneous figure for France as a whole." The per capita income, taking the country as a whole and in terms of 1938 prices, increased from 1,851 lire during 1861–1865 to only 1,885 in 1886–1890. The comparable figure for 1956 stood at 4,242 lire, when, in spite of heartening improvement, the Italian standard of living did not rank high among the countries of Western Europe.[22]

As far as can be determined on the basis of inadequate and defective data for the census years preceding 1901, during the three decades immediately after unification, no meaningful shifts occurred in the distribution pattern of the active population (as defined by Italian official sources, the active population differs principally from the labor force in not including persons seeking work for the first time) among the three principal divisions of the economic process: agriculture, goods-producing industries, and services. Those attached to agriculture continued to account for about 60% of the economically active population, while those engaged in goods-producing industries probably never exceeded 25%.[23] Indeed, the proportional predominance of agriculture persisted through the first five decades of the twentieth century. Not until May 8, 1957 did the percentage of Italians engaged in industrial activities rise to 36.3%, exceeding for the first time the proportion of those in agricultural pursuits.[24]

In reporting the gross internal product of the private sector of the economy for various years from 1860 to 1890, the Central Institute of Statistics calculated the share of the gross internal product which could be attributed to agriculture, goods-producing industries, and the services. Changes in this pattern of distribution between the beginning and the end of the thirty-year period confirm the impression of stagnancy in the industrial segment. The gross internal product — measured in current lire — increased from 7.4 billion lire during 1861–1865 to 10.1 billion lire during 1886–1890. Agriculture, forestry, and fishing, which accounted for 56.7% of the gross internal product during 1861–1865, fell to 49.5% during 1886–1890. Yet this decrease did not reflect an increase in the share apportioned to industrial pursuits. On the contrary, service occupations — transportation, communications, commerce, credit, insurance, banking, and other services — took up the loss sustained by agriculture: during 1861–1865, they accounted for 23% of the gross internal product and rose, by 1886–1890, to 29.7%. Industrial activities, which provided 20.3% of the gross internal product during 1861–1865, had increased by a mite to 20.8% during 1886–1890.[25]

By 1890, then, the goods-producing industries, so essential to the fullest development of labor unions, still provided work to only a minor part of Italy's active population and contributed an even smaller share to the gross internal product. But expand they did, if only very slowly and in minute fashion, according to the two measures of growth just cited. Did production increase as well? Alexander Gerschenkron set himself the task of answering this question. He accomplished the delicate and complex feat in the face of the most discouraging paucity of data. Despite admitted shortcomings in the indices constructed, he found it possible "to obtain a general view of the speed of the Italian industrialization in various periods and subperiods before 1914." The indices measure the relative output for six industries (with production in 1900 taken as 100) from 1881 to 1913: mining, metal-making, textiles, engineering, chemicals, and foodstuffs. Gerschenkron discerned a period of modern growth from 1881 to 1888, an interval of stagnation from 1888 to 1896, years of very rapid growth from 1896 to 1908, and a reduced rate of growth from 1908 to 1913. Thus, by 1890 Italy had barely completed its era of modern growth and had just relapsed into eight years of stagnation.[26]

Two additional indices, limited to manufacturing production, also attest to Italy's industrial retardation during most of the period between 1860 and 1890. *Industrialization and Foreign Trade*, a study by the League of Nations published in 1945, supplies data with which to measure Italy's relatively low estate and sluggish progress among the manufacturing nations of the world since 1870. Table 25 of Appendix A in this study demonstrates that as late as 1881–1885 Italy's manufacturing activities attained a proportionate magnitude comparable with the share of tiny Belgium. Even Russia, universally regarded as the most economically retrogressive of European nations, exceeded Italy's mark as early as 1870, while both France and Germany had left Italy far behind by that same year. The countries which Italy led with 2.4% of the world's manufacturing production, during the three decades under consideration, were Canada, Sweden, Finland, Japan, and India.[27] The second index of maufacturing production, prepared by the Central Institute of Statistics for its comprehensive study of the development of the Italian national income from 1861 to 1956, corroborates the conclusions drawn by Gerschenkron. Table 26 of Appendix A records a rise of 9 points between 1861–1865 and 1886–1890. While contemplating the unimpressive magnitude of Italian manufacturing production as late as 1890 — 30 in relation to 1938's 100 — it is still more sobering to realize that the index number of manufacturing production reached 203 in 1956 and to remember that Italy, notwithstanding such notable advance, did not figure as yet among the leading industrial nations of the world.[28]

Thus far, no calculations have fixed the actual number of men, women, and children who were engaged in those pursuits, apart from traditional occupations, which would respond most receptively to unionization: the goods-producing industries. Between 1860 and 1890, the government undertook only two official surveys to provide such information, namely, the statistical study of 1876 and the occupational census of 1881. Although the reliability of both series of findings is open to serious doubt, these data do suggest broad lines of development. They conform to familiar patterns of evolution encountered during the early stages of the industrial revolution in countries which experienced its demands both earlier and later than Italy.

The Ministry of Agriculture, Industry and Commerce undertook the first official survey of selected industries in 1876. The results, published in 1878, omitted statistics on mining, the metallurgical and mechanical trades, glass-making, ceramics, and the manufacture of chemicals. Vittorio Ellena based his famous pioneering study, printed in 1880, upon these admittedly limited figures. At the end of his analysis, Ellena attempted to furnish some measure of the importance of those industries not included in the 1876 survey by scraping together whatever information he could lay his hands on with regard to their location, production, and employment. However, the results, while more revealing than silence, supplied disappointingly small additional knowledge about industrial workers. In 1906, the Ministry of Agriculture, Industry and Commerce completed an extensive study on industrial conditions in 1903. Part I featured a comparison of industrial employment for 1876 with that for 1903.[29]

Before reviewing the employment data furnished by the 1876 survey, one of Ellena's sage precautionary remarks, made while discussing the meaning of the data, should be thoroughly absorbed. He wrote: "In every country, and more so in ours, the crafts employ a greater number of hands than the true factories." He implied that the 1876 employment figures of the so-called manufacturing industries should be utilized only with skeptical care since they disguised behind their terminology the prevalence of artisan-like production. Tremelloni has also warned that almost the entire group of workers designated as industrial by the 1876 survey might properly be assigned to the handicrafts since even factories at that time still operated along semiartisan lines.[30] Available evidence about to be presented would tend to substantiate the view that the predominance of handicraft activities before 1860 still remained a principal feature of manufacturing production in 1876 and lingered on as a consequential element of Italian industrial life well into the twentieth century.

The entire 1876 work force of 388,306 persons employed in the 15,202 establishments under survey constituted less than 2% of the total population ten years of age and above.[31] For every hundred persons engaged in these plants, 28.2 were adult men, 48.6 were adult women, and 23.2 were children.[32] The average firm employed 25 workers. This figure fell as low as 2 for the spirits industry, to cite the extreme case at the bottom of the scale, thus lending support to doubts about the extent of true factory production in 1876. Even where the average size of operation doubled, as in textiles, a considerable segment of the industry retained its handicraft nature.

The textile classifications of the survey (4 out of 23) accounted for almost 75% of all enumerated workers: silk, 51.6%; wool, 6.3%; cotton, 13.5%; and flax, hemp, and jute, 2.8%. The unrivaled hegemony of textiles within the manufacturing hierarchy of Italy at this early stage of the industrial revolution follows a pattern well established by economic history and still visible in awakening countries. Another strand common to past and present developing economies can also be discerned: of the 288,369 persons employed by the textile groups, 85% were women and children (56% women and 29% children). These textile plants alone utilized two-thirds of the country's motor horsepower. (Of a total of 55,336 units of motor horsepower, only 15,501 were derived from steam, while 39,835 were generated by hydraulic means.)

In examining evidence of the persistence of manufacturing operations with handicraft characteristics, the leadership of the silk industry among textiles should be noted. Silk production occupied all but 88,000 of the total number of textile workers. Only 15,692 of the 200,393 persons employed in the silk industry were men. The average establishment engaged 52 workers, as compared with the textile high of 84 workers in the cotton mills, which, less bound to tradition than the making of wool and less tied to seasonality than silk production, had advanced even before 1860 beyond other types of textile plants in size as well as technological progress. In the silk mills, although more than half of their motor horse-power came from steam, this fact in itself did not necessarily signify a high degree of mechanization. The use of steam, rather than the application of direct flame for the heating of boilers which were so vital to the reeling process, had marked the course of technical improvement before 1860 and continued to increase after 1860. But the reeling of filament from the steamed cocoons still remained a hand operation seasonally employing a large number of women and young girls. Additional evidence points to the persistence of hand operations in other branches of silk production as well. In 1876, only 445 mechanical looms were employed; these increased to 2,535 in 1891. But the use of hand or Jacquard looms continued to advance during this period, numbering 7,394 in 1876 and 10,580 in 1891.

Certainly, then, silk weaving still retained aspects of hand manufacture in 1876, nor did these characteristics disappear from the industry after 1890. Even the technologically more advanced cotton industry operated 14,300 hand looms in 1876 as against 12,478 mechanical looms. Only by 1900 had this relationship become 14,267 hand looms to 60,722 mechanical looms. Woolen mills ran 2,364 mechanical looms and 5,989 hand looms in 1876; by 1894 they used 6,507 mechanical looms and 3,760 hand looms. The linen-jute-hemp branch of the industry employed only 524 mechanical looms in 1876 while 4,854 hand or Jacquard looms still operated. Even as late as 1903, when the number of mechanical looms had increased to 4,523, there still remained 3,493 hand looms in action. Cottage industry production of silk, wool, cotton, linen, hemp, and mixed fabrics employed 205,789 hand looms in 1876 and 292,118 hand looms in 1903.[33]

Obviously, hand looms persisted as part of textile production beyond 1890. How, then, did Italy compare in this respect with other industrial nations? In the United States, hand looms disappeared from cotton mills after 1830, nor did they endure in England to any extent after 1860. But in France, as late as 1885, more than one-third of the cotton looms were run by hand. In Germany, only 9% of the cotton looms in 1861 were powered, while in 1908, 3,000 cotton hand looms still operated. Moreover, as late as the 1920's, Switzerland continued to use 4,500 hand looms in its cotton mills. In countries like France, Germany, and Switzerland, but particularly in Italy, the low cost of relatively skilled labor slackened the initiative of employers to introduce labor-saving machinery. "The lack of this incentive, the conservatism of the managers and of the workmen, and the greater cost of the more expensive power loom, have retarded the extinction of the hand loom. The Continental manufacturers have economized in capital; the English manufacturers, and to a great extent the American, in labor."[34]

In 1876, no other industry could compare in size with the textile groups: 75% of all surveyed manufacturing employment. The following industries trailed after textiles, but at a great distance, in the number of workers: paper mills (17,312), tobacco (15,654), tanneries (10,734), manufacture of spirits (10,118), ropeworks (8,372), government ship-yards (7,765), railroad and streetcar workshops (6,403), and the me-chanical laboratories, foundries, arms factories, and construction works of the Ministries of War and Navy (6,221). The paper plants in 1876 used some 25% of total motor horsepower (of this amount, 98% came from hydraulic sources). Consequently, the textile and paper industries alone accounted for about 92% of both steam and hydraulic motor horsepower during this era of Italy's industrial development. The 25 war and navy installations each employed an average of 250 workers, while the 4 navy yards each accommodated an average of almost 2,000 hands. The Italian government thus maintained the country's largest average concentration of workers in the industrial operations it ran. These establishments serve as yet additional illustrations of the lead often taken by the governments of industrially backward countries to bring into their struggling econ-omies advanced methods of production and improved arrangements of work. Nor was the dominant position assumed by Italian defense agencies in stimulating economically progressive undertakings for their own pur-poses — including railroad and highway construction — new to economic history, either before or after the Italian experience.[35]

The industrial survey of 1876 has stood the test of time as the more reliable of the two sources of information about manufacturing activities during the years from 1860 to 1890. Comparable statistics from the 1881 census merit only limited confidence. When viewed alongside the more trustworthy census counts of later years, they condemn themselves as in-flated, particularly with regard to the size of the industrial population. Nonetheless, the data presented by the 1881 census deserve cursory in-spection. For the period under consideration, they constitute the only body of information available after 1876 since the census due in 1891 never took place. Furthermore, overstated as the 1881 figures may be, they re-emphasize the impression left by the 1876 findings about the pre-dominance of particular kinds of industries during this phase of Italy's economic development. They also corroborate Roberto Tremelloni's view. The half century from 1861 to 1911 witnessed the establishment and growth of those industries which satisfied primarily consumer needs:

food processing, textiles, clothing, and shelter — activities which gave the period its principal industrial quality. After 1911 began the modern era of development when Italy fostered the metal-mechanical and chemical industries, as well as those which supplied sources of energy. (As late as 1893, only 3,275 workers in the entire country were employed in the chemical industry which was so pre-eminently suitable to the particular economic circumstances of Italy.)[36]

At the time of the 1881 census, 4,245,728 persons, or almost 19% of the population nine years of age and over, reported themselves as engaged in goods-producing industries. This figure seems exaggerated in view of the report by the 1901 census — two decades later and five years after 1896, when the period of Italy's very rapid industrial growth had begun — that the goods-producing industries employed only 3,989,816 workers. Of the 1881 total, 55.1% were classified as men and 44.9% as women. The textile industry alone purportedly employed the largest number of workers in 1881: 1,351,454. The comparable figure for 1901 fell to 783,253, probably reflecting both the more extensive use of power equipment within factories proper, as well as the declining relative importance of cottage production. The other important industrial activities, in descending order of size, for both 1881 and 1901, were:

Industry	1881	1901
Clothing and personal attirement	992,955	1,113,843
The building trades	586,790	564,798
Wood-working, straw products, and home furnishings	381,202	410,935
Food processing	323,553	314,500
Mineral, metallurgical, and mechanical	239,375	329,151

The confrontation of these two census years tends to support the suspicion that more than normal inaccuracy infected the classification of the industrial population for 1881 and to illustrate quite clearly the pertinency of Tremelloni's observations.[37]

The appearance in the 1881 census of a category specified as "mineral, metallurgical, and mechanical industries" invites immediate interest in the magnitude of production and employment in the most pivotal sector of these manufacturing activities: the basic iron and steel industry. Like mechanized textile production, its growth has everywhere served as an important measure of industrial evolution; its workers have usually been regarded in all countries as the very backbone of the labor movement, once they formed themselves into unions.

In 1861, Italy produced no steel at all, but it did turn out 26,551 metric tons of pig iron and 30,000 metric tons of iron. The governmental investigation of 1864 reported that Italy's entire output of pig iron, castings, and processed iron amounted to less than 0.50% of world production. By 1881, Italy managed to turn out 3,630 tons of steel. Production of pig iron had increased very slightly to 27,800 tons, but that of iron had more than tripled to 94,941. Steel output grew dramatically during the next decade and reached 107,676 tons by 1890. However, tonnage of pig iron had decreased to 14,346. In compensation, tonnage of iron increased to 176,-374.[38] The number of persons employed in the iron and steel industry remained slight, rising from 5,732 in 1881 to 8,560 in 1885, and then to 13,799 in 1890.[39]

Suffering from the lack of coal, iron, and investments adequate to its needs, Italy's iron and steel industry struggled on from one stage of insufficient technological development to another, always the dawdling darling of obsolescence. Although steel production abroad took place in large integrated plants by the end of the nineteenth century, not until 1905 did Italian entrepreneurs decide to build Italy's first integrated plant at Bagnoli. "Consequently the Italian steel industry differed from foreign industries owing both to the less economic processing systems employed and to the distribution of production among a few small works that could not afford to adopt the more up-to-date processing systems."[40]

The North and the South. Even before the advent of the Kingdom, Italy's incipient industrial life had concentrated in the North; there it continued to center after 1860, entrenching itself in the fertile manufacturing crescent of Liguria-Piedmont-Lombardy. This same tendency has disturbed the economic balance of most industrial countries, but Italy's entire economic, political, and social history conspired until quite recently to accentuate the disequilibrium between the North and the South.

Italian economists and historians, divided by their own mental Mason and Dixon line, have quarrelled acrimoniously about the causes of the greater industrialization of the North. Southerners have insisted that the State itself, dominated by Piedmont and northern interests, intervened to choke off the industrial life of the South. To support their indictment, they have cited discriminatory tariff policies, unfair division of national expenditures for public works, the monopoly of northerners in public administration, and unjust tax laws. Northerners have challenged this interpretation on two counts: the North had already reached a stage of industrialization superior to that of the South before 1860; the role of the State in economic affairs after unification had not been sufficiently large or intense to divert seriously the fundamental trend of economic development.

Despite these unsettled arguments, the chief elements of a moderately

145

satisfying explanation of the pattern of Italian industrial diffusion can be discerned.

1. The natural resources of the North, although meager indeed when contrasted to the wealth of the richer countries of Europe, excelled by far those of the South. The North, an area of active commerce, could also muster larger amounts of capital for industry since the consolidation of the public debt, high taxation, and the forced sale of ecclesiastical property had absorbed the available capital of the South. Proximity to sources of motor energy and low-cost transportation afforded by navigable rivers and canals, both absent in the South, at first dictated the location of early industries like textiles in the North. Then, the machine industry settled around Turin and Milan because of nearby iron ore deposits. The North possessed, too, the incalculably potent agricultural resource of the Po Valley, the most extensive stretch of fertile land in all the peninsula, close to its industrial centers.

2. Even in Italy, the economic axiom held true that, to those areas which already had, more would be given industrially. To be sure, iron ore supplies served to attract the machine industry to Piedmont and Lombardy, but at this early phase of Italy's industrial revolution, the presence and dominant position of textile manufactures also influenced its location there, for the textile plants were the principal buyers of machinery. Soon, the railway equipment industry found encouragement in the availability of metal, developing markets, and existent, if modest, capital funds. Later, Milan as the industrial capital attracted rubber manufacturers because other industries needed rubber products.

3. The North, blessed by geography, communicated easily — as a result of friendship, conquest, or commerce — with those regions of Europe which had experienced the revolutionary impact of new industrial techniques, commercial institutions, and advances in transportation. Piedmont under Cavour's guidance established early economic and financial relations with France, England, and Belgium. The first railways in Piedmont connected Turin with Paris. The Alpine tunnels facilitated rail traffic between the northern industrial centers and Paris. The regions of Lombardy and Veneto had maintained, even when under Austrian control, close economic relations with more advanced industrial areas, especially with Switzerland and Germany. Foreign names abound in the economic history of Lombardy and Veneto. Swiss entrepreneurs became so numerous at Bergamo that they formed a colony which has survived to the present day. The Falcks came from the Rhineland to develop their metallurgical activities in the Como region. Northern leaders found it natural to look beyond the Alps for guidance. They sought out the eco-

nomic and technical literature of England and France and introduced new concepts and methods into North Italy. The rule of the North by the government of Austria, as contrasted to the Bourbon domination of the South, distributed a fuller share of administrative experience among a larger number of individuals in the North than in the South. Public works, which had enriched the North even before the establishment of the Kingdom, expanded there afterward in the name of military defenses. Italy's land borders lay wholly along the northern frontiers.

4. Attitudes toward economic activities, of ancient Italian lineage, distinguished the North very markedly from the South. Obviously, northern Italians did not possess the fierce initiative of Victorian merchants and factory owners, but they did show much greater drive than southerners to improve their material welfare. Proud of the cultural achievements of Venice, Genoa, Milan, and Florence during the Middle Ages and Renaissance, they freely acknowledged the fundamental importance of economic activities in securing the intellectual and artistic prestige of these cities. Consequently, when men managed to lay hold of wealth through trade and industry, such acquisition carried more prestige than social stigma. As the economy of the North shifted from its agricultural moorings, sons of noble families invested capital in commercial and industrial ventures. Count Cavour made of himself a distinguished example of such enterprise. In the South, instead, the owners of extensive real property continued the attitudes of the old landed nobility and disdained any form of commerce or manufacturing. They either turned back into farming, profits garnered from the soil, or used these savings to pay the costs of leading lives of wealthy leisure. The other classes had little capital to invest in anything; nevertheless they absorbed the mannerisms of their economic betters. They too opposed fresh approaches and new methods in business and industry. Naples could not advance under the burdens imposed on progress by these antiquated notions about proper economic behavior. The metropolis also suffered from the backwardness of venture capital, the new railroads which pulled away the surrounding agricultural areas toward Rome and Emilia, and the devastating effects of the united Kingdom's reduced tariff rates upon her formerly protected industries.[41] Although ousted from her position as capital and proud commercial center, Naples found no means to transform herself into an industrial port city. Deprived of an economic future, Naples grew into an extraordinarily busy political market place for the education of practitioners, the exchange of favors and patronage, and the emission of letters of introduction to the highly placed.

Statistical evidence records only too well the ever-growing economic imbalance between the North and the South. Already by 1876, 62% of all persons covered by the survey of principal Italian industries worked in Lombardy (42.2%) and Piedmont (19.7%). An additional 22% were employed in three other northern regions, Veneto (9.6%), Liguria (3.4%), and Emilia (3.1%), and in one central region, Tuscany (6.2%). Therefore, six regions of North and Central Italy accounted for over 84% of all industrial workers in 1876. The Campania region of South Italy, with Naples as its principal center, gave employment to 7.6% of all industrial workers. Sicily, the southern region with the next highest share, reached only 1.8%. The northern regions of Lombardy, Piedmont, Veneto, and Liguria, along with Tuscany in Central Italy, exploited 81% of all motor horsepower. Campania in the South employed 11%, while all other Italian regions utilized but 8%.[42]

Even the unreliable census of 1881, which exaggerated the number of industrial workers by including peasants producing cottage textiles among the industrial population — thus probably distorting the count in favor of the South — reported 1,197,150 persons, or 28.2% of goods-producing workers, as employed in Lombardy (16.1%), Piedmont (9.1%), and Liguria (3.0%). With the addition of Veneto (7.0%), Emilia (6.5%), and Tuscany (7.2%), the share of these six regions reached almost 50%.[43]

Shepard B. Clough and Carlo Livi, in their succinct and highly informative article, *Economic Growth in Italy: An Analysis of the Uneven Development of North and South,* have supplied additional pertinent indices to demonstrate that the economic gap between the two parts of the country widened steadily after unification and had not narrowed as recently as 1953. For the moment, only that portion of their evidence which concerns the period from 1860 to 1890 will be presented.

1. Southern Italy had a much higher birth rate than North Italy. Although its pace of emigration was also higher, a rate of natural increase superior to the North nevertheless prevailed there. This demographic pattern burdened the South with a larger proportion of unproductive age groups, especially the youngest when dependency is almost complete. In addition, the boon of emigration saddled Italy, and the South in particular, with the cost of supplying full-grown people of working age absolutely free for the economic development of other countries. While the expense of providing ready-made labor to the world fell heavily upon the regions of origin, account must be taken of the partial return of this outlay in the form of remittances from abroad.

2. In 1871, 59% of the population in the North over six years of age were illiterate; in the South, this proportion stood at 84.1%.

3. From 1871 to 1880, the South, with 41% of the nation's land area

and almost 40% of the population, accounted for only one-third of the total local tax revenues of the country. Its per capita local revenue reached only 75% of the per capita average for the rest of the country. Although the South collected 43.5% of total provincial revenues during this period, it paid only 30.4% of national taxes, including direct and indirect taxes on consumption and business.

4. From 1860 to 1890, the corporation represented an institutional innovation and the prevalence of its use can be taken as a measure of entrepreneurial zeal. In proportion to its population, the North fostered more incorporated enterprises than the South, drew to itself more corporate investments, and could boast more corporate capital for each industrial worker.

5. In 1877, the South held 7.1% of savings banks accounts in the nation; in 1878, it was credited with only 27.5% of all bank discounts; it made 5.5% of nongovernment bank loans during this time; it could boast of but 16% of joint-stock banks in 1876; and it represented a mere 12% of the capital in corporations in 1887.[44]

The State and the Economic Order. According to Alexander Gerschenkron, during the course of European industrialization, countries with very backward economies usually exhibited an initial period of relatively intense growth. These countries tended to foster the development of industries which turned out producers goods because at that time rapid technological improvements had most benefited this segment of manufacturing activities. These advances enabled backward nations to enter upon heavy industrial production with the newest equipment. Under such circumstances, private banking interests and public agencies combined to push forward as far as possible the first major industrial effort. Where economic conditions were extremely retrogressive, the State assumed the most affirmative and strategic role in the process of industrialization, as in Russia during the 1890's under the strong guidance of Count Witte.

Gerschenkron draws careful attention to some of the more noteworthy economic activities of the Italian government. The State aided in the establishment of extensive steel works at Terni in 1884; it provided subsidies for shipbuilding and navigation through legislation passed in 1885 and 1896; it waived its royalties from iron ore mined on the island of Elba; it attempted unsuccessfully to compel railroads to grant preferential rates to domestic users; and it sometimes utilized government orders to influence the development of industry. Gerschenkron maintains, however, that these public efforts suffered from three grave defects: they lacked sufficient intensity; they diminished when they should have increased during the crucial period from 1896 to 1908; and, in establishing tariff policy, they mistook the proper industries upon which to lavish protective benefits. Because the Italian tariff became the principal device of state intervention, its success or failure in advancing economic growth becomes the hinge upon which Gerschenkron turns his case.[45]

Before reviewing Gerschenkron's argument, the expenditures of the Italian State in developing both the railway and public road systems of the peninsula demand attention. Particulars on these costs, not provided by Gerschenkron, serve to portray the government of Italy as far from sluggish in at least one very vital sector of the economy.

In 1861, Italy could count only 2,773 kilometers of railroads. Ten years later, this total had grown to 6,710. By 1881, the railroad system had expanded to 9,506 kilometers. In 1891, the total increased to 13,964, an expansion of 400% in thirty years.[46] No part of Italy remained untouched by the extension of the railroad system. In 1861, with the exception of the area around Naples which possessed 184 kilometers of railroads, the entire South, the Islands, and the region of Abruzzi and Molise on the Adriatic Coast were innocent of a single kilometer of trackage. In contrast, by 1886, these formerly neglected areas of Italy could boast of 4,022 kilometers of railroads, a remarkable fiscal as well as engineering feat. This kilometrage constituted almost 36% of the total for all of Italy in 1886: 11,202.[47]

This network of rails stretched from the Alps to the Straits of Messina and provided modern transportation, as well, for Sicily and Sardinia. So, by the time that the St. Gotthard Tunnel opened in 1882, Italy possessed direct communication with Western and Central Europe. Moreover, goods from India, after passage through the Suez Canal, could journey overland from Brindisi to various parts of the continent.

The Italian government had assumed the entire burden of providing this essential basis for industrial development in the face of mounting unrest against its tax and fiscal policies. In 1873, state expenditures for railroad construction (costs of maintenance, operation, supervision, and research have been omitted) amounted to 4.5% of total national government disbursements, including both ordinary and extraordinary outlays. By the fiscal year 1888–1889, this percentage had risen to 14. During the previous fiscal year, the proportion reached almost 19%.[48]

State intervention in the building and operation of railroads took place amid stormy national debate, while its later withdrawal provoked equally bitter controversy. Private companies had received concessions when railroad construction first started in Italy. However, Silvio Spaventa (1823–

1893), the Minister of Public Works in the second Minghetti cabinet (1873–1876) kept urging nationalization despite the hostility of commercial interests in North Italy, especially in Lombardy. Spaventa supported his policy with economic arguments concerning efficiency and economy and with patriotic pleas concerning the safety and dignity of the State. He won his case and the railways of Rome and the South came into the possession of the government in 1873 and 1875. Meanwhile, negotiations went ahead regarding the nationalization of the railroads of North Italy. Those who wished to maintain the integrity of private ownership continued to fight the Spaventa policy. First, they triumphed in principle, and later in practice, with the compromise agreement of 1885, but not before a series of investigations and commissions of inquiry had intervened. In 1885, Parliament decreed that the state railroads would be let out in concession to three private companies for sixty years. Under the agreement, the State had the right to terminate the contract with the private companies at the end of twenty years or forty years. The State also retained title to the greatest part of the permanent right-of-way, granting only its use to the contracting companies. To the companies went the task of operating and maintaining the railroads, in return for which they received a share of the proceeds, calculated in relation to the running expenses of the railroads under state management.

By the time of Italy's era of very rapid growth between 1896 and 1908, the golden age of feverish railroad construction had passed into history. Gerschenkron ascribes the relative weakness of Italy's expansion in these years to the absence of railroad construction which, during Russia's comparable era of industrial outburst, served as the central influence upon economic development. There, from 1886 to 1900, the railroad gridiron increased more than 70%, while it grew less than 10% in Italy from 1896 to 1908. Although Italian legislation of 1885 had provided for special investment funds, the terms of the act virtually dictated hesitant expansion policies by the concessionary companies during the years just prior to the possible expiration of the agreement in 1905. The railroads did, in fact, revert to the State in that year, but the plans for new development by the government became tracks and equipment too late to influence the period of very rapid growth which ended in 1908. The time was out of economic joint for Italy in other respects as well. Since the main spurt of railroad building had occurred prior to 1896, it would be logical to suppose that capital funds released from that task would have found their way into industrial investment. This shift did not take place because of the proclivity of many large Italian investors

151

for safe government bonds and the parallel attraction of those with small savings to cooperative banks or the government's postal system.[49]

At the same time that the Italian State intervened to provide Italy with an extensive network of railroads, the exigencies of nationhood had imposed those more usual and inescapable financial obligations already mentioned: the establishment of a peninsula-wide system of government administration; the creation of an army, navy, and merchant marine; the installation and management of postal and telegraph facilities; the improvement of education and public health services; and the promotion of public works. Certainly the extension and modernization of the country's highways had to accompany the spread of railroads if the total impact of efficient transportation upon economic development were to be realized. Yet this necessity imposed an additional burden upon the Italian government's limited resources. Nonetheless, the State launched a more than respectable highway program. Between 1862 (important legislation concerning national and provincial roads dated from 1862, 1869, and 1872) and 1885, 4,356 kilometers of national and provincial highways were built. From 1868, when requirements for the obligatory maintenance and construction of communal roads were enacted, to 1890, some 13,000 kilometers of local roads were laid down. By the end of the period under consideration, the full extent of national roads open to vehicles measured 7,891 kilometers; the whole provincial network covered 34,778 kilometers; and the complete system of obligatory communal roads traversed 36,965 kilometers, or an over-all sweep of 80,000 kilometers, about 28 kilometers for each 100 square kilometers of territory.[50]

State expenditures for all public works, including highway and railroad construction and maintenance, totalled 1,002,681,000 lire during the decade from 1871 to 1880 and rose, almost doubling, to 1,769,039,000 lire during the next ten years. During the first period, 45.6% of these outlays went to the South; during the second decade, 29.8% ended there.[51]

In final economic lament for the years from 1860 to 1890, this review of industrial development must now turn to Italy's tariff policy. It bore the marks of that cursed spite which dogged Parliament and hindered Rome from ever setting its actions right. With unification, the free trade principles of Piedmont had spread forth to bless the entire nation. Despite the severest economic dislocations, especially in the South, which attended the easy entry of foreign goods into Italy (heaped upon the damage wrought by free internal trade to regional economies formerly protected), the followers of Cavour held steadfast to their low tariff convictions. After the political upset of 1876, their victorious opponents to the Left found that the demands of the budget prompted customs reform. In 1878, Parliament introduced a modified system of protection. Then, in

1887, Italy repudiated its commercial treaties with France and the disastrous trade war between these two neighbors began. The protective tariff system of Italy dated from these incidents.

Gerschenkron frankly admits the difficulties inherent in the attempt to measure the influence of tariff policies upon industrialization. In some instances, the abandonment or reduction of the tariff encouraged industrialization; in other instances, governmental measures of more direct impact than the tariff provided the necessary push. Withal, Gerschenkron is willing to assert that "it would seem difficult to attribute much positive influence to the tariff structure that existed in Italy during her big industrial upswing. In fact, it is more reasonable to regard the tariff as one of the obstacles in the road of the Italian industrialization."[52]

Italian tariff policy centered upon the protection of three chief products: grain, cotton textiles, and iron and steel. Parliament first raised the tariff on grain from a nominal level in 1887. It acted against its better judgment which had been formed by the findings of Count Jacini's agrarian inquiry. After the increases of 1895, Italian wheat became the most sheltered among Europe's principal nations, thus subjecting "the tender plant of its industrial growth to the rigors of a protectionist climate in agriculture."[53]

The wisdom of Italy's tariff policy in regard to industry must be judged with the price of coal — then the keystone of economic growth — firmly in mind. Italy, without that resource, paid twice as much for coal as countries which mined their own. Therefore, Italy should have avoided those industries which used large quantities of coal and fostered, instead, lines of endeavor, especially those pioneering in new products, where such expenditures were relatively small. According to Gerschenkron, the "vast and variegated area of engineering offered the greatest promise in this respect."[54] He might have added that the highly developed talents of Italian artisans fitted them admirably for work in that type of industry. Italian tariff policy should have embraced this kind of rational purpose, especially since Italy's strategic railroad system could not reduce its consumption of high cost coal.

The tariff of 1878, on the contrary, gave protection to cotton textiles and the production of ferrous metals. The latter industry utilized coal in large quantities. Although the tariff covered various engineering items, the rates were not high enough to compensate, except partially, for the protection which iron and steel enjoyed. The duties on machinery increased generally in 1887, offering a degree of protection. But Gerschenkron maintains that, if this margin is computed *ad valorem*, the amount of protection emerges as almost negligible. The tariff on textile and agricultural machinery hardly exceeded the duties on steel. The low rates on machine parts encouraged the assembling but not the production of machines in Italy. Moreover, "nonspecified" machinery was lightly protected, a policy which Gerschenkron regards as greatly mistaken because this grouping represented "the very area of innovations. . . ."

To summarize, Italian parliamentarians, like lawmakers elsewhere at this time, favored existing industries with protection and ignored the future. They advocated free trade principles only for the engineering industry without realizing its potential importance. Worse still, when commercial treaties were negotiated, following the 1887 legislation, the duties on machinery became the special objects of concessions and were reduced or removed entirely. Nor did the government evidence the slightest foresight about the chemical industry, a field of activity especially fitted for success under Italian conditions. Gerschenkron feels justified in concluding "that the main action of government policies in the field of Italian industrialization was likely to retard rather than promote its development."[55]

FOOTNOTES – CHAPTER IV

[1] Croce, cited above, pp. 77–78.

[2] Appendix A, Table 7 of this volume.

[3] United Nations Educational, Scientific and Cultural Organization, *Monographs on Fundamental Education—XI*, "World Illiteracy at Mid-Century," pp. 38–41.

[4] Appendix A, Table 7; *Annuario statistico italiano 1886*, p. 954; *Annuario statistico italiano 1895*, p. 166.

[5] *Annuario statistico italiano 1895*, p. 129.

[6] *Annuario statistico italiano 1886*, pp. lxiv–lxv; *A Cyclopedia of Education*, Paul Monroe, ed., "Italy," Vol. III, pp. 501–502.

[7] *Annuario statistico italiano 1886*, p. 957; *Annuario statistico italiano 1905–1907*, p. 94.

[8] *The New York Times*, January 11, 1959, p. 13.

[9] *Annuario statistico italiano 1895*, pp. 880–887, 912–915; Appendix A, Table 11.

[10] Appendix A, Table 8.

[11] *Annuario statistico italiano 1886*, pp. lxxv, ccxliv–ccxlv; *Sommario . . .*, cited above, p. 149; *Annuario statistico italiano 1895*, pp. 880–887.

[12] Michels, *Storia critica . . .*, cited above, p. 188.

[13] *Annuario statistico italiano 1895*, pp. 880–887, 912–915.

[14] Croce, cited above, pp. 54–55, 60–61.

[15] *Annuario statistico italiano 1886*, pp. lx–lxi.

[16] *Sommario . . .*, cited above, p. 65; *Annuario statistico italiano 1886*, pp. l–li.

[17] Appendix A, Table 3.

[18] Leonetti, cited above, p. 37.

[19] Rigola, cited above, p. 82; passage translated by M. F. Neufeld.

[20] The same, pp. 84–85.

[21] Croce, cited above, pp. 54–55; *Atti della Giunta per la inchiesta agraria e sulle condizioni della classe agricola*, Vol. XV, Fascicolo I, "Relazione finale sui risultati dell'inchiesta redatta per incarico della Giunta dal Presidente, Conte Stefano Jacini." The commission issued its 15 volumes in 24 parts through the Forzani publishing house in Rome between 1881 and 1886. The synoptic-analytic index of the proceedings and studies, published as Vol. XV, Tomo II, was compiled by Leopoldo Meini. The commission members were: G. A. Angeloni, A.

Bertani, A. Branca, A. Damiani, F. de Siervo, S. Jacini, F. Meardi, E. Morpurgo, F. Salaris, L. Tanari, G. Toscanelli, and F. Vitelleschi Nobili.

[22] Alexander Gerschenkron, "Notes on the Rate of Industrial Growth in Italy, 1881–1913," *The Journal of Economic History*, Vol. XV, No. 4 (December 1955), p. 360. The work of Maffeo Pantaleoni which Gerschenkron consulted is: "Delle regioni d'Italia in ordine alla loro ricchezza ed al loro carico tributario," *Scritti varii di economia*, Serie III. For a discussion of the theoretical aspects of the relation between Italian economic development during the 20–25 years following unification and the political and social character of the *Risorgimento*, centering in speculation concerning the primitive accumulation of capital, see Gerschenkron's review article on Rosario Romeo's *Risorgimento e Capitalismo* (Bari, 1959): "Rosario Romeo e l'accumulazione primitiva del capitale," *Rivista Storica Italiana*, LXXI, No. 4, pp. 557–586. For the per capita income figures cited, see "Indagine statistica sullo sviluppo del reddito nazionale dell'Italia dal 1861 al 1956," *Annali di statistica*, Anno 86, Serie VIII, Vol. 9, p. 42, Table 6, B; see also, Appendix A, Table 30.

[23] Appendix A, Table 13. For the census years before 1901, an attempt was made to approximate whenever possible the category definitions used by the Central Institute of Statistics for data concerning the economic process after 1901. "Agriculture" includes agriculture, forestry, fishing, and hunting. "Goods-producing industries" comprises extractive and manufacturing industries, building and construction, and the production of electric, gas, and water power. "Services," designated as "tertiary" by the Institute, groups together commerce, hotels and tourist trades, transportation, communications, credit, banking, insurance, and other services.

[24] *Annuario statistico italiano 1958*, pp. 306–307.

[25] *Indagine statistica . . .*, cited above, p. 36; see also, Appendix A, Table 32.

[26] Gerschenkron, cited above, pp. 361–364; see also, Gerschenkron, *Description of an Index of Italian Industrial Output, 1881–1913*, Russian Research Center, Harvard University, 1955. For the specific meaning of Gerschenkron's terms, see this study, p. 301 below.

[27] League of Nations, Economic, Financial and Transit Department, *Industrialization and Foreign Trade*, p. 13. Mining was included in the indices for France up to 1898, for Belgium to 1902, and Italy to 1913.

[28] *Indagine statistica . . .*, cited above, p. 99. The Central Institute of Statistics defined "manufacturing industries" in the following terms: (1) agricultural-manufacturing (food and beverages, tobacco and tobacco products, textiles, clothing, fur and leather, wood-working and wood products); (2) extractive-manufacturing (metallurgical activities, mechanical industries, processing of nonmetal-liferous minerals); and (3) chemicals and allied products, paper, rubber, printing and publishing, photo-phono-cinematographic products, and miscellaneous manufacturing.

[29] The official survey entitled, *Notizie statistiche sopra alcune industrie*, was published in Rome in 1878 by the Ministry of Agriculture, Industry and Commerce. Ellena's study, "La statistica di alcune industrie italiane," was published as Vol. 13, *Annali di statistica*, Serie 2a, in Rome in 1880. The study published in 1906 by the Ministry of Agriculture, Industry and Commerce in three parts was entitled: *Statistica industriale. Riassunto delle notizie sulle condizioni industriali del Regno*.

[30] Tremelloni, *Storia recente dell'industria italiana*, cited above, p. 18, footnote 1.

[31] All figures concerning industrial employment in 1876 have been taken from the 1906 volume, *Statistica industriale. Riassunto . . .*, Parte I, pp. 8–9. For details on Ellena's statistics, which vary slightly from the official data published in 1906, see his study, cited in footnote 29, pp. 29–37. Ellena listed a total of 382,131 men, women, and children employed in the industries covered, in contrast to the total of 388,306 cited by the 1906 official publication, which in turn, was at variance

with the total of 460,000 mentioned by Roberto Tremelloni with reference to the same survey (see work and page cited in footnote 30).

The total population of Italy in 1871 was 26,801,200, of whom 6,013,500 were under ten years of age. See *Sommario di statistiche storiche italiane,* cited above, p. 40.

[32] *Statistica industriale. Riassunto . . .,* cited above, p. 10.

[33] The same, pp. 8–9; *Annuario statistico italiano 1905–1907,* pp, 448, 450, 452, 454, and 455.

[34] Melvin Thomas Copeland, *The Cotton Manufacturing Industry of the United States,* pp. 90–91.

[35] *Statistica industriale. Riassunto . . .,* cited above, pp. 8–9.

[36] Tremelloni, *Storia recente . . .,* p. 58; *Annuario statistico italiano 1905–1907,* p. 446.

[37] *Annuario statistico italiano 1886,* p. 96; *Annuario statistico italiano 1905–1907,* p. 111.

[38] *Sommario . . .,* cited above, p. 129.

[39] *Annuario statistico italiano 1895,* p. 423.

[40] Ernesto Manuelli, "Situation and Prospects of the Italian Steel Industry," *Review of Economic Conditions in Italy,* Vol. XII, No. 6 (November 1958), pp. 567–568.

[41] Shepard B. Clough and Carlo Livi, "Economic Growth in Italy: An Analysis of the Uneven Development of North and South," *The Journal of Economic History,* Vol. XVI, No. 3 (September 1956), pp. 337–343. For a comparison of Neapolitan tariff rates before unification with those of the Kingdom of Sardinia and of the Kingdom of Italy, see Ferdinando Milone, *L'Italia nell'economia delle sue regioni,* p. 750, footnote 1.

[42] Ferdinando Milone, cited above, pp. 51–52.

[43] *Annuario statistico italiano 1886,* pp. 95–96.

[44] Clough and Livi, cited above, pp. 335, 343–349. Clough and Livi defined the South as including the following regions: Abruzzi and Molise, Campania, Puglia, Basilicata, Calabria, Sicily, and Sardinia; Central Italy as including the regions of Tuscany, Umbria, Marche, and Lazio; the North as including the following regions: Piedmont, Liguria, Lombardy, Trentino and Upper Adige, Venetia, Venetia Julia, and Emilia. The calculation of the South's share of the total population in 1881 was made by M. F. Neufeld. See *Annuario statistico italiano 1892,* pp. 72–77.

[45] Gerschenkron, cited above, pp. 361, 367.

[46] Appendix A. Table 9.

[47] *Annuario statistico italiano 1911,* p. 186.

[48] The railway construction costs and total government expenditures for the years indicated were as follows:

Expenditures in Lire

Year	Railway Construction	Total Government Costs
1873	54,077,584	1,136,248,589
1887–88	297,879,386	1,572,855,138
1888–89	235,784,102	1,735,212,458

See *Annuario statistico italiano 1895,* pp. 880, 887.

[49] Gerschenkron, cited above, pp. 370–371.

[50] *Annuario statistico italiano 1892,* pp. 630–632; see also, Appendix A, Table 10.

[51] Clough and Livi, cited above, p. 349.

[52] Gerschenkron, cited above, pp. 367–368.

[53] The same, p. 368.

[54] The same, p. 369.

[55] The same, p. 370.

V

The Pull of History: 1860 to 1890

The Slow Rise of Organized Labor Resistance

AVAILABLE evidence of economic growth and change during the nineteenth century has indicated quite clearly that Italy did not experience its initial phase of modern industrial development until the 1880's. Not until then, as well, did Italy first learn of its chronic agricultural poverty. Nor had a thriving commercial life throughout the peninsula counterbalanced these dark deficiencies with energy, initiative, and opportunity. Inevitably, the triple economic backwardness which prevailed during most of the years from 1860 to 1890 imposed harsh suffering upon both urban and rural workers. Discontent remained a fixed part of life, like hunger, and erupted sporadically, as of old, into unorganized, violent protest.

By the end of the first decade after unification, the Italian countryside seethed with revolt. The artisans and factory workers in the cities participated in the earlier phases of these uprisings, but the aroused peasants and agricultural laborers demonstrated the greatest fervor and the fiercest persistence. Then, as the second decade of the Kingdom came on, open discontent disappeared under harsh governmental reprisals and the folk on the land relapsed into their wonted, stolid, and dangerous calm. By now, the conservative working-class organizations — mutual aid societies and cooperatives — which had taken their start earlier, entered their season of large growth and prosperity. At this time, too, the inaugural Catholic congresses assembled to debate emerging issues of social life, including the proper forms of worker and employer associations. Meanwhile, militancy slowly increased among workers everywhere and even mutual aid societies sometimes made economic demands upon employers and countenanced withdrawal from work. Strikes increased in number, intensity, and scope. Simultaneously, the first permanent labor unions established themselves at the local level. They soon moved toward city-wide and provincial federations. A few craft groups next strove for regional and national forms of organization.

Destitution guided the main course of Italian labor development in the years before 1890. Earlier, this narrative traced the infiltration into Italy of those transmontane radical doctrines which came to influence a small advanced segment of workers, largely through the efforts of educated missionaries from the upper classes. These ideas have continued to form such a large part of the mental and spiritual baggage of the Italian labor movement after World War II that any endeavor to depreciate their persuasive power (as distinguished from their fitness or truth) among Italian workers must end in failure. Yet it would be equally futile to minimize the force of unabating poverty and — what can be much more dangerous socially — near-poverty. They supplied these imported revolutionary ideas with staying strength since radical programs never advanced in Italy beyond the stage of promising an end to human suffering at some future time. But if persistent poverty and near-poverty kept the appeal of socialism in its various guises fresh and always plausible, they also served the cause of organized labor resistance by making it impossible for workers to forget their manifestations: long hours of toil, pauper wages, and the ever-rising cost of living.

Hours of Labor, Wages, Living Costs, and the Standard of Living. In the early 1860's, men, women, and children labored 11 and 12 hours a day in all those crafts and industries which did not function on a piece-work basis. In some instances, the working day reached 14 hours. Rarely, it rose to 16 hours. It descended just as seldom to 10 hours, and hardly ever to 8. Among peasants, the normal workday in spring and summer extended for 12 hours, while it lasted 15 hours at harvest time. During the winter months, hours of labor decreased with the shortened period of daylight at the very time when work itself grew scarce.

Statistics on wage rates between 1860 and 1890 may be assembled from two principal sources: (1) the data carried by the official statistical yearbooks of the Italian government, and (2) information garnered from a host of independent studies, both contemporary and of later origin.

The official calculations of average hourly wage rates have the merit of continuity and homogeneity. They run from 1862 beyond 1890. They report earnings from 30 occupations in 18 different plants and mines, owned by 14 separate firms. However, they suffer from at least two telling limitations. First, the preservation of homogeneity necessarily limited the scope of inquiry to the 18 plants and mines originally selected, thereby freezing the sample within the primitive pattern of Italian industry for 1862. Second, the tabulated data excluded the wages of women and children, since they were regarded as too low, and also ignored those wages of men which appeared exceptionally high or depressed. The so-called average hourly rate, therefore, bore not even a slight resemblance to the concept of a prevailing wage weighted in proportion to the number of workers in each category of earnings. This official approach, which might have been either professionally naïve or politically sophisticated, greatly exaggerated the level of hourly wage payments since 12 of the 18 establishments in the sample formed part of the textile industry. Here, as we have learned, women and children constituted at least 85% of all workers as late as 1876 and earned pittance wages even when compared with the low enough compensation of men in the mills. Yet the earnings of this overwhelming majority were excluded from the official calculations.

The findings of the independent studies are tainted by at least five defects, also applicable, in part, to the official statistics: (1) the obvious diversity of working conditions in a kingdom but recently contrived of seven states, each laden with deeply ingrained local habits; (2) the paucity of data for industrial workers, who, in any event, formed a small portion of the total labor force; (3) the inaccessibility of information concerning the wages of artisans who plied their crafts in numerous small and scattered establishments; (4) the lack of precision due to limited knowledge about scattered maximum- and minimum-wage figures without adequate data on the number of workers involved in each category; and (5) the nature of available evidence — heterogeneous, impressionistic, and largely applicable to industrial workers.

In 1861, according to estimates made by assembling the information unearthed by independent studies, the average daily wage of selected craft and industrial workers ranged from 1.20 lire to 1.50 lire (or from 109 to 134 thousandths of a lira per hour based upon an 11-hour day).[1] Variations from this average daily wage may be gathered from the following summary:

Less than 1 lira a day: Paper mill workers in Lombardy.
Unskilled textile workers in Lombardy and Biella.
Sardinian miners.

1 to 1.5 lire a day: Some textile workers in North Italy and Naples.
Building laborers in Piedmont and Lombardy.
Unskilled workers in railroad shops.
Ribbon and leather workers in Milan.
Certain categories of sulphur workers in Romagna.

Maximum rates for skilled workers:

Textiles	2.86
Building Trades	2.42
Paper Mills	2.00
Mining	3.39
Shipyards	3.25
Railroad Shops	5.25

As compared with the average daily wage rate derived from the independent surveys — 1.30 lire, or 122 thousandths of a lira per hour — the official estimate for 1862 stood at 146 thousandths of a lira per hour, or 1.61 lire a day.[2]

How, then, did the average craft and industrial worker — still a relatively rare specimen in Italy's overwhelmingly agricultural economy — fare on this wage, however estimated? He and his family lived intimately with constant privation. In the absence of reliable data concerning all items which comprised the cost of living in 1862, available data on the retail cost of wheat have been marshalled since bread and pasta constituted the principal staple of the average worker's diet. According to calculations made in the 1860's, each Italian consumed 282 pounds of wheat a year. (This estimate perhaps shot somewhat high for well-to-do individuals, since they could afford to balance their meals with fruits, vegetables, and meat. It probably hit somewhat low for workers who had to subsist almost wholly on the cheaper farinaceous foods.) In 1862, 220 pounds of wheat (1 quintal) cost 28.5 lire. If the head of a family of four persons earned an average of 1.30 lire a day, he would have had to expend the wages of 111 days — 145 lire — to purchase enough wheat (5.1 quintals) to satisfy his own needs and those of his dependents. If the obviously inflated official rate of earnings is utilized instead — 1.61 lire a day (146 thousandths of a lira per hour for 11 hours) — he would have had to spend 90 days working for this same supply of wheat. Had he escaped unemployment and held on to his job for 300 days during the year, under one estimate he would have devoted 37% of all working hours for this purpose and, under the second, more favorable estimate, 30%.

But wheat is not yet flour, nor surely bread. Even so, a third or more of the income of an average family head disappeared with the purchase of this bare necessity alone. When he earned less than the average daily wage here assumed, or when he faced the all-too-familiar trials of unemployment, a substantially higher proportion of his income had to be expended for wheat. The families of workers, especially in the North, often subsisted on cornmeal, cheaper than wheat, but less nourishing and palatable. Even with this sacrifice, they found it difficult to feed, clothe, and house themselves. Geisser and Magrini, who figure among the leading Italian authorities on industrial wages in the second half of the nineteenth century, observed at the conclusion of their researches that wages in the 1860's appeared to have been caught in a frightful state of depression. The *Inaugural Address* of Karl Marx, written in 1864 for the International Workingmen's Association, reflected the economic knowledge garnered by Marx from the Blue Books, reports, inquiries, statistics, and tax studies he had patiently unearthed at the British Museum; it extended the stricture of Geisser and Magrini to all of Europe:

> In all countries of Europe it has now become a truth demonstrable to every unprejudiced mind, and only denied by those whose interest it is to hedge other people in a fool's paradise, that no improvement of machinery, no appliance of science to production, no contrivances of communication, no new colonies, no emigration, no opening of markets, no free trade, nor all these things put together, will do away with the miseries of the industrious masses; but that, on the present false base, every fresh development of the productive powers of labour must tend to deepen social contrasts and point social antagonisms.[3]

Official government statistics indicated a rise of 25% in hourly wage rates between 1862 and 1873. Despite this increase, which, it must be recalled, applied only to the more fortunate workers in the plants under survey, the average family head had to work 94 days in 1873 to acquire the same amount of wheat — 5.1 quintals — for which he had labored only 90 days in 1862, according to the same official source of information.[4]

Moderates and conservatives, not radicals alone, now began to discover the truth which lay behind the riots of 1868 and 1869: the worsening ability of wages to cover even the most basic wants of working-class families. During the hearings conducted by the Commission of Inquiry on Italian Industry in the early 1870's, all representatives of the various chambers of commerce who testified characterized wages as either "low," "limited," or "small." Again, an independent investigator of this same period remarked: "It is impossible to deny that wages are generally inferior to the needs of the worker, especially after the recent increase in the price of basic necessities and rent." Another writer emphasized the implicit irony of Italy's social condition. The poor now enjoyed greater juridical status than ever before in modern history and were seemingly better compensated for their labor. But, neither these civic rights nor these higher wages, sucked dry by advancing prices, had been able to create in them a happier state of mind and spirit.[5]

The most meaningful Italian wage data for any year within the entire period under study appeared, surprisingly enough, at the end of the 1870's in the United States of America. On April 11, 1878, the Acting Secretary of State, F. W. Seward, addressed a circular to the consular officers of the United States in Great Britain, France, Germany, Belgium, Italy, Spain, the Netherlands, Sweden and Norway, and Denmark. He called attention to an earlier request for information about the condition of American trade with foreign countries. Now, he called upon the various consular officers to furnish the following additional information: (1) wage rates paid to all classes of laborers, but especially agricultural and mechanical laborers and those engaged on public works and railroads; (2) an estimate of the cost of living for working-class families, or lists of the actual prices paid for the necessities of life; and (3) a comparison of present wage and cost-of-living rates with those which had prevailed during the preceding five years. Other questions concerned the activity of commerce, "business habits and systems," and the monetary situation.

The State Department gathered together the subsequent consular reports and the House of Representatives published them in 1879 under the title, *State of Labor in Europe: 1878.*[6]

The Letter of Transmittal from the Secretary of State, William M. Evarts, to the Speaker of the House of Representatives, Samuel J. Randall, left small doubt that the investigation of 1878 into the economic welfare of European workers drew its force from the fears and perplexities suffered by middle-class Americans in the wake of the first modern and nationwide industrial upheaval in the United States: the railroad strikes and riots of 1877. Near the conclusion of his Letter of Transmittal, the Secretary of State wrote:

> It is unfortunate that so many who have escaped from the bondage and travail of European labor, and become citizens of the United States, should so soon forget the wages, food, and condition from which they sought release through emigration, and show such small appreciation of their new and superior surroundings and condition as to seek, by strikes and organized violence — European methods of remedying European evils, and totally foreign to and subversive of republican institutions — to introduce strife, where none of old existed, between employers and employés, where harmony and mutual reciprocity should alone prevail. It is equally deplorable, and more unaccountable, that so many native-born

Americans should accept the teachings of the very worst school of Europe by countenancing or abetting strikes and communism.[7]

Earlier, the Secretary of State had warned that the ruling classes of Europe, who could dominate their own working population only by force, looked for the imminent destruction of the American Republic at the hands of its own workingmen. As a result,

> all strikes and riots in this country are hailed in Europe as so many outbursts foreboding the final dissolution of the Republic. The report from the consul at Prague, which will be found in the appendix, giving an account of the feeling which prevailed in Europe in regard to the railroad strikes and riots of 1877, is a good illustration of this important point.[8]

The comparative national wage rates and costs of necessities, as summarized in Tables 34 and 35 of Appendix A reproduced from *State of Labor in Europe: 1878*, placed the American worker at the top and the Italian worker at the bottom of the economic welfare hierarchy. Table 34 estimates the weekly rate of wages for given categories of labor in seven European countries, New York, and Chicago. Table 35 assembles the retail prices of necessities in an equal number of European countries, New York, and Chicago. These synopses point to the following conclusions: (1) Italian wage rates in 1878 amounted to less than one-third those in the United States. Wage rates in Spain, also compared with those in the United States, held to the same low Italian levels. Those in Denmark, France, and Germany reached one-third the wage rates in the United States, while those of Belgium achieved a magnitude of somewhat less than one-half those in the United States. England and Scotland produced the highest European wage rates: two-thirds those of the United States. (2) The prices of vital food items, soap, starch, and coal were lower in the United States than in any of the European countries. In commenting on the relatively high standard of living enjoyed by American workers, the Secretary of State observed that, if they had been content to live on the same meager and unvaried diets as European workers and if, in addition, they had been willing to practice the same degree of frugality as Europeans, they could live as cheaply.

These official thoughts formed the first statement of a logical sequence of propositions. American mechanical appliances had placed the United States, productivity-wise, 25 years ahead of Europe. Consequently, the average American workman could perform one-and-one-half to twice the amount of work, in a given period of time, as the average European workman. However, steamships were annihilating ocean distances. Unless American manufacturers found it possible to extend their markets and

163

undersell foreign producers, American workers could no longer expect steady work. The conclusion of this argument came swiftly: "Under no consideration must we have strikes; under no consideration must our factories lie idle. If our manufacturers cannot run their establishments profitably — and capital will no more remain permanently invested unprofitably than will labor work for nothing — and pay the prevailing wages, our working people must help them to make profit by consenting to a reduction of wages."[9]

The wage rates and working hours arrayed for the present study in Table 36 of Appendix A represent hitherto ungathered pertinent items which were scattered throughout the individual consular reports prepared for five districts in Italy: Piedmont, Genoa, Florence, Rome, and Messina. Selected crafts and industries include agricultural and common laborers, blacksmiths, bricklayers, carpenters, machinists, shoemakers, tailors, tanners, textile workers, and tinsmiths. Merely a glance across Table 36 will establish the diversity of wage rates from region to region for the same craft or industrial category. Table 36 therefore serves as a reminder of diversity which the summary averages in Table 34 necessarily obscured. The cost-of-living items listed for Italy as a whole in Table 35 also concealed, perforce, existing regional variations. Therefore, the wage rate columns of Table 36 must be supplemented by information concerning regional living costs. Fortunately, the consular reports furnish some enlightenment.

In Piedmont, agricultural workers earned from 24 cents a day for a 9-hour day to 40 cents for a 12-hour day during the spring, summer, and fall if and when work were available. They had to spend from 16 cents to 20 cents a day for food. Although the rural worker could occasionally afford to eat some sausage, his daily food consisted mostly of polenta, a form of cornmeal mush. He varied this diet with rice bread, in areas where rice grew, and with soups thickened with flour, containing rice, garden vegetables in season, and sometimes a little lard as a touch of luxury. Cheese, greens, and chestnuts, when available, supplemented this fare. Mechanics in Turin earned an average of 65 cents a day, while silk spinners received 24 cents and railroad laborers from 32 to 60 cents. Most workers had to spend more than half of their daily wage for food. Because rents were high, whole families dwelt in a single small room. Wages were so inadequate that children "at a tender age [had] to work early and late to obtain a scanty subsistence and necessary raiment."[10]

In the Genoa area, agricultural laborers were reported as averaging about 40 cents a day; daily food cost them from 12 to 20 cents. In the city, common laborers earned 46 cents a day, but the cost for food ranged from 25 cents to 35 cents a day. The consul described the constant diet of the Genoese Italian laborer as consisting mostly of bread, boiled chestnuts, polenta, and the thick soup called minestrone. Occasionally a bottle of ordinary wine, stockfish, or cheese relieved this monotony. Only during holidays or gala festivals did the laborer or peasant enjoy fresh meat.[11]

Ordinary field hands in the Florence district averaged about 40 cents a day, while common laborers in the city of Florence received a like amount. Board came to 57 cents a day ($4.00 a week) for men and 43 cents a day ($3.00 a week) for women. Four rooms in a tenement cost an average of $60 a year. Clearly, only those categories of workers in Table 36 who earned well beyond the figures cited for common laborers could have met such expenditures. In his report, the consul at Florence stated that the city could not be considered "either a commercial or a manufacturing center when compared with cities of the same size and population in countries like France, England, and some parts of Germany; and although it is making advancement in both directions every year, yet the deplorable state of its finances, high rate of taxation, and general poverty of its inhabitants, render the investment of capital here at the present very questionable. . . ."[12]

In the Rome area, agricultural workers earned from 26 cents to 60 cents a day, including lodging. They had to pay from 12 to 20 cents a day for food. In Rome itself, common laborers in manufactories earned 60 cents a day, while women received half that sum. The daily cost of food for city workers ranged from an estimate of 30 cents to 50 cents a day. The ordinary worker's diet in the Rome district consisted of coarse bread, cheese, and raw onions in the morning. For lunch, he ate vegetables and macaroni, with pork fat or olive oil added. An alternative to this dish was polenta. In the evening he again ate bread and cheese, with onions or a salad as a side dish, sometimes varied by stockfish. Very rarely did an ordinary worker eat mutton or goat meat washed down by common wine.[13]

Porters, laborers on public works, and workers by the day in the Messina area earned from 30 to 70 cents, while "mechanics" received from 70 cents to $1.00 for a 12-hour day. Until the time of the consular report, "mechanics" in Messina were principally French and English, but because of the high rates of wages demanded by them, they were discharged and Sicilian workers substituted. In commenting upon the cost and standard of living in the Messina area, the consul observed: "The laboring classes are frugal and industrious; very rarely do you find destitution among them. They are contented with little, and live upon what our workmen would despise. The living expenses of a mechanic with a family of three,

165

including tenement, clothes, &c. amounts to $4.90 per week." The level of living implied by these figures would obviously have excluded all but the most skilled workers listed in Table 36.[14]

Time brought determinable, limited relief at least to that part of the labor force covered by the official Italian surveys of hourly wage rates already described. During the 1880's, the price of wheat declined, while hourly earnings of these selected workers gradually rose. Whereas the head of a family had labored 90 days in 1862 and 94 days in 1873 to satisfy his own wheat needs and those of his dependents, the necessary number of days had fallen to 69 by 1880 and to 43 by 1885 and 1890. Thus, within thirty years, the number of required working days had halved. This decrease certainly represented a blessing, but did not assuage the great nutritional evil of Italy, as the statistical yearbook for 1892 ingenuously revealed while reporting, with congratulatory satisfaction, the boon of lower wheat prices and higher wages: "With respect to wine, meat, and oil — articles which have a very minor importance in the nourishment of the Italian worker as compared with cereals — we have seen that the prices of these items do not have a tendency to diminish."[15]

The Uprisings of 1868. The workers of Italy during the immediate years after unification suffered from poverty of the depth just described, as well as from the deflation of grandiose political illusions which the heady atmosphere of the *Risorgimento* had bred. Discontent exploded, at the end of the decade, in a series of uprisings both in cities and countryside. The government of the new Kingdom had been pursuing an upright policy of balancing the budget by cutting governmental expenses and raising taxes. By 1868, the country lay in full crisis: the bad harvest of the preceding year had dealt Italy a cruel blow; the devaluation of the currency had brought about stagnation in commerce and industry; basic commodities had risen in price; the tax on real property had soared to 16.25%, while the personal property tax, weighing most heavily upon wage earners, mounted to 8%; the purchasing power of wages remained at the lowest level.

Although protests against the personal property tax among workers and peasants threatened to go beyond clamorous verbal protest, and although workers refused to pay it, the government, nothing daunted, proposed another regressive levy: a tax upon the milling of grain. Between January and March 1868, Parliament discussed the milling tax. The deputies of the Left tried to warn the majority group against driving the great mass of Italian workers and peasants to desperation. Francesco Crispi went so far as to declare: "When the government steps beyond the law, I recognize the right of the people to resist."[16] Later, in March, he defined the milling tax ironically as a progressive tax, not in proportion to wealth, but in proportion to poverty. He reminded Parliament that bread formed nine-tenths of the diet of the poor, while it formed but one-tenth or less of the food of the rich. He pointed out that the price of bread had increased after 1860 due to political and economic conditions in Italy, rising even more after 1866 following the issue of paper money. He warned the lawmakers that if the proposed law were passed, bread, so important to the poor, would become a precious commodity, difficult for workers and peasants to buy with their limited and meager resources.[17]

The democratic press and workers groups — political leagues of republican persuasion, mutual aid societies, and budding craft unions as yet far from numerous or important — sought to direct the weight of public opinion against the passage of the law. Editorials predicted that the milling tax would lead to grave disorders. Responsible leaders of the Left, though indignant at the government, feared that popular revolt might endanger not only the monarchy, for which they had no love, but also the unity of Italy itself. The Central Council of the Italian Workers Societies, which served as the permanent body between congresses (see Chart, page 118), circulated an appeal in March 1868 to all its constituent organizations to join in a collective protest against the tax upon "proletarian hunger." During this controversy, Mazzini made one of his wisest observations in a letter to his friend, Andrea Giannelli: "Growing poverty, the milling tax if approved, etc., will increase discontent; material reasons have created uprisings, but never revolutions."[18]

Despite protests, threats, warnings, gloomy press predictions, and working-class restiveness, Parliament approved the tax measure in March 1868. At the start of the new year, 1869, the government proposed to collect 2 lire on every quintal (220 pounds) of wheat, 1.20 lire on every quintal of oats, 1 lira on every quintal of corn and rye, and 0.50 lira on every quintal of dried vegetables and chestnuts — all staples of prime quantitative importance in the workers' diets.[19] Just how harshly the new impost bore down upon workers in the new year can be seen with specific clarity from a letter written by a shoemaker to La Nazione (The Nation), January 11, 1869: "I earn 2 lire a day, have 8 small children, and consume 18 pounds of bread daily (because there is nothing else). This amounts to 540 pounds in a month. Now, with the increase in both the consumption and milling taxes, I pay an increase of 2 centimes a pound — this amounts to 10.80 lire a month — in a year this comes to 129.60 lire; how do you think it is possible for poor people like me to pay the tax?"[20]

But the poor did not await the actual application of the tax to protest its injustice. Urban artisans and workers, especially in the North, reacted against the approval of the tax immediately and vented their anger by organizing demonstrations, intensifying group efforts, and demanding wage increases. The strikes in the larger centers of population differed from those of earlier years. They showed a novel tendency to spread beyond one trade or industry to others in the same locality. For example, in Turin at the beginning of April 1868, the workers at the arsenal struck in protest against the personal property tax. This strike spread to the railroads and tobacco factories. The provincial prefect settled the strike rapidly by promising to suspend collection of the tax. However, the authorities confiscated the April 4 issue of *L'Avvenire dell'Operaio* (*The Future of the Worker*), published by the Turin General Society of Workers (organized in January 1868 in order to unite all workers in the city), on the grounds that it had excused the strike as the pitiful expression of people pushed to the limits of patience. Then, in May, the leaders of the strike lost their jobs and had to depend upon a fund established by their fellow workers.[21]

Meanwhile, a general strike had broken out at Bologna. It lasted for two days, April 14 and 15. The printers distinguished themselves by walking out in full force; those who worked for the newspaper, *L'Amico del Popolo* (*The Friend of the People*), remained at their jobs, for it alone had defended the strikers. *La Nazione*, in commenting on the Bologna strike, exploited a special fear which Adolphe Thiers, the French Minister of the Interior in the first Nicolas Soult cabinet, had manipulated so well a generation earlier. Just before his brutal suppression of the workers' insurrections at Paris and Lyons in April 1834, Thiers wrote to the prefect of the lower Rhine: "I advise you to take the greatest care to furnish your share of documents for the great forthcoming investigations. The correspondence of all anarchists, the intimate connections between events in Paris, Lyons, Strasbourg, and, in a word, the existence of a vast conspiracy embracing the whole of France — all this must be made entirely clear."[22] Now listen to *La Nazione* in 1868:

> The disorders of Bologna appear to be, in character and procedure, an episode in that sad drama that for some time has been unfolding in England, France, Belgium, Switzerland, Bavaria, and, it is possible to say now, in every part of Europe. By chance, the revelations which the newspapers of Geneva contain these days are able to throw some light upon this episode. They report that the strike in the canton continues and attribute it exclusively to the wretched devices of the International Workingmen's Association established there. . . . The accounts of the disorders in Bologna might be read with the Geneva

strikes in mind to see whether or not the events in both countries do not resemble each other.

The article continued by stressing the duty of urgent inquiry in order to learn

> if among the evils of political character there were not hidden one much more terrible, one which had to be unrelentingly resolved should catastrophe be averted, and about which one cannot think without horror: the social question.[23]

Exactly a month later, *L'Unità Cristiana* (*Christian Unity*), a democratic newspaper in Turin, expressed a less hysterical and more constructive point of view:

> The disease which today torments the Italian people is discontent. From this discontent arise strikes and riots, riots and strikes; in a word, general despair. The poor, who live from day to day, see the possibilities of work diminish day by day, and they lack bread to eat.

The article warned that if the government and the ruling classes did not find a remedy for the discontent and needs of the people, "they would hurl Italy upon a slippery road of agitation, ruinous struggles and repression without end."[24]

As the date for applying the tax drew near, apprehension seized officials in Rome. On December 24, the Minister of the Interior sent a telegram to the prefects of all provinces. He called attention to the financial and political importance of the law and forewarned the prefects that they could expect trouble from the parties of the extreme Left. They were urged to prevent all disorders and to frustrate the subversive designs of the radicals. These anxieties proved well founded. However, the uprisings at the end of December 1868 and during the early months of 1869 flared up in the rural areas, in contrast to the urban nature of strikes in the earlier part of 1868.

Day laborers constituted the largest and most degraded element among the peasants. They worked under even less favorable conditions than unskilled workers in the cities, for they lived far apart from each other and at great distances from centers of population. Moreover, the parties could condemn them to political isolation with impunity, since they still lacked voting rights. Consequently, agricultural workers could join together only with enormous difficulty to resist wage cuts or unreasonably long hours through the force of numbers. Nor could they expect the aid of deputies or local councilmen. They also suffered greatly from the vicissitudes of good and bad harvest years. An unknown timorous conservative, who had no reason to exaggerate the plight of agricultural laborers, recorded in his diary that reapers who came down from the mountains were willing to work for 0.20 lira a day, a wage level he had never witnessed before. The highest point reached by wages during that same month, June, was 0.60 lira a day.[25] Although the diary recorded statistics for 1871, the data may be considered roughly applicable to immediately preceding years since conditions had not changed substantially. Nor had discontent spread only among day laborers. Due to conscription and increasing severity of taxation, unrest also took hold of small property owners, renters, and sharecroppers. The clergy, once the moderating influence in favor of peasant resignation on earth, now seemingly failed to discourage feelings of revolt in the hearts of the faithful. The Church openly regarded the new government as so hateful that the higher ecclesiastical authorities were accused of actually fostering rather than disapproving this spirit among the clergy.

The first disorders took place on December 26, 1868 among the peasants in the province of Verona. The revolts spread rapidly to Lombardy, Piedmont, Veneto, and Emilia. *La Gazzetta Ufficiale* (*Official Gazette*), of January 1, 1869, in order to counteract the disturbing reports from the countryside, stated that the milling tax had gone into effect in 12 provinces without any disorders. True, it admitted, turmoil followed in other provinces, but without serious consequences. Despite these authoritative reassurances, the public began to hear of violent deaths in the province of Reggio Emilia. In January 1869, the situation worsened. The grain millers, who had to exact a higher price for their services because of the tax, either sided with the revolting peasants in many communities or, in order not to arouse their ire, closed down their mills. In some places, the populace referred to the demonstrations as the strikes of the millers. In Emilia, bands of peasants invaded town halls and mills. They rushed into the city of Parma in droves to the tolling of church bells. At Pavia, all bakers received a circular from a revolutionary committee which invited them to refuse any kind of agreement with the authorities and to desist from any type of negotiation if they did not wish to suffer later consequences. Bloody riots took place in the vicinity of Pontassieve and in the provinces of Turin and Bologna. The disturbances grew more serious in the provinces of Reggio Emilia and Parma. In some communes, the peasants began to build barricades. *La Gazzetta Ufficiale* of January 4 noted meetings and demonstrations in the provinces of Cuneo, Verona, Pavia, Cremona, Piacenza, Modena, Bologna, Lucca, and Arezzo. On January 5, the government issued a decree placing General Raffaele Cadorna (1815–1897) in full military charge of the provinces of Bologna, Parma, and Reggio Emilia. On that same day the Secret Republican Committee of Milan distributed a flyer which ended with these words: "Whoever senses the dignity of being an Italian citizen, whoever feels that Italy was made by the people and for the people, should clean his rifle and keep his powder dry."[26]

On January 6 at Verona, the rioting peasants cried: "Down with the rich!" Parma was in full insurrection on January 7 and troops engaged in battle with large numbers of peasants. At Ancona, a wall poster read: "Do not pay the tax if you wish to have a Republic." At San Giovanni in Persiceto near Bologna, 2,000 peasants invaded the public offices, set fire to records, ransacked private homes, and saw death and wounds inflicted upon themselves and the forces of law and order. The same kind of disorders took place at Cento, at Pieve, and other small communes. At Carmignano near Pistoia in Central Italy, 300 mountaineers took over the city hall, burned official records and the portrait of the King, and then put their demands in writing. In Milan city and province, a poster appeared which betrayed a different spirit, a nostalgia which some citizens felt for the days before the Kingdom. It called for the downfall of a government which took bread from the mouths of its people, robbed them of religion as well, and killed their children in useless wars. Next, it acclaimed the former Austrian authority, the Pope, and bread without a milling tax, and finally called for revolution if Italians were not to be completely lost.

South Italy suffered the milling tax much more tranquilly than North and Central Italy since that kind of tax had the stamp of long familiarity there. Still, the millers struck at Potenza, at Trani, and at Molfetta on January 6. The next day women demonstrated their ire at Terra di Lavoro near Alife, and at Campobasso the peasants rioted, crying: "Long live Vittorio Emanuele; down with City Hall and communal taxes; we would like to pay them, but how can we." In some small communities of Abruzzo and Calabria, resistance to the tax law grew more severe toward the middle of the month.

Although the riots began to simmer down after January 15, 1869, new disturbances broke out a month later, especially in Emilia province at Reggio, Pian di Voglio, and Imola. The events at Reggio resembled armed revolt. The two Manini brothers, sons of the head of the Republican Party in Reggio, united with the rebels in the countryside to form a revolutionary company. With the Manini brothers as leaders, the group invaded the mills, recaptured the tax monies, and redistributed them to the peasants. In the course of this daring action, the band had to confront both soldiers and *carabinieri*. After three days of fighting, most of their number, sensing themselves isolated, turned discouraged and headed for their homes. However, the Manini brothers and a few faithful followers refused to surrender; they fled to the mountains whence they molested the *carabinieri* and the soldiers. Finally, with the arrest of their father, the brothers allowed themselves to be captured. They served prison terms until the amnesty of October 1870.

Italy paid heavily for these uprisings in human life and social bitterness. In Emilia, 26 peasants were killed and 55 peasants and soldiers were wounded. In the vicinity of Bologna alone, 1,127 arrests had taken place. In Emilia, the authorities brought 129 cases against 2,226 defendants. Of 2,172 accused persons for whom occupational information was available, 108 were landowners, 261 were artisans, 569 were sharecroppers, and 1,234 were day laborers. According to the statistics which appeared in various newspapers throughout Italy, the total number of deaths due to the disturbances of 1868 and 1869 came to 257, while 1,099 persons had been wounded, and 3,788 individuals had been arrested.[27]

The national crisis precipitated by the institution of the milling tax drew into bold relief the states of mind among government officials, members of Parliament, conservative, moderate, and radical members of the middle class, and urban and rural workers. The prefect of Parma, in a report to General Cadorna, represented the uprisings as concerted mass movements. He reasoned that the riots had arisen rapidly and had spread quickly from community to community. This meant, logically, that they had required planning and travelling to prearranged places of contact. Moreover, these preparations had been consummated without knowledge of the authorities. The prefect stressed the dreadful novelty of this development among the working classes.

These inferences, based more upon the fears aroused by the riots than upon concrete, ascertainable facts, took another form in Parliament. There, the deputies raged against the menace of socialism and the role of the socialists in stirring up these revolts. The facile illation strayed far from the truth. Bakunin's followers had played no part in the uprisings. Indeed, Bakunin occupied himself outside of Italy in 1869. Not until the next year did he become concerned with the upheavals as historical events. He considered them completely spontaneous in origin. Although he claimed no credit for the Bakuninites, he nevertheless took ideological pleasure in the rural character of the riots. It appeared to prove his contention that a natural insurrectionary socialist spirit existed among Italian peasants, for, in contrast to Mazzini, he had laid great stress upon the primacy of their revolutionary role.

The conservatives and moderates laid major responsibility for the revolts upon the republicans. The accusation had no basis in fact, since

Mazzini had steadily pointed out the futility of such insurrections and had expressed clear opposition to them. Responsible elements among the republicans neither encouraged nor backed the riots, although younger and more emotional members did act without authorization.

The direct nature of the charges by radicals and republicans against the clergy also lacked validity. While they might have demonstrated that during the years immediately before the tumults of 1868 and 1869 the clergy failed to calm the mounting discontent among the peasants, they possessed little proof that ecclesiastical enmity toward the new State had resulted in actual incitement toward riot. The influence of the clergy, like that of republicans, radicals, and socialists, had operated indirectly and with minor consequence as compared to the spontaneous reaction of the tax-laden poor to the misery of poverty and hunger.

The predominance of peasant participation in the movement constituted a unique feature of these events. Only during the earlier part of 1868 did urban workers rebel against the proposed milling tax. Later, the largest and most violent revolts reflected peasant dissatisfaction. Unexpectedly, too, the most active peasant demonstrations occurred in North and Central Italy rather than in the more impoverished South. The most plausible explanation of this meridional passivity takes into account the sheer exhaustion of southern peasants following numerous uprisings before 1868. After the proclamation of the Kingdom, the old ruling classes of South Italy and Sicily resisted the new State with every resource at their command, including willingness to condone peasant revolts. By the time that North and Central Italy seethed with protest, the peasants of the South had spent their outrage.

Spontaneous and unorganized, the riots, strikes, and insurrections of 1868 and 1869 must not be twisted to represent a leap ahead toward the permanent organization of peasants into militant unions. Their beginnings still awaited future fulfillment. As yet, no firm and continuous action by peasants foreshadowed the most unique feature of the Italian labor movement: large, combative agricultural unions. But the future Italian labor movement benefitted, nonetheless, from the riot years because they shook the comfortable classes free of any euphoria which they managed to retain after the unification of Italy. They might still attempt to place the blame for the country's ills upon radicals, republicans, socialists, and Bakuninites, but in vain. Men of good will found it hard to understand what had happened to impair their exemplary intentions. Their perplexity comes through in a letter which appeared in *La Nazione*. The writer, after describing the uprisings in Parma, broke off with these desperate questions: "To what end have served the kindergartens, the many schools, the workhouses, and the numerous charities devoted to the working class? Our generation has worked so hard, has spent no inconsiderable sum in behalf of the children of the people, but with what recognition or love?"[28] Betimes, their intellectual and radical sons would come to think that they had found the true answer, free of paternalism, in the labor and socialist movements which they both sponsored and directed.

Mutual Aid Societies. From 1860 to 1890, mutual aid societies exhibited remarkable powers of survival and growth. Limited in purpose and moderate in philosophy, these societies reproduced on the Italian scene the very type of organization which had appeared in other countries during their transition from handicraft to factory production. They merit attention and honor because the societies ushered in the first influential phase of modern development in the history of Italian labor. They served the cause of later, more militant unionism by tiding artisans, mechanics, and skilled workmen over difficult years of trial and error, while, at the same time, providing them with a partial platform for occasional aggressive action. To these ends, the societies provided aid to sick and disabled members, pensions to the aged, subventions to the unemployed, as well as education to brother workers and their families. They also sponsored producers, consumers, and credit cooperatives. When assembled in congress (see Chart, p. 118), their delegates raised questions of principle which remained under debate, although in different outward forms, long after unions replaced the societies as the most representative organizations of labor: Should the societies stick to the tasks of mutual aid for which they were created and for which they received middle-class backing, or could they properly make wage and hour demands upon employers and back up their claims through strike action? Should the societies debate political issues and take up political stands, thus risking internal division and impairment of their primary function?

The accompanying table illustrates the rapid growth of mutual aid societies between 1862 and 1885, the latest year in the period under discussion for which official data had been collected. This expansion can be attributed, in part, to the conviction among the more liberal elements of the middle class — a feeling composed partly of fear and partly of sincere concern — that the encouragement of moderate mutual aid societies provided the only ready insurance against threats to the economic, social, civil, and political order. They had noticed that many societies of workers, formed without the surveillance of men of superior education and talents, thought only in extreme political terms and succumbed easily to unsound theories and vague, fantastic social and humanitarian aspirations. These middle-class liberals therefore felt it necessary to counter the growing number of strikes, the propaganda of the International, and the shocking uprisings of urban and rural workers with proper orientation and guidance which they willingly provided. In 1862, when mutual aid societies had a known total membership of 111,618, about 10,000 persons held honorary status. These personages included landowners, officials of political parties, police chiefs, and even the King himself. By 1885, the number of honorary and meritorious associates — largely from outside the ranks of labor — rose beyond 50,000.[29]

Italian Mutual Aid Societies, 1862–1885.

YEAR	No. of Existing Societies	Societies Revealing Number of Members			Societies Revealing Amount of Resources	
		No. of societies	No. of members	Average no. of members per society	No. of societies	Amount of resources in lire
1862......	443	417	111,618	268	371	2,715,749
1873......	1,447	1,146	218,822	191	1,095	9,351,580
1878......	2,091	1,981	331,548	167	1,949	21,141,662
1885......	4,896	4,821	791,296	164	3,520	32,200,840

Source: For the year 1862, *Annuario statistico italiano 1886*, pp. 1024–1025; for the years 1873, 1878, and 1885, *Annuario statistico italiano 1905–1907*, p. 786.

The largest number of societies and members developed, as in earlier decades, in North and Central Italy. There, the regions of Lombardy, Piedmont, Emilia, Tuscany, and Veneto ranked highest. In the South, Campania, with Naples as its principal center, Sicily, and Apulia predominated.[30] The societies flourished among artisans, skilled workers, agricultural labor, and even the professions.[31] By 1888, railroad workers had combined into eight consortia of over 80 societies with a membership of close to 60,000. The railroads checked off the dues of their employees and helped to keep the societies solvent by making substantial contributions to their treasuries.[32] These organizations recall the conservative behavior and dedication to mutual benefit activities of the railroad brotherhoods in the United States during the earliest years of their existence.

The total resources held by all Italian societies in 1885 — 32,200,840 lire — attained respectable dimensions indeed, but a mere listing of the services rendered illustrates the financial pressures under which they operated: benefits to aged and incapacitated members and to those otherwise unable to work; aid to families of dead members; compensation for industrial accidents; payments to unemployed workers; monetary encouragement to members travelling in search of jobs; burial expenses; nursing and maternity care; sponsorship of cooperatives; and the provision of educational opportunities for members and their families, including schooling at night and on Sundays, elementary instruction, training in drawing, arts, and crafts, circulating libraries, along with the distribution of books and supplies needed in classes.

The experience of other countries, and contemporary Italian evidence as well, warrant the assumption that many societies, founded with eagerness and hope, failed to survive for long, especially when they reached the crucial test of having to pay old-age pensions. Unfortunately, official statistics never fully enumerated the number of societies which appeared for the first time and which expired in any given year. Therefore, no precise birth and mortality tables can be established. The accompanying table approximates this need, only partially to be sure, by listing the number of societies which survived the years of their birth from 1860 to 1890 and lived to distribute benefits in 1904. It also reveals that the period, 1880–1884, brought forth an unusually large number of robust societies. Since Parliament did not accord to mutual aid societies the privilege of applying for juridical status as benevolent associations until April 15, 1886, these statistics would also seem to bear witness to the eternal truth that democratic deliberative bodies eventually recognize the inevitable. Public law 3818 proffered legal status to organizations which had already increased and prospered without the blessing of government.[33]

Mutual Aid Societies Existing on December 31, 1904 According to Period or Year of Foundation.

Period or Year	Total Number of Societies
1860–1864	286
1865–1869	367
1870–1874	518
1875–1879	696
1880–1884	1,199
1885	213
1886	219
1887	168
1888	163
1889	156
1890	183

Source: Annuario statistico italiano 1905–1907, p. 789.

The Rise of Cooperatives. Like mutual aid societies, Italian cooperatives grew out of the conservative principle of self-help and endeavored to better the lot of their members without seeking drastic changes in existing economic arrangements. This characteristic endeared them to Mazzini who knew as a result of his repeated exiles in England the achievements of the Rochdale Society of Equitable Pioneers and the movement they sparked. Through letters, articles, and speeches, he preached the gospel of cooperation along with a heavy sprinkling of his other concerns. He applauded the formation of cooperatives in Italy and encouraged them in their moments of trouble and doubt: "Do not allow the early difficulties to weary you. The cooperation of all will triumph over them. You have in your hands the most sacred cause in existence: the independence of labor."[34]

Italian cooperatives must be regarded as the second most tempering force in the troubled lives of workers from 1860 to 1890. They warrant careful consideration in the history of labor, first, because they focus attention upon the conservative side of Italian workers, too easily overlooked too often. Never dominant after 1890, this quality persisted, in spite of the provocations of Italian history, as a residual influence of no negligible power. Secondly, the cooperatives, while maintaining their organizational and political independence during the first two decades of the twentieth century, established close fraternal ties with the more aggressive labor and socialist movements. This intimate relationship, already evident after 1860, had its roots neither in chance nor in altruism. In a country abounding with one principal resource — manpower to excess — the lack of economic development and opportunity, unemployment, the fear of losing jobs, the tormenting behavior of business cycles, and black lists drove mutual aid societies and unions to the desperate hope of providing work through the creation of every imaginable type of cooperative. At their moment of greatest success, Italy's people's banks were judged inferior to those of Germany; its agricultural cooperatives never equalled their counterparts in France and Germany; and its consumer cooperatives, far too numerous and dispersed, could not compare in quality and soundness with the societies in Great Britain. But the variety of cooperatives in Italy made that country unique in the world of cooperation. That enthusiastic disposition to develop in every branch of service must be ascribed, certainly in part, to the spur of the unions pushed to the limits of ingenuity.

Cooperation, both in concept and practice, came to Italy from abroad with the single exception of dairy cooperatives which alone were native. The first cooperatives to spread among workers provided small sums of credit. To be sure, indigenous organizations called *monti frumentari* developed after 1860 in South Italy and provided aid in kind to poor peasants who needed wheat, corn, and barley for the next year's sowing.

But true credit cooperatives took their start only after 1862 when Luigi Luzzatti (1841–1927), who had studied cooperation in England and Germany, published his book, *The Spread of Credit in Italy*. Luzzatti — the father of Italian cooperation, often referred to as the Hermann Schultze-Delitzsch of the peninsula, and a pioneer in social reform, labor legislation, and profit sharing as well — founded the first people's banks (*banche popolari*) at Lodi and Asola in 1864. Under Luzzatti's leadership, groups in Milan and Brescia created similar banks and the movement began to spread beyond its northern cradle. Between 1865 and 1871, the number of people's banks and cooperative credit societies increased from 4 to 64. By 1881, they had risen to 171 and subscribed capital had expanded from 26,640,440 lire in 1871 to 43,449,670 lire ten years later. In 1890, 738 societies and banks operated with a subscribed capital of 97,556,938 lire. The most important regions, in terms of the number of banks, subscribed stock, and credit operations, were Lombardy, Campania, Emilia, Veneto, Apulia, Piedmont, and Sicily.[35] Mutual aid societies also advanced credit to their members, either directly from their normal funds, or indirectly by creating separate loan agencies (*casse prestiti*) or savings and loan agencies (*casse depositi e prestiti*). In 1885, 981 out of 3,768 responding mutual aid societies reported themselves as engaged in these kinds of credit activities.[36]

The first cooperative rural bank (*cassa rurale*) appeared in 1883 at Loreggia in the province of Padua, the result of the educational efforts of Leone Wollemborg (1859–1932). The banks purposed to bring to the isolated countryside the kinds of services provided by the people's banks in the towns and large agricultural villages. They grew in number from 6 in 1884 to 44 in 1890. Even after the spread of rural banks, the people's banks continued to supply agricultural credit; in fact, they often came to the aid of the rural banks which owned no capital, especially in the first years after establishment, and depended upon the savings deposits of members and nonmembers for their ability to make loans.[37]

Producer and labor cooperatives took early and varied forms. In 1861, the savings bank at Bologna aided in the formation of the first known cooperative for the construction and improvement of workers' homes. By the end of 1889, 69 building cooperatives of this kind operated in Italy, primarily in the regions of Tuscany (19), Emilia (12), and Liguria (11).[38]

Typographical workers in Genoa founded the Shop of Printing Artists in 1863, and bakers at Ferrara established the Social Bake Shop. The next year, the Society of United Workers of Alessandria subscribed to a fund to inaugurate a cooperative workshop for the fashioning of furniture. In August of the same year, workers in Genoa started their own production of beer and carbonated water. The Artisan Brotherhood of Florence, after instituting a people's bank, granted a considerable loan to the Cooperative Society of Masons in 1865. The Bologna Printers Cooperative, fathered by the mutual aid society of printers there in 1868, enjoyed marked success in the following years. The ribbon workers in Milan founded a cooperative in 1869. Other producer cooperatives continued to spring up in Bologna, Lodi, Genoa, and other communities.[39] At the end of 1889, the official government count recorded 109 producer cooperatives of this "industrial" type. They concentrated largely in the regions of Piedmont (29), Lombardy (25), and Emilia (20).[40] The Italian economy, backward as it was, proved no more friendly to producer cooperatives than more advanced countries; few survived their first years of experimentation. Of 52 cooperatives examined by Ugo Rabbeno in 1888, only 20 were found by that famous student of Italian cooperation to be more than four years old; none, except the famous pioneering society at Altare, dated its foundation before 1873.[41] Those which managed to linger on had to content themselves, before as well as after 1890, with artisan work and products of small manufacture.

In 1870, peasants in the Lomellina district and in the province of Brescia had formed agricultural producer cooperatives on the Danish model; during the 1880's, producer cooperatives also sprang up among peasants who specialized in the breeding of livestock as well as those who raised berries. But the most distinctively Italian agricultural producer cooperatives appeared among the dairy peasants, on the mountainous slopes of northeast Italy near the Austrian border. They first came into being in 1872, inspired by the zeal of a local priest, among the villages near Agordo in Belluno province and in the Friuli district near Udine. In those areas, small landholdings and limited individual production imposed the pooling of activities and resources as a necessity if profits were to be realized. The cooperatives took the charming name of social dairies (*latterie sociali*). By the end of 1889, of 208 dairy cooperatives recorded for all of Italy, 174 operated in the region of Veneto and 30 in the region of Lombardy. Thus, they prospered most in the very areas where they had taken root.[42]

The famous labor societies, which created a unique place for themselves among producer cooperatives, also dated from the 1880's. Unskilled laborers in the Po Valley formed cooperatives and petitioned the government for direct contracts to level the embankments and dig irrigation canals, so avoiding the use and cost of middlemen. Since cooperatives lacked clear legal status as yet, and since many persons questioned the ability of simple laborers to administer the execution of public works, grave preoccupation arose concerning the serious financial losses which the government might suffer in the event of project failures. However, the law of 1889 authorized the formation of labor cooperatives. Laborers, diggers, quarry workers, carters, and porters received the right to take part in the bidding for public works contracts which amounted to less than 20,000 lire. At the end of 1889, 49 labor cooperatives existed, primarily concentrated in the regions of Emilia (25), Veneto (12), and Lombardy (7). In the same year, of 43 cooperative societies of masons, which also sought public works contracts, 32 centered in the regions of Emilia (10), Tuscany (9), Lombardy (7), and Veneto (6).[43]

Still another variety of producer cooperative enterprise dated from 1883, springing up as an offshoot of a labor society. In that year, Nullo Baldini, (1862-1945), a member of Parliament and a strong protagonist of cooperation, organized the day laborers of Ravenna as a work cooperative. The next year, they contracted to drain the marshes of Ostia and other areas in the Campagna district of Rome. Once they had completed this heavy task, the society rented the reclaimed lands to farm on its own. Although their project failed, to these unskilled workers must be given the honor of inaugurating the system of collective rental (*affittanza collettiva*). Lombard peasants also applied the same technique in 1889 and the practice spread during the following years.[44]

The advance of consumer cooperatives proceeded slowly after their initial start (the pioneering society at Pinerolo dated from 1849; the General Society of Workers in Turin opened its store in 1853; another cooperative started at Alessandria in 1854, while the railroad workers of Turin established their society in the same year). Nor did progress achieve true vigor until the 1880's. The extreme economic fragility of the early cooperative ventures into retail enterprise induced intellectuals of the middle class like Luigi Luzzatti, Francesco Viganò (1807–1891), Enrico Fano (1834–1891), Gerolamo Boccardo (1829–1904) to direct their knowledge and trained attention to the experiences of other countries. Thereupon, they patiently educated Italian enthusiasts not to vend their stock at cost to the detriment, not the good, of all concerned. As a consequence of these efforts, two stores founded on the Rochdale principle — the sale of wares at market price and the division of the surplus, above costs and a small reserve, proportionately among members according to the size of their purchases — opened at Sampierdarena and Como in 1864.[45]

Estimates vary concerning the number of consumer cooperatives before the 1880's. In 1865, *Il Giornale degli Operai* (*The Workers Journal*) mentioned 58 operating consumer cooperatives. Viganò listed 40, while another writer counted 54 in the same year. Some of the organizations began to show steady strength. The society of railroad workers in Turin attained a turnover of more than 1,000,000 lire at this time. (In 1899, this cooperative would join with the prosperous cooperative founded by the General Association of Workers in 1853 to form the Turin Cooperative Alliance, for long one of the model cooperative achievements in the world.) In 1867, the Cooperative Consumer Storehouses, modelled on Rochdale principles, took their start in Milan. According to Fano, 30 consumer societies in 1869 faithfully followed cooperative practices; however, the number of societies which sold necessities to workers without profit reached 100. Viganò maintained that mutual aid societies had sponsored and supervised the best of the consumer cooperatives.[46]

Between 1867 and 1869, Luzzatti and his collaborators published the first Italian periodical dedicated to the cooperative movement: *Cooperazione e Industria* (*Cooperation and Industry*). The Italian Industrial Association, founded in Milan, sought to encourage industrial ventures, people's banks, mutual aid societies, and producer and consumer cooperatives. It also engaged in stimulating the establishment of industrial associations in other communities.[47]

The pace of organization now quickened and by 1889 more than half of the 1,242 recorded cooperatives operated among consumers: 681. Except for 60 elsewhere on the peninsula, they concentrated in the regions of North and Central Italy: Piedmont (347), Lombardy (90), Tuscany (81), Veneto (39), Emilia (36), and Liguria (28).[48]

Meanwhile, the urge toward federation in ferment among other organizations of workers manifested itself among cooperatives as well. The National Association of Italian People's Banks appeared in 1874. Then, in December 1885, the Archimedes Cooperative Society of Milan urged a country-wide congress. The next year, 130 delegates representing 201 separate cooperatives responded to the call. At the beginning of 1887, the first issue of *La Cooperazione* came from the presses. Later, in November, the second national congress of cooperatives met at Milan and created the Federation of Italian Cooperatives (Federazione delle Cooperative Italiane). The Fifth Congress of the Federation in 1893 changed its constitution and altered its name to become the National League of Cooperatives (Lega Nazionale delle Cooperative). Until the end of World War I, the League stood independent of political parties, but worked actively with labor unions and mutual aid societies. This

181

common stance came to be known after 1906 as the Triple Alliance of Labor.[49]

The Catholic View of Social Action. The gradual modernization of Catholic social thought and its application to economic activities constituted the third conservative force to emerge between 1860 and 1890. Catholic influence among workers certainly remained small as compared with the size, prestige, and affection gained by mutual aid societies and cooperatives. Yet this period served as the time of preparation, of testing new ideas against traditional concepts, of debating Catholic ways to meet successfully the blatant challenges of industrial life and socialist thought. It pushed the Church forward toward the eventual role it would assume in the labor movement after World War I and especially after World War II.

In 1865, partisans of the Church formed the Catholic Society for the Defense of Liberty and the Church in Italy. This organization, approved by Pius IX, came to an early end since it provoked the hostility of the State. On June 1, 1867, Giovanni Acquaderni (1838–1922) founded the Society of Italian Catholic Youth and became its first president. The new group took as its task the defense of Christian society and adopted as its motto: "Prayer, Action, Sacrifice." Seven years later, under the inspiration of Count Acquaderni, it brought about the establishment of the Institute of Catholic Congresses and Committees of Italy (Opera dei Congressi e dei Comitati Cattolici d'Italia) which, for thirty years, assumed the role as the central clearing body for the entire Italian Catholic social movement. The Institute sought "to reunite Italian Catholics and Catholic associations in common and concordant action for the defense of the rights of the Holy See and of the religious and social interests of Italians, in conformity with the desires and instigation of the Supreme Pontiff and under the guidance of the Episcopate and Clergy."

In order to realize these ends and in response to the Pontifical Brief of September 25, 1876, the Institute created a division within its own organization dedicated to works of charity. Three years later, the division divided into two groups, one called Charity and the other Christian Economy. In 1887, the Christian Economy segment changed its name to Christian Social Economy and set up an ambitious research program dealing with the state of Catholic mutual aid societies, the moral and economic condition of agricultural workers, the practical results of the Jacini agrarian inquiry, the possibility of organizing corporative workers organizations, and the methods for establishing more effective mutual aid societies among peasants and farmers.

The proceedings of the national congresses called by the Institute reveal the deep conservatism of most Catholic thinking at this time. The first of these Italian congresses assembled in Venice from June 12 to June 16, 1874. The second section of the congress, which dealt with insurance and assistance, discussed the painful subject of mutual aid societies. The country's democratic-liberal elements of Mazzinian persuasion had won a virtual monopoly over these organizations through their zeal in sponsoring them; small wonder, then, that the societies assumed an anticlerical attitude. This development naturally aroused deep concern among Catholics. They feared that the freemasons were converting the societies into political instruments for use in the electoral campaigns from which Catholics still abstained. The congress of Venice recognized the grievous fault of Catholics in neglecting mutual aid societies and concluded that they should be organized among Catholic workers, inspired by Christian principles and modelled upon the medieval guilds of arts and crafts. The congress also approved a pious resolution which advocated a day of rest for workers. The Florence congress of 1875 and the Bologna congress of 1876 discussed mutual aid once again and the more militant participants stressed the dangerous consequences of excessive hours of work, the use of women and children in heavy labor, and night shifts. However, the reforms proposed remained either vague or impractical.

The fourth national congress at Bergamo in October 1877 witnessed, for the first time, the crystallization of social attitudes into concrete ideas which could be transformed into specific action were there agreement and the desire to do so. These noteworthy discussions preceded the encyclical of Leo XIII, *Rerum novarum,* by fourteen years. The Marquis Achille Sassoli-Tomba, who published shortly two important books expounding the liberal Catholic position, *Sull'organamento cooperativo del lavoro e del miglioramento delle abitazioni degli operai (On the Cooperative Organization of Work and the Improvement of Workers Housing,* 1878) and *La questione sociale nelle nostre campagne (The Social Question in Our Countryside,* 1879), affirmed his advanced views at Bergamo. His thoughts, daring for the time, aroused grave apprehension among the predominantly conservative delegates. Sassoli-Tomba formulated the most far-reaching concepts about labor unions and the relation of Catholics to them. They found acceptance only after World War II: (1) the necessity of organizing workers into nonconfessional, "free unions" in order to insure their solidarity; (2) the prime importance of gaining legal recognition for unions; and (3) the need for union representation in Parliament.

Sassoli-Tomba's wise proposals did not prevail and the congress passed, instead, a resolution which set the theme of subsequent Catholic thought on the question of labor. It proposed that Catholic workers form Christian associations to protect their material and moral interests. These organizations, inspired by the medieval guilds of arts and crafts (*corporazioni*), would include both workers and employers who required no compulsory legislation to insure free and spontaneous agreement. Succeeding congresses reaffirmed the corporative principle, destined to become a pervasive Catholic view of labor relations. Despite this cautious approach to labor organization, most Catholic employers rejected the proposal to encourage workers leagues or unions. Fear induced some Catholic laymen to request their prohibition by the Vatican itself.

At the congress of Modena, held in 1879, Sassoli-Tomba repeated his radical doctrines and then spoke in favor of agrarian reform and the creation of institutions to aid the unemployed. The sixth congress at Naples in 1883 approved the creation of regional federations of mutual aid societies and workers circles, to be followed by the institution of a national body. The resolution insisted that these groups were to be confessional in nature, free of any political character. Conferences, classes, lectures, and Catholic publications would re-enforce their religious spirit and sentiments. The congress also declared that contacts between Catholic societies of workers and those which espoused contrary principles were dangerous. They had to be avoided at all cost.

The seventh congress at Lucca, which did not take place until 1887, reflected the fears stirred up among conservative groups by the success of socialist agitation throughout the country. The congress again addressed itself, as at Bergamo, to the "social question" and mixed Christian guilds of employers and workers. A notable address delivered by the Marquis Lorenzo Bottini concerned the corporative approach: *La questione operaia e la corporazione cristiana* (*The Labor Question and the Christian Guild*). The Lucca congress went on record in favor of social studies which conformed to the principles of Christian philosophy. However, it warned students of labor problems to proceed with utmost caution lest they aroused the passions and undue claims of workers, or led them to believe that scientific investigation favored the revival of restrictive measures, contrary to legitimate freedom and the needs of modern industry.

Meanwhile, Catholic mutual aid societies grew in number. They continued on as confessional organizations under the surveillance of ecclesiastical authorities: local parochial committees supervised by diocesan committees. But the phraseology of certain resolutions approved by the eighth congress at Lodi in 1890 indicated a growing awareness that either

184

mutual aid societies had to concern themselves with the full range of day-to-day shop problems, or Catholic workers had to form other associations suited to these broader purposes. The need so formulated later gave rise to the Catholic labor leagues (*leghe cattoliche del lavoro*). The Lodi congress reconfirmed its approval of legal recognition for mutual aid societies, but made clear the distinction it drew between such recognition and the granting of legal status to labor unions. The congress also considered the propriety of state interference in economic affairs for the purpose of regulating the work of women and children. The delegates approved of state intervention so long as government limited its purpose to the labor of women and children in industrial establishments alone.[50]

Strikes and the Growth of Militancy. Although the period from 1860 to 1890 must be characterized as the golden age of mutual aid societies, it also witnessed the rise of workingmen's organizations which ceased to emphasize beneficial aims alone and stepped beyond the line of moderate behavior, no longer with cap in hand, to make demands upon employers for higher wages, better working conditions, and shorter hours. Often, workers had to forestall the attempts of employers to lengthen hours and to lower wages by forming leagues of resistance. Under the pressure of decreasing real wages, even mutual aid societies sometimes acted like leagues of resistance.

Contemporary accounts either ignore completely or exaggerate the actual strength of labor groups and the size of the strikes they called. After February 1861, when the Mazzinians in Florence organized the Artisan Brotherhood (Fratellanza Artigiana), the movement spread out from the city into Tuscany and established strong groups in Leghorn and Lucca. The Brotherhood proposed the federation of all workingmen's societies in Italy. *La Nuova Europa* (*The New Europe*) of Florence claimed in November 1861 that the Workingmen's Society of Naples, then a center of radical ferment, had 2,860 members belonging to 20 different crafts. There must have been veritable giants in the Neapolitan earth in those days since the whole province in 1907, almost 50 years later, could count little more than 18,000 unionized industrial workers![51] We do know with certainty, however, that the militancy of the Naples arsenal workers, whose strike in 1861 spread beyond their ranks, offended the sensibilities of the local Mazzinians. Through their newspaper, *Il Popolo d'Italia* (*The People of Italy*), they denounced the February strikes as the handiwork of reactionary elements who wished to aid the enemies of liberation and unification.[52]

In 1862, women workers in Milan created their own Association of Mutual Benefit and Instruction. The next year, 1863, not only saw the organization of new societies of women workers at Siena and Cremona, but also witnessed a strike of printers at Milan in which almost the entire craft engaged. That same year, the carpenters and masons of Turin struck in a body. In Naples, 800 metallurgical workers left their jobs. A serious clash occurred between the strikers and the military forces in which the director of the plant was wounded.

The most important strike of 1864 took place in the Biella district of Piedmont. There, at least 3,000 workers in the woolen industry demanded impressively modern improvements in factory regulations: all dismissals had to be judged legitimate by a committee of workers; only children of workers could be hired as apprentices; a working foreman who did not join the Mutual Aid Society of the Woolen Weavers had to be fired. The strike ended through the arbitral good offices of Pasquale Stanislao Mancini (1817–1888), a respected jurist and politician. Mancini, in his award, established new regulations and these were accepted by both parties. These new rules represented the first example in Italian labor history of a collective bargaining contract between workers and their employer. Mancini's role also represented a pioneering step in the use of third-party arbitration, apart from government officials — a practice not yet widely accepted in Italy today.

Militant printers societies, like those which had been set up earlier in Milan, Turin, and Genoa, appeared in Florence and Naples in 1864. At Alessandria, a society of carpenters demanded a reduction in the hours of work and also insisted upon the closed shop. In the course of the same year, 500 railroad workers struck in Florence. In Genoa and Nervi, as if to deride easy generalizations about the orderly evolution of human institutions, the spaghetti workers established a mutual aid society *after* demanding improvements in their contract and *after* taking strike action. During 1865, the railroad workers of Apulia and Sardinia went on strike. Unemployed workers invaded a woolen plant in Arpino and destroyed its machinery. In Piedmont, the hatters threated to strike unless they received an increase of wages.[53]

The urban strikes in 1868 which preceded the imposition of the milling tax have already been rehearsed. The next year, important strikes among port and arsenal workers occurred in Naples; 1869 also witnessed there the establishment of the first strike fund on record. Following these strikes, the police began to persecute the local section of the International Workingmen's Association which, under Bakunin's leadership, purportedly numbered about 3,000 members.

In 1870, a group of tailors in Bologna, after they had established a cooperative shop, summoned the first congress of an Italian brotherhood of tailors. Delegates from Turin, Milan, Florence, Venice, and Padua answered this call. The same year, when 40 furriers in Naples lost their jobs, and after a delegation of protest had received no satisfaction from the employers, the furriers went on strike. The Naples section of the International pledged the payment of strike benefits. The police broke into strike headquarters and arrested the president and secretary of the International, a lawyer, and two strikers. On the basis of documents picked up during the search of the premises, four of these men were convicted. The next year, strikes flared up among the sulphur miners at Cesena, the bricklayers of Rome, the railroad workers and tailors in Milan, the bakers at Turin, and the women tobacco workers at Venice.[54]

In 1871, the workingmen's societies which adhered to Mazzini's Brotherhood Pact clashed at the XII Congress of Workingmen's Societies in Rome with those associations which followed the policies of the International, as guided by Bakunin in Italy. The Mazzinians won a Pyrrhic victory, for the more radical groups, which opposed Mazzini's doctrines of cooperation between workers and employers, broke away from the Artisan Brotherhood. They called themselves either *fasci operai* (workers bands) or sections of the International. The most notable *fasci operai* developed in Tuscany and in Romagna, with their largest concentrations of members in Bologna, Rimini, and Florence. The Fascio Operaio of Florence claimed 5,000 adherents. The masons, with a membership of 1,700, constituted the largest element; the shoemakers numbered 700, and the mechanics 500. These *fasci operai* took both politics and economic reform as their province. In this respect they resembled the various sections of the International. At the time of the split after the Rome congress, the Artisan Brotherhood, on its own count, numbered 87 local branches and 5,000 members. Later, when competing with the *fasci operai*, it claimed an increase of membership and 300 affiliated societies. Nonetheless, the Artisan Brotherhood by 1879 had lost so many followers that the Mazzinian newspaper, *Il Dovere* (*Duty*), ceased publication.[55]

Fresh peasant revolts, despite the repressions of 1869, broke out during 1871 in Lombardy, Veneto, Mantua, and the environs of Rome. Throughout Italy, peasants were crying out for land. In the midst of these disturbances, fearful government officials, police, and newspapers ascribed almost supernatural influence to representatives of the International. Meanwhile, the printers and the railroad engineers and firemen quietly began to break out of their local organizational shells and to grope for alliance with their fellows elsewhere. Eventually, the two skilled crafts founded the first national unions in Italy. They drew their courage and ability to resist employers from the membership solidarity and security which mutually financed benefits created. Thus, these pioneering Italian organizations resembled, in the character of their development, the English trade unions, the German *gewerkschaften*, and the American craft unions of the 1870's and 1880's for which the Cigar Makers International Union of Samuel Gompers and Adolph Strasser had set the example.

In 1868, Italian printers — their ancient guilds had found reincarnation in pious unions; these, in turn, had evolved into mutual aid societies — assembled for the first time at Feltre where they proposed to bind themselves together nationally. Not until December 1872, however, did the printers meet again at an unheralded congress in Rome where they created the Association of Italian Typographical Workers. In 1874, the Association published the first issue of its national organ, *Il Tipografo (The Printer)*, which bound members throughout the peninsula more closely and kept them informed concerning conditions and trends within the trade. By 1878, the Association reported 27 affiliated societies and 2,268 members. In 1880, its representatives attended the International Typographical Workers Congress at Brussels. There, delegates discussed the importance of solidarity among printers of all countries, strike funds, unemployment, travelling members, apprenticeship regulations, employment of women, pension funds, and producer cooperatives. In 1880, too, the Association conducted a successful strike in Milan which lasted three and one-half months, but which won for the printers a substantial wage increase. In 1890, the printers negotiated a collective bargaining agreement for the entire region of Veneto. Then, in 1893, the Association changed its name to the one now linked with the honor of designating the oldest permanent craft union in the country: the Federation of the Book (Federazione del Libro).[56]

The origins of national federation among railroad workers reach back to the mutual aid society of engineers and firemen of North Italy, founded in 1877. The engineers and firemen employed by the southern and Calabria-Sicily lines organized a mutual aid society in 1883. Two years later, 650 engineers and firemen representing the railroads of North Italy, South Italy, and Rome organized the Mutual Aid Society of Italian Railroad Engineers and Firemen. The association became the Railroad Band (Fascio Ferroviario) in 1890, the League of Italian Railroad Workers (Lega dei Ferrovieri Italiani) in 1894, and finally the Italian Railroad Workers Union (Sindacato Ferrovieri Italiani).[57]

Only among the highly skilled printers and railroad engineers and fire-men did the beginnings of national federation antedate the decades before 1890. The workers in the woolen industry, despite an ancient guild tradition, remained cloistered within the confines of local cares and ignorant of conditions in other woolen centers. In 1877, for example, during the bitter strike in the Biella district, the employers imported scabs from the Bergamo area. These strikebreakers, unaware of true conditions in the province of Biella when hired, suffered humiliating indignities and disappointments there. In all countries, this kind of experience eventually led to the beginning of wisdom and national federation. For the time being on the Italian scene, it stirred up extreme militancy among the mutual aid societies of woolen workers, especially those in the Weavers Association of Croce Mosso. The Biella strikes had started as far back as 1861 and had recurred almost annually down through 1877 when the factory owners, with the police as their collaborators, established an effective black list. The authorities also banished 40 strikers to enforced residence elsewhere, an Italian police practice known as "*confino.*" Unrest among the woolen workers, marked increase of strike activity elsewhere, and the ill-starred uprising attempted by Bakunin's followers at Benevento in 1877 impelled the Minister of the Interior to propose the appointment of an investigating committee to seek the causes of strikes and their prevention and cure. Count Francesco Bonasi (1830–1897) served as chairman of the committee after its formation in February 1878.[58]

The committee found information about 634 strikes that had taken place between 1860 and the first six months of 1878. More than 65% of these strikes occurred in four regions: Lombardy (161), Piedmont (131), the Neapolitan provinces (66), and Emilia (56). The committee discovered the causes of 427 strikes. Of this total, 233 broke out over demands for wage increases. No other single cause could compare with the issue of wages, for delays in the payment of wages resulted in the next highest number of strikes, 23. A listing of the other causes emphasizes, once again, the perennial and universal nature of certain friction areas in modern industrial life: demands for lower hours of work, prevention of wage cuts or increase in hours, hostility toward the introduction of machinery, either opposition to or insistence upon the hiring of more workers, disputes concerning piecework or timework methods for fixing wages, need for more work, charges of employer dishonesty with regard to wage payments in kind, and controversies over factory regulations and discipline. The committee's findings concerning the crafts and industries where strikes occurred reconfirm the predominantly handicraft nature of the Italian economy during the years from 1860 to 1878.[59] The 452 strikes for which information could be obtained took place among the following workers:

Textile and dyeing	108
Mechanics and blacksmiths	22
Bricklayers	35
Brickmakers and glassworkers	12
Sulphur and other miners	22
Papermakers	6
Bakers	27
Carpenters	21
Hatters and tailors	10
Tanners	6
Tobacco workers	12
Printers	25
Farm hands, railroad laborers, porters	90
Other crafts	46
More than one industry	10

The decade from 1880 to 1890 is memorable in the annals of Italian labor history because the peasants of North Italy, once they were organized into mutual benefit societies and cooperatives, rose in protest against the degrading lives they led.[60] In the province of Rovigo, in the Polesine district, malaria infected the marshy countryside. Except during harvest time, when the peasants could sometimes afford to eat bread, they subsisted on cornmeal. A family of five persons, all working, rarely earned more than 1.15 lire a day with which to provide themselves with food, clothing, and shelter. The peasants built their homes, especially in Basso Polesine, of marsh reeds plastered with earth. Senator Stefano Jacini declared that no peasant anywhere in Italy suffered such neglect as the peasant of the Polesine. Jacini described him as constantly battling for his own existence. His relations with others outside his class debased him and showed him the inferiority in which they held him and in which they meant to keep him. Baron Sidney Sonnino reminded the Chamber of Deputies that the peasant in the lower valley of the Po occupied one of the most fertile and highly productive agricultural regions of the country. Despite this gift of nature, even in years of good harvests, when profits and land rents soared, the peasant enjoyed neither wage increases nor improvements in the conditions of his work. An army major, dispatched to the Polesine during the flooding of the Adige in 1882, brought away with him two indelible memories: the hard hearts of the nobility and property owners and the squalid poverty of the abject peasant. He remarked that he knew the poverty of the shepherds of the Sila in Southern Italy and of the peasants in Sicily, but he had never witnessed poverty equal in degradation to the poverty of the Polesine. Despite their prevailing misfortune, the peasants at last found their apostle when the government named the humane Dr. Nicola Badaloni as the medical officer of the commune of Trecenta. That self-sacrificing native of Recanati near Potenza in South Italy spent his days and nights trying to cure his charges of poverty and pellagra. He refused to leave them in later years, after a long life dedicated to their service, even when offered higher posts because of his scientific achievements.

Toward 1880, the Polesine counted two political tendencies: the conservatives who controlled the entire province and the progressives who constituted a very small minority. In trying to better the lot of agricultural workers, the progressives inaugurated mutual benefit societies among the peasants. Their headquarters became the centers of the first political assemblies and conferences held in the area. When, in 1880, liberal elements of the middle class began to demand the extension of suffrage, Dr. Badaloni and Alberto Mario (1825–1883), the Mazzinian reformer, bent their efforts in the Polesine toward that goal. After the widening of the vote in 1882, workers of the Polesine helped to elect as their representative in Parliament Agostino Bertani, the deputy who had first called for an investigation of agricultural conditions in Italy.

During the June harvest season of 1880, without any preparation, foreknowledge, or intent, the reapers suddenly left the fields of the Polesine. They struck against age-long poverty and oppression in an instinctive movement of despair. The revolt of the peasants ended disastrously when the police arrested several hundred of them. During the trial at Rovigo, the court meted out severe sentences. Beaten and more debased, the peasants returned to their starvation wages of 0.40 or 0.50 lira a day. The conservative forces in the communities unleashed the fiercest accusations against the progressives; they laid upon the liberal leaders, as subverters of the peasants, the entire blame for the general strike. They even brought Dr. Badaloni to trial and involved Jessie Mario, Alberto Mario's wife, in the proceedings, although the Minister of the Interior had assigned her to investigate the situation in the area. Despite the persecution of the progressives, the elections of 1886 gave the ultimate victory to them. Dr. Badaloni, along with three other friends of the agricultural workers, was elected to the Chamber of Deputies.

The peasants in the province of Mantua in Lombardy suffered harsh reverses when the small farms of the area fell into bankrupcy and the large landowners, who had grown aware of the economies inherent in rational farming, acquired them. Even widespread emigration could not alleviate the plight of the peasants. They also attempted to improve their position by forming mutual aid societies. But these first attempts at organization could not accomplish what the workers most needed: high-er wages. The demand for wage improvements reached its climax in 1884 after the landlords, who had turned down every peasant request since 1878, again refused them any concession. At this time, the work of two men of good will from the middle classes resulted in the launch-ing of two fresh movements. Eugenio Sartori, an engineer, through his own publication, *Libera Parola (Free Speech)*, inspired the formation of a new coordinated mutual benefit society among the peasants near Mantua and in the Oltrepo district. Captain Francesco Siliprandi, who had served valorously with Garibaldi in the patriotic wars, encouraged and founded the General Association of Italian Workers, using as the mouthpiece for the diffusion of his ideas the newspaper, *La Favilla (The Spark)*. This Association organized the peasants in that area of the province of Mantua which touched upon the province of Cremona. A third newspaper, *Il Pellagroso (The Pellagrous One)*, also worked in behalf of the Mantuan peasants.

The two organizations sought to raise peasant wages by establishing rates in each village which served as the basis for uniform demands in that particular locality. The young movement, driven to desperation by hunger, burst out of the bounds of orderly militant action and rose up to the cry of "La boje." The meaning of this phrase has never been ex-plained. As the slogan of people in revolt, it connoted ire as well as the desperate conviction, "Now, let us make an end to it all." Riots, demonstrations, intemperate language, and clashes with the police fol-lowed their inevitable course. The strike ended, as strikes during the early days of organization usually end, in the dissolution of the peasant associations in the spring of 1885. Their leaders went to prison to await prosecution. Fear covered the countryside again and wages remained at the same level as before. The victory of the landowners now seemed complete. The leaders of the uprisings remained in the jails of Mantua and Venice until they stood trial in February and March 1886. The Venetian jurymen set them free and declared that they saw no crime in joining together for the moral and economic redemption of those who suffered most.

After the trials at Venice, organizational silence prevailed in the province of Mantua. Due to emigration, especially to Brazil, periodic un-employment diminished since fewer workers crowded the labor market. Wage rates began to increase. Then, at the same time that the coopera-tive movement began to develop strongly, Dr. Romeo Romei formed the Mantuan Federation of Workers and Peasant Societies in October 1891. The Federation hoped to better the life of peasants and workers by drawing together into one organization all cooperative associations, mutual aid societies, workers resistance leagues, workers education societies, and workmen's circles dedicated to political action.

The Polesine had its Dr. Badaloni, Cremona its Leonida Bissolati, and Modena its Gregorio Agnini (1856–1945). Reggio Emilia claimed Camillo Prampolini. He embraced socialism at the University of Rome when one of his professors declared that the right of property did not admit the right of labor. In 1886, a strike broke out among the masons and day laborers of Reggio Emilia who demanded an increase in wages. The unexpected strike shocked the conservatives. With Prampolini at their head, the socialists gave the strike guidance and inspiration. The masons, the day laborers, the ditchdiggers, and the rice workers all received increases in wages. The settlement fixed the working day at 13 hours, with two hours of rest.

The cooperative movement in Reggio Emilia, taking its inspiration from the organizations founded in Mantua during 1884 and 1885, favored consumer and labor societies. Professor Vinsani, an engineer, aided by Giacomo Maffei, encouraged and aided them. Professor Vinsani had left the army, where he served as an artillery officer, to join Garibaldi at Mentana. The ideals of the French Revolution stirred him more than socialism. His theory of cooperation was simple: since it was obviously futile to crack one's head against the hard wall of central power, one necessarily had to move in the opposite direction toward the periphery, acquiring control over the state, little by little, by means of consumer cooperatives. Professor Vinsani ran the cooperative of Reggio Emilia in completely individualistic fashion. He never called a membership meeting, nor did he seem particularly interested in increasing their numbers. He sought, instead, to create good will among all workers. His organizational ideal ran toward an alliance of workers, an embryonic form of the later chambers of labor, for he wished to unite in the group he had founded all associations: mutual aid societies, cooperatives, Garibaldian veterans, socialist circles, and republican leagues. Meanwhile, the cooperative acquired steeper and steeper debts. Called upon to battle constantly with the competing shopkeepers, it finally came to an end in 1887 or 1888. In contrast, the labor cooperative prospered during these years among the masons under the leadership of Luigi Roversi. It gained new strength after 1889 when the law launched by Giacomo Maffei in Parliament to encourage labor cooperatives went into effect.

During these years, Prampolini became the editor, reporter, and columnist of the weekly newspaper, *Reggio Nova* (*New Reggio*), founded by Professor Vinsani and Maffei in 1885 as a weekly with the intention of transforming it as soon as possible into a daily newspaper. A year later, Prampolini changed the title of the newspaper to *La Giustizia*. Its simple subtitle read: "Defense of the exploited." The renamed weekly soon enjoyed large distribution in Italy and Prampolini helped greatly to orient Italian workers toward Marxism and social democracy. He insisted particularly that the peasants had to organize themselves. In Reggio Emilia, more than elsewhere, socialism became a mystic faith. Referring to Prampolini, Rigola observed: "The peasants collected around the Master as the early Christians around Jesus." Rigola went on to say that Prampolini, with his beautiful saintly head, often talked to the peasants in the form of parables and allegories. Unlike so many Italian radicals, he stood clear of the slightest trace of fanaticism. His mind was luminous, positive, and rational. His influence among the masses of workers and peasants stemmed completely from his ability to make them understand his thoughts. Once Prampolini founded the League of Peasants, all the rest followed: Reggio Emilia became the Mecca of Italian socialism and merited designation as the "laboratory of social experiences," for that area attempted all experiments in the endeavor to redeem labor.[61]

While the workers of Reggio Emilia gathered socialism to their hearts, the workers of Lombardy embraced economic action. The Labor Party in Lombardy, after participating in the national elections of 1882, had gone into decline, but managed to encourage the formation of a new organization, the Sons of Labor, as its economic arm. By 1883, the Sons of Labor began to organize not only sections of mixed trades and crafts according to locality but also sections of separate trades and crafts. Expanding out of Milan to other parts of Lombardy, the Sons of Labor emphasized action leading to immediate economic gains. In the view of Rinaldo Rigola, the organizational structure of the Sons of Labor provided the essential basis for the later chambers of labor which assembled into one territorial grouping all workers of a locality regardless of craft or industry. The undogmatic willingness of the Sons of Labor to approve sections organized by particular trades or industries as well, anteceded the establishment of communal and provincial branches of the national category unions at a later period.[62]

Events now moved rapidly toward the establishment of chambers of labor, destined to become the nerve centers of the new Italian labor movement. In 1889, Osvaldo Gnocchi-Viani journeyed to the Paris Exposition, accompanied by a delegation of Milanese workers. They visited the *bourse du travail* of that city, founded two years before. On his return to Italy, Gnocchi-Viani proposed to create similar institutions in his own country.

On the eve of its emergence as a national force, Italian labor exhibited itself as weak indeed. Mutual aid societies and cooperatives aside, after thirty years of agitation and martyrdom, workers had created, with the untiring aid of middle-class friends, occasional resistance leagues which still acted, when they did, within the narrow limits of a single locality and a single craft or industry; a few community-wide associations; the Sons of Labor which had accomplished the remarkable feat of spreading out from the city of Milan into the province; and two national federations of printers and railroad engineers and firemen. They had also engaged in spontaneous and violent strikes. Unfortunately, all too often the sound and fury of these uprisings, the pathos of needless human suffering, and the astonishing range of man's cruelty diverted the attention of their leaders and sympathizers away from crucial questions: Of what order of magnitude were these events? Did they concern workers by the thousands, tens of thousands, or hundreds of thousands?

The investigation which examined strike activities from 1860 to 1878 provided information on the number of known strikes, the crafts and industries where they occurred, and their determinable causes. However, the survey could throw no light on the number of workers annually involved in strikes. From 1878 onward, however, official government publications began to report these yearly details. Tables 39, 40, and 41 of Appendix A provide a measure of the strength of Italian labor from 1878 through 1890 in terms of the action workers took to improve or preserve wages, hours, and working conditions.

During all of these 13 years, a total number of 911 known strikes — agricultural strikes were excluded from the official figures — involved only 230,703 craft or industrial workers. In 1890, 38,402 workers struck — the highest number for any of the years under survey. Almost 63% of all strikes for the entire period lasted three days or less and only 12% endured for more than 10 days. The largest proportion of strikes took place among common laborers (25%); textile workers (22%); metallurgical, mechanical, and mineral workers (11%); and a motley category which included carpenters, glassworkers, coachmen, conductors, boatmen, carters, and porters (11%).

From 1878 through 1890, 1,550,467 man-days were lost in strikes. Only 17.5% of this total resulted in favorable terms, while 62.3% brought about partly favorable terms and 20.2% ended with unfavorable terms. Of the 17.5% of total man-days lost which procured favorable terms, almost 80% related to demands for higher wages. Of the 62.3% of total man-days

195

lost which obtained partly favorable terms, almost 71% related to wage demands. Of the 20.2% of total man-days lost which issued in failure, 57% related to wage demands.

The ability of this relatively small number of strikers to wrest concessions from employers may be gauged from the following data, based upon Table 41, concerning the specific causes of strikes expressed in terms of total man-days lost from 1878 through 1890:

Total Man-Days Struck for Higher Wages: 1,078,608

Favorable	20%
Partly favorable	63%
Unfavorable	17%

Total Man-Days Struck for Reduction in Hours: 39,179

Favorable	53.2%
Partly favorable	16.4%
Unfavorable	30.4%

Total Man-Days Struck to Resist Reduction in Wages: 79,112

Favorable	13.3%
Partly favorable	56.6%
Unfavorable	30.1%

Total Man-Days Struck to Resist Increase in Hours of Work: 11,441

Favorable	16.7%
Partly favorable	74.4%
Unfavorable	8.9%

Total Man-Days Struck for Other Causes: 342,127

Favorable	6.4%
Partly favorable	65.1%
Unfavorable	28.5%

In marked contrast to the weakness of militant labor organizations among Italian workers, the success of mutual aid societies and the steady advance of cooperatives would indicate that neither the character of the people, nor their tragic history, nor the poverty of their country's soil and resources necessarily condemned them to receive as gospel the doctrines of revolutionary Marxism. Certainly before 1890, the voices of moderation among enlightened elements of the middle class had appealed sympathetically to Italian artisans and peasants. Nonetheless, the increase in strike activities, the formation of resistance leagues, and the spread of disorder in rural areas after 1880 dramatized the inability of temperate forces in the body politic to break out of the toweringly difficult problems which rose up all about them. Despite mounting emigration, Italy's soil could not feed the population, nor could its economy provide steady and adequate employment. Yet that economy, balanced only by well-distributed weaknesses everywhere, had to support the minimal but costly accoutrements of state: an effective central administration in Rome, roads, railways, port improvements, a modern navy and merchant marine, an efficient army, a nationwide system of schools, and local and provincial governments.

Small wonder, then, that the conservative governments before Depretis, at a time when statesmen did not yet realize that moderate inflation blessed more than it bled, chose the way of the balanced budget and high taxation, only to bring misery to the masses and political downfall upon themselves. The inflationary policies of the so-called radical governments under Depretis and Crispi proved equally disastrous, nor did patriotic adventures overseas reduce the treasury's plight. Radical leaders, once they came to power, bristled whenever peasants and workers attempted to call attention to their grievances through demonstrations or strikes. Poverty lay over Italy. But the intense hatred between the two leading moral forces of social moderation — the Church and the Mazzinian republicans — poisoned the life of the nation even more. Here moved tragedy: the embittered Church abhorred the new régime, but execrated the republicans and the freemasonry they brandished; Mazzini and his disciples, for their part, bore a plausible, but irrational and implacable, aversion toward the Church. The Vatican, proud and plundered by change, dug in its heels and lost the spirit of many of its faithful. The Mazzinians, intransigent and bigoted with modern enlightenment, failed the people even more for they had once been closer than the Church to the working masses. So it came to pass after 1890 that workers and their sympathizers in Italy, the historical guardian of traditional Western values, turned toward a philosophy of class violence to bring a better world to birth.

FOOTNOTES — CHAPTER V

[1] Rosselli, cited above, pp. 24–27. See especially, p. 25, footnote 1, for a discussion of the extensive sources of Rosselli's wage data.

[2] *Annuario statistico italiano 1886*, p. cxlviii.

[3] Rosselli, cited above, p. 28, for the statement by Geisser and Magrini; G. M. Stekloff, *History of the First International*, p. 442, for the passage cited from the *Inaugural Address* of Karl Marx, reproduced in the Appendix, "Address, Preamble, and Provisional Rules of the International Workingmen's Association, Founded in London, September 28, 1864," pp. 439–448.

[4] *Annuario statistico italiano 1886*, p. cxlviii.

[5] Rosselli, cited above, pp. 253–255. The Italian title of the published reports of the Inquiry mentioned in the text is: *Atti della inchiesta sulla industria italiana*. They were issued in 8 volumes at Florence from 1872 to 1874.

[6] U.S. Congress, House of Representatives, 46th Congress, 1st session, Executive Document No. 5, *State of Labor in Europe: 1878*.

[7] *State of Labor in Europe: 1878*, p. 39.

[8] The same, p. 35.

[9] The same, p. 38.

[10] The same, p. 293.

[11] The same, p. 288.

[12] The same, pp. 286–288.

[13] The same, pp. 298–300.

[14] The same, p. 290.

[15] *Annuario statistico italiano 1892*, p. 543; passage translated by M. F. Neufeld.

[16] Rosselli, cited above, p. 215; passage translated by M. F. Neufeld.

[17] The same, p. 215.

[18] The same, pp. 215–217; passage translated by M. F. Neufeld.

[19] The same, p. 218, footnote 1.

[20] The same, p. 254, footnote 3; passage translated by M. F. Neufeld.

[21] The same, p. 218.

[22] Quoted in Marc Bloch, *The Historian's Craft*, p. 92.

[23] Rosselli, cited above, p. 220; passage translated by M. F. Neufeld.

[24] The same, p. 220; passage translated by M. F. Neufeld.

[25] The same, p. 229, footnote 1.

[26] The same, p. 232; passage translated by M. F. Neufeld.

[27] The same, pp. 233–236; quoted passages translated by M. F. Neufeld.

[28] The same, p. 248, footnote 2; passage translated by M. F. Neufeld.

[29] *Annuario statistico italiano 1889–1890*, p. 304.

[30] *Annuario statistico italiano 1886*, p. 257.

[31] *Annuario statistico italiano 1889–1890*, p. 305.

[32] The same, p. 307.

[33] *Annuario statistico italiano 1905–1907*, p. 789.

[34] Rosselli, cited above, p. 129; passage translated by M. F. Neufeld.

[35] *Annuario statistico italiano 1895*, pp. 778, 752.

[36] *Annuario statistico italiano 1889–1890*, pp. 311–312.

[37] Giulio Costanzo, "The Principal Types of Co-operative Society in Italy," *International Review of Agricultural Economics*, New Series: Vol. 1, 1923, pp. 54–55; *Annuario statistico italiano 1905–1907*, p. 752.

[38] *Annuario statistico italiano 1889–1890*, pp. 320–321.

[39] Rosselli, cited above, pp. 127–130, 252–253.

[40] *Annuario statistico italiano 1889–1890*, pp. 320–321.

[41] Ugo Rabbeno, *Le società cooperative di produzione*, pp. 280–304.

[42] *Annuario statistico italiano 1889–1890*, pp. 320–321; Bolton King and Thomas Okey, *Italy To-Day*, p. 187.

[43] *Annuario statistico italiano 1889–1890*, pp. 320–321.

[44] E. A. Lloyd, *The Cooperative Movement in Italy*, p. 3.

[45] Rosselli, cited above, pp. 34–35, 128. For a list of contemporary books on the relationship among cooperatives, mutual aid societies, and workers groups by the writers mentioned in the text and others as well, see Bulferetti, cited above, p. 190, footnote 280.

[46] E. A. Lloyd, cited above, p. 1; Rosselli, cited above, pp. 127, footnote 3, 251–252. For various kinds of cooperative ventures initiated and run by mutual aid societies and workers groups, see Salvatore Fenicia, *La cooperazione in Piemonte*, pp. 237–256.

[47] Rabbeno, cited above, pp. 11–12.

[48] *Annuario statistico italiano 1889–1890*, pp. 320–321.

[49] Lloyd, cited above, p. 5; Meuccio Ruini, "The Italian Cooperative Movement," *International Labour Review*, Vol. V, No. 1 (January 1922), pp. 17, 19; Por Odon, *Guilds and Co-operatives in Italy*, p. 101.

[50] Francesco Magri, *Dal movimento sindacale cristiano al sindacalismo democratico*, pp. 5–8; Luisa Riva Sanseverino, *Il movimento sindacale cristiano*, pp. 106–118.

[51] Rosselli, cited above, p. 66; *Annuario statistico italiano 1905–1907,* p. 803.

[52] Rosselli, cited above, pp. 68–69.

[53] Gualtieri, cited above, p. 63; Leonetti, cited above, pp. 40–43; Rosselli, cited above, pp. 131–133.

[54] Gualtieri, cited above, pp. 79–80, 98; Leonetti, cited above, pp. 46–47.

[55] Rigola, cited above, pp. 59, 61.

[56] Leonetti, cited above, pp. 53, 55, 58; Rigola, cited above, pp. 226–228.

[57] Rigola, cited above, p. 228.

[58] Gualtieri, cited above, pp. 128, 138, footnote 19; Rigola, cited above, p. 225.

[59] Gualtieri, cited above, pp. 127–129.

[60] The following account of the uprising of the peasants in North Italy in the 1880's has been primarily based upon Rigola, cited above, pp. 81–95. See also, Gradilone, cited above, III, 1, pp. 299–309.

[61] Rigola, cited above, pp. 94–95.

[62] The same, p. 77.

VI

The Drive toward the Future:

1890 to 1926

The Modernization of Italian Politics

FOR three decades before World War I, Italian socialists laid political claim upon their country in the name of the proletariat. As their members and parliamentary representation increased, the inability of the socialists to choose decisively between gradual reform and revolutionary change forced upon their leaders a Hamlet-like refusal to assume political responsibility. Giovanni Giolitti, who served as Prime Minister five times during his notable career, outmaneuvered the paralyzed socialists through the reforms he enacted and domesticated their right wing through carefully devised favors. Of these, the most inspired benefit dispensed government aid to cooperatives, the life-giving economic and political base of moderate socialism. That tall, solid, broadshouldered, shrewd, dispassionate, calculating, untheatrical, realistic Piedmontese — who combined attributes which Italians in general and socialists in particular lacked — dominated Italian public life from 1903 until the outbreak of World War I. Upon his ascendency, by catering to the socialists because he recognized in their demands the logical consequences of the industrial revolution, Giolitti modernized Italian politics and drew Italy, at last, into the family of democratic and progressive nations. So well did he succeed that during a short interval before 1912 Italy showed signs of transforming itself into a stabilized liberal state, supported by moderate socialists who accepted the Constitution. But neither they nor Giolitti had counted upon the recalcitrance of a new generation of radicals who did not accept the ideas of orderly progress stretching in a straight line from fathers to sons. Instead, weary of positivism and its constraints, they returned to a more passionate blend of revolutionary fervor: Bergsonian *élan vital,* irrationalism, glorification of violence, and the enthronement of the will.

During the years of Giolitti's dominion, before Mussolini had taught political rhetoricians and innocents the hard meaning of tyranny as the substance of everyday life, Giolitti's detractors exercised the liberty which Giolitti assured them by assailing him as Dictator or Minister of the Underworld. According to their rigid and confused views — not as yet given tolerant perspective and clarity by later tragic events — he perfected into art that Machiavellian system of government by advantageous deals which Depretis first devised and Crispi improved. True enough, under Giolitti the three gears of *trasformismo* meshed lubricously to assure continuity of progressive government, so essential to the welfare of Italy at that time: (1) order and ability in the administration of the affairs of state; (2) delicate manipulation of political factions, regional cliques, and economic interests inside Parliament with such persistence that the process took on a special vitality of its own and often seemed unrelated to the realities of Italian life; and (3) favoritism, the peddling of jobs and influence for proper election returns, and outright corruption, bribery, and even violence, especially in the South. The critics of Giolitti's methods were numerous, vocal, and often brilliant. But they never suggested concrete alternatives to the Giolitti formula. How might Italy — a country with no experience of widespread democracy; still feudal, poverty-stricken, and illiterate throughout broad stretches of its territory; and astonishingly diversified in regional sentiments and ways of life — otherwise escape the curse of reaction or one short-term ministry following another? Nor did they consider deeply enough Giolitti's gift to the free and relatively prosperous age which now bears his name: ever-expanding political democracy and liberty.

Giolitti founded his control of Parliament upon the absence of party organization. As we have already seen, the political parties of the *Risorgimento* represented little more than tendencies, currents, groups, or makeshift associations. After unification, until 1876, when the Cavourian liberals of the Right lost the national election to the so-called Left, Italy had managed to maintain some semblance of a two-party system, based upon the ability of the conservatives to govern through shifting alliances of interests — a device then known as the *consorteria* or *connubio.* Even so, political conflict drew life from the play of conservative and progressive forces in Parliament, rather than from the opposition between organized rival branches of these alignments in communes throughout the country. These did not exist. Once Victor Emmanuel II called Agostino Depretis of Piedmont to assume political power and once Depretis contrived the device of *trasformismo*, boundaries between parliamentary tendencies, faint as they had already become, simply disappeared. By 1887, when Depretis died, *trasformismo* had accomplished its mission so well that those Italians who contemplated the labors and parliamentary records of their representatives could readily believe with ample justification that all Italians had become liberals. Not only Giolitti and Giuseppe Zanardelli, but Sidney Sonnino and Antonio Salandra as well — each eventually became Prime Minister — considered themselves liberals to a man. But the term itself had lost real meaning. Sonnino and Salandra represented the liberal tradition of the Cavourian Right. Aristocratic and conservative in philosophy and distrustful of progressives and socialists, they opposed the democratic policies of Giolitti, the liberal. But Sonnino and Giolitti represented distinct extremes. For the most part, the liberal-conservatives vied for political power without espousing clearcut policies and programs. Soon it grew impossible to draw distinctions of principle between one faction and another. Not without logic did those who backed a particular liberal-conservative government in office come to be known later as ministerialists (*ministeriali*), in contrast to those who opposed it, the antiministerialists (*antiministeriali*).

After 1898, three parties formed a combined opposition to the liberal-conservatives: the republicans, the radicals, and the socialists. Together they acquired the designation, Extreme Left (*Estrema Sinistra*). Of these three, the republicans claimed the oldest ancestry. Although they prided themselves upon their Mazzinian inspiration, strong divisions outnumbered agreement in their ranks. They achieved consensus only in opposing the monarchy. To their consternation, this republican passion found difficulty in gaining adherents in a country which not only enjoyed both King and regal institutions but also associated with them the sentiments of patriotism and the very concept of nationhood itself. The dwindling number of republicans held on primarily in the Romagna in North Italy, in the Marches in Central Italy, and in Apulia in South Italy. Perhaps elementary truth inspired the remark that the Republican Party, after the death of Mazzini, held on to life as a council of the elect, reflecting only "the echo of a name and the shadow of a ghost."[1]

The radicals also claimed a Mazzinian patrimony in the Party of Action which those opposed to the *trasformismo* of Depretis had formed in 1878. They advocated the widest possible suffrage, government fully responsible to Parliament, decentralization, limited state action, and a foreign policy adapted to the limited resources at the command of the Italian State. They found strongest support among the middle and lower middle classes and skilled artisans in Lombardy, Veneto, Emilia, and Tuscany. In 1900, the radicals won 34 seats in the Chamber of Deputies and increased that number to 70 by 1913.

The organization and character of the Socialist Party were unique for Italy at this time: national and democratic. These qualities influenced Italian political life incalculably after 1890. Local associations selected delegates to regional congresses and to annual or biennial national conventions on the basis of membership strength. The conventions chose the chairman, secretary, and central committee of the Party. The central committee, often referred to as the directorate (*direzione*), named the permanent staff, including the editor of the Party's newspaper. Membership dues supplied the organization with limited funds. The Italian Socialist Party could not compare in financial well-being with its French and German counterparts. Since deputies in Italy served without pay until 1912 and since the Party could not supply funds to workers with political ambitions, professional men and intellectuals had to represent the proletariat in Parliament.

Once the Socialist Party turned into an electoral force of alarming proportions to the conservatives, the traditional political currents called parties could no longer rely upon the easy ways of their past life. The vibrant and ubiquitous socialist press, calling out to the downtrodden, made it impossible for the liberal-conservatives, radicals, and republicans to exploit public opinion at will in the strongholds they once commanded without contest. The carefully articulated socialist form of hierarchical organization also prevented the older parties from counting with assurance any longer upon groups hastily assembled at election time, only to be dispersed after they had served their purpose, or upon the personal followers of politicians.[2] Although the conservative-liberals, the radicals, the republicans, and even the emerging Catholic currents in time heeded the example of the socialists, perforce, they learned the obvious lesson but partially. They could not match the integrated organizational arrangements of the socialists, nor did they ever form labor and cooperative alliances of the magnitude achieved by the socialists. History destined Benito Mussolini, a socialist of richly fluctuating persuasions, to build upon the example of his former comrades and to outstrip their feat by adding force and fear to organizational skill in building the Fascist Party.

The Violent Decade: 1890 to 1900. After the fall of the first Crispi ministry in January 1891, the Marquis Antonio Starrabba Di Rudinì (1839–1908) replaced him in 1891–1892. Then followed the first ministry of Giovanni Giolitti in 1892–1893. In December 1893, Francesco Crispi returned to power and remained in office until March 1896. From that time until June 1898, the second Di Rudinì ministry governed Italy on the basis of an understanding with Felice Cavallotti, the radical leader and dramatist. General Luigi Pelloux (1839–1924) succeeded Di Rudinì as Premier and governed until June 1900.

During this period, the established conservative-liberal politicians refused to believe that popular unrest, triggered by the social and economic frictions which tormented the progress of Italy's industrial revolution, could not be downed and eradicated by force. Since middle-class professional men and intellectuals led the newly formed Socialist Party and spoke violently in the name of the exploited proletariat, upon their heads descended the full strength of governmental opposition and coercion. In these years, the Socialist Party passed through its heroic period of repression, imprisonment, and martyrdom to emerge at the dawn of the new century as a major power in Italian politics.

The Magi of both international and national events attended the birth of the Italian Socialist Party. In 1890, May 1 had been proclaimed as the international day of labor by European socialists assembled at Bordeaux. This declaration inspired Italian socialists. They also noted, at the opposite end of the political spectrum, the revolutionary shift of attitude implied by the presence of Italian government representatives at an international congress which assembled that same year on the call of the German emperor, William II, at Berlin to study the social question "with a warm heart and a cool brain."[3] Meanwhile, during 1890 and 1891, fresh and ardent socialists like Filippo Turati banded together in the Socialist League of Milan (Lega Socialista Milanese). Its program, in contrast to the more modest and attainable demands of the Workers Party, betrayed the inflated yearnings of young people not yet levelled by the down-to-earth rigors of politics. Their aims were coterminous with the economic, political, social, educational, religious, and moral universe. But such lavish demands must be expected at the beginning. However, another aspect of the program which cropped up under the heading, Method, quite abruptly robbed the future of all surprise since it appeared so early in the history of Italian socialism: the need to compromise the apocalyptic and violent dogmatism of revolutionaries with the evolutionary doctrines of reformists. The proponents of these two basic socialist views of life who, in the name of working-class unity, forbore to separate but who could not learn to live amicably together, in the end succeeded only in paralyzing the socialist movement and inviting its ultimate collapse. The League stated its germinal compromise in the following terms:

> Scientific socialism does not believe in a miraculous renewal of the social organism as a result of decrees from on high and uprisings from below. It judges the following question as idle and leaves it unanswered: whether the process of attaining the great goals of economic and political evolution will render necessary, as has happened thus far in history, violent and bloody conflict between clashing interests and between the classes which represent them? For scientific socialism, the social revolution does not fulfill itself in a given moment of time, but spreads out through an entire period of time; it attracts to itself all the activities of evolution, reflecting itself in facts and thoughts and also availing itself of even the most hostile forces; they become, each in turn, aids of socialism. But the revolution is not able to fulfill itself if the new principle which animates it has not taken over and penetrated on its own all the most vital organs and strata of the old structure; thus, the new organism might already find in the environment around it all the forces and all of the elements necessary to maintain its life.[4]

During 1891, Turati and Anna Kulishov founded *Critica Sociale* (*Social Criticism*) at Milan. Until 1925, when Mussolini repressed it, this fortnightly review served as the most influential and highly respected mouthpiece of moderate socialism in Italy. In the same year, the Workers Party in Lombardy and Piedmont beat down its former aversion to dealings with the middle class and intellectuals (most probably the purer sons of toil had fallen away as members) and consented to meet with leaders of the Socialist League of Milan in order to choose delegates to the International Socialist Congress in Brussels later in the year. The joint deputation, in an obviously symbolic gesture, selected Giuseppe Croce, the glovemaker, and Filippo Turati, the brilliant barrister and intellectual, to represent the two faces of Italian socialism. At Brussels, the European socialists defeated the anarchists in their midst. This experience prepared Croce and Turati for the task of vanquishing the anarchists in Italy itself when all those summoned to defend the interests of the working class met together on August 14, 1892 at Genoa for the first congress of the Party of Italian Workers. (The 1891 meeting at Milan between the Workers Party and the Socialist League is sometimes treated as the first, sometimes as the preliminary congress, of the new Party of Italian Workers.)

The delegates represented all shades of left-wing opinion and all varieties of workers groups, including the recently organized local chambers of labor. The four hundred delegates split apart, physically, over the issue of legalitarianism. The Marxists espoused the use of parliamentary elections for socialist ends, while the anarchists rose up in outrage against such heresy. Each of the separate meetings passed resounding resolutions in the name of the Party of Italian Workers. The anarchists' session did not produce permanent results since the true anarchists went back to the manufacture of bombs and the planning of assassinations, while those who discovered in the course of debate that they were socialists after all gradually returned to their proper fold. In the other hall, the Socialist League of Milan took control, established the new Party on a permanent basis, and spurred the conference on to the adoption of a program. First designated the Party of Italian Workers, then known as the Socialist Party of Italian Workers, it finally became the Italian Socialist Party in 1895. To the chambers of labor and other unions, the program assigned the immediate task of improving hours, wages, and factory regulations. To the Party, on the other hand, the program entrusted the economic emancipation of the working classes through the conquest of political power. Although a reasonable person might interpret the terminology, "the conquest of political power," as permissive of participation in local and parliamentary elections, the program nowhere specifically mentioned the word, "elections." Consequently, the militant revolutionaries could just as easily appeal to the program for assurance that the Party had approved the conquest of political power through violence and force.[5]

The tactical need to vanquish the anarchists at Genoa had stayed the zeal of the more radical-minded and intellectual Marxists there. The composition of the central committee reflected the triumph of the moderate forces: Enrico Bertini, a printer; Giuseppe Croce, the famed glovemaker; Carlo Dell'Avalle, a printer; Annetta Ferla, a representative of the Sons of Labor of Milan; Giuseppe Fassati, a mechanic; Costantino Lazzari, a bookkeeper and one of the founders of the Workers Party whose name would appear in the future during every phase of the socialist descent toward communism and fascism; and Antonio Maffi, the type-caster who had been elected a deputy from Milan on the Workers Party ticket in 1882. Milan became the logical headquarters of the Socialist Party.

Roberto Michels (1876–1936), the eminent sociologist and historian of the Italian Socialist Party, did not regard the constituent assembly of socialists at Genoa in 1892 as the truly inaugural congress. He assigned this honor to the Socialist Party congress at Reggio Emilia in 1893 because the socialists met there for the first time without interference from the anarchists. The program adopted at Genoa held out to socialists the possibility of winning effective political power. The congress at Reggio Emilia dashed this hope of the moderates. The delegates approved an Order of the Day which bristled with irreconcilable Marxist injunctions against class collaboration:

> Since political powers are nothing but the organization of the bourgeois class with which that class sustains its battle against the proletariat, and since no durable and substantial reform or concession for the benefit of workers will ever be accomplished through these political powers as long as they are composed of a middle-class majority . . . , socialist deputies in their parliamentary utterances will emphasize the declaration that the Socialist Party has no faith in the efficacy of adulterated reforms which the middle class, in the interest of maintaining the status quo, is able to concede . . . and, moreover, socialist deputies in their conduct will always need to conform to a program of action and to party propaganda that are in fact and in essence revolutionary.[6]

The policy of absolute intransigence in national and local elections and avowed hostility to middle-class reforms took strength from the following circumstances: (1) the fear that even temporary collaboration with other parties for common objectives would result in a confusion of both theory and practice and in the eventual degeneration and death of the Party; (2) the fierce hostility of the State toward socialists imposed upon the new Party a compensatory attitude of unswerving adherence to rigid principles which served them almost as a bulwark of self-protection; (3) the earliest exposure of Italians to socialism came through the International Workingmen's Association. That early heritage of political inflexibility could not fail to influence later generations of socialists.

Even the national newspaper authorized at Reggio Emilia reflected in its name the prevailing spirit of the congress, *Lotta di Classe* (*Class War*), a title inspired by the cries at Genoa which had accompanied the separation of the Marxists from the anarchists: "Class War!" and "Collectivism!" The new publication appeared in Milan under the editorship of Camillo Prampolini. The purity of doctrine espoused at Reggio Emilia matched the brilliance of the names among the three hundred delegates. Among those who sent letters of solidarity were Cesare Lombroso (1835–1909), the world-famous criminologist, and Edmondo De Amicis (1846–1908), a writer as renowned as he was sentimental, whose book, *Cuore* (*Heart*), became one of the most widely read Italian publications. Two of Europe's outstanding socialists, the Belgians Emile Vandervelde (1866–1938) and Louis De Brouckére, attended the sessions. On the last day of the congress more than three thousand peasants paraded in front of the theater where the fateful resolutions had been debated and approved.[7]

Very soon the doctrines of the revolutionary Marxists clashed, head on, with political reaction. Events found them wholly wanting. For the next ten years, Italian socialism learned, "to its cost," in the words of Turati, "the inescapable necessity of liberty and the prudent tactics of alliances."[8] Political crises rubbed the lesson in without mercy. In 1893, the Banca Romana scandals, which revealed fraudulent administration and unsecured loans to members of Parliament, brought about the fall of the first Giolitti ministry. (During Giolitti's stay in office, Parliament passed, in June 1893, a law providing for the conciliation of industrial disputes. Its terms will be described at more length elsewhere. But at this point it is revealing of Giolitti's approach toward the realities of industrial society to observe that the *probiviri* legislation marked the first time that the Italian government had intervened in disputes between capital and labor.) Zanardelli then tried to put a ministry together, but failed. Even while Giolitti still headed the government, Sicily had stormed with flashes of revolt, yet the authorities had failed to restore order. With turmoil increasing on the Island, the country turned to Crispi once more for salvation. His second ministry lasted from December 1893 until March 1896.

By 1893, social unrest exploded in Sicily, but anxiety pervaded all parts of Italy. Although poverty remained part of the daily lives of most workers, its intensity had diminished because the cost of bread had grown cheaper despite the government's imposition of heavier duties upon imported wheat in its efforts to placate the agrarian interests. In the North, after the depression which had followed the speculations of the 1880's, industry began to take hold again. In the South, the economy, still stunned by the blows which followed the severance of commercial relations with France in 1887, also moved slowly toward recovery. But the great mass of workers and peasants no longer seemed willing to accept their lot meekly, without protest, for the modernization of life had educated them and widened their horizons. Railroad construction had not only created the beginnings of a national market and the wants which products new to backward areas arouse, but had also, like a latter-day miracle, facilitated easy communications between formerly isolated parts of the country. Young peasants, conscripted into the army and the navy, learned to read, write, and think upon their past disadvantages; they received better food, clothes, and shelter than they had ever known before. Letters from friends and relatives in South America and the United States bore welcome remittances and they also described the superior tenor of life in the New World. Francesco Saverio Nitti summarized this transformation of attitude: "There is a general discontent, not because things have grown worse, but because we have grown better and are less tolerant of wretchedness." Crispi's denunciation of the commercial treaties with France had ruined many members of the lower middle classes. They and the large mass of workers and peasants associated government with heavy taxes, currency depreciation, a continuously adverse balance of trade, bank scandals, rumored alliances of politicians with the Maffia and the Camorra, and the juggling of tariffs and bounties to enrich a small segment of the population at the expense of the people at large. In this atmosphere of distrust, the ambitious socialists found willing ears. Since they confined their own expression of violence to words, they did not foresee the disasters which were to follow upon their appeals for the overthrow of bourgeois society.

The South, in conformance with its destined role in Italian history, supplied the detonating charge. To understand the events of 1893 and 1894, it would be well to return momentarily to the period after 1860 when Sicilian peasants and sulphur miners associated themselves in organizations of Mazzinian inspiration. In sharp contrast to Naples and its provincial environs, Sicily showed no disposition to encourage either the socialism of Bakunin or of the internationalists during the 1870's and 1880's. Nor did it respond to Benoît Malon's efforts in 1874 to diffuse the ideas of moderate and evolutionary socialism through the launching of *Il Povero* (*The Poor One*). Napoleone Colajanni (1847–1922), a university professor and ardent republican disciple of Mazzini, first turned the tide with the publication of his influential book, *Il Socialismo* (*Socialism*), in 1884. Colajanni had treated his subject in a manner best suited to attract the young republican intellectuals and scholars of Sicily who heretofore had considered socialism a retrogression toward utopianism and social despotism. Giuseppe Giuffrida De Felice (1859–1920), a former clerk in the Catania prefecture, then supplied the push toward organization. Fervid, independent-minded, impatient of authority, feverishly active, and filled with hatred against injustice, he founded the Workers Band of Catania (*fascio dei lavoratori*) in 1891 with the intention of establishing other *fasci* elsewhere and of eventually uniting them in a single Island association. The iniquitous economic arrangements and social retardation of Sicily provided the third force which goaded the peasants and miners into rebellion.

Thirty years of constitutional government had stirred the construction of roads, railway lines, and schools and had marked the organization of public services and the advance of public security. But the spirit of feudalism still prevailed and new Don Rodrigos made the communes, provinces, and private charitable institutions their fiefs on the little altered scene of the Sicilian Vespers. The great estates of Sicily, the *latifondi*, served as focal concentrations of discontent and gave perpetual lie to the vows of Italian ministries since 1860 that they would reduce economic and social injustice on the Island. The nobles who owned these vast tracts either resided outside of Sicily or, when they remained there, lived at a distance from the peasants, avoiding intimate sight of their ceaseless labor and suffering. The system of working the land exploited both soil and peasant. The owners leased their lands to others who, in turn, rented the land to yet a third set of operators. Nothing prevented them from subleasing the land once again. Greedy beyond the least concern for social peace, the aristocratic landowners also insisted upon continuing the feudal practice of collecting taxes directly from the peasants. Only a small portion of these levies reached the coffers of government. Moreover, as Sidney Sonnino had demonstrated conclusively in his famous studies of Sicilian conditions, the entire structure of taxation leaned most heavily upon the very poorest element of the population, leaving the rich virtually untouched. Thus hardpressed, the peasants and miners already had reasons enough to resent bitterly the perverse economic and social despotisms which enslaved them. But in the years immediately after 1890, they felt the new lash of a marked decline in wheat production, in addition to disastrously falling prices and unemployment. World-wide depression had cut the demand for wine, sulphur, and citrus fruits, Sicily's principal exports. The price of wine sank from 40 or 50 lire for 26.4 gallons to 10 or 20 lire, while the price of sulphur per ton fell from 112 lire in 1891 to 55 lire in 1894.

The *fasci* soon spread throughout the Island as though by contagion and their leaders claimed from 120 to 300 branches and 200,000 to 300,000 adherents. Colajanni, in his history of the subsequent uprisings and the role of the *fasci, Avvenimenti in Sicilia (Events in Sicily)*, published in 1895, doubted that total membership had ever exceeded 200,000. Rinaldo Rigola, many years later, questioned the true value of the *fasci,* despite their fantastic growth, since the weaknesses they betrayed during the violence which engulfed them indicated to Rigola that positive and scientific socialism had not yet taken hold of their thoughts and action. The inner life of the *fasci,* while charming in its melange of activities and loyalties, plainly indicated the contradictory qualities detected by Rigola. The *fascio* of Palermo boasted 10,000 enrolled workers. In the large assembly hall of its headquarters, where inscriptions from the works of Bovio, Marx, and Louis Blanc substituted for decoration, members recited socialist dramas, often composed by them, and held their numerous meetings and conventions. In another hall, red gonfalons covered the walls, each ensign representing one of the 63 trades and crafts associated with the *fascio*. Here, a bust of Marx stood enthroned on a red base, while statues of Garibaldi and Mazzini (who had found no health in the author of the *Communist Manifesto*) flanked the father of modern socialism. In the corridor of the Palermo head-quarters, tailors, producers of pasta, barbers, cheesemongers, shoemakers, and other affiliated groups offered their wares and services at reduced cost. Nor did the *fascio* neglect mutual benefit activities. A decurion (the term gave ancient Roman dignity to the task) headed each group of ten members. He took on the responsibility of watching over his fellow-workers and acted as a father to them. In times of emergency, he came to their aid, and collected money to provide another mule, for example, to a member who had lost his essential beast of burden. The programs and activities of *fasci* elsewhere might differ in scope and complexity from those of Palermo, but for the most part they undertook similar en-deavors. In the headquarters of some *fasci*, the crucifix occupied a place of honor along with pictures of Marx, the King and Queen of Italy, Lassalle, and Victor Hugo. During street processions, a likeness of the Madonna often led the parades, followed by banners dedicated to the saints of the republican and socialist pantheon.

The *fasci*, as part of their program of action, called for the abolition of local excise taxes on foodstuffs, the establishment of consumer co-operatives, and the restoration to peasant use of usurped crown lands. The leaders of the movement — Giuseppe De Felice, the pioneering socialist organizer; Bernardino Verro, a landowner; Garibaldi Bosco, a bookkeeper; Nicola Barbato (1856–1923), physician and member of Parliament; Giacomo Montalto, a lawyer; and some members of the aristocracy, like Prince Alessandro Tasca of Cutò, formerly the socialist deputy from Sciacca — endowed these demands with a tone of apparent control, unity, and strength. Actually, as subsequent events proved, the *fasci* most lacked these very qualities. The disturbances which swept across Sicily during 1893 and 1894 owed less to the influence of the *fasci* than to the age-old alternation of abject resignation and sudden recourse to fierce revenge. This pattern had manifested itself in 1860, even during the high enthusiasm of the nationalist uprising, when bloody revolts in Pace, Collesano, Bronte, and Missoria erupted to the cry: "Death to the gentlemen! Down with the hatted ones!", for the becapped peasants saw themselves at war with those superior beings who had money enough to spend for hats.

211

As the same spirit of unrest which had filled the northern peasants of the Polesine, Mantua, and Reggio Emilia in the 1880's infused the Sicilian peasants after 1890, landowners and their agents evidenced their apprehension by denying work to members of the *fasci*. They equated requests for higher wages — day laborers earned 0.80 lira a day during the winter and 2.50 lire for 14 to 15 hours of work during the summer — as threats of violence and summoned the police. These fears grew into panic after the turbulent strikes of the sulphur miners in November 1892. Then, on January 20, 1893, in the commune of Caltavuturo near Palermo, a band of about twenty soldiers, policemen, and rural guards fired, without provocation, upon the peasants of the village when they returned from the fields where they had taken possession of the royal demesne which, they reasoned, belonged to the community.

When Parliament reassembled on January 30, Colajanni and other progressive deputies castigated the massacre as unconscionable aggression by public forces against unarmed citizens. Giolitti, in his reply, promised to establish responsibility for the outrage, punish the guilty, and take measures to prevent its recurrence. Giolitti made good his promise to investigate by sending the Director General of Public Safety, Sensales, to Sicily. Most of the deputies from the Island, unlike Colajanni and his few confederates who had voiced indignation, represented the vested interests there and wanted the *fasci* abolished outright. Although Giolitti did not agree with them, he needed their votes and hoped that perhaps the *fasci* might consent to their own dissolution. Sensales and co-operative local officials understood their instructions perfectly. A policy of pinpricking irritations ensued: small provocations, house searches, prohibitions against meetings, breaking into *fasci* and socialist meetings when held, trials, police frameups, frequent admonitions, and the use of *agents provocateurs* to discredit the work of the *fasci*. Withal, new agrarian strikes broke out again in the provinces of Palermo and Caltanisetta in May and June of 1893. Nor did the efforts of Sensales and his allies prevent the leaders of the *fasci* from urging members to participate in the local elections of 1893. Because local taxes, crown lands, and the behavior of officials and police were of pivotal importance to the welfare of Sicilian workers and peasants, their leaders believed that they would derive considerable benefit from the control of communal administration. Indeed, the economic and political activities of the *fasci* impressed the gentry deeply.

When the *fasci* from everywhere on the Island assembled in congress at Corleone in 1893, they demanded both wage concessions and agrarian reforms. In some provinces, the fearful landowners granted wage increases and many proprietors signed all provisions of the farm agreements (*patti colonici*) set forth by the congress. At Corleone, the delegates also approved a resolution calling for eventual government ownership of the subsoil and for immediate royalty and tax relief to mine operators. They hoped that the savings gleaned from these reforms would redound to the benefit of the miners. The congress went on to demand the abolition of the work usage whereby pickax miners virtually bought children (*carusi*) from their parents for a pittance and worked them unmercifully. The delegates proposed that the mine operators employ the *carusi* as they would other labor and pay them directly. The time, place, and desperate need for work made the complete abolition of child labor unthinkable even to socialists in Sicily.

The leaders of the *fasci* attempted to guide them toward peaceful methods for enforcing their demands. Although the largest and best organized *fasci*, those in Palermo, Messina, and Catania, avoided the descent into violence, revolt seized the rest of Sicily, just as Garibaldi Bosco had truly predicted at the socialist congress of Reggio Emilia when he declared: "Soon Sicily will go up in flames." In October and November, peasant strikes and demonstrations against increased municipal taxes shook the countryside, but without bloodshed. Then, between December 1893 and January 1894, the conflagration began. On December 25, the police arrested a sulphur miner at Valguarnera for expressing subversive sentiments during a speech. When a *carabiniere* fired his pistol at the crowd after it had requested the orator's release, the angered mob tore down telegraph lines, freed prisoners, sacked stores and dwellings, and then burned the mayor's house, police headquarters, and public offices. At Monreale, tumult, assaults upon the tax office, and incendiarism lasted several days. In trying to placate the crowds at Mazzarra, the city government abolished the tax on flour only to have the bakers increase the price of bread the next day. The population answered this provocation by devastating and burning private as well as public property. The uprising at Castelvetrano lasted from the last days of December to the first days of January and, because of its duration and the city's size, wreckage and arson outstripped devastation elsewhere. Goatherds led the remonstrances at Partinico against the municipal tax on consumers goods although discouraged by the local *fascio*. On December 10 at Giardinelli, a crowd formed after Mass and shrieked for the abolition of local taxes and the overthrow of the city hall. They then proceeded to burn it down. In a subsequent encounter with police reinforcements, eleven demonstrators fell dead. Other revolts took place at Lercara Fridi and Termini Imerese where the subprefect, addressing the demon-

213

strators who had sacked and burned the tax collection offices, barely escaped with his life. Eleven citizens died during a later battle with the police. The number of communities where workers rose in savage resentment against their brutal and heartless exploitation by the dominant cliques of Sicilian society lengthened until the entire Island took on the color of flame.

"Who," wrote Rigola many years later, "would put an end to this insurrection of suffering and vendetta?" The nation, as represented in Parliament, chose Francesco Crispi, the Sicilian, as its savior. When he became head of the government on December 10, 1893, he at first called for conciliation and spoke of agrarian reforms. But Crispi, ever ready to believe tales of French conspiracy, soon succumbed to fictions fabricated by the police. They could demonstrate that Amilcare Cipriani, a renowned hero of the Paris Commune, had visited Sicily early in 1890 to bring off an insurrection there. The authorities imprisoned him the next year and he did not return to France until the middle of 1893. Taking up again his revolutionary designs for Sicily, he arranged to meet Giuseppe De Felice at Marseilles in August. He abandoned that encounter when he learned that the police knew of his plans. From these pieces of intelligence and others less accurate, Crispi's informants concocted the fantastic fable that the French were financing the socialists and leaders of the *fasci* in a design to separate Sicily from Italy and to set up a republic under the protection of France and Russia. The police also purported to possess evidence that the Church, ever willing to aid in the destruction of the Italian State, favored the conspiracy. Crispi did not hesitate to propound these absurdities later in the Chamber of Deputies itself.

On January 4, Crispi declared a state of siege in Sicily and dispatched General Morra di Lavriano there as Commissioner Extraordinary with plenary powers and 50,000 troops. Sicily remained under martial law for seven months. The general and his collaborators destroyed the *fasci*. Their leaders, including De Felice, Barbato, Bosco, and Verro of the central committee, were herded into custody. Then, later in January, the police seized 1,000 individuals and imprisoned them on the volcanic islands off the Sicilian coast. On April 7, 1894, the leaders of the now obliterated workers movement appeared before the special military tribunal in Palermo. During their trial, the court charged them with international conspiracy. The police officer who advanced this testimony could produce no concrete evidence, but insisted that he possessed "metaphysical certainty" of the truth of his accusation. Not even the military court could bring itself to believe his declaration, but nevertheless went ahead to mete out justice on May 30 by sentencing the accused to heavy prison terms ranging from five years for a student to eighteen years for De Felice.

Meanwhile, in January 1894, violence exploded in the Lunigiana of northwestern Tuscany where the republican and anarchist tradition still prevailed among the workers of the Massa and Carrara areas. In natural sympathy with their comrades in Sicily, the quarrymen and other partisans suddenly armed themselves and overran the countryside and mountain slopes. Faced with this new emergency, Crispi sent General Heusch to deal with the marble workers. The general put an end to the insurrection, but attempted, afterwards, to aid the population in bettering their conditions.

Benedetto Croce has not spared criticism of Crispi's impetuosity and hallucinations of international conspiracy. He also acknowledged that Crispi had made no attempt, either before or after the imposition of blind repressive measures, to rectify long-standing abuses through salutary reform. He conceded that General Morra di Lavriano was vain, ungenerous, narrowminded, and harsh. Nonetheless, the benign historian of Italian liberalism could evaluate the fateful role of Crispi and the leaders of the *fasci* with the following calm pronouncement:

> Whatever may have been his sins of commission and omission, Crispi had cut short a movement which did not contain within itself the seeds of life and which had no future before it . . . . It was an attempt to delude men into revolt, which even in a good cause can never produce good results; based on deception, it deserved to be destroyed by force.[9]

Crispi now moved in for the kill. He presented to the Chamber of Deputies proposals to amend the public security law. They subjected to punishment all those who aroused class hatred and endangered the public peace. When asked directly by Enrico Ferri (1856–1929), the socialist deputy, who was a famous lawyer and criminologist, whether the proposed extraordinary legislation was aimed against labor unions, Crispi assured the Chamber that the measures were designed to combat the anarchists. The emergency laws went into effect on July 19, 1894 and were to continue in force until December 1895. The socialists began to feel the scourge of Crispi's enmity even before he let loose the full force of his attack. Already in early September 1894 the prefectural authorities prohibited the third national congress from meeting at Imola. The congress did not assemble until January 1895 in Parma after the socialists had bethought themselves to meet as a private group. On October 22, 1894, while Parliament was still in recess, Crispi ordered the suppression of the Socialist Party and of all groups associated with it. At Crispi's instigation, the Ministry of the Interior began to level charges against individuals throughout Italy, to find them guilty of trivial acts (the police exiled a lawyer to enforced residence (*domicilio coatto*) for singing the *Workers Hymn*), to imprison many victims of official hysteria, to close down newspapers for attacking Crispi's policies, and to expunge from the parliamentary election lists the names of those who had attracted Crispi's disfavor. Then, at the close of the parliamentary session, Crispi ordered the arrest and imprisonment of all socialist deputies. Behind bars, the socialists had time to ponder upon the first lesson offered by experience. Because of the uncompromising stand taken by the socialists assembled at Reggio Emilia the year before, socialist deputies had been enjoined from voting confidence in any bourgeois government. Consequently, in November 1893, they had refused to support Giolitti, justifying their political blindness with noble principles. Smugly defiant, they had eased the way for the return of Crispi and the irresponsible reaction he visited upon Italy.

The very excesses of Crispi's brutal policies defeated his purposes as liberal, conservative, and even Catholic sentiment turned in favor of the socialists. University professors, government officials, and the very military officers assigned to defend the accused showed open sympathy for the socialists on trial. During the by-elections, voters elected socialists in prison as deputies. Later, as a result of the general elections of 1895, the socialists drew 80,000 votes (31,500 from Lombardy and Piedmont alone, while Sicily's illiteracy of 81% enabled the Island to supply only 5,000 votes) and won twelve seats as compared to the eight seats they had previously held. The Chamber of Deputies, still under Crispi's spell, failed to feel the temper of public opinion and cancelled the election of all imprisoned socialists. As a mark of protest, their constituents reelected them to Parliament.

Crispi's passion for the grandiose led presently to the ignominious colonial defeat of Italy since his foolhardy ambitions had assured the transformation of minor skirmishes with Abyssinian tribal bands into full-scale warfare by the end of 1895. The persecution of socialists through the institution of special tribunals and house arrests now went unnoticed by the public at large which was preoccupied with news from Africa. The harassed socialists nevertheless denounced the war against the Negus Menelik as an imperialistic adventure which Crispi had undertaken in a desperate effort to distract attention form his unpopular policy of repression at home. Italy's disastrous defeat at Adua on March 1, 1896 — when two generals and 4,600 officers and men were killed, 2,000 wounded, and 1,500 taken prisoner — assured the downfall of Crispi's second ministry on March 5.

The socialists now could savor the sweet taste of revenge as Crispi suffered humiliating defeat. Although he had failed to wipe out the socialists with his own brand of Bismarckian May Laws, he left them sober and changed, for Crispi unintentionally caused the profound transformation of many socialist leaders as a consequence of his implacable assault upon them. Just as the critical study of Marxism in the universities would tend to alter both socialist and liberal thinking, so the persecution of the socialists had brought the liberal forces of Italy to their side, paving the way for a new alignment of Italian politics, the *Estrema,* and freshening the atmosphere at Montecitorio for Giolitti's experiments with advanced legislation. After 1896, despite heady official resolutions, many thoughtful socialists would find it impossible to sneer at bourgeois doctrines of civil liberties since courageous representatives of the middle classes had risked their own freedom to protect socialists in their right of association, free speech, free press, and fair trial. Nor could socialists honest with themselves henceforth picture the army as a tool of the capitalists after its officers had risked their careers to defend with zeal prisoners to whom they were assigned as counsel.

The second Di Rudinì ministry, based on an understanding with Felice Cavallotti, the radical leader, lasted from 1896 to 1898. Di Rudinì, a Sicilian of unblemished character and natural sobriety, began propitiously enough. He sought at once to liquidate Crispi's African fiasco. To pacify Sicily, he appointed a royal commissioner of moderate views and manner. Although the commissioner refused to recognize the right to strike and would not countenance either socialist or Catholic unions, he encouraged the organization of sulphur miners along nonpolitical lines. He also managed improvements in local government administration, including the tax system. Di Rudinì mended diplomatic relations with France, dealt forthrightly with the fiscal deficits, and released nearly half of those confined to *domicilio coatto.* Everywhere, in the first year of Di Rudinì's ministry, tensions relaxed along with the memory of emergency legislation and penal settlements. The socialists not only regained their liberty and volubility, but became strong enough to publish their first daily paper, *Avanti!,* at the end of December 1896. Political prisoners soon obtained their freedom through amnesty in time to vote in the general elections of 1897. Out of a total of some 500 seats, the socialists obtained 20, an increase of eight deputies, while the republicans and radicals won 47. The country continued to move forward despite the return of violence and repression to Italy in 1898, after so short a lease of freedom. The very government which resorted to fresh reprisals nevertheless sponsored two pioneering social security measures. In March 1898, Parliament made workmen's compensation insurance for industrial workers compulsory — thus abandoning the voluntary feature of the 1883 legislation and establishing an important principle for future social legislation. Moreover, departing from the German and Austrian systems which served as models, the Italian law placed the entire cost of insurance upon the employer. Later, in July 1898, after periodic and futile attempts since 1877 to legislate on pensions, the Chamber created the National Workers Insurance Fund for Invalidity and Old Age. This move spelled victory for those who supported a central national fund in contrast to those who urged state subsidies for mutual aid societies and savings banks.

For all his statesmanship and gentlemanly qualities, Di Rudinì could neither alter fundamentally the social and economic plight of the country, nor could he escape government by national intrigue in Parliament and by mutual favors, bribery, and corruption at the communal and provincial levels. Import duties on grains rose again. The integrity of law enforcement agencies came under serious public doubt when a political offender, Frezzi, died in prison. Although the circumstances of his death aroused grave suspicions, the government brushed the scandal aside. The conservatives kept plaguing Di Rudinì for his "pitiful toleration" of the extreme parties. To placate them, he made the republicans slightly uncomfortable, but shook up the socialists more forcibly. Again, the singing of the *Workers Hymn* subjected men to imprisonment; those who aided workmen on strike were either brought to trial or harassed. In addition to forbidding socialist meetings, the government sent its agents to trail socialist deputies and tampered with their telegrams. After the election of socialists to two municipal councils, the government dissolved them. It sat idly by when a prefect decreed the end of three chambers of labor. When the Cremona Agricultural Workers Union attempted to revive itself, the government intervened; it also took action against a group of tenants in Sicily who had organized to defend their interests. By the end of 1897, the reputation of the government, tarnished by the Frezzi scandal, grew more discolored at the disclosure of another bank fraud at Como. The socialists, in good voice under their comparative freedom, sprang to the attack. The clericalists, always ready to find the source of Italy's ills in the Constitution, joined them. The propertied classes, ever alarmed, lived in greater fear. Baron Sidney Sonnino, who, as a younger man, had seen the only resolution of Sicily's misery in revolution, gave voice to these conservative anxieties a year before. He declared in a famous article which appeared under the signature, "A Deputy," in the

Nuova Antologia (*New Anthology*) of January 1, 1897, that socialism and clericalism menaced the Italian State. As a bulwark against these twin autocracies, he set forth his provocative "Return to the Constitution." He argued against the system of ministerial responsibility to Parliament and the maneuvering implicit in the so-called democratic process. Instead, he urged an increase in the power of the executive by making the ministers of government servants of the sovereign. As clearly as Mosca and Pareto, Baron Sonnino distrusted and denigrated parliamentary government and advocated drastic constitutional reform.

By the end of 1897, renewed riots tended to illustrate the Sonnino thesis that a constitutionally all-powerful Parliament showed only feeble incapacity to cure or alleviate Italy's persistent social and economic malaise. The climax of this fresh upsurge of unrest took place in Milan from May 6 to 9 and soon occupied a place of honor in the dolorous annals of Italian labor history: the May Events (*Fatti di Maggio*). Poor Italian harvests and, later, the Spanish-American war pushed up the price of bread. The government should have foreseen and cushioned the distress caused by this unexpected rise in the cost of the chief staple in the diet of workers and peasants, especially those in the South who lived a half day from starvation. Yet, it lifted no hand to alleviate their plight. The socialists did not fail to exploit the advantage so negligently offered to them by the government. The ancient arguments and demands concerning communal lands once again flared up into heated discussion. In January 1898, the Marches, Apulia, and Sicily rose in rebellion, and rioting continued there until April. The crowds vented their spleen against the grain dealers, who had raised the price of wheat, and the mayors and members of the communal councils, who had imposed the tax on flour or denied to the peasants their share in the communal lands. Soldiers used force to restore order, but by the end of January the government in Rome saw the wisdom of reducing the duty on wheat by one-third until April 30. Mob fear induced the abolition of the local tax in many communes of the South. By the end of April, violence had spread to the North. Crowds stormed the bakery shops at Forlì. The populace fought with the police near Ravenna and at Piacenza and Parma. The government alerted 80,000 reserves. On May 4, it finally suspended the duty on wheat until June 20, 1898.

In Milan, the industrial center of Italy, workers knew want, but did not experience deep and continuous deprivation. However, during 1898, the springs of politics in Milan, always taut, now contracted even more. Lombard and Venetian peasants, in their search for factory work, had shifted from quiet village life to an urban atmosphere of political turmoil.

These countrymen, without willing it, upset the social equilibrium of Milan. When the city celebrated the fiftieth anniversary of the "Five Days of Milan," March 18 to 22, which marked the time in 1848 when the city rose against Austrian rule, feelings ran so high that the republicans, the socialists, and the monarchists each organized a separate procession. When a conservative deputy killed Felice Cavallotti in the last of many duels to which that impetuous radical deputy had been addicted, the same political bitterness manifested itself at his funeral.

The Milanese poor held justified grievances against the wealthier classes. Moderates controlled the Milan municipal council. At times they allied themselves with the clericalists, but they had a sufficient majority to govern on their own. While they furnished the city with excellent administration, local taxes burdened the people excessively. When, after years of debate by the council, it looked as though a new law on local finance would impel Milan to push its boundaries into the growing industrial suburbs, unrest seized the owners and workers of factories there. They protested against the implied extension of Milan's heavy taxes on basic commodities to the outlying districts which the city proposed to annex. They refused to believe that these imposts might be reduced or even cut down completely. Against this background of local agitation and political vituperation, the socialists, the republicans, the radicals, and the clericalists staged their attacks upon the national government. The *Osservatore Cattolico* (*Catholic Observer*) of Don Davide Albertario (1846–1902) belittled both Savoy's princes and policies; Luigi De Andreis (1857–1929), the republican deputy from Milan, defined the vote and the carbine as the chief weapons of the people; the socialists committed themselves to spreading discontent which needed little encouragement.

On May 5, the police in Pavia killed a student, Muzio Mussi, the son of the radical deputy from Milan, when they fired upon a crowd which had assembled to protest against an increase in the price of bread. After the news reached Milan, the Socialist Party printed an inflammatory handbill. During lunch hour, a group of workers at the Pirelli plant distributed these leaflets, but the police interfered and arrested three of them. Other workers tried to intervene. The police, outnumbered, withdrew to their barracks with one of the arrested men. Excitement increased in the next few hours after the authorities refused to release the man held by the police. Turati and another socialist deputy, Dino Rondani, spoke directly to the Pirelli workers and urged them to remain calm. They refused this advice, gathered additional cohorts at the Stigler plant, and then advanced upon the police barracks where soldiers, summoned as reinforcements, had already taken their stand. The police and soldiers eventually fired into the crowd, killing two workmen and wounding fourteen. A policeman also fell dead when he failed to remove himself fast enough from the line of fire. A rain storm halted the first phase of violence.

The next day, protesting workers from the Pirelli, Stigler, Vago, De Angeli, Roth, Bocconi, Prinetti, Suffert, Silvestri, and Grondona factories jammed the streets. Some demonstrators attempted to reach the chamber of labor, but the authorities had blocked off the street, and the crowd moved toward Porta Venezia. Without provocation, cavalrymen rode into their ranks. The demonstrators seized streetcars and converted them into barricades. Others broke windows and mounted to the roofs of buildings in order to rain tiles down upon the streets. After initial fear and hesitation, the government declared martial law. More troops, under the command of General Fiorenzo Bava-Beccaris (1831–1924), rushed to Milan. For three days, soldiers and police searched out demonstrators in their houses, shot them down, and used the city roofs as points of vantage for taking aim. On May 9, an artillery officer mistook for rebels a group of beggars who had come for their usual plate of soup to the Capuchin monastery of Monforte. He ordered his soldiers to batter down the walls of the monastery and to search the den of anarchy. Suffering from the heat of the hunt, the soldiers pulled at the monks' beards in full faith that they had at last captured disguised insurgent leaders. (Subsequently, the government sought to interdict Paolo Valera's *L'Assalto al convento* (*The Assault on the Monastery*) which described this unbelievably fantastic incident.) In all, the May Events cost Milan the lives of two policemen and eighty citizens. Moreover, four hundred and fifty persons were wounded. These figures represented the official count. Many believed that the true toll ran much higher.

Di Rudinì outstripped Crispi in meeting the threat to public order. He extended martial law from Milan to Naples, Florence, and other troubled areas on the peninsula. The government again set up military tribunals, resorted to house arrests, closed down more than a hundred left-wing papers, and dissolved chambers of labor, unions, and cooperatives. Nor did it scruple from venting its wrath upon the benevolent Società Umanitaria of Milan which Mosè Loria (1814–1892) had established by bequest to aid the unemployed to form cooperatives and to train themselves for useful occupations. With purblind insensitivity to popular feelings, Di Rudinì allowed the King to decorate General Bava-Beccaris as an unprecedented reward for services rendered during civil strife. The King went so far as to thank the general in a personal letter to him.

The government imprisoned hundreds of political offenders, including distinguished socialists like Filippo Turati, Anna Kulishov, Leonida Bissolati, Andrea Costa, and Costantino Lazzari; republicans like Luigi De Andreis; radicals like Carlo Romussi (1847–1913); and priests like Don Davide Albertario. Of 828 persons brought to trial, including 224 minors and 36 women, 688 received sentences which totalled 1,390 years of imprisonment, 90 years of house detention, and 307 years of surveillance by the police. Fines amounted to almost 34,000 lire. Some prominent socialists like Professor Arturo Labriola (1873–1959) — not to be confused with Professor Antonio Labriola, the pioneering Italian Marxist and teacher of Benedetto Croce — avoided persecution by escaping to Switzerland, where they found hospitality with Vilfredo Pareto (1848–1923). To those Italians with historical memory, the May Events and their aftermath brought back to their thoughts the times of Mazzini when patriots suffered either flight abroad or imprisonment at home.

In June 1898, Di Rudinì's second ministry fell. General Luigi Pelloux succeeded him. Like Di Rudinì before him, Pelloux began his stewardship with a display of wisdom and liberality. He brought an end to martial law and military tribunals by August. In January 1899, the King granted grace to those political prisoners who had received the lightest sentences. Anna Kulishov, seriously ill, left prison to become a legend. Like Costa and Turati, she had met adversity with patience, gentleness, and fortitude. Later in January — after Parliament received a petition in favor of amnesty signed by 400,000 Italians and after Turati and De Andreis, who had lost their parliamentary status when jailed, were re-elected by their constituents through plebiscite — the government pardoned all those not convicted of common crimes. It did not confer general amnesty until June 1899.

At a time when the Dreyfus Affair kept France in turmoil and when Italian sympathies quite naturally lay with Emile Zola and those who cried out for justice in the teeth of reaction, Pelloux decided to introduce, on February 4, 1899, legislation which, he thought, would prevent the kind of violence which had flared up into rebellion twice in the course of five years. The bills provided for the banishing of political prisoners to penal settlements, prohibited outside meetings without prior permission of the police, forbade strikes by state and local government employees, enabled the courts to dissolve any organization which sought "through overt action to subvert the social order and the Constitution of the State," allowed the suspension of any newspaper whose editor had been convicted of false and seditious statements or incitement to violence, and, finally, gave the police the power to review each issue of a newspaper after its editor had been convicted for a third time.

Now the socialists abandoned their policy of parliamentary abstention and isolation and adopted Turati's "prudent tactics of alliances." The famous coalition, the *Estrema*, fought against Pelloux's "barrack-room" policies under the leadership of Matteo Imbriani (1843–1901) for the radicals; Giovanni Bovio (1841–1903) and Salvatore Barzilai (1860–1939) for the republicans; and Turati, Costa, Ferri, Prampolini, Bissolati, and De Felice for the socialists. The reactionary and conservative members in the Chamber could muster enough votes to approve the Pelloux measures, but the government ran through the pretense of hearing proposed amendments, only to reject them in the end. This obdurate behavior provoked the liberals into uncompromising opposition and men like Zanardelli and Giolitti added the weight of their prestige to the righteous indignation of the *Estrema*. Pelloux, following the lead of Crispi in Africa, attempted to divert the mind of the nation by recklessly plunging into the international scramble for concessions in China. He ordered the Italian fleet to occupy a bay off the province of Chekiang (Che-Chiang Sheng) with the purpose of wresting a port from the Chinese government. The enterprise smacked of neither sense nor hope, for Italy had no trade or emigration interests in China. Giolitti, speaking for the opposition, expressed the feelings of the country when he implored Pelloux not to risk the nation's credit on so rash a venture. Parliament, sensing that the people dreaded a repetition of the African disaster, refused consent to the occupation. Pelloux recalled the navy, but the gamble had sapped the country's limited financial resources needlessly. Pelloux then resigned, reorganized his cabinet to demonstrate its purely conservative character, and relying heavily on Baron Sonnino for inspiration and guidance, introduced a refurbished and more severe public safety bill.

The outraged and embattled *Estrema* introduced into Parliament, for the first time in Italian history, persistent and determined obstruction, employing filibustering techniques and disorder, including the seizure and destruction of the ballot urns. The conservatives proposed to prevent obstruction by specific countermeasures: closure and the guillotine (fixing the times when parts of a bill had to be voted on). The *Estrema* filibustered against the guillotine with even more energy. Since the situation seemed hopeless, Pelloux resorted to a stratagem: in June 1899, he adjourned that session of Parliament and tried to endow the measures he sponsored with legal life through royal decree. To be effective, a royal decree needed parliamentary approval within a month. When the Chamber reopened, the debate on the bills continued amidst bedlam, for many members outside the *Estrema* resented the promulgation of laws by royal decree when Parliament was still in session. When the opposition had reached the point of exhaustion and voting appeared inevitable, they destroyed the ballot urns. Pelloux again adjourned Parliament. During this recess, the Court of Cassation, the highest tribunal of the Italian judicial system, in considering a case concerning an anarchist, declared Pelloux's action unconstitutional and the decrees void. In February 1900, Pelloux presented his proposals again. Not only the *Estrema* and nearly all left-wing liberals, but the Di Rudinì conservatives as well, opposed the measures, leaving the government with a majority of only 27. Again amendments flooded the Chamber and again the *Estrema* fought the good fight with interminable and raucous speeches. Now, the constitutional crisis in which the nation found itself reached its height. The government suggested the appointment of a committee to draw up new Standing Orders for the Chamber of Deputies. Whatever recommendations the committee offered were to be provisionally accepted without the approval of the Chamber. All parties in the Chamber, including the *Estrema,* agreed about the necessity for stricter rules and procedures, but the opposition refused to concede that the Chamber should have no voice in promulgating them. The motion therefore gave rise to new obstruction. At the end of March, in the midst of great confusion, the president of the Chamber declared the amended motion passed. The opposition protested the decision of the president as illegal, but to no avail. Four days later, the entire opposition left the Chamber and the remaining deputies approved the new Standing Orders. Parliament then went into recess for six weeks.

When the Chamber reassembled on May 15, 1900, the municipal elections at Milan had conferred impressive victories upon the socialists. The country at large had also found excuses for the obstructive tactics employed by the *Estrema:* violence often had to be met with violence; or, more subtly, the restricted suffrage in Italy justified the parliamentary Left, a minority, in using whatever means it found effective against the reactionary forces since it really expressed the will of the majority in the nation. Gabriele D'Annunzio (1863–1938), who, as the Member for Beauty (so dubbed by his esthetic devotees), sat on the far right, dramatically crossed the Chamber at the opening of the session and took his place among the members of the *Estrema.* Earlier, he had made an astonishing appearance before a meeting of the obstructionists and had declared: "I realize today that on one side there are many who are dead and howling, and on the other side a few who are alive and speaking. As a man of intelligence I am ranging myself on the side of life." In this charged atmosphere, the president of the Chamber tried to govern himself along the lines of the new Standing Orders. He invited shouts, epithets, and the singing of *Garibaldi's Hymn*. On the following day, he resigned and Pelloux dissolved Parliament and decided to appeal to the voters on June 3 and 10, 1900. Baron Sonnino, who had authored the misguided policies of the government and who refused to interpret correctly the obvious signs of dissatisfaction throughout Italy, remained firm in his conviction that the *Estrema* would be wiped out in the elections.

The country made its opinions crystal clear at the polls. The *Estrema*, which had remained in alliance during the electoral campaign, increased its representation from 67 to 95 seats. The socialists gained 12 seats, now possesssing 32 deputies as against their former 20. Government candidates, in fact, had been able to muster no more than 60,000 votes over opposition candidates. Despite his repudiation by the country, Pelloux hoped to retain power, but when Parliament reopened he found his position untenable. Giuseppe Saracco (1821–1907), a moderate politician, became Prime Minister and served in that capacity until February 1901. During Saracco's stay in office, an anarchist, but recently returned from America and still burning with rage against Italy's sovereign because of the personal letter of congratulation that monarch had written to General Bava-Beccaris for his part in stamping out the rebellion at Milan, assassinated King Humbert at Monza on July 29. Victor Emmanuel III (1869–1947, king 1900–1946), the new King, declared himself, in his proclamation of August 2, as dedicated "to the guardianship of liberty and the defense of the monarchy. . . ." In February 1901, that liberty moved closer into sight when Giuseppe Zanardelli became Prime Minister and Giovanni Giolitti assumed the key role of Minister of the Interior.[10]

The Giolittian Era. The Sicilian rebellion of 1893–1894, Crispi's reprisals, the May Events, and the calamitous aftermath of the *annus terribilis*, 1898, uncovered with startling clarity dangerous flaws in the political life of a country new to nationhood and self-government. These defects, as they stiffened into stubborn error, eventually allowed Benito Mussolini to turn aside the democratic evolution of Italy, and perforce, of its labor movement. Italy, then, like many awakening countries in the world of the 1950's, could trace the source of its blunders to the absence of a large, ubiquitous, respected, responsible, democratic, and public-spirited middle class. Without this moderating social and political conductor of extreme tendencies, whether to the far left or to the far right, the nation stood constantly exposed to the lightning shocks of sudden tumult and disorder, followed by the inevitable recoil into police terror and autocratic retrogression.

The conservative and reactionary members of Parliament took their directions from the businessmen and industrialists of North Italy, especially Lombardy, and from the large landowners of the agricultural South. Both economic groups insisted upon acting out doomed despotic roles in a time of democratic change. They revealed themselves as completely incapable of providing apt leadership to a people who were moving very slowly out of their feudal past and were asking only for enough work and food to keep alive and for decent recognition of their rights as citizens in a constitutional monarchy. At the extreme left, neither the republicans nor the radicals could present an affirmative program of action which recognized the role of the modern state in an industrial society. The socialists had the insight and ability to devise such a program. However, their ideological rigidities estopped them from ever fulfilling their proposals through legal enactment. Marxian preconceptions forced the Party to substitute turbulence for constructive policy and uncompromising parliamentary opposition for democratic cooperation. Under these circumstances, it fell to Giovanni Giolitti to create the conditions of a truly liberal régime without the presence or aid of a numerous and responsible middle class.

In his youth, Giolitti had turned in surfeit against the theoretical emphasis of his classical education and had come to measure the success of an enterprise not "at all by the theatrical grandiosity of the ways and means through which it is achieved." He valued, instead, "the sober use made of the means adapted for its attainment." In setting out to construct a liberal system, "semi-revolutionary in appearance," but conservative in its ultimate goals, Giolitti had to employ available resources as he found them. Realistic and scornful of sentimentality, he accepted regional variations in literacy, democratic traditions, and political intelligence. He kept his tactics in North Italy free of the corruption and force which his agents employed in South Italy. Although eminent enemies like Gaetano Salvemini (1873–1957) denounced these devices for securing Giolitti's program of national liberty as unconscionable, they were so hot in pursuit of spiritual perfection that they never stopped to ask one basic question: Could Giolitti's policy of freedom and progress be maintained in Italy by acting upon a false concept of democracy and leaving the long-corrupted, feudal, ignorant, and poverty-ridden South to its own devices?

Many years later, Salvemini wrote: "Looking back at the work of the crusader after thirty years, I find that I have nothing to regret. I must acknowledge, however, that I would have been wiser had I been more moderate in my criticism of the Giolittian system." Mussolini, Hitler, Stalin, and actual experience of European and American democracies pounded enough humility into Salvemini, the historian of freedom, to make him realize and admit that socialist criticism "did not help to direct the evolution of Italian public life toward less imperfect forms of democracy, but rather toward the victory of those militarist, nationalist, and reactionary groups who had found even Giolitti's democracy too perfect." Until Mussolini enslaved Italians, Giolitti's foes to the left were maimed by their temperaments, zeal, and bigotry from understanding his mission: the renewal of Italy's economic and social life, and the emancipation of Italians from the tyranny of their own history and geography.[11]

The assassination of King Humbert I raised the hopes of industrialists and landlords that young Victor Emmanuel III would urge the return of General Pelloux. Instead, when Saracco's majority vanished after six months, he summoned the finest and most respected representative of Italian liberalism, Giuseppe Zanardelli. Zanardelli had not only risen repeatedly in Parliament to decry the repressions of both Crispi and Pelloux, but as Minister of the Interior in 1889, had also tested his convictions by allowing civil liberties full reign, to the embarrassment and disgust of three ministerial colleagues who resigned from the government in protest. Moreover, he proposed and accomplished the revision of the old Legal Code which originated in Piedmont and replaced it with the enlightened Zanardelli Code. He himself sponsored the laws concerning freedom of combination which became part of the Code of 1889. The Piedmont Code of 1859, inspired with the spirit of laissez-faire, enjoined employers from uniting together with the intent of reducing wages unjustly; it also prohibited workers from stopping or interfering with production or causing an increase in the price of goods without reasonable cause. Since only the courts could determine reasonable cause, each strike had to pass the test of thorough scrutiny, logically, in a criminal proceeding. The absurdity of this situation became clear to Crispi when he served as Minister of the Interior, and he fostered in 1878 the creation of the Francesco Bonasi Commission of Inquiry into strikes, combinations, and the laws regulating them. The commissioners, far from radical, had recommended the legal sanction of the right to organize by both employers and workers; they also urged that strikes, except those given to violence, be made legal. Depretis embodied these recommendations in a bill which he introduced into Parliament in 1883, but the Chamber defeated his measure. Finally in 1889, Zanardelli succeeded in this endeavor.

Under the national emergencies declared by Crispi, Di Rudinì, and Pelloux, the new rights lapsed. But at the turn of the century, with Zanardelli as Premier and Giolitti as Minister of the Interior, workers and socialists felt certain that the government would respect their right to organize and to strike peaceably. Indeed, when strikes increased throughout the Po Valley in 1901 and Giolitti found himself importuned to replace the strikers with soldiers, he refused. He also declared that he would use force only against strikers who themselves resorted to violence. In refusing to dissolve workers organizations, Giolitti introduced into the discussion of the issue the important distinction between associations of workers organized for legal purposes and those same groups when they exceeded legal bounds.

During Giolitti's ministries, the Italian Socialist Party entered upon its golden age. Despite the strength it gathered between 1900 and the beginning of World War I, it ultimately destroyed itself through internecine warfare among its various currents, for each tendency felt morally certain of espousing the only true and orthodox Marxian principles and tactics. After the 1893 socialist congress at Reggio Emilia, subsequent events permitted but two congresses until 1900. The clandestine congress of 1895 at Parma abolished group membership in favor of individual membership and gave the Party its permanent name. The next year at Florence, the Party adopted an agrarian program and declared the small independent farmer an economic anachronism destined to disappear.

The 1900 congress of Rome, held from September 8 to 11, derived its fame from the maximum and minimum programs it proclaimed. The maximum program bristled with rhetorical declarations of principles and revolutionary aims. It employed the universal verbiage of socialist pronunciamentos: proletarian struggle, bourgeois oppression, and the economic and political expropriation of the ruling class. In contrast, the minimum program dealt with attainable economic, social, fiscal, educational, and administrative reforms: the referendum, universal suffrage, full responsibility by the State for its actions at all governmental levels, salaries for deputies in Parliament, freedom of speech and assembly, and government neutrality in struggles between capital and labor. The twin programs were intended to mollify the conflict between the moderates and the revolutionaries within the movement. Present from the very birth of the Party, after 1900 the partisans of revolution and intransigence could appeal for justification of their convictions to the maximum testa-

228

ment of faith, while the equally true believers in evolution and democracy could settle their claim to orthodoxy by pointing to the minimum program.

In a speech which he delivered at the end of June 1901 while Minister of the Interior, Giolitti demonstrated his remarkable ability simultaneously to give the conservatives the true measure of their policies, to grasp the appeal of the socialists, to taunt them for their chief weakness, and, fascinated by their program, to see the sense of absorbing their most reasonable demands into his own schedule of reforms:

> It is my profound conviction that socialism can be fought against only on the field of liberty; the other road has been tried and you have seen the results! . . . The truth is that the Socialist movement has an exclusively economic basis. A little study of parliamentary geography will prove it. Take away from the Socialist party all those who are elected in the Emilia, at Mantua, at Rovigo, at Bologna, all those from that plain where the suffering of the peasants is greatest and then tell me what is left of the Socialist party . . . .[12]

In these four sentences, Giolitti pointed out the political and economic failure of the conservatives in the regions where the Socialist Party held strongest sway. But he also deftly probed the principal defect of socialism itself: the careful nurture by the Party of the Genoa-Milan-Ravenna triangle and the neglect of workers outside those areas, especially the great mass of peasants in the South. With craft, Giolitti turned the tables upon the socialists and reproached them with the very criticism they usually levelled against bourgeois governments for their unfeeling abandonment of the South.

In October 1903, when Giolitti became Prime Minister, the Socialist Party claimed only 33,686 members. Giolitti's desire to cater to this small minority group particularly infuriated his conservative and reactionary opponents. Of total socialist membership, 42.3% were urban workers, 14.9% were artisans, 15% were rural laborers, and 14.3% were members of the lower middle class. Only 3.8% were students or belonged to the liberal professions. (The remaining 9.7% were occupationally unidentified.) The political consequences of illiteracy and the unpaid status of deputies emerged from another set of statistics. Of the 33 socialist members of Parliament in 1903, 28 were university graduates from middle-class or upper-class families and constituted 84.8% of the total; three sprang from the lower middle class, or 9.1%; and two could claim birth among the authentic proletariat, or 6.1%. The class origins of the 81 socialist deputies in the German Reichstag offered sharp contrast to the Italian pattern: 65.4% started out in life as true workers, 18.6% stemmed from the lower middle class, and 16% were university graduates of middle-class derivation. The situation in Holland more nearly resembled the Italian scene since half of the eight socialist deputies were educated men, while the Belgian proportions approached those of Germany since 53.5% of the 28 socialist deputies possessed proletarian ancestry.[13]

At the time that Giolitti named the members of his cabinet in October 1903, the moderate followers of Turati had presumably won the day on the floor of the socialist congress at Imola in 1902. Did not Ivanoe Bonomi (1873–1951) pilot through successfully a resolution which permitted socialist cooperation with other parties during local elections as a parallel to the alliance of the *Estrema* during the national elections of 1900? But victory at one moment of a socialist congress could never establish consistent subsequent action or determine the run of feeling at another time. Now that the socialists could no longer be tapped on the shoulder suddenly and hustled off to jail, thoughtless, turbulent, and irresponsible individuals felt free to reassert their extreme dogmas. At the far left clustered the syndicalists who believed in direct revolutionary economic initiative by the proletariat and abhorred political action. Arturo Labriola, the eloquent professor and journalist from Naples whose forceful personality merged economic knowledge and Nietzschean psychology, led this faction. Its dogma held undertones of Bakunin's anarchism and loud overtones of Marx's more furious pronouncements. Just to the right of the syndicalists ranged the hard-shelled Marxist revolutionaries, headed by that perennial Jack-of-all-immoderate-notions, Costantino Lazzari. The impulsive Enrico Ferri, who never held to one position for long, lined up with the syndicalist-revolutionary wings against the reformists. In the madhouse atmosphere which prevailed at Imola, the same delegates who voted for the Bonomi motion, the quintessence of reformism, also found it possible to preserve outward harmony by agreeing upon a resolution which recognized the existence of two irreconcilable currents within the Party! Labriola ascribed this confusion to Turati's superficial persuasive genius, while Turati and his disciples sincerely believed, as always, that they were acting in the supreme interest of socialism by maintaining formal unity even at the expense of logic.

The fiction of harmony ended when Ferri, as editor of *Avanti!*, seized the opportunity to embarrass the moderates, whose cooperation Giolitti sought, by attempting to create a national scandal out of the purported deeds of Giolitti's newly appointed Minister of Finance during the time of Crispi's persecution of the socialists. The revolutionaries and syndicalists took up the cry and hoped to discredit the provisional ministry. When Pietro Rosano (1847–1903), an intelligent and highly respected public servant, committed suicide on the very day of his designation as a result of the accusations against him, public opinion throughout the country turned against the socialists. Ferri's journalistic devices merely succeeded in strengthening the conservative parliamentary forces to whom Giolitti had to turn for support.[14]

In April 1904, at the regional congress of Brescia which preceded the national assembly of socialists, a coalition of extremists framed and passed a resolution which repudiated parliamentary activity as a degeneration of the socialist spirit and approved the use of any tactics, including violent ones, in the struggle with the bourgeois state. Consequently, at the national socialist congress held in Bologna from April 8 to April 11, the precarious formal unity established at Imola seemed on the verge of collapse. Turati and Bissolati headed the reformists, while Labriola and Enrico Leone led the syndicalist current. Ferri, perhaps seeing himself as the savior of the Socialist Party, abandoned the revolutionaries and emerged as the leader of a new center group. Once again Labriola repeated his double incantation which denied that true socialism consisted of a series of reforms, and that parliaments must be used to create socialism. "Reformism is not a manner of substantiating socialism, it is rather its most violent negation." Turati had begun to despair of preserving even a semblance of outward solidarity when Ferri, now turned compromiser, introduced his unity motion, won its passage, and established an uneasy armistice.[15]

The syndicalist predictions of Labriola found substantiation in September 1904 when the first successful general strike in world history occurred. Again, the peasants of the South and the Islands rebelled against continuing poverty and intolerable taxes. At Cerignola, police killed two rioting peasants and wounded seven others in May. On September 4, harsh repressions followed an uprising at Buggerù. The Milan chamber of labor, stirred into action by Labriola and Walter Mocchi when it received news of another uprising at Castelluzzo, proclaimed a general strike on September 16. From Milan, hitherto the stronghold of socialist reformists and moderate labor unions, the strike spread to Genoa, Turin, Venice, Verona, Brescia, Rome, Naples, and the lesser cities of Italy. From September 16 to September 20, Italy seethed in the embrace of a syndicalist passion. The reformists could not openly repudiate the strikes in fear of alienating their electorate, yet these violent demonstrations ran counter to their fundamental beliefs. Labriola exulted at the end of the strike that "five minutes of direct action were worth as many years of parliamentary chatter." But he lacked the quiet imaginative capacity to foresee the influence of fright upon the middle classes.

Giolitti employed these fears to chasten the socialists in the general elections of November 6 and 13, 1904. He knew that the excesses of the syndicalists and the revolutionary fervor displayed during the general strike had perturbed Pius X (1835–1914, pope 1903–1914). Giolitti wished to neutralize the socialist vote by attracting Catholics to the polls, but the *Non expedit* stood between him and his plans for balancing political and social forces and trimming extremists down to manageable size.

Until September 1904, the official attitude of the Church toward that "sacrilegious usurper," the State, had remained firm against the participation of Catholics in national elections. Leo XIII had reasserted the abstention imposed by the *Non expedit* in a letter to the Cardinal Secretary of State on May 14, 1895. The Congregation of Extraordinary Affairs stressed the obligatory nature of the principle on January 27, 1902. During the following year, the Church did not hesitate to rebuke the devoted leaders of Italian Christian Democracy when they strayed beyond the tasks of social improvement assigned to them by the encyclical, *Graves de communi*, of January 18, 1901. Christian Democracy, still concentrated where it had begun in North Italy and Bergamo, remained the center of Catholic social endeavors. Vigorous forces within Christian Democracy hoped to transform its scattered groups into a movement united by common social and political principles and possessed of a definite program. When these aspirations received full voice at the Christian Democratic congress of 1903 at Bologna and the Catholic newspaper there, *L'Avvenire d'Italia* (*The Future of Italy*), endorsed them enthusiastically, a sharp official reply reiterated the continuing opposition of the Church to political activities. The long-standing prohibition formed the substance of the *Motu proprio* by Pius X addressed to members of Christian Democracy on December 18, 1903. Tension between Church and State increased at the end of April 1904. Following the visit of the French President to Rome on April 24, the Vatican Secretary of State, Cardinal Merry del Val, addressed a diplomatic note to the Catholic nations. The message stated that heads of those nations offended the Pope when they set foot in Rome and paid homage to the King "who against all rights retains his civil sovereignty" there. Jean Jaurès (1859–1914), the brilliant French historian and socialist leader, set off the explosion by publishing a copy of this letter in *Humanité* on May 17. Excitement gathered such force in Italian cafés, piazzas, and Parliament that on May 30 Giolitti found it imperative to rise in the Chamber to clarify the policy of the State by announcing his famous formula: "Our principle is this: that the state and the Church are two parallels which should never meet."

But nothing prevented intermediaries from functioning between the parallels. So they did in the wake of the September general strike. After Tommaso Tittoni (1855–1931), the Minister of Foreign Affairs, talked to loyal friends of Pius X from Bergamo, these men requested an audience with the Pope. Paolo Bonomi, their spokesman, described the threatening political situation in Bergamo and voiced the fear that radicals and freemasons might triumph in that stronghold of Christian Democracy unless the Pope relaxed the *Non expedit*. Pius X told his faithful followers to do as their consciences dictated. He recurred to the same phrasing when Bonomi asked whether he had understood His Holiness aright and whether the Pope's reply meant yes. Consequent to this relaxation, a Catholic from Milan and another from Treviglio won seats in the November elections. The next year, the Pope gave formal sanction to modification of the *Non expedit* in the encyclical, *Il fermo proposito* of June 11, 1905: if it seemed likely that a subversive candidate might be elected, bishops could request the suspension of the rule and, if granted, could invite Catholics to hold themselves in readiness to go to the polls.

Giolitti's maneuvers had worked to his will. The elections accomplished the loss of six socialist seats. Giolitti, who distrusted all extreme attitudes and actions because he had no faith in their social utility, hoped that the move of the country toward the right would teach the revolutionaries that "the Italian people . . . did not intend to permit certain limits to be exceeded by any side." Among the socialists, the reform elements, now hard pressed to justify their toleration of the general strike, charged that the syndicalists created a situation from which the moderates had found it difficult to extricate themselves. In retrospect, they also rationalized the general strike into discredit by asserting that an uprising without predetermined and precise aims necessarily turned into an abortive revolution and could only bring reaction, not socialism, to the struggling proletariat. During the next four years, the reformists appealed to reason, public order, and evolutionary progress under constant assaults from the revolutionaries.

The 1906 socialist congress at Rome lasted from October 7 to October 10. On October 9, the venerated Andrea Costa, looking out upon growing strife and disorder on the floor, threatened to resign as presiding officer. Since 1904, Enrico Ferri's center position had acquired a designation of philosophic sound, an endearing quality to Italians, regardless of precise meaning: integralism. The integralists insisted that socialist violence and evolutionary development were not, in essence, antithetical. Their Order of the Day balanced revolution against reform; it advocated both social legislation and direct action simultaneously by saving violence for a rainy day. The resolution won almost 27,000 votes, including those of the reformists, against some 7,000 votes registered for the other factions and abstainers. This curious vote merely confirmed the ambivalent character of the Socialist Party and did not contribute to improvement or cure. The congress itself invited deterioration by providing Enrico Leone with a forum from which to fling his anti-intellectual taunts against the Party — a radical aberration which later found its fullest expression in fascism and nazism. He mocked the Party, supposedly proletarian, for its representation in Parliament largely by intellectuals and professional men. Perhaps, he suggested, workers in Parliament might embarrass the socialists before the bourgeoisie by speaking in ungrammatical language.

Between the Rome and Florence congresses of the Socialist Party, the syndicalists had sharpened their ideas and conducted vigorous campaigns against the reformists through their lively newspapers in Rome, Milan, Mirandola, Florence, and Lugano. They conducted an agrarian strike in the province of Parma during the summer of 1908. After two months, the strike ended in failure and deep bitterness against the reformists because of their open opposition to the strike. Even before the delegates assembled at Florence from September 19 to 22, the syndicalists broke with the Socialist Party. Andrea Costa again presided at the convention; the reformists ruled the sessions on this occasion. The congress expressed its moderate philosophy in the resolution termed *Concordato*. The delegates roundly condemned the revolutionary syndicalists who had already departed from their midst. As a second rebuke to the syndicalists, they pressed for the closest relationship between the Socialist Party and the General Confederation of Labor which the chambers of labor and category federations had called into being as their national center at the end of September and the first day of October 1906. The reformist current predominated in the Confederation under the leadership of Rinaldo Rigola. The congress also favored legislation with regard to maternity aid, sickness benefits, old-age pensions, and progressive taxation; moreover, it voiced opposition to the general strike and strikes in the public services. On the last day of deliberations, Turati congratulated his comrades on the defeat of the syndicalists and the triumph of true socialism. But Gaetano Salvemini, ever mindful of the peasant South, still without voice because still without vote, chided the joyful reformists for leaving the all-important question of universal suffrage as the last item on the agenda.

The socialists next assembled nationally at Milan from October 21 to 25, 1910. Giolitti's long ministry from May 1906 to December 1909 had ended and Sonnino's second short ministry lasted from December 1909 to March 1910. By the end of October, Luigi Luzzatti would reach his eighth month as Premier. Meanwhile, socialist deputies had supported successful measures aimed at the improvement and strengthening of primary education. They had also backed legislation to reform the Senate and Luzzatti's bill for limited extension of the vote. Both projects failed of passage. These parliamentary activities of the reformists did not placate Salvemini. At Milan, he again smote them. He pleaded for the neglected South and especially for universal suffrage which alone could redeem it. He knew that the South needed to possess the precious vote to help itself, for both the Socialist Party and its strong ally, the General Confederation of Labor, had shirked that burdensome task. In 1910, of 8,000,000 organizable workers, only 844,000 had joined unions. Of this number, 390,000 belonged to peasant leagues, but only 100,000 of these organized agricultural workers lived in the predominantly agricultural South and the Islands. In answer to Salvemini, the reformists appealed to the record: the close relationship of the Party to the General Confederation of Labor, flourishing labor banks, social security benefits, protective labor legislation in behalf of women and children, the use of arbitration in settling industrial disputes, freedom of association, and the right to strike. This justification of the tactics of reform did not satisfy Salvemini, nor did it impress a more obscure delegate. Benito Mussolini (1883–1945), in declaring himself in favor of a revolutionary leftist resolution offered by Lazzari, pointed out that, despite universal suffrage and the most advanced social legislation in the world, neither Germany nor Austria approached true socialism. Although the opposition mustered almost 10,500 votes and nearly 1,000 delegates abstained, Turati's program received 13,000 votes. Its section on political action rested upon four principal demands: universal suffrage for both sexes, resistance to increases in the military budget and exertion for its future reduction, encouragement of socialist organizations at all levels through proletarian education, and the establishment of a complete state system of social insurance. Bissolati, who served as editor of *Avanti!* after the Florence congress, vacated his desk for Claudio Treves (1869–1933), Turati's closest collaborator.

Giolitti became Prime Minister again in March 1911. When he assumed office in 1903, he had invited Turati to join his cabinet. Through Bissolati, Turati replied that the times had not matured enough for a socialist to become a member of the ministry. The masses would misunderstand and condemn participation in a bourgeois government. In 1911, Giolitti again invited a socialist, this time Bissolati himself, to enter the Council of Ministers. Bissolati refused in much the same tone and for the same reasons as Turati had employed eight years before. Giolitti never hesitated to expose the weaknesses of adversaries and friends alike. On April 8, 1911, he admonished the socialist deputies: "I believe that all who are in this Hall must, at certain moments, assume responsibilities . . . ." He then went on intentionally to create consternation within the Chamber and indirectly to precipitate a crisis within the Socialist Party by declaring: "Eight years have gone by, the country has gone ahead, the Socialist party has greatly moderated its program, Karl Marx has been relegated to the attic . . . ." The shouts of approval and protest prevented him from ever finishing that sentence.[16]

Although the twelfth congress of the Socialist Party was not scheduled to meet until 1912, its convocation was advanced a year in order to meet a major crisis. In March 1911, Bissolati had met his old friend, Giolitti, refused official collaboration with the government, but consented to discuss with the King the political situation in Italy and to express his views on the government's program if called upon to do so. Giolitti moved fast and the King received Bissolati the following day. Although Bissolati had preserved the purity of his socialism by calling upon the King in soft hat, he had violated precedent flagrantly, for never before had a socialist deputy moved across the threshhold of the Quirinal Palace. The loud protests which immediately greeted this act issued, predictably enough, from the reactionary conservatives who felt betrayed by the King, and the revolutionary socialists, who felt betrayed by Bissolati. These outraged purists demanded that the special congress, set for Modena from October 15 to 18, decide definitively the official socialist stand concerning the Party's relationship to the bourgeois government. Yet, by the time the delegates assembled at Modena to deal with Bissolati's fall from grace, Giolitti had presented them with a fresh crisis. The reformist wing of the Socialist Party never recovered from the internal devastation it wrought. On September 29, 1911 Italy had declared war with Turkey over Tripoli.

That Giolitti, dispassionately devoted to domestic reform, should have risked the slow progress of the nation in the hazards of war can be explained only by seeking the wellsprings of his decision in psychological, diplomatic, and nationalistic sources. No nation — and especially

Italy which felt uneasy and deprived at not achieving that greatness in the world promised during the *Risorgimento* — could have lightly dismissed the ignominious defeat by the Ethiopians at Dogali in 1887 and the even more humiliating defeat at Adua in 1896. Of the 25,000 Italians in this campaign, those not killed had been captured and held for ransom. This national shame, imposed by black men upon the descendants of Dante and Leonardo da Vinci in one of the worst European colonial disasters of modern history, forced the Italians to sue for peace. The treaty of Addis Ababa recognized the independence of Ethiopia. Italy had now to content its colonial aspirations by falling back upon Eritrea. At this point it must be recalled that Italy had joined Germany and Austria in the Triple Alliance on May 20, 1882, after the frustration of Italian hopes in Tunis by the French in 1881. With the renewal of the Triple Alliance in 1887, Italy obtained a free hand in Tripoli. Italy reached similar understandings with England in 1890, with France in 1900 (in exchange for French liberty of action in Morocco), and with Russia in 1909. When France entered Fez, the capital of Morocco, in May 1911, despite German warnings, and precipitated an international crisis, the Italian government felt constrained to secure Tripoli for itself before the French established a protectorate in Morocco.

These developments gathered intense spiritual sustenance from the modern Italian nationalistic movement which found its voice during the first decade of the twentieth century. Vague, literary, and rhetorical, it despised liberalism, democracy, the freemasons, and above all, the socialists. The eminence attained by the most unique of all Italian nationalists, Gabriele D'Annunzio, cannot be explained without acknowledging his many accomplishments as poet, dramatist, novelist, artist, actor, politician, kiss-and-tell lover, and self-appointed apostle of Beauty. His inflated language, his hopped-up emotions, his Nietzschean praise of lust and violence, and his embroidered superficiality repel readers today, but he was the idol of an entire generation of Italians before and immediately after World War I. So celebrated a figure as Giuseppe A. Borgese (1882–1952), the philosopher, political scientist, and poet, had said in 1904, when he was twenty-two: "Yes, we love and admire Gabriele D'Annunzio more than any other modern poet of ours, living or dead, and from him we begin our art."

D'Annunzio markedly influenced Enrico Corradini (1865–1931), to whose nationalistic review, *Il Regno* (*The Kingdom*), Giovanni Papini (1881–1956) and Giuseppe Prezzolini (1882–   ) contributed during the two years of its existence from 1903 to 1905. So strenuously Italian were these young men that they rejected inspiration from foreign nation-

237

alists like Barrès, Houston Stewart Chamberlain, and Kipling. Did not Italy possess its own sources of light, the pioneering sociologists, Gaetano Mosca (1858–1941) and Vilfredo Pareto? They provided ammunition enough, especially to Prezzolini, for his antiparliamentarian forays. Prezzolini's contribution to nationalist theory, if his unsystematic views can be so graced, achieved historical importance because he made a firm distinction between the degenerate Italy of Parliament and the sound Italy of farm and factory. Other antisocialist nationalists, in their patriotic desire to increase the prestige of their country by reinforcing the strength of the middle classes, displayed open hostility to labor as the sworn international enemy of the bourgeoisie. Prezzolini's fusion of nationalism and syndicalism antedated by almost two decades the powerful propaganda of Mussolini during his rise to power. Both Papini and Prezzolini eventually abandoned the crude nationalism they espoused when associated with *Il Regno,* but joined forces again in *La Voce* (*The Voice*), founded by Prezzolini at Florence in 1908. This influential journal substituted for raucous nationalism a more constructive nationalism dignified with spiritual meaning. Gaetano Salvemini, Giovanni Amendola (1882–1926), and Benedetto Croce contributed to its prestige.

The new, refined, and cultural nationalism of *La Voce* did not replace the nationalism espoused by Corradini. This older nationalism, when it seemed most feeble, received fresh vigor from the irredentists. They shrilly demanded the return of Italian territory, still under the rule of Austria, to the flag of the Fatherland. Since they received little encouragement from liberals, clericalists, or socialists, they turned to Corradini's brand of nationalism for reassurance. This reinvigorated movement attracted some 230 persons to its first national congress at Florence between December 3 and 5, 1910. The rally asseverated the old nationalist slogans of power, authority, and the necessity and nobility of war. In a telegram addressed to the delegates, Giovanni Pascoli (1855–1912), the socialist poet from the Romagna, declared: "It is time to take up once again the heroic work: it is time that we set out to reconquer Italy for Italy!" The congress founded the Associazione Nazionalista Italiana (Italian Nationalist Party) and the new Party established its weekly newspaper, *Idea Nazionale* (*National Idea*), at Rome on March 1, 1911. Corradini completed the structure by supplying the gospel inscribed on its façade: "Just as socialism was the method utilized for the redemption of the proletariat from the bourgeois classes, so nationalism shall be for us Italians the method of redemption from the French, the Germans, the British, and the North and South Americans who are our bourgeois." Very soon nationalist propaganda, reaching out through newspapers and magazines published in Florence, Turin, Rome, and Naples, joined with diplomatic, psychological, economic, and social forces to glorify war as a means of winning colonies where the country's poor could emigrate to improve their fortune under Italian care without losing their nationality.[17]

Despite the Tripolitan War and the rise of nationalism, the socialists met at Modena in the middle of October 1911 and devoted their full energies to ceremonial ablutions. They concentrated upon the rites of cleansing themselves of the impurities which Bissolati's sins had brought into the inner sanctum of the Party. Bissolati's integrity and honesty did not make it easier for his friends to defend him. When accused of subservience to the government, he replied staunchly: "You may break me before I will pass to the opposition against the Government of Giolitti." Bissolati spoke out forthrightly although he knew that absolution would be denied him since only a small number of reformists on the extreme right were prepared to stand up in his behalf. The revolutionaries, the integralists, and the reformists to the left, including Turati, Rigola, Treves, and Giuseppe Modigliani (1872–1947), prepared themselves to censure Bissolati and to prevent future error through the enunciation of a guiding precept. They finally approved, after a second ballot and narrowly, the resolution introduced by Treves: "The congress . . . expresses the opinion that the socialist parliamentary group cannot and must not further systematically support, with its votes, the present cabinet." The wording abounded in the perennial vacillation of the Socialist Party and lacked injunctive prohibition, for the phrase, "expresses the opinion," did not carry the ring of command, while the adjective, "systematic," implied that socialist deputies might uphold Giolitti's ministry occasionally. Once more, the Party faltered from right to left and left to right because, as always, the even balance between the fundamental cleavages of opinion failed to produce an overwhelming majority for one or the other. Turati, who spent his life as a socialist laboring diligently in the aisles of compromise against threats of disunion, now saw that the resolution he had favored might, in the future, easily degenerate into decrees of excommunication. Socialists, themselves dissenters, instead of welcoming heterodoxies, might move to banish heretics from their realm. Turati's prophetic warning went unheard.

With the declaration of war in September 1911, the socialists proclaimed a general strike, but their bid to thwart the war effort met with indifference. Their obstructive, pacifist propaganda during the following months also failed as they learned that the proletariat, whose welfare they cherished and aimed to protect, treasured the imperialist war with all their hearts. Why not possess, reasoned the poor, a fertile, rich America, but closer at hand, easier and cheaper to reach? Somewhat more noble sentiments moved the reformists of the right to declare themselves in favor of the war: Angiolo Cabrini (1869–1937), Ivanoe Bonomi (1873–1951), Bissolati, Giuseppe Canepa (1865–1948), and De Felice, the veteran leader of the Sicilian Workers Bands. At Modena, Bonomi had said straight out: "There is a national solidarity that is not opposed to, but rather complements, class solidarity . . . . " Cabrini went so far as to insist that Italian socialists had a duty to wish for victory in Libya. Bissolati, not only at Modena, but also at the next congress at Reggio Emilia reasoned that responsible socialists must join the struggle to keep the nation from being strangled in the Mediterranean and to prevent, as well, the dangerous nationalist movement from exercising a monoply on Italian patriotism.

When the socialists assembled in Reggio Emilia from July 7 to 10, 1912, the revolutionary intransigents, under the leadership of Costantino Lazzari, Angelica Balabanoff (1876–   ), and Giovanni Lerda, dominated the proceedings. Benito Mussolini served as their spokesman. He had earned this privilege by thought and action: he published vituperative articles against the war in the weekly newspaper he edited in Forlì; with Pietro Nenni (1891–   ), the future left-wing socialist ally of the post-World War II communists, he organized railway raids and other disrupting forays and spent five months in prison for sabotaging the war effort. At Reggio Emilia, Mussolini, the young representative of the fundamentalist, Sorelian, and the revolutionary socialists, stood ready to impeach the right-wing socialists who had voted in February 1912 in favor of the government's decree of sovereignty over all Libya. Left-wing reformists led by Turati and Modigliani now occupied the Party's center position.

In his scathing speech, Mussolini, virtually an unknown figure in socialist ranks, excoriated the Tripolitan War, Giolitti, his reformist flunkies, democratic government, universal suffrage, the King, the Church, freemasonry, and the aristocracy. But he reserved his most vitriolic indictments for Bissolati, Bonomi, and their cronies. He assailed them not only as imperalist warmongers, but also as perpetrators of another unpardonable crime against socialism. On March 14, 1912, an unsuccessful attempt to assassinate King Victor Emmanuel III sent the Chamber of Deputies in a body to the Quirinal Palace to congratulate the King on his escape from injury. Three socialists accompanied the group: Bissolati, Cabrini, and Bonomi. In this act, Mussolini saw the beginnings of corruption and the end of socialism itself. On the motion of expulsion, Mussolini triumphed. Bissolati, Bonomi, and their followers founded the Reformist Socialist Party on the very night of the vote. It commanded little following and disappeared in 1917. Turati, Treves, and their adherents, still governed as in the past by a stale concept of proletarian unity, voted with the majority which removed them from positions of power. Lazzari headed the Party now and Mussolini succeeded Treves as editor of *Avanti!* The General Confederation of Labor, unwilling to stake its future upon either the official party or the Reformist Socialist Party, declared its autonomy.

When the last pre-World War I socialist congress met at Ancona from April 26 to 29, 1914, membership stood at almost 50,000 and the number of branches had reached 1,542. During the elections of October 26 and November 2, 1913, when Giolitti's extended suffrage law of June 30, 1912 increased the number of eligible voters from 3,000,000 to 8,500,000, a million Italians supported Socialist Party lists and elected 53 deputies. The Reformist Socialist Party and independent socialist candidates returned 22 adherents to the Chamber. Once again, Giolitti hedged possible socialist gains with Catholic victories, as he had in 1904. In 1909, Catholics voted under a strict formula laid down by the Vatican through the Italian Catholic Electoral Union (Unione Elettorale Cattolica Italiana) and returned 21 deputies to Parliament. Don Margotti's injunction of "Neither elected, nor electors" had suffered doctrinal change into "Deputies who are Catholics, not Catholic deputies" ("*Cattolici deputati, non deputati cattolici*"). In preparation for the elections of 1913, Giolitti arranged a pact with Count Vincenzo Ottorino Gentiloni (1865–1916), the president of the Italian Catholic Electoral Union. Expanding the rules of 1909, the agreement permitted Catholics to vote for liberal and conservative candidates if the government guaranteed to preserve freedom of conscience and religion, to leave private schools at peace, to grant parents of public school pupils the right to demand religious instruction for them, to prevent the passage of divorce laws, to accord equal treatment to all social and economic organizations regardless of their social and religious principles, and to strive for gradual tax reform. The Catholics elected 33 deputies and more than 200 constitutional liberals had been aided by Catholic voters in their election. Giolitti's underhand maneuvers had thus brought about the truest political unification in the history of modern Italy up to 1913 since large numbers of dissident and abstaining Catholics exercised their franchise in that year for the first time since 1870.

The revolutionists controlled the socialist sessions at Ancona completely. The most publicized controversy raged around the successful attempt of the revolutionaries to oust freemasons from the Party, thus protracting the inquisitorial practices initiated in 1910. To show their contempt for the reformists, they also whipped through a resolution which imposed absolute intransigence upon socialists in local elections. This less dramatic motion, which forced the withdrawal of socialists from alliances with progressive groups locally, had far-reaching repercussions because it established official policy which Italian socialism followed during and after World War I.

The moderate socialists saw the work of a lifetime destroyed at Reggio Emilia and Ancona by the Party's younger members. These newcomers engaged without mercy in the eternally recurring civil war between the generations: They sneered at the achievements of their elders as opportunistic, compromised, and unworthy; they felt invincible since they were fortified by that heavy dogmatism which a fresh reading of Karl Marx conferred and which served their inexperience as irrefutable answers to human economic, social, and political arrangements. Turati had staked his life on the belief that socialism could accomplish beneficent and important reforms through democratic parliamentary procedures. But the mythology of Marxism had so enthralled him that he never dared to risk proletarian disunity and the prospect of two independent socialist parties each with clear-cut principles. Years later, he declared openly in the Chamber of Deputies on November 24, 1920: "I know how to sacrifice my personal views, and that, which some ascribe to opportunism, is perhaps the greatest immolation one can make for the sake of one's ideal, for the cause of proletarian unity."[18]

By June 1914, when Red Week paralyzed the nation, Giovanni Giolitti had already surrendered the outward seal of office to Antonio Salandra and watched the rush of events from the sidelines where he retreated every now and then during chosen intervals of his career. That crafty master of statecraft might well have wondered whether all the reforms he espoused, piloted through Parliament, and prepared for the sovereign's signature; whether all of the liberties he championed and assured; whether all the encouragement and tolerance he extended to socialists and radicals had ended in failure. During his long domination over Italian politics and during years like 1905 and 1906 when he permitted others like Tommaso Tittoni, Alessandro Fortis (1841–1909), and Sidney Sonnino to rule nominally in his place, he had accomplished wonders of social amelioration. Government intervention had reduced illiteracy as evening schools and public libraries spread through the country. The Opera Nazionale per il Mezzogiorno, a predecessor in social purpose of its post-World War II namesake, had been created to resuscitate Sicily and the South after the devastations inflicted by the earthquake of 1908 in Messina and Calabria. During the first two decades of the twentieth century, Parliament, under the guidance and prompting of progressive ministries, decreed a weekly day of rest and closing on public holidays for stores and government offices, improved the health laws, provided for state sale of quinine and free salt to pellagra sufferers, reinforced the workmen's compensation funds, systematized legislation regarding the labor of women and children, made possible the building of low-rent workers homes (*case popolari*) through easing of the construction tax, regulated private charities, and extended the coverage of public relief. The government reclaimed waste lands to ease the condition of the peasants in the Campagna area near Rome and supplied loans to peasants in the Marches and in Umbria. Other laws sought to improve conditions in the Basilicata, Apulia, other southern provinces, and Sardinia. Luzzatti's ministry pioneered with a maternity fund for women workers and the central government pledged itself to assist communes by extending loans for the raising of public health and sanitation standards. The State, through a body of inspectors, assumed responsibility for the welfare of emigrants. The central government also asserted control over elementary education which showed the need for uniform standards and improved efficiency. Giolitti, ever mindful of the average citizen, nationalized life insurance in order to protect policyholders from the frequent bankruptcy of private companies, both foreign and domestic. Profits gained from this monopoly were pledged to strengthen the old-age pension and the workmen's compensation funds. The encouragement extended by Giolitti to Italian cooperatives, while not wholly disinterested, since local socialist cooperative administrators understood precisely the government source of their welfare, nonetheless helped to create one of the most extensive and cherished cooperative movements in the world.

These reforms and Giolitti's toleration of strikes, riots, and revolutionary socialist fervor led conservatives and reactionaries to accuse Giolitti of permitting the building up of a socialist state within the State. On Sunday, June 7, 1914, their fears materialized. An antimilitarist demonstration which started at Ancona soon swelled to insurrectionary size as the fiery propaganda of Mussolini, now the editor of *Avanti!*, inflamed the traditionally revolutionary regions of the Romagna and the Marches. Within a week, violence surged throughout Italy under the leadership of Errico Malatesta, the anarchist who had once apprenticed himself to Bakunin. Another general strike seemed inevitable, for the General Confederation of Labor gave its support to this hysteria. Although the *municipio* at Bologna had flown the red flag and the Marches and the Romagna had proclaimed a republic, by June 11 the tumult subsided as the upheaval ran its natural course. Then, in the words of Mussolini's *Avanti!*, an armistice was declared. During the disorders, Turati protested against the Salandra government's repressive violence and declared himself against mob violence as well; Claudio Treves tried to distinguish between mobism (*teppa*) and the orderly processes of socialism. But their sun had set. At the beginning of World War I, after years of compromise and twisted resolutions, Italian socialism took on again its original purpose: revolution.[19]

Neutrality, War, Anarchy, and the March on Rome. Through a rapid sequence of formal declarations issued between July 28 and the first days of August 1914, the major powers of Europe pushed the entire world into war and revolution which brought the nineteenth century to an end. On the evening of August 4, Edward, Viscount Grey of Fallodon, gazing out at St. James's Park from his window in the Foreign Office, said: "The lamps are going out all over Europe; we shall not see them lit again in our lifetime."

Italy had announced its neutrality the day before and guarded its technical honor by citing the provisions of the Triple Alliance which engaged Italy's intervention only in the event of defensive warfare, a definition not met by Austria's bombardment of Belgrade. From that moment until May 23, 1915, when Italy went to war with Austria, the Salandra government negotiated openly with the Central Powers and secretly with the Triple Entente. After Sidney Sonnino became Foreign Minister on November 3, 1914, he insisted that Article VII of the Triple Alliance entitled Italy to countervailing rewards should Austria extend its power in the Balkans. We shall see, presently, that this policy of territorial aggrandizement went beyond the long-sought redemption of the Trentino and Trieste to include dominion over the Adriatic. It so engrossed Italian diplomacy that in dickering over a local sea the nation squandered its moral opportunities to become a world power.

As the price of continued neutrality, Italy made demands which Austria at first refused to consider. Prince Bernhard von Bülow (1849–1929), the German Ambassador in Rome who headed a special mission to Italy at the end of December 1914, agreed to Italy's claims to the Trentino. The German government then pressed the reluctant Austrians to concur. When they finally assented in March 1915, they refused to grant more than the Trentino, but would not offer even that minimal prize until after the resumption of peace. By then, Italy's interventionists had driven thick wedges into the country's widespread approval of bargained neutrality. Sonnino, who had originally inclined toward strict adherence to the terms of the Triple Alliance — entering the war on the side of Austria and Germany — now took prompt advantage of this shift in the political climate of the piazzas. He insisted upon the immediate transfer to Italy of the Trentino and districts within Venezia Giulia, the creation of Trieste and its environs as a free state, and title to coastal areas and islands of the Adriatic which Italy had already partially occupied since the end of 1914.

Italy made steeper demands for active intervention on the side of the Allies: the territorial package already required of Austria, with the addition of Istria, the largest Dalmatian Islands, the southern portion of the province of Dalmatia, the Dodecanese Islands, a bit of the Turkish spoils in the Balkans, and extensions of territory in Libya, Eritrea, and Somaliland in the event that the Allies divided Germany's African colonies among themselves. Salandra characterized these interest-bearing negotiations with the Triple Entente, which also promised a substantial loan to Italy in addition to a share in eventual war indemnities, as expressions of "sacred egotism in the cause of Italy."[20]

Giolitti, who still controlled Parliament and regarded Salandra as a mere stop-gap in office, headed the advocates of neutrality. The socialists, *mirabile dictu*, found themselves ranged alongside of Giolitti. The warring leaders of the Party — Turati, Lazzari, and Mussolini — had finally united in pacifistic neutrality. Shocked beyond belief at the immediate patriotic readiness with which the German Socialist Party answered the call to defend the Fatherland against imperialists to the West and Russian barbarians to the East, Italian socialists, who had venerated their German comrades, closed ranks in pleased satisfaction that their own thoughts and action had remained doctrinally pure. The Vatican also stood aside, for Catholic France and Catholic Austria, past defenders of the Holy See against the trespasses of the Italian State, both held claims upon the gratitude and affection of the Church.

Mussolini found the Giolittian and Catholic company which the Socialist Party kept distasteful to his innermost convictions, dampening to his anarchistic temperament, and confining to his personal ambitions because these towering allies in neutrality dwarfed his own role among the socialists. Moreover, his genius conformed not to the shrewd and moderate arguments of neutrality, but to the emotional appeals of intervention. Very soon, during the early days of October 1914, Mussolini showed signs of impatience with the ideological restrictions under which he worked. His fierce diatribes against intervention, which had provoked him to label the revolutionary syndicalists, Filippo Corridoni (1887–

1915) and Alceste De Ambris (1874–1934), "subversive deserters," abated. His new arguments sounded like the syndicalist incantations of old: socialists must favor participation in the war since arms in the hands of comrades will help to destroy the bourgeois system when hostilities cease and the inevitable revolution follows. On October 18, he published an article, *From Absolute Neutrality to Active and Operative Neutrality,* which favored Italian intervention led by the Socialist Party. Two days later, at the Bologna meeting of the Socialist Party directorate, he found himself completely isolated and resigned as editor of *Avanti!* On November 15, the first issue of Mussolini's rival socialist newspaper, *Popolo d'Italia (People of Italy),* appeared in Milan. Its masthead carried a slogan of the dogged French revolutionary, Louis-Auguste Blanqui, "He who has a sword has bread," and another from Napoleon, "A revolution is an idea which has found bayonets." On November 24, the Milan section of the Socialist Party confronted him at a public meeting in the People's Theater and challenged him to justify his actions. Constant uproar made most of Mussolini's defense inaudible. When the assembly expelled him from the party "for moral and political unworthiness," Mussolini promised his judges, when his words could break through the din of shouts — "Get out!" "Leave!" "Traitor!" "Judas!" — dire revenge. He repeated these threats afterward in *Popolo d'Italia.*

The February 24, 1915 report of the Milan investigation commission exonerated Mussolini of the suspicion that he had perverted his views for personal profit. But the commission never thoroughly explored the auxiliary rumors that Mussolini's funds at the very beginning of his conversion came from Filippo Naldi, the interventionist editor of Bologna's famous newspaper, *Il Resto del Carlino,* nor did its members determine whether or not Naldi acted for himself or for third parties. Certainly the much discussed avenue of support, the beneficent publicity agency, served only as a screen. However obscure remained these points about the financial origins of *Popolo d'Italia,* the French source of money for the later interventionist campaign of Mussolini's newspaper never occasioned serious doubts: the Ambassador to Italy, Camille Barrère (1851–1940), and Marcel Cachin (1869–   ), the French socialist (later, a veteran leader of the Communist Party), acting in behalf of his government.

In the limbo of excommunication where he had driven his own victims in the past, Mussolini protested his continuing devotion to socialism. He made few converts to war among socialists or members of the General Confederation of Labor. The mayor of Milan, Emilio Caldara, represented Mussolini's outstanding socialist conquest, while Cesare and

Margherita Sarfatti became his closest collaborators. His isolation forced him to look elsewhere for support. He found ready associates among the noisy, impulsive, discontented syndicalists — now in, now out, of the Socialist Party — but lately abused by him. Corridoni and De Ambris joined Mussolini and brought along an organization of sorts. Adversaries of the General Confederation of Labor, they championed strikes not only for their immediate and tangible results, but also for the heroic qualities which they bestowed upon workers. Their followers, already formed as Bands of Revolutionary Action (Fasci di Azione Rivoluzionaria, also referred to as Combat Bands, Fasci di Combattimento) to agitate for intervention on the side of the Allies, joined Mussolini's followers at a national rally in Milan on January 24, 1915.[21]

Subtler forces of a constitutional nature also worked to destroy Giolitti's program of neutrality. Salandra slipped away from his master's control and became King Victor Emmanuel's man even while Giolitti continued to regard him as a temporary replacement. Under a strict reading of the Italian Constitution, the *Statuto*, the King possessed the right to name the government's ministers, make treaties of alliance, and declare war, but Italian monarchs had always aquiesced in the will of parliamentary majorities. The crisis in Europe between 1914 and 1915 altered the relationship between Salandra and Victor Emmanuel. Bound in strong friendship to Edward VII, late King of England, experienced in foreign affairs, and respected for his judgment, the King offered the privacy of his Court for the elaboration of diplomatic plans during a time when secrecy became urgent. Once Sidney Sonnino, long the champion of the "Return to the Constitution" doctrine of government, entered the cabinet as Minister of Foreign Affairs, the triumvirate of King, Salandra, and Sonnino displayed growing independence of Giolitti's parliamentary majority which opposed intervention.

Giolitti, secure in his control of the Italian bureaucracy and the Chamber of Deputies, underestimated the ability of interventionist forces to change public opinion. If Mussolini had felt ill at ease with the Church and Giolitti when he espoused the neutralist cause, he must have found the interventionists even more disturbing to his intellectual consistency and self-respect. They included the republicans, whose hatred of the socialists in Mussolini's native Romagna often sought release in violence and murder; the radicals; the Reformist Socialists whom Mussolini had ousted from the Socialist Party in 1912; and also the freemasons whom Mussolini had excommunicated in 1914. The crusading experience and zeal of this opposition should have given Giolitti cause for alarm. He could count upon the votes of the country's deputies, *La Stampa* of

247

Turin, *Il Mattino* of Naples, various Catholic and socialist local newspapers, and fresh publications aided by German advertising funds. But the interventionists, principally through their masonic connections, exerted influence over the important mass circulation newspapers of the country.

Still blunt in a month when sentiment was running in the direction of war, Giolitti thought that he could cut down Salandra's independence by publishing a letter on February 2, 1915 which urged the good sense of continued negotiation with Austria. He knew that Cavour had brought more important territorial prizes to Piedmont through diplomatic negotiations than Garibaldi and Mazzini had added through war and upheaval. Giolitti must have counted upon the evocative undercurrents of his appeal, for that past master of domestic bargaining and candor stated quite simply that Italy could acquire "a good deal" without going to war. To ardent interventionists, this suggestion, couched in the down-to-earth colloquial word, *"parecchio,"* seemed ignoble, for it extended to international affairs, at a time when men sacrificed themselves daily for their ideals on the battlefields of Europe, the shameless Giolittian system.[22]

The followers of Giolitti voted for the Salandra government even as late as March 1915. If Giolitti had reassumed control then, his well-known adherence to neutrality would have served as a signal to Austria that it would no longer be necessary to pay the price which Italy demanded. While he bided his time, the government pretended to bargain, still, with Germany and Austria, but signed a secret treaty with the Allies in London on April 26. On May 4, Italy repudiated the Triple Alliance. Giolitti has claimed in his *Memoirs* that Salandra kept him in ignorance of the commitment that Italy would go to war against the Central Powers a month after the signing of the treaty. Supposedly in ignorance of this already determined future event, Giolitti returned to Rome, after spending the Easter holidays in Piedmont, during the first part of May. To signify their intention of following his lead, 320 members of the Chamber of Deputies called upon Giolitti and left their visiting cards. This maneuver would open the way for Giolitti, once Parliament came into session again and before Salandra could plunge Italy into war, to cause the downfall of the government and to take over the premiership again. Giolitti would then negotiate with Prince von Bülow to acquire, without loss of life or property, Italy's territorial desires.

Salandra's interventionist policies now seemed doomed. But Giolitti, with the votes of an absolute parliamentary majority in his pocket, forgot that he had dominated Italian politics through his uncanny sense of shifts in the life of his time. True enough, the crowds at the railroad stations during Giolitti's trip from Turin to Rome had demonstrated against him and might have served as warning, but he probably judged these hostile group feelings as unrepresentative of Italian public opinion and less than spontaneous. He may also have deemed it unnecessary and unwise to consider the piazza rather than the Chamber of Deputies. Convinced that he knew best how to obtain the largest concessions for Italy at the least national expense, Giolitti discounted the power of eloquence, soft-headed idealism, and the ever-present compulsion among Italians to violent behavior. By May 5, he began to sense their force. On that day, D'Annunzio declaimed his oration, *Sagra,* at the unveiling of a commemorative monument to Garibaldi and his Thousand at Quarto near Genoa. D'Annunzio roused the crowd to a feverish pitch of enthusiasm. His example inspired Mussolini, Corridoni, and other nationalists to action on their own elsewhere in Italy during these last days before the declaration of war.

Although Parliament had not assembled as yet, Salandra knew its will and offered his resignation on May 11. Victor Emmanuel went through the ceremonial rites of interviewing various political figures to obtain advice concerning the composition of a ministry which would meet parliamentary approval. This ceremony lasted from May 11 to May 15. During this interval, D'Annunzio made a triumphal entry into Rome. The nationalists, who had filled the railroad station to hiss Giolitti at the beginning of May, now gave the patriotic Apostle of Beauty an adoring welcome and chanted for the death of Giolitti. Hostile crowds roamed the streets and invaded the Chamber of Deputies itself. In other cities, nationalist leaders employed the same techniques to incite the people against the neutralists. Giolitti and his followers, never before faced with the manifestations of violence against themselves, succumbed to the will of the streets. The Socialist Party, the labor unions, and the Church stood aside. The interventionists ruled everywhere. On May 18, Victor Emmanuel took action which forewarned the fascist future. For the first time since the foundation of the Kingdom, a monarch listened to the shouts of demonstrators, disregarded the parliamentary majority, and invited Salandra to remain in office as Prime Minister. Salandra then brought the Chamber of Deputies into session. Less than two weeks before, some 320 members had expressed firm loyalty to Giolitti. Now, on May 24, 1915, they voted overwhelmingly for the entrance of Italy into World War I on the side of the Allies.

Croce has described with his wonted eloquence the troubled months of Italy's neutrality. He could not dismiss the minority status of the interventionists, the blatancy and artificiality of their clamor, the flagrant manipulation of public opinion, the resort to rule by the mob, and the final thwarting of the will of Parliament. But he managed to impart nobility to these sordid events, thereby simultaneously satisfying both his urge to patriotism and the idealistic interpretation of Italy's modern history. According to him, Italy declared war "with the steadfast fervour of one who has at last chosen her predestined path, after being torn by doubts . . . ." Although he admitted the unsavoury conduct of the nationalists and D'Annunzio, Croce could still find the scholarly courage to write: "It was as if Italy were under an inspiration, which impelled her to play the part in the human drama assigned to her by the logic of history, or, as the popular language of the time put it, as if she were driven by fate."[23]

If the nationalists could have transformed their energy and ardor over-night into well-equipped, efficient Italian troops, and if the rugged battle front in the Alps could have lent itself to quick victories, the Salandra government might have retained the glittering reputation it amassed at the moment of triumph over Giolitti. Then, it rose up in the enthusiastic public mind as a fresh array of national forces against the stale parliamentary combinations and bureaucratic arrangements with which Giolitti had ruled the country for so long and so deplorably. But for two years, instead, Italian armies fought eleven battles on the Isonzo, never advancing toward the positions held by the Austrians at Gorizia and Tolmino more than ten or twelve miles. Military stalemate could not conjure up electrifying victories. Without them, the simple wear and tear of time exposed the Salandra government for what it was: a makeshift device without any firm hold upon the people or upon the principal organized groups of the nation.

The absence of Giolitti's maligned system now began to tell since nothing had been created, except words, to take its place. Many of Giolitti's prefects and subprefects still administered local affairs. The clergy showed no more enthusiasm for the war than Giolitti's provincial officials. Pope Benedict XV (1854–1922, pope 1914–1922), as early as July 30, 1915, appealed for peace and then followed up this early plea, which earned him a pro-German reputation, with informal approaches to the warring nations. Friends of the Vatican went beyond lack of enthusiasm for the war to agitate actively for peace. The socialists abided by the instructions which Lazzari, the head of the Party, had sent out to all branches when Italy declared war upon Austria: "Neither go along, nor sabotage" ("*Nè aderire nè sabotare*"). Discontent began to spread even among those who supported the war wholeheartedly, especially among patriots who wished to see Italy fighting for democratic principles and not for spoils. They regarded the policy of limited warfare firmly held by Salandra and General Luigi Cadorna (1850–1928), the commander-in-chief, as responsible for the growing national uneasiness about the war. Giolitti's deputies recovered their spirit and brought down the government in June 1916. Paolo Boselli (1838–1932), old, eloquent, and patriotic, became Prime Minister. On August 28, 1916, Italy finally declared war upon Austria's ally, Germany. Boselli retained Sonnino as Foreign Minister, but widened the character of his cabinet to include former neutralists, as well as a strong early interventionist, Leonida Bissolati, who insisted that Italy renounce any claims to territories occupied by peoples like the Jugoslavs who were fighting the common enemy. Bissolati's position created a new cleavage in Italian politics to replace the former rift between interventionists and neutralists: the renouncers (*rinunciatari*) and those who insisted upon the full measure of concessions granted by the Treaty of London. Its terms, while still presumably secret, offered excellent opportunity for heated public discussion. Among the most influential renouncers were Gaetano Salvemini, Giovanni Amendola, and G. A. Borgese, collaborators of the *Corriere della Sera* (*Evening Courier*), the world-famous newspaper of Milan.

By May 1917, Turati and Treves had re-established their influence among the socialists. The Party drew up a postwar program of astonishingly unrealistic moderation. It called for the establishment of an Italian Republic, a single house of parliament elected by universal suffrage, unhampered civil liberties, the election of judges, a full-scale system of social insurance, land reclamation, and widespread public works projects. The reformists might have foreseen that even conservatives — frightened by the inevitably heady aftermath of successful warfare when citizens feel their strength and demand their reward — could be expected to find these demands reasonable enough. Surely, it should have been apparent that such piecemeal and sensible proposals would have little psychological and economic appeal to Italian workers who had learned, for the first time during the prosperous war years, the daily meaning of steady employment. Then, too, in the event that Italy did not emerge from the war with a sure feeling of national accomplishment, its discontented masses would certainly toss aside with scorn programs for mild improvements.

Five months later, in October 1917, the disastrous campaign of Caporetto began. In that same autumn, a minority group of revolutionaries under Nikolai Lenin (Vladimir Ilyich Ulyanov, 1870–1924) grasped control of the Czar's empire. These two events dominated the course of Italy's future national life.

Reinforced by six divisions of German troops, nine Austrian divisions

251

broke through the Italian lines on the first day of the attack, October 24, 1917, and advanced ten full miles. The enemy forces had accomplished these gains through the use of poison gas under the cover of heavy fog. Within three days, they drove the demoralized Italian troops through the hill country and almost cut them off from crossing the Tagliamento River. The Piave River now became the fixed line of battle. On November 3 and 4, French and British soldiers joined the Italians to reinforce this stand. During the Caporetto campaign, the Italian army lost 300,000 men as prisoners and an even larger number deserted. Discipline broke down at the front when the Italian peasant-soldier, bored and exasperated by the tedium of long waits in the trenches broken only by bursts of action in inconclusive battles, fled from the scenes of rout, refused to stop, either at point of order or point of gun, and began his slow private retreat homeward. This national disgrace started with the dissension between General Luigi Cadorna, the stalwart clericalist, and General Luigi Capello (1859–1941), the foremost freemason in the Italian high command. Their friction persisted until the very eve of the enemy attack, with unbelievable disregard of full knowledge concerning Austrian-German preparations for battle. General Cadorna, perhaps seeking to minimize his own responsibility for the collapse of the Italian army, damaged Italy's pride and strained its none-too-compact social cohesion by referring to the demoralized behavior of the troops and deserters as a "military strike."[24]

On October 25, 1917, after the Caporetto disaster had plunged the country into despair, the Boselli cabinet resigned and four days later Victor Emmanuel Orlando (1860–1952), a former socialist from Palermo, became Prime Minister. Francesco Saverio Nitti, the brilliant economist and administrator, joined the cabinet as its most influential member. Giolitti resumed attendance at the Chamber of Deputies. The leading political figures of the country united to urge the nation to resist and to vindicate its honor. On November 7, the humane General Armando Diaz (1861–1928) replaced General Cadorna and set to work to restore the morale of the Italian troops. Turati himself did not hesitate to declare publicly that Monte Grappa, the pivot upon which Italian defenses hinged behind the Piave, was no less sacred to socialists than it was to other Italians. But Turati, on whose lips the word, *Patria* (Fatherland), had formed in an upsurge of patriotic feeling never expressed by socialists before, did not reflect the sentiments of all members of the Party. The war had precluded socialist congresses and the perennial factions of the Party had not shouted themselves into stalemated compromises for the sake of proletarian unity. The left-wing socialists, headed by

Lazzari and Nicola Bombacci (1879–1945), who, like Mussolini, came from the Romagna, held views diametrically opposed to those of Turati. They saw in Caporetto and the October Russian Revolution the hastening process of dialectical materialism and urged the Italian deserter, gun in hand, to follow the example of his Russian brother and to bring about the end of capitalism in Italy. This inflammatory message failed to arouse the fugitives who merely wished to escape from front-line boredom and discipline and not from capitalism. Early in 1918, the government imprisoned both Bombacci and Lazzari.

General Diaz restored the dignity of the Italian army through singular ability and shrewdness and at last snatched victory from the Austrians late in June 1918 when the enemy lost 100,000 men in a desperate effort to cross the Piave. Between October 24 and November 4, the Italians, after considerable Allied prodding, advanced to Vittorio Veneto, captured several hundred thousand prisoners, marched at last into Trieste, and occupied Fiume. Despite these final feats of arms, Italy could take no real pride in its military achievements at war's end. Wrangling between the renouncers and the strict adherents to the Treaty of London divided the country. The controversy emitted large drafts of irony. Regardless of the renouncers' high principles, or their opponents' appeal to realism in a grab-bag world, the most compelling argument belonged not to Italians but to their Allies who refused to take Italy's contribution to ultimate victory seriously. Disillusion also spread as the effort involved in restoring national honor after the disgrace at Caporetto lost its gleaming significance in the harsh pursuits of peace when Italians could no longer avoid the truth: the rejection of Giolitti's system of political accommodation left Italy the prey to chaos.

Giolitti's rule had been despised not merely by irresponsible elements of society which are always present in every nation, but also by the leading intellectuals and the freest spirits of Italy who had rejected Giolitti's philosophy of government as immoral at its very source and unworthy of a modern nation. A union of all Italians who believed in the strengthening of their own democracy through its reinforcement everywhere in the world might have replaced successfully Giolitti's substitute for a large and responsible middle class. The Socialist Party emerged as the dominant political force in Italy during the years from 1918 to 1920. Had the moderates within the Party prevailed, they could have supplied the very political cohesion which Italy most needed. But at this dangerous moment of history, the Socialist Party, always torn between reformists and revolutionaries, found itself even more rent by revolutionary zeal and loathing of democratic means. Despite clear triumph at the polls, the

Socialist Party disdained responsibility. In a final act of renunciation immeasurably more fraught with peril than their earlier rejections of Giolitti's invitation to share power in 1903 and 1911, they made "the great refusal" out of the same cowardice which Dante ascribed to Pope Celestine V in Canto III of *The Inferno:* senseless dogmatism which masked the deep fear of the revolutionaries to assume power. Mussolini did not impose fascism upon the Italian people. The failure of the socialists to offer them either revolution or reform invited Mussolini, or any other leader without scruples and with zest for power, to take over the government which lay waiting, unpre-empted.

In time of international peace, Italy found no domestic peace. The Treaty of London, which the Bolsheviks uncovered in the archives of the Russian Foreign Ministry and published, aroused the indignation of Woodrow Wilson (1856–1924), the champion of idealism in international relations. Orlando, the Prime Minister, insisted upon a literal interpretation of the treaty, while Bissolati, a member of Orlando's cabinet, headed Italy's renouncers. Sonnino, the Foreign Minister, remained the most consistent and ardent champion of Italy's full share of territorial gains as a reward for its war efforts. At the Peace Conference, which opened in Paris on January 18, 1919, the Big Three — Woodrow Wilson, David Lloyd George (1863–1945), and Georges Clemenceau (1841–1929) — rejected Italy's claims, now broadened beyond those of the treaty, on the ground that one of Wilson's Fourteen Points, the principle of national determination, precluded benefits in the Adriatic at the cost of the new Jugoslavian nation. At the various conference tables, during 1919 and 1920, Italy gathered up the South Tyrol, Trieste, Istria, part of Carniola, and several Dalmatian Islands from Austria and the Dodecanese Islands and Rhodes from Turkey. The Allies had to leave the question of Fiume, which Italy occupied, to direct negotiations between Italy and Jugoslavia since Wilson's support of Jugoslavia had caused Italy to withdraw from the Peace Conference for a time. As a result of the Treaty of Rapallo in November 1920, Fiume became an independent state and Jugoslavia received the entire Dalmatian coast except the town of Zara.

Throughout these international and national bickerings, Orlando and Sonnino had concentrated so intently upon islands, coastlines, and cities that they had utterly failed to think in terms of economic gains. They neglected to conclude advantageous trade treaties, especially with countries which exported iron and coal, so vital to Italy's expanding industries, and to stipulate favorable long-term loans. By renouncing its diplomatic claims to territorial concessions in exchange for economic benefits, Italy would have gained increased moral stature as well. Moreover, such evidence of international good will might have induced the world to recognize at full worth Italy's enormous wartime sacrifices. The nation lost 460,000 men in the war. Almost 950,000 had been wounded and 530,000 had been taken prisoner. This staggering expenditure of men and material wealth had left Italy deeply in debt and saddled with a cost of living which soared constantly upward. For her military efforts, bottomed upon motives no more sordid than those of her Allies, Italy received only 9,000 square miles of land with a population of 1,600,000.

On January 18, 1919, the very day when the Allied Powers met in Paris to forge the new peace, the Italian Popular Party (Partito Popolare Italiano), the first Catholic party to appear on Italian soil, launched an *Appeal* and published its program and constitution. The times were auspicious for initiating a Catholic party. The fear of revolutionary socialism compelled conservative Catholics to favor a nonconfessional party. Under normal circumstances, they would have insisted upon a strictly Catholic political organization. Although the Vatican itself did not actively support the formation of the Popular Party, it interposed no objections. The leader of the new Party, Don Luigi Sturzo (1871–1959), a brilliant Sicilian priest possessed of remarkable political acumen, did not allow futile discussions of dogma to endanger social and economic aims. In this purpose, Don Sturzo again found help in the mood of the times for the views of the Church on property had changed considerably during the past generation, largely as the result of the theoretical work accomplished by Monsignors Geremia Bonomelli (1831–1914) and Giuseppe Toniolo (1845–1918).

After 1895, these Christian thinkers had drawn a distinction between the divine right of property and the manner in which human beings employed that right in particular instances. Don Sturzo, both shrewd and keen, profited from the mistakes of Don Romolo Murri (1870–1944) and did not incur the displeasure of the Vatican by attempting to modernize the dogma of the Church for contemporary minds through a reinterpretation of basic creeds in terms of mystic symbolism. Rather, Don Sturzo concentrated on principles which did not run afoul of Leo XIII's *Rerum novarum* and other social, economic, and political pronouncements by the Church. The Popular Party pressed hard upon the hitherto exclusive position occupied by the moderate socialists. It called for civil and political liberties; universal suffrage, including the vote for women; proportional representation; an elective senate; and decentralization of government by leaving more power in the hands of regional and local authorities. The Party also favored freedom of religion, education, association, and economic enterprise. It believed that groups had the right to organize, even by class, a marked departure from the rigorous Catholic adherence, earlier, to corporative principles of collaborative economic organization; that the integrity of the family had to be maintained; that private property could best be perpetuated by strengthening small landholdings; and that the Church had to encourage the formation of labor unions. Internationally, Don Sturzo lined up the Party behind pacifism, for he was not unmindful of the revulsion to the war which now overtook the Italian people. At the first congress of the Popular Party in June 1919, the delegates denounced the materialistic spirit which had pervaded the sessions of the Paris Conference and arraigned the insurgent mood of nationalism which manifested itself everywhere. The Italian Confederation of Workers (Confederazione Italiana dei Lavoratori–C.I.L.), founded in March 1918, associated itself with the Popular Party in the manner of the General Confederation of Labor and the Socialist Party.[25]

On November 30, 1918, the directive council of the General Confederation of Labor proclaimed the principal demands of the Italian working class. The program foreshadowed the confusion and leftward shift which were to plague the labor and socialist movements in the coming months. Most of its features resembled the platform which both the Socialist Party and the C.G.L. had already approved in May 1917: a democratic republic; abolition of the Senate; direct, equal, and universal suffrage; freedom of association, assembly, strikes, and propaganda; a complete system of social security; wide extension of collective labor agreements; minimum-wage legislation; a vast program of public works; expropriation of uncultivated or inefficiently managed lands; immediate and simultaneous disarmament; abolition of tariff boundaries; and the foundation of an international federation of nations. But the resolution sponsored by the C.G.L.'s directive council in November 1918 did contain one wholly novel idea for socialist circles. It called for a Constituent Assembly (La Costituente), a cry also raised by the new-formed veterans organizations. The returning soldiers seemed to have in mind the Mazzinian and Republican dream of a supreme body, elected by universal suffrage, to articulate the future constitution of the Italian State as though it were the first day of creation. The C.G.L.'s concept, while unclear in precise meaning since the partisans of various socialist currents interpreted the functions of the Constituent Assembly in different ways, nevertheless anticipated a continuing national body comparable with the Chamber of Deputies in importance. The Assembly would assume responsibility for social and economic legislation. Based upon an ascending order of syndical organizations, of which the chambers of labor formed the most important links, the Assembly would strive for the gradual socialization of land with the aid of peasant cooperatives and for the eventual control of production by factory workers.

The program did not differ greatly, in substance, from the goals set by the Popular Party. Egalitarian pressures permeated the social climate. As early as 1916, when dissatisfaction assailed the troops grown restive during the stalemate in the fastnesses of the Alps, Salandra circulated a promise that peasants would receive land after they returned from the war. With demobilization, Popular Party leaders and priests did not hesitate to lead peasant veterans, disappointed not to find land awaiting them, in processions to occupy uncultivated *latifondi*. Moreover, in the elective Senate demanded by the Popular Party, the various administrative, intellectual, economic, and occupational groups of the nation were to have direct voice. Mussolini neither invented nor monopolized the medieval idea of the corporative structure of society now springing up, out of postwar chaos, as a radically new principle of human governance.

On December 12, 1918, the directorate of the Socialist Party, certain beyond even momentary pause of the imminent triumph of the international proletariat, issued an Order of the Day demanding the immediate creation of an Italian Socialist Republic under the dictatorship of the laboring masses. The resolution also called for the socialization of all means of production and exchange; the distribution of vital necessities through communal cooperative organizations; the abolition of military conscription; immediate disarmament; the municipalization of housing, hospitals, and other social services; and the transformation of government bureaucracy by placing it completely in the hands of its clerical staffs. Later, on December 22 and 23, the C.G.L. joined the socialist deputies, the League of Socialist Communes, and the Union of Railroad Workers at the large proletarian congress convoked by the directorate of the Socialist Party at Bologna. The delegates recognized the need to push at once for the Party's immediate program: demobilization, the withdrawal of Italian soldiers from revolutionary Russia, the restoration of civil liberties, and universal amnesty for political and military prisoners. As for the Party's call to agitate for its maximum program as well, the delegates resolved that their organizations alone possessed the competence to take action after the convocation of special congresses. The C.G.L. representatives still pressed for the Constituent Assembly.

In March 1919, the directorate of the Socialist Party severed its fraternal bonds with the Second International of Amsterdam and heralded its allegiance to the Third International, the Comintern of Moscow. During the parliamentary recess in April, the Turatian deputies who had

257

previously judged the program of the C.G.L. too extreme and had voted against it, reversed themselves and now demanded the creation of a body like the proposed Constituent Assembly. The resignation of the Orlando cabinet in June and the constitution of the first Francesco Nitti ministry failed to abate national unrest. A socialist conference at Southport, England, earlier in the year, had decreed an international general strike on July 20 and 21 to protest against Allied intervention in Russia. The strike hit Europe with less than fearsome force when the French Confederation of Labor failed to participate and the Italian railroad workers union also withdrew. The holiday spirit which invested the strike in Italy did not mean that the country had become less turbulent. On the contrary, throughout the month of July crowds everywhere demonstrated against the rising cost of living. In the Romagna and Tuscany, the inspiration of Russia led to the formation of soviets for the distribution of food. The central ambivalence of the Socialist Party manifested itself immediately. The General Confederation of Labor, far from revolutionary, remained in character when it warned the soviets against the fallacy of attempting to solve complex economic problems through the simple seizure of goods. However, *Avanti!*, the mouthpiece of the Party's revolutionary directorate which had voted to join the Comintern, took a surprising stand. It catered to the crowd by conceding that the mob had the right to gratify its wishes, but cautioned the masses that the rising cost of living could not be lowered through mob action. At a time when hungry families took the matter of eating into their own hands, the official voice of the Socialist Party, controlled by fervent left-wingers, lectured to them on the principles of economic orthodoxy. This predilection to confuse words with deeds, to love words and fear deeds, forecast the future inability of the socialists to translate the revolutionary situation of the autumn of 1920 into the new society of their inflamed rhetoric.

On March 23, 1919, Mussolini founded the Italian Combat Bands (Fasci Italiani di Combattimento) at a small meeting in a hall in Milan which faced the Piazza San Sepolcro. The anniversary of this event which, at the time, only Mussolini's *Popolo d'Italia* noted, became one of the principal holidays in the fascist calendar. The title, *Sansepolcrista*, later formed the highest fascist honor, reserved for the founding fathers of the New Italy. Mussolini designed a program for his sparse followers in 1919 not dissimilar to the reforms advocated by both the General Confederation of Labor and the Popular Party. The fascists declared themselves in favor of universal suffrage for both sexes, a Constituent Assembly, national syndical councils, partnership for workers in the management of industry, the expropriation of large estates, a capital levy, a tax of 85% on war profits, the reduction of the size of the army to guarantee its defensive character, and the confiscation of ecclesiastical wealth by the State. Obviously, Mussolini could not aspire to revolutionary distinction with these moderate demands. The fiery insurrectionists of the Socialist Party, led by Lazzari and Bombacci, far outstripped him in demagoguery by calling down the wrath of the workers upon all politicians who had supported the reprehensible war effort and by demanding the immediate installation of the dictatorship of the proletariat. To be sure, Benito Mussolini had not willfully shifted political allegiances and cut himself off from seemingly triumphant socialism only to reach the age of 36 in 1919 purged of all ambition to dominate Italian labor. Yet, in September 1919, it seemed clear that Gabriele D'Annunzio, the impetuous nationalist turned more feverish still, ruled the restless spirit of Italy.

Many countries dote on their adolescents and pamper them with leisure and comfort, but Latin countries, and Italy is no exception, indulge them by taking their youthful political notions and demonstrations seriously. In Italy during 1919, malcontent mounted among workers dismissed from war jobs which had evaporated in the sunlight of peace. To their disaffection, veterans, returning to find their former jobs occupied by men who regarded the entire war as a travesty of patriotism imposed upon fools, added their own. Deserters, who numbered in the scores of thousands, contributed their sense of guilt and hostility to the growing unrest. Then, too, there were the *Arditi,* those ardent and vain young men who had known special status in the Italian army. Used for sporadic but hazardous missions, during the intervals between exploits they enjoyed uncommon privileges and avoided the harsh discipline suffered by soldiers in the front-line trenches. Not only were they proud, self-important, and spoiled, but they were also idolized by adolescents who, during the war, had been too young for service. These hero-worshippers felt deprived, for fate had snatched from them the glory of fighting for their country. Filled with shame at the home comforts enjoyed while their brave brothers had risked their lives for the Fatherland, they took comfort from the daydream that, had they been old enough, they too might have been *Arditi.*

D'Annunzio easily exploited these tindery youthful elements in 1919 for he had publicized with the skill of a poet his exploits as a daredevil pilot. On September 12, 1919, D'Annunzio, who had gathered up a band of young volunteers with no property or privileges to forfeit by acting as rebels, seized Fiume. The Treaty of London had not included Fiume as part of the Allied bribe, but when the war ended, the Italian population of Fiume seized control of the city. Shortly thereafter, the Allied Powers designated Fiume an international city and French, British, and Italian troops moved in to garrison the port. D'Annunzio's coup met little resistance. Some ships of the Italian navy supported his venture, at the risk of treason to the Italian State. Once he marched into Fiume, the garrisons withdrew. D'Annunzio, with the born luck of a star performer, found ships in the harbor filled with food and other goods useful to the needs of the state he proposed to create. He installed himself in the finest Renaissance palace of the city. Although the Italian government disavowed his deeds, D'Annunzio's theatrical stratagem and subsequent experiment went unmolested for fifteen months because the Prime Minister, Nitti, held professorial views of government and power. He clearly recognized the destiny of the Socialist and Popular Parties as the two great mass forces of future Italian politics. He also accurately gauged the intensity of the nationalist fervor sweeping the country. Since the national elections scheduled for November 16 had not yet determined the proportionate strength of these parties and currents, and since Nitti believed that political action free of repression represented the only alternative to the Giolittian system, he allowed D'Annunzio to defy the government at Rome.

Europe and Italy laughed at D'Annunzio's excesses, but he succeeded in flouting constitutional government, never strong enough in Italy to risk ridicule in perilous times, and supplied Mussolini, unwittingly, with the future ceremonial accoutrements of fascism. He proclaimed the Constitution of the Province of Fiume, written in gibberish. Its mystical phraseology extolled the fullest liberty for the people and yet subjected them to "hierarchic organization and authority." In the *Statuto* of Italy's adored poet, lover, and pilot, the basic tenets of the Corporative State again asserted themselves, as they had already in the plans of the General Confederation of Labor, the parliamentary socialists, the Popular Party, and Mussolini's fascists. D'Annunzio provided for ten corporations. The first nine harbored recognizable groups like laborers, managers and technicians, and shopkeepers. But the tenth was "reserved for the mysterious forces of progress and adventure." The document concluded with these words: "In the pauses of music is heard the silence of the tenth corporation."[26]

Mussolini learned from the D'Annunzio adventure that sovereign government did not always affirm its authority even when clearly challenged. He declared immediately in *Popolo d'Italia*: "Our government is not at Rome, it is at Fiume."[27] This lesson, important enough, took secondary place to further instruction which widened Mussolini's demagogic vistas by broadening his techniques. Previous to Fiume, Mussolini had aroused his audiences through passionate oratory which churned the emotions. But he had never partaken of the fruit which revealed the psychological uses of ceremony and display. D'Annunzio had formed his ardent young men into legions, evocative of classic Roman glory, and had dressed them in uniforms which suited them to perfection: not so stiff as to be uncomfortable and to remind them of the discipline of war, but sufficiently laden with medals and insignia to impart dignity when called for and to overwhelm those not privileged to form part of this élite order. D'Annunzio had also taught his troupe the so-called Roman salute that he and Mussolini confused with the symbolic gesture of sculptured ancient orators in the act of arresting attention; ritual slogans which they repeated in chorus; an inflated rhetoric which sustained them; and the devil-may-care slogan, *Me ne frego!*, best rendered by the phrases, "To hell with it!" or "I don't give a damn!" D'Annunzio disguised operatic display as statecraft and appeared ridiculous to men of common sense (as the Commandant of Fiume, he sent fraternal greetings to Moscow), but Mussolini, a man of uncommon sense, discerned in D'Annunzio's half-mad catering to the emotional needs of the new generation the basic elements of a revolution which D'Annunzio himself would lack the ability to pull off.

The national congress of the Socialist Party met at Bologna from October 5 to 8, 1919 in the midst of social confusion engendered by economic dislocation, unemployment, the street brawls of black-shirted *Arditi*, the firing and destruction of the Milan office of *Avanti!* in April 1919, D'Annunzio's Heavenly City, the proclamations by all parties of grand designs for human affairs, and pervading the life and work of the entire peninsula, the far-off, unobserved, dimly understood, and electrifying Russian Revolution. In little more than a month after the socialist congress, the nation would be going to the polls to vote under the provisions of the 1919 electoral law. Don Sturzo had proposed proportional representation and both the General Confederation of Labor and the parliamentary socialists had approved this reform because they believed it would ward off the resurgence of Giolitti's despised arrangements for ruling nationally through local bargains. Since each party had to present a national list of candidates, the assembled socialists needed first of all to determine policy and then to select as candidates those men who espoused that policy.

The Russian Revolution and not the gradual disintegration of the Italian State ruled every turn of discussion at Bologna. Since the whole world stood on the brink of socialist salvation, the Genoa program of 1892, long the basic charter of Italian socialism, now appeared outdated and due for revision. The communist-abstentionists at the far-left wished to transform the Party into the Italian Communist Party and to join the Third International. This group also insisted upon a policy of complete intransigence and refused to participate in the general elections. The maximalist-unitarians stood at the right. They backed the maximum program of 1900, but also pleaded for the preservation of proletarian unity. Turati, although the foremost champion of the minimum program, allied himself with this group because of its desire to keep the Party from splitting asunder. His position was doubly anomalous because the maximalist-unitarians, while emphasizing matters of internal concern, did not venerate the Bolshevik revolution one *"Viva"* less than the communist-abstentionists. The maximalist-electionists formed the center coalition of the Party and won 48,411 votes, as compared to 3,417 votes for the left and 14,880 for the right. Stripped of Marxist jargon, the program of the center exhumed the old formula of compromise between the revolutionaries and the reformists. To please the revolutionaries, the majority program enunciated the doctrine that existing bourgeois institutions could not aid the socialist revolution; consequently, the Party had to set up parallel proletarian institutions, creating a state within a state. Since the maximalist-electionist resolution, as approved by the socialist congress, declared that "the proletariat must resort to the use of force to defend itself against bourgeois violence, to conquer power, and to consolidate revolutionary conquests," ordinary logic should have compelled the delegates to adopt the attitude of the communist-abstentionists and to eschew the elections completely. But to keep the Party intact, the revolutionaries gave way to the reformists and approved participation in the coming elections. Yet once again the socialists resorted to verbal acrobatics in the name of fictitious class unity; once more, the compromise resulted only in immobilization and abstention from action. As if to propitiate the revolutionary gods for the sins of concession, all factions voted by acclamation for the adherence of the Italian Socialist Party to the Third International. Nicola Bombacci became the Party secretary.[28]

The Socialist Party emerged from the November elections as the largest party in Italy. More than 1,840,000 voters sent 156 socialist deputies to Parliament. Experts estimated that if proportional representation had not obtained, the socialists might have captured some 70 more seats. The success of the Popular Party astonished the country. More than 1,175,000 Italians returned 100 popularists to the Chamber. The traditional bloc of men and parties which supported the liberal state lost its majority since it won only 239 of the 252 remaining seats. Mussolini also stood for election in Milan where the fascist list of candidates, the only one presented in all Italy, attracted 4,795 votes. Five years after the birth of Mussolini's interventionism and the *People of Italy*, and eight months after the foundation of the *fasci*, the movement still drifted through wilderness in search of political life. Several days following the elections, Nitti ordered the arrest of Mussolini on charges of plotting against the security of the State, but the authorities soon released him. At the opening of Parliament, when King Victor Emmanuel began to read the Speech from the Throne, most of the socialist deputies arose and left the Chamber singing *The Red Flag* (*Bandiera Rossa*). The socialists who stayed on showed their more respectful contempt for the Monarch by shouting: "Long live the Socialist Republic." The socialists enacted this scene, degrading to Parliament, in the fourth month of D'Annunzio's occupation of Fiume.

The Nitti government lasted on, without will or power, until June 1920. Prices continued to soar. Senseless violence became part of daily existence. Strikes broke out everywhere, without plan, pattern, or goal. These unopposed strikes won wage increases and steepened the inflationary spiral. D'Annunzio's neo-Roman circus continued on at Fiume. Italy's major crops failed. The state budget, already severely strained by war indebtedness, became seriously imbalanced when the government found it expedient to subsidize the importation of wheat in order to keep the price of bread down. Hard beset war-born industries, especially in the metal-mechanical fields, demanded state aid. The national council of the Socialist Party voted overwhelmingly for the immediate creation of workmen's councils to parallel the example of Russian soviets. The Nitti government gave legal approval to land seizure by the peasants, but a land reform bill, proposed by the Popular Party, never became law. The socialists fought the Popular Party's land reform program at every turn even though landowners in Veneto, the Po Valley, and North-Central Italy, where the popularists predominated, branded it as White Bolshevism. The socialists, who had the favor of Nitti and could have controlled him if they had merely consented to become part of his government, thereby bending Italy's entire future to their will, refused to act. They allowed anarchy to prevail, convinced that somehow, out of anarchy, socialist revolution would automatically flare up into reality. Already by March 1920, the vacuum created by the socialists began to fill slowly: a congress of industrialists resolved in favor of a government strong enough to maintain order and provide efficient service.

Nitti's position became daily more untenable. Don Sturzo has himself remarked that "Nitti had the Popular Party as his lawful wife and the Socialist Party as his mistress; it was a *ménage à trois.*"[29] On June 9, the popularists, surfeited with this one-sided arrangement, forced out of office the Premier who had given free reign to inflation, strikes, and the illegal spectacle at Fiume, while, at the same time, tripling the strength of the *carabinieri* and creating a new police corps, the Royal Guard (Guardia Regia), which incurred universal hatred. In this hour of crisis, when the Italian State seemed to be falling away, those who wished to rescue Italy for democracy implored the return of Giolitti. Now 78 years old, the master of parliamentary compromise took office and shrewdly included in his cabinet Ivanoe Bonomi, the interventionist, as War Minister; Count Carlo Sforza (1873–1952), a diplomat of ancient lineage with an intensely international view of world affairs, as Foreign Minister; and Benedetto Croce, the world-famous philosopher and man of letters, as Minister of Education. Giolitti proposed to reach a settlement with Jugoslavia regarding Italy's position in the Adriatic, to clear D'Annunzio out of Fiume, to strengthen the fiscal position of the State, to aid the war industries of North Italy, to deal effectively with disorder as it arose, to confiscate war profits, and to institute an inquiry into public expenditures during the war — a project bound to stir up popular approval in all countries.

The first emergency of momentous consequence to confront Giolitti burst upon the nation when metal-mechanical workers, encouraged by F.I.O.M., the largest union in Italy, and supported by the Socialist Party, took possession of 280 plants in Milan during September 1920. As the movement spread to other communities, it affected about 500,000 men and women. At first, Mussolini championed the movement and proposed to its leaders united action against three enemies: the industrialists, the government, and the communist unions. The overture was rebuffed. The workers not only continued to occupy the plants, but also maintained production as long as raw materials and cash-on-hand held out. Revolution seemed imminent. Leading political figures with authority saw in Turati the least of Marxist evils and assured him that democratic liberals and many industrialists as well would look upon the formation of a socialist government under his leadership as the best way out of the dilemma in the North. Unfortunately, the confirmed revolutionaries, while not quite sure of what the situation required each step of the way except the familiar and comforting phrases of rebellion, nevertheless knew by rote that they could not countenance a revolution arranged through class collaboration and democratic procedures. The longer the occupation of the factories continued, neither the General Confederation of Labor nor the Socialist Party had the audacity to go forward or the good sense to retreat in a gesture of magnanimity through strength. Giolitti, in his *Memoirs*, makes his own strategy clear:

> Personally I was convinced from the outset that this experiment could not fail to prove to the workers that it was impossible to realize their ends without the necessary capital, technical training and commercial organization, especially as regards the purchase of raw material and the sale of products. So as far as I was concerned, this episode represented in another form, a repetition of the famous experiment attempted by the general strike in 1904, which after having caused such alarm proved its own futility. Accordingly I thought that the government could not do better than adopt the same policy which it had done on that occasion, that is, to let the experiment continue up to a certain point, so that the workers might convince themselves of the impracticability of their conceptions and also in order to prevent the ringleaders from throwing on others the blame of their failure.[30]

After eight weeks, the unions received from Giolitti the promise to constitute a mixed commission to make proposals to the government for reorganizing the metal-mechanical industries "on the principle of the workers sharing in the technical and financial control or administration of industrial enterprises." The workers then evacuated the factories.

Long experience of life may offer too many possible parallels to fresh events and Giolitti deceived himself in believing that the upheaval of 1920 would repeat the pattern of 1904. But in 1920, Giolitti, sagacious as ever, had proved too cunning. His undramatic watchful waiting and intervention at the precise psychological moment of fatigue and doubt convinced Italy's men of property that conservatives could successfully resist violent socialist demands. Giolitti had not foreseen this stiffening of attitude by industrialists and financiers. He also erred in his estimate of the political temper of the people, for he fully expected that the voters would reprimand the socialists for their resort to violence, as they had in 1904. Instead, during the municipal elections in the fall of 1920, when the parties contested the control of local councils in some 8,000 communes, the socialists established themselves as the majority force in over 2,000 and swept into power in nearly half the provincial councils. The socialists campaigned on the tenets enunciated by the national council of the Party: revolutionary expropriation could best be consummated by gaining predominance over as many organs of power as possible and replacing them by communistic organs at the propitious juncture. Candidates pledged themselves to perpetuate socialist hostility toward the State by administering the communes and provinces according to proletarian doctrine and by disregarding local tax limits set

265

by the State. Although these notions did not prevail in most communes with socialist-dominated councils, they found application in enough of them to substantiate the worst fears of property owners and men of wealth. They began to look for ways of combating both the socialists and the popularists who demanded land for the peasants and other agricultural reforms. To his surprise, therefore, when Giolitti brought the crisis in the North to a meek close, he found neither conservatives nor socialists ready for bargaining and compromise.

Giolitti proceeded next to deal with D'Annunzio. The Premier had aroused the ire of the nationalists soon after taking office: he ordered the evacuation of Albania because harassment by the population of the Italian forces stationed there made the miserable troops yearn for home and because fresh garrisons, gathered at Ancona and destined for Albania, mutinied and refused to embark. To rob this incident of its sting, Giolitti then staged a massive patriotic spectacle on the second anniversary of the armistice in November 1920. At the altar of that monstrously white mountain of marble overlooking the Piazza Venezia, Giolitti stood at the side of the King, surrounded by generals, and celebrated Italy's military victory. In December, after the November 12 Treaty of Rapallo established Fiume as an independent state and reassured Jugoslavia that Italy had no intention of pressing the claims of the Treaty of London, Giolitti moved against D'Annunzio. Until the day before operations were to begin, not a single member of the cabinet knew of Giolitti's plans. Troops, as well as a naval unit, advanced upon Fiume, killed a few legionnaires, and rapidly cleared the city of both its commandant and his followers. D'Annunzio's unresisting surrender discredited him as the leading nationalist of Italy. His fall from prestige redounded to Mussolini's advantage. His fascists remained calm during the move against Fiume and Giolitti is said to have rewarded their good behavior by providing needed funds to the *People of Italy*. As D'Annunzio's legionnaires returned to Italian life, many sought out Mussolini's Fasci di Combattimento. So, too, complete demobilization created a reservoir of veterans who could not readjust themselves to civilian life. They found their needs answered by the semimilitary organization and the violent idealism which Mussolini offered.

Mussolini must have sensed that socialist power had reached its zenith in the factory occupations of September and October 1920. He also felt the panic of the middle classes and their desire for revenge. On Sunday, November 19, the fascists challenged socialist strength in its Bologna stronghold and fought it out in the streets without interference by the ostensible forces of law and order. The fascists exploited rubber

truncheons and castor oil as their primary weapons and beat the socialists into retreat. Giolitti offered no objections to Mussolini's action squads
(*squadre d'azione*) because he considered their attempts to destroy the
political and economic organization of the socialists necessary insurance
against revolutionary threats. He failed to foresee the more dangerous consequences to the State of surrendering the maintenance of the public
peace to a private army. But other interests understood these implications
at once. The dramatic demonstration of brute strength advertised to
industrialists and large landowners that fascist violence could be more
than an end in itself. It could serve to moderate the infatuated
Bolsheviks who called for the destruction of Italy's economic and social
way of life. If Mussolini did not openly invite financial assistance by
fascist deeds of daring at Bologna, he employed the simplest and most
effective alternative for securing it.

The Socialist Party convened in a specially summoned session at Leghorn in January 1921. The Comintern had presented a document to the
Italian Socialist Party which came to be designated as the Twenty-one
Points. It arrived from Moscow in September 1920 just when the Revolution knocked at Italy's main door in the North and socialist leaders failed
to answer the summons to full revolt. The Third International laid
down twenty-one conditions to be satisfied by the Italian Socialist Party
before it could adhere to the world federation. After they were published in *Avanti!* on September 21, many socialists expressed indignation at
the undisguised dictation of terms to a party about whose history and
present situation the International had no intimate knowledge. Nevertheless, the directorate of the Party accepted the Twenty-one Points by
a majority of 7 to 5. This approval was tentative, however, since only the
national congress could provide an authoritative answer.

The delegates at Leghorn in 1921 surely must have known that a split
in the Socialist Party would eventually expose the nation's fragile democracy to the most virulent evil it had ever encountered. They could
not have been innocent of the fascists' goal. In North and Central Italy,
the Black Shirts had administered beatings to all but a few local branches
of the Party. Plainly, the fascists meant to exterminate the largest party
in Italy. During lesser crises in the past, the Party always managed at
least the appearance of official unity. Now, when in mortal danger, it
failed itself and Italy. The delegates had the choice of three motions. One
faction moved the complete acceptance of the Twenty-one Points. The
unitarian communists, in contrast to the pure communists who felt no
reservations, wanted the Party to belong to the Third International, but
not at the cost of party unity and not on dictated terms. The concentra-

tionists on the right demanded that the policy of the Socialist Party be determined in Italy and not in Moscow. The pure communists received some 58,000 votes, the unitarian communists about 98,000 votes, and the concentrationists approximately 14,000 votes. The pure communists hastened to withdraw from the Socialist Party. On January 21, 1921, the day after the congress of the Socialist Party in the Goldoni Theater at Leghorn adjourned, the intransigents, assembled in another theater at Leghorn, formed the Italian Communist Party and nominated its first central committee. Among the founding fathers were young men of keen intelligence and tireless fervor: Ruggiero Grieco, Umberto Terracini, Antonio Gramsci (1891-1937), founder on May 1, 1919 of the famous communist paper at Turin, *Ordine Nuovo* (*The New Order*), and spokesman of the Fiat workers, and Palmiro Togliatti (1893-   ), the future leader of Italian communism after World War II. Nicola Bombacci also joined the communists, but later became a fascist who attained prominence only with the advent of the Salò Republic, fascism's last gasp. Meanwhile, the center and right groups of the Socialist Party remained uneasily united until October 1922.

The fascists' revolution by blood, as Turati called their resort to truncheons and beatings, had somewhat sobered the socialists and their revolution by words. In defense, they sought protection by appealing to law and order as though they had not themselves practiced violence. Yet even now they could not down their revolutionary appetites and still hoped for anointment by the Third International. Costantino Lazzari, the perennial left-winger from the time of the foundation of the Workers Party in 1882, set off on a pilgrimage to Moscow to plead for the Socialist Party. He returned without the grace he sought.

With the socialists losing ground, Giolitti decided to hold general elections on May 15, 1921. He considered the country ripe for the repudiation of revolutionary socialism. He must have felt capable of dealing with fascist violence in good time, for the government obviously closed its eyes to the private war of the fascists against the socialists and ignored the complaints of the socialists, undoubtedly justified, that the police actually supplied the fascists with arms. Certainly, the Royal Guards showed open hostility to the socialists in Milan and called their comrades to "prompt and bloody reaction" against them.[31] Moreover, Giolitti himself entered the game of violence in the North for the first time in his long career. He introduced into the electoral campaign of 1921 methods which he had previously confined to the South: infringement upon free speech, the irruption of rowdies into political meetings of opponents, the prevention of voters from exercising their franchise, and the disappearance of official voting reports. To assure the best results, he retained expert assistance. Giolitti included in the National Bloc — the electoral list under which he urged the voters of Italy to return candidates pledged to him — the liberals, who were moderately conservative; the conservatives, who were reactionary; the democrats, who could stomach neither the Socialist nor the Popular Party; and the fascists. In return for Giolitti's support, Mussolini employed measures which made the elections of 1921 the most turbulent ever held in Italy. This experience trained Mussolini for the terror he would let loose in 1924. When a British official seemed puzzled by Giolitti's fascist allies and questioned him, that poised and witty politician, bereft of illusions, replied that he regarded Mussolini's fascists as the Black-and-Tans of Italy.

The Socialist Party split and Giolitti's use in the North of fascist *squadristri* (irregular militiamen) as the equivalent of his *mazzieri* (men armed with clubs) in the South told in the election results. The number of deputies in the Chamber increased from 508 to 535 to include representatives from Italy's war-redeemed territories. Whereas the voters in 1919 had returned 156 socialists to the Chamber, in 1921 they chose only 122 socialists and 16 communists. Both Marxist groups suffered a loss of about 500,000 votes and returned 18 fewer deputies than in the previous national election. The popularists gained seven representatives, or a total of 107 deputies. The other parties won 290 seats, including 35 for the fascists (more than twice the number of communist deputies), 10 for the nationalists, seven for the republicans, four for the German-speaking areas, and four for the Slavic constituents. Mussolini sat among the newly elected fascists. His maiden speech to the Chamber indicated plainly that the future dictator had not decided as yet whether his destiny beckoned from the right or from the left. Mussolini forecast the alliance of the popularists, the socialists, and the fascists. He expressed friendship for the nationalists and the Catholics. Not averse to blackmailing the King, he remained silent only on the institutional question: monarchy or republic? Mussolini's career, thus far, established beyond doubt that for his ultimate mastery of Italy, he owed nothing to the gift of lucid vision which steadies ideals and purposes. He remained only a fraction less confused than the socialists and the politicians of the center and the right. Fortunately for him and his Black Shirts, if not for Italy, Mussolini's nature demanded of him neither scruples nor consistency. He felt no aversion toward seizing opportunistic advantages. Of most importance, he understood that beatings and murder brought hysterics and protest to a hush and clarified the more superficial aspects of human affairs.

Giolitti continued in office for a month. He enjoyed no support from either the socialists or the popularists. When in June the fascists also voted against him, Victor Emmanuel summoned Bonomi to form a new government. The popularists supported him and he replaced Giolitti as Prime Minister. On August 2, through the good offices of Enrico De Nicola (1877–   ), the president of the Chamber of Deputies, representatives of five groups signed the pacification pact which Tito Zaniboni (1883–   ), acting for the socialists, had arranged with spokesmen for the fascists: the socialist and fascist parliamentary delegations, the National Fascist Council, the Socialist Party, and the C.G.L. The socialists agreed not to incite the fascists and the fascists consented not to attack the socialists.

Mussolini soon discovered that the Fasci di Combattimento had outgrown his control as the organization extended its activities beyond Milan and other industrial centers, where he himself felt most at ease, deep into the rural areas. Sicily and South Italy, except for Apulia, had not waited for *squadristi* to resist land occupation by peasants and their popularist leaders. Until Mussolini achieved complete power, fascism did not spread below Rome, and the southern *latifondisti* managed very well without its aid. But in the North — the willing and impartial incubator of monarchism, liberalism, republicanism, all shades of conservatism, socialism, communism, and fascism, as well, in a final burst of talent — large and small landholders came to favor and admire the fascists. They had long resented the vast economic powers exerted by socialist-inspired agricultural and labor cooperatives, which prospered through government aid provided by Giolitti's legislation, and the agricultural workers leagues which derived strength from their affiliation with the General Confederation of Labor. The fascist leaders in the agricultural stretches between the Po and the Arno — Italo Balbo (1896–1940) at Ferrara, Count Dino Grandi (1895–   ) at Bologna, and Roberto Farinacci (1892–1945) at Cremona — refused to recognize the pact which Mussolini signed. He thereupon tendered his resignation from the national executive council of the Fasci di Combattimento. The council did not accept it. In the *People of Italy* of August 7, 1921, he announced: "Fascism no longer stands for liberation, but for tyranny; it is no longer the safeguard of the nation, but the defence of vested interests and of the most crawling, obscurantist Italian types."[32]

Mussolini had planned to make peace with the socialists and rid the

Party of the leaders he hated. Next, he hoped to come to an understanding with the General Confederation of Labor by separating it from the socialists, and then he desired to complete the triple alliance by consummating an agreement with the popularists. If his aims misfired through misjudging the strength of agrarian fascism, his defeat dissociated him, at least temporarily, from the most reckless elements among the fascists. Soon, in order to win new followers, he re-emphasized his republicanism, thereby alienating important generals and nationalists. To be sure, he did not long remain a simple member of his local *fascio,* for on November 21, 1921, he organized his followers, among whom he was already addressed as *Il Duce,* into a political party. Yet the incident illustrated with fresh emphasis how much chance, change, strategic shifts, and effrontery, rather than design and ability, influenced Mussolini's rise to power.

The socialists met at Milan in October 1921. Lazzari reported on his futile pilgrimage to Moscow. Once more the Party demonstrated its good revolutionary intentions by reaffirming its intransigence and by condemning all forms of collaboration by socialist deputies with the government in power. Mussolini assayed this decision: "It means that the National Right, in which the fascists are the majority, can be the arbiter of the life and death of governments, and that no government can govern without it . . . . Fascism now has before it a vast field of possibilities; it can do great things — things, not gestures, deeds, not words . . . ."[33] Despite this warning, when the moderate socialists urged their Party's national council in January 1922 to permit socialists to take action in the Chamber, the council reaffirmed the intent of the Milan resolution. Turati based his acquiescence upon Karl Kautsky's pronouncement that socialists could collaborate with bourgeois governments only when a united proletariat supported them. Since Italy did not fulfill this condition for a true believer, Italy's most notable socialist forgot that he was playing with the fate of his country's freedom and voted to abstain from responsibility.

At the end of January 1922, Pope Benedict XV died. When Bonomi led his cabinet to the Vatican to offer the government's condolences, the country, in the midst of smoldering civil war, could find no subject of more importance to debate than the propriety of Bonomi's action. Before Parliament reassembled in February, Giolitti's adherents voted to withdraw their support from Bonomi, forcing him to resign. During nine days of confusion, the word spread that Don Sturzo had vetoed Giolitti's return as Premier. If the popularist deputies had indeed followed Don Sturzo's lead with regard to Giolitti, they acted on their own when they

271

consented to cooperate in the new government which Luigi Facta (1861–1930) formed secretly. Facta, an inconsequential Giolittian of sorts, had performed this feat while the Chamber had been involved in a complicated debate: the deputies did not know whether they were voting for Bonomi, for Giolitti, for the ostensible points of the motion, or for the sake of ridiculing the entire performance. The fascists joined in supporting Facta for they knew perfectly well that under him parliamentary rule would approach its nadir.

The fascists now went to work upon the country with gusto. The nationalists, who never succeeded in attracting a mass following, had supported the agrarian fascists and their conservative allies against Mussolini in August 1921 because he astonished and outraged them with his intentions to placate the parties of the left. Without design, the sympathy of the nationalists resulted in the attachment of yet another group of fervent men to the fascist cause. Although Mussolini might have easily accepted their emphasis upon the sanctity of the nation, their veneration of the House of Savoy surely went against the traditional sentiments of his native Romagna and his own past. When he did absorb the nationalist credo into his program, he must have done so in the usual spirit with which men in public life make concessions to political necessity. Intellectually enriched by the nationalists, the fascists intimidated the tolerant officials of the Trentino by force and proceeded to teach its German-speaking inhabitants the nature of Italianization. On March 3, 1922, they also seized the government of Fiume and not until March 17 did Italian troops dislodge them by occupying the city.

The *squadristi* resumed their reprisals against socialists and popularists. They attacked workers and peasants in their homes in the middle of the night, broke up political meetings, wrecked union headquarters, sacked cooperative stores and warehouses, and destroyed newspaper plants. They knew that they were wiping out these organizations by crushing their spirits. During the spring of 1922, the fascists began to mobilize masses of followers in vast processions. Not fewer than 20,000 fascists assembled at Milan from all provinces of Lombardy on March 26 in an immense show of strength. On May 1, in answer to the general strike proclaimed by the socialists, thousands of fascist workers converged on Bologna and Rovigo; the fascist railwaymen kept many trains running. Throughout North Italy and in Brindisi that day, strife between socialists and fascists brought scores of deaths. In the smaller towns, the *squadristi* dispersed socialist meetings without opposition. On May 12, Italo Balbo ordered 40,000 rural workers to Ferrara from all parts of the province to force the national government to institute a public works program for thousands of unemployed peasants. He repeated this performance at Rovigo on May 20. But Balbo paraded his most terrifying display of fascist might — a preview of the March on Rome — during the last days of May at Bologna. Thousands and thousands of demonstrators from the countryside called for the dismissal of the prefect. He had not only curbed the fascists with his police, but had also persuaded the central government to prohibit the movement of unemployed agricultural labor from one province to another in search of nonexistent jobs. This infuriated the fascists who wished to infiltrate their followers from Ferrara among the peasants of the Bologna area, still a socialist stronghold although equally cursed by unemployment. As violence increased, Rome dispatched the director general of public safety to Bologna. He barred all access roads to the city and placed the zone under military authority on June 1. The commanding general then summoned Italo Balbo, the leader of the fascist hosts, and concluded a truce through him. The following day, the fascists began to depart, assured that the central government would transfer the offending prefect elsewhere.

On July 3, the *squadristi* of Apulia bore down upon Andria and took possession of its city hall. On July 13, Roberto Farinacci's Black Shirts, who had occupied the *municipio* of Cremona since July 5, wrecked the headquarters and property of all socialist and popularist organizations in that city and the rest of the province. They also destroyed the homes of two deputies, one the head of the Popular Party in Cremona. Roman *squadristi* invaded Viterbo on July 12, while those from Umbria marched on Tolentino in the Marches on July 17. During this very time, Novara and its environs suffered invasion by Black Shirts from Pavia and Monferrato; its citizens endured devastation, wounds, and fatalities. Magenta underwent particularly brutal treatment on July 24. The fascists now moved to destroy the cooperatives. On July 26, they went into battle against the republicans at Ravenna and left nine dead there. They visited the same ferocity upon Rimini, Pavia, Biella, and other centers in Piedmont. Meanwhile, the Labor Alliance — formed in February 1921 by the Socialist Party, the Republican Party, the Anarchist Union, the Italian Union of Railroad Workers, C.G.L., U.I.L., U.S.I., and the Federation of Port Workers — tried to intimidate the fascists and contain their continued advance through passive resistance in the form of local strikes.

National tension reached its peak during the disorders at Cremona and provoked a governmental crisis. Deputies rose in the Chamber to assail fascist outrages and the sack of homes of members of Parliament. Turati requested an audience with the King, received it, and gave his word, too late, to do everything within his power to snatch Italy from ruin. The Party's directorate immediately chastised Turati and those deputies who had encouraged him to consult the Monarch. It accused them of shattering the unity of the socialists. The intransigents insisted that the beleaguered local branches would never consent to class collaboration. On July 19, the Chamber voted no confidence in the Facta government. With folly enthroned everywhere, Victor Emmanuel again summoned Facta to form a ministry. The Premier presented his new cabinet on August 1.

Just at this moment, the Labor Alliance proclaimed a general strike throughout Italy. Turati designated it "legalitarian" because it purposed to affirm the authority of the State against the fascists. The strike endured officially from midnight on the last day of July until noon of August 2 and marks the final serious effort of Italian labor unions and socialists to block the advance of Mussolini. Don Sturzo has suggested that *agents provocateurs* instigated the strike to discredit its socialist and communist leaders, once and for all time, by its dismal failure. Subsequent events seemed to justify this surmise. The socialists had hoped that the strike would aid the formation of a ministry to the left. Instead, it insured Facta's return and isolated the socialists since the democrats and popularists refused, henceforth, to collaborate with them. The fascists emerged from the general strike as the true victors and the real rulers of Italy. Mussolini had not hesitated to stand up in the Chamber of Deputies and to present a deadline to the Prime Minister of Italy: either the strikers returned to their jobs within twenty-four hours, or else —! The government could not oblige him and he knew it. When the strikers continued their agitations, Mussolini let loose his *squadristi*. With the now traditional truncheon-and-castor-oil treatment (the forceful feeding of mauled victims), they set themselves to their familiar rounds of teaching submissive manners to the socialists and communists. Only the workers of Turin held out against the Black Shirts. Genoa, Ancona, and Milan fell to the fascists. Between August 3 and 4, the socialist government of the city of Milan, long in office and long resented by the middle classes, gave way to force. The fascists strode into control and D'Annunzio spoke from the balcony of city hall, the Marino Palace. On August 4, the fascists demolished the offices of *Avanti!*, their third attack since 1919. When the "legalitarian" general strike ended, the railroad workers withdrew from the Labor Alliance. The printers union and the General Confederation of Labor severed formal ties with the Socialist Party in an effort to save themselves.

In September, those socialists who were now known as concentration-ists, but who had borne other labels in the past — reformists, unitarians, minimalists, legalitarians, and gradualists — launched an appeal in behalf of collaboration with the government. They pleaded in vain. The nine-teenth national socialist congress meeting at Rome on October 1 ex-pelled Turati and his followers on the motion of Giacinto Serrati (1872–1926) and Lazzari. The vote went against the moderates, 32,106 to 29,119. Henceforth, until all opposition party life expired, Italy enjoyed the revolutionary luxury of maintaining one Communist Party and two socialist parties: the Maximalist Socialist Party, which contained the majority elements of the old Party and kept control of *Avanti!*, and the Socialist Party of Italian Workers (Partito Socialista dei Lavoratori Italiani) led by Turati and flanked by Treves and Giuseppe Modigliani. The young, courageous, and well-informed castigator of the fascists in Parliament, Giacomo Matteotti (1885–1924), acted as party secretary.

The Naples congress of the Fascist Party on October 24, 1922 served as a pretext to rally 40,000 armed *squadristi* from all parts of Italy in preparation for the March on Rome — a threat bruited about in Black Shirt circles for more than a year. The future hopes of many individuals and groups centered in that assembly. Emanuele Filiberto (1869–1931), the Duke of Aosta and cousin to the King, had commanded the Third Army during the war and was thought to covet Victor Emmanuel's crown. He maintained close connections with fascist leaders at Perugia. As fascist pretender to the throne, he served their purpose well: a silent threat for bargaining with the King. The Queen Mother, Margherita, maintained enthusiastic contact with fascist leaders and during the summer of 1922 engaged Count Cesare De Vecchi (1884–   ) in long conversations at Bordighera on the Italian Riviera. Not all industrialists, but most of them, wished desperately for fascist success since they thought primarily in terms of strike-breaking, lower wage costs, and pro-tection against Bolshevik outrages. Demobilized officers and frustrated youths whose education had brought them unemployment looked toward Mussolini as the savior of personal pride. Nationalists and conservative Catholic elements regarded the Black Shirts as the guardians of ancient traditions. Pius XI (1857–1939, pope 1922–1939) weakened the Popular Party and strengthened the fascist cause by enjoining bishops and clergy to avoid partisan politics. The chief of staff of the army, General Diaz, had not hesitated to address fascist demonstrators from the balcony of his hotel in Florence when he found himself in that city. Had not Bonomi, when Prime Minister, instructed the army to support the fascists? And, finally, many liberals like Salandra, Giolitti, Nitti, Bonomi,

Croce, and Luigi Albertini (1871–1941), the editor of the influential *Corriere della Sera,* had helped to push fascism forward by giving it respectability through their public favor.

At Naples Mussolini, who had already repudiated his republican convictions at a fascist gathering in Udine on September 29, reiterated his adhesion to the monarchy at Naples. With army and conservative backing assured, Mussolini retired to Milan. There, he perfected the last details of the fascist coup and waited for the royal summons to power. To direct the March on Rome, he left in Naples a quadrumvirate of his closest friends: Italo Balbo, Michele Bianchi (1883–1930), General Emilio De Bono (1866–1944), and Cesare De Vecchi.

As the mobilization of the *squadristi* continued, Paolino Taddei (1860–1925), the Minister of the Interior who had constantly pressed for action against the fascists only to be overruled by his colleagues in the cabinet, now renewed his pleas to defend the State. General Pietro Badoglio (1871–1956) and General Emanuele Pugliese (1874–   ), the commander of the army units in Rome, gave their assurance that they could suppress fascist rebellion and restore the country to civil order. Facta, fearful and incompetent, refused to stand up against Mussolini. On the evening of October 26, Salandra, acting as a go-between for De Vecchi and Grandi who had complete confidence in him and Orlando among the liberals, called upon Facta to deliver the fascist suggestion that he resign. Facta hesitated, but agreed to request the King to return to Rome from San Rossore near Pisa. Facta then called an emergency meeting of the cabinet and, at its close, had in his hands the resignations of all ministers. The next day, October 27, fascist importunities continued. From Perugia, where the Black Shirts established headquarters, mobilization orders were issued. That night, upon the advice of Giolitti, Facta went to the King and presented the government's resignation. Just before dawn on October 28, the government, angered by further ultimatums and fascist seizure of prefectures in North Italy, decided to resist. Facta declared a state of siege. The fascists, unused to firm action and counterattack, backed down that morning when the authorities in many localities proceeded against them. Then, at 12:15, the Stefani news agency issued a fateful release: "The King has refused to sign the proclamation declaring a state of siege."[34] A reconstruction of the sequence of events and decisions during these feverish days can never go beyond conjecture. Most authorities agree that the King probably gave verbal assent to the proposed proclamation during the night of October 27 and then withdrew his approval when Facta went to him for his signature early in the morning of October 28. Victor Emmanuel would never have reached a momentous political decision in constitutional defiance of his ministers unless profascist advisers at court had not played upon his fears. The generals in his entourage undoubtedly cast doubts upon the outcome of a clash between the fascists and the army which they represented as most sympathetic toward the Black Shirts. The attitude of the Duke of Aosta might well have frightened him. He certainly could be forgiven for having no confidence in Facta or his ministers who chose to resign at the most perilous moment of Italy's history as a nation.

Victor Emmanuel decided to rescue the country from chaos through a new government coalition to the right which would have represented less than one-fifth the members of the Chamber of Deputies: Salandra conservatives, fascists, and nationalists. Mussolini, still in Milan, insisted through intermediaries in Rome that he would not serve in any cabinet except one headed by him. He also stipulated that the call to assume office be directed to him at Milan and that his militia be permitted to enter Rome peacefully. (He wished to preserve the illusion of an armed occupation both for his Black Shirts and for the nation.) Else, he would not hold back the real March on Rome. The King sent a telegram to Mussolini offering him the presidency of the Council of Ministers, as the premiership is called in Italy. The fascist militiamen, mustered in readiness for action, began their trek by train to Rome. The first columns entered the Eternal City on the morning of October 30. Mussolini arrived by sleeper from Milan the same day at 10:30. After hurrying to the Quirinal Palace still attired in his Black Shirt and presenting the names of his cabinet members to the King, the new Prime Minister arranged for the quick but seemly departure of the Black Shirts from Rome lest their continued presence breed incidents and disorder. From 50,000 to 100,000 Black Shirts marched that day. They first rendered tribute to the Unknown Soldier at the Victor Emmanuel Monument. They then paid homage to the King at the Quirinal Palace. Thence, the fascists moved on to the Villa Borghese where they filed past Mussolini in review. They left that evening for home.

Mussolini began to govern.

Mussolini presented his first cabinet to the Chamber on October 31, 1922. To all outward appearances, the new government resembled one of the usual coalitions of the past, with fascists added: a general, an admiral, a Giolittian, a social democrat, two liberals, and two popularists. Mussolini addressed the deputies in the tones and attitude of a master sergeant. He reminded them that Parliament continued as an institution on his personal sufferance. "I could have made of this dull and deadened Chamber a bivouac of Black Shirts . . . ."[35] Parliament alone could decide, presumably through its own behavior, whether it would live two days or two years. When members urged Giolitti to defend Parliament, he replied: "I don't see any need; this Chamber has the government it deserves." Only 100 deputies, mostly socialists and communists, voted against that government.

On November 25, 1922, Parliament granted plenary powers to Mussolini until December 31, 1923 by a vote of three to one. He immediately appointed fascists as prefects and subprefects and replaced the membership of elective councils in the communes through executive authority. Gradually, Mussolini extended his rule. On January 12, 1923, he created the Grand Council of Fascism, which later became one of the most important organs of the State. On February 1, he disbanded the Royal Guard which once had taken action, at Nitti's command, against the fascists. To replace them, he transformed the *squadristi* into the officially militarized Voluntary Militia for National Security (Milizia Volontaria per la Sicurezza Nazionale). He now had at his disposal a large personal army maintained by the State without need of private contributions. Giovanni Gentile (1875–1944), the liberal philosopher who supplied fascism with the little intellectual content it ever achieved, also fashioned his pedagogical views, which favored State control over education to the disadvantage of the Church, into the Education Act of 1923 when he served as Minister of Public Instruction. Mussolini, not unmindful of his debt to the industrialists and the landowners, abrogated Giolitti's progressive tax measures which had sought to shift the burden of payments from the poor to the wealthier classes. He also asked the commission on wartime profits to wind up its investigation. The government reduced expenditures for social welfare. In August 1923, he demonstrated the national virility of Italy by ordering the bombardment and temporary occupation of Corfu.

Before his dictatorial powers expired, Mussolini obtained from Parliament on November 18, 1923, a new electoral law. Under the provisions of the legislation, that party list which secured the largest number of votes — as long as they constituted at least one-quarter of the total — obtained two-thirds of the seats in the Chamber. The remaining seats were then to be divided among the other party lists on a proportional basis. Large majorities approved this measure and voted the death of their own parties. In December, in accordance with the letter of the law, Mussolini graciously renounced the powers he no longer needed.

The opposition parties entered the elections of April 6, 1924 divided beyond the remotest hope of forging alliances. The national fascist ministerial list obtained 355 seats, while a joint nationalist-fascist list in four districts won 19 seats. With the aid of prefects, police, and militia, fascist candidates coerced 64.9% of the 7,021,551 valid votes cast. Of the 374 deputies now at the command of Mussolini, 275 belonged to the Fascist Party. The remaining 161 opposition deputies, who from the teeth of terror had captured 2,500,000 votes, belonged to the following parties, tendencies, or regional blocs: 15 independent liberals (98 candidates ran on seven lists), 10 representatives of Social Democracy (seven from Sicily), 39 popularists, 24 unitarian socialists, 22 maximalist socialists, 19 communists, seven republicans, 14 representatives of the constitutional opposition (two lists of national importance, one headed by Bonomi in North Italy and one by Amendola in South Italy and Sicily, and two minor lists), four representatives of the Piedmont Farmers list, two Sardinian party members, two Germans, two Slavs, and one dissident fascist. Salandra, Orlando, and Enrico De Nicola had campaigned for re-election on the fascist list. Giolitti's group had continued independent, but maintained an alliance with the fascists.

The violence directed against the enemies of fascism during the elections reached new depths of brutality. The country, unfortunately, had been well prepared for wholesale depravity. In the first year of fascist rule, Matteotti, the fearless general secretary of the moderate socialists, counted up 2,000 instances of assassinations, attacks, woundings, banishment from the community, and the wrecking or burning of printing presses, cooperative stores, union headquarters, offices, and private homes. He published his accusations and the book appeared in England under the title, *The Fascisti Exposed; a Year of Fascist Domination (Un anno di dominazione fascista)*. He also revealed the corruption of fascist officials and showed that their palms itched for public moneys. His charges could not be dismissed lightly. His lively intelligence and reputation in Parliament as a fiscal expert earned respect for the evidence he presented. After Parliament reopened on May 24, Matteotti dared to rise on the floor of the Chamber to question Mussolini about his conduct of the elections.

On June 10, 1924, Giacomo Matteotti vanished. The police authorities did not choose to find his mutilated body at Quartarella, outside of Rome, until August 15. Yet only two days after Matteotti's mysterious disappearance, Mussolini officially recognized him as missing under "circumstances of time and place not yet ascertained but such as to arouse suspicion of a crime which, if it had been committed, could but arouse the indignation and emotion of Parliament."[36] After that announcement, the country knew that Matteotti had been murdered. The entire nation felt deep resentment, and criticism of the fascists, hushed until now, broke out into the open. The inquiry which public opinion demanded led directly to government, police, and fascist officials of the highest rank and stopped just short of Mussolini himself. The Duce found it expedient to dismiss his comrade-in-fascist-arms, General De Bono, now the director of public security, the Roman superintendent of police, the under-secretary of the Ministry of the Interior, the chief of the Cabinet press office, his own personal secretary, and the administrative secretary of the Fascist Party. The police arrested Amerigo Dumini and Albino Volpi, who, along with Aldo Putato, constituted a triumvirate of thugs in the hire of the secret service and in closest touch with important police officials.

On June 27, the parliamentary opposition consisting of 150 socialists, popularists, and radical liberals under the leadership of Giovanni Amendola refused to attend the commemoration services for Matteotti inside the Chamber of Deputies and gathered outside to hear Turati's speech in honor of his dead comrade. Summoning up the historical memory of the secessions of the ancient Roman plebs from the life of the community to the Aventine Hill where they set up their own assembly and elected their own officers, he referred to the parliamentary opposition as those who "now stand on the Aventine of their own conscience . . . ."[37] The opposition also drew up a manifesto which demanded full investigation of the crime, the restoration of constitutional rights, the abolition of the fascist militia, guarantee of personal safety to deputies in the exercise of their duties, and the end of lawlessness and violence. The statement went to the heart of the matter when it declared: "And other clear indications have come to light of a vast tangle of corruption and trafficking, defiling the body politic; of the creation of a sinister association for the purpose of upholding by all and every means the positions of vantage and power which have been audaciously captured."[38] The newspapers called that organization the *Cheka* after its notorious Russian counterpart. The "tangle of corruption and trafficking" alluded to frauds in banking, exchange, and industrial transactions as well as to the trading by fascist government officials in permits, loans, protection, and even news.

The opposition members never returned to the Chamber, but withdrew, symbolically, to the Aventine. Once again, the dramatic Italian gesture defeated common sense, for this was the very time when the opposition should have been present in Parliament to denounce Mussolini in the highest public forum of the nation. Instead, they castigated fascism in Don Sturzo's *Popolo,* the maximalists' *Avanti!,* and Amendola's *Mondo*. Soon, in July, the government secured the passage of a press law which gave prefects the right to confiscate issues of papers considered seditious. By now, the opposition realized that only Victor Emmanuel could bring Mussolini to justice. But when the King saw the evidence on fascist criminality, he excused himself from taking action on the principle that the absence of a parliamentary opposition prohibited him from intervening. Meanwhile, the liberals in Parliament continued to vote confidence in Mussolini even after the Matteotti murder and several tarried on in the cabinet until the end of 1924. Orlando and Giolitti, however, turned against the government, but kept their seats. Croce, the savant, who had found excuses for unconstitutional methods and election violence, finally came to recognize the mortal danger which had engulfed liberalism. In December, Salandra himself broke with the fascists. When an association of war veterans, especially cherished by Mussolini, declared itself opposed to him, he threw out the directorate and replaced it with his own men.

Although the Matteotti Affair had at first tamed Mussolini's insolence, tarnished his reputation, and dampened his popularity, he found, as the months went by, that he had to contend face-to-face with only a dozen individual liberals and an equal number of communists in the Chamber of Deputies, while the Aventine opposition made no straightforward personal charges against him which required direct answer. In December 1924, the opposition secured a copy of a memorandum written by Cesare Rossi, the former chief of the Cabinet press department and one of Mussolini's most intimate collaborators. The press seized eagerly upon this document which not only detailed the events leading up to Matteotti's murder, but also exposed scores of other fascist crimes executed during the three preceding years. After six months of torment, public opinion at last felt certain that the moment had come when the King would have to demand Mussolini's resignation. But the Duce met the challenge head on. He rose in Parliament on January 3, 1925 and announced that he took upon himself full responsibility — not personal, but historical, moral, and political — for the illegal acts and crimes of violence perpetrated by his subordinates. Until then, he had sought to disown them. He announced that he would assume dictatorial powers and challenged the Chamber to impeach him under the force of Article 47 of the Constitution. He counterattacked the Aventine opposition by declaring them unconstitutional and seditious. They, in turn, broadcast a manifesto to the country on January 8. The terms of the moral issue now stood out more starkly than ever before. But Mussolini, and not his enemies, held the initiative, for the government "defended the régime" through the suspension of political liberties. The Aventine opposition lost its voice and its freedom of action and movement.

In February 1925, Mussolini insured unscrupulous vitality for his final assault upon civil freedom by installing Roberto Farinacci of Cremona, one of his most extreme disciples, as the general secretary of the Fascist Party. He ordered Farinacci to tighten up the organization and to direct it to uncompromising militancy. He chose the right man for the job. Almost alone among fascist leaders, Farinacci had never flinched or blanched during the period of fascist fright and indecision after the murder of Matteotti. He had insisted from the start of the national scandal that the fascists cease their defensive behavior and brazen it out to resume the offensive.

The last organized public expression of political opposition occurred in June 1925. The National Union, but recently established, met at its first and only congress at Rome from June 14 to 16. Led by men as intellectually eminent and spiritually courageous as Guglielmo Ferrero (1871–1942), Giovanni Amendola, and Carlo Sforza, the National Union embraced a policy of active rather than passive resistance to fascism and a program dedicated to the restoration of liberal parliamentary democracy. At the end of the month, from June 28 to 30, the Italian Popular Party assembled for its Fifth Congress. It approved the Party's gradual transition from conditional collaboration with the fascists to uncompromising, daily opposition to the régime. Neither the Italian Popular Party nor the National Union would ever meet again.

Mussolini and his cohorts could brook no criticisms; the kind of severely probing appraisal of the new order delivered by Amendola before the National Union infuriated them. On July 20, fascist ruffians forced Amendola, already assaulted once before in December 1923, to leave his hotel at Montecatini where he had repaired to take the cures of that famous spa. On the road near Pistoia, another fascist gang, posted on the highway, dragged him from his automobile, beat him, and left him severely wounded. Amendola died in a hospital at Cannes eight months later on April 7, 1926. While he still lived, the Aventine opposition crumbled. In September, the maximalist socialists cut loose; in October, the republicans; in November, the popularists. Yet they avoided Montecitorio.

Following the attack upon Amendola, on the last day of July 1925, the government, through a wide amnesty which halted all trials except those concerned with murder, reduced the still pending Matteotti case to the normal task of bringing ordinary criminals to justice. At the end of September, the authorities closed down *La Stampa* (*The Press*) of Turin and allowed resumption of publication only after they had forced Luigi Salvatorelli (1886–   ) to resign and Alfredo Frassati (1868–   ) to renounce control over editorial policy and then to surrender his property rights. The pace now quickened. Reprisals taken by the fascists of Florence against their adversaries at the close of October 4 turned that night into a horror of murder, beatings, wounding blows, and the firing of homes. A month later, the police disclosed that Tito Zaniboni had conspired to assassinate Mussolini on November 4. A supposed friend of the plotters kept the police informed of each stage of the plan. Since Zaniboni maintained close contact with the leading freemasons, the government seized all masonic lodges in Italy and the colonies. Since Zaniboni belonged to the Unitarian Socialist Party — the most consistently moderate and legalitarian of all Italian Marxists — the government order-ed its dissolution and suppressed its publication, *La Giustizia (Justice)*. Farinacci now took the offensive against Italy's world-famous news-paper in Milan, *Corriere della Sera (The Evening Courier)*. Already threatened by the fascist press, repeatedly seized by the police, and re-duced by the authorities to an editorial shadow of its formerly brilliant exposition of men and events, the *Corriere della Sera* still infuriated the fascists through the continued presence at its helm of Senator Luigi Albertini. In Parliament, he defended civil liberties with courage and persistence as outrages kept mounting. But the fascists prevailed. They persuaded the majority holders of stock in the newspaper to dissolve the society. On November 28, the newspaper published Luigi Albertini's farewell and the *Corriere della Sera* became another fascist sheet.

Toward the end of 1925, the fascists began to promulgate a series of laws which stultified discussion, limited the right of association severely, discouraged meetings and assemblies, and muzzled the free press. The Law on Associations of November 26, 1925 dealt ostensibly with secret societies — read, freemasonry. But its scope for mischief ran beyond this purported intention, for the legislation gave to police and prefectural authorities extensive powers of surveillance over all associations, societies, and institutes, including organized political parties, through the ability to require of them the most detailed reports concerning their finances, activities, and membership. Omissions or falsifications could draw the arrest of officers and the possible dissolution of the group. The law pro-hibited public servants, either civil or military, from belonging to secret societies on pain of dismissal. The law of December 24, 1925 authorized the discharge of state employees who revealed by their conduct inside and outside of office lack of faith in the political principles of the govern-ment. A group of professors who had publicly defended educational freedom soon felt the impact of this statute. The law of December 31, 1925 consolidated the provisions of the decrees of 1923 and 1924 concerning the press and added new restrictions. No printing establishment could operate without police authorization. The Ministry of the Interior controlled permission for the foundation of periodicals. All newspapers and other publications had to appoint a legally responsible editor, subject to the approval of the public prosecutor of the province. This official received a signed declaration each year naming the proprietor of each periodical. The prefect of every province could sequester publications if by false and misleading news they impeded the diplomatic relations of the country, lowered national prestige at home or abroad, incited the population unjustly, aroused class hatreds, induced disobedience of the law, interfered with discipline among civil servants, and belittled the Fatherland, the King, the Royal Family, the Pope, or the religion, institutions, and powers of the State and of nations friendly to it. The law of December 31 also contained provisions for the creation of a national register of professional journalists acceptable to the government. Soon enough, during the early months of 1926, fascist commissioners replaced the directive councils of regional associations of journalists; at the beginning of March, the executive committee of the Federation of the Press surrendered its responsibilities. The National Fascist Union of Journalists now remained in lone control.

The fascists did not rely solely upon legal methods of repression. On January 8, 1926, the deputies of the Popular Party decided to abandon their abstentionist tactics. When they appeared at Montecitorio to attend the sitting of the Chamber on January 16, fascist deputies manhandled them in the corridors. The next day, Mussolini declared from the government benches that those who wished to return from the Aventine had to recognize solemnly and publicly the accomplishments of the fascist revolution, acknowledge the errors of the Aventine, and sever all connections with those beyond the borders of Italy engaged in antifascist activities. Some days later, only three popularist deputies returned to confess their errors.

The five men accused of Matteotti's murder finally stood trial on March 16, 1926 at Chieti, a small provincial town in the Abruzzi and a site infinitely preferable to Rome for the dispensation of justice. Some months previously, Matteotti's widow, despairing of receiving justice, had withdrawn her civil suit. The brilliant legal defense by Farinacci, who declared that he spoke first as secretary of the Fascist Party, procured acquittal in two instances on March 24, while the court found Dumini and the two remaining defendants guilty "of nonpremeditated unintentional homicide extenuated by the subnormal physical resistance of Matteotti and by other circumstances."[39] The court remitted the sentences of five years, 11 months, and 20 days of imprisonment by four years in pursuance of the amnesty decree of July 1925.

On October 31, 1926, Anteo Zamboni, a boy of 15, attempted to assassinate Mussolini by pistol shot in Bologna. Fascists leaped upon him immediately and killed him by pummelling and strangulation. The opposition press felt the wrath of the fascists everywhere. They set flame to the headquarters of *Lavoro* (*Labor*) in Genoa and destroyed its presses. So violently did this demonstration rage that troops opened fire upon the crowd and left 20 wounded and three dead in the streets. The avengers also raided private dwellings, including the home of Benedetto Croce in Naples. Prefects suspended publication of *Il Mondo* (*The World*) and *La Voce Repubblicana* (*The Republican Voice*) in Rome; *Avanti!* (*Forward!*) of the maximalist socialists, *Unità* (*Unity*) of the communists, and *Battaglie Sindacali* (*Union Battles*) of the General Confederation of Labor in Milan; *La Stampa* (*The Press*) and *Ordine Nuovo* (*The New Order*), the organ of the Gramsci communists, in Turin; *Lavoro* at Genoa; *Il Gazzettino* (*The Gazette*) in Venice; *Giornale di Sicilia* (*The Journal of Sicily*) and *L'Ora* (*The Hour*) in Palermo; and other newspapers in Verona, Brescia, and Bolzano.

On November 9, the Chamber of Deputies approved a motion presented by the secretary of the Fascist Party which declared 120 deputies of the opposition deprived of their parliamentary mandate. At the same sitting, the Chamber received the draft of a bill for the defense of the State, prepared by Alfredo Rocco (1875–1935), the Minister of Justice. In the report which accompanied the proposed legislation, Professor Rocco justified the severity of the measure by appealing to fascist doctrine. The commission appointed to study the bill returned from its labors within an hour. Professor Rocco's compelling elucidation had made further discussion unnecessary. Only 12 deputies voted against the measure. The Senate discussed the draft bill and approved it on November 20, but with less haste. And 49 senators opposed the legislation. The Law for the Defense of the State, dated November 25, 1926, provided the death penalty for deeds directed against "the life, integrity, or personal liberty" of the King, the Queen, the Crown Prince, and the head of the State, as well as for plots against the independence of the country, revelation of military secrets, insurrection, and incitement to civil war. The statute prohibited the resurrection of associations, societies, and parties dissolved by the State, forbade membership in those bodies, and enjoined the espousal of their principles, programs, and policies.

Italians residing abroad who offended the Fascist State could suffer immediate loss of citizenship and confiscation of property; they risked imprisonment upon repatriation. To mete out punishment for the crimes listed in its eight articles the law established the Special Tribunal for the Defense of the State. The Tribunal followed wartime procedures and it pronounced final judgments. The Tribunal worked hand-in-cloak with the secret political police, the O.V.R.A. (Opera Vigilanza Repressione Antifascista), which also originated in 1926 at the initiative of Mussolini. Eventually, the O.V.R.A.'s 11 regional inspectorates, well-stocked with hidden funds, covered the entire country with a close network of informers. Almost immediately after the formation of the Tribunal, the O.V.R.A. discovered the existence of a communist center and arrested Antonio Gramsci, Umberto Terracini (1895–   ), Giovanni Roveda (1894–   ), and Mauro Scoccimarro (1895–   ). Palmiro Togliatti and Ruggiero Grieco escaped arrest.

Now, constitutional privilege of office no longer protected the most eminent figures of the opposition. Between 1921 and 1924, minor officials of the socialist and labor movements either recanted or sought safety abroad. They lacked sufficient prestige or status to guard them from harm. But even important men fled into exile between 1924 and 1927: Carlo Sforza to Brussels, Francesco Saverio Nitti and Giuseppe and Vera Modigliani to Paris, Togliatti to Moscow. Piero Gobetti (1901–1926), like Amendola, died of his wounds abroad. In 1927, Bruno Buozzi (1881–1944) reached Paris where, with the aid of the Confédération Général du Travail, he hoped to keep alive the meager remains of the General Confederation of Labor. Claudio Treves, Giuseppe Saragat (1898–   ), and Pietro Nenni escaped over the Alps. Carlo Rosselli (1899–1937) and Ferruccio Parri (1890–   ), the future leader of the Action Party and Italy's Prime Minister after the liberation of the North in 1945, engineered the escape of Filippo Turati, aged 70, by motor boat from Savona, thence to Corsica with the aid of fishermen, and at last to Paris. Don Sturzo went first to Paris and then to London.[40]

So ended, in comforting freedom from opposition and choice, Cavour's liberal monarchy, Mazzini's republican hopes, Garibaldi's kaleidoscopic aspirations, Giolitti's earth-bound vision of a modern industrial democracy, Turati's confused but humane socialism, and the dialectical hallucinations of the maximalist and communist bigots.[41]

FOOTNOTES – CHAPTER VI

[1] Arcangelo William Salomone, *Italian Democracy in the Making: The Political Scene in the Giolittian Era 1900–1914*, p. 31.

[2] Rigola, cited above, pp. 126–127.

[3] Croce, cited above, p. 184.

[4] Rigola, cited above, pp. 107–114; passage translated by M. F. Neufeld.

[5] Gualtieri, cited above, pp. 159–167; Manacorda, cited above, pp. 290–331; Michels, *Storia critica del movimento socialista italiano,* pp. 125–126; Rigola, cited above, pp. 118–123.

[6] Michels, cited above, pp. 126–127; passage translated by M. F. Neufeld.

[7] The same, pp. 127–129.

[8] Filippo Turati, *Trent'anni di "Critica Sociale,"* p. 71, as quoted in Salomone, cited above, p. 44.

[9] For accounts of the uprisings in Sicily and the Lunigiana, see Napoleone Colajanni, *Gli avvenimenti di Sicilia e le loro cause;* Croce, cited above, pp. 186–188; Giovanni Giolitti, *Memoirs of My Life,* pp. 85–90; Gradilone, cited above, III, 1, pp. 341–372; Gualtieri, cited above, pp. 172–183; King and Okey, cited above, pp. 81–87; Michels, cited above, pp. 159–166; Rigola, pp. 127–139; and Salvatore F. Romano, *Storia dei fasci siciliani.*

[10] For accounts of the May Events (*Fatti di Maggio*), the constitutional crisis which ensued, and the parliamentary battles, see Croce, cited above, pp. 204–213; Gradilone, cited above, III, 1, pp. 373–390; Gualtieri, cited above, pp. 228–243; Hilton-Young, cited above, pp. 40–43; King and Okey, cited above, pp. 87–110; Rigola, cited above, pp. 177–189; and Napoleone Colajanni, *L'Italia nel 1898: tumulti e reazioni.*

[11] Salomone, cited above, pp. 102, footnote 2, 107, xv.

[12] The same, pp. 47–48.

[13] Roberto Michels, *Le prolétariat et la bourgeoisie dans le mouvement socialiste italien,* pp. 87–88, 119–120.

[14] Giolitti, cited above, pp. 159–161.

[15] Salomone, cited above, pp. 66–67.

[16] The same, p. 59.

[17] The same, pp. 86–101.

[18] Hilton-Young, cited above, p. 71.

[19] The classic accounts of the development of Italian socialism to 1911, in the first case, and 1906, in the second case, still remain Roberto Michels, *Storia critica . . .,* cited above, especially Parts IV and V, pp. 211–344, for the years of the twentieth century contemplated in this chapter, and *Le prolétariat et la bourgeoisie dans le mouvement socialiste italien.* For the most pleasantly detailed account in English of both socialist and Catholic developments during the Giolittian Age, see Salomone, cited above, pp. 34–85, from which all quotations, not separately footnoted, were taken. For other treatments of socialist developments, see Giolitti, cited above, pp. 162–163, 171–178, and 224–226; Gualtieri, cited above, pp. 269–301; and Rigola, cited above, pp. 250–272, 299–305, 372–376, 391–398, and 406–413. For the larger, less systematically arranged, and often curiously attenuated aspects of political developments, see Croce, cited above, pp. 214–236, 256–269. For Giolitti's role in restoring Catholics to the political life of the nation, see Giovanni Spadolini, *Giolitti e i cattolici.*

[20] Croce, cited above, p. 274.

[21] The same, pp. 278–280; Luigi Salvatorelli and Giovanni Mira, *Storia d'Italia nel periodo fascista,* pp. 46–48.

[22] Sprigge, cited above, pp. 126–127.

[23] Croce, cited above, pp. 286–287.

[24] Sprigge, cited above, pp. 144–145.

[25] Luigi Sturzo, *Italy and Fascismo,* pp. 91–97.

[26] Sprigge, cited above, pp. 174–175.

[27] Hilton-Young, cited above, p. 96.

[28] Rigola, cited above, pp. 440–443.

[29] Sturzo, cited above, p. 98.

[30] Giolitti, cited above, p. 437.

[31] Hilton-Young, cited above, p. 124.

[32] Pentad, *The Remaking of Italy,* p. 208.

[33] Hilton-Young, cited above, p. 127.

[34] Pentad, cited above, p. 212.

[35] Benito Mussolini, *Opera omnia di Benito Mussolini,* Eds., Edoardo and Duilio Susmel, Vol. XIX, p. 17. "Potevo fare di quest'aula sorda e grigia un bivacco di manipoli . . . (vivi applausi a destra; rumori; commenti; Modigliani: 'Viva il Parlamento! Viva il Parlamento!'; rumori e apostrofi da destra; applausi all' estrema sinistra) . . . potevo sprangare il Parlamento e costituire un Governo esclusivamente di fascisti. Potevo: ma non ho, almeno in questo primo tempo, voluto."

[36] Sturzo, cited above, pp. 178–179; *Dizionario enciclopedico italiano,* Vol. VII, "Matteotti, Giacomo," p. 506.

[37] Hilton-Young, cited above, p. 138; *The Cambridge Ancient History,* Vol. VII, Chapter XIV, pp. 450–456. Tradition recalls five secessions. Two, those of 494 B.C. and 449 B.C., are regarded as possibly historical. A third, that of 287 B.C., is generally accepted as unquestionably historical.

[38] Sturzo, cited above, pp. 182–183.

[39] *Encyclopaedia Britannica* (1957), Vol. 12, p. 801, column 1.

[40] Hilton-Young, cited above, pp. 150–151.

[41] For further details concerning the period from August 1914 to the consolidation of fascist power, see Carleton Beals, *Rome or Death;* Giuseppe A. Borgese, *Goliath: the March of Fascism* (antifascist); Benedetto Croce, *A History of Italy 1871–1915,* pp. 270–288; Guglielmo Ferrero, *Four Years of Fascism* (antifascist); Panfilo Gentile, *Cinquanta anni di socialismo in Italia,* pp. 135–203; Giovanni Giolitti, *Memoirs of My Life,* pp. 377–448; Denis Mack Smith, *Italy,* pp. 289–387; Pentad, *The Remaking of Italy,* pp. 175–256 (antifascist); A. Rossi (Angelo Tasca), *The Rise of Italian Fascism* (antifascist); C. J. S. Sprigge, *The Development of Modern Italy,* pp. 112–203; Luigi Sturzo, *Italy and Fascismo* (antifascist); Luigi Villari, *The Awakening of Italy* (profascist); and W. Hilton-Young, *The Italian Left,* pp. 76–147. See, especially, Luigi Salvatorelli and Giovanni Mira, *Storia d'Italia nel periodo fascista,* pp. 15–362. For a critical review of the most recent historical works concerning the origins and accomplishments of the fascist movement, see Ugo Azzoni, "Fascismo e antifascismo," *Il Mulino,* IX, N. 1, February 1960, pp. 7–28.

VII

The Drive toward the Future:
1890 to 1926

Social and Economic Advance in the Age of Giolitti

FOR twenty-five years before World War I, unparalleled social progress and economic prosperity attended the turmoil of Italy's political life. The validity of Giolitti's grand design for the nation — so seemingly opportunistic and disjointed, but actually so coherent when viewed from historical distance — hinged upon the conviction that steady industrial expansion would confer upon Italy ever-increasing material benefits and, sequentially, growing national tranquillity. Yet the patient master of reasonable purpose became the victim of his own excess of sanity: he underestimated the time he had at his disposal. He seemed to forget that the social and economic welfare of Italian workers and peasants had to improve at a rate so fast and steep that it would neutralize the inherited virulence of mounting class rancor. Had Italy been a national laboratory controlled only by the logic of social and economic melioration, Giolitti's common sense might have triumphed over socialist and fascist fantasies. Indeed, all contemporary evidence, except the unfathomable data of the very human Italian heart, supported the image of a slowly emerging industrial democracy.

Social Progress. The population of Italy increased from an estimated 31,421,000 in 1891 to 37,452,000 in 1921. During these three decades, the population density per square kilometer mounted from 106 to 126 despite net losses recorded during the war years and notwithstanding the beneficent drain of massive emigration.[1]

The flight of the poor from Italy, especially from the South and the Islands, attained heroic proportions during the period from 1901 to 1910 when the annual average number of emigrants stood at 602,669. Although the annual average for the next decade declined to 382,807, during the single year of 1913 alone, 872,598 Italians left their homeland for other countries. Not only did this prodigious siphoning of population act as a giant safety valve for the release of economic and social pressures which admittedly defy precise measurement, but it also bestowed tangible and easily determined benefits upon the nation. During the period 1891–1895, of the total amount of depositor credits in postal savings, those of emigrants accounted for 0.5%. This proportion rose to 20.9% in 1910 and 18.4% in 1920. By 1920, too, remittances to Italy from emigrants which passed through the Bank of Naples amounted to 980,756,383 lire, of which 878,349,654 lire arrived from the United States.[2] (During the fiscal year 1920–1921, all expenditures of the national government for education and fine arts totaled less than these emigrant remittances: 907,092,289 lire.)

Table 3 of Appendix A shows the average annual magnitude of total emigration for selected years. It also illustrates clearly that during the period from 1891 to 1921 (1) emigrants of working age formed a high proportion of all emigrants and that (2) during the years of heaviest emigration, the number of workers and artisans who left Italy exceeded by substantial thousands the number of peasants and agricultural laborers who sought their fortunes elsewhere.[3]

The emigration of men and women of working age would seem to represent, when viewed in the abstract, a heavy economic drain for the nation which exports manpower. This loss appears especially unfortunate and ironic in the case of a country on the verge of accelerated industrialization which, at a juncture so crucial, must suffer the departure of artisans and workers from its shores. That Italy actually subsidized the rearing of ready-made workers for other countries cannot be contested. Nor can it be gainsaid that Italy expended little-to-be-spared sustenance upon millions of children only to see them leave when they reached their prime of life to enrich other nations with their labor. But it is equally true that Italy could not have continued to sustain them without risking social upheavals more ruinous still than those which exploded even after the safety valve of emigration had already released enormous pressures. Moreover, the remittances and savings which emigrants poured into the debtor mother country year after year must be regarded as substantial compensation for theoretical economic loss. (During the 1950's, the drain of manpower from the South continued, but flowed not outward but toward the industrial North.)

The health of the nation improved markedly. Italy's general mortality rate fell from 27.3 per thousand of total population during 1881–1885 to 17.4 during 1921–1925. The accompanying table compares Italy's achievement in the first quarter of the twentieth century with the record of Spain and France; it illustrates, as well, Italy's persistent lag when contrasted with more industrially advanced countries like England, Germany, and the United States.[4]

General Mortality Rates per 1,000 Population.

Years	Italy	Spain	France	England and Wales	Germany	United States
1901–05	22.0	25.9	19.6	16.0	19.9	16.4
1911–13	19.5	22.2	18.2	13.9	15.9	14.0
1921–25	17.4	20.2	17.2	12.1	13.3	11.8

The number of deaths in Italy due to infectious and parasitical diseases more than halved between 1891 and 1921. The rate almost halved in the case of deaths from respiratory ailments during the same period. The battle against typhoid and paratyphoid also showed remarkable results as the number of reported cases decreased from 178.9 per 100,000 of total population in 1891 to 96.3 in 1921; comparable figures for pellagra recorded a drop from 9.1 in 1905 to 0.5 in 1921. However, the incidence of malaria per 100,000 of total population worsened: 544.2 in 1902 to 725.6 in 1921.[5] Available data concerning the expenditures of the national government for public health purposes demonstrated slow and uneven improvement: 0.05% of the total budget in 1889–1890, 0.12% in 1901–1902, 0.58% in 1910–1911, and 0.46% in 1926–1927.[6]

The increase of the average daily amounts of available nutritive substances, expressed in terms of calories per inhabitant, provided an additional measure of the relative welfare and prosperity of the Giolittian era. The average for the decade 1891–1900, 2,119 calories, spurted to 2,617 calories during 1901–1910. These first ten years of the twentieth century have remained the period of most rapid advance since the comparable average for 1911–1920 rose to only 2,694 calories. From then onward, the average declined, except during 1921–1930 when the average attained the all-time high of 2,834. In the five-year period from 1951 to 1955, the average stood at 2,691.

Of the total average number of available calories for each inhabitant during 1891-1900, 319 were of animal origin; during the next decade, the comparable figure declined to 311, while it rose sharply during 1911–1920 to 360. Despite these signs of modest gains, carbohydrates continued to predominate among the foodstuffs available to Italians. The accompanying table records the pattern of the average daily available supplies of carbohydrates, proteins, and fats, expressed in terms of grams per inhabitant. It should be noted that the largest gains took place in the golden decade of Italian life, the pre-World War I years from 1901 to 1910.

Average Daily Available Amounts of Nutritive Substances in Grams.

Nutritive Substances	1891–1900	1901–1910	1911–1920
Carbohydrates	322.9	420.7	428.2
Fats	54.6	57.3	60.1
Proteins	72.7	90.3	95.5

Table 5 of Appendix A lists, in kilograms, the average annual amounts of selected available specific foodstuffs per inhabitant; it clearly demonstrates marked advance for the era between 1891 and 1921 in the case of two basic elements of the Italian diet: wheat and unpolished rice. Improvement in the third basic element, corn, proved less steady. The claim of progress also holds true for fresh vegetables and citrus fruits. The data with regard to meat, fish, and olive oil — the chief sources of proteins and fats — reveal either negligible improvements or actual declines between 1891 and 1921.[7]

As beneficent shifts of population relieved the pressure of Italians upon available land and jobs, as emigrants poured savings and remittances into their homeland, as public health improved, and as food supplies increased, all means of communication expanded. Although the most notable period of Italian railroad construction occurred before 1896, nevertheless later increases in the kilometrage of railroad lines remained impressive. Especially after 1905, when the State once again assumed control of the system, the government modernized operations and equipment and extended trackage as well. The data at hand reveal, indeed, a steady growth of kilometrage from 13,964 in 1891 to 20,556 in 1921.[8]

The network of national, provincial, and communal vehicular roads also developed rapidly. National highways increased from 7,891 kilometers in 1890 to 10,336 kilometers in 1921. No data for provincial and communal roads were available for 1921, but between 1890 and 1910 provincial road kilometrage grew from 34,778 to 44,671, while communal roads mushroomed from 36,965 to 95,406 kilometers during this interval.

The number of total highway and road kilometers per 100,000 inhabitants rose from 264 in 1890 to 432 in 1910.[9]

Expenditures by the national government for all public works, including the cost of constructing and maintaining the national highway and railroad systems, increased from 3.9% of total disbursements in 1889–1890 and 3.7% in 1901–1902 to 8.7% in 1910–1911. By 1920–1921, the percentage had reverted to the magnitude of earlier years, 3.7%.[10]

The number of licensed motor vehicles, automobiles, and trailers more than doubled between 1914 and 1921, expanding from 42,629 to 87,939. Merchant marine tonnage also demonstrated formidable development: that operating under mechanical propulsion increased from 199,945 in 1891 to 1,075,200 in 1921. Conversely, tonnage under propulsion by sail decreased from 625,812 in 1891 to 191,182 in 1924. The tonnage of goods arriving in Italy by means of water transportation almost doubled between 1891 and 1921, increasing from 8,486,000 to 16,164,000. The tonnage of goods leaving the country by means of water transportation reached its highest peak in 1911 when it ascended to 7,529,000; for the other years under consideration, the figures remained between the limits of 4,000,000 and 5,000,000 tons.[11]

Growth in other forms of communication which affected the daily lives of vast numbers of people in the most direct fashion showed comparable vitality. Correspondence handled by post offices throughout the nation increased from 397,000,000 pieces in 1891 to 1,808,000,000 in 1921. The number of telegrams sent by private persons mounted from 8,300,000 in 1891 to 20,700,000 in 1921. While in 1891 Italy could boast only 12,093 telephone subscribers and 42 public telephone stations, by 1921 the number of subscribers reached 116,922 and stations multiplied to 3,181. The proportion of the national budget devoted to postal, telephone, and telegraph services increased slightly from 3.6% in 1901–1902 to 4.7% in 1910–1911. However, it decreased to 2.7% in 1920–1921.[12]

The decline in illiteracy between 1881 (no official census statistics were gathered in 1891) and 1921, while very substantial, still left more than a quarter of the population without the ability to read or write. Among Italians six years of age and above, illiteracy declined from 62% in 1881 to 27% in 1921. Although the region of Venezia Tridentina showed an illiteracy rate of only 2% in 1921 and the regions of Piedmont, Lombardy, and Liguria rates of 7%, 9%, and 10% in that same year, more than half of the population of Calabria and Basilicata were illiterate, and just under 50% of the population of Sicily and Sardinia could neither read nor write in 1921.[13]

Among children from 6 to 12 years of age, illiteracy decreased from 64.1% in 1881 to 35.3% in 1911. By 1921, the percentage had decreased to 29.

Percentage of Children between the Ages of 6 to 12 Who Were Illiterate, 1881, 1901, 1911, and 1921.

	1881	1901	1911	1921
Boys	61.8	45.1	34.5	28.0
Girls	66.5	48.1	36.2	29.0
Both	64.1	46.6	35.3	29.0

Two other sets of data measure in more detail the improvement of educational services in the nation: (1) the proportion represented by children between the ages of 5 and 15 enrolled in elementary schools, with relation to all children of that age group; and (2) the proportion represented by children between the ages of 5 and 15 enrolled in elementary schools, with relation to every 1,000 of the total population of Italy. While there were only 80 elementary school pupils for every 1,000 of total population in 1891, by 1921 there were 112 pupils for every 1,000 of total population. The proportion of all children between 5 and 15 years of age who were enrolled in elementary schools grew from 39.3% in 1901 (adequate data for 1891 were not available to derive the percentage needed) to 45.2% in 1911 and 51.8% in 1921. Enrollment in the middle schools grew from 2.5 for every 1,000 of total population in 1891 to 10.2 in 1921. Comparable figures for those pupils pursuing higher education rose from 6 for every 10,000 of total population in 1891 to 13 in 1921.[14]

Admittedly, Italy faced labors of enormous fiscal, administrative, and social difficulties in pushing the frontiers of education out to the remote villages of the peninsula and islands and in attempting to reduce illiteracy among the overwhelming majority of people to whom it seemed less a curse than the immemorial way of life. Yet national expenditures for education and fine arts stood at 2.4% of the total budget in 1901–1902 and remained at that same point in 1920–1921; in 1910–1911 it had risen only to 4.3%. In contrast, governmental disbursements for the army, navy, and merchant marine rose from 19.8% of total outlays in 1901–1902 to 30% in 1920–1921.[15] In this respect, Giolitti's age resembled only too closely earlier decades. The consequence of its failure to assign primary importance to the education of all Italians, at least at the elementary school level, becomes immediately obvious when another set of contrasting statistics is scanned. In 1901, 48.5%

of Italy's population over 6 years of age could neither read nor write; in 1900, only 10.7% of the comparable segment of the population in the United States lacked the ability to read or write. A decade later, when the degree of illiteracy had fallen to 7.7% in the United States, the Italian ratio still registered very high: 37.6%. By 1920, the American rate of illiteracy descended to 6%. However, Italy's rate in 1921 stood at 27%, not only far above the proportion for the United States, but considerably in advance of the percentages registered for the leading countries of Western Europe as well.[16]

The most arresting aspects of Giolitti's design to transform Italy into an industrial democracy centered in his dramatic extension of political suffrage and the widening of both the character and coverage of social security and protective labor legislation. Table 8 of Appendix A illustrates the striking numerical rise in the electorate from 2,750,000 eligible voters in 1890 to almost 8,500,000 voters in 1913 as a consequence of the electoral laws of that year and 1912. Giolitti championed these measures against severe opposition. They represented the first major changes in electoral qualifications since Zanardelli's reform legislation of 1882 and proposed to extend the vote even to illiterates who had reached the age of 30. Giolitti has recorded his unswerving confidence in the social and economic benefits which would flow liberally from "the elevation of the lowest class to the dignity of full citizenship . . . ." He firmly believed that its rise "to a higher grade of civilisation was . . . a most urgent problem . . . . The security of our social structure required it, since exclusion of the workers from the bureaucratic and political life of the country has always had the effect of exposing them to the suggestions of the revolutionary parties and their subversive ideas. This is so because the revolutionaries have always one formidable argument ready. They point out that, owing to this exclusion, only one means of defence lies open to the masses against the impositions of the governing classes, and this is the use of violence . . . ." Moreover, Giolitti acted on the faith that economic prosperity demanded political liberty and the fullest participation in civic affairs: "The general conditions of civilisation . . . showed that only the nations in whose progress the masses took an active part – nations such as England, Germany, France and the United States – were economically powerful . . . . Nor is this difficult to understand, when one thinks of the mass force of intelligence, will and working capacity lying latent in the great industrial centres in the towns and among those scattered over the country."[17]

After 1890, the quickening pace of industrialization in North Italy and the gradual spread of modern production systems elsewhere on the peninsula forced Parliament to recognize the harsh and often brutal concomitants of factory life in the country's expanding urban centers. Measures to protect the health and shore up the economic security not only of city workers, but of miners and agricultural laborers as well, began to appear on the stately columns of the statute books alongside traditional legislation. Workmen's compensation, which had been instituted on a voluntary basis through law 1473 of July 8, 1883, became compulsory in 1898 through law 80 of March 17, 1898. The legislation applied to employers of five or more persons in all those industrial processes, including mining and quarrying, where machinery was utilized. Law 1450 of August 23, 1917 extended the benefits of workmen's compensation to agricultural workers and sharecroppers. The following statistics illustrate the steady growth in the number of workers who came to be insured against accidents which occurred while at work:[18]

Total Number of Workers Enrolled in the National Insurance Fund for Workmen's Compensation.

1884	443
1891	113,923
1901	310,969
1905	540,850
1911	660,056
1921	1,002,589
1925	1,221,833

The National Fund for Workers Invalidity and Old-Age Insurance had been first established on a voluntary basis on July 17, 1898 through law 350. It began to operate in October 1899. By 1911, 394,456 persons insured themselves with the Fund whose assets stood at 136,393,963 lire. Decree law 603 of April 21, 1919 transformed the National Fund for Workers Invalidity and Old-Age Insurance into the National Fund for Social Insurances (Cassa Nazionale per le Assicurazioni Sociali). After January 1, 1920, insurance with the Fund became compulsory except for stated categories of workers. By 1921, the number of insured persons had risen to 712,155 and the Fund's assets had increased to 1,018,485,931 lire.[19]

As early as February 11, 1886, law 3657 of that year sought to regulate child labor by prohibiting the employment of children below 9 years of age in factories, quarries, or mines. For underground work, the minimum employing age was set at 10. Law 242 of June 19, 1902 raised the minimum age for the employment of children in various kinds of industrial and construction labor to 12, while that for work underground was advanced to 14. The act also extended various forms of legislative protection to women workers. The law of July 17, 1910, number 520, introduced maternity insurance for those women workers covered by law 818 of November 10, 1907.[20]

A compulsory day of rest for working people came into effect through law 489 of July 7, 1907. Night work for bakery and pastry workers was prohibited through law 105 of March 22, 1908. Comprehensive legislation establishing the 8-hour day and 48-hour week for all workers and clerks in industrial and commercial establishments did not appear in Italy before law 692 of March 15, 1923 was enacted.[21]

Unemployment insurance and employment offices were established through decree laws 2214 of October 19, 1919 and 3158 of December 30, 1923. Those covered by the Fund who received unemployment compensation in 1922 numbered 1,107,598; the number had declined to 230,777 by 1925.[22]

Economic Development. We have already noted, statistically, that as compulsory elementary education grew more effective through improved legislation and enforcement, and as new facilities and teachers advanced into the remote areas of the country, a larger proportion of children between the ages of 5 and 15 was drawn into the schools and, consequently, out of the labor market. In addition to limiting the employment of children, protective labor legislation enacted by Parliament served, as well, to siphon from the labor market groups of women affected by special provisions of the law. Social security measures and rising real income also helped to reduce, very gradually, the percentage of the total Italian population engaged in economic pursuits.

By experiencing this diminution in the percentage relationship between the economically active population and the total population, Italy conformed, if most belatedly, to the pattern of development already achieved by those countries which had felt the impact of the industrial revolution earlier and more intensively than the peninsula. Moreover, Italy followed a process which has continued to operate in most of those nations which began their economic development later than Italy. Thus, whereas in 1881 (Italy undertook no census in 1891) 15,152,000 Italians, or 53.2% of the total population, were classified as economically active, this proportion fell to 47.6% in 1921.[23]

At first glance, Italy's economic growth and prosperity after 1900 seem substantial indeed, especially when contrasted to the sluggish nature of the country's industrialization before the turn of the century. Certainly, the domestic progress recorded during the years of Giolitti's hegemony stands unchallenged so long as only internal measurements of achievement are employed. But the serious lag and vital flaw in Italy's economic development become immediately apparent when Italy's percentage distribution of the active population among the three principal sectors of economic activity is viewed, in historic procession from decade to decade, alongside comparable percentage distributions for other countries. The three major divisions are: (1) agriculture, forestry, and fishing; (2) goods-producing industries (manufacturing, construction, and extractive); and (3) services, including transportation and communication.

In 1901, when the proportion of those engaged in agricultural pursuits stood at 8.7% in Great Britain and 33.1% in France, Italy recorded a comparable measure of 59.8%, somewhat below India's figure of 64.2% and a fraction above Japan's 59.4%. Thus, at the beginning of the twentieth century, Italy remained firmly among the ranks of predominantly agricultural countries whose economies, in less enlightened times than ours, were frankly characterized as retarded or backward, but which are now dubbed as underdeveloped. Forty years earlier, in 1860, the United States exhibited for the last time a percentage of agricultural employment, 59.9%, of the same magnitude as Italy's in 1901. Also of striking interest is the proportion of the 1860 work force of the United States occupied in goods-producing industries and in services: 20.1% and 20%. These figures complete the resemblance to Italy's pattern for 1901 when goods-producing industries accounted for 23.8% and services for 16.4% of the active population.

An important goal in the progress of expanding economies is reached when countries achieve either a balance between the proportion of workers attached to agriculture and those employed in goods-producing industries, or, better still under most circumstances, a predominance of goods-producing industries over agriculture. Italy failed to reach even the stage of simple balance between agriculture and goods-producing industries until May 8, 1957 when those engaged in goods-producing industries accounted for 36.3% of the work force, while those in agriculture fell to 33.8%. As late as 1921, more than twice as many persons in Italy engaged in agricultural activities as in industrial endeavors: 56.2% as against 24.3%. This persistent ascendancy of agriculture over goods-producing industries contrasted sharply with the economic history of other countries. The percentage of those in the industrial work force equalled or eclipsed the proportion of those who devoted their labors to agriculture as early as 1882 in Prussia, 1901 in France, and 1910 in the United States. Great Britain offers the most dramatic contrast to Italy. There, as early as 1841, nearly twice as many Englishmen were engaged in goods-producing industries as in agriculture: 45.5% as against 23.1%. Therefore, Italy's economy in 1921 presented a relationship between agricultural and industrial employment almost the reverse of the English pattern eighty years earlier.[24]

Forgetting, for the moment, the sluggish nature of Italian industrial development when compared with the dynamic economies of England and the more advanced nations of Western Europe, we must address ourselves to the fond memory — prevalent in Italy today among older men and women whose recollections flow back into the first three decades of the twentieth century — of the Giolittian age as years of unparalleled prosperity. In relation to Italy's own economic past, they were. Yet the simple chronicling of the distribution of the active population among agriculture, industry, and services will miss this central fact. The statistics, forthright enough given their limited nature, show that agriculture descended from its graphic heights by only 3.6 percentage points between 1901 and 1921 and that the industrial sector reached its highest point in 1911, only 26.9%, and then sank to 24.3% in 1921, merely 0.5 points more than the percentage for 1901. However, an analysis of the changing pattern of the constituent elements of the gross internal product (as measured in current lire for each period) during these same years demonstrates that the sunny impressions of memory possessed the glow of truth. The gross internal product for the *private* sector of the economy, when divided into proportions attributable to agriculture, goods-producing industries, and services, reveals enlightening gains and losses. Agriculture, which accounted for 62.2% of the active population in the *private* sector of the economy in 1901 and 49.2% of the gross internal product during 1901–1905, still claimed 59.2% of the active population in 1921 — a loss of 3 percentage points — but could gather up only 40.6% of the gross internal product during 1921–1925, an 8.6 point drop. Industry, meanwhile, advanced only 0.8 percentage points from 1901 to 1921 in the proportion of the active population mustered into its ranks, but registered a gain of 9.8 percentage points in its share of the gross internal product between 1901–1905 and 1921–1925. The services, while gaining slightly in their proportion of the active population, actually suffered slight losses in their proportion of the gross internal product.[25]

Other indices of industrial activity in Italy from 1900 to the years immediately following World War I confirm the basic conclusions derived from the foregoing analysis of the gross internal product. Table 25 of Appendix A indicates that during this period Italy figured sixth among the nations of the world in terms of manufacturing production. To be sure, this standing did not place Italy in a position of signal honor since medieval Russia outranked Italy, while Belgium, Sweden, Finland, and even Japan and India did not lag far behind. Nonetheless, Italy's share of world manufacturing production advanced sufficiently to demonstrate that the years from the turn of the century to 1914 indeed constituted the golden age of Italian industrial progress: 2.4% before 1896, 2.7% during 1896–1900, 3.1% during 1906–1910, 2.7% for 1913, and 3.3% during 1926–1929. Although these proportions do not loom large in terms of world output, they represent remarkable achievement for the Italian economy when viewed in terms of its own past.[26]

A second index, with industrial production from 1896 to 1900 serving as the base of 100, shows an increase from 123 during 1901–1905 to 208 during 1921–1925, or an advance of 85 points. Of these 85 points, the years from 1901 to 1915 accounted for 60, while the years from 1901 to 1910 alone contributed 44 points, or more than half of the entire growth for the 25-year period.[27] A third index of manufacturing production – calculated upon the basis of the years from 1925 to 1929 as 100 – again confirms the outstanding importance of the first ten years of the twentieth century to Italy's industrial development. This third measure of growth records an increase from 22.6 in 1891 to 58.8 in 1921, a rise of 36.2 points. The upward swing, however, did not progress evenly, for the index advanced 14.4 points between 1891 and 1901, 20.3 points between 1901 and 1911, but only 1.5 points between 1911 and 1921.[28] Still another computation of manufacturing production which used 1938 as the base year shows an advance from 29 during 1891–1895 to 67 during 1921–1925, a rise of 38 points. Of this total increase, the period from 1901 to 1915 accounted for 21 points.[29] A fifth series, which traces the growth of Italian trade in manufactured articles and takes as its point of departure values reckoned at 1913 prices, once more reaffirms the vitality of Italian manufacturing during the first decade of the twentieth century.[30]

Alexander Gerschenkron, in his intensive study of industrial growth in Italy from 1881 to 1913, concluded that Italy's "big industrial push" took place between 1896 and 1908. His aggregate index of output by six industries (mining, metal-making, textiles, engineering products, chemicals, and foodstuffs), in which 1900 served as the base year, implied the following annual average rates of growth:[31]

Annual Average Rates of Growth of Italian Industrial Output for 1881–1913 and Subperiods.

Period	Percentage Change	Characterization
1881–1888	4.6	Modern growth
1888–1896	.3	Stagnation
1896–1908	6.7	Very rapid growth
1908–1913	2.4	Reduced rate of growth
1881–1913	3.8	Over-all growth

According to Gerschenkron, four notable traits distinguished Italy's period of rapid expansion from 1896 to 1908. (1) It weathered the depression of 1900 — severe economic adversity visited the continent, especially the countries of Central Europe which had become Italy's chief associates in trade since the disastrous tariff war with France — almost untouched. (2) The proportion of producer goods to the total production registered by the six index industries mounted swiftly: 28% in 1896, 43% in 1908, and 47% in 1913. (3) Italy, where industrialization lagged for decades, failed to fulfill the expectation which the history of other developing countries has established: the later that large industrial expansion surges forward, the more vigorously it pushes on. In contrast to Italy's highest average annual rate of advance from 1896 to 1908, 6.7%, Sweden increased its industrial production by almost 12% yearly between 1888 and 1896, Japan achieved an annual growth rate of 8.5% between 1907 and 1913, while Russia expanded more than 8% annually during the 1890's. Even Germany, which had moved well beyond its inaugural spurt of most rapid development during the last decade of the nineteenth century, still progressed industrially at a rate of almost 5.5% each year — a pace less rapid than Italy's most advanced degree of change, but not markedly so. (4) As compared with the period of maximum forward drive in other countries, Italy's dynamic turn from 1896 to 1908, "while free from any severe setbacks, seems to have proceeded in a less uniform and more jerky fashion, denoting perhaps a more delicate state of public confidence and greater entrepreneurial uncertainties and hesitations."[32]

The discussion in Chapter IV of the Italian government's role in the economic life of the nation between 1860 and 1890 has already called attention to Gerschenkron's conviction that official policies on industrialization could best be characterized as maladroit and that the tariff measures adopted during those decades illustrated this ineptitude most tellingly. Gerschenkron also describes additional circumstances after 1890 which he considers especially pertinent in accounting for the slower rate of Italian industrial growth as compared with the more energetic pace set by other countries. First, he recalls that the most powerful spurt in the building of railroads on the peninsula took place before the pivotal economic expansion from 1896 to 1908. Not unexpectedly, additions to the Italian railroad system in those years amounted to less than 10%. In contrast, during Russia's era of most intensive industrialization from 1886 to 1900, the railway network increased by more than 70%. Secondly, the legislation of 1885, which transferred the management of the state-owned railroads to three private companies, also provided for possible repossession by the government after twenty years. This stipulation virtually insured uncertain investment policies by the operators for a decade before 1905 when, indeed, the railroads passed back to the State. To be sure, after the turnover, modernization and expansion plans were drawn up, but they materialized into trackage and rolling stock too late to influence either the magnitude or nature of industrial development before 1908. Thirdly, the "veneration of 4 per cent," to borrow Professor Giulio Einaudi's angry phrase, estopped the possible flow of capital released by reduced railroad construction into industrial ventures. Many large investors preferred the safety of bonds guaranteed by the government, while small investors tended to concentrate their savings in the postal system and the cooperative banks. These funds ended up either as short-time commercial credit or as loans to communes and provinces for the construction of public works. Not surprisingly, therefore, the years from 1896 to 1908 witnessed a large-scale recall of Italian securities held abroad. Fourthly, profound political and economic unrest before Giolitti came to power, and the strikes which ensued each year after his policy of social reconciliation assured the neutrality of government in labor-management controversies, precluded the possibility of tranquil economic growth. Unlike Italy, most countries managed to enjoy a measure of social and industrial tranquillity during the years when they sustained their most intense economic expansion. Afterward, they tended to adjust upward the standard of living of their workers. Granted this breathing spell by favorable fortune, they avoided disturbing strikes during the most energetic phase of their growth, whereas in Italy the period of rapid advance and industrial disorder came simultaneously. Gerschenkron concludes: "Had the industrial upsurge in Italy taken place one or two decades earlier, in all likelihood it would have been much less disturbed by industrial strife . . . . Along with the advantages of being late, there are also some definite disadvantages to being very late — a point that may deserve special attention with regard to the underdeveloped countries of our time."[33]

These four conditions interfered with the realization of the highest possible industrial upsurge in Italy. Gerschenkron believes, however, that the constructive and possibly saving role assumed by the large Italian banks toward the end of the century shielded industrial activities, at least partially, from the full potential effects of those obstacles. The banks brought off this feat by abandoning limited French practices which dominated investment banking in Italy and adopting those methods which German banks had evolved to quicken their own industrial revolution. They reached beyond conventional loans and advice concerning stock flotation to provide manufacturing enterprises with technical aid, business counsel, and firm fatherly guidance. The transformation began when German leadership and capital, augmented by an admixture of Austrian and Swiss resources, established the Banca Commerciale Italiana in 1894. Although neither this institution nor the other banks which followed its pioneering example could wholly escape the distrust of all financial institutions which the banking catastrophes of 1889–1894 had created in the public mind — most notably the Credito Mobiliare and the Banca Generale disasters — and although the very origin of these innovations aroused fears of foreign economic penetration, the times were not wholly unpropitious for the acceptance by the business community of the wide array of services now offered. Many enterprises, weakened by depression, willingly took advantage of them. With time, Italian industrialists grew dependent upon the aid of the investment bankers, nor did they grow restive under these arrangements, as did German entrepreneurs after 1900, during the entire period before World War I.[34]

Thus far, attention has lingered upon the over-all expansion of Italian industrial output as represented by six separate statistical measures of growth. Each series tended to corroborate the national memory of a golden age of industrial development and prosperity between the closing years of the nineteenth century and World War I — the Giolittian era. Now, the influence of this paramount economic event upon the character and fortune of the Italian labor movement must be determined. For this purpose, indices of production necessarily give way to indices of employment. Four aspects of this additional inquiry immediately suggest themselves: (1) At stated intervals after 1890, how many persons were engaged in industrial employment and what was the magnitude of change over the years? (2) What shifts took place in the distribution of workers among the constituent categories of employment? (3) Did employment continue to concentrate in the famous industrial triangle of the North: Piedmont, Liguria, and Lombardy? (4) How did Italian labor fare, economically, under conditions of industrial development? Did real wages rise and did hours of work decline?

In seeking these facts, the Furies of the Greeks, the Erinyes, come to mind. They served as the ministers of the vengeance of the gods against guilty mortals. Ancient legend and drama agree that they moved with dispatch and perception. But the passage of the centuries has certainly impaired their powers of discernment. They pursue relentlessly those earthly creatures who would compare the findings of one official census with another and leave unscourged those desk denizens of government enumerating bureaus who, year after year, conspire to rob successive inquiries of simple comparability. The most patient diligence finally must yield in the attempt to align their wayward handiwork. Yet they continue on, unpunished, nay refreshed, over the decades while the Furies unleash their hounds of conscience upon those who would gather fresh figs of meaningful data from statistical thistles.

The decennial censuses might seem to offer fixed sources of enlightenment concerning the number of persons employed in the different subdivisions which constitute each of the principal industrial segments: mining, construction, manufacturing, and the production of electricity and gas. The limitations upon this hope have proved severe. First, the government conducted no census in 1891. Secondly, the classifications employed in 1911 differ markedly from those used in 1901, just as those used in 1921 vary from the 1911 classifications. Due to the lumping of elements and the absence of sufficient detail in the printed sources, it is impossible to match categories across the years with moderate confidence of accuracy, short of delving into the working files themselves — a time-consuming prospect which would not automatically insure success. Thirdly, Italian experts agree that the population censuses tended to enumerate many persons who had no real industrial connections, even when industry is defined widely to include the handicrafts. Among these intruders, to name only the most obvious examples, were those who performed auxiliary work for various industries in isolated small workshops, or at home; those who answered the census taker by expressing a hoped-for rather than an actual attachment to industry; and those who once worked in industrial establishments, but who had long since been separated from them. Defects of this character, but of more exaggerated proportions, had so infected

the census of 1881, as we have already discovered, that it would be misleading to utilize its findings in the absence of data for 1891. Therefore,
the number and the percentage distribution of the industrial population
among its various branches of activity for 1901, 1911, and 1921 must
suffice.[35]

The shifts in industrial employment revealed by the census data should
be traced alongside Gerschenkron's revelations about the rates of growth
in output for specific industries. According to his calculations, chemicals,
metal-making, and engineering products registered the largest gains in
production for the entire run from 1881 to 1913 and contributed most
heavily to the country's record performance from 1896 to 1908.
Chemicals attained an annual average rate of growth of 13.7%, metal-
making 12.4%, and engineering products 12.2%. Textiles, which had
reigned during most of the nineteenth century as the country's leading
industry, registered at 2.5% for the entire span of years under survey
and at only 3.5% from 1896 to 1908. The production of foodstuffs out-
paced textiles with annual percentage changes of 3.1% from 1881 to
1913 and 5.5% from 1896 to 1908. Mining managed to eke out a rate
of but 1% for the full course and not more than 1.8% for the shorter
period of the main forward push.[36]

The population census figures, for all their limitations, recorded the
sharpest rise of employment in those very industries which Gerschenkron
cited as experiencing the most rapid growth in production. The number
of employees in the chemical industry increased almost four and one-
half times in the ten years between 1901 and 1911; those in the mineral-
working, metal, and mechanical industries more than doubled in
count; and those in industries using the products of agriculture, forestry,
and fishing grew more than one and one-half times larger during the
decade. Meanwhile, both the absolute and relative numbers of workers
in the clothing and textile industries declined. Employment in clothing
fell by 1911 to less than two-thirds its strength in 1901 and that of
textiles diminished to about four-fifths its former size. Between 1911
and 1921, a recession year, over-all industrial employment had increased by less than 200,000 and slight reversals took place in the
direction of employment indicated between 1901 and 1911. Employment in the chemical industry fell by one-fourth. Those occupied in
industries using agricultural, hunting, and fishing products decreased
slightly in number. Whereas attachment to the clothing and allied
trades grew somewhat in both absolute and relative terms, employment in textiles continued its downward trend, dropping from 14.7%
of all industrial workers in 1911 to 12.3% a decade later. Workers engaged

in the mineral-processing, metal, and mechanical trades registered gains of 20,000, but declined fractionally in relative position.

The expansion of employment in producer goods industries, even though considerably checked between 1911 and 1921, as compared with the decade between 1901 and 1911, should not obscure the truth about Italy's economy: the soft goods industries, printing, and construction — where handicraft methods, small shops, and homework continued to thrive — still offered the greatest opportunities for so-called industrial employment in 1911 and 1921. They accounted for 3,370,531, or 77.2% of the 4,368,095 persons classified as industrial in 1911, and for 3,252,552 workers, or 71.3% of the 4,559,582 workers classified as industrial in 1921. By contrast, the chemical, extractive, and mineral-working, metal, and mechanical industries could claim only 964,719 workers, or 22.1% of all industrial employees in 1911, and fewer yet in 1921, when postwar retrenchments in the heavy industries still prevailed: 945,895, or 20.8% of all industrial workers. (See Appendix A, Table 15.)

Fortunately, the general trends which these findings indicate can be checked against the more precise data brought to light through the industrial investigation of 1903 and the industrial censuses of 1911 and 1927. These counts surveyed industrial firms and did not rely upon an individual's judgment about the nature of his own employment. Where the census of population classified almost 4,000,000 workers as industrial in 1901, the 1903 investigation covered only 1,275,100 workers. The 1911 census of population regarded almost 4,370,000 workers as industrial, but the industrial census of that year placed but 2,304,500 in that category. The industrial census of 1927 counted 3,302,400 factory workers.[37]

According to the 1903–1911–1927 series, which presumably reflected the number of workers engaged in true factory production more accurately than the population census figures of 1901–1911–1921, employment in chemicals grew 45% between 1903 and 1911, but almost doubled between 1911 and 1927. Those employed in the mineral-working, metal, and mechanical industries increased in numbers more than 135% between 1903 and 1911, but only by one-third between 1911 and 1927. Workers in food production and allied trades showed more modest gains: 30% between 1903 and 1911 and 12% between 1911 and 1927. Contrary to the picture of both absolute and relative decline among workers in clothing and allied industries as rendered by the census of population figures, the industrial censuses indicated a rise of 342% from 1903 to 1911 in the number of workers engaged in the clothing, skin, and leather industries. They continued to gain by over 80% between

1911 and 1927. Although the number of textile workers increased from 411,100 in 1903 to 495,200 in 1911 and then experienced a spurt to 642,900 in 1927, the industry declined in relative importance from 32.1% of the total number surveyed in 1903 to 21.5% in 1911 and then to 19.4% in 1927. The construction crafts indicated a steady rise in the number of workers. From 1901 to 1911, according to the population census, employment increased by almost 24%; it grew over 170% between 1911 and 1927, according to the industrial censuses.

With the single exception of clothing and allied industries, the two series of data, though unlike in coverage, diverse in classification, and unequal in magnitude, reached substantial agreement about the nature of industrial growth between 1901–1903 and 1911. The 1927 statistics indicated, in addition, that the basic trends established during the first decade of the twentieth century continued on into the early years of the fascist era.

The 1903–1911–1927 industrial series also confirmed the conclusion drawn from the population censuses: the soft goods industries and construction continued to provide the largest share of industrial employment. Yet, when the proportions obtained from the population censuses are placed alongside those shown by the industrial series, it becomes clear that true factory employment, which the industrial series reflected more accurately than the population censuses, favored the producer goods industries. To be sure, the consumer goods industries and construction still dominated employment even in the industrial series, but less imperiously so than in the population censuses. Regardless of this meaningful difference between the two sets of data, little doubt remains that despite impressive advances in the chemical, metallurgical, mechanical, and metal-working industries, the industrial segment of Italy's economy — still widely overshadowed by agricultural employment, it should be recalled — remained predominantly consumer-oriented in character as late as 1927. (See Appendix A, Table 15.)

Within this pattern of industrial development for the country as a whole, did the various regions fare equally well? The figures presented in Table 22 of Appendix A indicate clearly that the industrial triangle of the North — Piedmont, Liguria, and Lombardy — and especially Lombardy, not only retained their long-established lead over the rest of the peninsula, but also slightly strengthened their position. In 1901, the industrial population of the three northern regions constituted 35.4% of the entire industrial population of Italy, while Lombardy alone accounted for 20.2%. By 1911, comparable proportions had grown to 38.9% for the three regions and 21.9% for Lombardy.

These increases, however, concealed losses by the three regions in the proportion of national employment they could claim among the producer goods industries. They compensated for these declines through substantial advances in the share of national employment among the consumer goods industries and construction. While the average share of producer goods employment alloted to the three regions as a whole for 1901 stood at 37.4%, the comparable figure for 1911 had fallen to 32.3%. So fared Lombardy as well: 20.5% of total national employment among the producer goods industries in 1901 and 15.1% in 1911. Yet, in none of the producer goods industries did the number of workers for the three regions as a whole comprise less than 16% of national employment in 1911; in the mineral-working, metal, and mechanical industries that year, they comprised almost 45% of total employment. Moreover, the three regions so improved their composite share of national employment in the consumer goods and construction industries that their proportion for textiles reached 60.2% in 1911 as against 45.5% in 1901. The minimum proportion for any of these industries in 1911 stood at 30.2%, a slight decline from the minimum for 1901, 32.5%. The dominant role of Lombardy in the industrial development of the nation can be gathered from a review of its share of the country's total employment. Disregarding the extractive industries, employment for any industrial branch never fell below 15.5% of the national total in 1901, while textiles reached 32.4%. In 1911, again disregarding the extractive industries, Lombardy's minimum share stood at 16.5%, while the maximum, for textiles, shot up to 41.5%.[38]

The arrayal of regional industrial densities in 1927 demonstrates that the triangle of the North continued to retain its traditional hegemony over the other sections of Italy. Lombardy stood highest, with 195.1 industrial workers for every 1,000 inhabitants. Liguria came next with a density of 159.5, and then Piedmont with a density of 156.4. Tuscany ranked fourth with 114.3 industrial workers for every 1,000 inhabitants. Comparable figures for Campania, with Naples as its center, diminished to 62.3, while they descended still more for Sicily, 49.2, and for Basilicata, 39.8, the lowest density in the entire country. The following table illustrates dramatically the progressive diminution of the density of the industrial population in moving from the North to Central Italy and then on to the South and the Islands.

The percentage distribution of workers enumerated in the 1927 industrial census, both by regions and among the various branches of in-

Number of Industrial Workers for Every 1,000 Inhabitants according to Regions, 1927.

Region	Density	Region	Density
Piedmont	156.4	The Marches	66.4
Liguria	159.5	Lazio	81.2
Lombardy	195.1	Abruzzi and Molise	44.2
Venezia Tridentina	79.7	Campania	62.3
Veneto	78.3	Apulia	52.4
Venezia-Giulia	113.3	Basilicata	39.8
Emilia	78.8	Calabria	50.8
Tuscany	114.3	Sicily	49.2
Umbria	71.1	Sardinia	64.1

Source: Annuario statistico italiano 1928, pp. 142–143.

dustrial activity, revealed that the early predominance achieved by the industrial triangle of the North, and especially by Lombardy, continued after World War I. In 1927, Piedmont, Liguria, and Lombardy accounted for 48.3% of all industrial workers included in the survey of that year (more limited in coverage, but also more accurate than the industrial employment data of the population census), while Lombardy alone employed 28.8%. The calculated percentage distributions also demonstrated forcefully that despite the eminence achieved by these three regions in the producer goods industries — they accounted for 52.7% of national employment in the mineral-working, metal, and mechanical industries and for 54.3% in the chemical industry (Lombardy's respective proportions were 28.6% and 32.6%) — even the most intensively industrialized areas of all Italy still afforded most employment in the consumer goods industries as late as 1927. Whereas workers in the producer goods industries accounted for 29.4% of all industrial employment in the three regions as a whole, the consumer goods industries provided jobs for 68.7% of all industrial workers.[39]

Thus far, statistical analysis has indicated that Italian industry experienced its period of sharpest growth between the last years of the nineteenth century and 1911; the share of producer goods in the total industrial output increased rapidly during those same years. Over the longer period from 1901 to 1927, North Italy enjoyed the major portion of the nation's industrial progress, while Central Italy, the South, and the Islands had to content themselves with the inadequate remains. Moreover, as late as 1921, agriculture still occupied twice as many people as industry. The industrial census of 1927, in turn, found employment concentrated in the consumer goods industries and construction. These developments — substantial in comparison with Italy's own past, but limited in both extent and quality from the vantage point of Italy's future and the pattern of growth in the more advanced industrial nations of the world — have been emphasized because they offer important clues to an understanding of the character of the Italian labor movement and, consequently, to the comparable ideological dangers which beset newly emerging labor movements in the world today. Did economic advances improve the welfare of Italian workers fast enough and tangibly enough to engage their sympathies in the established social, economic, industrial, and political systems of the country?

The estimates of real per capita national income from 1891 to 1925 suggest steady but very modest advance. Based upon 1938 prices, the real per capita national income, expressed in lire, rose from 1,888 during 1891–1895 to 2,741 during 1921–1925. But if the historical eye seeks out the record for the years which preceded 1891, the most arresting figures come into view. In 1861–1865, the real per capita national income stood at 1,851, merely 37 lire below the 1891–1895 average. Moreover, the 1876–1880 average, 1,919, had topped the 1891–1895 figure by 31 lire. These comparisons suggest a 20-year period of improvement from 1861 to 1880 and then two decades of retreat and stagnation since the per capita income did not rise well beyond the 1876–1880 level until 1901–1905. The years from 1896 to the beginning of World War I — the time of the dramatic spurt in industrial production — witnessed the most consistent and rapid rise in real per capita national income: 501 lire.[40]

The real per capita income figures just presented possess the ability to establish the pace of Italy's accomplishment during the twentieth century in contrast to its own past, but they cannot measure Italy's position and progress against the contemporaneous records set in other countries. This limitation created the necessity to find a meaningful and comparable gauge of real per capita income for Italy, for countries more advanced than Italy, and for less industrialized nations. The device employed by Colin Clark in *The Conditions of Economic Progress*, "International Units" (I.U.), although far from ideal, provides this standard. As defined by Colin Clark, "One I.U. of real income was taken as the quantity of goods exchangeable in the U.S.A. for $1 over the average of the decade 1925–34."[41]

Italy's real per capita income, expressed in I.U., increased from 132 in 1901 to 196 in 1926, an increment of 64 I.U. in 25 years. Although Great Britain advanced only 12 I.U. and Germany 2 I.U. during this same span of time, the United States added 271 I.U. and France 160

I.U. to their real per capita incomes. Even backward Greece bettered its performance by 38 I.U. in the fourteen years between 1913 and 1927, while Japan supplemented its real per capita income by 36 I.U. in the 13 years between 1913 and 1926. Italy's mediocre gains placed that country in the class of Greece and Japan; its record appears even more lackluster when the lowly grade of Italy's real per capita income in 1901 and 1926 is contrasted to the elevated levels of other countries. At the beginning of the twentieth century, Great Britain's real per capita income measured 3.7 times that of Italy. Comparable figures for the United States were 3.1; for Germany, 2.2; and for France, 1.7. Twenty-five years later, the real per capita income of the United States attained 3.5 times the size of Italy's, while the figures for Great Britain, Germany, and France stood at 2.6, 1.5, and 2 times the size of Italy's real per capita income. Finland's I.U. in 1926 equalled Italy's; Greece lagged behind Italy, but not by far; Japan came within easy calling distance.[42]

Within the limitations imposed by the depressed level of Italy's real per capita income and its uneven economic growth, what behavior characterized the course of real wages for workers? In 1907, the National Workmen's Compensation Fund surveyed the earnings of insured members and estimated the average daily wage at 3.53 lire for the Kingdom. Rinaldo Rigola calculated that a worker who attained this average wage for a ten-hour day could earn enough in one hour to buy one of the following items: 2.2 pounds of bread, 6.6 pounds of potatoes, not quite 9 ounces of meat, or 3.5 ounces of butter. Although Rigola admitted that tuberculosis and the other diseases of poverty still struck with devastating force among workers and their families, and although he conceded that rents had soared for housing which did not meet the most elementary tests of hygiene and decency, he concluded, nonetheless, that the standard of living among workers, especially with regard to nutrition, had improved considerably over the level of the previous decade.[43] Rigola's prudently cheerful view must be discounted, at least in part. He felt constrained to demonstrate that real wages had risen perceptibly in order to confound traditional conservatives, economic liberals, and devotees of the cooperative movement who united for once in insisting that the benefits in higher wages and lower hours obtained by workers as a result of union action were surrendered, in the long run, through higher prices. Rigola's impression can be checked in some measure by extending to 1907 the measure of real earnings utilized for the period from 1860 to 1890: the number of working days required to earn enough money to satisfy the needs in wheat of a family of four persons. In 1890, the average worker devoted 43 days to this requirement. In 1907, the number of days had fallen to 37.5. This decrease, far from striking, nevertheless indicated that the early years of the twentieth century brought increased purchasing power to the average working-class home for at least the basic ingredient of its highly farinaceous diet.[44]

Antonio Fossati has presented the case for a most modest evaluation of the rise of real wages. According to him, between 1899 and the outbreak of World War I, "real wages constantly tended toward improvement." This judgment expresses with euphemistic indirection the disagreeable truth that in all those years wages never caught up with the rise in the cost of living. The average nominal wage for a working day of nine and one-half hours increased, according to Fossati's calculations, from 2.33 lire in 1899 to 2.48 lire in 1901. It then mounted to 2.96 lire in 1907 (this average would rise to 3.11 lire if based upon a ten-hour day in order to compare it with the figure of 3.53 estimated by the National Workmen's Compensation Fund for that same year) and 3.30 lire in 1911. By 1914, it stood at 3.53. However, the price of foodstuffs basic to the worker's diet increased so frequently that the cost of living outran nominal wages constantly from 1899 to 1920, except for one year, 1909.[45]

In 1925, when the index of real wages reached 111.81 and the lot of the Italian worker had supposedly turned less harsh, a carpenter had to labor 38 minutes in Rome and 41 minutes in Milan to earn enough money to pay for a kilo of flour (2.2 pounds). His counterpart in London had to work only 17 minutes, while his comrade in Berlin labored but 29 minutes to buy the same amount of flour. An unskilled laborer in Rome had to work 53 minutes to acquire a kilo of flour, but his fellow worker in Milan labored 1 hour and 5 minutes to achieve the same end. Comparable figures for London and Berlin ran 23 minutes and 37 minutes. Table 37 of Appendix A details the amount of time a skilled and unskilled worker had to labor in 1925 to purchase a kilo of white bread, potatoes, bacon, flour, cheese, and rice in Rome, Milan, London, and Berlin. In all instances, the improved fortunes of the worker in Rome and Milan found him at a distinct disadvantage when compared with the life of the workingman in London and Berlin.

The creeping pace of improvement in real wages between 1899 and 1920 suggests the thought that Giolitti might have conferred the extended franchise, the benefits of social legislation, and government tolerance of strikes upon Italy's impoverished workers not only as immediate requital for the harshness of bare subsistence, but also as enlightened devices for wresting future gains from the economic and political systems. The decline in real wages from 1923 to 1926, after the spurt of the postwar years, and the restricted purchasing power of the Italian worker's hour of labor, as measured against English and German standards, suggest the further thought that the economic process, deaf to resounding promises, forced the fascists to bestow national pride and empire upon resurgent Rome's industrial and agricultural masses as a substitute for the first down payments due upon a truly meliorating rise in wages. This obstinate drag for decades upon the purchasing power of the meager income of workers and the sure-fire ability of Marxian propaganda to invigorate perennial class hatreds frustrated Giolitti's long-minded plans for pushing Italy into the twentieth century and insured the rule of violence, vindictiveness, disunity, and chaos in the labor movement. Like an instrument of fate, Mussolini rampantly pursued the quiet tread of index numbers. When he finally broke into the main avenue of Italian history, he plastered a new base year upon monuments, politics, economics, social life, and international affairs. For unions, too, time retook its start with the fascist *Anno I.*

FOOTNOTES – CHAPTER VII

[1] Appendix A, Table 2.

[2] For emigration figures, see *Sommario . . .*, cited above, p. 65; for postal savings and remittance figures, see *Annuario statistico italiano 1905–1907*, pp. 779–780; *Annuario statistico italiano 1911*, p. 241; *Annuario statistico italiano 1919–1921*, pp. 409, 414. The totals, in lire, upon which the postal savings percentages are based, follow: 1891–1895, total depositor credits 333,683,978, total emigrant credits 1,829,483; 1910: 1,773,578,777 and 369,981,924; 1920: 6,979,838,448 and 1,285,493,162.

[3] *Sommario . . . ,* cited above, pp. 65, 68.

[4] For the 1881–1885 mortality rate in Italy, see Fossati, cited above, p. 660; for the figures listed in the table, see World Health Organization, *United Nations Epidemological and Vital Statistics Report,* Vol. 7, p. 308, with the exception that the figure shown for the United States on the 1901–1905 line covers only the year 1901 and is taken from U.S. Department of Commerce, Bureau of the Census, *Historical Statistics of the United States 1789–1945,* p. 47.

[5] Appendix A, Table 4.

[6] *Annuario statistico italiano 1905–1907*, pp. 859, 876–887; *Annuario statistico italiano 1911*, pp. 301–307; *Annuario statistico italiano 1919–1921*, p. 464; and *Annuario statistico italiano 1932*, p. 430. In Chapter IV, the reported governmental expenditures for given services during the period from 1860 to 1890 included provincial and communal, as well as national, disbursements. The percentages cited in Chapter IV were calculated from these combined totals. Comparable totals and percentages could not be calculated for the period from 1890 to 1926 since the *Annuari* from 1911 to 1914 provided figures for selected provincial costs, but none at all for the same communal items. For the post-World War I period, the 1919–1921 and 1922–1923 *Annuari* fail to give any information about communal and provincial expenditures. The *Annuario* for 1927 provides communal

expenditures for certain services in 1925, but supplies no functional expenditures for the provinces. For these reasons, the discussion in Chapter VII of governmental expenditures for the services cited during the period from 1890 to 1926 covers only *national* outlays. However, since both the *Annuario* for 1919–1921 and the *Annuario* for 1922-1925 did not break down the national expenditures of the Ministry of the Interior into separate classifications for public health and public security, it was necessary to resort to the *Annuario* for 1932 which contained 1926–1927 national expenditures for public health.

[7] For all caloric, nutritive, and foodstuff data cited in the text and the tables, see *Sommario . . .,* cited above, pp. 229–233, and Appendix A, Tables 5 and 6.

[8] Appendix A, Table 9.

[9] Appendix A, Table 10.

[10] See footnote 6 for sources of data.

[11] *Sommario . . .,* cited above, pp. 137–139; Appendix A, Table 11.

[12] Appendix A, Table 11. For the sources of data on government expenditures, see footnote 6.

[13] Appendix A, Table 7.

[14] For the percentages given in the table concerning children between the ages of 6 and 12 who were illiterate, see *Annuario statistico italiano 1905–1907,* p. 245; *Annuario statistico italiano 1914,* p. 107; *Annuario statistico italiano 1927,* p. 67 For the various statistics needed to compute the proportions given in the text, see *Sommario . . .,* cited above, pp. 39–40, 76–78.

[15] For the sources of data on governmental costs, see footnote 6.

[16] Statistics for the United States were taken from Eli Ginzberg and Douglas Bray, *The Uneducated,* p. 21.

[17] Giolitti, cited above, pp. 237–238; see also, pp. 236, 239–247.

[18] For the text of the 1883 legislation and for a description of the 1898 and 1917 statutes, see Enrico Roselli, *Cento anni di legislazione sociale 1848–1950,* Vol. II, pp. 228–231, 109–111, 142. For the sources of data in the table, see *Annuario statistico italiano 1905–1907,* p. 796; *Annuario statistico italiano 1914,* p. 329; *Annuario statistico italiano 1919–1921,* pp. 422–423; and *Annuario statistico italiano 1922–1925,* pp. 314–315.

[19] *Annuario statistico italiano 1914,* p. 325; *Annuario statistico italiano 1919–1921,* pp. 417–418; *Annuario statistico italiano 1927,* p. 272, footnote (a).

[20] Rosselli, cited above, pp. 232–233, 249–253 (text of the 1902 legislation), 262–264.

[21] The same, pp. 257–260 (text of the compulsory day of rest law), 261–262 (text of bakery and pastry shop law), 264–266 (text of the 8-hour law of 1923).

[22] *Annuario statistico italiano 1922–1925,* pp. 293, 309.

[23] Appendix A, Table 13. The active population, as defined by official Italian sources, differs from the labor force, apart from other minor causes of divergence, because it does not include those seeking work for the first time.

[24] Appendix A, Table 12.

[25] Appendix A, Table 14.

[26] Appendix A, Table 25.

[27] Appendix A, Table 16.

[28] Appendix A, Table 27.

[29] Appendix A, Table 26.

[30] Appendix A, Table 28.

[31] Alexander Gerschenkron, "Notes on the Rate of Industrial Growth in Italy, 1881–1913," *The Journal of Economic History,* Vol. XV, No. 4 (December 1955), pp. 363–364. A geometric rate of growth between the first and the last years of the specified periods was assumed.

[32] The same, pp. 365–366.

[33] The same, pp. 370–373.

[34] The same, pp. 373–375.

[35] Appendix A, Table 20.

[36] Gerschenkron, cited above, p. 364. A geometric rate of growth between the first and the last years of the specified periods was assumed.

[37] Appendix A, Table 21.

[38] Appendix A, Table 22.

[39] Appendix A, Table 23.

[40] Appendix A, Table 30.

[41] Colin Clark, *The Conditions of Economic Progress* (1957 Edition), p. 18. Colin Clark himself raises the question of the aptness of the decade chosen as a standard of comparison. "It was perhaps defensible at the time, as including 5 years each of the very different trading conditions of the 1920s and of the 1930s. In due course it will have to be replaced; but it does not appear that we have yet an alternative base which will give us the possibility of an improvement big enough to justify the not inconsiderable labour of converting all previous data to a new base." (The same, p. 18.)

[42] Appendix A, Table 29.

[43] Rinaldo Rigola, cited above, pp. 378–383.

[44] The *Annuario statistico italiano 1911*, p. 141, gives the price of a quintal of wheat of average quality as 25.98 lire. A family of four required 5.1 quintals to sustain itself. Given the average daily wage in 1907 as 3.53 lire, the number of days required to buy this amount of wheat came to 37.5.

[45] Appendix A, Table 33.

VIII

The Drive toward the Future:
1890 to 1926

The Labor Movement

WITHIN the brief span of a single generation — between 1890 and 1926
— Italian workers broke through the confining barriers of isolated workshops and fields, organized assemblies of factory unions and agricultural
leagues within the bounds of a commune or district, extended their vision beyond provinces and regions to form national federations of distinct crafts and industries, created a dominant confederation where most
unions in the Kingdom found voice and response for their common concerns, participated in crescively bitter doctrinal disputes, answered without hesitation politically inspired calls to redress their grievances through
frequent and violent general strikes, abetted the eventual development
of four central bodies and independent groups which claimed more than
4,000,000 members in 1920, scaled the heights of power that year to occupy the plants of North Italy in a bid for full partnership in factory
control, and then soon afterward, as though exhausted by the very intensity of their past militancy of thought and action, allowed Mussolini's
bullies to truncheon them into stunned inertia, silence, and final submission.

From the very beginning of this tragic cycle, almost insurmountable
economic, social, political, cultural, and psychological obstacles impeded
the formation of stable unions endowed with the will to improve the
conditions of labor through wresting small, attainable concessions from

employers day by day. First, large regional and provincial variations in economic and social development created such substantial divergencies among the labor markets of the country that the basic requirements of workers shifted markedly from one area to another and even from one commune to the next. Confronted by this formidable handicap, the pioneers of the modern Italian labor movement needed to invent institutions and methods flexible enough to respond readily to the singular call of hundreds of crafts, industries, and agricultural pursuits in all sections of the long peninsula and the islands, each progressing or stagnating in different phases of economic development. For men and women alien to pragmatic ways of thought and action and most at home in the certitudes of sweeping doctrines, the actual dimensions of the task, formidable enough, loomed immense and encouraged millennial solutions.

Secondly, Italy's predominant rural manpower imposed upon the young and straitened labor movement the burdensome obligation to organize agricultural workers. But these sharecroppers and day laborers — impoverished, desperate, and never fully employed — constituted the very segment of the country's entire labor force, with the possible exception of Sicily's sulphur miners, who could least afford to pay adequate dues and to build strong and enduring unions. Among all laborers, but especially among agricultural workers, social retardation and illiteracy added discouraging handicaps for labor organizers. Misery and frustration might easily push these forgotten people into strikes which all too often caught the ferocity of rebellion. But these peasants lacked broad enough understanding of the forces which enslaved them to become disciplined members of stable unions. In 1901, almost 50% of the population six years of age and above neither knew how to read nor to write, while a decade later national illiteracy still stood at almost 40%. By 1921, when the proportion of illiteracy had fallen to 27% for the country as a whole, in no region of South Italy and the Islands had this ratio fallen below 40%. In Calabria, 53% of the population over six years of age still lived in ignorance of the printed word.

The low level of earnings, especially among agricultural workers, and the sluggish rise of real wages, when joined to chronic unemployment, underemployment, and the fear of discharge, acted as the third brake upon the pace of organization. They also undermined the stability of unions and endowed the Italian labor movement with its violent and volatile character. Sheer want often provoked employed workers into bitter, prolonged, and futile strikes. Inexperienced leaders mistook this initial enthusiasm and militancy for lasting dedication to the cause of unionism. But after rounds of disaster, the more realistic organizers came to realize that these summer soldiers served merely to set in motion high periodic waves of temporary membership which hard-pressed local assemblies found difficult to accommodate and impossible to control as these newcomers rushed into and out of the labor movement. Since many unions carried a high proportion of unemployed on their rolls, they found themselves saddled with adherents who contributed nothing to the financial support of their struggles, but who agitated for aggressive action, unmindful of realistic strategy or public opinion, since they had neither jobs nor wages to lose.

The determined resistance of employers, first as individuals and then belatedly in association — they had neglected to organize themselves at first since they regarded labor unions as pathological phenomena with doubtful chances of survival once a benighted government ceased its policy of benevolent neutrality and came to its senses — also stunted the sound growth of permanent unions of moderate persuasions.

The Herculean difficulties imposed upon the labor movement by regional diversity, the overwhelmingly agricultural nature of the work force, the subsistence level of income, the dogging spectre of unemployment, and the obduracy of industrialists and landowners discouraged faith in the possibility of gradual improvement and deepened already chronic mass despair. This sense of hopelessness and betrayal opened the minds of workers to every drift of revolutionary political dogma. With simple faith learned from their traditional religion, they believed implicitly that they could earn economic justice for themselves by hastening a foreordained fiery day of social judgment. Consequently, the most eloquent pleas of socialist and labor reformists could never disabuse their proletarian followers of the conviction that only the forcible overthrow of capitalist governments could liberate them. Neat logic moved in next to subordinate unions and their limited aims to the supreme *political* purpose of founding the new order.

The Italian labor movement pressed debate against this version of its historical role, periodically asserted its institutional independence, and tried in vain to elude the stresses, strains, and doctrinal civil wars within the Socialist Party. The charged atmosphere of perpetual internal strife bestowed upon union life the appearance of serious activity and, when sterile disputes temporarily simmered down, of accomplishment itself. Political passion simulated vitality and lent to labor organizations a glow of strength which Mussolini eventually reduced to the fiction it had always been. Most historians of the Italian labor movement have perpetuated this illusion, first, by neglecting the painful, year-in-year-out efforts of unions to administer to the unheroic needs of their members — an understandable defect in the competence of writers without intimate experience of the daily parade of grievances, wage demands, controversies over job rights, and entreaties for work. Unconscious Marxists, when most charitably characterized, they further unbalanced their chronicles by emphasizing the drama of general strikes and confusing these unplanned uprisings with labor strength. Moreover, they obscured the truth even more by bogging down their narratives in a mire of national and international socialist wrangling. For purposes of clarity, this study has pulled asunder what man in Italy hath inextricably joined together and has treated socialist follies in chapters devoted exclusively to conservative, liberal, as well as left-wing, political aberrations. This approach should raise into distinct relief the struggle of union members and leaders to establish vigorous permanent economic organizations without depreciating the grave importance of political factionalism which divided and weakened the Italian labor movement.

The adopted procedure of analysis therefore searches out the specific services rendered to workers, as workers, by the succession of union institutions devised by the far from unlettered statesmen of Italian labor. After their formation in the 1890's, the pioneering chambers of labor, like the central local labor bodies which first appeared in the United States in the late 1820's and 1830's, grouped together all workers on the communal or provincial level. They served as their exclusive representatives until the emergence of national craft and industrial organizations, often called federations or category unions. But even after the category unions appeared on the scene, the chambers of labor continued to command the warmest affections of Italian workers. Nonetheless, as wage bargaining became more widespread, local chambers could no longer perform with dispatch and adequate knowledge certain tasks which necessity had thrust upon them in the earliest stages of union development. They could not possess, by any stretch of effort or feasible increase of personnel, detailed information about hundreds of crafts and industries. Despite the technical skills which industrial growth demanded, in some areas of even the most advanced industrial regions, chambers of labor had to continue to serve workers too remote from their own category unions or too limited in numbers to warrant the attention of their still weak and hard-beset craft or industrial organizations. In other places, chamber officials, prodded by ambition and zest for power, refused to yield jurisdiction to available category officials or to cooperate with them. Inevitably, strife arose between those who advocated the primacy of the chambers of labor and those who championed the cause of the category unions, the federationists.

This controversy involved the most basic questions of administrative policy and procedure, but it also possessed political overtones and undertones as well. The chambers of labor, less concerned than the category unions with the specific needs of any one craft or industry, emphasized the requirements of the entire local labor movement. Very often the satisfaction of these demands rested with communal or provincial officials and councils who responded only to strong political pressures. Success, instead of encouraging chamber members to seek redress within the limits of practical reforms, urged them on to scale the heights of revolutionary exactions. In contrast, the category federations, which attracted adherents by winning immediate and tangible improvements, cherished their earth-bound aims and refused to subordinate them to the so-called higher goals of Marxian theory. In answer, the chambers accused the category federations of creating pockets of privileged workers among the proletariat, thus stripping them of their zeal for revolution. The category federations replied by taunting chamber leaders with the charge of irresponsibility: they manipulated with impunity unskilled and jobless workers who risked nothing by indulging in futile strikes and demonstrations. The two main union currents avoided open hostility and formal separation by constituting the Central Secretariat of Resistance where they attempted to coordinate their activities and to compose their differences of outlook. The habit of conference, the continuing usefulness of both geographical and category forms of organization, the hardening of public opinion toward labor unions after the general strike of 1904, the temporary obloquy suffered by the revolutionary elements as a result of that event, and the marked decline in membership due to internal strife dictated the creation of the General Confederation of Labor. The first truly national center of organized workers on Italian soil harmonized in its structure, government, and operations the enthusiasm for general issues and labor unity generated by the chambers with the sobering knowledge of industrial complexity possessed by the federations and their branches.

The quest for labor union viability goes back to 1889 when Osvaldo Gnocchi-Viani, the distinguished socialist organizer of Lombardy, led a delegation of workers from Milan to Paris where they visited the celebrated Exposition. Among other wonders, they inspected the *bourse du travail* which the city of Paris had established two years earlier as a focal point of contact for workers seeking jobs and employers in need of labor. Very soon, the *bourse du travail* developed from a free employment exchange into the central headquarters of Parisian unions. The delegation from Italy reacted to this pioneering operation with enthusiasm. Soon after its members returned to Milan, the Federation of the Book, the organization of printers which enjoyed the longest continuous history of any national union on the peninsula, took official action in favor of establishing a replica of the Parisian *bourse* in Milan. By 1891, Milan, Turin, and Piacenza had formed chambers of labor (*camere del lavoro*). In calling these bodies chambers of labor rather than following the French terminology, labor exchanges, the Italian unionists sought to lend dignity to their organizations by designating them as the nominal counterparts of the chambers of commerce which represented the interests of employers.

The supreme authority of each chamber of labor rested with the general council composed of one or more delegates from each of the constituent local sections or leagues, according to their size. While the general council exercised wide supervisory, judicial, and policy-making functions, the more compact executive commission, elected by all members of the chamber, served in an administrative capacity and carried out the program approved by the general council. The control commission of three to five members, elected by either the general council or the entire membership of the chamber, watched over the activities of the executive commission and participated in its sessions without vote. Specialized commissions headed the services provided by the larger and better organized chambers: strike control, conciliation of industrial disputes, and settlement of controversies between members and their unions; organization and propaganda; workers education; medical and legal assistance; employment; and research and statistics.

On July 1, 1893, representatives from 12 chambers of labor met in Parma, thereby calling into session the First Congress of Italian Chambers of Labor which also came to be regarded as the First Congress of Societies of Resistance. Under the presidency of Angiolo Cabrini, the socialist founder of the original chamber of labor in Milan, the Parma Congress adopted a program which equated the functions and responsibilities of the chambers of labor with the widest range of industrial, economic, social, and political problems. Milan became the central headquarters of the new organization, but the lean years brought on by the depression of 1893 prevented the Congress from becoming strong and independent. Like the National Trades' Union of 1834 in the United States and the later National Labor Union of 1866, the Congress of Italian Chambers of Labor failed to collect sufficient dues to function with even modest authority. Poverty forced the Congress to live on the charity of the Milan chamber of labor and upon the financial good will of those unionists who constituted the central committee of the national organization. Despite its destitution, the Congress lived on and kept alive the idea of a national confederation of union members.[1]

The number of chambers rose to 16 in 1894 as a result of financial aid received from communal councils, chambers of commerce, provincial authorities, workers savings funds, and people's banks. Yet by October of that year, they ceased to exist. In retaliation for the uprising of the Sicilian *fasci*, Francesco Crispi ordered the dissolution of all chambers. Later, on November 12, 1896, the Council of State forbade municipalities to subsidize the chambers. Nevertheless, by early 1898, the number of reborn chambers had increased to 25. Within months, the government avenged the May Events with such fury that only four chambers survived. Two years later, when Milan played host to the Third Congress, delegates from 19 chambers attended the session. At the end of 1904, the official count by the National Labor Office in Rome showed 90 chambers in existence with a total membership of 340,228, a gain of 50,000 members since 1902.[2] The National Labor Office published information about 85 chambers claiming 2,974 branches and 392,889 members during the first half of 1907. Piedmont, Liguria, and Lombardy accounted for 33 chambers, 834 branches, and 110,845 members. Because of the traditional zeal of the peasants in Emilia for collective action, that region could boast 13 chambers, 1,229 branches, and 151,544 members. Thus, the industrial triangle of the North and Emilia contained more than half the chambers of labor and almost 70% of both the branches and members of the entire country.[3]

The National Labor Office limited itself to specific reporting dates and supplied no information about the rise and decline of chambers during the intervening years. Additional sources, however, stress the sensitivity of many short-lived chambers to the twists and turns of the business cycle. The perennial reluctance of Italian workers to pay dues regularly starved others out of existence. Still others learned, almost at the brink of extinction, that indiscriminate growth more often spelled disaster than vigor. Like the assemblies of the Knights of Labor during the Great Upheaval of 1885–1886 in the United States, the chambers in many localities found that they alienated their stable membership through neglect when large numbers of new adherents, filled with sizzling but temporary strike enthusiasm, monopolized their attention. In time, chastened leaders closed down inactive chambers or made them dependent branches of chambers in large nearby communities. Eventually, the chambers located in the provincial centers of the nation began to exert the authority of prestige over smaller chambers in the surrounding communes.

Even with the rise of the national category unions after the turn of the century and the establishment of the General Confederation of Labor in 1906, the chambers of labor, through their chief provincial seats of influence, continued on as the heart of the Confederation and of the labor movement. Of all labor institutions, they uniquely held the affection and fulfilled the needs of Italian workers. The provincial chambers achieved their hegemony by rendering services and assuming responsibilities which the communal bodies, estopped by geographical limitations, could not undertake. They provided regional employment centers and coordinated the movements of unskilled and semiskilled workers who frequently shifted from one industry to another, as job opportunities dictated, and, hence, from one category union to another. The category federations could not perform these services. Moreover, as collective bargaining and strikes spread beyond the limits of the single community, the provincial chambers assumed leadership in the formulation of contract demands and in the direction of strikes. They initiated various kinds of workers insurance and self-help projects, more economically and efficiently operated on the larger territorial basis of the province than the commune. The predominance of agricultural workers, even in North Italy, also assured the sway of the provincial chambers. Their ability to guide and coordinate activities over broad geographical areas provided the only logical and effective means for organizing widely scattered land workers. This same faculty elevated them to positions of pivotal political importance. In a labor movement steeped in politics from its very inception, the locus of union power inevitably shifted from its original communal base to the strategic provincial level.

Because workers felt close to the nearby chambers and turned to them during times of stress, these organizations interested themselves in the enactment and proper application of labor and social legislation. They chose representatives from their midst to serve on official and civic study commissions. They became advocates of workers housing and improved standards in personal and social hygiene. They also conducted preparatory educational activities for emigrants who were seeking temporary work abroad and for those who had decided to leave Italy permanently. To the chambers fell also the task of supervising the election of workers trustees (*probiviri*) in accordance with the arbitral law enacted by Parliament on June 15, 1893.

This legislation provided for local conciliation services through boards of trustees (*collegi dei probiviri*, literally, colleges of honest men) derived from the French *conseils des prud'hommes*. It marked the only successful governmental attempt between 1890 — when Article 165 of the Criminal Code provided penalties against the restriction of industrial or commercial freedom through the use of violence and intimidation, or through the incitement and prolongation of strikes and lockouts — and World War I to deal with the relationship between labor and capital. As early as 1878, when a board of trustees already operated successfully in the silk industry at Como, an investigating committee of Parliament recommended the creation of local boards of trustees to conciliate differences between workers and employers. Domenico Berti (1820–1897), the Minister of Agriculture, Industry and Commerce, attempted to give legislative embodiment to this proposal, but Parliament rejected the bill. Other equally unsuccessful attempts to regulate labor disputes and strikes received the attention of Parliament between 1883 and 1893.

Precise regulations to govern the structure and procedures of the local boards of trustees followed, by a year, the legislation of June 1893. The Minister of Justice and the Minister of Agriculture, Industry and Commerce could create boards of trustees for a single industry, or for groups of industries, in order to conciliate disputes between employers and journeymen or apprentices, or between journeymen and their apprentices. A chairman and 10 to 20 members composed each board. The chairman, or president, appointed by royal decree, had to be either a judge or an individual who possessed the qualifications necessary to be a justice of the peace (conciliatore). Employers, at a meeting of their own, chose half the members of the board from a previously prepared list of employer candidates. Labor followed the same procedure in electing their representatives from a list of foremen and workers. The regulations authorized the possible inclusion of women on either of these lists. Once the board assumed office, the employer members chose a vice-chairman by secret ballot from among the worker members. The worker members selected a second vice-chairman from among the employer members of the board. This procedure guaranteed the acceptability to both sides of the two vice-chairmen.

Each board established a conciliation office and a jury. The chairman of the board, or one of the two vice-chairmen, in rotation, presided over the conciliation office with the assistance of at least two members, one representing the employers and one representing the workers. The jury included the chairman and four members, two representing employers and two representing workers. Employers and workers might call upon the conciliation office, the court of first resort, to settle disputes over the following issues: (1) wage rates already fixed or in need of setting for the future; (2) wages for work already done; (3) working days established or in need of determination for the future; (4) compliance with special agreements concerning work; (5) defects in work performed; (6)

adjustment of wage rates due to changes in materials or methods of work; (7) damage to materials, tools, or other forms of property for which workers were responsible and industrial accidents for which employers were responsible; (8) compensation to workers when the employer shut down the factory or discharged workers before the job had been completed or the term of the agreement had expired; and (9) the cancellation of contracts with journeymen or apprentices. No case could be brought before the jury, or if the nature of the controversy exceeded the jurisdiction of the jury, before any court of justice, unless an attempt had first been made to settle the dispute through the conciliation office. The jury had the authority to decide conflicts in which the sum of money involved did not exceed 200 lire.[4]

The creation of this system of boards of trustees not only represented the initial intervention of the Italian government in disputes between capital and labor, but also placed Italy among pioneering nations like France, Australia, New Zealand, and individual states in America which dared to experiment with the techniques of conciliation and voluntary arbitration as civilized substitutes for strikes and lockouts. Moreover, the legislation of 1893 marked the victory of industrial unrest over long-standing parliamentary reluctance to interfere with economic processes. The Chamber of Deputies finally recognized the industrial revolution. Indeed, during the last decade of the nineteenth century and the first decade of the twentieth century, the intense industrial upsurge in Italy and the widening of both product and labor markets forced workmen to look beyond their local craft or factory unions and their communal or provincial chambers where they felt most at home. Scattered, autonomist, local groups found themselves incapable any longer of protecting the interest of their members. The new forces of industrialization drove them to federate and to form national unions in self-defense.

The compositors and typographers, like printers in all countries, including the United States where they established the oldest of all permanent national unions in 1850, formed Italy's first national category federation in 1872. However, they did not confer upon their association its permanent name, the Federation of the Book, until 1893. The organization of the second oldest category federation reaches back to 1877, but it did not become the Union of Italian Railroad Workers until after 1898. Workers in the state tobacco monopoly, the navy yards, the army arsenals, and other government services created the third oldest national union of consequence in 1898, on the initiative of the tobacco workers of Turin. Two years later, 300 craftsmen, organized in eight locals, set up the Italian Federation of Building Trades Workers. By the end of 1901, the

Federation counted 30,000 members and 230 leagues. The next important federation arose in 1900 among clerical workers in private employment.[5]

The metal-mechanical workers, who eventually assumed militant leadership over the entire Italian labor movement, did not form a lasting national federation until 1901. Before the strike of metallurgical workers in 1891, only isolated mutual aid societies existed among them. Following the strike, the metallurgical workers organized into leagues, but the reprisals after the May Events of 1898 drove them from the scene. Yet by December 1899, 5,000 metallurgical workers had established 18 local groups. By December 1900, the number of workers had tripled and the number of branches had risen to 67. From June 16 to 18, 1901, representatives of 80 leagues and 18,000 unionized workers met at Leghorn to constitute themselves into a country-wide federation. Delegates to the Milan congress of 1902 represented 50,000 organized metallurgical workers.[6]

The year 1901 registered the high point in the foundation of national category federations and the reorganization and strengthening of those established earlier. This burst of unionizing energy found its source in the success of the general strike at Genoa in 1900. That event established the *de facto* liberty of unions to organize and to form associations free from government interference. In the past, the longshoremen of the port, which constituted Genoa's most lucrative economic asset, had joined together into improvement leagues ever since the law of May 29, 1864 abolished their ancient guilds and left them open to exploitation by intermediaries (*confidenti*) who wormed their way into positions of trust between the longshoremen and their actual employers. In November 1900, the various longshoremen's organizations, which had won the loyalty of 4,000 of the 6,000 workers on the docks, concluded a collective agreement with the contractors who loaded and unloaded goods. Suspiciously soon thereafter, the prefect of Genoa dissolved the chamber of labor through a decree dated December 18, 1900. The chamber had suffered this indignity twice before, in 1896 and 1898. The decree of 1900 established the right of officials to search the premises of the chamber and its constituent organizations. As might have been expected, it also authorized the seizure of the membership lists of the longshoremen's improvement leagues. Immediately after the publication of the decree, the two secretaries of the chamber published a vigorous protest. On the morning of December 20, all workers of the port struck in full force. The strike then spread rapidly from the porters and longshoremen to the metallurgical plants, the shipyards of Genoa and nearby communities, and to most of the other trades and industries. At its height, the strike withdrew 18,000 to 20,000 persons from work. Public opinion in Genoa sided with the strikers. Provincial authorities, who had not expected such unified and vehement opposition, found themselves in a perturbing dilemma. In trying to explain his action to correspondents of *La Stampa* and the *Corriere della Sera,* the prefect exhibited the range of his social vision by declaring that the cowardice of the ruling classes had forced him to his decision. He explained that employers kept yielding repeatedly to the might of the chamber of labor, an obviously subversive organization since seven members of its executive commission were socialists, while the eighth member was an anarchist.

The Prime Minister, Giuseppe Saracco, intervened almost immediately and urged negotiations; they were soon begun in Genoa as well as Rome. The strikers made known their demands at a huge open-air rally and at meetings called by individual unions: (1) the restoration of all seized archives and documents belonging to the various locals and leagues of the chamber; (2) the right to elect a commission which would proceed to establish a new chamber of labor; and (3) the federation of the various improvement leagues of the port into one inclusive union. During negotiations at the prefecture, labor representatives also called for a meeting of workers to elect a representative committee charged with the task of discussing the permanent interests of Genoese workers with delegates from the chamber of commerce. The item highest on the agenda for these deliberations concerned the creation of a board of trustees to settle controversies between capital and labor. The city authorities granted office space to the committee when it was constituted and the prefect agreed to restore all documents taken from the liquidated union organizations. The signal victory won by the workers of Genoa eventually found fit expression in the comfortable and decorous headquarters furnished to the new chamber of labor by the city of Genoa. But the Prime Minister of the nation supplied a gift of wider and more lasting consequence than the generous restoration of Genoa's chamber of labor. When the unabashed prefect insisted that the eight former members of the old chamber's executive commission be excluded from candidacy for office in the reconstituted chamber, Saracco declared that organized workers had the right to elect anyone who seemed best suited to serve their needs. On Saturday, December 22, over 9,000 workers voted for the new executive commission of the resurrected chamber. Municipal officials arranged and supervised the balloting. On the afternoon of the next day, Genoa observed an impressive ceremony at the Carlo Felice Theater. Six members of Parliament, including Leonida Bissolati, celebrated the liberty of association and the right to strike won by the workers of the city.[7]

The list of category federations organized during 1901 and 1902 betokened the encouragement felt by workers throughout the peninsula as a result of the victory at Genoa. The woodworkers set up the first national organization under the new régime of freedom; it grew rapidly to include 6,000 members and 50 locals. Milan saw the inaugural congress of the Federation of the Textile Arts in March 1901. In September, the public illumination workers as well as the hatters federated on a national scale. The hat workers claimed 3,500 adherents grouped into 38 locals. At the end of October, the chemical workers joined forces. In December, the streetcar employees and those working for secondary railroads, a total of 4,000 members, held their founding congress in Milan. The next year, 1902, witnessed the country-wide organization of hospital attendants and shoe workers. In June, the unlicensed personnel of the merchant marine laid the foundations at Naples for the Federation of the Workers of the Sea.

The creation of the National Federation of Land Workers merits special consideration because the extensive unionization of agricultural day laborers and other rural workers rendered the Italian labor movement unique. The Federation not only surpassed comparable organizations of other countries in its ability to attract the peasantry, but it also assembled a national agricultural association larger in membership than any industrial or commercial union in Italy itself. Provincial and district federations preceded the birth of the national coalition. Between May and August 1901, the provinces of the Po Valley bustled with union fervor. Federations sprang up in Verona, Mirandola, Modena, Cremona, Ferrara, Polesine, Guastalla, Reggio Emilia, Piacenza, Gromello, Bologna, Parma, Alessandria, Pavia, and Lomellina. In the Romagna region, during 1900 and 1901, union leagues of sharecroppers and day laborers arose in Forlì, Ravenna, and Cesena. Central and South Italy also felt the impact of this resurgent spirit among agricultural workers. The Marches fostered two leagues and Tuscany quickened with the beginnings of unionization during 1901. In July, day laborers organized in Rome and in Apulia. Thousands of peasants joined agricultural leagues in Foggia and Bari during the autumn of 1901. The provincial socialist congress held at Corleone in Sicily decided to launch a peasant federation, The Sicilian Land. In October, organized peasants of Marsala, after obtaining a rent reduction, formed themselves into the Agricultural Federation.

The leaders of the most important provincial federations understood the need for coordinated and informed activities throughout the country. They issued a call to attend a National Congress of Land Workers on November 24, 1901. Over 700 leagues, representing more than 150,000 members, sent delegates. The inaugural convention, among its other demands, pressed for the socialization of land. Due to the grinding poverty of the peasants and to the multiformity of land cultivation, the national federation did not undertake to call strikes, organize agitation, or subsidize resistance to oppression. It served, instead, in a directive capacity to encourage organization, to assist local federations in collective bargaining, to promote interprovincial congresses and meetings concerned with mutual interests or internal conflicts, to ward off the ill effects of internal migration of workers seeking jobs by encouraging agreements among host areas and by pressing for the establishment of employment offices, and, finally, to maintain constant relations with other labor organizations in Italy and abroad and to encourage reciprocal international agreements for the protection of emigrants.[8]

As a result of this unprecedented growth of category federations during the opening years of the twentieth century, by the end of 1902, 24 national organizations of industrial, commercial, agricultural, and transport workers claimed 480,134 members. Of this total, the National Federation of Land Workers accounted for 240,000, or half of all workers organized into category federations.

The government and administrative structure of the category federations varied, necessarily, from industry to industry, craft to craft, and service to service. Nonetheless, a pattern of organization evolved which, in its essentials, fitted all federations. The form and function of institutional arrangements from commune to national headquarters established an hierarchical tradition of such strength that it survived the deepfreeze of fascism to reassert itself in the labor movement of the midtwentieth century. At the communal level, workers in the same industry, craft, or service formed a communal branch, section, league, or union. With the growth of these local bodies, it often became necessary for the central office of the federation to establish regional, provincial, or zonal offices to coordinate and supervise the work of the communal unions. As in all unions throughout the industrial world, the periodic national congress of delegates from the constituent local bodies functioned as the ostensibly supreme authority. It received the reports of the federation's officers and administrative agencies, served as the chief legislative control, revised the constitution when necessary, and appraised the financial and moral state of the federation. The central committee consisted of a set number of delegates chosen either by the congress directly or through a referendum vote of the local communal unions.

During the formative years, the only nationwide bodies were the congress and the central committee. Gradually, the delegates added the national council to the federation's hierarchy. The composition and major responsibility of the national council had precluded its existence during the federation's early years of limited resources. The national council, made up of one or more delegates from each local union, depending upon its size, met upon call whenever vital problems arose. These questions usually concerned wages. The council also supervised the activities of the central committee and discussed and acted upon all matters not specifically reserved to the congress itself. The central headquarters of the federations varied in size and complexity with the responsibilities which the state of their treasuries allowed them to assume. When the parent body paid strike benefits, unemployment insurance, sickness allowances, and travelling subsidies to members seeking work, the required personnel and administrative machinery bestowed upon the central office the appearance and character of a business enterprise. But even under the most reduced circumstances, the national headquarters of federations needed a skeleton force of executive officers, inspectors, and clerical assistants. The larger federations, even when not prosperous, needed additional staff and funds for statistical research, publications, and economic and industrial studies.[9]

In January 1902, the Italian Federation of Chambers of Labor began to publish its monthly bulletin, *La Cronaca del Lavoro* (*The Chronicle of Labor*). The definitive constitution of the federated chambers, approved by the 1901 congress at Reggio Emilia, provided for a propaganda committee. It included, among others, all parliamentary deputies who belonged to chambers of labor. Members of the propaganda committee soon realized their inadequacy. They could not cope, first of all, with the rivalry and confusion of jurisdiction between chambers of labor and category federations. As the federations gained adherents, they began to assume responsibilities which previously had resided in the chambers. This development created two hostile camps in the labor movement: the chamberites and the federationists. Nor did friction abate when the category federations added political insult to organizational injury by extending their influence among political leaders, especially those in the Socialist Party. The federations sought the aid of deputies and other influential public figures because they not only came to distrust their effectiveness in dealing alone with the ever-present scourge of unemployment, but they also began to fear for their very survival. The communal branches of the federations could not assume the crushing burden of relieving unemployed members, but the central headquarters of category unions, however deeply conscious of their obligations, soon reached the end of their own resources during periods of protracted unemployment. They therefore concluded that the problem could be met only through national legislative measures. To disseminate this view, the federations decided to influence Parliament through written and oral propaganda.

Because of the waxing dissension between the chamberites and the federationists and because of the urgency for finding a solution to unemployment, the federal committee, which directed the affairs of the federated chambers between conventions, urged the transformation of the propaganda committee into a central secretariat of resistance, endowed with adequate funds and a responsible paid staff. A referendum on convening a joint congress of delegates from chambers of labor and the federations to discuss the suggestion of the federal committee received overwhelming approval from the federated chambers. The congress met in Milan on November 1 and 2, 1902. It devised a program as well as rules and regulations for the new Central Secretariat of Resistance. Angiolo Cabrini became the director of the Secretariat. Among other responsibilities, the congress entrusted him and his colleagues to encourage closer understanding between the chambers and federations in order, principally, to avert jurisdictional disputes; to coordinate the organizational efforts and the institutional resources of the federations and to serve as a catalytic agent in their development; to take the lead in urging legislative action after consulting the wishes of each federation; and to represent the Italian labor movement at international congresses.[10]

The two main conflicting forces within Italian labor both drew their inspiration from a common source, socialism. The dedication of socialism to generous ideals and to a professedly secular but psychologically sacred mission drew young idealists of the middle class and the most intelligent scions of the working class to the side of the neglected, impoverished, and illiterate agricultural and industrial workers. Socialism both animated these natural leaders and, at the same time, poured enthusiasm, hope, and a sense of liberation into the spirit of wage earners. In 1902, this enthusiasm coursed to its zenith at the socialist congress of Imola. Roberto Michels could only characterize the fervor there as exalted. In that city, where socialists had won municipal control, men and women of all classes, not merely workers, joined the thronged socialist procession that wound through the streets during the Feast of the Madonna. Thousands upon thousands of workers, intellectuals, students, and middle-class citizens marched behind the red flag to the martial tune of the *Hymn of the Workers*.[11]

Yet, for all this ardor, intestine strife between the reformist and revolutionary socialists embroiled the congress at Imola in harsh debate. These swirling eddies of principled strife spilled over into the day-to-day affairs of the labor movement. Revolutionary zeal pervaded the chambers of labor. The champions of more gradual reform held their ground in the category federations. Stripped of theoretical pretentions, the essential conflict between the reformists and revolutionaries centered, as in all other European countries with strong socialist movements, in the divergent roles which these two currents assigned to labor unions. The revolutionaries sought to transform all unions into hubs of political agitation. The reformists wished to mold unions into efficient instruments of economic conquest. Unlike the reformists, the revolutionaries depreciated the efficacy of parliamentary action and refused to cooperate with government agencies or consultative bodies even when they dedicated their efforts unquestionably to the welfare of labor. The revolutionaries abused the strike weapon continually by converting it into a political instrument. They stirred up wage controversies without the consent and against the best judgment of the federations. In threatening strikes against employers, the revolutionaries raised the club of working-class solidarity. When they lost these ill-advised and unplanned strikes, they blamed their defeats upon the lack of collaboration by the reformists.

The life of the XXI Legislature lasted from June 1900 to October 1904. The federated chambers, the category unions, and local sections and leagues throughout the country debated and passed judgment upon parliamentary acts concerning emigration, limitations upon the work of women and children, workmen's compensation, the creation of a National Labor Office, and the establishment of the Superior Council of Labor. Although the congress of the federated chambers at Reggio Emilia in October 1901 had approved Zanardelli's project for creating a National Labor Office after ten years of parliamentary discussion, the question of cooperating with the Superior Council of Labor precipitated years of hard debate. Many socialist union leaders precluded any form of collaboration with the bourgeois state, while others, especially those also active in labor and consumer cooperatives, favored participation since it would bring close contact with public figures. These influential men could induce favorable legislation, public contracts, and subventions.

To complicate the issue still more, many socialists, although well disposed toward the Council, fought the admission of representatives of the Christian social movement. In fact, a decade elapsed before delegates of the Catholic cooperative federation entered the Council.

The organization of the Superior Council of Labor deserves attention because it embodies the earliest official expression of a persistent idea which has fascinated Italian socialists, syndicalists, and nationalists for decades: the parliament of functional occupational groups rather than of geographical entities. Even the corporative experience under fascism did not weaken its hold. During World War II, at the First Congress of the restored General Confederation of Labor, the delegates called for the reconstitution of the Superior Council of Labor. Later, the 1948 Constitution of the Republic provided for its revivification. After nine years of delay, the Italian Parliament implemented the intention of the Constitution by approving law 33 of January 5, 1957 creating the National Council of the Economy and Labor at the insistence of all segments of the contemporary labor movement.

The original Superior Council of Labor, which began its operations in Rome on September 25, 1903, numbered forty-three members. The Minister of Agriculture, Industry and Commerce presided over its deliberations. The Senate and the Chamber of Deputies each elected three members. The chambers of commerce and the agrarian assemblies of the Kingdom were entitled to four members each, while the National League of Italian Cooperatives, the Association of People's Banks, and the Italian Federation of Mutual Aid Societies were each assigned three representatives. Since industrialists were not as yet organized into associations and since unions were not legally recognized, the government itself chose six employer representatives from agricultural, industrial, commercial, and mining enterprises, as well as an equal number of labor representatives from the ranks of miners, port and maritime labor, peasants, and industrial workers. Government officials, economists, and social scientists constituted the remaining members of the Council.

Neither industrial expansion, nor the growing preoccupation of the Italian State with social and labor reform, nor the good offices of the national government in creating consultative bodies where representatives of all social and economic classes met to discuss issues of mutual concern, could dam the rush of proletarian violence which periodically engulfed the peninsula. The general strike of 1904, already properly detailed as an important episode in Italy's political history, marked the triumph of the revolutionary forces within the Milan chamber of labor, the most powerful union organization in all Italy. It also manifested the temperamental propensity of Italian workers to give themselves up wholly to excitation by romantic insurrectionists. These extremist leaders, loyal only to the apocalyptic demands of the last barricaded judgment, believed with utter conviction that to them fell the sacred revolutionary duty of whipping Italian workers into mutinous, stone-showering demonstrations since centuries of servitude had sapped them of will power. This form of economic and social protest became increasingly common during the closing years of the nineteenth century and the early decades of the twentieth century. Although the Bakuninites had elevated violence into a passion and Arturo Labriolo had clothed it with dialectical respectability by extracting revolutionary syndicalism out of Karl Marx through the courtesy of Georges Sorel (1847–1922), Socialist Party congresses had always rejected the general strike as an effective weapon of victory in the proletarian arsenal. Despite this stand, political strikes exploded in Italy more frequently before World War I than in those countries where the syndicalist-inspired working class had officially hailed direct action and general strikes as the means to expropriate the ruling classes.

The general strike of 1904 ended in political defeat for the socialists in the national elections which Giolitti called for November 6 and 13, 1904. The unions, too, already hard beset by unemployment, financial stringency, and intensified employer resistance, suffered the consequences of internecine warfare. In Milan, where the reformists and revolutionaries battled most ardently, the chamber of labor in 1904 could report only 130 constituent organizations and 19,082 members, in contrast to 163 sections and 43,292 adherents in 1902. During this time, the category federations lost 150,000 members, especially among peasants, textile workers, and metal-mechanical workers. Some federations in the early stages of their development, like the newspaper venders, found continued growth impossible, while others went out of existence. Still others merged with sister federations in order to survive. According to the vital statistics of the National Labor Office for the entire labor movement in 1904, the chambers of labor and category federations with socialist sympathies counted 450,000 members; the non-Marxist unions of clerks, government employees, teachers, and professional persons, which felt close to the radical and republican parties, claimed 100,000 members; the customs workers, actors, orchestral instrumentalists, and clerks, who professed no political preferences, numbered 20,000 members; and the Social Christian associations totalled 100,000 members.[12] (More attention will focus upon the Social Christian movement later. This early, the strength of Christian Democracy consisted not in its

unions, which organized small landowners and artisans, but in its cooperatives and mutual aid societies — a phase of development experienced by the Catholic labor movement of Chile during the 1950's.)

As a result of serious reverses, particularly among the peasants, the
Central Secretariat of Resistance urged the chambers of labor to work
closely with consumer and producer cooperatives. Irony accompanied
this turn of fortunes because, as late as 1901, the Congress of the Federated Chambers of Labor debated the question of admitting mutual aid
societies and cooperatives to the chambers of labor. The pure unionists
argued that, while the chambers fought against capitalism, the cooperatives forestalled the day of reckoning by basking under the illusion that
they could substitute cooperation for private capitalistic enterprise. The
more rational unionists countered this objection by pointing out that the
Marxian workers of Reggio Emilia based their unions upon labor and
consumer cooperatives. They asked pointedly what function a chamber
of labor in Reggio Emilia could serve if it ousted the cooperators. The
Congress finally declared that class-conscious organizations might properly admit mutual aid societies and cooperatives to membership. The
central body of the cooperative movement, the National League of Cooperatives, organized in 1886, also thoroughly debated the nature of the
most suitable relationship between the cooperative and labor movements. Since the League welcomed cooperative groups of all political
persuasions — liberal, republican, socialist, and Social Christian — the
decision of the XIII Congress at Genoa in October 1903 to cooperate
closely with the predominantly socialist labor movement illustrated, of
course, its own socialist predilections, but also revealed the practical
good sense of the League.

The moral and financial support of the cooperative movement proved
of particular salvation to the besieged agricultural leagues. Class-conscious unions of peasants had not spread beyond Lombardy, Emilia,
Umbria, Lazio, Apulia, and Sicily. The peasants and agricultural day
laborers of Liguria, Tuscany, Abruzzi, Basilicata, Calabria, Sardinia,
and Piedmont, except in the province of Novara, remained almost completely outside the influence of the labor movement. Yet in the very
areas where agricultural organization had reached its apogee, disastrous
strikes in 1902 brought about a fall in membership as swift as its rise.
On February 7, 1904, the National Federation of Land Workers had
a financial balance of 62 lire. Consequently, the executive committee and
representatives of the constitutent organizations of the Federation met in
Mantua that month. They decided to change the character of the national
body into a Central Secretariat of Provincial Organizations. Thirteen

provincial units with 101,200 members joined the new decentralized organization. Some 60,000 peasants belonging to local leagues which had not federated on a provincial basis also entered the Secretariat.

Thus, within two years, agricultural unionism had lost almost 90,000 adherents. Firmer resistance and stronger reprisals by landowners, internal dissension, inexperience, and the failure of agricultural workers to understand the strategic aspects of strikes undoubtedly contributed to this precipitate decline. But other economic and social realities shared even more heavily in this process. Although the capital invested in agricultural production did not decline during these early years of the twentieth century, it did not increase at a rate fast enough to absorb the total available manpower. Moreover, the higher that agricultural unions raised wages, the more disposed were landowners to introduce labor-saving machinery. The obvious answer lay in the reduction of the work force. Emigration from the Po Valley helped in allaying peasant distress, but it did not attain sufficiently large proportions to constitute a long-term solution. The unions then turned to the cooperatives and to the government for aid. Although consumer cooperatives helped peasants and laborers to cut down their daily expenditures, they needed labor and agricultural cooperatives to provide them with wages. Beginning in 1903, the collective rental of land for cooperative cultivation, which had first appeared in 1886 at Ravenna and Cremona, spread into Emilia, Romagna, and Mantua. After Parliament in July 1889 had sanctioned the right of labor and producer cooperatives to bid on government contracts, these forms of self-employment also spread throughout the North.[13]

The Fifth Congress of the federated chambers and category federations met at Genoa in January 1905. The delegates from the revolutionary Milan chamber presented a motion which accused the socialist, radical, and republican members of Parliament of neglect of duty both before and after the general strike of 1904. The Congress did not approve this resolution, but the atmosphere of schism already bore down heavily upon the assembly. Sharp boundaries of thought between the revolutionaries and the reformists had not completely asserted themselves, since many revolutionaries had still not forsworn parliamentary action. But the Road to Damascus for the extreme left-wing lay nearby. Already, socialist periodicals had been dispensing the revolutionary syndicalist ideas of Georges Sorel and Hubert Lagardelle, the editor of *Mouvement Socialiste*. These men purported to propound an entirely new theory of the role of the proletariat. Impatient with the delays and ineptitudes of parliamentary governments and with the pace and disorder of political compromise, they saw in direct revolutionary action, unfettered by parties, the only hope for the fulfillment of the Marxian prophecy. Sorel's masterpiece, *Violence,* found publication at Palermo in 1905 before the French edition appeared. But, as yet, most of the Italian left-wing socialists with syndicalist predilections remained within the Party. However, Enrico Leone abandoned the Party to found his magazine, *Il Divenire Sociale* (*The Social Future*) in Rome during 1906.

At the end of the sterile debates, the Genoa Congress approved measures of policy which revealed the internal disorder to which strife between the chambers and the federations had led. The Congress declared that the chambers had to inform the federations at once about the organization of new groups of workers within their craft or industrial jurisdictions. Moreover, the chambers had to assume responsibility for the enrollment of these members in appropriate federations within a year after they joined the chambers. The motion also urged the federations, in turn, to direct their local unions to affiliate with the chambers of labor. The Central Secretariat of Resistance received the mandate to organize new category federations and to mediate disagreements between the chambers and federations. These decisions and the deliberations which preceded them had the merit of attempting to clarify organizational principles and lines of authority even though they proved powerless to preserve labor unity. Just as the national craft unions in the United States discovered in the 1870's and 1880's that they risked the very life of their organizations by leaving locals unchecked in their freedom to negotiate wage agreements and to declare strikes, so the Italian federations insisted that the chambers cease to aid local craft or industrial groups which remained outside the federations or which belonged to the federations but did not respect their decisions. The national federations also maintained that they alone, and not the chambers, had sufficient knowledge to judge when and if their locals should demand improvements in wages and conditions of work or, in the absence of satisfaction, should risk strike action. Among the delegates who favored this trend toward organizational clarity and administrative efficiency were representatives of Umanitaria, Italy's most illustrious privately endowed institution dedicated to the welfare of workers. It contributed remarkably to the preparation of leaders in labor, cooperative, and other social institutions. Its educational goals resembled those of Ruskin College at Oxford and the schools for leadership training established by the Christian and socialist unions in Germany.

Syndicalist theory received testing in practice the next month, February 1905. After the Chamber of Deputies declared itself in favor of the return of the railroads to public control, and at the same time that the Minister of Public Works presented a draft law covering new arrangements under state administration, the agitation committee of the railroad workers organizations — which represented Railroad Redemption (Riscatto Ferroviario) and the Federation of Railroad Unions — demanded twenty principal reforms to safeguard their interests. They included a unified set of regulations to cover all government lines, the promotion of temporary employees to the permanent staff after six months of probation, a working day of eight hours, and ten days of leave with pay. These demands appeared reasonable enough, but the method chosen by the railroad workers to enforce them surprised not only the nation, but the labor movement itself. In 1902, the railroad workers had won a major victory over the concessionaire companies by the skillful use of reformist tactics and the exertion of pressure upon members of Parliament since the government still owned the railroads. Now, in 1905, the same workers shifted to direct revolutionary action to win their demands. At the end of February, they applied the operating rules meticulously. By obstructing and impeding travel, they alienated public opinion from the start. The entire press, except for the socialist newspapers, fulminated against the railroad workers and incited the government to action.

On March 4, Giolitti resigned from office with his entire cabinet, alleging ill health. This move delighted the railroad workers and seemed to prove to the revolutionary syndicalists that pure trade union action had brought the government low. Unhappily for the union leaders, they now found that they had no excuse to delay strike action promised for April 16, the very day when the new Prime Minister, Tommaso Tittoni, opened debate in the Chamber on the proposed railroad law. Members of Parliament regarded the strike as a test between railroad union workers and the dignity of the Italian government. Since the strikers had eschewed political lobbying in favor of revolutionary direct action, they now faced the prospect of standing alone or securing the aid of the entire labor movement. The Central Secretariat of Resistance refused to call a general strike. After four days, the railroad strike, which had secured the participation of less than half the workers, ended.

This defeat injured the railroad unions and the entire labor movement as well. It also terminated the usefulness of the Central Secretariat of Resistance. The revolutionaries taunted the Secretariat with responsibility for failure because it had refused to involve all unions in the strike. On April 29, 1905, the central committee of the Secretariat resigned from office.

The incessant factional quarrels wearied the rank and file and helped to empty their faith in labor unions. Between 1904 and 1906, the number of chambers declined from 90 to 82 and membership fell from 340,228 to 318,446. The number of affiliated organizations dropped from 3,328 to 2,733. The loss in membership affected particularly Piedmont, Lombardy, and Campania. Moderate elements within the labor movement recognized the need for immediate, strong action.[14]

In February 1906, the Secretary of the Italian Federation of Metallurgical Workers, who also enjoyed membership on the Superior Council of Labor, proposed to other category federations that they convene in Milan to discuss the formation of a national confederation of Italian unions. This proposal found favor and nineteen category federations met in Milan on March 4. After considerable discussion, the delegates resolved to summon a nationwide meeting of local union delegates later that year in Milan. This convention would serve as the constituent assembly for the proposed confederation. Since the delegates did not wish to offend the Central Secretariat of Resistance, they urged full cooperation with the Secretariat upon the preparatory committee. These good intentions proved difficult at first since the revolutionaries had gained control of the Secretariat after the resignation of the central committee. However, as soon as the revolutionaries realized that they could never revive the Secretariat, they offered no strong objections to the creation of the new confederation. Thus, initiative passed into the moderate hands of the preparatory committee.

The constituent assembly, which became the First Congress of the General Confederation of Labor (Confederazione Generale del Lavoro — C.G.L.), met from September 29 to October 1, 1906 at the headquarters of the Milan chamber of labor which had now returned to the control of the reformists. The Congress drew 500 delegates from 700 local unions and leagues representing 250,000 members. Since the reformists had taken the initiative in convoking the constituent assembly, a group of revolutionaries refused to participate in the proceedings, but enough syndicalists, republicans, anarchists, and local unions without political or ideological commitments did attend the sessions to insure long disputes of stormy verbosity. Both the moderate majority and left-wing minority agreed upon the formation of the General Confederation of Labor, but quarreled violently about its policies, functions, and powers. Compromise became impossible since the revolutionary minority groups insisted that all decisions of the constituent assembly, including the proposed constitution, be submitted to the referendum vote of each affiliated local union and league. After the critical majority resolution won by twice the number of votes received by two minority proposals, the syndicalist, republican, and anarchist delegates absented themselves from the morning session on October 1. These factions announced through a representative that they would not participate in the final deliberations of the assembly; they added loftily that they would abide by the decisions of the proletariat once it expressed its views on the proposed General Confederation of Labor through direct interrogation by referendum. The assembly received this message of the first outright cleavage in the Italian labor movement with silence. It proceeded to elect officers and governing committees. It named Turin as the central seat of the Confederation. The prominence accorded to the first paragraph of article 3 of the constitution, which detailed the principal duties of the Confederation, gave evidence to the importance attached by the experience of the delegates to the saving principle it enunciated: "The Confederation will undertake the absolute general direction of the agricultural and industrial proletarian movement without any considerations whatsoever of political distinctions."[15]

All constituent unions in the national category federations and chambers of labor could seek membership in the C.G.L. Unaffiliated independent groups might also join the C.G.L. if no suitable category federations existed for their crafts or industries and if no chambers functioned in their areas of activity. The constitution entrusted the execution of confederal policies and responsibilities to the directive committee composed of seven members elected by the national congress. The directive committee chose two of its own members to constitute the executive secretariat. The constitution also provided for a vigilance committee composed of thirty members. Among other tasks, it had the power to summon a national congress more frequently than every two years if considered opportune.[16]

On January 1, 1907, *The Confederation of Labor* began to appear regularly. Two weeks later, the directive committee nominated Rinaldo Rigola as the general secretary of the Confederation and editor of its paper. He served in this capacity until his resignation in 1918. The directive committee also chose an administrative secretary. Central headquarters remained at Turin until 1911 when it moved to Milan.

Less than a month after the constituent assembly had completed its work, representatives from the C.G.L., the National League of Cooperatives, and the Italian Federation of Mutual Aid Societies convened in Milan on November 23, 1906. While each organization retained its own autonomy, they drew up an agreement to act in concert for the defense of their common interests. The executive or directive committees of the three national organizations arranged to keep in close communication through their general secretaries.[17]

Shortly before the establishment of the C.G.L., 75 employers in various branches of manufacturing inaugurated the Piedmont Industrial League in Turin on July 19, 1906. As early as 1864, the entrepreneurs of the leading industry in Turin had constituted themselves as the Society of Woolen Cloth Manufacturers in order to deal uniformly with their employees. But the Piedmont Industrial League of 1906 represented the first attempt of Italian employers in more than one industry to band together to protect themselves against their workers by defending the principle of liberty of contract. The already existing chambers of commerce did not qualify for this distinction because they included commercial as well as industrial firms and did not concern themselves exclusively with problems of labor relations. Industrialists and landowners in other parts of Italy soon followed the example set by Turin. The most noted agricultural association, the National Agrarian Confederation, evoked particular attention for its activities in the provinces of Emilia between 1908 and 1914.

Why did Italian employers delay so long in creating industrial associations to protect liberty of contract, to aid fellow employers when strikes shut down their plants, and to insure uniformity of policy and action in dealing with unions? Rinaldo Rigola, the most perceptive as well as the most comprehensive and knowledgeable of all Italian labor historians, suggested that industrialists at first looked upon unions as pathological manifestations which could not long endure. In their estimation, labor organizations and social legislation did not emerge out of basic economic and industrial conditions, but out of government demagoguery and fear of demonstrations in the piazzas. They therefore regarded these transient manifestations with forbearance as another sign of the iniquities of the age. Granted, they reasoned, the government had the right to encourage freedom of union action by assuming an attitude of benevolent neutrality, but employers also retained the right not to deal with organizations of their workers. Upon the rock of this logic, elaborated into a principle of economic progress, they later erected their industrial associations.

The doctrine of laissez faire found champions among the unions as well whenever it suited their requirements — an attitude not unknown to the American Federation of Labor in the time of Samuel Gompers and William Green. Three events in 1907 illustrated this aspect of the mentality of the Italian labor movement. In January 1907, *The Confedera-*

tion of Labor discussed in its pages projected legislation concerning collective bargaining then under study by the Ministry of Agriculture, Industry and Commerce. The Minister himself had come to realize the difficulties of formulating a law applicable to all industries. He therefore intended to present to Parliament a series of laws tailored to the character of individual industries or groups of allied industries. Repeating the widespread opinion of Italian unions about legislation on collective agreements, the C.G.L.'s mouthpiece reminded the Ministry that labor had not sought or encouraged the proposed law. The Confederation asked, instead, for changes in the existing statute creating boards of trustees in order to expand the jurisdiction of these informal conciliation tribunals. The newspaper continued: "The collective labor agreement is rendered possible and becomes a fact through the formation of labor organizations on the one hand, and the concentration of industry on the other hand. Therefore, the law should not intervene, except to secure and assure the results of free contractual relations between the two groups: owners and workers."[18]

The voice of the C.G.L. then cited the recently stipulated contract between the Italian Federation of Metallurgical and Mechanical Workers (Federazione Italiana Operai Metallurgici e Meccanici — F.I.O.M.) and Itala, the automobile plant in Turin. It hailed that agreement as splendid confirmation of the virtues imparted to collective bargaining by workers aided not by governmental enactments but by practical tactics derived from their class-conscious instincts. This Marxian tribute to free collective bargaining should not impair appreciation of the wholly extraordinary character of the Itala contract — remarkable for Italy or for any other industrial nation of that era. It stirred up lively controversy, criticism, and even indignation. The epochal document set forth rules governing wages, hours of work, incentive rates, and discipline. The company agreed to hire all workers through the employment office which F.I.O.M. had established in Turin. The firm received the right to have two representatives in that office. All workers had to be union members, or had to join the union within a month of employment. If a worker were expelled from the union, he had to be laid off without dismissal pay. The terms of the contract were to endure for three years. F.I.O.M. guaranteed to the company freedom from strikes during this period and deposited 100,000 lire as a performance bond. In compensation for this guarantee, the company granted pensions to certain workers. It also obligated itself to contribute enough capital for the construction of 3,000 rooms in a cooperative housing project in accordance with the terms of the law of May 31, 1903. Advanced as these provisions were, they were overshadowed by the creation of a grievance committee for the plant. All grievances and controversies funnelled through the grievance committee. If the problem could not be settled, it was appealed to a specially instituted arbitration commission with the power of final judgment. The workers were not to suspend operations during the course of the resolution of grievances. In turn, the firm obligated itself, in the case of firing a worker for reasons which were not beyond its control, to pay an indemnity equal to 70 days of wages.

Although F.I.O.M.'s metal workers constituted the vanguard of the Italian labor movement and although they approached the world with relatively moderate political and social views as contrasted with those of many other unionists in the North, this unusual contract did not survive three years. Neither the officials of F.I.O.M. nor the workers had had sufficient preparation in union and industrial life to aid them in maintaining their obligations. F.I.O.M. itself and the modern Italian labor movement had but recently come into existence. Both the union and the company had telescoped decades of factory give-and-take to arrive at a position in collective bargaining so advanced. Certainly the union had obtained undeniable advantages and ironclad guarantees. Nevertheless, more revolutionary colleagues in other unions taunted F.I.O.M. with binding workers to their masters and stifling their combative spirit. Since not even F.I.O.M. possessed the stature to assume the responsibility of carrying out a complex collective agreement, the metal workers reestablished their so-called freedom of action and returned to the old system of memorializing their employers. However, they did not abandon one feature of the forward-looking collective contract with Itala, the grievance committee. Even more, in the years between 1907 and 1914, the creation of grievance committees became a general goal of the wider labor movement — a prize to be won in the heart of the factory. It constituted "the object of the greatest aspirations and claims of the working classes."[19]

In discussing the failure of the F.I.O.M. — Itala contract, Rinaldo Rigola, a moderate socialist, felt strongly that unions would have denaturalized themselves in following the strict terms imposed by the agreement. By becoming responsible for the adherence of all members to contractual obligations, unions would have transformed themselves into business organizations for selling labor under monopoly conditions. The prospect of this development — the logical outgrowth of the desire of all unions in all countries to control the labor market either before or after hiring — repelled even the most reformist of socialist labor leaders. But

343

they also rejected another consequence of mature collective bargaining: the legal recognition of unions.

At the very time that the Ministry of Agriculture, Industry and Commerce attempted to frame suitable legislation on collective agreements, the Superior Council of Labor projected legislation to confer juridical personality upon labor organizations. Recognition by the State would have devolved through the simple act of registration. Once enrolled, unions acquired the right to send representatives to official consultative bodies and boards and to consummate collective contracts enforceable in the courts. To guarantee the fulfillment of union obligations under the contract, the proposal required the posting of a bond equal to one-fifth of the union's financial resources. As a further guarantee of union responsibility, the draft law required the approval of the wage provisions of the collective agreement by at least two-thirds of the workers concerned. A notary or police official had to verify the results of the vote and then the agreement had to be filed at communal headquarters or printed in the bulletin of the prefecture. Since even those unions which could not be suspected of syndicalist aversion to state initiative in social and economic affairs harbored both Marxist suspicions of middle-class motives as well as unacknowledged laissez-faire proclivities for freedom of action, the labor movement opposed the recommendations of the Superior Council of Labor.

Perhaps, on a plane clean of ideologies, union officials simply feared their inability to maintain contractual engagements, given the political volatility of union membership. The draft law also opened up another source of concern to the unions by making them responsible not only for their own members, but also for unorganized workers in the plant under contract. Although then, as now, unions already suffered from frequent contractual violations by employers and although the projected legislation would have given them recourse to the courts, labor officials dreaded their responsibilities under the proposals more than they desired the security offered to legally recognized unions. They rationalized their opposition by maintaining that notarized documents, court litigation, and procedural delays could never foster constructive labor relations — a refrain loudly familiar to more recent times and happier lands. Consequently, the suggestions of the Superior Council of Labor returned to its files. The unions and employers continued their freedom of action to conclude, or not, simple wage agreements; when the contracts grew in complexity, the employers insisted upon specific guarantees for contingencies and the unions determined, in each case, whether they could meet these additional requirements.[20]

In working for legislation desired by labor, the directive committee of the C.G.L. took seriously the constitutional provision enjoining the Confederation from favoring any one political philosophy. The committee therefore considered it mandatory to clear its legislative demands with the three parties of the Extreme Left: the radicals, the republicans, and the socialists. To this end, it assembled representatives of these parliamentary groups at Bologna in April 1907. The delegates examined carefully the major proposals of the C.G.L. As an earnest of political impartiality, the spokesmen for the C.G.L. invited the parties of the Extreme Left to send representatives to the congresses of the Confederation. Despite these good intentions, the C.G.L.'s leadership found itself ever more closely bound to the Socialist Party, but troubled by its proprietary attitudes. Misunderstandings between the two organizations lasted throughout 1907 and 1908 as the C.G.L. sought to stave off interference, to insure for itself the management of labor affairs, and to limit party concerns to political activities. The controversy continued on until the Congress of Florence in September 1908 stilled the din of oratory. Common sense and good will moved the reformists, now in command of the Party after the expulsion of the syndicalists, but a ukase from on high also made for peace. The international socialist movement had purportedly resolved this troublesome issue through its all-things-to-all-men Stuttgart declaration: the Party and the unions must regulate their own affairs independently of each other, but in the overriding interest of the class struggle, the relation between the Party and the unions must grow increasingly more intimate without compromising the unity of the labor movement.[21]

In Italy, the very existence of the labor movement, not its unity alone, stood in mortal danger from outside political interference. The precipitate rise in the number of strikes, often instigated without the knowledge of the parent federations, and the more and more frequent resort of Italian workers to the politically motivated general strike brought level-headed socialists to the realization that labor leaders had to possess unquestioned control of their own organizations. They knew that, unless unions learned to discipline strike action, Parliament would eventually limit the use of this life-giving weapon for them. The proliferation of strikes during this period cannot be wholly ascribed to revolutionary political agitation, but must be traced in part to the friendly neutrality of the government under the inspiration of Giolitti, the exceedingly slow rise in real wages, the financial depression of 1907 and 1908, and the decline of building activities with the ensuing rise of rents for housing. Nevertheless, the clash between the chamberites and the federationists, between the politically minded localists and the more moderate union-oriented national category and C.G.L. leaders, revealed the catalytic importance of political considerations in precipitating strikes both locally and throughout the country. The frequency and size of ordinary strikes and the recurrence of general strikes forced the C.G.L. to assert its authority by withholding aid from manifestations which alienated public opinion and could end only in disaster.

The statistical record of strike action from 1891 to the outbreak of World War I illustrates the dimensions of the institutional problem which plagued the C.G.L. In 1891, 132 strikes occurred among some 35,000 industrial workers, while 24 strikes occurred in agriculture and affected almost 8,000 workers. Only a decade later, the number of industrial strikes had risen to 1,042 and involved close to 200,000 strikers, while the number of agricultural strikes had increased to 629 and idled nearly 223,000 peasants. In 1907, 321,500 industrial workers conducted 1,881 separate strikes. That year, agricultural workers did not linger far behind their factory brothers when 254,131 took part in 377 strikes. By 1911, the number of industrial strikes had decreased to 1,107 and the number of strikers to 253,000; the number of agricultural strikes and strikers had decreased to 148 and 133,000. However, two years later, although only 810 industrial strikes occurred, the number of strikers reached the all-time high of 384,725. In agriculture, the scene remained comparatively calm with but 97 strikes and 80,000 strikers.[22]

After the general strike of 1904, the principal labor disturbance to arouse public opinion throughout the nation and to give second thoughts to labor leaders occurred at Turin in May 1906. The police attempted to invade the chamber of labor there during a demonstration. When this action met classically inevitable resistance, one worker was killed and others were wounded. Without awaiting the approval of the Central Secretariat of Resistance (the C.G.L. had not as yet been organized), or seeking prior agreement with other chambers of labor, the Turin group proclaimed a national general strike in protest against police violence. The strike soon extended to other cities and led to grave disorder especially in Bologna and Rome.

Little more than a year later, on October 10, 1907, the gas workers strike in Milan, after lasting several days, came to a satisfactory end. As part of the settlement, the union insisted that Italian and foreign strikebreakers return to their homes. While a train filled with scabs passed the vicinity of the Miani and Silvestri factory the next day, a stone hurled against the train smashed one of its windows. The train ground to a halt and *carabinieri* left their cars and approached workmen who were standing in front of the factory. This encounter first resulted in commotion and then in gunfire; several workers fell wounded. On October 12, the following day, a general strike swept over Milan and other cities as well. The state railroad workers decided to join the general strike, despite the provisions of article 49 of the regulations which forbade strikes on pain of dismissal. Leaders of both the Socialist Party and the C.G.L. directed the railroad workers not to follow their inclinations. They refused this guidance. Two hours after they left their posts, the government dismissed or arrested a total of 500 railroad employees. The firm stand taken by the Socialist Party and the C.G.L. against unadvised, irresponsible action by local hotheads as well as against strikes in the public services naturally widened the breach between the revolutionaries and reformists within both movements.[23]

The next general strike took place in the province of Parma. During 1907, the Parma chamber of labor became the center of the dissident movement which had stalked out of the constituent assembly of the C.G.L. in 1906 and had espoused without reservations the principles of revolutionary syndicalism. Since that doctrine regarded each strike as a vital fraction of the general strike for liberation, the Italian disciples of Sorel sought to multiply and intensify strike activities by inciting workers on to turbulent demonstrations. Syndicalist chambers of labor and local agricultural leagues beyond the province of Parma grouped themselves around the chamber at Parma to form a center of revolutionary syndicalism. This wider group created the Committee of Resistance which eventually became the Italian Syndical Union (Unione Sindacale Italiana).

In 1908, the Parma chamber, under the leadership of its secretary, Alceste De Ambris, claimed 12,000 members belonging to 200 leagues. Only one-sixth of this total worked in industry; agricultural laborers and sharecroppers constituted the bulk of the membership. The Agrarian Employers Association of Parma counted 3,000 members and opposed the chamber with financial strength and dominant influence over local government officials. On April 30, the chamber proclaimed a strike of agricultural day laborers in retaliation against the proprietors who had violated the terms of the contract concluded the preceding year. The Association responded to this threat by importing strikebreakers from surrounding areas. For two months, the strikers resisted exceptionally well and their numbers increased from 11,000 to 30,000. Although the C.G.L., the Federation of Land Workers, and the Socialist Party espoused and aided the cause of the day laborers, they placed little faith in the judgment of the syndicalist leaders who directed the strike. In

June, the Parma chamber justified their fears and doubts by decreeing a general strike for the entire city. The police immediately invaded and occupied the premises of the chamber. Oltre Torrente, the working-class section of Parma, fought the police for three days. After government forces ended the strike in Parma itself, agitation continued in the countryside, but began to wear down by July and finally collapsed.

The strike had offered dramatic moments when sympathizers opened common kitchens to feed the strikers and their families and when the children of strikers left the province to live with people who could care for them — a move employed four years later by the Industrial Workers of the World during the famous textile strike in Lawrence, Massachusetts. But, in the end, Parmese revolutionary syndicalist fervor had ended in complete failure: the dismissal of all striking day laborers and the absence of any contract whatsoever. This misfortune, as well as the series of earlier events at Turin and Milan, led directly to the September 1908 Florence pact between the Socialist Party and the C.G.L. on jurisdictional prerogatives, as blessed by the Stuttgart encyclical.[24]

Despite the pact of Florence, while leaders of the Socialist Party and the C.G.L. remained uncertain during October 1909 about the form of their protest against the visit of the Czar of All the Russias to Italy, the execution in Spain of Francisco Ferrer touched off a spontaneous general strike throughout Italy. Workers in Paris also protested, by means of a general strike against the political policies of the Spanish government and the strike spread to other large cities in France. The desecration of the general strike, by invoking it for purely political ends, so disgusted the master-dogmatist of French unionism, Sorel, that he felt constrained to abandon completely his concern with the labor movement.[25]

During 1910 in Romagna, a furious battle broke out between agricultural day laborers and sharecroppers for the possession of reaping machinery. This spectacle, which belied the Marxian solidarity of workers, caused difficulty and embarrassment to the C.G.L. Yet consternation increased to shame when it became apparent that the struggle between the sharecroppers and day laborers disguised, in reality, political warfare between socialists and republicans.[26]

The next summer, in 1911, the automobile workers of Turin, who had succumbed to the influence of revolutionary syndicalist leaders, went on strike to obtain lower working hours and an increase in wages. The strike lasted for more than three months and ended in defeat shortly before Italy prepared to occupy Libya. F.I.O.M. directed the 1912 strike of metal workers in Turin. After three months, the more moderate union achieved partial satisfaction of demands. Although the workers had asked for a

55-hour week and a half-day on Saturday, the three-year agreement established a 59-hour week until the end of 1912 and a general wage increase of .01 lira an hour (laborers received .30 to .40 lira an hour, while semiskilled workers received .60 to .70 lira an hour). The company agreed to reduce the work week to 58 hours in 1913 and to 57 hours in 1914; it also obligated itself to increase wages during 1913 by .01 lira an hour and by a similar additional amount in 1914.[27]

The bloody repression of a meeting in Rimini by the police triggered another general strike in November 1913 as a protest against repeated interference of armed official patrols with popular demonstrations.[28] This troubled, prewar era of local, regional, and national general strikes, invoked seemingly at will by a revolutionary minority, ended in the national tumult of Red Week during June 1914. That minor revolution, when rioting demonstrators battled the police throughout the peninsula, paralyzed the country. Chapter VI has already detailed the political aspects of this event.

The readiness of Italian workers to resort frequently to the use of the general strike found partial explanation in the festering accumulation of economic and social resentments which Marxism in its more radical forms sought out for exploitation. Unemployment and underemployment among all workers, but especially among the agricultural day laborers, also accounted, in part, for this phenomenon. Certainly, men and women without jobs or prospects gained emotional release and suffered no loss through militant action, no matter how frequently strikes occurred. In part, too, the proclivity to mass action in the piazzas stemmed from the spirit of intense cultural localism which manifested itself in the labor world by the deeper loyalty of workers toward the chambers of labor than toward the category federations. Yet only the national craft and industrial unions had the potential ability to build a disciplined, dues-paying movement out of Italy's working class. Eventually, this central defect of orientation and control left the ardent but fragile labor organizations at the mercy of the fascist Black Shirts.

Despite the turmoil of general strikes and the rise of a revolutionary syndicalist federation, the C.G.L. grew in numbers under moderate leadership. Emerging Catholic unions and the cooperative movement, which mirrored the forward-looking conservative forces ever present in Italian economic and social life, also gathered strength. The Second Congress of the C.G.L. (also recorded, historically, as the Seventh Congress of the Societies of Resistance) met at Modena from September 6 to 9, 1908, two weeks before the decisive Socialist Party congress at Florence.[29] Between 1907 and 1908, the membership of the Confederation rose from 190,422 to 306,957, representing 176,957 industrial workers and 130,000 peasants. Since official government statistics showed 934,369 organized workers in the Kingdom at the beginning of 1908, C.G.L.'s membership represented 33% of all organized labor.

The Second Congress approved an urgent measure regarding sympathetic strikes. To insure the utilization of this tactical weapon only after due deliberation and close regard for all elements in the situation, the Congress ruled that national and international appeals for solidarity had first to be addressed to the General Confederation of Labor as the chief representative of the unionized proletariat. The C.G.L. would then determine its position and initiate necessary procedures. Later, the delicate task of delineating the character of the relationship which should properly prevail between the C.G.L. and political parties divided the delegates between those who took the Confédération Générale du Travail as their model, rejecting all political links, and those who desired them. However, among those who approved some form of alliance with political parties, the precisionists wished to know the identity of the particular parties to be favored. An amendment to the majority resolution settled all doubts by singling out "the Socialist Party and those other parties which accept the method of the class struggle and the program and methods of the General Confederation of Labor." The Congress also voted administrative changes by amending the constitution. The membership of the directive council was increased from 7 to 11, including the general secretary. Two of these members, along with the general secretary, composed the newly created executive committee. The national vigilance council now selected three auditors and two alternates from its own ranks. It met at least once a year to review the C.G.L.'s past performance and to approve the proposed program for the future. Its members also served as trustees of the Confederation for the centers they represented. The Congress itself chose both the national vigilance council and the directive council by secret ballot.[30]

When the General Confederation of Labor met at Padua from May 24 to 28, 1911 for the Third Congress, its paid membership for 1910 numbered 302,400, or 4.3% of 7,000,000 organizable workers. During that same year, the total of all unionized workers, except those in Catholic leagues, came to 817,034, a loss of 117,335 adherents since 1908. Industrial workers accounted for 52% of all organized workers, while agricultural laborers and sharecroppers represented 48%. The union members of the nation constituted 11.7% of all organizable workers. The industrial triangle of the North—Piedmont, Liguria, and Lombardy—claimed 219,607 union members, including agricultural workers, or 27% of the entire labor movement. Moreover, these three regions accounted for 158,218 organized industrial workers, or 37% of the national total. The official statistics for 1910 also demonstrate that the chambers of labor remained the most representative organizations in the Italian labor movement. The National Labor Office ascribed 501,941 adherents to them. Independent unaffiliated leagues and local unions showed 320,286 members, while the non-Catholic national category federations claimed 166,156 members grouped in 2,394 local organizations.

The weakness of the category federations can be grasped from a review of another phase of these statistics. The National Federation of Land Workers had to disband, as we have seen, very soon after its formation. By 1910, of the 390,851 supposedly organized agricultural workers, 267,689 belonged to independent leagues, while only 123,162 joined chambers of labor. The Italian Union of Railroad Workers, which followed the syndicalist banner and remained outside the C.G.L., claimed the highest membership of all national category federations, 44,961. The Federation of Building Trades Workers came second with 42,220 members; the Federation of the Book stood third with 12,400 members; then followed the metallurgical workers with 11,330 members, the textile workers with 9,491 members, the hatters with 5,802 members, and the maritime workers with 5,765 members.[31] Other data, pertaining to 1907, provided additional evidence of the central defect of the Italian labor movement: its inability to organize substantial proportions of those industries which afforded most employment into national category federations. The highest percentages of organized workers occurred in small-scale endeavors: headwear, 46%; printing 40%; state-run industries, 40%; ceramics, 30.8%; and fur and leather, 26.7%. By contrast, of the 503,013 workers in the textile industries, mostly women, only 4.7% were organized. In the clothing trades which employed 324,116 workers, again predominantly women, only 1.6% joined unions. Organized workers in wood-working industries represented only 6.5% of those employed, while union members in the shoe industry comprised only 6.2% of all workers. Workers in the metal trades showed more ability to organize, for 21.6% had joined unions, even though most of them had not cast their lot with F.I.O.M. The building trades workers showed similar union interests, although only 16.7% of their numbers had organized.[32]

The Padua Congress of the C.G.L. revised the governmental structure of the Confederation once more. Under the constitutional arrangements adopted at Modena three years previously, the Congress elected the national vigilance council on the basis of electoral lists derived by nominations from the floor. Apparently, the cautionary statement in article 6 of the constitution, which urged voters to propose candidates representative of the various regions of the country while also considering the importance of these areas to the C.G.L., did not achieve its purpose. Therefore, the 1911 Congress decreed that the national vigilance council would bring together one representative chosen by each affiiliated national category federation and one representative selected by each affiliated chamber of labor. Council members from the chambers of labor would speak only for those who did not belong to national category federations. Through this amendment, the C.G.L. improved its capacity to consider both geographical and trade interests during deliberations between congresses. The second major constitutional change concerned the directive council. The Congress no longer elected its members. Instead, the national vigilance council chose 14 individuals from among its own ranks to form the directive council. The council also selected the general secretary and two vice-general secretaries from its own members. The three secretaries constituted the executive office of C.G.L.[33]

Four months after the C.G.L.'s Congress at Padua, the Italian government declared war against Turkey and began its Libyan adventure. The leaders of the Socialist Party and the C.G.L., taken unawares, met at Bologna on September 25, 1911 and took up the gauntlet against imperialism by proclaiming a general strike of 24 hours for September 27. What they expected to accomplish defies imagination. Preparations for war had already begun. Not even socialists could have seriously thought that their gesture would halt the projected landings in Tripoli. The general strike, like their obstructive and pacifist propaganda during the course of the war, met with indifference. The masses cherished the retrieval of national honor and the prospect of land. The failure of the party of the proletariat to unite its class-conscious followers during a time of crisis preceded by a year the first major schism in the labor movement, formalized through the foundation of a national syndicalist federation to rival the C.G.L.

When the minority factions at the constituent assembly of the C.G.L. in 1906 at Milan left the proceedings and retired to a hall of their own, they drew up a constitution replete with syndicalist concepts. But after the rump sessions closed and the secessionists departed for home, syndicalist leaders could never secure approval of the constitution by a majority of their reputed followers. Of more importance, dissension reigned even among those who professed to embrace revolutionary syndicalism. Meanwhile, beginning in 1907, the chamber of labor of Parma had become the center of the revolutionary syndicalist movement, known as the Committee of Resistance, and had eventually attracted isolated leagues and chambers in other parts of Emilia, in Turin, and in Massa-Carrara and the Marches where the anarchist tradition survived. These groups of syndicalists and their sympathizers met at Bologna in April 1909 under the denomination, Direct Action. They debated the feasibility of a mass return to the C.G.L. in order to grasp control from within, but found that the high dues and constitutional provisions of the Confederation hindered their aspirations. The second congress of Direct Action took place again at Bologna in December 1910. Delegates represented 10 chambers of labor, 19 independent groups, and the Italian Union of Railroad Workers — a goodly company, said to have totaled 150,000 members. They still discussed the merits and evils of participating in political activities. They also brought up again for serious consideration the hope to rejoin the C.G.L. as undercover conquerors. The verbal project once more came to naught. In 1912, the third assembly of Direct Action, reduced in numbers but more united ideologically, convened at Modena. The delegates proclaimed the foundation of the Italian Syndical Union (Unione Sindacale Italiana), the second national center on the peninsula, which named its publication *Guerra di Classe* (*Class War*). The Italian Union of Railroad Workers, although anarcho-syndicalist in thought, remained autonomous. Thus, in 1912, two schools of unionism competed for the loyalty of Italian workers: the General Confederation of Labor, oriented toward reform socialism as typified by the German labor movement, and the Italian Syndical Union, dedicated to revolutionary syndicalism, as typified by the unions of France and Holland. Unlike the French revolutionary syndicalists who headed the majority labor group, the Italian Syndical Union represented a minority of workers.[34]

Almost 200 delegates representing 102,000 members in over 1,000 local leagues and unions met at Milan on December 4–7, 1913 as the Second Congress of the Italian Syndical Union. The delegates recommended that the central committee of the U.S.I. concentrate its fire upon those regions where reformist political attitudes ranged undisturbed. The Congress also approved of sabotage as the only effective response of agricultural workers to the provocation of landowners. The executive officers of the U.S.I. received a mandate to prepare for an agricultural general strike. The assembly went on to affirm the necessity for exalting more strenuously the idea of the general strike and authorized a special subcommittee of the central committee to study the most potent techniques for mobilizing the entire proletariat in a general strike. The syndicalists then castigated the national category federations by characterizing them as centralized, bureaucratic, and limited in vision and goals. The delegates, while leaving for the next national congress the task of delimiting the proper relationship of the national category unions to local organizations, decided emphatically that the national federations must not interfere with the activities of the Italian Syndical Union! Finally, the Congress passed a resolution that urged the U.S.I. to devote broad, constant, and special attention to antimilitarism.[35]

The General Confederation of Labor gathered its delegates at Mantua for its Fourth Congress in early May 1914. Its membership had declined from the high point of 1911, 383,770, to 309,671 in 1912; by 1913, the C.G.L. had recouped some of its losses, for its membership stood at 327,312. The severe economic crisis of 1912–1913, the counteroffensives of employer associations, and revolutionary syndicalism helped to retard the steady progress of the Confederation. Unemployment mounted to exceptional heights at the same time that almost 900,000 emigrants left Italy. That total for 1913 alone set the annual record in Italian history. The Federation of the Book reported that it had paid out 245,000 lire in unemployment benefits for 1913 as compared with 54,818 lire for 1909. The scarcity of jobs served to harden the attitude of employers during the widespread industrial strikes which involved 384,725 workers in 1913, the largest number reported from 1881 until the outbreak of World War I. Three years earlier, employers in the most heavily industrialized part of Italy, Lombardy, had inaugurated the Lombardy Federation of Employers Associations to deal with labor unions. Official government reports listed 48 agricultural employers associations in 1911. Known membership reached almost 13,500. Revolutionary syndicalism, the third cause of decline in union membership, cast a depressing spell upon the entire labor movement through its "cyclone" tactics. After workers had suffered the vicissitudes of a violent and futile syndicalist experiment, "skepticism followed and many workers ended up by not wishing to have anything to do any more with either reformism or with syndicalism."[36]

Government statistics for all organized workers, whether or not affiliated with the C.G.L. or U.S.I., showed, at first glance, a steady rise from the total of 817,034 in 1910 to 971,667 in 1913. The comparable figure for 1914 fell but slightly to 961,997. However, while membership in agricultural leagues purportedly increased without break from 390,851 in 1910 to 488,705 in 1914, unionized industrial workers fared less well. Their numbers ascended from 426,183 in 1910 to 502,698 in 1913, but suffered decline to 473,292 in 1914. Reported membership in the non-Catholic national category federations fell from 210,621 in 1911 to 111,546 in 1914. Therefore, agricultural workers in 1914 represented 51%

of all organized labor, as contrasted to 48% in 1910. The discrepancy between the union fortunes of agricultural and industrial workers — equally buffeted by economic depression, employer resistance, and syndicalist tactics — can perhaps be explained best by the tendency among unions of industrial workers to drop those delinquent in dues payments from the rolls. On the other hand, since the abysmal poverty of agricultural workers made the collection of dues either sporadic or completely impossible, agricultural union membership records reflected active membership less accurately than the books of unions in the industrial segment of the economy.

Of the 961,997 organized workers in 1914, 682,002 belonged to organizations affiliated with chambers of labor, the C.G.L., or the U.S.I., while 176,669 remained independent. The balance, 103,326, belonged to Catholic unions. The Catholic labor movement, like Catholic political life, advanced slowly in finding philosophical principles and tactical measures acceptable to the Church, but it had nevertheless persevered to provide firm roots before 1914 for its phenomenal growth after World War I.[37]

For 30 years after 1874, its founding date, the Catholic social movement of Italy centered in the Institute of Catholic Congresses and Committees (Opera dei Congressi e dei Comitati Cattolici d'Italia). At the time of the Seventh Congress at Lucca in 1887, the predominant tone of discussion reflected conservative fears concerning the success of socialist agitation throughout the country. The official stand of the Congress warned against arousing the passions and the undue claims of workers which might interfere with industrial freedom. Although in 1890 Catholic mutual aid societies still operated as confessional organizations under the guidance and vigilance of ecclesiastical authorities, the Eighth Congress in Lodi that year betrayed growing awareness that Catholic workers needed to form groups which were free to deal realistically with day-to-day industrial problems. The delegates also approved of state intervention in economic affairs, but only under very special and restricted circumstances. At the Ninth Congress of Vicenza in 1891, the progressive forces maintained that Catholic mutual aid societies, which still adhered to the corporative principle of including both employers and workers, should be gradually transformed into organizations to defend the rights of workers and to improve their lot. At Vicenza, Group II of the Opera dei Congressi — its interests centered on Christian social economy and charity from headquarters in Bergamo — presented the first statistics ever gathered on the extent of Catholic social organizations. The report revealed the existence of 284 workers societies with 73,769 members living in 1,554 parishes. All but 10 were mutual aid societies. Of these 284 societies, 247 operated in four regions: Piedmont, Liguria, Lombardy, and Veneto. Lombardy alone claimed almost one-third. Of the 52,449 members in the four regions, 23,735 dwelt in Lombardy. These organizations usually banded together to set up regional, provincial, and diocesan federations. Some of them, moreover, created auxiliary savings banks, credit unions, and consumer and producer co-operatives.[38]

Advance toward Catholic unions of workers separated from their employers received impetus from the momentous encyclical of Leo XIII, *Rerum novarum,* in 1891. Although the Tenth Congress at Genoa in October 1892 still discussed seriously the establishment of rural unions with both landowners and peasants as members (mixed unions), other addresses and observations indicated that the delegates realized only too well that Catholic workers were finding the new class-conscious leagues, locals, and chambers of labor attractive. Two years later, at the Eleventh Congress in Rome, influential speakers still insisted that mixed unions conformed most closely with Christian principles of social harmony. But they also realized that Catholics might have to encourage unions limited to workers alone (simple unions) if they were to stem the swelling tide of socialist labor unions. Subsequent congresses kept worrying the issue, but the proceedings at Pavia in 1894, Turin in 1895, Fiesole in 1896, Milan in 1897 (the government temporarily dissolved the Opera dei Congressi in 1898, the *annus terribilis*), and Ferrara in 1899 placed more emphasis upon the founding of rural banks, credit unions, and cooperatives — ventures more pleasing to conservative Catholics who feared "simple" unions as breeders of class antagonisms.

After 1900, industrial, social, and political pressures forced the conservative old guard (*partito dei "vecchi"*) of the Catholic movement to debate the urgency of creating attainable Christian associations like labor unions, frankly committed to safeguard and advance the economic interests of workers, instead of supporting the lost cause of an organic reconstruction of society into corporative institutions steeped in pseudo-medieval religious, economic, and social harmony. The conservatives met the challenge presented by the young progressives (*partito dei "giovani"*) with heavy reluctance and pious hostility, for they refused to concede the possibility of dissension among Catholics. The new orientation, Christian Democracy, represented a veritable revolution in Catholic thought and action. Three men led the liberal forces within the Opera dei Congressi in adapting Catholic doctrine and works to the requirements of modern life: Giuseppe Toniolo, Professor of Economics at the University of Pisa, the first and leading systematic theorist of

Christian Democracy; Don Romolo Murri, who believed that Christian Democracy had to open up a road to the future intermediate between liberal laissez faire and socialism, but who went on to espouse increasingly unorthodox views which ultimately led to his excommunication by Pius X fifteen days after socialist votes in 1909 elected Don Romolo as the deputy from Fermo; and Filippo Meda (1869–1939), the disciple of Toniolo, who worked for the reconciliation of Church and State and emphasized political and parliamentary activities.

At the Seventeenth Congress held at Rome in 1900, Professor Toniolo again voiced the fears of the young progressives that the Church would forfeit the loyalty of Catholic workers to the socialist chambers of labor unless Catholics themselves organized competing labor unions. The Congress of Taranto in 1901 re-emphasized the need for separate workers unions. At Bologna in 1903, the delegates even abandoned the binding, universal, confessional character of labor leagues and deferred to the discretion of local directors. The statistics of organizational success placed before the Congress strongly confirmed the validity of Christian Democratic thought and tactics. Catholic-inspired rural banks (*casse rurali*) increased in number from the single pioneering experiment of 1890 to 759 in 1903. The number of mutual aid societies grew from 274 in 1891 to 825 in 1903. Catholic unions, both "simple" and "mixed," mounted in number from 54 in 1900 to 229 in 1903.[39]

Catholic unions won adherents, but Christian Democracy paid temporarily heavy tolls for its move forward. As a result of rising discord between the progressive and conservative currents, evidenced by the impossibility of cooperation between the young group and the old guard within the permanent general committee of the Opera dei Congressi on July 28, 1904, Pius X, who had succeeded Leo XIII to the papal throne in 1903, suppressed the Opera dei Congressi on July 30. However, Group II, which concerned itself with Christian social economy and charity, continued to operate out of Bergamo. Until 1906, it called itself Group II for Christian or Democratic Christian Catholic Action. Then, on March 24, 1906, Group II became the Economic-Social Union for Catholics of Italy. Between 1907 and 1909, inspired by the leadership of the Union, the different groups associated with it constituted themselves into four federations: the Federation of Mutual Aid Societies, the Federation of Agricultural Cooperatives, the Federation of Rural Banks, and the General Secretariat of Workers Unions which, since its foundation on March 20, 1909, carried the responsibilities of a true labor center. Finally, the new constitution of the Union, granted by the Holy See on February 15, 1911, created four General Secretariats: labor unions and employers associations, cooperatives and agricultural institutes, mutual aid societies, and credit institutions. The carefully detailed deliberations of the Twentieth Catholic Congress of Modena, held in October 1910, had inspired these constitutional arrangements.[40]

In 1910, Catholic labor unions claimed 104,614 members organized into 374 local bodies. Of this total, 67,466 worked in industry and 37,148 in agriculture. The overwhelming majority of Catholic union members concentrated in North Italy; more than half of them, 57,870, lived in Lombardy. Although the constitutions of four local unions permitted employers to join, only workers comprised their membership. Of the 374 local organizations, 270 grouped workers of a single category, while 104 assembled workers of various categories, but subdivided them by craft or industry. The bylaws of these locals openly affirmed their confessional character. Despite their devotion to Catholic principles, the Christian unions sanctioned strikes, but disapproved of violence and sabotage. During 1910, 112 unions participated in 175 disputes affecting 78,856 workers. Only two Catholic category federations appeared on the national scene. Achille Grandi (1883–1946), the most exalted figure of the Italian Christian labor movement, founded the Italian Textile Union in 1908 with 1,630 members. Two years later, the federation counted 6,047 members divided into 34 locals; 32 functioned in Lombardy. Its central offices in Milan published the federation's newspaper, L'Organizzazione Tessile (The Textile Organization). In 1909, Italo Mario Sacco (1886–   ) led in the formation of the Union of Railroad Workers. The federation published its newspaper, Il Direttissimo (The Express), at its headquarters in Florence. By 1910, the Union boasted 2,225 members located in 13 locals. Between 1911 and 1914, Catholic workers formed national category federations among shop clerks and salesmen, postal and telegraph personnel, and metallurgical workers. At the approach of World War I, official statistics showed 40,009 industrial workers and 63,317 small landowners, renters, sharecroppers, agricultural workers, and day laborers organized into Catholic unions, almost a direct reversal of the industry-agriculture proportions of 1910.[41]

On the eve of World War I, vigorous mutualistic and cooperative associations flanked Italian workers on every side with their rich offerings of self-help. The venerable mutual aid societies, first among these groups in age, prospered on. With the rise of militant unionism, the mutual aid societies reverted wholly to their original functions of succoring workers with timely aid against insurable perils of life. They provided their members with these vital services at a time when the Italian government did not. Workmen's compensation insurance became compulsory in 1898 for certain categories of industrial workers, but agricultural laborers and sharecroppers remained outside the range of these benefits until 1917. Obligatory maternity insurance first appeared on the statute books in 1910. The government did not begin to administer life insurance as a state monopoly until January 1913. Old-age and invalidity insurance for workers continued as voluntary until January 1920. Nor did workers receive unemployment insurance or public placement services until 1920. Health insurance waited for government sanction until 1929, but even then depended upon the terms of collective agreements. Guaranteed health insurance did not arrive until 1943. Consequently, mutual aid societies well earned the gratitude of Italian workers.

Leagued together since 1900 in the Italian Federation of Mutual Aid Societies, the associations numbered 6,535 at the end of 1904 and reported 926,026 members. Total assets amounted to 72,395,544 lire. Of the mutual aid societies enumerated in the comprehensive survey of 1904, 1,548 had received legal recognition, while 4,987 functioned without juridical approval. By 1914, the number of legally recognized societies had increased to 2,241. The regions of Piedmont, Liguria, and Lombardy claimed 36.5% of all mutual aid societies in 1914. Calabria led the other regions with 8.2% of the societies, while Veneto followed with 7.5%, Tuscany with 7.2%, and Campania with 7.1%. The classification of mutual aid societies in existence at the close of 1914, according to the year of their foundation, brings into relief the periods of greatest development. Of the 2,241 societies, 4.4% originated between 1895 and 1899, 6.7% between 1900 and 1904, and 13.8% between 1905 and 1909. Thus, 25% of all mutual aid societies operating in 1914 traced their time of birth to the period of Italy's strongest industrial upsurge from 1896 to 1908.[42]

Other mutualistic endeavors also flourished. Although landowners, manufacturers, businessmen, and professional people held shares in people's banks (*banche popolari*), agricultural, industrial, and clerical workers dominated their membership rolls. Since the cost of shares varied from 5 lire to a maximum of 100 lire, even the poorer elements of the population could participate in ventures which made credit accessible to them. In 1876, when Luigi Luzzatti founded the Association of Italian People's Banks, the 111 banks then in existence possessed paid-in capital of 35,322,526 lire. By 1893, the number of banks had grown to 730 and the amount of paid-in capital had increased to 89,949,527 lire. The most complete official coverage of people's banks dated from 1908 and remained the best source of information before World War I. That year, 736 banks with paid-in capital and reserves of

155,664,387 lire, advanced almost 500,000,000 lire to agricultural clients. Banks in centers like Milan, Bergamo, Cremona, Bologna, Novara, Lodi, Mantua, and Pavia enlarged their jurisdictions in time and became regional in scope. They absorbed banks in smaller communities and turned them into branches. These wealthy institutions extended credit to agricultural consortia, rural banks, dairies, vineyards, and other agricultural, industrial, and labor cooperatives. Many of the people's banks assumed important civic functions by facilitating irrigation projects, land improvements, and other public works.[43]

The rural banks (*casse rurali*) received savings deposits from both members and other customers and made loans in amounts varying from 50 to 1,000 lire. When the size of deposits did not enable them to meet the demand for credit, rural banks obtained necessary capital from people's banks and ordinary savings banks. Their numbers grew from 44 in 1890 to 973 in 1900. In 1905, 1,386 rural banks reported paid-in capital and reserves of 1,200,522 lire. By December 1912, the number of rural banks had increased to 1,652 with paid-in capital and reserves of 4,011,535 lire.[44]

Law 89 of February 27, 1908 authorized the establishment of institutes for the construction of housing for low income families (*istituti per case popolari o economiche*). The legislation exempted those projects which qualified under its terms from the building tax. By December 1914, 660 institutes had come into existence. Of this total, cooperative societies sponsored 548. As of the same date, 3,333 houses had qualified for exemption from the building tax. Tuscany led all other regions with 990 houses, while Emilia followed with 715, Veneto with 506, and Lombardy with 402.[45]

The cooperative movement, apart from credit institutions, also made prodigious forward strides. Between December 1889 and the end of 1901, the number of consumer, producer, and labor cooperatives increased from 1,242 to 2,126. Of the 1901 total, 1,638 had obtained legal recognition, while 488 operated as *de facto* institutions. They reported 567,450 members and total assets of 74,121,047 lire. The regions of Piedmont, Liguria, Lombardy, Veneto, Emilia, and Tuscany claimed 84% of the members and 92% of the assets. By the end of 1910, the number of legally constituted cooperative societies, except those providing credit, had mounted to 5,064. Although still heavily concentrated in North and Central Italy, Italian cooperatives had spread to other regions as well. In contrast to 1901, the six regions mentioned before could now claim only 76.1% of all societies, 74.2% of total membership, and 87.8% of paid-in capital and reserves. National membership rose to 817,529 and assets increased to 125,350,250 lire. Housing cooperatives, which accounted for merely 7.5% of all societies in 1910 and 6.1% of the entire membership, held 34.4% of paid-in capital and reserves. Consumer cooperatives formed 38.4% of all societies and attracted 42.4% of all cooperators. However, their paid-in capital and reserves amounted to only 18.2% of all co-operative funds. Comparable figures for agricultural cooperatives were 19.6%, 19.7%, and 12.5%; for cooperatives in industrial production, 9.4%, 8.6%, and 14.6%; for insurance cooperatives, 2.4%, 5.9%, and 10.5%; and for labor cooperatives, 17.9%, 11.6%, and 3.5%. The 1,623 consumer co-operatives held assets in the amount of 22,868,709 lire. Their sales totaled 105,698,894 lire. The pre-eminent six regions of North and Central Italy accounted for 80.4% of all consumer cooperatives in the country, 84.4% of their paid-in capital and reserves, and 80.9% of their total sales.[46]

The Federation of Italian Cooperatives, founded in 1886, became the National League of Cooperatives at its Fifth Congress of Sampierdarena in 1893. Despite pretensions of political neutrality, the League, along with the General Confederation of Labor and the Italian Federation of Mutual Aid Societies, formed the economic base of the socialist movement and provided its reformist leaders with political power as well. Representatives of these three organizations conferred in Milan at the end of November 1906 and formed a working relationship, the Triple Alliance of Labor. The League and the Italian Federation of Mutual Aid Societies enjoyed particularly close relations. The Como Congress of the League in 1899 had urged the union, on a national scale, of mutual aid societies. Encouraged by the League, interested societies founded the Federation in 1900. Antonio Maffi, the general secretary of the League until his death in 1912, also served as president of the Federation. Moreover, both organizations maintained headquarters in the same building at Milan.

Under the constitutional arrangements of the National League of Co-operatives, individual groups could affiliate with the League either directly, or indirectly, through local cooperative federations. In 1886, the year of its birth, 68 cooperative societies and federations belonged to the League. This number rose to 229 in 1896 and to 1,280 in 1906. By 1916, the total mounted to 2,189. If this figure had included societies indirectly affiliated with the League through their local federations, it would perhaps have doubled.[47]

When the Fourth Congress of the General Confederation of Labor assembled at Mantua on May 5, 1914 to define the most effective program and plot the most direct course of action for achieving labor unity, unlike the assemblies of the mutualistic and cooperative movements, it received reports of membership losses: almost 7,000 between 1913 and 1914 — slight, but disturbing, since C.G.L. still lacked 63,000 members merely to resume its position of 1911. The bitter debates repeated the theoretical quibbling of past socialist and C.G.L. gatherings and fore-shadowed the tragedy of the future. Rinaldo Rigola who, from 1906 on-ward, had invited Catholic unions to join the Confederation as an earnest of political neutrality, wisely took the offensive in his report as general secretary to the Congress. He summarized the position of the C.G.L. with irony and precision:

> We have no friends; certainly, not the syndicalists; not the reform socialists who accuse us of being bound too closely with the official Socialist Party; not the official socialists who say that they do not want the economic organizations to become the place where the contraband of reformism is manufactured.

He then proceeded to challenge directly the revolutionary delegates and left-wing representatives of the Socialist Party:

> But the labor movement is not able to be intransigent because it is only a way of achieving successive reforms . . . . Whoever believes that the emancipation of the proletariat must come only through catastrophe cannot be a labor organizer . . . . If our action has been tepid and reformist, I promise you the same course of action in the future because only thus is revolutionary work accomplished. We do not wish to conduct other experiments until the time when we have a great proletarian army behind us.

In deriding the futility of contemplating revolutionary changes in the economic and political structure of Italian society when the C.G.L. had organized little more than 320,000 workers out of a potential total of 7,000,000, Rinaldo Rigola, like Filippo Turati in the Socialist Party, as-sumed the task of Cassandra in the labor movement. Workers, unpre-pared either morally or technically for authority, would attempt within six years to run the factories of the nation and would falter and then fail.[48]

A week before Italy's declaration of hostilities against Austria on May 23, 1915, the directorate of the Socialist Party invited its deputies in Parliament, its regional leaders, and officials of the C.G.L. to as-semble at Bologna on May 16. There, these men searched for measures within their power to prevent the oncoming catastrophe. They were meeting during D'Annunzio's "Radiant May," when the interventionist mobs ruled Rome, and soon recognized that they had no choice but to accept the coming war as inevitable. The C.G.L., along with the Social-ist Party, adopted the attitude expressed by Costantino Lazzari, the

Party's revolutionary secretary, of neither approving the war nor sabotaging it.[49]

Unlike so many other socialist declarations which lacked detectable meaning, this formula had the virtue of leaving people to their own devices. The unions joined in the war effort wholeheartedly and collaborated intently with the industrial mobilization committees. Although wages failed pitiably to keep up with the rising cost of living, despite periodic increases determined on the basis of official government statistics — with 1913 as the base year, the index of real wages for 1914 stood at 99.7, for 1915 at 93.4, for 1916 at 85, for 1917 at 73.1, and for 1918 at 64.6 — the average number of strikers between 1915 and 1919 decreased markedly.[50] The four-year average for industrial strikers registered at 146,000 as contrasted with 385,000 in 1913. The comparable average for agricultural strikers fell to 17,000 from the 1913 total of 80,000.[51] Undoubtedly, feelings of patriotism contributed to this strangely peaceful Italian wartime record. In addition, relief at having any job at all certainly impelled many workers to suffer the inadequacy of their wages without resorting to strikes. Upon the outbreak of war in 1914, hundreds of thousands of workers who had emigrated to find jobs returned in haste to Italy. This sudden blow to Italy's weak economy swelled the lines of the unemployed to half a million. But once Italy joined the Allies a year later, war industries not only absorbed repatriated workers, but also drew women into factories where they had never worked before. These elements in the work force probably nursed their grievances patiently and tended their new-found jobs with gratitude.

But specially instituted arbitral and conciliation services — the first additions since 1893 to the limited probiviral system, which suffered from doubts concerning its legal ability to constitute even voluntary arbitration courts in collective disputes — must claim the major credit for shrinking the wartime volume of industrial strife. Regulation 1377 of August 22, 1915 made arbitration compulsory for all economic or disciplinary controversies arising in establishments subject to the rules governing industrial mobilization. As the government judged more and more industries vital to the prosecution of the war, the scope of the regulations extended to them. The seven Regional Committees of Industrial Mobilization supplied the administrative machinery for the initial arbitral steps, while the Central Committee of Mobilization in Rome acted as the ultimate appeals board. For those undertakings located in the "war zone" which produced necessities of life, or fulfilled vital economic needs, but fell outside the jurisdiction of the regulations, the government inaugurated conciliation procedures for both individual and collective disputes. Later, these services applied to enterprises of this kind in all parts of the country. Still later, the conciliation committees came to act as voluntary arbitration courts for all remaining industries lying outside the "war zone." The acceleration of economic emergencies forced Parliament to extend the machinery of arbitration and conciliation to all collective disputes in agriculture.

Finally, the Chamber enacted decree 1672 of October 13, 1918 which decree 1098 of July 31, 1921 extended indefinitely. The measure provided for the establishment of new probiviral courts and widened the jurisdiction of both the old and the new courts to cover collective controversies which concerned the administration of existing contracts as well as collective disputes which involved the alteration of agreements still in force or setting new conditions of employment. The court attempted conciliation on application from one or both parties, from the prefect in disputes confined to one province, or from the Minister of Commerce, Industry and Labor in cases of interprovincial controversies. If conciliation proved successful, the chairman of the court recorded the terms of agreement and these minutes took the force of evidence and contract. In the event of failure, the court then rendered its own judgment. This opinion, very far indeed from advisory, possessed the full force of law. Appeals from probiviral judgments went to the Permanent Committee on Labor Questions. Order 25 of September 14, 1919 provided conciliation and arbitration services for collective disputes in agriculture through provincial committees made up of a magistrate who acted as chairman and two representatives each of the parties to the dispute.[52]

During 1916, C.G.L.'s membership fell to 201,291 from its total of 233,863 for 1915. It then climbed to 237,560 in 1917 and reached 249,039 in 1918.[53] Clearly, the Confederation barely held its own during the war, but found time to plan for peace. At a meeting on May 1, 1916, representatives from the French, British, Belgian, and Italian labor movements decided to call an international conference to formulate the general conditions of peace from the viewpoint of the working class. The meeting took place at Leeds in July, attended by French, Belgian, and English delegates. Disregarding the commitments made by the Italian mission in May, which had included Rinaldo Rigola, the executive committee of the C.G.L. rejected the idea of official representation at Leeds. Therefore only three C.G.L. members, including Angiolo Cabrini, presented themselves at Leeds along with two delegates from the Italian Syndical Union, including Alceste De Ambris.[54]

In May 1917, the directorate of the Socialist Party, socialist members of Parliament, and leaders of the C.G.L. published a joint statement of demands for the months immediately following peace and the postwar period as well. This program endured through the first half of 1918 and marked another public demonstration of the increasingly close relationship which the war had sealed between the Socialist Party and the C.G.L. During May, too, the beginning of popular discontent with the war manifested itself as demonstrations, notably in Milan. Later in the year at Turin, workers from many factories struck on August 21 in protest against bread shortages. They assembled, according to the habit of Italian strikers, at the Turin chamber of labor. The police intervened and strife followed. The next day saw the beginnings of a general strike throughout the city; it rapidly turned into insurrection complete with barricades. The fighting continued for five days. The Alpine troops, called in to combat the strikers, allowed themselves to be disarmed by the populace. Other soldiers replaced them and their intervention ended in massacre. The strikers left 500 dead and 2,000 wounded in the streets of Turin.[55]

By 1918, the Italian labor movement began to stir again with its wonted ferment. During the first days of March 1918, the head of the General Secretariat of (Catholic) Workers Unions summoned representatives of all Christian labor organizations to Rome for the purpose of creating the Italian Confederation of Workers (Confederazione Italiana dei Lavoratori — C.I.L.). Delegates from national category federations in industry, agriculture, commerce, and the public services, as well as from unions of labor (the Catholic equivalent of the chambers of labor), participated in the deliberations. The constitution of the new Confederation provided for a national council composed of 12 members from the category federations and 26 members from the unions of labor. The constitution also provided for an executive commission and a general secretary. Giuseppe Corazzin (1888–   ), who, along with Achille Grandi, Giovanni Battista Valente, Giovanni Gronchi (1887–   ), the future President of the Italian Republic, and Italo Mario Sacco stood high among the leaders of the Christian labor movement, became general secretary with headquarters at Milan. The national council elaborated a program of action at its first meeting in Rome on September 29, 1918.

The Christian unions could not have selected a less felicitous moment in Italian history to launch their venture. First, they had to clarify their relationship with Catholic Action, and secondly, with the Popular Party which announced its formation on January 18, 1919. Cardinal Pietro Gasparri (1852–1934), Pope Benedict XV's Secretary of State, resolved the first issue by his celebrated letter of September 25, 1919. The message, addressed to the president of the Popular Union (Unione Popolare) freed C.I.L., as well as Catholic mutual aid societies and cooperatives, from both supervision and legal control by Catholic Action. Achille Grandi placed the second issue before the First Congress of the Italian Popular Party at Bologna on June 14, 1919. The Congress approved a motion which established "a reciprocal autonomy from the technical point of view, that is, in the respective union or political sphere, and interdependence in all overlapping functions." This pellucid formula kept jurisdictional peace as effectively as the Florence declaration of 1908 established clear-cut spheres of action for the Socialist Party and the C.G.L.[56]

The dissidence of revolutionary dissent now infected the syndicalists. In May 1918, the Italian Labor Union (Unione Italiana del Lavoro — U.I.L.) became the fourth confederation in the country after the Italian Syndical Union expelled its right-wing for favoring Italy's intervention in the war on the side of the Allies. U.I.L., gathering inspiration from its patron saint, Filippo Corridoni, one of Mussolini's chief collaborators who died under arms, declared its complete independence of any political party, pledged its determination to eradicate capitalism, advocated the direct administration of production and distribution by the working class, and asserted that sentiments of international solidarity among workers should never transcend devotion to Italy's own welfare and liberty. Edmondo Rossoni (1884–   ), who would later head the National Confederation of Fascist Syndical Unions, and Alceste De Ambris, who had inspired the 1908 agrarian strike as secretary of the Parma chamber of labor, piloted the U.I.L. The Confederation's newspaper, *Italia Nostra* (*Our Italy*), carried the catchwords: "One does not deny the Fatherland, but conquers it" — a slogan which could have fitted comfortably on the masthead of Mussolini's *People of Italy*.[57]

On October 1, 1918, Rinaldo Rigola, after serving for twelve years as the first general secretary of the Confederation, resigned. Since 1906, under his guidance, socialist leaders of the most representative assembly of unions on the peninsula had fought valiantly to preserve the C.G.L.'s policy of stressing organizational and economic gains against the political demands of shifting Socialist Party doctrines. His departure marked the passing of a unique interval in the entire history of Italian labor. Ludovico D'Aragona (1876–   ), who had worked in an important post at central headquarters for a decade, replaced Rigola. In anticipation of increased future responsibilities in the postwar period, the Confederation decided to issue its publication once more on a weekly basis and to change its title to *Battaglie Sindacali* (*Union Battles*).

In 1917, as we have seen, the Socialist Party and the C.G.L. collaborated publicly on peace proposals. Then, in 1918, the directorate of the Socialist Party vetoed participation by the C.G.L. in a government commission empowered to study all postwar problems. Plans for the commission's membership envisaged large union representation; labor organizations would have named their own representatives directly. The socialists in Parliament and C.G.L.'s leaders looked upon this potentially vital undertaking with favor, but the Socialist Party refused to grant its approval. The C.G.L. accepted the decision. Despite the Stuttgart Declaration and the 1908 Pact of Florence, events were now coursing too rapidly for the C.G.L. to stop to draw fine lines of jurisdictional distinctions. Nonetheless, on November 30, 1918, the directive committee of the C.G.L. urged the convocation of a Constituent Assembly, organized along syndical lines, as part of its principal postwar demands for the Italian working class — an enthusiasm not universally shared by all factions within the Socialist Party. On December 12, 1918, the directorate of the Socialist Party issued an Order of the Day demanding the immediate creation of an Italian Socialist Republic under the dictatorship of the laboring masses. Later in the month, on December 22 and 23, the C.G.L. joined the socialist deputies, the League of Socialist Communes, and the Union of Railroad Workers at the large proletarian assembly convoked in Bologna by the directorate of the Socialist Party to consider its Order of the Day and then to act upon it. There, the C.G.L. continued to press for the creation of a Constituent Assembly, with prestige comparable to that of the Chamber of Deputies, to assume complete responsibility for social and economic legislation. These moves served well as prelude to the revolutionary years of 1919 and 1920 and to the Corporative State which they spawned.[58]

During 1919 and 1920, the readjustment of Italy's war-tumid industries to the lean demands of peace returned tens of thousands of women to their homes and sent tens of thousands of men into the streets. Tens of thousands of returning veterans also took their places among the unemployed. Inflation sent prices skyrocketing. The inevitable scarcity of goods during a period of massive economic readjustment exhausted the patience, already sorely tried, of Italy's industrial and agricultural workers. The Russian Revolution, the Bolshevik coup in Hungary under Béla Kun, the Spartacist revolts in Berlin and the Ruhr mining districts, and the charged expectation throughout the rest of Europe that deep social changes would at last unfold the Marxist dream of universal peace and prosperity aroused Italian political passions to the full. Throughout 1919 and 1920, masses of striking and demonstrating people filled the avenues, squares, and plazzas of Italy. Peasants, goaded by war-time promises of the government itself, invaded uncultivated lands and claimed them, after centuries of hungering for them, as their own. Workers occupied the plants of North Italy in the firm belief that the revolutionary day of reckoning had at long last arrived.

These bitter and fierce attachments to the ever-verdant promises of Utopia to the Left — perhaps beyond the placation of human government — outshone and outshouted the less obtrusive and quieter forces of progressive and constructive reform. The government, during the course of the war, had extended compulsory workmen's compensation to agricultural labor in August 1917. Now, in April 1919, the State provided for compulsory old-age and disability insurance by reorganizing the National Fund for Workers Invalidity and Old-Age Insurance into the National Fund for Social Insurances. Later, in May, Parliament set new standards of factory hygiene and stipulated penalties for their violation. Then, in October, legislation established compulsory unemployment insurance and created a national system of employment offices. While Parliament sought to satisfy the yearnings of the people for social justice, the employers, perhaps also reasoning that present concessions might stave off future convulsions, granted wage increases of immediate benefit to workers. The index of real wages, taking 1913 as the base year, soared from the lowest point it had reached during the war, 64.6 in 1918, to 93.1 in 1919. Then, in 1920, the index shot up to 114.4 and kept rising until it reached 127 in 1921.[59]

Inflationary prosperity, happily, spurred the indices of real wages on to unprecedented heights. When combined with the atmosphere of great expectations which pervaded the entire country, these larger earnings brought into the ranks of organized labor millions of adherents, including clerical and technical workers, who could never pay dues before, or if they could, saw no reason to do so. Transported by enthusiasm far greater than that which swept hundreds of thousands of Americans into the Knights of Labor during 1885 and 1886, Italian workers stormed the portals of the chambers of labor and the category federations. Membership in the General Confederation of Labor leaped within a single year from 249,039 members in 1918 to 1,150,062 paid-up members in 1919. Nor did this fervor abate. By 1920, the C.G.L. reached the topmost peak of membership when it soared to 2,200,100. Even as it declined in 1921 under the assaults of the fascist Black Shirts, membership still stood at 1,128,915.[60]

The Italian Confederation of Labor (C.I.L.) made equally astonishing gains among Catholic workers. By 1919, it counted 500,000 organized workers, while in 1921 its membership advanced beyond 1,500,000. These adherents belonged to 16 local unions (chambers) of labor and 14 national category federations. The largest among them, the Italian Textile Union, claimed 131,252 members in June 1920. C.I.L.'s publication, at first called *Confederazione* (*Confederation*), became *Il Domani Sociale* (*The Social Future*) under the editorship of Giovanni Battista Valente. The new periodical absorbed the bimonthly organ of the former Economic-Social Union, *Azione Sociale* (*Social Action*).[61]

The cooperative movement, also a strong force for social moderation, prospered in unprecedented fashion during and after the war. Due to increased demands for every variety of supplies, cooperative societies allied with the National League of Cooperatives increased both their reserves and their membership. In 1918, 2,321 societies affiliated directly with the League. This number grew to 3,840 in 1920 and then reached 4,302 in 1921. In that year, the League attained a membership of 1,050,000 and the total extent of business turnover soared to 2,500,000,000 lire. The National Credit Institute for Cooperation (Istituto Nazionale di Credito per la Cooperazione), founded by royal decree on August 15, 1913 (a conscious device by Giolitti to encourage economic and social progress and to obviate the need for radical change) held 280,000,000 lire in capital, of which 260,000,000 lire originated from state grants (another conscious device by Giolitti to wed cooperative leaders to bourgeois governments).[62]

Following the foundation of C.I.L. in 1918 and the Popular Party early in 1919, came the establishment, also under Catholic sponsorship, of the Federation of Mutuality and Social Insurances (Federazione Mutualità e Assicurazioni Sociali) and the Italian Cooperative Confederation (Confederazione Cooperativa Italiana). At its congress in Treviso on April 2 and 3, 1921, the Italian Cooperative Confederation reported among its membership: 3,200 consumer cooperatives grouped into 68 local consortia and federations, 2,116 credit cooperatives or banks (*casse rurali*) united in 57 local federations, 694 labor cooperatives joined in 33 provincial consortia, 800 agricultural unions associated into 64 local unions, 40 fishermen's cooperatives which formed part of a national consortium, and 525 veterans cooperatives.[63]

Still other moderate influences sought to sanify the body economic. Rinaldo Rigola maintained that the myriad schemes which flourished during the war and the reconstruction years — profit-sharing, ownership by labor of stock in the companies where employed, the formation of worker cooperatives to redeem capitalistic enterprise, and countless additional variations on these themes — never captured the imagination of workers even when translated into legislative projects. He insisted that workers remained faithful to simple and tangible goals: increased wages, the eight-hour day, and obligatory social insurance. Guided by this line of reasoning, the General Confederation of Labor refused to abandon its program of positive earthly reforms in favor of the Heavenly City.

At the beginning of 1919, C.G.L. inaugurated the campaign for the eight-hour day. It considered the realization of this aim feasible since many category workers indicated their willingness to discard former prejudices against scientific management and Taylorism in exchange for the eight-hour day. These unions quite neatly demolished the argument that the institution of the eight-hour day would damage the general welfare of the nation by lowering productivity. C.G.L. officials met at the beginning of February with leading industrialists in Genoa. These industrialists accepted the confederal proposal and assumed the responsibility of introducing the eight-hour day in their plants to the greatest possible extent. On February 20, 1919, the Federation of Metallurgical Workers (F.I.O.M.) and employers in the metallurgical industries signed the first agreement on the eight-hour day. In consequence, 500,000 workers came to benefit from this reform after thirty years of effort. Negotiations in other industries, particularly textiles, proved more difficult, but gradually the eight-hour day prevailed as normal in most factories. The study conducted by the International Labour Office a few years later — it surveyed the hours of work fixed for industrial establishments through collective bargaining during the years from 1919 to 1923 — amply justified Rinaldo Rigola's claims. The details of the I.L.O. study also identified the saving process of collaboration between unions and management which continued to operate during these fateful years of political clamor and social violence.[64]

More sinister developments in 1919 outran the quest for reasonable solutions to economic and social problems. They ushered in the political tragedy of that year. Mussolini officially launched the Italian Combat Bands (Fasci Italiani di Combattimento) in March 1919. Between March and December, 11 military classes demobilized into an economy stripped of excess jobs by the termination of war production. Industrial strikes numbered 303 in 1918 and involved 158,036 workers. In 1919, 1,049,438 industrial strikers participated in 1,663 separate actions. While in 1918 only 675 agricultural workers had joined in 10 strikes, but one year later, 208 agricultural strikes involved 505,128 peasants.[65] By the end of June 1919, all of Italy took to the streets in protest against the high cost of living and impelled by the general feeling, not unfounded, that the war had brought enormous earnings to the war profiteers ("*i pescicani*," literally, the sharks). These demonstrators vented their discontent in strikes, the pillage of markets and shops, and vandalism. Without thought of consequence, they took action against hunger and scarcity which could only result in fattening these evils.

The disorders started at Forlì on June 30, rushed on to La Spezia, covered most of the Lunigiana, and then spread to Florence and the other major cities of Tuscany, Romagna, and Emilia. They reached out to Rome, Naples, and Milan, where, on July 6, the crowds sacked more than two hundred shops. Everywhere, mobs not only assaulted private shops and magazines, but also cooperatives. The chambers of labor enjoyed the confidence of the people and became arbiters for the entire community. Many proprietors handed over the keys of their warehouses to them. In some localities, soviets sprang up, inspired by the Russian Revolution. In the valley of Bisenzio, near Florence, the people established a republic of soviets. Despite popular enthusiasm, after three days the troops dissolved the republic without resistance. During this national turmoil, the authorities often found it useless to invoke the aid of troops on a large scale because the soldiers fraternized with the mobs. The government decided to allow popular rancor to run its course. Officials in Rome urged communal executives to maintain peace as best they could, to seize available supplies for the benefit of the population, and to repress the cornering of foodstuffs. The government, like all governments in similar circumstances, instituted a consultative commission to study the cost of living.

No sooner had the tumults of early July abated, when fresh chaos threatened. The international socialist and labor movements had planned a general strike for July 20 and 21 to protest against the intervention of the Allied governments in the Russian civil war. However, the French withdrew and this supposedly world-wide event found the Italian masses not only exhausted by the revolts they had mounted against the high cost of living several weeks before, but also disappointed by the stubborn continuation of high prices and scarcity of food.[66]

Italy now pressed rapidly toward the factory occupations of 1920. During World War I, F.I.O.M. had tried to re-establish official recognition for grievance committees (*commissioni interne*), but met resolute refusal by the industrialists. The wartime government, for its part, never recognized grievance committees as legal institutions, but advised their adoption without making it compulsory.[67]

At the F.I.O.M. Congress of Rome in November 1918, Bruno Buozzi, the leader of the metal-mechanical workers, reaffirmed the Federation's claim that the union must discuss directly with industry, or through grievance committees, all questions concerning wages and the distribution of work. He held that this experience would eventually lead to the sharing of technical administration within the plant by workers and management. At the same meeting, Emilio Colombino, a colleague of Buozzi, advanced the thesis that grievance committees would prove most useful to labor unions not because they resolved issues of importance to workers, but because they placed the ablest comrades in contact with industrial reality. This experience would train them for eventual operation of the country's factories when Italian workers appropriated them for the common use. He stressed the futility of placing private enterprise under socialistic control only to lose it through technical ignorance. Pursuing this theme, Colombino sounded completely pessimistic about the future of grievance committees. He even doubted the value of preserving them. He recalled that fifteen days or so after workers elected a grievance committee, they would send it packing, accusing all its members of betrayal and collusion with management. "We have many theories in our head," he said, "but we have to admit that we are not always infallible." Colombino had the insight of a prophet.[68]

At the beginning of 1919, the Automobile Employers Association at Turin recognized grievance committees in a contract negotiated with F.I.O.M. During the coming months, industrialists in other industries ratified agreements containing many new and special provisions, including the creation of grievance committees and a system of voting for them which guaranteed representation for minorities within the plant. In these unsettled days, hardly an industrialist breathed who would have dreamed of refusing the establishment of a grievance committee in his factory. In climax, F.I.O.M. and the powerful Mechanical and Metallurgical Employers Association of Milan signed a contract, duplicating the Turin precedent, in February 1920.[69]

The appearance of grievance committees brought on interminable controversy about their proper role in plant and nation. The moderate socialists, the "maximalists," the communists, the labor reformists, the revolutionary unionists, the Catholic confederationists, and the omnipresent defenders of dozens of other shades of opinion advanced their views in print and speech. Although danger inheres in falsely simplifying a complex and calamitous union of ideas and events which resulted in the factory occupation movement of 1920, two principal currents of thought about grievance committees deserve particular attention. Moderate labor leaders looked upon grievance committees as agencies of decentralized union activity. The committees exercised specific and limited functions agreed upon by both industry and labor. This view seemed to prevail from the end of 1918 until August 1919. Then moderate attitudes gave way to revolutionary enthusiasms — an inevitable shift under the prevailing internal organization of the labor movement. The chambers of labor still tended to absorb the more radical notions let loose upon the country. Yet, the sole countervailing forces within the labor movement, the category federations, possessed neither effective local administrative machinery in most communities nor factory institutions founded upon the national union's permanent constitutional arrangements. Their recently acquired grievance committees took life, in contrast, from the sporadic uncertainties of Italian collective bargaining. With no formal and intimate control over their members in the community or plant, the distant category union leadership looked on helplessly while firebrands in the chambers of labor and factories determined policy for the Italian labor movement.[70]

The drive for factory control by workers drew its primary strength from Turin. It began there, and even after it had penetrated the entire industrial North, Turin maintained intellectual and political hegemony over the course of its development. The group called the New Order — it took inspiration from Antonio Gramsci and name from the publication of the extreme left-wing of the Socialist Party at Turin which he founded, *Ordine Nuovo* — accomplished this ascendancy. Gramsci rose up from a Sardinian family of the most modest connections and means. He pursued his studies at the university despite poverty and infirm health. Quite early, the unyielding certainties of Marxian dogma attracted him. When he turned to journalism, Gramsci devoted himself tirelessly to the espousal of orthodox communism, emphatic of disciplined tactics and eventually subservient to the Russian lead, as contrasted to the more emotional Neapolitan brand represented by Amedeo Bordiga. He launched *Ordine Nuovo* in 1919, antedating the formal establishment of the Communist Party in January 1921. Upon the discussion groups which the incipient communists had organized in Turin, where the most famous classes took hold among the workers in the large and important Fiat works, Gramsci exerted notable force. (With the publication of Gramsci's copious prison notes in 1947, *Lettere dal carcere*, composed during his incarceration by the fascists and preserved by the Communist Party underground, the most casual comment of the prolific patron saint of the Italian Left has come to enjoy unrivalled prestige.)[71]

Radicals within and outside the labor movement, especially those guided by communist ideology, now insisted openly that grievance committees must serve merely as the instrumentality to obtain worker control of the factories — they represented but the first step on the road toward total expropriation. In August 1919, at the Fiat plant in Turin,

373

the initial move occurred in the transformation of grievance committees into factory councils (*consigli di fabbrica*). A new grievance committee, which replaced one dismissed by the same workers who had elected it, took the initiative in providing for the election of a representative, called a commissioner, from each department of the plant. When these commissioners met together, they formed the factory council. By October, almost all metal-working shops in Turin had departmental commissioners. With an understandable but still curious want of logic, the revolutionary leaders in the Turin plants put forward the proposition that grievance committees (the only agencies actually recognized by management) commanded only minor responsibilities, while factory councils possessed the power to metamorphose the nature of existing union institutions and then to substitute themselves entirely for them. In due time, factory councils would prepare for the "expropriation of industries in favor of the proletariat."[72]

By mid-October 1919, enough factory councils had formed to warrant an assembly of commissioners in Turin. Despite the movement's growth, industrialists still ignored the councils in their own enterprises, while labor unionists themselves harbored mixed feelings about them. Some of them fought the councils actively, fearing supersedure by them as radical theory frankly proclaimed. Others supported them. Nevertheless, labor leaders united in seeking to restrict the eligibility to serve as commissioners, as well as the right to elect commissioners, to organized workers. Eventually the various currents of opinion reached a compromise by decreeing that all workers had the right to vote for commissioners, but that only labor unionists had the right to stand for election.[73]

The conflict between the moderates and the radicals over the transformation of grievance committees into factory councils and the proper relationship of the councils to the labor movement continued into 1920 against a background of mounting unrest and violence. The strike of state postal and telegraph workers started on January 13. It did not succeed in mustering all employees because members of the Catholic federation continued on the job. Notwithstanding its limited efficacy, on January 20, the national government not only granted the demands of the strikers and promised not to take punitive measures against them, but also agreed to pay them for the days they spent on strike. The Catholic civil servants reaped ridicule and professional injury as a result of their loyalty. The former strikers taunted them as scabs and, because they refused to work beside scabs, C.I.L. members had to transfer to other posts in the agency. Following the strike, Filippo Turati reported that departmental heads in the Ministry of Posts did not dare to enforce discipline or demand work of their subordinates, fearing punishment by them.

The railroad workers strike began on January 20, manipulated by an anarchist minority. The officials of the Socialist Party and the socialists in Parliament, while declaring sympathy with the strikers, betrayed reservations by revealing that they had had no direct knowledge of their plans. The C.G.L. took more forthright action and placed all constituent organizations on guard against joining local strikes of solidarity with the railroad workers. The Association of Veterans opposed the strike directly, while the Catholic railroad workers refused to participate and battled it vigorously. Mussolini befriended the strikers and devised the cry: "The railways for the railwaymen." The government proceeded to treat with the strikers who resumed work on January 29 under conditions which returned all of them to their former posts. Following the lead of the postal clerks and telegraphers, the railroad workers also demanded compensation for the days they marched on the picket lines. They gave ground by graciously allowing the railroad administration to contribute the amounts due them to a fund devoted to low-cost housing for railroad workers.

Strikes of industrial workers also gained momentum. The textile workers of Bergamo and the Sicilian sulphur workers left their jobs at the beginning of February, while the Genoese metallurgical workers struck from February 18 to 20. During the second half of February, when the Ilva plant at Naples announced that it intended to close down due to lack of fuel, the workers went on strike. The strikers and police engaged in bloody conflict. In Milan, on March 1, workers proclaimed a general strike as a mark of solidarity with the streetcar workers. The streetcar workers had left their posts the day before to protest against the death of one of their comrades in a scuffle which followed a meeting of the Proletariat League of Wounded War Veterans. When the general strikers tried to return to work on March 2, groups of anarchists and the milling mobs attempted to prevent them by force. At the end of February and the beginning of March, agricultural strikes broke out in the province of Ferrara and larger strike movements soon engulfed the provinces of Vercella, Novara, Pavia, and Lomellina.[74]

The Fifth Congress of the General Confederation of Labor met at Leghorn at the end of February and the beginning of March 1920 for the first time since the Mantua Congress of May 1914. Representatives of 2,200,100 affiliated members assembled at a time of extended class warfare and deep national crisis. They found that unprecedented numerical strength did not blind their leaders to internal defects which were seriously weakening Italy's largest alliance of organized workers. The report of the general secretary and the agenda of the Congress stressed the need to amend the constitution to provide the confederal labor movement with greater powers of rigorous discipline. The officials of C.G.L. were asking the Congress quite plainly to limit the autonomy of category unions since recent strikes in the public services and among many craft, industrial, and white-collar workers indicated that the category federations were placing the interests of their own adherents above the welfare of the country at large. The experienced moderate leaders of the Confederation properly feared that the sympathies of some segments of the middle classes for the plight of the nation's workers and the neutral tolerance of other sectors might well turn into panic and then stiffen into support for the self-proclaimed champions of law and order, the fascists. Already, in the countryside, members of cooperatives and chambers of labor witnessed this reaction and saw the painfully constructed handiwork of years of toil burned down by the fascists before their very eyes.[75]

The revolution on the land itself, in full swing early in 1920, had begun during the summer of 1919. The source of these disorders went back to 1916 when Italy's peasant-soldiers were still fighting the tedium of trench warfare. Salandra, the Prime Minister, to bolster morale, had promised them land upon their return to civilian life. When the government lagged in keeping its word, the peasants of South Italy and Sicily, without the benefit of socialist leadership, occupied uncultivated lands. Violence often accompanied these events, but just as frequently ceremonial processions lent them dignity. Nor did priests, veterans, and leaders of the Popular Party wholly absent themselves from the manifestations. Mussolini, not to be outdone, wrote in the *People of Italy*: "We are for the land for the peasants. The State is a thing that the peasant does not know. The peasant wants the land and must have his land." The Ribera incident near Palermo in February 1920 shocked the middle classes and came to symbolize for them the lawlessness which had overtaken even rural society. The peasants of the Duke of Bivona seized his castle and imprisoned him there for days until he consented to their demands. Neither the Visocchi decree-law of September 2, 1919 nor the Falcioni decree-law of April 22, 1920 could check the momentum of this movement since the later legislation imposed more rigid conditions upon granting land to peasants than the earlier statute. Under its terms, the government aided only cooperatives, associations, or comparable bodies already organized for the joint cultivation of land. The government had actually foreshadowed this policy in 1919 by allotting to the National Veterans Aid Society (Opera Nazionale dei Combattenti) capital funds in the amount of 300,000,000 lire for the purpose of acquiring land. The legislation of 1920 also limited its jurisdiction to lands not cultivated or insufficiently cultivated.[76] Although betrayed by Parliament, the peasants of the Po Valley refused to surrender entirely their craving for land ownership. Out of defeat, they snatched partial victory by devising the system of manpower obligations (*l'imponibile di mano d'opera*). In almost all agricultural collective agreements in the Po Valley, this arrangement, which had no industrial precedent within the Italian labor movement, laid down minimum requirements for the number of laborers necessary for each measure of land under cultivation. At the end of the sixth decade of the twentieth century, legislation still kept this system in force.[77]

In March 1920, the Italian Confederation of Industrialists, which had its start at Turin in 1910 where it primarily served the interests of northern manufacturers, moved its headquarters to Rome and altered its name to the General Confederation of Italian Industry (Confederazione Generale dell'Industria Italiana — Confindustria). Confindustria claimed to include not only the chief industries of Italy, but also three-quarters of the smaller enterprises. Its membership still concentrated, naturally enough, in North Italy. Confindustria established close bonds with the Association of Joint Stock Companies. As part of a complete plan of operations, it devised methods for resisting unions and counteracting their demands. In April, the Confederation won its first victory by crushing the general strike at Turin. Ostensibly called to force the recognition of factory councils, the strike had actually begun as an emotional protest on the part of workers against instituting daylight-saving time. Since the change had started during the war, which itself had turned unpopular among workers, they looked upon daylight-saving as yet another manifestation of capitalist and governmental tyranny. In August, the General Confederation of Agriculture announced its formation and won wide membership among holders of diverse kinds of agricultural property.[78]

Social pressures now mounted to the pitch of explosion. The old order seemed to be falling apart. But the socialists, dominated by their dogma-ridden and do-nothing majority which waited with confidence for the revolution to fulfill itself miraculously, lacked the will to create a new one. The fatal experiment in the administration of industry by factory councils of workers now drew near. In August 1920, F.I.O.M., backed up by the Catholic unions, presented demands for new wage increases. The companies refused these demands.[79] The leaders of F.I.O.M. now faced a dilemma. During 1919, the employers of Piedmont had granted F.I.O.M.'s minimum-wage demands, but the industrialists of Liguria, Lombardy, Emilia, and Tuscany forced the metal-mechanical workers into protracted strikes which lasted sixty days. With the treasury of the union empty in the summer of 1920, F.I.O.M. did not wish to precipitate new strikes which might last for many months, exhaust the workers, and end in failure. Its heads now proceeded to experiment with seemingly safer substitutes for enforcing their demands.

At first, they stopped overtime work in selected plants. Then, on August 17, they decided that three days later F.I.O.M.'s members would slow down at their benches or insist upon the faithful observance of all work rules. The employers refused to resume negotiations, as requested by the Minister of Labor, Labriola, who convinced himself that the industrialists were deliberately inviting a showdown when they hoped to saddle the government with the necessity of using force against the metal-mechanical workers. Instead of meeting with their employees, the owners determined to answer the union's obstructive tactics with lockouts and so drive the workers into the very type of normal strike action which F.I.O.M.'s officers were trying to avoid. On August 28, the management of Alfa Romeo in Milan closed down its shops after repeated incidents of violence and sabotage. Confronted by this unexpected turn of affairs, F.I.O.M. ordered all members on August 30 to occupy the factories they worked in, night and day, to prevent further lockouts.[80]

The occupation of plants by workers to enforce their demands, or to stave off unemployment, had begun as early as March 1919 although it never developed into a concerted movement. Members of the national syndicalist U.I.L. at Dalmine forestalled a lockout then by occupying the factory where they worked, hoisting the tricolor flag of the Fatherland, and electing an administrative committee to run the plant.[81] During the first six months of 1920, instances of plant occupation multiplied. Workers took over the Ansaldo shops at Viareggio in February; the Mazzonis cotton mills at Pont Canavese and at Torre Pellice at the end of February; a woodworking factory in Asti, closed down by bankruptcy proceedings on court order, at the beginning of March when the workers raised the Red Flag and resumed operations on their own; the mechanical shops of Miani and Silvestri at Naples during the second part of March; and the Spadaccini plant at Sesto San Giovanni outside Milan and the Ilva plant at Piombino during the first part of June. The public authorities emptied the Miani and Silvestri plant in Naples by force at the cost of one death. A general strike followed and lasted for two days. Government authorities resolved the situation in the Mazzonis cotton mills by requisitioning the factories. The government remained in legal authority until April 9 when the firm signed a satisfactory agreement with its workers.[82]

After F.I.O.M. authorized the factory occupations at the end of August 1920, workers held hundreds of plants in Milan alone. However, the most renowned event in the entire movement occurred in Turin where the metal workers, lost to F.I.O.M.'s control as a result of domination by Gramsci's communist New Order group, took over the management of the large Fiat plant. Such violence accompanied their action that the nation recoiled in shock. The occupation of factories then spread to other industries and to other parts of Italy. It seemed to most Italians that the revolution had begun. By the end of the year, 1,267,953 industrial workers would have participated in 1,881 strikes, while 1,045,732 agricultural laborers would have left their fields in 189 demonstrations of their discontent.[83]

The factory occupations continued from September 1 until September 20, 1920. Writers differ, according to their political and social predilections, about the efficiency of the factory councils in administering the plants under their control. A report published by the General Confederation of Italian Industry in 1947 concluded from available evidence that factory councils bungled their directives and sit-in strikers accomplished little or no work in the plants.[84] Opposing this conservative view with his own socialist appraisal, Angelo Rossi stated that the factory councils maintained production surprisingly well, considering the absence of engineers, technicians, and clerical workers from the plants. They created guards, enforced discipline, and secured universal respect for property. He admitted that, as the occupation went on, the difficulty of replenishing raw materials and obtaining money for wages brought some sense of reality into Utopia. Moreover, the new-dawn enthusiasm of the early September days faded as workers began to chafe at the boredom of spending most of their time in the factories. Toward the last, leaders did not permit them to leave the shops at all for fear that they might never return.[85]

Meanwhile, the battle between the labor unions and the communist currents continued. The communists insisted that the factory occupation movement constituted the beginning of rapid sovietization. The trade unionists, while not rejecting the idea of eventual full industrial control by workers, countered with the doctrine that the movement represented the first step of a progressive replacement of employer authority by the rule of workers. Later events stripped the blowhard communist dicta down to their hard core of claptrap. Workers felt neither technically nor morally equipped to assume factory control. When Senator Giovanni Agnelli (1866–1945), the president of Fiat, formally offered to turn over the management of that enterprise to its revolutionary work force organized as a cooperative, they refused.[86]

But before that moment of truth unfolded, the time arrived when the C.G.L. and the Socialist Party could no longer defer action by issuing pronunciamentos. Workers controlled the factories of North Italy. Either they obtained full legal right to administer these plants or the millennial socialist dream of two generations would come to an abrupt end overnight. On September 5, the C.G.L. listed three alternative courses of action. The factory occupation movement could confine its scope and consolidate its strength in the metal-mechanical industries. Or, secondly, the C.G.L. could encourage the broader movement throughout Italy. Or, thirdly, the workers could transform factory occupation into a revolution. The Socialist Party then spoke its equally divided mind: without committing itself to any specific program, it offered to take charge of the movement. Socialists thus avoided again the necessity of applying loudly cherished Marxian principles to a particular instance of crisis. Instead, they called for Parliament, then in recess, to convene.

Meanwhile, Giolitti, the Prime Minister, had waited for time to educate the workers. He knew socialist leaders too well to fear any revolution of their making. Consciously thinking of his successful procrastination during the 1904 general strike, he delayed action until mid-September and then took himself to Turin, the center of his native Piedmont. He talked to everyone reasonably and insisted that employers meet with union representatives. He finally induced employers to consider specific requests made by the unions relating to wage increases, holidays, and severance pay. The General Confederation of Italian Industry and the General Confederation of Labor also pledged to confer on factory control by workers and to resolve the crisis. By a decree dated September 12, 1920, Giolitti established a commission of representatives from the two Confederations. They possessed the authority to prepare a draft law covering the participation of workers in the technical, financial, and administrative control of enterprises.

The commission, of course, could not achieve any meeting of minds. The C.G.L. proposed the creation of an elected workers control council in each factory with extensive powers: command over administration and management; supervision of the formation, increase, and reduction of capital; direction of banking transactions; and the regulation of the technical processes of manufacture. The recommendation also called for trade union authority in each branch of industry, exercised through supreme control agencies — further Marxian variations on syndicalist, Catholic, and D'Annunzian corporative notions.[87]

The proposals submitted by the General Confederation of Italian Industry centered on the obligatory creation of grievance committees in all factories. Their suggested responsibilities went far beyond the duties they performed under then prevailing collective bargaining contracts. For example, grievance committees would strive for increased efficiency and productivity and would have access to all information necessary to this effort. To preclude the possibility that labor and management might find themselves ignorant of the causes of critical shifts in the business cycle, the recommendations of the industrialists also called for nation-wide control commissions in each industry. These commissions would consist of representatives from labor unions, employer organizations, and government. They were to consider particularly questions relating to raw materials, supplies, economic and financial developments, industrial trends, productivity, and social insurance.[88]

To lend more color to diversity, the Catholic C.I.L. presented a scheme of its own devising. It resembled in part C.G.L.'s plan, but, in addition, it championed the notion of shareholding. Workers were to receive part of their employer's profits to buy stock in the company and would be represented on the board of directors.[89]

In view of these conflicting ideas, the government presented a compromise draft-law of its own to the Chamber of Deputies on February 8, 1921. Both employers and unions rejected this bill which provided for industry-wide control committees of workers. The employers insisted that the legislation impeded their freedom of action and destroyed their prerogatives with regard to the technical and economic development of their industries. The unions protested that the bill ignored the fundamental demands and aspirations of workers. The communists denounced the plan in bitter terms. Parliament took no action during that session, but the government again presented this legislation on June 20, 1921. Not surprisingly, the Chamber of Deputies did not discuss, much less approve, the bill during the succeeding months which brought economic collapse, unemployment, and reinvigorated fascist attacks on the headquarters, periodicals, and property of the Socialist Party, the labor unions, and cooperatives. Parliament ceased to function.[90]

During 1921, the incurably divided labor movement made valiant efforts to maintain a united stand against the stiffening attitude of employers inspirited by fascist warfare against bolshevism in all its forms. In contrast to 1919 and 1920, the unions found themselves hard-pressed to preserve their wage scales and the eight-hour day. Already in December 1920, the C.G.L. had called a conference of transport and communication unions in Rome with the purpose of initiating and guiding a defensive alliance of the Italian Union of Railroad Workers, the Federation of Workers of the Sea, the National Union of Workers on Secondary Railroads (Sindacato Nazionale dei Ferrovieri Secondari ed Internavigatori), the Streetcar Workers Union, the Federation of Port Workers, and the Federation of Postal and Telegraphic Unions. But these category unions, although deeply concerned with preserving the hard-won favorable terms of their collective agreements, could not escape the leadership jealousies, political dissensions, and ideological strife which infused each decision on policy or tactics.

As the menace of fascism swelled, on January 25, 1921, the Popular Party and C.I.L. drew up a pact of cooperation, paralleling the close accord which now obtained between the C.G.L. and the Socialist Party of Turati. Then, in February 1921, the Italian Union of Railroad Workers urged the widest possible defensive coalition to include itself, the Socialist Party, the Republican Party, the Anarchist Union, C.G.L., U.I.L., U.S.I., and the Federation of Port Workers. From this proposal emerged the Labor Alliance, intent upon protecting political freedom, union rights, and the eight-hour day. The Labor Alliance also hoped to heal the ideological and programmatic rifts which weakened the labor movement and left it progressively more helpless before increasingly brutal fascist assaults.

At the end of April 1922, the C.G.L., apparently desperate with concern about the ability of the Labor Alliance to resist the fascist onslaughts then in violent advance, used intermediaries to win the protection of D'Annunzio. C.G.L.'s leaders remembered his greetings to Lenin at the time he commanded Fiume. D'Annunzio graciously consented to talk with Ludovico D'Aragona, the general secretary. The result of D'Annunzio's efforts in behalf of the C.G.L.: he sent a bust of Dante to the General Confederation of Labor and received that organization's warm thanks. *Avanti!* publicly frowned upon this gratitude.

After the widespread fascist destruction of socialist, republican, popularist, and labor headquarters and property during the late spring and summer of 1922, culminating in the July outrages at Cremona, Novara, and Ravenna, the Labor Alliance roused itself to meet mounting violence with the passive resistance of local strikes. Then, just as Luigi Facta, who had resigned the premiership on July 19, presented his new cabinet on August 1, the Labor Alliance proclaimed a general strike of national scope. Because the Alliance had mounted this extreme action to end, once and for all time, the violation of civil liberties which "must find aid and security in the rule of law," Filippo Turati designated it "legalitarian," thereby investing the general strike, presumably, with the moral strength to move mountains. But it lacked necessary physical force and the entire enterprise ended in disaster. Inspired by the Socialist Party to push the government to the left, the general strike insured Facta's reinstatement and alienated the democrats and popularists from the socialists. It also prepared even greater political defeat for socialism by convincing the middle classes, the army, the navy, the police forces, and civil service officials that fascist excesses supplied indispensable safeguards against bolshevism. Finally, the general strike shattered both the Labor Alliance and the labor movement after Mussolini unleashed the fury of his Black Shirts. The Italian Union of Railroad Workers started the exodus from the Alliance, next U.I.L. withdrew, and then U.S.I. The Federation of Port Workers left the C.G.L. The C.G.L. and the printers severed all ties with the Socialist Party in order to husband their waning strength. Thousands upon thousands of humiliated, mauled, and disillusioned workers fled their unions for safety.

Statistics confirm the grim proportions of this tragedy. During the rest of 1922, the full evil which the fascists could not work, unemployment completed. Official government statistics reported a minimum of 304,242 and a maximum of 606,819 persons unemployed in 1922.[91] After the fascist demonstrations and punitive expeditions during the spring and summer of that year and the March on Rome at the end of October, strike fervor abated. In 1921, 1,045 industrial strikes had called 644,564 factory workers from their benches, half the number of strikers in 1920. Only 79,298 agricultural workers engaged in 89 strikes. By 1922, industrial strikes declined to 552 and strikers to 422,773. Agricultural strikes fell to 23 and strikers to 25,146. Industrial peace reigned in 1923: 200 industrial strikes and 66,103 industrial strikers; one agricultural strike and 110 strikers. Membership in the C.G.L. declined from 1,128,915 in 1921 to 401,054 in 1922. When delegates to the Sixth Congress of the General Confederation of Labor, its last one, assembled at Milan in December 1924, its adherents had fallen away to 201,049.[92] The delegates reaffirmed the responsibility of the labor movement to the working class, repudiated revolutions brought off by minority factions of the proletariat, once more avowed its political independence and its sympathy for all parties sharing its own principles, declared its approbation of the common ownership of the means of production, and again amended the confederal constitution so that it now carried 56 articles.[93]

As C.G.L., C.I.L., and U.S.I. lost ground, the fascist unions moved rapidly forward. Not until the failure of the factory occupation movement did Mussolini's lieutenants attempt to organize labor groups beyond the few agricultural districts of early fascist success. At the end of 1920, they founded the Farmers Brotherhood (Fratellanza Colonica) in Tuscany and the short-lived Italian Confederation of Economic Unions (Confederazione Italiana dei Sindacati Economici) in Romagna and Emilia. The fascists now began to attract industrial workers. Dino Grandi established the first fascist chamber of labor at Bologna in January 1921 and fascists formed their first association of railroad workers on October 7, 1921. The movement also gained momentum in provinces outside the fascist cradle. It aroused the enthusiasm of nationalists like Alfredo Rocco (the distinguished professor of law who fused Catholic labor theory and national syndicalist blood-thinking in his system of corporative society) and Enrico Corradini (one of the early organizers of the Nationalist Party in 1910 and editor of *Il Regno* (*The Kingdom*), where he and his associates created the Italian nationalist myth), and former socialists like Oliviero Olivetti and Sergio Panunzio.

On January 24, 1922, less than three years after the foundation of the first *fascio* at the Piazza San Sepolcro in Milan on March 23, 1919, and little less than three months after the foundation of the National Fascist Party on November 7, 1921, the first national congress of fascist labor organizations took place at Bologna. Representatives of 250,000 organized fascist workers proceeded to institute the National Confederation of Syndical Unions (Confederazione Nazionale delle Corporazioni Sindacali). Five occupational groups, designated as corporations, united within the new Confederation: industrial labor, agricultural labor, commerce, seafarers, and the intellectual and middle classes. The congress selected Edmondo Rossoni, the leader of the national syndicalist U.I.L., as general secretary of the Confederation and proclaimed April 21, the mythological date of the founding of Rome, as the anniversary of Italian labor. To crown their deliberations, the delegates resolved that however important labor loomed in national economic life, the various social classes had to subordinate "their rights and aspirations . . . to the superior interests of the nation as a whole." On April 1, following the inaugural congress, the daily newspaper of the C.N.C.S., *Il Lavoro d'Italia* (*Italian Labor*), appeared. By the time that the Confederation's second national congress took place from June 4 to 6, 1922, membership had increased to 458,284. Almost 500 delegates converged upon Milan from 52 provinces.[94]

By 1923, Rossoni's National Confederation of Syndical Unions, which had added "Fascist" to its name in December 1922, claimed 850,000 adherents at a time when C.G.L. membership sank to 211,016. The end of free cooperatives also drew near. The Italian Union of Cooperatives (Sindacato Italiano delle Cooperative), founded by the fascists early in 1921 as the center of their cooperative ventures, met in convention for the first time at Milan on June 17, 1923. The president announced to the delegates who represented 1,341 societies that two important consortia had joined their Union: the Consorzio delle Cooperative Carniche, which engaged in large works of reconstruction in devastated areas, and the Consorzio Operai Metallurgico, which operated in the iron and steel industries. For the second half of 1923, the Union reported 1,846 affiliated societies, 348,270 members, capital in the amount of 42,750,000 lire, and business turnover totalling 650,000,000 lire. A year later, these figures had mounted to 2,570 societies with capital set at 60,450,000 lire and business turnover calculated at 840,000,000 lire.[95]

The fascists now took steps to deal constructively with the conditions of labor. Since February 1920, the Chamber of Deputies had been considering a bill to regulate hours of work, but could not reach agreement for three years. Decree-law 692 of March 15, 1923 and the administrative regulations of September 10, 1923 set the maximum number of hours of actual work at eight per day and forty-eight per week. The provisions applied to all commercial and industrial enterprises and to casual agricultural labor.[96] Then, in December 1923, Mussolini advanced the government's announced policy of "class collaboration in the national interest" by inviting representatives of fascist unions and employers associations to meet with him at the Chigi Palace in Rome. Both groups agreed to abandon the disastrous methods of the class struggle in treating with each other and to settle conditions of labor through peaceful negotiation based upon industrial knowledge. The National Confederation of Fascist Syndical Unions, which had hitherto admitted employers to membership, consented to limit its adherents to labor. The organization of employers became the prerogative of the General Confederation of Italian Industry.[97]

The assassination of Giacomo Matteotti in June 1924 and the isolation with which the horror of the country enveloped the fascist government slowed down Mussolini's program for inaugurating "integral" fascism. At the end of August 1924, C.G.L., C.I.L., U.I.L., the Confederation of Bank Employees of Italy (Confederazione dei Bancari d'Italia), and the

National Union of Clerical Workers of Italy (Sindacato Nazionale Impiegati d'Italia) united to form, at Milan, an interconfederal committee to defend the free labor movement against fascist terror and attack. But the bond which drew these organizations together proved fragile indeed and raveled when Mussolini again resumed the initiative. On January 31, 1925, the government appointed the Commission of Eighteen, or the Commission of Solons as popularly designated, to prepare plans for the constitutional bases of the Fascist State. Senator Giovanni Gentile, Italy's most famous contemporary philosopher after Benedetto Croce, presided over the Commission, just as he had headed the earlier Commission of Fifteen which the Fascist Party named in September 1924 to accomplish the same mission. The final report of the Commission of Eighteen, submitted on June 24, 1925, contained the full report of the Committee of Fifteen as an appendix.

The Commission recommended increased powers for the executive as a check against the weaknesses of Italian parliamentary government. It also urged the legal recognition of separate syndical associations of employers and workers in fulfillment of fascist theory. A National Corporative Council in Rome would replace the Chamber of Deputies. Although members of the Commission failed to agree upon the details of the plan, release of the report resulted in extensive public discussion and fascist groups began to advocate juridical status for syndical organizations. This movement attained its end at the Vidoni Palace on October 2, 1925. Italian industrialists, represented through the General Confederation of Italian Industry, recognized the National Confederation of Fascist Syndical Unions as the sole representatives of Italian workers. In turn, the unions recognized the Confederation as the sole representative of Italian employers. A few days later, at the meeting of the Fascist Grand Council on October 6, 1925, Alfredo Rocco espoused the logical sequel to the declaration at the Vidoni Palace.

The Fascist State would permit no strikes or lockouts in the public services, nor would it allow strikes and lockouts in private enterprises unless labor courts, subsequently to be created, first declared them justified. On December 18, 1925, the Chamber of Deputies passed the syndical law establishing the "juridical discipline of collective labor relations." The Senate approved the measure on March 11, 1926 and the King signed it as law 563 on April 3. On July 1, the government published regulations 1130 which elaborated the administration of the law. Only existing fascist employer and labor organizations received legal recognition and the exclusive right to represent their occupational interests. Strikes and lockouts became criminal offenses. Collective agreements bound all workers and employers in the economic sphere covered by the contract and not merely members of the syndical associations. To provide against the breakdown of bargaining between the parties, the law created labor courts for the adjudication of collective disputes. Fascist syndical, economic, and social policy found summary expression in the Fascist Charter of Labor, solemnly proclaimed on April 21, 1927 by the Fascist Grand Council and vaunted as one of the fundamental statements in world history concerning the ordering of human affairs.[98]

Bruno Buozzi, F.I.O.M.'s dynamic leader, succeeded D'Aragona as general secretary of the C.G.L. in January 1926. He attained this office only to preside over the Confederation's doom. After the attempted assassination of Mussolini in Bologna by Anteo Zamboni, a boy of 15, on October 31, 1926, the Fascist Party and the government employed terror, now with the force of law, against all resistant political and economic organizations.

At this moment, the entire cooperative movement — the socialist National League of Cooperatives, the Catholic Italian Cooperative Confederation, the societies inspired by the liberals, especially the large network of people's banks, the consortium of labor and producer cooperatives created by unionists in the province of Parma, the consortium of agricultural and industrial cooperatives under republican leadership in the Romagna, the agricultural and industrial cooperatives established by the National Veterans Aid Society, and other groups, including the fascist Italian Union of Cooperatives — counted 6,481 consumer societies, 7,643 producer and labor groups, 1,534 credit cooperatives, and 3,719 mixed and miscellaneous associations. Except for the fascist cooperatives, they now operated without legal status, subject to the whims and harassments of the authorities. On December 30, 1926, the democratic cooperative and mutualistic societies received their coup de grâce when the royal decree of that date established the National Fascist Institute of Cooperation, a government agency empowered to coordinate, assist, and develop the work of cooperatives and mutual aid societies.

Although the Black Shirts invaded and sacked the central headquarters of the C.G.L. at Milan on November 1, 1926 and the authorities followed soon thereafter to seal its doors, these same officials restored the keys after three weeks and insisted that the government had not dissolved the Confederation. Mussolini played a waiting game. He knew only too well that the C.G.L. still maintained intimate contact with the international labor movement and that the I.L.O. recognized it as the national labor center of Italy. He wanted this Genevan prestige for the fascist labor movement and realized that official government destruction of the General

Confederation of Labor would shatter that hope as well. Mussolini's patience soon rewarded him. After grave deliberations, the directive council of the C.G.L., at its final sitting during the beginning of January 1927, determined to close down the crumbling headquarters of the free labor movement in Italy. Bruno Buozzi left his homeland for Paris where he kept alive, with the encouragement of the Confédération Générale du Travail, the memory of Italy's moderate, progressive, and responsible General Confederation of Labor. So ended the C.G.L. on French soil.[99]

On January 16, 1927, just after the dissolution of the C.G.L., a group of formerly influential leaders of the Confederation met in Milan under the chairmanship of Rinaldo Rigola, now blind, but once the renowned organizer of Biella's textile workers and the C.G.L.'s independent and temperate voice during its first twelve years of life. These surviving friends made their peace with the régime. The *Stefani* news service published the text of their declaration on February 2. Among the chief signers of the statement were Rigola himself, Eugenio Azimonti, Umberto Calda, Emilio Colombino, and Ettore Reina. Ludovico D'Aragona denied that he had ever set his name to it. The document took time to make its theoretical and practical points. The statement admitted that the working class of Italy had immobilized itself through its collectivist ideology and enmity toward capitalism, for it stood neither for the State nor against the State. Without disavowing socialism, which the manifesto defined as a tendency of society, it recognized that this dualism between unions and the State could not continue for long: either the State must absorb the unions or the unions must destroy the State. The declaration then affirmed the social bonds which united all useful factors of production and the limited right of both workers and employers to class self-defense. The climax and purpose of the long, involved, and not undignified statement now came clear:

> The fascist régime is a reality and reality must be considered . . . .
> We can cite all our reservations about the methods and aims of the fascist intervention, but since an intervention has taken effect, we are interested in following its developments at close hand.

Consequently, they offered no opposition in principle to the exclusive legal recognition of fascist unions, controlled collective bargaining, and the labor courts. Nor did they voice objection to the Corporative State and to the Charter of Labor. They let live in order to live. They wished to utilize their labor union experience by proposing to found a research center. They did indeed establish the Association for the Study of Labor Problems (L'Associazione per lo Studio dei Problemi del Lavoro) at

Milan and issued a small review which featured serious and well prepared articles, *Problemi del Lavoro* (*Problems of Labor*). Both the Association and its publication remained faithful to the spirit of the declaration of January 1927 and did not refrain from uttering temperate criticism of both *de facto* and fascist unions. Their activities exerted the most restricted influence in Mussolini's police state although *Lavoro* (*Labor*) of Genoa, considered the daily newspaper voice of the Association, possessed a larger audience. So ended the General Confederation of Labor on Italian soil.[100]

FOOTNOTES – CHAPTER VIII

[1] Gualtieri, cited above, pp. 194, 167–168; Leonetti, cited above, p. 75; Rigola, cited above, pp. 157–162, 234–235; Italo Mario Sacco, *Storia del sindacalismo,* pp. 75–78, 245–248.

[2] Rigola, cited above, pp. 158–159, 282.

[3] *Annuario statistico italiano 1905–1907,* pp. 802–803.

[4] For the most detailed description in English of the boards of trustees, see Gualtieri, cited above, pp. 148–151.

[5] Rigola, cited above, pp. 157, 226–229; see also, this study, Chapter V, pp. 187–188.

[6] Rigola, cited above, pp. 228–229.

[7] The same, pp. 192–199; Luigi Einaudi, *Le lotte del lavoro,* pp. 69–104.

[8] Rigola, cited above, pp. 229–233.

[9] The same, pp. 227–230.

[10] The same, pp. 244–249.

[11] Roberto Michels, *Storia critica* . . ., pp. 251–255.

[12] Rigola, cited above, pp. 272, 281–284.

[13] The same, pp. 271–280.

[14] The same, pp. 287–295.

[15] The same, pp. 306–310.

[16] For the complete text of the constitution of the C.G.L., see Rigola, cited above, pp. 309–313. For the major portions of the constitution, drawn up by the seceding minority groups, which is permeated with syndicalist revolutionary philosophy, see also, Rigola, cited above, pp. 313–314.

[17] The same, pp. 315–316.

[18] Rigola, cited above, p. 323. By 1912, 242 boards of trustees had been established in Italy. During that year, 35,771 industrialists and 220,683 workers participated in the elections stipulated by the law. The total number of controversies brought before 116 boards in 1912 reached 5,413. Of the 6,114 separate causes of controversy, 4,816, or almost 80%, concerned discharges and wages. Within the five-year period, 1909–1913, 749 industrialists and 25,721 workers were involved in the controversies brought before the boards, either in their role as conciliators or as juries. See *Annuario statistico italiano 1914,* p. 316.

[19] Francesco Magri, *Controllo operaio e consigli d'azienda in Italia e all'estero: 1916–1947,* pp. 184–185; Confederazione Generale dell'Industria Italiana, *I consigli di gestione,* Vol. II, p. 7; Mario Guarnieri, *I consigli di fabbrica,* p. 19. The experience of the unionized hat workers and employers in Monza, while also unique, contrasted sharply with that of F.I.O.M. – Itala. In 1902, the Italian Federation of Hat Workers, headed by Ettore Reina, and the Association of Hat

Manufacturers concluded an agreement which not only dealt with wages, hours, and working conditions, but also provided for grievance procedures, an intermediate appeals commission composed of industrialists and workers, and final resort to arbitration in order to avoid strikes. Amicable relations continued under this contract for some time. See Sacco, cited above, pp. 256–257.

[20] Rigola, cited above, pp. 325–327.

[21] Michels, *Storia critica* . . ., pp. 342–343; Rigola, cited above, pp. 342–348.

[22] Appendix A, Table 38

[23] Rigola, cited above, p. 371; Leonetti, cited above, pp. 102, 105.

[24] Rigola, cited above, p. 371; Leonetti, cited above, p. 107.

[25] Rigola, cited above, p. 375; Leonetti, cited above, p. 109.

[26] Rigola, cited above, p. 383; Leonetti, cited above, p. 111.

[27] Leonetti, cited above, pp. 113, 116–117.

[28] The same, p. 118.

[29] The Second Congress of the C.G.L. held at Modena in 1908 may be designated as the Seventh Congress of the Societies of Resistance if the following system of enumeration is followed: the Congress of the Federated Chambers of Labor at Parma in 1893, I; the congress of these organizations at Piacenza in 1897, II; the congress of these organizations at Milan in 1900, III; the congress of these organizations at Reggio Emilia in 1901, IV; the first congress of the chambers of labor and the national category federations at Genoa in 1905 after the formation of the Central Secretariat of Resistance, V; and the constituent assembly of the C.G.L. in Milan in 1906, VI.

[30] Rigola, cited above, pp. 366–371.

[31] *Annuario statistico italiano 1911,* pp. 212–215.

[32] Michels, *Storia critica* . . ., cited above, pp. 308–311. In agriculture, which employed the vast majority of Italy's workers, only 4.9% of 5,693,080 laborers and sharecroppers, were organized.

[33] Rigola, cited above, pp. 395–398.

[34] The same, cited above, pp. 333–334; Leonetti, cited above, pp. 103, 105, 109, 111, 116.

[35] Rigola, cited above, pp. 406–407.

[36] The same, cited above, pp. 410–411; *Annuario statistico italiano 1914,* p. 298.

[37] *Annuario statistico italiano 1914,* pp. 296–298. Neither the maritime workers federation nor the Italian Union of Railroad Workers reported 1914 membership figures to the National Labor Office of the Ministry of Agriculture, Industry and Commerce. However, the National Labor Office did receive information for 1913: the maritime workers federation, 53,857 members, an incredible increase over its 1910 membership of 5,765; the Italian Union of Railroad Workers, 49,000 workers, an increase of almost 5,000 over its 1910 membership.

[38] Magri, cited above, pp. 7, 26; Luisa Riva Sanseverino, cited above, p. 214.

[39] Magri, cited above, pp. 27–33; Sanseverino, cited above, pp. 216–244.

[40] Magri, cited above, pp. 34–45; Sanseverino, cited above, pp. 244–255; Rigola, cited above, pp. 414–416.

[41] Magri, cited above, pp. 47–59; Sanseverino, cited above, pp. 255–257; *Annuario statistico italiano 1914,* pp. 296–297.

[42] Oscar Spinelli, *La mutualità in Italia e all'estero,* pp. 45–46; *Annuario statistico italiano 1914,* p. 334. The National Life Insurance Institute (Istituto Nazionale delle Assicurazioni) administered life insurance as a state monopoly from January 1, 1913 to December 31, 1923 in accordance with law 305 of April 4, 1912 and the royal decree regulation 939 of August 5, 1912. Law 966 of April 29, 1923 abolished the state monopoly, beginning on January 1, 1924, and permitted both domestic and foreign private companies to conduct business in Italy under set guarantees.

[43] Giulio Costanzo, cited above, pp. 52–54; *Annuario statistico italiano 1905–1907*, p. 750; *Annuario statistico italiano 1911*, p. 279.

[44] *Annuario statistico italiano 1905–1907*, pp. 752–753; *Annuario statistico italiano 1914*, p. 349.

[45] *Annuario statistico italiano 1914*, p. 332.

[46] The statistics on cooperatives presented in the text were calculated from data found in the following sources: *Annuario statistico italiano 1889–1890*, pp. 320–321; *Annuario statistico italiano 1905–1907*, pp. 758–759, footnote (c); *Annuario statistico italiano 1911*, pp. 265–266.

[47] E. A. Lloyd, cited above, pp. 4–6; Spinelli, cited above, pp. 45–46.

[48] Sacco, cited above, pp. 267–272.

[49] Rigola, cited above, pp. 426–427.

[50] Appendix A, Table 33; Rigola, cited above, pp. 427, 431–432.

[51] Appendix A, Table 38.

[52] International Labour Office, Studies and Reports, Series A (Industrial Relations) No. 34, *Conciliation and Arbitration in Industrial Disputes*, pp. 425–428. For a description of 1907, 1908, and 1911 special legislation and regulations concerning individual and collective disputes in the rice fields and for an account of special legislation in 1906, 1912, 1913, 1919, and 1920 to insure equitable treatment for employees of privately owned public transportation (streetcars, light railways, and inland navigation services) who could not legally strike, see pp. 429–430.

[53] John Clarke Adams, cited above, p. 427.

[54] Leonetti, cited above, p. 125.

[55] The same, pp. 127–128. For details concerning the joint peace proposals of the Socialist Party and the C.G.L., see this volume, p. 251.

[56] Magri, cited above, pp. 69–75; Sanseverino, cited above, pp. 346–354. For details concerning the program elaborated at the September 29, 1918 meeting of the national council and definitively approved by the executive commission on February 3, 1919, see also, Sacco, cited above, pp. 284–287.

[57] Sacco, cited above, pp. 293–295.

[58] Rigola, cited above, pp. 437–438, 430. For details on the November 1918 proposal of the C.G.L. and the Socialist Party's proposals of December 1918, see this study, pp. 256–257.

[59] Appendix A, Table 33.

[60] John Clarke Adams, cited above, p. 427.

[61] Sanseverino, cited above, pp. 348–349.

[62] Lloyd, cited above, pp. 6, 97–98; Ruini, cited above, p. 16.

[63] Sanseverino, cited above, p. 348, footnote 4.

[64] Rigola, cited above, p. 438. *Hours of Labour in Industry — Italy*, Studies and Reports, Series D (Wages and Hours) No. 8, November 1923, of the International Labour Office provided the following information about hours of labor as stipulated in collective bargaining agreements:

The agreement between F.I.O.M. and the metal-working employers of Lombardy (Consorzio Lombardo Fera Industriali Meccanici e Metallurgici), dated February 20, 1919, fixed the working week at 48 hours for engineering, shipbuilding, and iron and steel works. Previous weekly hours of work had averaged 55 to 60 in engineering (figures for Fiat were 60 in 1913, 58 in 1914, 57 in 1915, and 55 in 1916) and 72 in iron and steel works. The new schedule went into effect for engineering and shipbuilding plants on May 1, 1919 and for iron and steel mills on July 1, 1919. The association of employers in the metal industries of Liguria also reached a similar agreement with F.I.O.M. on February 20, 1919. On March 24, 1919, employers in Naples followed suit. Overtime could be temporary and not permanent. Special arrangements were made for continuous process work and fixed rates for overtime pay were established in the contracts. The April 1922 survey of the metal industries, published in the *Bollettino del Lavoro* of October 1922, showed the 48-hour week in force among 96.9% of all workers and among 99.4% of automobile workers. It applied to only 93.4% of workers in precision and precious metals industries. The 48-hour week was exceeded in relatively small engineering works which averaged 35 workers per plant and in iron and steel works which averaged 65 workers per plant. In all, these shops accounted for only 3.1% of all workers employed in the metal-mechanical industries. (See I.L.O. report, cited above, pp. 16–19).

During 1920, the 48-hour week was introduced into the textile industry — the first in Italy to regulate hours of work through agreement — by collective contracts concluded between employers in the cotton, silk spinning, wool, jute, linen and hemp, and dyeing industries and C.G.L.'s Italian Federation of Textile Workers and C.I.L.'s Italian Textile Union. The national agreement in the cotton industry was signed on April 7, 1920. Subsequent agreements of February 12, 1921 and August and September 1921 maintained the 48-hour week. These cotton agreements, like the other textile agreements except the silk spinning contract of February 1922, provided definite schedules for overtime pay and establishment of weekly maxima for hours of overtime. In 1919, the 8-hour day went into effect in some silk spinning mills in various parts of Italy, but not until December 1920 did the Association of Silk Manufacturers (Unione Industriali Sereci) sign an agreement with the two textile unions. The subsequent agreements of September 1921 and February 1922 contained no provisions for overtime pay. Only 30,000 silk weaving workers of the Como district were assured the benefits of the 48-hour week (first introduced in May 1919) under the agreement signed between the Association of Silk Manufacturers (Associazione tra i Fabbricanti di Seterie) and the two textile unions in April 1920. The agreement of February 1921 continued these provisions, but that of March 25, 1923 appeared to limit the regulation of working hours to mills in the cities and to omit those in the countryside. The national agreement of July 17, 1920 in the wool industry set limits of 2,400 hours per annum, or 8 hours a day for 300 working days. It did not establish maxima for hours of overtime, but prohibited overtime unless there was no unemployment in the trade where overtime was requested. The agreements of February 1921 and December 1921 continued these provisions. However, local agreements for Vicenza and Biella at the end of 1921 and in 1922 related only to wages. A separate agreement with an independent union was concluded in Prato on November 17, 1921. Provisions similar to those established in the cotton agreements were written into the national linen and hemp industry agreements of February 3, 1920 for the C.G.L. textile workers and of May 10, 1920 for the C.I.L. textile workers. The agreement for the jute industry dated from 1920 and its provisions on hours also resembled those in the cotton agreement. The agreement of July 7, 1922 continued these provisions. The agreement of July 23, 1919 for the ribbon industry of Milan, Monza, and the Lake Maggiore districts set the work week at 48 hours. The subsequent agreement of February 2, 1922, signed by the employers and the C.G.L. and C.I.L. textile workers, introduced the annual average of 2,400 hours, distributed on the basis of 48 hours a week. The December 25, 1921 agreement for dyeing, finishing, and silk printing established the 48-hour week, but was cancelled at the end of 1922. The agreement of April 7, 1923 increased the amount of permissible overtime and reduced overtime pay. (See I.L.O. report, cited above, pp. 19–26).

The Lombardy division of the Association of Italian Wood Working and Allied Manufacturers (Associazione Italiana Industriale del Legno e Affini) concluded an agreement on June 11, 1920 with the Italian Federation of Wood Workers (Federazione Italiana Lavoranti in Legno) fixing the work week at 48 hours and providing a Saturday half-holiday, particularly for workers living in towns. Overtime was limited to 10 hours per week, excluding Saturdays, and overtime rates ranged from 25% to 50%. These provisions remained in the agreements of 1921, 1922, and 1923. At its congress in April 1922, the Italian Confederation of Wood Workers called for the extension of the terms of the Lombardy agreement to local agreements elsewhere. (See I.L.O. report, cited above, pp. 26–27).

The national agreement of November 20, 1920 for the chemical industry established the work week at 48 hours of actual work. The agreement of November 20, 1922 altered these provisions to provide for a maximum of 10 hours of overtime per week. Special consideration was also given to overtime problems in continuous process establishments. Overtime pay rates were established according to length of overtime for working days, holidays, and night work. (See I.L.O. report, cited above, p. 27).

The agreement of July 30, 1920 between the Italian Federation of Glass, Crystal, and Mirror Manufacturers (Federazione Italiana Industriali Vetri, Cristalli, e Specchi) and the National Federation of Workers in the Mirror and Allied Trades (Federazione Nazionale Lavoranti in Specchi ed Affini) limited actual hours of work for all grades of labor to 48 hours per week and included provisions for free Saturday afternoons. These terms remained in the agreement of September 4, 1922 although changes were made in provisions concerning overtime pay. The agreement of September 1923 continued the terms concerning hours of work. (See I.L.O. report, cited above, pp. 27–28).

The working day was set at 8 hours in the national agreement of March 1919 for the building industry. The agreement was abrogated by the employers federation (Federazione Nazionale Costruttori Edili) in December 1921. The employers demanded a total annual number of working hours amounting to 2,496 to allow for time lost during inclement weather. The workers rejected this proposal. Negotiations failed. The ensuing strike lasted for several months. The strike ended through local agreements since no national agreement could be concluded. (See I.L.O. report, cited above, pp. 29–32.)

The national agreement of April 27, 1920 between the Association of Paper Manufacturers and the Federation of Bookbinders, Paper Workers, Technicians, and Related Workers (Federazione Italiana Legatori, Cartai, Cartotecnici ed Affini) set the working day at 8 hours, established maximum overtime at 12 hours a week, and provided for graduated overtime rates of pay for holidays over the 50% stipulated for normal overtime. The agreement was abrogated on April 17, 1922 and agreements including 8-hour day provisions were concluded on a local basis for Rome, Milan, Turin, and Florence. (See I.L.O. report, cited above, p. 32.)

Local agreements provided the 48-hour week for workers in the printing and allied trades of Milan, Bergamo, Turin, Alessandria, Venetia, Caserta, and Bari. (See I.L.O. report, cited above, pp. 32–34.)

[65] Appendix A, Table 38.

[66] Luigi Salvatorelli and Giovanni Mira, *Storia d'Italia nel periodo fascista*, pp. 82–85; Rigola, cited above, pp. 438–439.

[67] Magri, *Controllo operaio . . .*, p. 186; Confederazione Generale dell'Industria Italiana (Confindustria), *I consigli di gestione*, Vol. II, p. 7. Some American writers prefer to translate *commissioni interne* as "internal commissions." This designation has the doubtful virtue of being literal, but means little or nothing to an American reader since it does not signify the nature of *commissioni interne*. These same writers insist that the duties of the *commissioni interne* differ from those of American grievance committees and are also broader. This objection demonstrates basic unfamiliarity with the severely limited functions and powers of *commisioni interne* in practice, as well as with the extensive range of factory issues, formerly reserved by management as part of its prerogatives, which now enter grievance procedures in the United States.

[68] Magri, *Controllo operaio* . . . , pp. 186–187.

[69] Magri, *Controllo operaio* . . . , p. 187; Confindustria, cited above, p. 8.

[70] The clearest summary of these tendencies, not always easily distinguishable, can be found in Magri, *Controllo operaio* . . . , Chapters V, VI, VII, VIII, and X.

[71] John McKay Cammett, *Antonio Gramsci and the "Ordine Nuovo" Movement: A Study in the Rise of Italian Communism,* Ph.D. Dissertation, Columbia University, 1959; Hilton-Young, cited above, pp. 142–143; Magri, *Controllo operaio* . . ., p. 187.

[72] Confindustria, cited above, p. 8; Magri, *Controllo operaio* . . . , p. 188.

[73] Confindustria, cited above, pp. 8–9.

[74] Salvatorelli and Mira, cited above, pp. 123–125; Sturzo, cited above, p. 101.

[75] Rigola, cited above, pp. 460–463.

[76] Salvatorelli and Mira, cited above, pp. 125–126; Lloyd, cited above, pp. 100–101; Sturzo, cited above, p. 101.

[77] Rigola, cited above, pp. 464–467.

[78] Angelo Rossi, *The Rise of Italian Fascism, 1918–1922,* pp. 67–70.

[79] Confindustria, cited above, p. 9.

[80] Salvatorelli and Mira, cited above, p. 145.

[81] Sacco, cited above, p. 295.

[82] Salvatorelli and Mira, cited above, p. 125.

[83] Rossi, cited above, pp. 75–76; Rigola, cited above, pp. 447–454; Appendix A, Table 38.

[84] Confindustria, cited above, p. 9.

[85] Rossi, cited above, pp 76–77.

[86] Rigola, cited above, pp. 464–465.

[87] Confindustria, cited above, p. 9; see also, Document No. 3, pp. 28–32.

[88] The same, Document No 4, pp. 32–34.

[89] The same, Document No. 5, pp. 34–40; see also, Giovanni Battista Valente, *Il regime associativo delle aziende.*

[90] Confindustria, cited above, Document No. 6, pp. 41–46. For details concerning the intellectual and political influence of Antonio Gramsci on the chief developments in the factory council movement, see Cammett, cited above, Chapters III and IV.

[91] *Annuario statistico italiano 1927,* p. 245.

[92] Appendix A, Table 38; Adams,cited above, p. 427.

[93] Rigola, cited above, pp. 480–481.

[94] William G. Welk, *Fascist Economic Policy,* pp. 46–48.

[95] Lloyd, cited above, pp. 109–110.

[96] International Labour Office, *Hours of Labour in Industry — Italy,* Studies and Reports, Series D (Wages and Hours) No. 8 (November 1923), pp. 5–15.

[97] Welk, cited above, p. 50.

[98] Finer, cited above, pp. 497–498, 502–503; Rigola, cited above, pp. 481–486; Welk, cited above, pp. 51–55, 62–63. For the texts in English of the following documents, see Welk, cited above, on the pages indicated: Law on the Corporate Organization of the State as Proposed by the Commission of Eighteen, pp. 253–258; law 563 of April 3, 1926, pp. 258–266; regulations 1130 of July 1, 1926, pp. 266–285; and the Charter of Labor, as published in the *Gazzetta Ufficiale,* No. 100 of April 30, 1927, pp. 287–292.

[99] Gradilone, cited above, III, 2, p. 232, footnote 14; Rigola, cited above, pp. 484–488.

[100] Salvatorelli and Mira, cited above, pp. 378–380.

IX

The Future Unfolds:
1926 to the Invasion of Sicily

The Promise of Fascism: Italy on Parade

MUSSOLINI has himself established the measure for judging his accomplishments. He regarded the creation of the Corporative State — the alternative in the twentieth century to both capitalism and communism — as his prime achievement. Upon this pyramid of statutes, decrees, regulations, syndical organizations, collective agreements, labor courts, bureaucracy piled upon bureaucracy, and official verbiage, his reputation for inventive genius in the development of modern polity must rest. Certainly, he and his associates exhibited neither originality nor unusual success, as compared with other contemporary leaders and experts of Western Europe and the United States, in contriving devices to stabilize the currency, to aid failing banks and faltering industries, to encourage economic self-sufficiency, to program public works as an answer to depression and unemployment, to manipulate population growth and internal as well as external migration, and to extend an already ramifying system of protective labor legislation, public welfare, and social security. Since these endeavors shared very common features with ventures elsewhere, Mussolini's claim to singularity in the realm of statecraft must necessarily cling to the superior ability of the corporative system, as distinct from ordinary capitalist economic enterprise aided by interventionist acts of government, to increase productivity, national income, the standard of living for workers, and the common good.

History insists upon the irony of human affairs. From the time he took power until World War II, when his star descended, Mussolini scored his most brilliant successes neither in working economic miracles, nor in merely strengthening the Italian economy, but in the ancient art of consolidating his political strength at home and abroad. He restored social order to the country and gave Italians new self-confidence. From D'Annunzio he had learned the value to Latin leaders of large gestures and romantic display. He kept Italians constantly on stage, where most of them wanted to be, in a perpetual national enactment of the first act of *Aïda*, replete with the blare of trumpets, pomp, panoply, trappings, processions, and outcries of triumph. Highly organized from the cradle to the grave, they paraded frequently in uniform and shouted fiery slogans in response to Mussolini's own barking from balconies on high. Thus, the Duce diverted energies formerly expended by fomenting useless disorder in the piazzas into useless, wide-swinging, martial displays of national pride and discipline. Almost 8,662,000 Italians participated in the elections of March 24, 1929, or 89.9% of all eligible voters, while 10,060,426 Italians cast ballots in the elections of March 25, 1934, or 96.5% of all eligible voters. Only a few thousand voters protested against the single national list in either election. Granted, the penalties against dissent discouraged its display on a larger numerical scale, but not even Mussolini's bitterest political enemies and severest critics ever adduced substantial evidence to prove that the fascist plebiscitary dictatorship did not enjoy the confidence of most Italians.[1]

Both at home and abroad, Mussolini secured middle-class admiration and the public praise of distinguished figures by suppressing ordinary crime more thoroughly than any other Italian government, by waging total war upon the Maffia in Sicily, by improving the highways of the country, by electrifying the railroads and forcing them to run on precise schedule, by driving beggars and dirt from the streets of Italian cities, by steadily publicizing his campaigns against illiteracy, disease, and other social ailments through the proclamation of special weeks dedicated to their public eradication, and by finally freeing the ruins of the Roman Forum from the squalid tenements which less imperially minded governments had permitted to infest that splendid site. (To be sure, this enthusiasm for the past cut into the remains which blocked the newly opened Via dell'Impero, transferred antique glories from one site to another, and successfully blocked serious explorations.)

Illiteracy fell from 27% of the population six years of age and above in 1921 to 21% in 1931, a 6 point drop of less than notable dimensions when compared with the unheralded decrease of 11 points between 1911 and 1921. As for the proportion of illiteracy revealed in the population census of 1936, by 1943 the government had still not published a single figure on that subject. The statistics on school enrollment presented more impressive gains. Of the total number of children between the ages of 5 and 15 in 1921, 51.8% had enrolled that year in elementary schools, a gain of 6.6 percentage points over 1911. By 1930–1931, of the 4,936,734 children between the ages of 6 and 14, 88.8% had registered in elementary schools, while 77.9% took their examinations. Ten years later, those enrolled in elementary schools had increased to 89.6% and those examined to 79.2% of the 5,574,310 children between the ages of 6 and 14. Although the number of students attending the middle schools had decreased from 10.2 per 1,000 inhabitants in 1921 to 9.2 in 1931, this proportion rose to 21.5 in 1941. Similarly, students at institutions of higher education numbered 13 per 10,000 inhabitants in 1921 and fell to 11 in 1931, but rose rapidly to 32 in 1941.[2]

During the years, 1911–1920, the number of deaths from all causes per 100,000 of population averaged 2,057.7, as compared with 2,158.5 for the previous decade. Improvement during the fascist period progressed rapidly: 1,663.3 during 1921–1930 and 1,394.2 during 1931–1940. Although the incidence of deaths per 100,000 of all inhabitants from infectious and parasitical diseases had increased by 61.9 points from 1901–1910 to 1911–1920, the steep decline from 1911–1920 to 1921–1930 amounted to 143.4 points; the fall continued by 86 points during the succeeding decade so that the number of deaths stood at 177.3 during 1931–1941 in contrast to 406.7 for 1911–1920. The fascist decades showed similar advance with regard to the incidence of deaths from respiratory diseases. They declined from 404.4 per 100,000 inhabitants during 1911–1920 to 301.5 in the next decade and then decreased to 259.3 during 1931–1940. The fascists hardly distinguished themselves in lowering the incidence of typhoid and paratyphoid cases per 100,000 inhabitants — an average fall of about 8 points during each of their two decades of control, as contrasted to a decline of 23 points from 1901–1910 to 1911–1920. The number of malaria cases actually increased from 584.2 during 1911–1920 to 591 during 1921–1930, but their incidence dropped by 261 points during the next decade to a low of 330 per 100,000 of the total population.[3]

The fascist government carried forward its program of railroad electrification with impressive efficiency. The index of advance (1922 = 100) mounted from 101.7 in 1923 to 285.2 in 1934 when 4,179.1 of the nation's total kilometrage, 23,123.2, operated by electric traction. At the end of 1938, the kilometrage of electrification reached 6,678.7 in relation to the country's total kilometrage, 23,221.1. Whereas by the end of 1934 neither the State nor private railroad companies had electrified one kilometer of rail in the regions of Lucania, Calabria, Sicily, and Sardinia, by the end of 1938, the State had electrified 400 kilometers of track in Calabria, although the other three regions continued in their wonted neglect. The extension of the railroad system as a whole under the fascists did not depart from the pattern of progress established under previous governments: total kilometrage in 1901, 16,451; 1911, 18,394; 1921, 20,556; 1931, 22,571; and 1941, 23,062. In highway construction, however, they broke radically with past performance. The fascists not only constructed their famous showpiece *autostrade* but also expanded the national highway system from 10,336 kilometers in 1921 to 20,692 in 1931. This burst of activity then halted during the next ten years since total kilometrage stood at 21,111 in 1941. The number of licensed motor vehicles increased from an average of 45,215 for 1911–1920 to 192,802 in the following decade and then soared to 454,369 during 1931–1940. Other avenues of communication also widened during the fascist decades. The magnitude of correspondence handled by the post office increased from 1,851 million pieces during 1911–1920 to 2,546 million pieces during 1931–1940. The number of telephone subscribers during this same time-span grew from 96,016 to 395,886, while the number of public telephones multiplied from 2,534 to 15,191.[4]

But Mussolini earned his greenest peacetime laurels when he performed the miracle withheld from other Italian governments: reconciliation with the Vatican. Mussolini's nurture in the Romagna among Italy's most devout republican and anarchist unbelievers and his subsequent dedication to atheistic socialism could hardly have prepared him for this role. Moreover, the Fascist Party, with its complex genealogy, itself contained strong secularist and anticlerical elements. Still, Mussolini, not one clause less realistic than Pius XI, did not pretend to count his beads, but calculated, instead, the good which would flow to him and to fascism by concluding the Lateran Treaties of February 11, 1929 with the papacy. These pacts, officially ratified on June 7, 1929, recognized the temporal rule of the Pope over the full extent of the state of the Vatican City: 108.7 acres. The concordat between the government and the Holy See regulated the status of the Church and religion in Italy. Moreover, the State paid 750,000,000 lire in cash and 1,000,000,000 lire in consolidated bonds to the Pope in compensation for Church property seized in 1870.

Although a favorite son of the Church now, Mussolini did not grant the Vatican complete independence. In the realm of education, Catholic instruction could not offend against fascist dogma. He permitted Catholic Boy Scout organizations to encamp, but only within Balilla (the fascist youth organization) preserves. The fascists calumniated Catholic Action in the controlled press, the police moved with unison throughout the country to suppress affiliated groups, and Party members in uniform, guided by Carlo Scorza (1897–   ), Amendola's chief assailant, used violence against its associations. They forced Catholic Action to transform the nature of its functions and drastically limit the scope of its varied activities. For his part, Pius XI found plain words to castigate fascist persecution of Catholic Action in the encyclical, *Non abbiamo bisogno*, of June 29, 1931. He rightly viewed the oppressive measures of Party and State as pretexts "to tear away from the Church, the young, and all the young. . . ." Yet many members of the Catholic hierarchy supported Mussolini and his government with continued zeal.[5]

With striking unoriginality, Mussolini also utilized wars and diplomatic alliances to recharge personal authority among his own people. He had predicted that the twentieth century would be the century of fascist power and that Italy would return for the third time in history to act as the motivating force in human civilization. In 1934, just as the country began to pull out of severe economic depression, Mussolini ordered preparations for war. In May, the navy and air force increased their supplementary estimates by thousands of millions of lire; the government decided to lay down two 35,000-ton battleships; the Fascist Party decreed military instruction for all boys in the Balilla over six years of age. Once committed by the bellicose threats of rampant nationalism, first, and then by war itself, to a policy of armed might, Mussolini chained impoverished Italy to staggering expenditures. In the immediate postwar year of 1920–1921, before fascist rule, 30% of the national budget went to satisfy the needs of the army, navy, and merchant marine. In 1931–1932, the percentage of the total budget devoted to the Ministries of War, Navy, and Air fell to 21.7%. By 1935–1936, this percentage soared to 38.6 to meet the costs of the Abyssinian War, but even later, in 1938–1939, on the eve of World War II while Italian troops still lingered in Spain, the proportion declined but slightly to 35.5%. In 1931–1932, the government expended 6.2% of the national budget for education and 0.2% for public health. These percentages dropped to 4.9 and 0.1 in 1938–1939.[6]

Mussolini's road to war started on August 2, 1928 when Italy signed a treaty of friendship with Ethiopia. By fascist design, on December 5, 1934, Italian and Ethiopian troops exchanged fire on the disputed Ethiopian-Somaliland frontier. Mussolini refused to arbitrate the boundary question involved in the clash at Ualual since he needed a pretext for the invasion of Ethiopia. Early in January 1935, the Ethiopian government appealed to the League of Nations. To postpone still further the

League's delayed action, Italy agreed to arbitration in May. After futile negotiations at The Hague, and after belated gestures by the League to investigate the controversy directly, Italian forces crossed over into Ethiopia on October 3, 1935. With the capture of Adua three days later, they retrieved Italy's honor, so shamed in 1896 after ignominious defeat at Adua by the black troops of black Emperor Menelik. On October 7, the League Council declared Italy the aggressor. On November 18, 1935, 52 member nations of the League joined in prohibiting the import of Italian goods and establishing an embargo on arms and financial assistance. The move failed from the very beginning, but especially after February 1936 when these countries disagreed on extending sanctions to include shipments of oil to Italy.

Mussolini rallied the nation politically by characterizing the attempted economic ostracism of Italy, led by Anthony Eden of imperialistic Britain, as the attempt by the wealthy and powerful colonial empires to cut off the poorer countries of the world from desperately needed overseas territorial possessions. He also met the economic test imposed by sanctions remarkably well. The government, like many others during the early 1930's, had instituted import restrictions as depression measures. Once, therefore, the League declared sanctions against Italy, already existing machinery could operate to apply even more stringent restrictions. The government then paralleled this device with a rigidly enforced system of price controls upon articles of general consumption. Four other circumstances aided Mussolini even more importantly in weathering the crisis: the period of sanctions did not last long enough to harm Italy's economy irreparably; the vital supply of oil had never ceased to flow; 27 nations kept trading with Italy; and, finally, the war against Ethiopia moved rapidly, aided by the Italian people who supported the war with enthusiasm, even to the extent of offering up their gold wedding rings for the cause. Addis Ababa fell on May 5, 1936. Italy proclaimed the annexation of all Ethiopia on May 9 when Victor Emmanuel III, playing Victoria to Mussolini's latter-day Disraeli, assumed the title of Emperor of Ethiopia.

On July 4, 1936, the League Council voted to discontinue sanctions, an act which marked the end of the League as a political institution capable of maintaining peace. Two weeks later, on July 18, the explosion of civil war in Spain compelled Mussolini to aid the Franco cause as support for his own prestige. The man who claimed to have rescued Italy from bolshevism and earned by that service the gratitude of conservative forces throughout the world could not tolerate the vision of a "communist" power in the Mediterranean under the democratic, freemasonic,

"Popular Front" influence of France. The drain upon the national ex-
chequer for dispatching from 50,000 to 75,000 "volunteer" troops to Spain
and maintaining them there until June 1939, when added to the cost of
the Ethiopian campaign and the steadily mounting rearmament program,
obligated the government to devaluate the lira on October 5, 1936 and to
institute forced loans of 5% on all real estate.[7]

Since Italy's adventure in Spain excited French and British fears and
raised international stress in the Mediterranean, Mussolini turned to nazi
Germany as an ally. His pact of October 26, 1936 with Hitler regarding
Austria marked the beginning of the Rome-Berlin Axis. During 1937,
Italy strengthened its position in the Danube basin, concluded agreements with Great Britain and Jugoslavia, and to the renewed consternation of France and Great Britain, assured the Arabs of Roman friendship during Mussolini's impressive visit to Libya in mid-May when he
assumed the mantle of protector to the Moslem world. On November 6,
1937, Italy triangulated the Nazi-Japanese anti-Comintern accord and
withdrew, a month later, from the League of Nations. On March 13, 1938,
the nazis annexed Austria and brought Germany to the Brenner Pass.
Mussolini accepted this betrayal of the Italian-German agreement on
Austria with outward calm since Italy had already sacrificed its military
mobility through heavy commitments in Ethiopia, Libya, and Spain.
From that moment on, he had to serve out his destiny as the junior partner to his friend in arms, Adolf Hitler.

Mussolini now sought to hold Italy under the spell of a perpetual verbal revolution. He attacked golf, first-class compartments on trains, and
pacifists as symbols of bourgeois degradation and scorned all those who
preferred prosperity and personal ease to national glory and power. The
Duce even announced measures to split up the large estates, the *latifondi*, of Sicily. Despite the recognition by Britain of the conquest of
Ethiopia as a result of the Anglo-Italian pact ratified on November 16,
two weeks later, the Italian Chamber of Deputies, under orders, clam-
ored for the Italian conquest of Nice, Corsica, Tunisia, Jibuti, Malta,
and Suez. After strengthening its bonds with Jugoslavia in January 1939
with the hope of reconciling Jugoslavia and Hungary, Italy invaded and
conquered Albania on April 7. Albania became part of Italy. The Pact of
Steel with Germany, calling for the closest political and military collaboration, followed on May 22. Italian troops left Spain at the end of
May and early in June, after the surrender of Madrid and Valencia in
late March.

During the long dispute between Germany and Poland, which culminated in the Danzig-Polish crisis from August 20 to September 1, 1939,

401

the Italian press strongly supported Germany. The German-Russian pact, signed in Moscow on August 23, undermined the anti-Comintern pact when Japan withdrew. After Germany attacked Poland on September 1, Italy proclaimed its neutrality on September 2 with the thought of serving Germany as a channel for necessary supplies. Great Britain and France declared war on Germany the following day. For nine months, Italy enjoyed potential bargaining advantages vastly superior to those of World War I, but Mussolini considered gains bartered for glory unworthy of an heroic nation. In less exalted moments, he feared that Hitler's resounding march of victories might make Italian intervention superfluous unless Rome joined the nazis very soon. Uncomfortable and restless in neutrality, Mussolini finally brought Italy into World War II on June 10, 1940. The Fascist Party had plastered the walls of Italy with the slogan: Mussolini is always right (*Mussolini ha sempre ragione*). Convinced of this truth himself, the Duce brushed aside the doubts of his generals and admirals about the country's industrial and military preparation for combat. This foolhardy man lived to earn for his unprepared nation the contempt of its own allies. He could not admit weakness and therefore could not see that a repetition of the debacles of World War I would mean the end of him and fascism since he had destroyed all opposition where he might have plausibly directed blame.[8]

The Economics of Fascism. At a loss for a distinctive fascist program until 1926 when his followers devised heady corporative principles for organizing economic affairs, Mussolini afterward allowed his pride in this wonder for all the ages to blind his judgment. The costly, bumbling, and sterile apparatus of Rube Goldberg intricacy, far from achieving prodigies of fascist production, merely concealed behind its enormous bureaucratic façade the persistence of techniques prevalent everywhere for inducing fiscal, industrial, commercial, and agricultural health. Had Mussolini carefully reviewed during the spring of 1940 the country's economic history since 1922, he might have hesitated to rush so loyally to Hitler's side. During his first twelve years in power, Mussolini found himself engaged in economic holding operations, first against the ravages of World War I and then of world-wide depression. His experts adopted remedies which preceding Italian governments had already employed or introduced new devices already at work in other countries of the West. Up to April 3, 1926, these restoratives could not contain corporative ingredients since the vague syndicalist ideas bandied about in fascist circles did not find concrete expression until the passage on that date of the law concerning the legal discipline of collective labor relations. Even after the epiphany of this legislation, its ancillary regulations, and the Charter of Labor a year later, the economic and social measures utilized by fascist officials without fanfare continued to resemble the contrivances rigged up by other countries still suckled on creeds outworn.

In 1921, a year before the March on Rome, two of Italy's largest met-allurgical complexes, Ilva and Ansaldo, collapsed of their own war-swollen weight and called for rescue. Other industrial firms tottered on the brink of disaster. Already toward the end of 1914, the president of the Bank of Italy had led in the creation of a consortium for financing indus-trial enterprises, the Consorzio per Sovvenzioni su Valori Industriali (C.S.V.I.). The ties with the Bank of Italy remained so strong that they marked the C.S.V.I. as virtually a branch of the Bank itself. Through the C.S.V.I.'s endeavors, the country's banking system came to hold stocks and bonds of overexpanded industrial ventures in consequence of loans extended to them. As contracting markets paralyzed production, the banks lost more and more liquidity. When, at the end of 1921, the Italian Discount Bank (Banca Italiana di Sconto), one of the nation's four largest banks, failed, the government hastened to arrange the formation of an institution to intervene between the Banca and its creditors: the Special Autonomous Section of the C.S.V.I. (Sezione Autonoma Speciale). This new rescue agency, at first limited in its functions and funds, had to expand its activities immensely when the banking crisis deepened and the Bank of Rome also threatened to sink into bankruptcy. For a decade between 1922 and 1932, the Special Autonomous Section and the Insti-tute of Liquidation (Istituto di Liquidazione), which replaced it in 1926, persisted in their salvaging operations throughout Italy, especially among those banks and small credit institutes closely associated with the Italian Discount Bank and the Bank of Rome. These activities endowed the State with the unnegotiable industrial securities formerly held by the immobilized banks.

With the advent of world-wide depression, the Italian government realized the need to grant even greater financial assistance to both indus-trial firms and banks. The Italian Credit Institute (Istituto Mobiliare Italiano) took form on November 13, 1931. It possessed 500,000,000 lire in authorized capital and the government guaranteed its bonds. The Insti-tute extended loans to commercial and industrial enterprises against the security of their stocks and bonds. The Italian Financial Society (Società Finanziaria Italiana), an entity created soon afterward and controlled by the government, began its mission to the banks by aiding the Italian Commercial Bank (Banca Commerciale Italiana), the nation's largest institution of this class. Deliverance from insolvency involved the transfer of depreciated industrial securities from the banks to the Italian Financial Society.

Through all of these financial transactions, extending back to the early post-World War I years, the Italian government had possessed itself of such large blocks of industrial stocks and bonds that it decided to exert more direction and control over the firms it virtually owned through the creation on January 23, 1933 of the Institute for Industrial Reconstruction (Istituto per la Ricostruzione Industriale — I.R.I.), a body similar in many of its functions to the Reconstruction Finance Corporation formed in the United States at the end of the Hoover administration. To make feasible its task of coordination, I.R.I. organized large portions of its holdings into economic sectors: telephones in 1933, Società Torinese Esercizi Telefonici (S.T.E.T.); shipbuilding in 1936, Società Finanziaria Marittima (F.I.N.M.A.R.E.); and steel in 1937, Società Finanziaria Siderurgica (F.I.N.S.I.D.E.R.).[9]

The fascist government did not limit its restorative endeavors to the renewal of public confidence in the nation's banks and industries. Mussolini's first Minister of Finance, Alberto De Stefani (1879–   ), pursued other laudable improvements which would have delighted the liberal economists of the nineteenth century. He reformed the tax system and successfully urged the repeal of those special measures which Giolitti designed to confiscate war profits. He cut government expenditures severely and reorganized the public bureaucracy. He balanced the budget which had run a deficit of over 3,000,000,000 lire in 1922–1923. He transferred government monopolies like the telephone system to private enterprise. Both Mussolini and his Minister of National Economy also stayed well within the bounds of unoriginal acceptability when they urged Italian industrialists to cut costs and raise production by adopting the principles and techniques of Frederick Winslow Taylor, then so highly publicized in the United States. The Italian Scientific Management Institute (E.N.I.O.S.) received their encouragement. Manufacturing production seemed to respond magnetically to this wealth of governmental reassurance. One set of index numbers (1913=100) revealed the following steady upward push: 1921, 98.4; 1922, 108.1; 1923, 119.3; 1924, 140.7; 1925, 156.8; and 1926, 162.8. The index for the world as a whole rose from 81.1 in 1921 to 126.5 in 1926. Another series (1922=100) showed changes in production levels for individual Italian industries: metallurgical, 119 in 1923 to 190 in 1926; chemicals, 117 in 1923 to 155 in 1926; building construction, 147 in 1923 to 263 in 1926; textiles, 112 in 1923 to 145 in 1926.[10]

Brisk credit expansion and speculative ventures accompanied these industrial gains. The number of Italian joint stock companies increased from 6,850 in 1922 to 12,134 in 1926. The total value of share capital jumped from 21,395,000,000 lire in 1922 to 40,413,000,000 lire in 1926.[11] The artificial silk industry where the huge billion-lire corporation, Snia Viscosa, took firm hold, the chemical industry now dominated by the second of Italy's new corporate giants, Montecatini, and shipbuilding began to show symptoms of over-rapid growth. When De Stefani attempted to curb these inflationary tendencies, he incurred the hostility of the free-riding commercial, industrial, and financial communities. Mussolini replaced him by Count Giuseppe Volpi di Misurata (1877–1947) who espoused the cause of Big Business. The liberal credit policy of the government continued and Count Volpi reinforced his reputation for financial acumen when he secured from Great Britain and the United States favorable settlements of Italian war debts. However, in mid-1926, after the Italian currency showed unmistakable signs of infirmity and credit weakened, Mussolini himself sprang to the breach and pledged to stabilize the lira in his famous speech of August 18, 1926 at Pesaro.

Until this point in their history, the fascists had concentrated almost all energy in stiffening internal political power and destroying every vestige of organized opposition. The government stimulated business activity and corrected defects in the banking system, but did not press beyond the liberalistic concept of preparing a fertile seedbed for economic exploitation by private interests. Now, the government intervened harshly with direct measures to rout the inflationary evil. It reduced the total note circulation in the country from its peak of 21,400,000,000 lire in 1925 to 16,800,000,000 in 1929. At the end of 1927, the Italian lira, which had declined in value to 25–26 lire to the dollar, stabilized at 27.25% of its pre-World War I value at 19 lire to the dollar. Mussolini had promised to defend the integrity of the lira "to the last drop of blood." So he did. The stabilization program proceeded so thoroughly that serious deflation resulted, followed by temporary industrial and commercial stagnation. Because of higher costs and prices, exports declined by 4,863,200,000 lire between 1925 and 1929. Imports fell by 3,426,700,000 lire during the same period.[12] Unemployment, which reached a maximum of 156,659 and a minimum of 72,211 in 1925, shot up to a maximum of 489,347 and a minimum of 193,325 in 1929.[13]

The government pointed the most orthodox ways toward recovery. At the time of deflation, it reduced grain imports, ordered more intense wheat cultivation, imposed a uniform type of bread upon consumers, decreed the use of Italian minerals in steel production, enjoined the mixture of wine-derived alcohol with gasoline, limited the number of pages in newspapers to conserve cellulose, prohibited luxury or new government construction, ordered consolidation of services and personnel in public administration (never achieved), and authorized private employers to increase daily working hours from eight to nine. Employers also began to readjust wages, but prices refused to budge. Their rigidity forced the Fascist Grand Council in October 1926 to halt this policy until prices moved downward. Count Volpi, at the end of 1926, announced to the Senate a budgetary surplus of 2,268,000,000 lire, an achievement repeated during the next few years. The Council of Ministers, in February 1927, reaffirmed the government's policy of deflation which predicated reductions in wages and prices. But prices persisted in their stickiness.

Finally, in early May 1927, the secretary of the Party started a rush of masochistic zeal by lamenting in a speech at Brescia that retail food prices remained high because agricultural employers found it impossible to lower farm wages. Immediately thereafter, the fascist peasant unions of Brescia announced a voluntary wage reduction of 10%. Peasants in Pavia, maritime workers in Genoa, and wage earners in Bologna soon broadcast news of similar sacrifices. On May 24, the officers of employer and labor organizations in the textile industries announced wage cuts of 10%. At the end of May, the Chamber of Deputies, not to be outdone in economic patriotism, cancelled the salary jump it had voted itself in March. In May, too, the Council of Ministers eliminated the cost-of-living bonus enjoyed by state employees and curtailed local government pay scales. The Council also warned industrialists, farmers, and businessmen that prices had to drop. During the campaign to realize this goal, the Fascist Party organized national and provincial labor-management committees to direct the Battle of Prices. After prodding by the government, the national federation of landlords reduced housing rents from 10% to 20%. Nonetheless, on July 1, the government prohibited rent increases or rents which amounted to four times their prewar levels. On July 7, 1927 *Lavoro d'Italia* (*Italian Labor*) declared: "After so many rivers of ink, after so many tons of protests and an equal tonnage of promises, nothing has been accomplished, and if things go on as they have, nothing will be done." During July, too, the president of the General Fascist Confederation of Industry admitted that the cost of living had declined but fractionally in comparison with the level of prices. That summer the government reduced postal, telegraph, and railroad rates. In the end, the age-old formula prevailed: on October 3, 1927, the fascists authorized wage reductions ranging from 10% to 20%.[14]

By 1929, Italian industry revived and succeeded in recapturing its international markets. It accomplished this feat as a result of the felicitous conjuncture of external events and internal developments largely dominated by government initiative. Tariff revisions gave extra protection to those sectors of production which felt the intrusion of foreign goods most keenly. The construction industry benefited particularly from the government's policy of augmenting public services and instituting broad public works programs. Officials encouraged cartel-like understandings among industrialists — a bit of German invention long admired from afar — to eliminate internal competition. Between 1927 and 1929 this behavior permeated the most important areas of Italian industry. To reduce costs and promote technological progress, royal decree law 1206 of June 23, 1927 and royal decree law 406 of March 8, 1928 offered temporary tax favors to those firms which consolidated their facilities. From 1919 to 1927, an average of only 19 mergers took place annually. In 1928, 266 companies effected 105 mergers, while 245 companies participated in 102 mergers the next year.[15]

Despite the persistence of unemployment, industrial activity rapidly recovered its pre-1926 stride. The general index of manufacturing production (1913=100) inclined slightly from 162.8 in 1926 to 161.2 in 1927, but reached 175.2 in 1928 and 181 in 1929, the highest point achieved in Italy's history until 1937. The indices for selected industries (1922= 100) showed similar trends: metallurgical production fell from 190 in 1926 to 170 in 1927, but shot up to 226 in 1929; building construction dipped from 263 in 1926 to 249 the next year, but soared to 440 in 1929; textiles advanced slowly from 145 in 1926 to 153 the following year and then achieved the high mark of 176 by 1929. The index of gas and electrical production never ceased to move upward. From 173 in 1926, it developed to 180 in 1927, reached 197 in 1928, and scaled 212 in 1929. Only chemical production suffered stagnation; it plodded on from 155 to 156 between 1926 and 1927 and then sank down to 153 in 1929.[16]

When the depression of 1929 paralyzed economic life throughout the world, Italy had barely emerged from Mussolini's trial by deflation and could marshal few reserves of strength to withstand its debilitating attacks. The country's index of manufacturing production (1913=100) descended from its high point of 181 in 1929 to the nadir of 123.3 in 1932. It did not again achieve the magnitude of 1929 until 1937 when it climbed to 194.5. The index for the world as a whole dropped from 153.3 in 1929 to 108.4 in 1932, a loss of 44.9 points as contrasted to Italy's loss of 57.7 points. Moreover, the world index recovered its 1929 position by 1935, two years earlier than Italy, when it reached 154.5. The index of production in the metallurgical industries (1922=100) stood at 226 in 1929, sank to 149 in 1932, and did not regain its 1929 position until 1935.

The chemical industry, already sluggish since 1926, sank from 153 in 1929 to 119 in 1932, but roused itself to arrive at 164 by 1934. Building construction had shot to unprecedented heights of 440 in 1929, then plummeted to 234 in 1932, and recovered only to the point of 419 by 1935. Textile manufactures slid from 176 in 1929 and declined to 137 in 1932; it started to rally in 1933, yet managed to reach only 158 by 1935. The production of gas and electricity withstood the depression with ever-expanding energy: the index climbed steadily from 212 in 1929 to 218 in 1932 and then zoomed to 272 in 1935.[17]

Italy's imports of manufactured articles, expressed in terms of 1913 prices, fell from $175,000,000 in 1930 to an average of $126,000,-000 during 1931–1935. Exports declined from $224,000,000 in 1930 to $189,000,000 during 1931–1935. The value of all imports and exports, expressed in terms of the 1938 lira, dropped from an annual average of 33,760,000,000 lire, or 836 lire per capita, during 1926–1930 to 20,876,-000,000 lire, or 496 per capita, during 1931–1935. The tragedy inherent in these indices of perishing production and trade found clear voice in other figures. The number of totally unemployed workers shot to 1,006,-441 in 1932, increased to 1,018,953 during 1933, and declined lightly to 963,677 in 1934. The last official unemployment statistics for May 1935 showed 755,344 persons as totally unemployed. After that date, the government published figures on unemployment insurance, but provided no statistics on the number of unemployed even though the armed forces mobilized 1,000,000 men in the spring of 1935 and the Ethiopian War quickened industrial activity.[18]

The Italian government intervened in this new and deeper crisis, but once again by-passed the corporative machinery so laboriously erected in 1926 and refurbished in 1934. Ever since the end of World War I, the Italian State had hit upon the device of creating semigovernmental bodies called *istituti* or *enti nazionali* to aid principal sectors of the economy in serious difficulties. These agencies received direct government grants or subsidies. Already by 1926, the Istituto Nazionale per l'Esportazione had begun to promote export trade and the Ente Nazionale Serico had arisen to reorganize the silk industry, badly damaged by severe competition from rayon. The government also organized the Ente Nazionale Italiano per l'Organizzazione Scientifica del Lavoro (E.N.I.O.S.) to introduce Taylorism and scientific management to Italian commerce and industry. In 1927, the Ente Nazionale Italiano per le Industrie Turistiche came into operation to coordinate the development of the tourist trades. The promotion of rationalized methods and standard practices in industry became the responsibility of the Ente

Nazionale per l'Unificazione dell'Industria, while the Ente Nazionale per l'Artigianato e le Piccole Industrie took as its province the encouragement of small industries and handicraft workers and artisans. The next year, 1928, saw the formation of the Istituto per il Credito Navale to subsidize and reorganize the merchant marine.

The depression forced the government to set up the Italian Credit Institute, the Italian Financial Society, and I.R.I. under circumstances already described. Entrepreneurs also experimented with remedies of their own. Italian manufacturers, who had entered into formal production and marketing agreements between 1927 and 1929 to counterbalance the dislocations set off by devaluation, now formed voluntary consortia, inspired by Germany's cartels, to coordinate their activities, avoid overproduction, and divide shrinking opportunities among themselves. Legislation dated June 16, 1932 placed these group arrangements under government control, antedating the N.R.A. in the United States by a year. Consortia with compulsory membership could organize whenever more than 70% of the establishments within a segment of production elected to join together and received the approval of appropriate corporative associations and unions. The Italian Cotton Institute, first constituted on a voluntary basis in 1933, became a compulsory consortium in March 1934. It typified the purposes of all consortia: reduction of output, allocation of production quotas among its members, lowering of production costs, and increase of sales abroad.[19]

On January 12, 1933, the logical sequel to the law on consortia took legislative form. To order the anarchy of competition still more by preventing the building of unneeded additional facilities and to encourage, as well, emphasis upon pioneering ventures and industrially undeveloped areas, the government required all enterprises which wished to establish new plants, or to expand old units, to obtain licensed permission from a special commission in the Ministry of Corporations. Theoretically, the commission's decisions waited upon investigations conducted by provincial and national officials of the corporative bureaucracy. Actually, the vital aspects of the procedure fell chiefly under the control of the General Fascist Confederation of Industry. From its first year of operation, 1933–1934, to 1940, the commission accepted 6,854 applications for building new plants or adding to old ones and approved 5,046 of these requests. Of the total number authorized, only 3,753 went into construction — 385 in South Italy and the Islands, 395 in Central Italy, and 2,973 in North Italy — and eventually gave employment to 118,309 workers — 11,134 in South Italy and the Islands, 16,723 in Central Italy, and 90,452 in North Italy. The competitive situation accounted for the discrepancy between approved projects and those effectuated: the larger industrial combines placed applications before the commission with the sole intent of scaring off newcomers to their internal markets.[20]

The Italian government also adopted the usual practice of other countries during the depression by increasing the size and scope of its public works program and encouraging large-scale private improvements through subsidies or other forms of enticement. It intensified the pace of land reclamation (between 1922–1923 and 1927–1928, the annual cost of completed public and private projects reached a minimum of 244,900,000 lire and a maximum of 388,000,000 lire, while comparable figures for the years between 1928–1929 and 1939–1940 ranged from the low of 726,800,-000 lire to the high of 1,207,200,000 lire), power development (the annual production of hydroelectric power increased from 9.4 billion kilowatt hours in 1928 to 14.4 billion in 1937), electrification of railroads, construction of highways, and erection of public buildings in the grand fascist style. Expenditures by the national government for all public works had amounted to 3.7% of total government outlays in 1920–1921. By 1931–1932, these expenditures rose to 11% of the total national budget for that year.[21] The government also sought to relieve suffering through unemployment insurance established before the advent of fascism to power, control of internal migration through the state employment services also organized under prefascist auspices, curtailment of the work week, and special appropriations for distressed areas.[22]

Not until 1934 did Italy succumb to the inspiration of other European countries and devise an elaborate system of import licenses, quotas, exchange controls, and other trade restrictions which soon poured their blessings upon the peninsula. The sanctions applied by the League of Nations against Italy on November 18, 1935 therefore found the country already regulated and well prepared to defend itself against the world by giving another tightening twist to the machinery it had perfected as a depression measure to control foreign commerce. The government not only instituted rigid price controls, but also set about to exploit domestic resources and conjure up substitutes for products Italy lacked. Castor oil, in large supply since the gagging of political opposition, now became a lubricant for gasoline engines. The newly established Italian Coal Authority (Azienda Italiana Carboni) pushed the production and distribution of domestic coals, particularly those found in the Arsa Basin and in Sardinia. Special union-management committees and additional *enti* and consortia multiplied in the fuel, glass, ceramic, wool, silk, cellulose, paper, leather, mineral oils, and scrap-iron industries to increase efficiency and spur production. By the time that the League of Nations

410

abandoned sanctions in early July 1936, Mussolini had fixed economic autarchy as a principal goal for the near future. Then, on October 5, 1936, Italy, along with other European gold block countries, lowered the gold content of the lira by about 40%. Although economic self-sufficiency and military preparedness still remained high on the list of national objectives, the currency devaluation, liberalized import duties, and new trade agreements began to stimulate foreign commerce and also saved the Duce from exorbitant rises in the cost of living.[23]

The lifting of depression, the assorted array of economic, financial, and administrative contrivances and cures employed by the Italian government to turn the business cycle upward, the Ethiopian War, and preparations for future war pushed the general index of Italian industrial production (1928=100) from 102 in 1935 to 123 in 1939. War itself proved unkind. The index sank slightly in 1940, but plummeted to 105 in 1941 and to 91 in 1942. While textile production never quite recovered from the shock of the depression, rising from 77 in 1935 to 92 in 1940 and then rapidly declining to 59 in 1942, the construction industry suffered the most telling war blows. Its index reached 162 in 1935, but fell to 91 in 1938, recovered momentarily in 1939 to reach 121, and then declined to 83 in 1940 and to 36 in 1942. The chemical industry, however, rose from 100 in 1935 to 163 in 1939 and then began to trail off from that peak, reaching 157 in 1940 and 121 in 1942. The index for the metallurgical industries climbed from 112 in 1935 to 122 in 1939, but sank to 109 in 1942. The industries which engendered energy, heat, and light continued to show their persistent tendency to rise. Their index increased from 136 in 1935 to 208 in 1942.[24]

While the combined activities of fascist ministries and parastatal economic institutions, abetted by the Abyssinian War, succeeded in raising the indices of industrial production between 1922 and the onset of World War II, they could not alter the fundamental features of the distribution of industrial employment or tellingly divert trends already much in evidence before the triumph of fascism. The 1931 population census classified 5,224,130 persons as goods-producing industrial workers compared with 4,559,582 so designated in the 1921 population census. The 1936 population census (World War II eliminated the 1941 population census) identified 5,154,325 workers as goods-producing, a statistical loss of about 70,000 between 1931 and 1936. Employees in industries using agricultural, hunting, and fishing products had accounted for slightly more than one-fourth of all industrial workers in 1921. This percentage fell off but slightly in 1931 and then showed a more rapid decrease in 1936. The numbers of workers assigned to the clothing and allied trades produced the same proportional vagaries between 1931 and 1936 as they showed between 1901, 1911, and 1931 — inconsistencies of development most probably due to variations in the definitions of the classification from year to year. Although the percentage of textile workers with regard to the total number of industrial workers increased slightly in 1931 as compared to 1921, the long-term trend of decrease reasserted itself in 1936 when the proportion dropped to its lowest point in history: 10.9%. The persistent proportional rise or retention of position during earlier decades by workers engaged in the construction trades, chemicals, and the mineral-working, metal, and mechanical industries continued during 1931 and 1936. The magnitude of these increases did not mark the fascist period as unusual. The percentage of workers in the metal-mechanical occupations had doubled between 1901 and 1921 to reach almost 17% of all goods-producing workers although a slight decline had set in between 1911 and 1921. Between 1921 and 1931, as between 1931 and 1936 as well, the percentage rose by 2.8 points. Whereas the proportion of workers engaged in the chemical industries had tripled between 1901 and 1921, despite a decline from 1911 to 1921, by 1931 the percentage amounted to 3.4 and rose to 5.1 in 1936. The construction trades grew from 15.7% in 1921 to 19.7% in 1931 and receded but fractionally to 19% in 1936.[25]

The percentage distributions of workers among various branches of goods-producing industrial activity according to the 1927 and 1937–1939 industrial censuses substantiate the pattern of trends already indicated by the percentage distributions derived from the population censuses of 1921, 1931, and 1936.[26] Between 1927 and 1937–1939, the proportion of textile workers to all industrial workers dipped from 19.4% to 15.1%. Unlike the erratic falling behavior of percentages cast up by the population censuses for workers in the clothing trades, those of the industrial censuses revealed steady rise through 1927 and then decline to 12.6% in 1937–1939. The trend in the mechanical trades continued upward. They accounted for almost one-fifth of the total number of industrial workers in 1937–1939. In 1903, the proportion had stood at 8.5%, reaching 11.2% in 1911 and 14.5% in 1927. In contrast, the percentage of workers in the metallurgical industries declined from the high point it achieved in 1911, 6.2%, to 2.5% in 1937–1939. The nonmetallic minerals industries showed a gradual but steady decline from 1903 onward, falling from 8.1% that year to 5% in 1937–1939. According to the industrial censuses, the number of workers in the construction trades increased along with their proportions among all industrial workers, pushing upward from 5.3% in 1911 to 13.4% in 1937–1939. The proportional rise in the chemical industries proceeded very slowly; it augmented by only 0.3 percentage points between 1903 and 1937–1939.

Under fascist tutelage, Italy's industrial economy still remained predominantly oriented toward consumer goods although both the industrial and population censuses indicated slight proportional gains for the producer goods industries after 1935. Even then the consumer goods industries, printing, and construction gave employment to 60.6% of all industrial workers in 1937–1939, according to the industrial census, and to 68.4% of all industrial workers according to the population census of 1936.

The fascist government, for all its protestations of devotion to the development of the neglected South, did as little to correct the imbalance of industrial employment opportunities between the North and the South as did the liberal ministries of the nineteenth and twentieth centuries. The census for 1927 surveyed 3,338,071 workers engaged in purely industrial pursuits. Of this total, 2,224,339, or 66.6%, worked in enterprises located in North Italy. Of the 4,058,170 industrial workers surveyed in the census of 1937–1939, 2,651,975, or 65.3%, worked in establishments in North Italy.[27]

The fascist régime exhibited as limited ability to expand the proportion of Italy's manufacturing production in relation to all other countries as it mustered capacity to influence bold departures from long-term trends in the distribution of workers among industrial categories, the consumer goods-producer goods ratio, or the North-South industrial disequilibrium. True, Italy's share of world manufacturing production rose to 3.3% during 1926–1929, as compared to 2.7% in 1913. However, it fell again to 2.7% during 1936–1938. Moreover, the 1926–1929 record could not claim distinction since Italy's percentage of world manufacturing production had already stood at 3.1% during 1906–1910. Nor could the fascists maintain the 1926–1929 level during 1936–1938, the very years when their government enjoyed the highest security and popularity. Yet the share of Russia, Mussolini's bête noire, ascended from 4.3% to 18.5% between 1926–1929 and 1936–1938; Japan's improved from 2.5% to 3.5%; and even backward India's increased slightly from 1.2% to 1.4%.[28]

The proportional distribution of the active population in Italy between 1921 and 1936, according to economic activity — agriculture, fishing, forestry, and hunting; goods-producing industries (manufacturing, construction, and extractive); and services — evidenced more disposition than other measures of economic change to break with the trend established between 1901 and 1921. The population census for 1921 counted 56.2% of the active population employed in agriculture. This percentage fell to 51% in 1931 and 48.2% in 1936, a marked decline of 14 percentage points in 15 years, as contrasted to the drop of 3.6 percentage points for the 20 years from 1901 to 1921. The ratio of the active population engaged in industrial pursuits increased by 3.8 percentage points between 1921 and 1936. Comparable gain for the longer period between 1901 and 1921 registered at 0.5 percentage points. Services, too, moved lightly upward between 1921 and 1936 by 4.2 percentage points, as compared with the increase of 3.1 percentage points between 1901 and 1921.[29]

Comparison of the distribution of the labor force in Italy, India, Japan, France, Germany, Great Britain, and the United States indicates that only Italy and India still remained overwhelmingly agricultural in 1931. That year, in contrast to Italy's record of 51%, only 36.2% of Japan's total labor force engaged in agriculture. Although both Italy and Japan showed the same percentage of their work forces attached to goods-producing industries, Japan's proportion engaged in the services, 36.7%, contrasted markedly to Italy's 21.8%. Japan's proportion in agricultural pursuits fell during the following decade to 28.6% while Italy's still ranged high at 48.2%. Moreover, Japanese industry employed 34.8% of its labor force; Italy's, 28.1%. This industrial percentage, when placed alongside comparable figures for other countries of the West during the same period, brings into relief the degree of Italian industrial retardation: France, 36.1%; Germany (including Austria and the Sudetenland), 47.1%; Great Britain (1931), 46.5%; and the United States, 33.1%.[30]

The percentage distribution of the active population among agricultural, industrial, and service pursuits in the *private* sector of the economy, when compared with the distribution of the gross internal product in the *private* sector of the economy among these categories, reveals that the fascist régime distinguished itself by increasing markedly the contribution of the services to the gross internal product. During the years between 1901–1905 and 1921–1925, while the proportion of the total active population engaged in agriculture declined by 3 percentage points, the share of agriculture in the gross internal product diminished by 8.6 percentage points. In contrast, industry increased its ratio of the active population by only 0.8 percentage points, but augmented its part of the gross internal product by 9.8 percentage points. The service occupations gained 2.2 percentage points of the active population, but sustained gross internal product losses of 1.2 percentage points. Under fascism from 1921–1925 to 1936–1940, despite the Battle of Wheat and the billions of lire spent upon reclamation projects, the percentage of the gross internal product ascribed to agriculture fell by 11 percentage points as its proportion of the active population decreased by 8 percentage points. Industry gained only 3.1 percentage points of agriculture's loss in the gross internal product and 4.3 percentage points of its diminution in the active population. The services expanded their gross internal product and active population proportions by 7.9 percentage points and 3.7 percentage points.[31]

To bring off the feat of reducing agriculture's share of the total active population by 8 percentage points and cutting its contribution to the gross internal product by 11 percentage points, while achieving the most modest gains in the industrial segment of the economy, the fascist régime had set in motion a giant program of land reclamation and launched the Battle of Wheat which symbolized the government's will to modernize the agrarian life of the nation. Law 3134 of December 24, 1928, the Mussolini Act, provided the basis for the reclamation of 2,300,000 hectares of swampland — 7% of Italy's total land area — at a contemplated cost of 6,823,000,000 lire. The government undertook to furnish 4,010,000,000 lire of this sum. The following figures dramatize the vast extent of the fascist plan as it developed beyond the bounds set by the original legislation: the cost of all authorized government reclamation projects and private undertakings subsidized by the State, as expressed in terms of 1927 gold lire, totalled 3,017,600,000 lire for all the years between 1870 and 1921, but mushroomed to 8,697,100,000 lire from 1921–1922 to July 1, 1936. Authorized expenditures from 1936–1937 to 1939–1940 amounted to 3,119,800,000 current lire. By July 1, 1940, of 9,761,029 hectares of land subject to reclamation, improvements had moved to completion or lay in the course of fulfillment on 6,115,621 hectares, while work had yet to begin on the remaining 3,645,408 hectares.[32]

Important agricultural reforms preceded Mussolini's Battle of Wheat "to free the Italian people from the slavery of foreign bread." The law of July 29, 1927 reconstructed the agrarian credit system and created the National Consortium for Agrarian Credit. The act of December 13, 1928 prepared the way for the establishment of new agricultural schools and colleges, experiment stations, research centers, and extension services, the *cattedre ambulanti d'agricoltura.* To foster both the extension of wheat cultivation and the improvement of yield per hectare, the government not only promoted research, but also encouraged the sowing of high-quality seeds and the use of mechanized farm equipment. Upon official urging, peasants competed for prizes offered for outstanding achievements. The plan worked. Mussolini won the Battle of Wheat. Old fields grew more grain and the Duce dislodged Minerva and Bacchus from olive groves and vineyards and installed Ceres there. The average number of quintals of wheat produced per hectare rose from 11 in 1921 to the post-World War I high of 16.3 in 1938. The importation of wheat dropped from 27,998,000 quintals in 1921 to the post-World War I low of 2,905,000 quintals in 1938. Italian production rose from 51,084,000 quintals in 1921 to 81,838,000 quintals in 1938, the highest yield ever attained in Italy until 1953.[33]

While technically successful, the Battle of Wheat resulted in higher retail prices for bread. They rose from 1.41 lire per kilogram in 1921 to 1.91 in 1938 and soared as high as 2.50 lire in 1926. Even during the depression, the 1921 cost remained lower than that for any year except 1934. The price of pasta per kilogram advanced from its lowest point during the post-World War I period, 2.14 lire, to 2.43 in 1938. It had reached as high as 3.42 lire in 1926. During the decade from 1921 to 1930, the average annual production of wine totalled 44,898,000 hectoliters and the yield of olive oil reached 2,490,000 quintals. During the succeeding decade, 1931–1940, these figures fell to 38,944,000 hectoliters and 2,174,-000 quintals. However, the price of both items fell considerably during the 1931–1940 period.

Data with regard to the availability (not the actual consumption) of nutritive substances indicate that the average daily number of calories available to each inhabitant of Italy climbed to fresh heights during the decade from 1921 to 1930 before the land reclamation program and the Battle of Wheat could have attained momentum: 2,834 calories as compared to 2,694 during the previous ten years. However, the average fell below the 1911–1920 level during 1931–1940 when it registered at 2,641 calories. The statistics also indicate that the 1921–1930 decade provided Italians with the possibility of consuming, were means at hand, the highest average daily amounts of all three principal elements of diet as compared with the preceding and following decades: fats, proteins, and carbohydrates. The decade from 1931–1940, the time of Mussolini's most persistent and costly agricultural efforts, accomplished less, for the most part, than the two preceding decades. In terms of the annual average number of kilograms per capita, the availability of the following foodstuffs increased during 1921–1930, but decreased during 1931–1940: wheat, fresh vegetables, beef, olive oil, sugar, and coffee. The availability of the following foodstuffs declined during both decades as compared with 1911–1920: tomatoes, fresh fruit, dry fruit, pork, sheep and goat meat, bacon, lard, and wine. The availability of the following foodstuffs rose both during 1921–1930 and 1931–1940: potatoes, fresh beans, fresh and preserved fish, eggs, milk, cheese, and butter. Mussolini's agrarian decade, 1931–1940, distinguished itself, as compared with the previous ten years, by augmenting the availability of the following foodstuffs:

corn, rice, barley, oats, dry beans, and citrus fruits (which still lay far below the level of 1911–1920).[34]

Mussolini paralleled the Battle of Wheat with the Battle of Births. He proposed to bolster the declining birth rate itself, to control migration from country districts of high birth rates to urban areas of low birth rates, and to discourage even the severely limited remaining opportunities for emigration after 1921 when the United States and other countries closed their ports to immigrants. In December 1925, the government founded the National Institute for the Protection of Motherhood and Infancy (Opera Nazionale per la Protezione della Maternità e dell' Infanzia). The agency aided pregnant women, particularly destitute and abandoned mothers; served as an educational clearing house for pre-natal and infant care; intervened in the cases of poor, afflicted, orphaned or homeless children; and worked with local agencies in combatting children's diseases through the organization of maternity clinics and hygiene classes. In 1939, the Institute expended 133,340,000 lire in assisting over 1,670,000 mothers, infants, and children.[35] To assure these services a copious future, Mussolini levied a flat tax upon bachelors in 1926 and raised the income taxes of bachelors and the heads of families with few children. He rewarded the heads of large families with special allowances and tax exemptions. They also received particular consideration for posts in public employment and for apartments in housing built with government aid. The law sternly prohibited propaganda in favor of birth control, the sale of contraceptives, and abortion. As further encouragement, the royal decree law of August 21, 1937 provided loans for newly married couples with limited incomes. They had to repay these grants in full if they struggled on without children after four years. However, whenever a fourth child blessed fruitful marriages, the government cancelled the debt.

In December 1928, the prefects of provinces received the power to regulate migration to urban centers. They could return to their former places of residence all persons who arrived in cities without means of support and remained unemployed. As a by-product of official desire to achieve balance between fertile rural areas and urban centers of low birth rates, between 1929 and 1938, the newly constituted office of the Commissioner for Internal Migration and Colonization brought increasing order to the quest of the unemployed for jobs by directing the movement of 3,500,000 workers from their homes to regions which offered greater industrial or agricultural opportunities. The commissioner also supervised the settlement of families from the mainland in African colonies or Sardinia. Although the fascist régime frowned upon emigration as a loss of manpower and soldiery unworthy of an ascendant world power, the depression forced the government to modify its policy. Nonetheless, emigration remained insignificant in comparison with the titanic exodus of earlier years, especially 1913 when 872,598 persons left Italy. During the decade from 1921 to 1930, an annual average of 257,844 Italians departed, while 137,814 returned from abroad. The annual average for 1911–1920 registered at 382,807, while average annual emigration reached the all-time high of 602,669 during the decade, 1901–1910. However, during the Mussolini decade *par excellence*, 1931–1940, only 70,265 persons left, while 58,986 found their way back to Italy. As in earlier decades, between 1921 and 1930, the number of workers and artisans who emigrated exceeded the number of agricultural workers. Of the 225,943 emigrants with known occupations, 116,595 were workers and artisans, while only 56,789 were agricultural workers. During the next decade, emigrants with known occupations numbered 58,021; the number of workers and artisans totalled 28,054, as compared to 6,355 agricultural workers.[36]

The patriotic decline in emigration affected adversely Italy's balance of international payments. Whereas postal savings deposits of emigrants constituted 34.2% of all postal deposits in 1920 and 24.1% in 1921, this proportion fell to 7.6% in 1931 (a year of deep depression), but declined even lower in 1939 when it sank to 1.2%. Remittances from emigrants through the Bank of Naples, as recorded by checks paid by the post offices, dropped from 345,349,000 lire in 1928 to 128,389,000 lire in 1935. After 1935, the government withheld official statistics for emigrant remittances except from workers who had colonized East Africa.[37]

Despite the campaign to increase Italy's population at the expense of its standard of living, neither marriage nor birth rates responded warmly to these blandishments. Between 1921 and 1941 the population of Italy grew from 37,452,000 to 44,357,000, while the density of population increased from 126 inhabitants per square kilometer to 148. As compared to the average annual arithmetic increase of 6.8 per thousand persons between 1911 and 1921, the rate between 1921 and 1931 rose to 8.4, but actually declined slightly between the 1931 and 1936 censuses when Mussolini's Battle of Births should have exploited its conquests most fully.[38] The Duce's chosen thoughts on population increase illustrate the economic and social wisdom of the Head of the State who controlled the destiny of 45,000,000 souls: "In a Fascist Italy in which land has been reclaimed, cultivated, irrigated, in which discipline and order prevail, there is room and bread for an additional 10,000,000 people."[39]

This necessarily brief review of the leading economic developments in

Italy between 1922 and the advent of World War II has attempted to illustrate the basically orthodox quality of the fascist economic order. Traditional habits of mind certainly prevailed during the early years of Mussolini's rule when conservative forces within the Party hoped to salvage the liberalistic elements of capitalism and exploit them in a favorable atmosphere cleared of working-class militancy and strikes. Later, when runaway speculation, inflation, and depression forced the government to intervene in the economic life of the nation as a more active partner, the fascist system, vaunted by its founders as the universal future form of human governance, exhibited few inventive economic skills or talents for institutional arrangements not already possessed by previous Italian governments or evolved by other countries of the West. But even if Mussolini had possessed an original mind, he could not have contributed to this particular branch of statecraft. Although once a socialist, he had neglected the disciplined study of economics for fiery utterances and destructive revolutionary zeal. His restless spirit, vanity, and devouring ambition bent him toward the public forum of journalism, politics, and oratory. The dips of the business cycle provided him with anticapitalistic propaganda, not with occasion for analysis and understanding. His closest fascist lieutenants shared his ignorance of economics and indifference toward its mysteries. Small wonder, then, that the bankers, large landowners, and captains of industry who had financed fascism proposed to take their reward by operating the economic system along conventional capitalist lines, or that their colleagues and experts in the government at Rome diligently supported these policies and plans. These hard-headed men of affairs placed what song the Sirens of economic change sang beyond all conjecture. But the radicals within the Fascist Party did not. They knew that tune by heart. They kept hearing in silence the music of progress and adventure once poured forth by the Tenth Corporation of D'Annunzio's constitution of the District of Fiume, the *Carta della Reggenza Italiana del Carnaro*, that operatic inspiration for the Corporative State.

Mussolini's vanity and Napoleonic concern for the judgment of history assured his good will and eventual enthusiasm for the series of projects which anchored the national stage where the Corporative State, in more and more ornate costumes, acted out its shifting roles: (1) *Reports and Proposals of the Presidential Commission for the Study of Constitutional Reforms*, submitted to the government by Professor Giovanni Gentile's Commission of Eighteen on June 24, 1925; (2) the Pact of the Palazzo Vidoni between the General Confederation of Italian Industry and the National Confederation of Fascist Syndical Unions, concluded on October 2, 1925 under the auspices of Roberto Farinacci, the general secretary of the Fascist Party; (3) law 563 of April 3, 1926 on the Legal Discipline of Collective Labor Relations; (4) royal decree 1130 of July 1, 1926 on the Regulations for the Enforcement of Law 563 of April 3, 1926; (5) royal decree 1131 of July 2, 1926 on the Establishment of the Ministry of Corporations; (6) royal decree 401 of March 17, 1927 on the Organization of the Ministry of Corporations; (7) the Charter of Labor, published in the *Gazzetta Ufficiale* on April 30, 1927; (8) royal decree 1003 of March 29, 1928 on the National Regulation of the Demand and Supply of Labor; (9) law 1019 of May 17, 1928 on the Reform of Political Representation in the Italian Kingdom; (10) royal decree 3222 of December 6, 1928 on Rules for the Application of Royal Decree 1003 of March 28, 1928; (11) law 2693 of December 9, 1928 on the Organization and Powers of the Fascist Grand Council; (12) law 206 of March 20, 1930 on the Reform of the National Council of Corporations; (13) law 163 of February 5, 1934 on the Establishment and Functions of the Corporations; (14) royal decree of December 27, 1934 on Changes in the Membership of the Central Corporative Committee; and (15) law 129 of January 19, 1939 on the Establishment of the Chamber of Fasci and Corporations.[40]

In presenting the Corporative State to Italy and the world, the fascists should have placed the Corporation at the very center of the proscenium. The term came from the medieval Italian name for guilds of arts and crafts, *corporazioni delle arti e dei mestieri*. Twentieth-century ideas about the Corporation combined modern fantasy about medieval economic life with Catholic doctrines on the interdependency of social classes. To these speculations, the anarcho-syndicalists and guild socialists had added their fears of the bureaucratic state of nationalized industries and had proposed, instead, the direct control by organized workers over all production and services. The fascist syndicalists dosed the entire brew with strong potions of nationalism and distilled from these drafts the elixir of corporativism: self-governing bodies of organized workers and employers associated together to direct without class conflict the economic system of the country. Logically, corporations of workers and employers in the cultivation of olives, or the textile industries, or the construction crafts, or the metal-mechanical trades, or the railroads, should have each governed output and its distribution from the local shop and factory, on through intermediate communal and provincial associations, up to the national level. Corporative organizations of wider jurisdiction could then have established coordination among related economic activities. Finally, these corporations would have joined together to systema-

420

tize the largest segments of the economy: agriculture, industry, and the services. The voices of both logic and political drama demanded this self-governing system of production and distribution from the lowest to the highest levels, but fascism never truly implemented its alternative to capitalism and communism.

Authentic syndicalist corporations would have monopolized Italian economic life and threatened the monolithic nature of the fascist political dictatorship. They would also have absorbed powerful employer organizations like the General Confederation of Italian Industry and the Confederation of Agriculture. These groups, as well as the more conservative members of Party and government, had once regarded the fascist corporations as bulwarks against communism, but now came to fear the universal organizational appetite of Edmondo Rossoni's National Confederation of Fascist Syndical Unions. At the time of the Palazzo Vidoni Pact, he had agreed with reluctance to limit the Confederation's jurisdiction, which potentially covered all employers and actually included landowners within its agricultural precincts, only to workers. By 1926, the General Confederation of Italian Industries took the lead in opposition to mixed corporations and forced the question. The final recommendations of the Commission of Eighteen and the law of April 3, 1926, prepared by the Minister of Justice, Alfredo Rocco, compromised the issue and supported separate organizations of workers and employers.

The Rocco legislation opened up the eventual possibility, if not the probability, of establishing two great all-inclusive confederations in Italy, one for employers, the other for workers. By consenting to less than truly corporative syndical institutions, Rossoni hoped to retain intact control, within his single confederation, of workers in industry, commerce, the professions, and agriculture. He courted disillusion. Employer organizations, independent too long, refused to merge into one great national confederation; their recalcitrance forced Rossoni's eclipse as the outstanding labor hierarch in 1928 when the National Confederation of Fascist Syndical Unions split into units paralleling the employer associations. The employers dragged their feet on other roads as well. Although the Rocco law stated that the "Corporation constitutes the unit of organization of one field of production and represents its interests as a whole," not a single joint corporation graced the fascist landscape until 1930 and even then it hardly resembled the ideal of syndicalist dreams. There emerged from the eloquence of the statute and the hopes of the radical reformers a rearrangement, grouped with false military precision, of the time-honored system of category and geographical unions of workers and associations of employers, culminating in separate national labor and management confederations. As a result of the nine-days-wonder propaganda, the productive forces of the nation found themselves divided into thirteen legally recognized national confederations: six syndical organizations of employers for industry, agriculture, commerce, land transportation and internal navigation, credit and insurance, and maritime and air transportation; six syndical groups of workers disposed in the same fashion; and the National Confederation of Fascist Syndicates of Professional Men and Artists. Outside of these legally recognized entities, the government permitted the creation on August 5, 1926 of five national associations of public and semipublic employees: government workers; school teachers; postal agents; state railroad workers; and postal, telegraph, and telephone employees.

The General Confederation of Italian Industry became the national syndicate of industrialists in the new order and added "Fascist" to its title. Logically, according to legislation and regulations, six confederations of Italian workers should have immediately replaced Rossoni's one national labor center. Instead, humoring his desires and ambitions for the moment, the government legally recognized the National Confederation of Fascist Syndical Unions on September 26, 1926. Its old corporations, which grouped individual category federations into five vocational orders for industry, agriculture, commerce, seamen, and the intellectual and middle classes, disbanded and their members reassembled within the six newly classified ranks. Two years later, these six federations under Rossoni's domination emerged as independent national confederations when the royal decree of November 21, 1928 dissolved the National Confederation of Fascist Syndical Unions and ended Rossoni's visions of grandeur.

As in the unenlightened days of the liberal state, both workers and employers formed their own category associations at the communal level. These local groups then established two kinds of provincial workers and employers organizations. Local textile unions, for example, combined into provincial textile unions; these, in turn, affiliated themselves into the national textile federation. The national syndicate of textile workers then took its place within the national confederation of all industrial workers. The regulations mustered employer groups into the same structural pattern. In addition to duplicating the constituent elements of the dissolved C.G.L.'s labor federations and of the prefascist employer category associations of iron and steel manufacturers, or shipbuilders, or rice producers, the new corporative dispensation established geographical units which reproduced the chambers of labor, the chambers of commerce, and the communal and provincial branches of the General Confederation of Italian Industry, the General Confederation of Agriculture, and other national employer associations — bodies which grouped all categories within a geographic jurisdiction. Thus, at the communal level, the syndicate of metal-mechanical workers joined other local industrial syndicates to form the communal syndicate of industrial workers. These communal syndicates sent delegates to the provincial industrial syndicate. Labor syndicates in agriculture, commerce, land transportation and internal navigation, credit and insurance, and maritime and air transportation also united within each of these large segments to erect communal and provincial organizations. Employers and professional men and artists of all categories also allied themselves geographically. The individual national category federations of employers and workers within each of the six broad classifications, together with their apposite geographical entities, constituted the twelve national labor and employer confederations. So waxed the confederation of professional men and artists.

The structure of the corporative system carried no novel features except two: instead of one labor confederation which united all workers, including those in the professions, seven confederations now shared their dues; instead of freedom of association, fear and compulsion ruled. Indeed, the unique aspects of fascist labor relations rested firmly upon constraint, however disguised by political oratory or the subtle involutions of labor law, so dear to the Latin mind. The dictatorship recognized only one labor and employer syndicate for each locality and for each craft, trade, industry, or profession. The legally constituted associations of workers and employers drew up collective agreements, usually at the national level, supplemented by provincial wage bargains which reflected differentials in the cost of living. The terms of these accords covered all workers and employers, regardless of their membership or nonmembership within the organizations under contract. Since nonmembers paid the same amount of dues as members, simple justice called for this principle of *erga omnes*. Since grievance committees disappeared from Italian industrial life and the right to strike or to engage in lockouts became punishable criminal offenses, the law balanced its harshness by creating the *magistratura del lavoro*, special labor courts to settle collective disputes arising out of the negotiation or interpretation of labor agreements. Individual disputes went before regular magistrates aided by one labor and one production expert. Fascism could not claim originality for the labor courts it fathered since Australia and New Zealand had pioneered with them at the end of the nineteenth century. Moreover, it left the final resolution of thousands upon thousands of individual grievances to costly and time-consuming normal court procedures. Alfredo Rocco must have realized the corporative system's poverty of invention except for that primal element of distinction, complete government control. He resorted to soporific rhetoric when he presented the regulations for the law of April 3, 1926 to the Fascist Grand Council in June of that year:

> The new organization of labor . . . is developing in a twofold direction: one vertical and the other horizontal. The vertical organization is being realized outside the state but under the control of the state, and comprises syndicates of a single category or trade grouped into superior organizations, federations or confederations. The horizontal organization is being realized within the state, and comprises all the factors of production for each branch of industry. Thus the corporation is being organized within the state, including employers, workers and artisans.[41]

Rocco, the brilliant legal authority, knew well enough that mixed self-governing corporations of workers and employers, endowed with real power in the productive process, could never feasibly enter into the evolving schemes of the fascist régime. Instead, the government itself assumed the dominant role in labor relations by creating the Ministry of Corporations on July 2, 1926. At first limited to syndical affairs, the Ministry of Corporations absorbed the functions of the Ministry of National Economy in 1929. Its jurisdiction and responsibilities resembled, at a minimum, the authority and duties of the Mediation and Conciliation Service combined with the competence and tasks of the Departments of Labor and Commerce in the United States. The Ministry supervised and controlled the activities of all labor and employer associations, registered and enforced all national and provincial collective agreements, conciliated collective disputes between workers and management, planned and conducted educational programs, gathered and published statistics, watched over fascist welfare organizations, and maintained close factory inspection services through the Corporative Inspectorate. The Inspectorate's widely dispersed offices also availed, in part, as the Ministry's communal and provincial eyes and ears. Too, the Ministry kept in touch with local syndical and economic developments through the quasi-official provincial economic councils which replaced all chambers of commerce on April 18, 1926. On June 16, 1927, the government established provincial economic offices to operate as secretariats for the provincial economic councils and as local branches of the Ministry as well. Each province also set up special advisory committees representative of local syndical groups; these pyramided upward to a national labor-management committee in Rome.

This provincial administrative jungle cried out for simplification. On June 18, 1931, the fascist régime accomplished this feat by a series of name changes. The provincial economic council acquired augmented powers, equal labor-management representation, putative independence, and a new tag, the Provincial Council. The provincial economic offices turned into the Provincial Offices of Corporative Economy and represented, locally, the Ministry of Corporations. In Rome, the National Council of Corporations, made up of leading government bureaucrats and syndical officials of both labor and employer organizations, advised the Ministry of Corporations and proved of minor importance.

The Fascist Charter of Labor, elaborated by the Ministry of Corporations, won the approval of the Fascist Grand Council on April 21, 1927, the very anniversary dedicated to labor. The Council commended it to the Italian people as "this fundamental document of the Fascist Revolution." That enactment offered "the best short description of the aims and aspirations of the Fascist syndical movement and . . . the best single, authoritative statement of the Fascist attitude on the fundamentals of economic and social policy."[42] Then followed, the next year, on May 17, 1928, the law which transformed the Chamber of Deputies into an assembly of syndical representatives. Although the character of the Italian Senate remained untouched (the King nominated its members for life), labor and employer organizations, principally, but recognized cultural and welfare groups as well (disabled veterans, state employees, universities, and scientific academies), selected the deputies of the metamorphosed Chamber, now healthily geared to the productive forces of the reinvigorated nation and no longer dominated by degenerate political interests. Once again, elaborate procedures followed ostensibly democratic principles only to stumble into a final morass of autocratic control. The syndical associations designated eight hundred candidates, while the cultural and welfare organizations selected two hundred. The Fascist Grand Council received these lists and culled out six hundred names. At elections, the voters of Italy could accept or reject this single slate of four hundred candidates.

Since the corporative Chamber voiced its views as freely and functioned as parliamentarily as the controlled Chamber it replaced, fascists enamoured of pure corporativism, without admitting the defects of the corporative Chamber, insisted upon the need for yet another institution to coordinate the syndical system and order the economic life of the country. Since the National Council of Corporations had led an openly mediocre existence, the law of March 20, 1930 sought to insert into the corporative arch its missing keystone, the corporation. The more radical fascists, frustrated in their yearnings for true self-governing corporations of workers and employers, hoped to approximate their ideal by creating

425

national joint bodies where labor and employer representatives of the principal areas of productive activity could resolve economic differences, supervise the larger aspects of labor relations, and discuss problems of mutual concern. The new legislation reorganized the National Council of Corporations into seven separate sections: six combined the six employer and six labor confederations, while the seventh acted for professional men and artists. These sections, in turn, could contain subsections. For example, the section on industry and handicrafts contained two subsections, one for industry, the other for handicrafts. Under approved conditions, the subsections might exert powers equal to those of the sections and would act independently. When questions of mutual concern came under discussion, the sections and subsections met in common session. Twice annually, the National Council of Corporations drew the members of the seven sections together in general assembly. The assembly could discuss policies concerning syndical controls, labor relations, and the coordination of employment. In theory, it could also exercise strategic control over economic life by devising rules for meshing the plans, programs, and activities of the seven branches of national production. To facilitate its work, the National Council designated special and permanent commissions. Epitomized by Mussolini as the economic general staff, this supreme arbiter of Italian production actually functioned through its Central Corporative Committee which encompassed important government officials and the presidents of the thirteen syndical confederations. The meetings of the Central Corporative Committee took place under the presidency of Mussolini, the head of the State and the Minister of Corporations.

The 31 meetings of the Central Corporative Committee from May 1930 to September 1932, the 82 meetings of the seven sections, and the 8 meetings of the general assembly could not convince the most ardent fascists that authentic corporations had appeared on Italian soil. Mussolini admitted that the corporative system still remained in its syndical phase, a rationalization reminiscent of the cant employed by contemporary Marxists who have justified the Russian failure to abolish economic class distinctions by differentiating between the impure socialist period and the final communist stage of the revolution. Clearly, the situation once more demanded costume changes. In May 1933, he announced that the Central Corporative Committee had received from the government plans for the creation of true corporations. After approval by the Committee, the Fascist Grand Council, and Parliament, the design passed into law on February 5, 1934. It provided for corporations where "various branches of economic activity" joined forces. Each corporation consisted of an equal number of worker and employer representatives from the pertinent syndical confederations, public officials, technical experts, and leaders of the Fascist Party. The law empowered each corporation to extend economic counsel to government agencies upon request, attempt to settle collective labor controversies through its corporative conciliation board, and regulate production, competition, and remuneration for consumer goods and services sold under conditions of special privilege or under circumstances where syndical agreements could not determine wages. All rules, decisions, and price and wage determinations formulated by the individual corporations required the approval of the National Council of Corporations before they acquired the force of law. The Minister of Corporations, Mussolini himself, assumed the presidency of each corporation.

Three months after the passage of this legislation, the Ministry of Corporations and the Central Corporative Committee devised an integrated vertical system of organization for the corporations. Each corporation encompassed all activities of a complete production cycle. The royal decree of May 29, 1934 established eight corporations in Group I which involved agricultural, industrial, and commercial operations: (1) grains, (2) vegetable, flower, and fruit growing, (3) viticulture and wine production, (4) edible oils, (5) sugar beets and sugar, (6) animal husbandry and fishing, (7) wood and wood products, and (8) textile products. The royal decree of June 9, 1934 formed eight corporations in Group II which concerned only industrial and commercial operations: (9) building and construction, (10) metallurgy and machinery, (11) clothing, (12) glass and ceramics, (13) chemicals, (14) paper and printing, (15) the extractive industries, and (16) water, gas, and electricity. The royal decree of June 23, 1934 set up six corporations in Group III which pertained solely to services: (17) the professions and arts, (18) internal communications, (19) sea and air transportation, (20) tourist and hotel trade, (21) credit and insurance, and (22) the theater and public entertainment. On November 10, 1934, Mussolini swore into office the 824 members of these 22 corporations at the hall of Julius Caesar on Michelangelo's Campidoglio in Rome. Despite the pretentions of legislation and Mussolini's boast that "the self-regulation of production under the aegis of the producers. . ." formed the basis of the entire corporative system, the corporations born in 1934 functioned as mere advisory councils where representatives of employers, workers, the Fascist Party, and the régime passed the time of day in discussion.

Since article 7 of the law of February 5, 1934 assured the autonomy of all labor and employer organizations in each corporation, the Ministry of

427

Corporations and the Central Corporative Committee issued a series of decrees on August 16, 1934 which once more reorganized the syndical system. The category federations of employers and workers received full independence and legal recognition. They could now conclude collective agreements formerly negotiated only through the confederations. Although the communal, provincial, and interprovincial syndical groups did not receive legal status, they continued to serve as the local representatives of the separate national category federations of workers and of employers. The still legally blessed confederations licked their wounds by catering to the common concerns of affiliated federations, thinking up over-all services for them, exercising fiscal surveillance over their books, and coordinating (a word synonymous in all languages with bureaucratic impotency) their residual and marginal activities: social welfare and education. Collective agreements stipulated by the autonomous category federations went first to the confederations for transmission to the proper government agency for publication. All these efforts the confederation shared with their provincial and interprovincial offices, now no longer annointed with legal position. The shorn confederations, once thirteen in number, squeezed down to nine: (1) agricultural employers, (2) workers in agriculture, (3) industrialists, (4) workers in industry, (5) merchants, (6) workers in commercial enterprises, (7) credit and insurance enterprises, (8) workers in credit and insurance enterprises, and (9) professional men and artists.

The administrative organization of the independent, separate category federation of either employers or workers continued the traditional structure of prefascist economic institutions: a general assembly, a council, an executive committee, and a president or secretary. Members of communal groups affiliated with a federation met in local assembly to elect representatives to the provincial assembly. These delegates chose the president or secretary of the provincial body. These provincial officers, when gathered together, constituted the general assembly of the national category federation. The general assembly usually met once every three years. It served as a deliberative body for discussing common organizational concerns, debated the policies of its leaders, and elected members to its council. The council, which convened once a year, attempted through its membership to represent the various federational groups and interests. It elected, from its own ranks, the executive committee and an auditing board. Among its other duties, the council considered the annual reports of the executive committee. The executive committee managed the federation with the aid of the president or secretary elected by the general assembly. Like members of the council and the executive committee, this officer held his post for three years. The nine confederations also functioned within this organizational pattern. The presidents or secretaries of affiliated autonomous national category federations formed the council of the confederation. The council then named the president, the executive committee, and the board of auditors. The Ministry of Corporations, always in closest touch with national and provincial headquarters of the Fascist Party, approved all elections and appointments of the autonomous syndical federations and confederations.

At the end of 1939, employers had organized four confederations of agricultural, industrial, commercial, and credit and insurance enterprises; 92 autonomous employer category federations held membership in these four confederations. Workers duplicated the confederations of employers; professional men and artists added the ninth. Labor formed four autonomous agricultural federations, 20 industrial federations, eight commercial federations, and six federations among credit and insurance enterprises. Professional men and artists constituted 24 national unions and 1,058 zonal associations. Membership in the employer syndicates at the end of 1939 numbered 2,922,231: agriculturists, 1,500,472; commercialists, 748,321; credit and insurance heads, 7,970; 103,469 directors and officials of industrial enterprises, 443,916 handicraftsmen, and 118,083 factory proprietors. Membership in fascist labor organizations totalled 8,507,300 at the end of 1939: 4,299,026 agricultural hands, 3,374,564 industrial operatives, 602,285 commercial workers, and 81,646 employees in credit and insurance establishments. The ninth confederation included 149,779 professional men and artists. Dues paid by members and nonmembers of the nine confederations — an employer's annual dues could not exceed a total equal to one day's wages for each person in his employ and a worker's annual dues (collected by check-off) could not go beyond his wages for one day although syndical bylaws could authorize supplementary dues as well — amounted to 590,486,000 lire at the end of 1939, of which 373,630,000 came from employer associations and 216,856,000 came from labor organizations. The State claimed 10% of all dues collected and placed that sum in a special account of the Ministry of Corporations.[43]

What did this laboriously piled-up mountain of bureaucratic endeavor accomplish?

First, the Ministry of Corporations, the Provincial Offices of Corporative Economy, the National Council of Corporations, the Central Corporative Committee, the 22 corporations, the nine confederations, the 154 syndical federations, the hundreds of communal and provincial syndical branches, and the Provincial Offices created thousands of jobs for the fascist economy. During the fiscal year 1931–1932, the cost to the central government alone of its corporative activities, 77,168,000 lire, represented 0.3% of the total national budget as compared to 0.2% devoted to public health. By 1938–1939, these expenditures increased to 319,637,000 lire, while their proportion to total outlays that year rose to 0.7% of the national budget as compared to 0.1% expended for public health. These disbursements cared not only for the novel corporative aspects of administration, but also for the normal services provided by conventional ministries of labor, ministries of industry or commerce, and their regional offices.

The corporative bureaucracy fostered a new generation of civil servants with considerable proficiency in areas of labor relations long neglected by former governments. Together with the group of technicians developed by the corporations, confederations, federations, and communal and provincial syndicates, these young men emerged, for the first time in modern Italian history, as a trained corps of experts in the details of collective bargaining, mediation, contract interpretation, grievance procedures, social security, workers education, protective labor legislation, prices, wages, incentive systems and payments, the statistics of production, the vicissitudes of the labor market, and labor law.[44]

Secondly, the Corporative State revolutionized collective bargaining and left its enduring imprint upon the Italian system. Before World War I, the scope of collective agreements (*concordati collettivi*) had not reached beyond provinces, groups of provinces, regions, or at its widest extent, groups of regions. F.I.O.M. and employers in the metal-mechanical industries signed Italy's first nationwide agreement, which established the eight-hour day and standard work rules, in 1919. Other national agreements followed in the paper, marble, textile, glass, clothing, chemical, and gas industries. Yet the record of the membership-bloated Italian labor movement after World War I in stipulating so few industry-wide agreements, which set uniform conditions of work and minimum-wage scales, ranked as less than impressive. Mussolini robbed Italian workers of free unions — a resource which they had not yet learned to exploit for full economic yield under the liberal state, but tapped, instead, for political gushers — and gave them as compensation national collective labor agreements. By the end of 1939, Italian syndical associations had deposited copies of 338 national and interprovincial collective labor agreements at the Ministry of Corporations: 25 for agriculture, 210 for industry, 63 for commerce, 31 for credit and insurance, and 9 for the professions and arts. During the same year, labor and management groups concluded 3,085 provincial agreements: 158 in agriculture, 2,482 in industry, 367 in commerce, 76 in credit and insurance, and 2 in the professions and arts.[45]

Did the extended scope of collective bargaining under Mussolini increase the material welfare of the average Italian worker? Once again, Mussolini has provided the measure of judgment. In commending the proposed corporations to the General Assembly of the National Council of Corporations on November 14, 1933, the Duce characterized the corporations as the instruments "through which Italy's laboring classes will improve their standard of living."[46] The third and most central possible achievement of the Corporative State should, therefore, have embodied the fulfillment of this prophecy since it might have endowed the whole elaborate superstructure with human dimensions, mitigated the harsh curbs upon freedom, and released the régime from suspicion of economic and social hypocrisy.

In assessing the closely articulated fascist system of collective bargaining as the inspired medium to improve the lot of Italy's laboring masses — according to Mussolini, the depression of the 1930's meant "the end of liberal capitalism, the economic system. . ." which emphasized "the individual profit motive. . ." and marked "the beginning of a new economy. . ." which stressed "collective interests," in short, the Corporative State — the specter of continuing unemployment must haunt all calculations.[47] Although the real per capita national income, measured in terms of 1938 prices, increased from 2,741 lire during 1921–1925 to 2,902 lire even during 1931–1935 and then climbed to 3,191 lire during 1936–1940, the index of unemployment might suggest that the Duce sacrificed "collective interests" for the prosperity of the wealthier classes: agricultural unemployment rose from 100 in 1929 to 221.3 in 1934, while the index of industrial unemployment grew from 100 in 1929 to 357.6 in 1935. Total unemployment attained the unprecedented height of 1,018,953 persons in 1933. After 1935, the government ceased publication of unemployment statistics.

These facts alone could not indict the fascist system of catering to powerful economic groups at the expense of labor's desperate needs. But major wage cuts and boomeranging reductions in hours of work have furnished additional evidence for the brief. Notwithstanding the wage reductions of 10% to 20% in private employment and the equally drastic lowering of salaries among public and parastatal employees after the devaluation of the currency in 1927, on November 18, 1930, the government ordered a 12% salary slash for all state employees and dependents of other public and semipublic agencies. Private employers did not hesitate long in following this lead. The government again diminished wages by 6% to 20% on April 14, 1934. Employers soon caught up with the State.

On October 11, 1934, employer and worker syndicates agreed to reduce weekly hours of work from 48 to 40 as a measure of stemming unemployment. When the trial period ended, the government ordered the permanent institution of the 40-hour week. The diminution in hours, unfortunately, also meant pay cuts as high as 16% in many cases. However, the State also established price and rent controls to counterbalance wage losses. Too, in the autumn of 1936, the régime authorized wage increases ranging from 5% to 11% and on April 30, 1937 the Central Corporative Committee, on Mussolini's proposal, authorized the augmentation of wages and salaries by 10% to 12% (inclusive of the 1936 gains) to offset the consequences of the Ethiopian War, sanctions, rising world prices, and the second devaluation of Italy's currency on October 5, 1936.

These half-hearted or tardy efforts proved barren. In 1927, the year of the Charter of Labor, the index of real wages in Italy, taking 1913 as the base year, stood at 120.79. By 1930 it fell to 119.04. As the depression lifted, the index rose to 124.16 in 1934, but decreased to 108.76 in 1936 and then sank to 100.53 in 1938. The index then rose to 105.68 in 1939. During the war years, the index precipitated from 100.24 in 1941 to 68.80 in 1943 and then to 22.30 in 1945. Thus, after their glorious African conquests, the fascists failed to lift the real wages of that part of the population which could find jobs, appreciably above the 1913 levels of the despised Giolittian era. The war which Mussolini thought craven to avoid finally pushed down the level of real wages to the borders of starvation.[48]

Not even the inability of the corporative system to raise real wages beyond 1913 levels or to prevent their steep descent during World War II could provide conclusive proof of its failure to improve the standard of living of the working classes. Against the decline of real wages must weigh the manifold social services, national insurances, welfare provisions, and educational and recreational facilities of the Fascist State. The Charter of Labor and subsequent legislation granted definite privileges to workers through mandatory clauses of collectively bargained agreements between syndical associations. These stipulations entitled workers to an annual vacation with pay, usually a week. In the event of death or discharge beyond the blame of workers, they or their families received compensation in proportion to their years of service. When ownership changed, workers retained their full rights, while prior claims held good against the new employer. Illness could not justify dismissal unless its duration exceeded the specific period named in the contract. Employers could not fire workers who left to fulfill their patriotic obligations in the armed services or fascist militia. Most of these benefits, as well as contractual and legal regulations regarding hygienic conditions of labor, also accrued to workers who engaged in home production. As a result of the royal decree of May 6, 1928, all collective agreements had to deal in precise terms with discipline, probationary periods, wages and salaries, sickness benefits, and all other matters covered by law. In addition, the government, implementing the Charter of Labor, expanded the services of the employment centers established before fascism. As a result of the royal decree of March 29, 1928, employers could choose workers only from among those enrolled at the employment centers. Moreover, the employer had to extend preference to members of the Fascist Party and the fascist unions according to priority on the registration lists. After January 10, 1935, only wage earners who possessed workbooks (*libretti di lavoro*) could claim the privilege of enrolling at employment offices. These *libretti* contained details about each worker's background, training, experience, and past affiliations. All wage earners, not merely those in search of jobs, had to possess workbooks.

The National Fascist Institute of Social Security, which replaced the National Fund for Social Insurances in October 1935, administered old-age, disability, and survivors insurance; unemployment insurance; tuberculosis insurance; maternity insurance; and family allowances. At the end of 1939, the Institute recorded 619,555 invalidity, old-age, and survivors insurance pensions in force, including special groups of beneficiaries: public-service transport employees, workers in the merchant marine, industrial accident victims, and the sulphur miners of Sicily. During the depths of the depression in 1932, the Institute paid out close to 55,500,000 daily unemployment insurance subsidies amounting to 186,212,000 lire; in 1939, the number of daily payments had not declined, but had risen to almost 56,335,000 totalling 167,180,000 lire. Decree law 2055 of October 20, 1927 brought compulsory tuberculosis insurance into effect; the government extended its benefits to sharecroppers by decree law 761 of March 19, 1936. The Institute extended assistance to 60,116 insured workers and members of their families in 1932. This total grew to 86,830 persons in 1939. The number of women covered by obligatory maternity insurance increased from 675,465 in 1923 to 1,409,353 in 1938. Royal decree 636 of April 14, 1939 converted maternity insurance into marriage and birth insurance. Birth insurance, no longer limited to working mothers as before, now protected all persons in the social insurance system, including wives; marriage insurance benefited these individuals and their daughters. The ancillary activities of the National Institute for the Protection of Motherhood and Infancy have already received attention in the description of Mussolini's Battle of Births.

The National Fascist Institute of Social Security also administered family allowances (*assegni familiari*). The practice had originated in the collective agreement drawn up between the General Fascist Confederation of Industry and the Confederation of Workers in Industry on December 1, 1934. The Institute at that time assumed responsibility for administering the national family allowance fund established by the contract. The decree law of August 21, 1936 substituted public responsibility for private contractual arrangements after October 5 of that year. The original August decree benefited only industrial workers, but at the end of 1936 and throughout 1937, the government moved ahead to include employees in commercial, credit, and insurance companies, as well as agricultural labor. Heads of insured families received small weekly grants of 4 lire for each dependent child under 14 years of age. Contributions by workers, by employers, and by the State financed the fund. The average monthly number of heads of families assisted in 1939 totalled 1,418,204; of this total, 1,000,501 worked in industry. The allowances that year aided an average monthly number of 3,067,064 children.

In 1939 the administration of the National Fascist Institute for Workmen's Compensation, reorganized by royal decree 1765 of August 17, 1935, effective April 1, 1937, insured 324,592 industrial workers (the 1936 population census enumerated 5,154,325 employees in the manufacturing, extractive, and construction branches of industry). Separate funds protected public employees, maritime workers, and agricultural labor. The fascist régime did not create the National Institute for Workers Sickness Assistance (Istituto Nazionale per l'Assistenza Malattia ai Lavoratori— I.N.A.M.) until 1943. Administered by the National Fascist Institute for Workmen's Compensation, it aimed to coordinate separate, special funds long operative in industry, agriculture, commerce, banking, and insurance. They had developed out of funds originated by the venerable mutual aid societies, but expanded rapidly under the compulsory sickness insurance features of collective agreements from 1929 onward. After 1943, I.N.A.M. unified all services except the industrial fund which remained financially autonomous. In 1938, the six mutual funds for industry claimed 3,103,264 members, the two agricultural funds insured 5,263,939 persons, while the fund for commerce covered 373,398 employees. Finally, in 1939, public assistance and charitable institutions aided 3,051,584 needy citizens of the proud and conquering fascist empire.[49]

Beyond doubt, Italian workers recovered part of the loss they suffered through the decline of real wages during the fascist period by benefits reaped from social insurance programs inherited from previous liberal régimes and then amplified or augumented by the Corporative State. But most democratic industrial nations of the world also afforded similar, and often superior, aid without the loss of personal, civic, and economic free-doms. Another disturbing reservation: in addition to contributing direct-ly to certain social insurance funds, Italian workers also subscribed in-directly to the system when their syndicates made regular payments to the National Institute for the Protection of Motherhood and Infancy, to the National Fascist Institute of Social Security, and to the National Service for Leisure Time (Opera Nazionale Dopolavoro) which replaced the educational and recreational activities previously offered by the free workers circles. Moreover, 10% of all syndical dues collected and then deposited at the Royal Treasury Office of each prefecture ended up in a special account of the Ministry of Corporations. William G. Welk, a care-ful scholar who judged the economic aspects of the fascist experiment with scrupulous care, wrote at the end of the 1930's:

> Disregarding such benefits as are implied in extended social insur-ance and the social welfare activities of the regime, our general con-clusion about the condition of Italian labor under Fascism as measured by prevailing wage and employment conditions must be that on the whole it has not only failed of improvement but has been made worse — certainly in agriculture, and most probably in in-dustry.[50]

If the vast pyramidal machine of fascist economic organization ground slowly but surely only to satisfy fewer material needs of Italian workers than the far less ordered system of the liberal monarchy, Mussolini's corporative régime, buttressed by the O.V.R.A. and the Special Tribunal for the Defense of the State, did bring industrial peace to the nation. Un-der fascism, strikes and lockouts became criminal offenses. If employers closed down their establishments without justification, or with the intent to force their employees to change the terms of the labor agreement then in force, the law of April 3, 1926 subjected them to fines ranging from 10,000 to 100,000 lire. The law also forbade employees, in groups of three or more, from quitting their jobs by agreement, or remaining at their benches but interfering with the regular flow of work, in order to compel the employer to modify the terms of the labor agreement. Fines against employees might range from 100 to 1,000 lire. The law also imposed jail sentences of not less than one year nor more than two years, in addition to the fines, upon leaders and promoters of strikes and lock-outs. Employees and administrators in government offices and public utilities and services could suffer imprisonment, temporary loss of position, and severe fines for abetting strikes or suspension of work. In 1929, 77 criminal strikes and lockouts occurred; the total sank to 16 in 1932; it rose to 70 in 1935, but declined to 45 in 1938. The next year, criminal strikes and lockouts numbered 22. Whereas almost 450,000 workers and peasants still participated in the 575 strikes recorded for 1922, despite fascist terror, the number of strikers after 1926 diminished to negligible proportions.[51]

With strikes and lockouts precluded as the ultimate weapon for winning agreement during disputes between workers and employers, the fascists found it necessary to elaborate a substitutive procedure of conciliation, appeals, more conciliation, special courts, further conciliation, and, finally, judicial decisions. In the event that collective disputes between labor syndicates and employer associations came to pass, either in the course of interpreting contracts then in force or of formulating the provisions of new contracts, the corporative conciliation boards established by the legislation of 1934 attempted to settle the conflicts. For example, in early 1935, the conciliation board of the Corporation of Metallurgy and Machinery took up the controversy between labor and management at the Fiat plants in Turin over the workers' demand that the company throw out the Bedaux system of scientific management, long protested by them. The conciliation board recommended its discontinuance on February 19, 1935 and the company accepted its decision. If Fiat had refused the board's advice, the labor syndicate could have appealed to the Ministry of Corporations where important fascist functionaries acted as mediators. Without benefit of magic formulae, they settled most collective controversies at this point. In 1939, the Ministry of Corporations handled 106 collective controversies. Officials conciliated 63 and failed in 11 instances. The remaining 32 disputes represented abandoned or remanded cases.[52]

The syndicates presented unresolved collective disputes before special sections of the 16 courts of appeals in their guise as labor courts (*magistrature del lavoro*). Three professional judges and two labor and production experts heard each case. The provincial economic council proposed the names of these experts and arranged them according to groups and subgroups of economic activities. Every year, the president of the court designated from the list for each group and subgroup on the biennially revised panel the names of the experts who might serve on cases concerning those kinds of enterprises. In accordance with the law, the president of the court always attempted to conciliate the labor dispute before the court rendered its decision. Only legally recognized syndicates could bring action in behalf of employers and workers. During 1939, the Court of Appeals heard 60 cases of collective controversies. In 28 instances, the parties abandoned litigation. The court conciliated four disputes. It passed judgment on 28 cases.[53]

Workers with individual grievances about hours of labor, wages, incentive rates, job classifications, work assignments, efficiency evaluations, discipline, fines, discharges, and severance pay, first brought them to the attention of their union officials since shop stewards had disappeared from Italian plants. The appropriate labor and employer syndicates then attempted to resolve the questions at hand. The disposition of individual grievances at this stage of the procedure attained impressive statistical stature. The Fascist Confederation of Agricultural Workers reported that during 1938 the unions under its administrative care received 304,875 cases and processed 200,891. Of these, the petitioners either abandoned or the syndicates failed to resolve 144,989, while the syndicates settled 54,142 favorably and 1,760 unfavorably. They sent 103,984 individual grievances to the courts. Of this total, 99,220 were abandoned or remained unresolved, 4,487 enjoyed favorable outcomes, while 277 suffered adverse decisions. During 1939, the syndicates within the Fascist Confederation of Industrial Workers accepted 144,662 individual grievances. Of this number, they resolved, at syndical headquarters, 52,205 disputes which benefited 495,056 workers to the sum of 47,549,000 lire. However, 21,174 grievances gave rise to negative recommendations, while 26,756 were abandoned. The syndicates referred 38,119 cases to their legal offices. There, 8,537 grievances found positive solutions: 15,397 workers recovered 7,044,000 lire. The syndicates within the two smaller labor confederations for commercial workers and for employees in credit and insurance establishments, as well as in the confederation of professional men and artists, also pursued actively, although on a limited scale in contrast to agriculture and industry, the resolution of individual grievances.[54]

Since the fascists abolished the probiviral arbitration boards in 1928, when syndical efforts to conciliate grievances failed, the union, if it judged the grievance trialworthy, or the association, if it considered the issue important enough to contest, or the individual on his own (the syndicates bore no automatic obligation to assist its members) could carry the case to the *preture* (courts of first instance) or the *tribunali* (courts in the larger communities). Again, the judge first attempted conciliation. If he failed, he tried the case under regular legal procedures. Labor and production experts did not advise the courts unless the parties to the dispute demanded their presence at the very start of the trial. In cases which involved more than a fixed amount of money, the losing party could appeal to the labor courts. Individual grievances kept the dockets of the *preture* and *tribunali* full. A large proportion of these cases involved severance pay, not only because the law permitted generous settlements, especially for clerical employees, but also because unemployed workers had more than ample time to devote to litigation. In 1939, of the 20,240 cases brought before the *preture*, the parties abandoned 8,140 and the courts conciliated 3,673. Of the remaining cases, the courts agreed with the petitioners in 5,978 instances, rejected their claims in 2,106 cases, and declared themselves incompetent on 343 occasions. During the same year, of the 8,190 cases handled by the *tribunali*, the litigants abandoned 2,585, while the courts conciliated 539. The courts agreed with the claimants in 2,851 cases, rejected their demands in 1,199 cases, and declared themselves incompetent in 224 instances. Of the 2,027 cases of individual grievances carried to the courts of appeals in 1939, the grievants abandoned 142 and the courts conciliated 132. The courts revoked or annulled the appealed decision in 143 cases, confirmed the decision in 784 cases, and amended the decision in 826 cases.[55]

Although the courts could undoubtedly handle individual grievances with substantial justice, especially those complaints which did not involve the setting of broadly applicable precedents, decisions on collective controversies necessarily reflected political considerations. The famous case of the rice workers in the Po Valley illustrated admirably the concern of the Labor Court with national economic policy rather than with pure justice. The Confederation of Fascist Agricultural Syndicates and the Fascist Confederation of Agriculture concluded an agreement in March 1927. After the devaluation of the lira and the fall of world prices for rice that year, the employers demanded a 30% reduction in wages. Representatives of the workers refused to accept this decision. When attempts at conciliation failed, the case went before the Labor Court. The court heard both sides of the issue, consulted its own experts, and finally decided to grant the employers only a 5% decrease in the daily wage. However, the court imposed this seemingly small cut after the government had already decreed a general wage reduction of 10%. Thus, the relation of 5% plus 10% to 30% spelled out the right-down-the-middle wisdom so endemic to the arbitration of labor disputes everywhere.[56]

The large number of individual grievances processed at the syndical level and the record of the *preture* and *tribunali* in disposing of complaints which reached the courts, while impressive, could not compensate Italian workers for the loss of grievance committees elected directly by them. Intimate, omnipresent, and sensitive to the needs of their constituents, the committees had begun to offer, during the era of free unions, an informal, knowledgeable, and potentially rapid alternative to the involved, lengthy, and costly system elaborated under fascism. Employers, despite the efforts of fascist unions to reinstate shop stewards, resisted these demands until 1939 when shop stewards (*fiduciari di azienda*) and departmental representatives (*corrispondenti di reparto*) reappeared on the industrial scene. The collective agreement of October 12, 1939 extended to them the special considerations afforded union officials and leaders in case of transfer or dismissal. But the new brand of shop stewards had no direct contact with management. Appointed after Fascist Party approval by fascist union officers from among members who also belonged to the Fascist Party, the shop stewards merely transmitted grievances and decisions between the factory and the union or Fascist Party headquarters.

Another approach to swifter resolution of important factory issues at the plant level stemmed from the 1937 regulations on piecework. Based upon the provisions of the national agreement on piecework which prohibited every kind of incentive wage except piecework, they permitted the creation of joint technical committees (*collegi tecnici*), composed of labor and management syndical representatives and a government labor expert who served as the impartial chairman. The joint technical committees handled grievances over piecework and possessed exclusive authority to render decisions. Other joint technical committees, especially constituted for the purpose, dealt with individual complaints about job classifications. Late additions to the corporative structure, the committees represented the most direct participation ever achieved by fascist unions in the administration of collective agreements and labor legislation within the plant. But these essentially democratic responses to the exigencies of modern factory life could not withstand the prior claims of the Fascist State. Under the code of civil procedure enacted in 1941, the dogma of the "exclusive jurisdiction" of the judiciary over civil matters celebrated its triumph, and even the joint committees for the settlement of piecework disputes were stripped of all decision-making authority. The last stone had thus been added to the construction of a formally perfect judicial system which, despite its actual ineffectiveness, has nevertheless persisted up to the present day.[57]

The power of the nation's courts necessarily expanded under the state-controlled corporative system of labor relations and the atmosphere of open fascist scorn for democratic principles and procedures. Indeed, by 1939, the Duce found that he could no longer tolerate an elected Chamber of Deputies even though Italian voters merely designated their choice, on a take-it-or-leave-it basis, from the single list of 400 names carefully culled by the Fascist Grand Council from 1,000 nominees. Law 129 of January 19 called for an appointed Chamber of Fasci and Corporations. Mussolini wished to discourage the faintest notion, which controlled elections might still possibly foster, that the people retained ultimate political power. Under these circumstances, grievance procedures could hardly escape autocratic centralism and focus in the shops among the people who worked there. Despite the antidemocratic spirit which infused all aspects of the corporative system of labor relations in accordance with Mussolini's philosophy of the State, fascism managed to bequeath to the Republic of 1946 more than its concept of the judiciary's paternalistic role in maintaining industrial peace. It also surrendered rich stores of labor legislation, so often confused in Latin countries with the actual accomplishment of statutory purpose, and its trained corps of experts, as innocent of the meaning of everyday democracy as they were astute in the survival tactics of bureaucratic services. Moreover, fascism handed down, virtually untouched, its system of industry-wide collective bargaining.

Under fascism, industrial bargaining units broadened as the category federations decreased from 60 during 1921 to 47 during 1926 and then to 20 by 1939 in consonance with Italy's economic structure and labor markets. Then, too, after the establishment of syndical confederations for whole segments of the economy — industry, commerce, agriculture, credit and insurance, and the professions and arts — these inclusive associations negotiated interconfederal accords like the family allowance accord of 1934 which covered all industrial establishments in the nation and the accord of December 20, 1937 which laid down regulations on piecework payments throughout industry and served as the basis for the piecework provisions in articles 2100 and 2101 in the Civil Code of 1942. These interconfederal accords were to gain as wide acceptance under the Republic as the category agreements which catered, under fascism, to the needs of particular branches of industry, like textiles, the building trades, and the metallurgical and mechanical crafts. The category-wide collective agreements usually concentrated on fringe benefits, apprenticeship rules, hours of work, holidays and vacations, seniority, overtime pay, disciplinary procedures, layoffs, and discharges. These terms restated, in part, existing legislative clauses. Supplementary provincial labor agreements determined wages since the cost of living varied widely among different areas of the country. At times, provincial agreements also encompassed minor local usages. Notwithstanding these formal procedures for the provincial determination of wages, the central government inevitably dictated the real decisions. Gino Giugni has admirably summarized the entire process of labor relations under the Corporative State:

> Bargaining developed along bureaucratic and legalistic channels, followed a flat regional, zonal, or national pattern, and by establishing

minimum rates and standards suited to the least efficient producers, came to act as a protective device for marginal enterprises.[58]

To achieve this niggardly end while Italian labor suffered both from unemployment and decline in real wages, the corporative system forced the democratic knowledge and skills of the factory to give way entirely before the fascist bureaucracies of unions, of Party, and of State. The resurgence of political democracy after World War II restored free unions to Italy, but could not eradicate the hankering of feeble labor organizations for shortcuts to progress: national interconfederal accords, category-wide agreements, highly centralized union administration, and crucial weakness at the very heart of the movement — the workshop, yard, and plant.

FOOTNOTES — CHAPTER IX

For a succinct discussion of the theory and practice of fascism, Mussolini's foreign policy, the drift toward war, and Italy's military and political defeat, see Mack Smith, cited above, pp. 389–492.

[1] Appendix A, Table 8, of this volume.

[2] Appendix A, Table 7; see also *Annuario statistico italiano 1932*, pp. 88–89, 92; *Annuario statistico italiano 1933*, p. 73; *Annuario statistico italiano 1942*, pp. 140–141; *Sommario* . . ., cited above, pp. 77–78.

[3] Appendix A, Table 4; *Sommario* . . ., cited above, pp. 69–75.

[4] For the index numbers given on railroad electrification, see Welk, cited above, p. 203, and for the actual kilometrage cited for 1934 and 1938, see *Annuario statistico italiano 1935*, p. 94 and *Annuario statistico italiano 1939*, p. 122. For the national highway figures cited, see Appendix A, Table 10; *Annuario statistico italiano 1943*, p. 104. For other data enumerated, see Appendix A, Table 11; *Sommario* . . ., cited above, pp. 136–137, 149, 151.

[5] Freemantle, cited above, pp. 243–249; Jemolo, cited above, pp. 634–666; Salvatorelli and Mira, cited above, pp. 419–505.

[6] For the data upon which the 1920–1921 data were based, see *Annuario statistico italiano 1919–1921*, p. 464. For 1931–1932 data, see *Annuario statistico italiano 1933*, pp. 341, 346. For 1935–1936 data, see *Annuario statistico italiano 1937*, p. 206. For 1938–1939 data, see *Annuario statistico italiano 1941*, pp. 239, 242. The costs for all years, except 1935–1936, included ordinary, extraordinary, and capital movement expenditures. In 1935–1936, due to the exigencies of war, of a total budget of 66,923,399,000 lire, 33,866,477,000 lire consisted of capital movement expenditures; 33,471,258,000 lire of this latter sum were charged against the Ministry of Finance. By including this element, distorting because of its unusual size, the proportion of the national budget devoted to the army, navy, and air force calculates out to but 19.1%, as against the more realistic figure, 38.6%, when expenditures for capital movements are omitted.

[7] Salvatorelli and Mira, cited above, pp. 776–844.

[8] The same, pp. 844–999.

[9] Confindustria, *L'Industria italiana alla metà del secolo XX*, pp. 164–166, 184; Gualberto Gualerni, *La politica industriale fascista*, Vol. 1, pp. 75–98; Felice Guarneri, *Battaglie economiche tra le due grandi guerre*, Vol. 1, pp. 305–318; Welk, cited above, pp. 168–169.

441

[10] Appendix A, Tables 17 and 27; see also, League of Nations, *Industrialization and Foreign Trade*, p. 134.

[11] Welk, cited above, p. 162.

[12] Guarneri, cited above, p. 154.

[13] *Annuario statistico italiano 1930*, p. 254.

[14] Salvatorelli and Mira, cited above, pp. 355–357, 382–385.

[15] Gualerni, cited above, p. 13; Guarneri, cited above, pp. 160–161.

[16] Appendix A, Tables 17 and 27; see also, League of Nations, cited above, p. 134.

[17] Appendix A, Tables 17 and 27; see also, League of Nations, cited above, p. 134.

[18] League of Nations, cited above, p. 160; Confindustria, cited above, p. 137; Welk, cited above, pp. 165–166, 231–232.

[19] Welk, cited above, pp. 167–170.

[20] Gualerni, cited above, pp. 52–74, 135–137.

[21] For the annual costs of land reclamation projects, see *Annuario statistico italiano 1941*, p. 96. For hydroelectric power production data, see Welk, cited above, p. 200. For the figures upon which the calculations for total public works expenditures were based, see *Annuario statistico italiano 1919–1921*, p. 464 and *Annuario statistico italiano 1933*, p. 341.

[22] Guarneri, cited above, pp. 287–297.

[23] Welk, cited above, pp. 171–179.

[24] Appendix A, Table 18.

[25] Appendix A, Table 20.

[26] Appendix A, Table 21.

[27] See Appendix A, Table 15, for consumer-producer goods proportions of employment. The North-South calculations for 1927 were based upon the figures of the industrial census of October 15, 1927 presented in the *Annuario statistico italiano 1928*, pp. 142–143. The regions comprising North Italy were: Piedmont, Liguria, Lombardy, Venezia Tridentina, Veneto, Venezia Giulia and Zara, and Emilia. The following classifications were excluded from the totals of the regions just named and from the grand total for the nation as a whole: fishing; hygienic, sanitary, and urban sanitation services; and transportation and communication. The total obtained upon this basis, 3,338,071, differed slightly from the Confindustria 1927 total of 3,302,400 used to compute percentage distributions among various industrial classifications. For the 1937–1939 statistics, see Confindustria, cited above, p. 83. This total also differed slightly from the 1937–1939 total Confindustria itself used to compute percentages of distribution among various industrial classifications — 4,058,170 as against 4,162,500.

[28] Appendix A, Table 25.

[29] Appendix A, Table 13.

[30] Appendix A, Table 12.

[31] Appendix A, Table 14.

[32] Welk, cited above, pp. 191–192; *Annuario statistico italiano 1941*, p. 96. As early as 1923, the National Forest Act, enacted that year, stimulated the State's program for the preservation and extension of the country's forests.

[33] *Annuario statistico italiano 1944*, Supplemento N. 1, "Agricoltura e Foreste," September 1944, p. 12; *Sommario . . .*, cited above, pp. 106, 159; Welk, cited above, pp. 191–195.

[34] *Sommario . . .*, cited above, pp. 110, 196, 198, 229–233; see also, Appendix A, Tables 5 and 6.

[35] *Annuario statistico italiano 1941*, p. 278; Welk, cited above, pp. 184–185.

[36] For internal migration statistics, see Welk, cited above, p. 187; *Annuario statistico italiano 1937*, p. 174; *Annuario statistico italiano 1938*, p. 191; and *Annuario statistico italiano 1941*, p. 209. For emigration statistics, see *Sommario . . .*, cited above, pp. 65, 68. See also, Welk, cited above, pp. 182–187, and Appendix A, Table 3.

[37] The total of postal savings deposits in 1920 amounted to 3,882,303,481 lire, while emigrant deposits that year amounted to 1,326,570,469. See *Annuario statistico italiano 1919–1921*, p. 409. Comparable figures for 1921 were 3,797,612,074 and 915,734,031. See *Annuario statistico italiano 1919–1921*, p. 409. The figures for 1931 were 5,589,891,000 and 424,915,000. See *Annuario statistico italiano 1933*, p. 371. For 1939, the comparable figures were 8,788,834,000 and 109,687,000. See *Annuario statistico italiano 1941*, p. 224. For the figures on emigrant remittances for 1928 and 1932, see *Annuario statistico italiano 1933*, p. 376. For remittance figures for 1935, see *Annuario statistico italiano 1936*, p. 160.

[38] Appendix A, Table 2; *Annuario statistico italiano 1919–1921*, p. 30; *Annuario statistico italiano 1934*, p. 8; *Annuario statistico italiano 1955*, p. 19.

[39] Welk, cited above, p. 189.

[40] For English translations of these documents, or summaries of their principal contents, except for law 129 of January 19, 1939, see Welk, cited above, pp. 253–329.

[41] Herbert W. Schneider, *Making the Fascist State*, p. 191. For accounts concerning the legislative and administrative basis for the corporate system of labor-management relations and for detailed descriptions of the operation of the system, see the following publications: Confederazione Fascista dei Lavoratori dell'Industria, *Organizzazione sindacale e ordinamento corporativo*, Serie B, N. 1; G. Lowell Field, *The Syndical and Corporative Institutions of Italian Fascism;* L. Rosenstock-Franck, *L'Economie corporative fasciste en doctrine et en fait: ses origines historiques et son évolution;* Herbert W. Schneider, *Making the Fascist State*, pp. 138–214, *The Fascist Government of Italy*, pp. 66–100; William G. Welk, cited above, pp. 43–155, and the documents, regulations, and legislation reproduced in English in Appendix I, pp. 253–329.

[42] Welk, cited above, p. 63.

[43] *Annuario statistico italiano 1941*, p. 205; law 563 of April 3, 1926, article 5; royal decree 1130 of July 1, 1926, section III, articles 23 to 28.

[44] *Annuario statistico italiano 1933*, pp. 341, 346; *Annuario statistico italiano 1941*, pp. 239, 242.

[45] *Annuario statistico italiano 1941*, p. 205.

[46] Welk, cited above, p. 117.

[47] The same, p. 117.

[48] Appendix A, Tables 30 and 33; Welk, cited above, pp. 178, 232–233, 238, 240, footnote 14, 241.

[49] *Annuario statistico italiano 1934*, pp. 191, 193; *Annuario statistico italiano 1941*, pp. 256–267; Roselli, cited above, Vol. 1, p. 421; Welk, cited above, pp. 96–99, 242, footnote 15.

[50] Welk, cited above, pp. 241–242.

[51] Law 563 of April 3, 1926, section III, articles 18–23; Welk, cited above, p. 89; *Annuario statistico italiano 1940*, p. 94; *Annuario statistico italiano 1941*, p. 320.

[52] Welk, cited above, p. 145; *Annuario statistico italiano 1941*, p. 208.

[53] Law 563 of April 3, 1926, section II, articles 13–17; *Annuario statistico italiano 1942*, p. 178.

[54] *Annuario statistico italiano 1941*, pp. 206–207.

[55] *Annuario statistico italiano 1941*, p. 318.

[56] Welk, cited above, p. 84.

[57] Gino Giugni, "Bargaining Units and Labor Organization in Italy," *Industrial and Labor Relations Review*, Vol. 10, No. 3 (April 1957), pp. 428–430.

[58] Gino Giugni, cited above, p. 431.

X

The Future Unfolds: Allied Military Government to Postwar Boom

The Wages of Freedom

THE Allied armies first waded through the clear invasion waters of the Mediterranean onto the mined beaches of the southern coast of Sicily on July 10, 1943. Nearly 100 American military government officers, armed with 12 proclamations and general orders designed to restore peace and freedom to Italy, landed with the 1st, 3rd, and 45th Divisions and Seventh Army Headquarters at Gela, Licata, and Scoglitti, while civil affairs detachments of the Eighth Army went ashore near Catania. On July 22, after a breath-taking dash across the Island, General George Patton entered unresisting Palermo. In Rome, the Fascist Grand Council, after a meeting which started during the late afternoon of July 24 and ended at 2:40 a.m. on Sunday, July 25, supported Count Dino Grandi's resolution by a vote of 19 to 7 (the president of the Senate abstained and Roberto Farinacci supported his own proposal). The motion advocated the King's resumption of his constitutional position as supreme commander over the nation's armed forces on land and sea and in the air. The nominal supreme source of fascist power, the Grand Council, which Mussolini had not called into session since December 1939, surmised that the Allies might more reasonably endure moderate fascist representatives of the King, should Italy sue for peace, than deputations branded with the militancy of classic fascism. Nor did the Grand Council underestimate the political advantage of associating the King with the Party's calamitous war. But the Grand Council acted in haste and could not foresee the extreme crisis it would provoke since it had heard rumors about the palace plot against the Duce without fully realizing the determined strength and scope of that conspiracy.

At five o'clock on Sunday afternoon, July 25, Mussolini reached the Villa Savoia; King Victor Emmanuel III received him shortly thereafter. That weak King, Mussolini's creature since 1922, boldly informed the Prime Minister of his dismissal and of the appointment of his successor, Marshal Pietro Badoglio. After the audience ended and Mussolini emerged from the palace, *carabinieri* took courteous and protective charge of him. They carried the Dictator off in a Red Cross vehicle for imprisonment first on the island of Ponza, then on the island of Maddalena, and finally in the fastness of Campo Imperatore on Monte Corno, the highest peak of the Gran Sasso in the Apennines. He remained prisoner at this holiday resort high above Aquila in the Abruzzi until Captain Otto Skorzeny, at the head of a German mission sent expressly by Hitler, rescued him on September 12 in a glider operation of daring imagination.

At the moment when Badoglio took office, he, his colleagues, and the King recognized two dangers and feared their certainty: resistance to the new government by loyal fascists and, simultaneously, revolutionary uprisings by antifascists. The action of the Grand Council should have intimated that the protracted war and the Allied victories in Africa and Sicily had demoralized more than the fascist masses. Certainly, their leaders had demonstrated no faith in the capacity of fascism to save either the nation or their own superior necks. By contrast, anxiety over left-wing insurrection at first seemed justified. Important elements of public opinion held the fascist hierarchs, who had saluted Mussolini until the last hour of crisis, responsible for the country's disaster and also refused to absolve the King and his private counselors from sharing that guilt. When the clandestine antifascist political groups met openly on July 26 for the first time in twenty years, they instinctively reanimated the joint bodies which had sought so tardily to defend liberty against dictatorship in 1924. The new committees of national liberation included representatives of the Christian Democrats, the Democracy of Labor (by and large, the successors of the radicals), the republicans, the socialists, the liberals, the communists, and the disciples of the Party of Action, the heirs of the Justice and Liberty movement. Carlo Rosselli had organized that defiant operation in exile at Paris and strove, until Mussolini's thugs assassinated him and his brother, Nello, the historian, to reconcile the liberal and socialist traditions in the transcendent synthesis of liberal socialism. Of these six parties, the communists, the socialists, and the adherents of the Action Party vigorously opposed the monarchy and advocated a republic.

The appeal of the Milan Committee of National Liberation, published at the end of its inaugural meeting on July 26, epitomized the spirit of the antifascist parties throughout the country. It called for the complete extermination of fascism and its oppressive institutions; an honorable peace; the restoration of civil and political liberties, especially freedom of the press; immediate amnesty for political prisoners; the re-establishment of a scrupulous system of justice untainted by summary proceedings, but severely fair when dealing with those responsible for fascist crimes; and the abolition of the racial laws. Although the left-wing parties of the Milan committee, particularly the communists, demanded the immediate formation of a government representative of all the antifascist parties, other committees elsewhere, led by Rome, recognized the wisdom of leaving Marshal Badoglio in temporary command to arrange for the withdrawal of Italy from the war. However, Ivanoe Bonomi, the head of the committee at Rome, counselled Badoglio against a completely non-political ministry. Nonetheless, Badoglio yielded to the fears of the King and named a cabinet of technicians.

Italians wanted an end to war and confusion. They yearned for peace instead of revolutionary uprisings. Under Badoglio's uninspired leadership, a synthetic philosophy, an elaborate administrative system, an empire, and an operatic new social order — the entire Fascist Revolution — quietly and ignominiously dissolved. In a series of decrees issued between July 29, 1943 and August 7, 1943 the government abolished the Special Tribunal for the Defense of the State, the Fascist Grand Council, the Chamber of Fasci and Corporations, and the National Fascist Party. To insure public order, the authorities prohibited the formation of political parties, enjoined the publication of new newspapers, and continued press censorship. Royal decree 718 of August 9, 1943 transformed the Ministry of Corporations into the Ministry of Industry, Commerce and Labor, and royal decree 721 of the same date abolished the National Council of Corporations, the Central Corporative Committee, the corporations, and their entire spawn of subordinate bodies. It also abrogated those sections of law 563 of April 3, 1926 and of the regulations contained in royal decree 1130 of July 1, 1926 which furnished the legal basis for labor relations under the Corporative State. The mediation of labor-management disputes could no longer await the initiative of the conciliation committee of each corporation, as fixed by the legislation of February 5, 1934. Instead, the government empowered the Ministry of Industry, Commerce and Labor to constitute ad hoc conciliation boards for industrial controversies suited to their individual natures. Labor unions and employer associations could continue to conclude collective bargaining contracts. These agreements assumed the force of law not only with regard to the signatory syndical associations, but also with reference to individual employers and workers within the covered categories whenever the Council of Ministers recommended a royal decree to specify approval.[1]

Meanwhile, Badoglio and the King applied consummate ineptitude to their almost hopeless mission of shifting Italy's war allegiance without assuring German seizure of the peninsula. They squandered precious days in strategic procrastination by refusing to recognize that Italy possessed neither the spiritual strength nor the material resources to continue at war and could not bargain realistically with the Allies for less than unconditional surrender. Their pride, illusions, caution, and blind hope to deal with the British and Americans as equals slightly surpassed the folly of Allied inability to act wisely and with generosity toward enemies who had complotted but recently in their imminent destruction. Arduous wartime difficulties of communications, misunderstandings, hesitations, and delays piled up to strengthen the Germans. Badoglio described his failure to establish consolidated positions of defense as a ruse to deceive the nazis, but they never doubted for a moment that Badoglio aimed to bring his country into the war on the side of the Allies. Immediately upon Mussolini's fall, they pushed additional troops into Italy, but could only hope, at first, to mass their forces behind an imaginary line stretching from Pisa to Rimini. Then, during the five weeks which elapsed between Badoglio's first contact with the Allies and September 3, the day his emissary finally signed the armistice document, the gift of time served the Germans well. By September 8, when Badoglio addressed the nation by radio at 7:30 that evening and told of the peace he had achieved, the nazis had funneled enough manpower through the Brenner Pass to lay hold of Rome shortly afterward and to offer stiff resistance, later, to the Allied landings south of Naples. During the early morning hours of September 9, as American troops struck the beaches at Salerno, the royal family, its entourage, the Premier of Italy, and his officials left Rome by motor convoy. Upon arrival in Pescara on the Adriatic, they sailed for Brindisi where the government first found seat before it moved, next, to Bari and, subsequently, to Salerno.

In the North, the German troops protected another Italian government. In a series of six Orders of the Day issued between September 15 and 17, Mussolini Unbound brought the fire of a fresh brand of fascism to his beloved people and installed himself, with Hitler's contemptuous support, as the head of the Social Republic of Salò on Lake Garda. Now,

Italy endured triple rule. North and Central Italy suffered the puppet régime of the nazis. In the South and the Islands, the Badoglio government held sway only over limited areas which the Allied Control Commission handed over to form King's Italy. But even in those provinces, the Allied Control Commission exercised prior sanction over all laws and decrees. Elsewhere, the British and American military government officers ministered directly to the civil needs of the population.

In King's Italy, the syndical confederations and federations of workers and employers escaped the drastic purge applied to other fascist institutions and retained legal life. Badoglio wished to place the membership, property, and funds of these organizations under the supervision of government functionaries. However, Bruno Buozzi, the former leader of the metal-mechanical workers before Mussolini's triumph and the last general secretary of C.G.L., had smuggled himself into Italy from exile during World War II. He now opposed Badoglio's plan by protesting that civil servants would have neither the will and capacity to de-bureaucratize the fascist labor federations, nor the prestige among workers to convert these organizations into a free labor movement. Achille Grandi, the leader of the Catholic textile workers in pre-fascist days and the last general secretary of C.I.L., who represented the Christian Democratic forces, and Giovanni Roveda, who spoke for the communist current, supported their socialist colleague in full accord. Since both Marshal Badoglio and the King knew that fascism had tainted them and that they could flourish no greater warranty of their devotion to democracy than the restoration of free labor unions, they heeded Buozzi's admonitions. The government appointed Bruno Buozzi as commissioner of the Confederation of Industrial Workers, while Roveda and Gioacchino Quarello (1892–   ), the leader of the pre-fascist Christian metal-mechanical workers, became vice-commissioners. Then followed the designation of Achille Grandi, Giuseppe Di Vittorio (1892–1957), Oreste Lizzadri (1896–   ), and Guido De Ruggiero (1888–1948) as commissioners and vice-commissioners for the Confederation of Agricultural Workers, the Confederation of Commercial Workers, and the Confederation of Professional Men and Artists. By serving in responsible positions of authority within these huge associations, the veteran labor leaders aimed to hold intact their membership and machinery of organization. They also aspired to conserve the wealth acquired by the fascist unions during the twenty years of Mussolini's rule in the form of property, liquid funds, and economic, welfare, and recreational institutions. Their expectations proved too sanguine, for the largest share of labor dues and riches concentrated in North and Central Italy where the Republic of Salò soon took command. Nonetheless, the successful collaboration in this venture among the three principal political currents of the antifascist labor movement stirred fresh hopes for gain beyond estimate or price: the formal unity of the Italian labor movement.[2]

Marshal Badoglio must have counted upon his gesture of friendship toward the antifascist labor leaders to recommend the monarchy to the favor of northern workers. In factories at Turin and Milan, they had struck ten times between August and December 1942 despite corporative prohibitions. In January and February 1943, 11 more strikes threatened to disrupt the fascist war economy. Then, on March 5, 1943, the first significant strike of the war, ordered by the Communist Party and led by Giovanni Roveda, broke out at the Fiat Mirafiori plant in Turin. It spread to other large factories of Piedmont, Lombardy, Liguria, and the lower Po Valley. In Milan, the strike shut down the factories of Pirelli, Breda, Borletti, and Marelli. The fascists made their peace with the strikers by conceding the wage increases demanded by them. However, as food supplies contracted, as the cost of living mounted, and as the government insisted upon the continuation of work during factory air attacks by the Allies, more severe strikes agitated North Italy in the autumn. The massive bombardment of the Villar Perosa plants and the deaths it bestrewed touched off the complete cessation of work at Mirafiori, S.P.A., and Michelin in November. All Turin took to the streets to demand a 100% increase in wages, the doubling of rations for soup ingredients, a daily liter of milk for children, and the right to cease work during aerial assaults. The authorities granted inadequate concessions and the workers soon resumed strike action. In Milan and in the manufacturing centers of Liguria, artisans joined their factory brothers to demonstrate their class solidarity. To a man, they staged these protests in the teeth of fascist and nazi bayonets. In South Italy, Badoglio and the King must have viewed with mingled respect and fear the militant spirit of these northern workers. To what lengths would such men and women not go when free, unless they had sure evidence that the government of liberation respected their rights as well as their strength?[3]

Shortly after the free trade unionists assumed their roles as commissioners of the ex-fascist labor organizations, the Badoglio government, in August 1943, urged the officers of the General Confederation of Italian Industry and the Confederation of Industrial Workers to seek industrial peace by re-creating those factory institutions which might encourage cooperation. Under the auspices of the Minister of Industry, Commerce and Labor, the representatives of the employers, Giuseppe Mazzini and Fabio Friggeri, met with commissioners Buozzi, Roveda, and Quarello.

449

Together, they worked toward an agreement which would give concrete expression to the fresh spirit of national unity as well as to the principle of labor-management alliance in the face of the twin enemy: fascism and nazism. On September 2, 1943, six days before Badoglio announced the armistice, these men placed their names upon the first voluntary inter-confederal accord concluded after two decades of economic dictatorship. It provided for the rebirth of grievance committees (*commissioni interne*) in the nation's industrial plants. The signers of this pioneering document, known as the Buozzi-Mazzini accord, scheduled the agreement to remain in force for three years.

The 1943 accord conferred upon grievance committees more duties than they had performed in earlier days. The relatively short and general statement entrusted to the committees responsibilities for collective bargaining as well as the adjustment of disputes attendant upon the application of the agreement. The terms of the document also urged the committees to propose possible improvements in production methods, enabled them to participate in the administration of jointly financed insurance and social institutions within the factory, and encouraged them to formulate proposals for the improvement of technical instruction and welfare services.[4]

Outside of King's Italy, in those areas of the South still under the authority of Allied Military Government, the conduct of labor relations and the character of unions differed sharply from the developments associated with the policy adopted by the Badoglio government at the suggestion of Bruno Buozzi and his colleagues. On October 1, 1943, A.M.G. razed the entire fascist corporative structure in Sicily. In democracy's name, the Allies decreed, overnight, freedom of association and the labor market. With the elimination of all fascist agencies which had supervised the corporative treasure-trove of labor laws, administered social security measures, and provided job placement services, the Allies found themselves constrained to create provincial and regional labor offices and to permit the resuscitation of the pre-fascist chambers of labor. Since the Armed Forces needed Italian manpower and constituted the only substantial employer in South Italy, the labor offices acted as public employment bureaus and as the field representatives of the Ministry of Industry, Commerce and Labor. In addition, labor office personnel busied themselves with labor relations, the collection of statistics, and the details of social security. Under the guidance of A.M.G. officers, they also sought to revive the free labor movement.

At the end of 1943, and during the first half of 1944, the Badoglio government attempted to reconstruct, as best it could, the administrative framework of the State. Among other tasks, it caused public insurance and assistance institutes to resume their functions, decreed wage increases on December 28, 1943 to all workers on permanent payrolls covered by collective bargaining agreements, and nominated a royal commission on March 15, 1944 to study the forms of insurance and social security preliminary to undertaking basic changes in the legislation then in force.

During the German occupation of Rome, Buozzi and Grandi, at peril to their lives whenever they came out of hiding, continued the efforts initiated by Giovanni Gronchi in 1941 and 1942 and pressed for agreement among communist, socialist, and Christian Democratic labor leaders. In the liberated South, unity did not prevail everywhere. Although the labor movement of Apulia managed to avoid schisms, in Naples, where the Party of Action inspired the General Confederation of Labor, the Christian Democratic workers remained apart. Toward the end of 1943, 370 labor delegates gathered at Bari, deliberated the establishment of a free labor organization, and appointed a provisional committee to lay the bases of its foundation. In February 1944, two congresses met at Salerno. One, under socialist and communist inspiration, revived the C.G.L. originally founded in 1906. The other, under Christian Democratic guidance, brought the C.I.L. back to life. Nevertheless, on March 11, 1944, the leading groups in South Italy agreed upon provisions for coordinating administration and membership drives.[5]

From his tiny capital by the waters of Lake Garda, safe from the perils of Italian life everywhere else in 1943 and 1944, Mussolini prepared to stir up mass faith in his salvaging operations. He now emphasized the socialistic bent of republican fascism, for he hoped to attract the allegiance of the industrialized North's class-conscious workers. Mussolini announced that the constitution of Salò would affirm the right of workers to participate in the management and profits of industry. But his newfound socialism emerged stillborn. The Salò constitution never evolved into an effective instrument of government; most decrees published under its authority received whole numbers and the most fractional enforcement. Despite the disjointed time, the Salò Republic tried frantically to popularize itself into respectability. Point 12 in the Eighteen-Point Declaration presented to the National Republican Fascist Party at its meeting in Verona on November 18, 1943 authorized the creation of councils of administration (*consigli di gestione*) in all private, public, and parastatal industrial plants. Representatives of technical employees, workers, and the government would serve on these councils. Unlike most of the ephemeral schemes proclaimed by the Salò Republic, the idea of councils of administration, already embedded in the minds of Italian workers since 1919 and 1920, stirred, stretched, and moved forward to derange the period of reconstruction after the liberation of the North in 1945.

Mussolini need not have encouraged these ventures gratuitously since they aided only his bitterest adversaries and failed to spare him or his régime. Under the noses of the nazis and fascists, provisional labor committees, largely dominated by the highly disciplined communists and left-wing socialists, and necessarily appointed from political heights since they had to operate clandestinely, organized strikes and demonstrations, perpetrated acts of successful sabotage against production vitally needed by the Germans, and laid plans for the establishment of chambers of labor and category unions immediately after Allied victory. (Months after the enemy had departed, many provisional labor committees of revolutionary bent refused to disband even when peace called for their democratic election.) The general strike of March 1, 1944, remarkable in its daring, attested to the underground efficiency of the committees. It brought out of factories, plants, shops, stores, and offices 70,000 workers in Turin, 150,000 men and women in all Piedmont, and over 1,000,000 participants in North Italy.

Up to the end of 1943, Badoglio's government still consisted wholly of technicians since the King feared that the inclusion of representatives of even the most conservative parties would provide communism with a logical wedge to force its way into the cabinet. The Allies came to realize, slowly and reluctantly, for they had grown fond of Badoglio despite his doubtful past, that the government needed a broad political basis if it ever hoped to stir the imagination and loyalty of the large mass of Italians. Six parties had acquired the foremost political authority then present at Naples although, clearly, the South could not boast party leaders of national renown and stature since most of them concentrated in Rome and the North. The communists, socialists, Action Party members, Christian Democrats, Democracy of Labor adherents, and liberals formed the popularly esteemed Committee of National Liberation where they cooperated closely. When they requested permission to hold a national convention in Naples on December 20, the Allied Military Government authorities refused, since their regulations prohibited political meetings in A.M.G. territory. Therefore, the Allied Control Commission, anxious to infuse the Italian government with the prestige commanded by the Committee of National Liberation, persuaded Marshal Badoglio to allow the congress to take place at Bari in King's Italy. There, the first free political assembly in twenty years met on January 28, 1944.

Under the stimulus of its most distinguished participants, Benedetto Croce and Count Carlo Sforza, the congress went into opposition and demanded responsible party government and the abdication of the King. Having spoken its collective mind, the convention adjourned, and the parties waited.

During the winter and the spring of 1944, when British and American soldiers scored hardly perceptible gains south of Rome at Anzio and Cassino, Victor Emmanuel also refused to budge. Since the Allies, under the influence of Winston Churchill's inflexible conviction, agreed to leave the Monarch undisturbed, certainly until the end of hostilities, the King alone could resolve the political stalemate. At the end of February 1944, Enrico De Nicola, while benefitting from Croce's constant advice, succeeded in ending the passive resistance of the King. Victor Emmanuel secretly agreed to turn over his powers, without formal abdication, to his son, Humbert (1904–   ), immediately upon the liberation of Rome. Two weeks later, Soviet Russia, ironically free of the scruples which prevented the six parties from serving the discredited Monarch, recognized the Badoglio government on March 14. Then, on March 26, Palmiro Togliatti, the chief commissar of Italian communism, arrived at Naples from Moscow. Countermanding the policy adopted by local communist leaders who had supported the other five parties in their attitude toward the King's continuance as the head of the State, on April 1 Togliatti brought into display the hard-headed realism imparted to him by his Moscow sojourn and insisted that the communists would accept office in any government in the overriding interests of the war effort.

The startling shift in the Party line left the second-string communist leaders embarrassed by the antipodal inconsistency from which they saw no escape. The spokesmen of the other five parties did retain freedom of choice, but they still lived in the shame of twenty years earlier, when their failure to cooperate made Mussolini supreme. Too, like many other Italians, they confused the strength of native communism with the strength of the Russian Red Army; they also magnified both the disadvantages to themselves of remaining outside the government and the benefits to the communists of holding a front-row seat. Instead of demonstrating political sagacity by placing the communists in an untenable position — an incongruous régime of the old King, the ex-fascist hero, Badoglio, and the proletarian communists — whence their countrymen and the rest of the world would have laughed them out of office, the other parties chose on April 6 to accept the King upon the basis of the De Nicola formula. On April 12, the King announced publicly his intention to comply with that proviso. The new six-party cabinet, with

Badoglio as Prime Minister, met on April 27 and announced that all political currents would prosecute the war effort in unison and would postpone the institutional question until the end of hostilities.

The Allied troops entered Rome on June 4, 1944. The King signed over his powers to Humbert who became the Lieutenant General of the Realm. To politically astute A.M.G. officers, and to most Italians, the fall of Rome meant the fall of Badoglio. On the façade of the Marshal's house in the Eternal City, Mussolini, who presented the palace to him as a mark of the nation's gratitude, had emblazoned the words, for all Rome and the world to see, that Badoglio, at the head of his troops, had entered Addis Ababa on May 5, 1936. In contrast to that warrior's record of beneficial accommodation to the buffets of fate, the National Committee of Liberation at Rome, under the presidency of Ivanoe Bonomi, went underground during the German occupation. Its patriotic dedication to organized resistance against the nazis exposed the committee's members to the daily peril of capture and endeared them to the people. Nonetheless, Lieutenant General Noel Mason MacFarlane, the Chief Commissioner of the Allied Council and the ablest individual ever to head that center of confusion, proceeded to Rome with Badoglio on June 8 under instructions to retain him as Prime Minister. The Marshal actually hoped to form a new government with representatives of the parties at Rome. General MacFarlane, who knew the realities of the political scene and recognized impossibilities, even if Churchill in London did not, yielded to the inevitable and the Allies accepted Bonomi. His ministry, announced on June 9, included members of the Rome Committee of Liberation, as well as Count Sforza, Croce, and other less notable figures of the South. The Allied Control Commission moved the seat of government to Rome on July 15.[6]

On June 3, 1944, the day before the first Allied soldiers reached the pine-silhouetted outskirts of Rome, Giuseppe Di Vittorio, Emilio Canevari (1880–   ), and Achille Grandi signed the *Declaration on the Realization of Labor "Unity,"* subsequently referred to as the Pact of Rome, for the communist, socialist, and Christian Democratic elements of the free labor movement now reborn as the General Italian Confederation of Labor (C.G.I.L.). Bruno Buozzi had not survived to place his name upon the agreement which crowned his long efforts and symbolized his most cherished hopes. Arrested and carted off with other prisoners for removal to the North, he fell into the hands of the Germans who shot him near La Storta, not far from Rome, on June 4.

The Pact of Rome limned out succinct structural and administrative guidelines for the resurgent unions: one confederation would league together all workers in Italy; labor in each class of economic activity would organize a national category federation; a single chamber of labor would serve each province and commune; one local and one provincial union for each recognized category would claim their own appropriate members in these geographical areas. The agreement also advocated democratic elections and proportional representation for minorities as guarantees of maximum freedom of expression by workers of every shade of political and religious conviction. Despite this pledge, the republican current did not sign the Pact because it opposed the key formula of representation by political factions. Since salvaging the wealth of the corporative unions figured prominently in the designs of the principals who formulated the Pact of Rome — vain hopes as long as those assets remained out of reach in the nazi-fascist North and while the Italian government and A.M.G. held on to that patrimony in the South — the labor leaders of the mass parties had excluded liberals and the Democracy of Labor from the agreement, although they participated in the national committees of liberation, on the ground that they had never engaged in union activities and could not claim traditional ties with the labor movement. Thus, only three organized political currents dominated the embryonic C.G.I.L.: the socialists, the communists, and the Christian Democrats. That euphoric and consentient political majority declared the Confederation independent of all parties, but reserved the right "to associate itself, whenever deemed opportune, with action of the democratic parties — the expression of the working masses — whether for the salvation and development of popular liberties, or for the defense of particular interests of workers and of the country." The *Declaration on the Realization of Labor "Unity"* also established a provisional directorate: a directive committee of fifteen members, five for each political group, and a general secretariat of three members, one from each political force: Achille Grandi, for the Christian Democrats, Giuseppe Di Vittorio for the communists, and Oreste Lizzadri for the socialists.[7]

During the second half of 1944, the reconstituted Confederation slowly began to mobilize its forces against harsh disadvantages. Di Vittorio summarized these obstacles in an address before the congress of labor organizations held in liberated Italy on September 15 and 16 at Rome. First, he observed, twenty years of dictatorship had dulled the political and union sensibilities of the people. Fascism and time had not only decimated the leaders of the free labor movement, but had also cancelled out an entire generation as a healthy source of replacements. Surviving officials of the old order saw only too clearly how distantly and faintly ran the parallels between the labor worlds of 1944 and 1919. Di Vittorio admitted that rank-and-file members with pre-fascist experience responded almost automatically to the call for participation in the revived unions. But the younger generation, who knew only the pseudo-unionism of the Corporative State, found the daily practice of democracy and its application to specific situations difficult to manage. War conditions, moreover, weighted these already heavy obstacles to organization by impeding communications between chambers of labor in even nearby provinces, as well as contact between the Confederation and its constituent bodies.

Di Vittorio then commented on the varied and contradictory legal arrangements of A.M.G. and the Italian government which enmeshed the labor movement. He called particular attention to King's Italy where provincial unions still functioned under their fascist officials and clerical staffs, while the fledgling democratic unions, desperately impoverished, could only envy the ample facilities and funds at the disposal of the corporative syndicates. Toward the end of his opening remarks on September 15, Di Vittorio spoke out prophetically against another weakness in the balanced growth of the Italian labor movement.

> Permit me, comrades, to hint at another defect in our organization which we have the duty to correct: this defect consists in the fact that while confederal chambers of labor sprang up immediately after liberation — and in many cases before liberation — we still have, in contrast, too few national category federations and the few which we have are far from being well organized or exercising regular functions. . . . Therefore, we must organize in a brief period of time national congresses of the most important branches of industry, agriculture, commerce, public services, and education in order to constitute national federations with a directive committee and a secretariat elected democratically by regional congresses of the interested unions.

Thus early, Di Vittorio forewarned the C.G.I.L. of a defect which later proved congenital.[8]

Black memories of fratricidal dissension before 1922, and the descent into exile or heavy homeland silence afterward, impelled the remnants of the free unions to close ranks. At the September Congress in Rome, the principle of unity drew the benediction of the international labor movement in the person of Walter Schevenels; of the British labor movement through the presence of Thomas O'Brien, a member of the executive committee of the Trade Union Congress, and Will Lawther, president of the National Miners Confederation; and of the labor movement in the United States through the participation of George Baldanzi of the Textile Workers Union of America, representing the C.I.O., and Luigi

Antonini, of the International Ladies' Garment Workers' Union, speaking for the A.F.L. Russia, emphasizing its own gesture of international good will toward unity in the Italian realm of labor, also despatched a trade union delegation to Rome. Between September 28 and November 14, 1944, the four Russian labor officials conferred with C.G.I.L. leaders, addressed assemblies called to welcome them, and visited unions in all parts of South Italy. By the time that the Inaugural Convention of the C.G.I.L. assembled at Naples on January 28, 1945, leaders of the American, British, Russian, and international labor movements, along with the chief figures in A.M.G., had, by their enthusiastic support, moved already fervent Italian unionists to transform the principle of labor unity into dogma. In that time of hope, the constitution adopted at Naples guaranteed that the Confederation would eschew every form of sectarianism and act independently of all political parties. Article 9 seemed assurance enough that the communists would respect the letter and spirit of the injunction:

> The independence of the unions from political parties and the State does not mean agnosticism of the unions with regard to all problems of a political nature. The C.G.I.L. will take a position on all those political problems which interest not merely this or that party, but rather the large mass of workers, such as the conquest and development of democracy and popular liberties, social legislation, and the reconstruction and economic development of the country, etc., and will defend solutions favorable to the interests of workers.[9]

The constitutional arrangements of the Confederation pledged joint participation in all major decisions by representatives of the three chief political currents and of the minorities as well. The formula of joint watchfulness applied at each level of C.G.I.L.'s hierarchical structure. Gradually, however, the communist secretaries and members of the directive committees and executive commissions succeeded in winning majority favor through their discipline, training, ability, single-minded dedication to the tasks at hand, and complete immunity from doubts or the moral restraints imposed by conscience. Achille Grandi, the Christian Democratic national secretary of C.G.I.L., for all his experience as the head of the Catholic textile workers in North Italy and as the general secretary of C.I.L. before fascism, could not match the hardened vigor of Giuseppe Di Vittorio. Grandi's age, virtue, and impaired strength, sapped by cancer, worked against him. Young Di Vittorio, flanked by communist cadres who, like himself, had mastered the Leninist skills of acquiring organizational control in the Italian underground and in the International Brigade during the Spanish Civil War, managed, within two years, to

457

capture the C.G.I.L. for the communists. The socialist national secretary, Lizzadri, who had participated bravely in the resistance movement, but brought to his office only limited union training, expressed the will of the members he served when he offered full cooperation to the communists. In the North, still held by the fascists and nazis, the communists also prevailed, not only through superior competence, but also through the simple expedient of attracting thousands of followers. They organized the largest partisan bands and through their bravery earned the respect of most citizens. In the factories, through the patriotic efforts of the provisional labor committees where the communists also displayed unusual courage and acumen, they won the loyalty of industrial workers. By the time that the Salò Republic crumbled and the Allies occupied the manufacturing centers of North Italy, communist prestige insured communist domination of the burgeoning unions there. When, on July 24 and 25, 1945, the First Congress of the Chambers of Labor of North Italy at Milan voted to affiliate with the C.G.I.L., the communists advanced firmly toward inevitable national command of the Italian labor movement.[10]

Before the liberation of the North, the Bonomi ministry had eased the position of the free unions under the jurisdiction of the Italian government by clarifying, if only negatively, their anomalous status. Decree law 369 of November 23, 1944 dissolved all fascist syndical organizations and abolished all association and union dues collected under the provisions of law 563 of April 3, 1926 and successive legislation. The decree also arranged for the nomination of liquidators to settle the affairs of those institutions and take charge of their assets. Happily inspired to avoid chaos, the decree preserved intact the provisions of collective agreements and accords, the judgments of the labor courts, and pertinent corporative rules and regulations, until modified by later government decision. Workers under the jurisdiction of the Lieutenant General of the Realm also won more tangible concessions of precedential influence: extra compensation for the high cost of living, the extension of the Christmas bonus to workers in private industry, and the provision of free or nominally priced meals at factory messes. But the redeemed union movement gained most signally when the government recognized its national importance by dividing the Ministry of Industry, Commerce and Labor and creating a separate Ministry of Labor and Social Insurance through decree law 377 of June 21, 1945, one day after Bonomi handed over the premiership to Ferruccio Parri.[11]

Meanwhile, in a desperate effort to win the loyalty of workers under the Salò Republic, Mussolini had not only encouraged the institution of councils of administration in industrial plants, but had also published a series of decrees between September 1944 and April 1945 which stipulated the eventual socialization of all enterprises with a capital of at least 1,000,000 lire or 100 workers. During this period, the Republic socialized 62 firms where the workers participated in managerial decisions and shared in the profits.[12] Mussolini's device, however unashamedly obvious, appealed even to nonfascist workers, for it rekindled their old hopes of 1919 and 1920 to control the factories of Italy. They had responded then, as if possessed, to political and social forces which aroused the aspirations of labor in all the leading industrialized countries of Europe, but most notably in Germany, where the Weimar Republic institutionalized the works councils, and in England, where postwar pressures assumed the more moderate form of the Whitley Council and shop steward movements. With the fall of the Salò régime after the German divisions capitulated to the Allied armies between April 29 and May 1, 1945, Italian workers once again acted out their part in the larger European drama. In Germany, codetermination took the lead. In England, the labor government nationalized basic industries and encouraged the extension of joint industrial councils. In France, where workers demanded plant committees and nationalization, the dénouement would closely resemble the eventual outcome in Italy. Caught up in this atmosphere of European working-class zeal and expectations, Italian socialist and communist labor leaders — this meant the C.G.I.L. itself — did not hesitate to make the establishment of councils of administration in every factory of the nation the major part of their post-World War II program. And so, within a generation, the aim of realizing immediate economic gains and defending collective bargaining agreements through the constructive use of grievance committees took on trivial guise as the seemingly momentous battle for the control by workers of Italian industry unfolded.

The cry of labor for factory control sounded with almost warranted appeal during the fervent days after the liberation of the North when partisans ruled the streets and commanded universal respect and favor. Secret committees of liberation had operated in the most important industrial plants under the sharp noses of the fascists and nazis. Very often, the committees acted with the consent of management. Alfredo Pizzoni (1894–1958), the banker-president of the Committee of National Liberation for North Italy, persuaded the Credito Italiano to extend loans to important companies like Falck and Pirelli. They, in turn, distributed these funds to the resistance movement. Enrico Falck (1899–1953), a Christian Democrat, encouraged the proliferation of communist cells among the 12,000 employees in his steel mills. Everywhere, factory committees of liberation, provisional labor committees, and organized political groups conspired to disrupt production schedules, to prevent the shipment of goods to Germany, and, like the Fiat workers in June 1944, to strike against German plans to remove the entire plant to the Reich — efforts of considerable consequence for the Allied war effort. They also exercised vigilance in those plants which collaborated with the enemy and collected evidence against them. In the final days before the nazi defeat, they saved many plants from destruction by the retreating Germans. As victory spread wing over the North, the factory committees of liberation, largely dominated by socialists and communists, emerged as the principal advocates of worker control. Indeed, large sections of the grateful population sympathized with their cause: those who saved the factories from harm should run them.

The zealous demand for councils of administration which seized the workers and labor leaders in the North contrasted strikingly with less industrialized Central and South Italy. There, grievance committees had continued to function in accordance with the Buozzi-Mazzini Accord of 1943; labor and management had conducted only somewhat vague discussions about wider participation by workers in factory operations.[13] But in the atmosphere of the North, thick with political and social rancor as well as with hope for a new economic order, grievance committees could not pursue the spirit of the contract which established them. They soon came to subserve party instructions. These instructions evidenced detailed interest in the future power of labor, but passed over grievance committees as ubiquitous reservoirs of daily strength. What politics failed to accomplish in eventually weakening the committees, the inevitable spread of postwar unemployment completed.

As early as April 17, 1945, the Committee of National Liberation for North Italy acted in haste, with the expectation that through haste it could present the Allies with an accomplished deed. It abolished the economic laws of the Salò Republic and declared inoperative those institutions created by Mussolini's legislation. However, the Committee reaffirmed the principle of worker participation in the profits and management of industrial concerns. It also conferred its blessings upon councils of administration and decreed the compulsory creation of new councils in those plants where none existed previously.[14] The Bonomi government in Rome had itself swept aside all provisions of the Salò Republic and did not recognize the Committee's decision of April 17. Nor, indeed, did A.M.G. acknowledge the Committee's action, once it occupied North Italy. This turn of events meant that councils of administration possessed no legal sanction. They could come to life only if the management of individual enterprises consented voluntarily to their establishment.[15]

Regardless of doubts about the legal status of councils of administration, the committees of liberation continued to function in almost all establishments, factories, and plants. They also took on fresh tasks with unabated moral, physical, and verbal force. The Allies, theoretically, had taken command, but regardless of A.M.G. decrees, orders, and proclamations, the committees of liberation not only controlled purges of fascists within shops and work places, but also tried to direct — and very often they succeeded admirably — the activities of the commissioners appointed by A.M.G. to supervise firms where managers and directors had tainted themselves through fascist and nazi collaboration. Within this environment of social and economic stress, the creation and operation of councils of administration became the leading political controversy of this chaotic period, so reminiscent of 1919 and 1920. The Communist and Socialist Parties, as well as the C.G.I.L., where left-wing leaders dominated their Catholic colleagues, strove to confer large powers upon the councils. They thought questions of cost and prices, productive capacity, employment and dismissal of workers, profits, investments, and even the use of raw materials, all proper subjects for discussion and control by workers. The Christian Democrats, on the other hand, while approving the councils of administration — in pre-fascist days, Giovanni Gronchi and Achille Grandi espoused the council idea as a powerful force to reduce social tensions, but did not contemplate the diminution of management's responsibilities and prerogatives — differed with the socialists and the communists on the degree of control which should be granted to them. They suggested labor-management councils which employers had to consult in the event of organizational and production changes, but they argued in vain. The loud demands for extreme measures drowned out their voices of moderation and submerged their terms of reasonable accommodation which alone possessed the possibility of acceptance by employers.

Meanwhile, the country awaited miracles of cleansing and invigorating endeavor from the Wind of the North, as represented by Ferruccio Parri's new government, installed at Rome on June 20, 1945. Instead of animating the State with moral authority, Parri and his ministers allowed political groups in the resistance movement to continue to usurp the powers and responsibilities of the central government. They also hesitated to act against military formations of partisans who refused to disband and permitted them, when they finally demobilized, to carry off arms and munitions for careful storage against the predestined day of revolution. The restless population, haunted by hunger and disappointment in the lagging pace of the millennium's arrival, staged frequent demonstrations and strikes. Late in 1945, the leaders of the Christian Democrats and liberals, their patience exhausted by constant socialist and communist attacks against them although they formed part of the coalition government, provoked a ministerial crisis. In resolution, Alcide De Gasperi (1881–1954), the head of the Christian Democratic Party, announced his first government on December 10, 1945. Both before and after this event, the socialists and communists, as members of the Parri and De Gasperi coalition governments, pressed for the legal recognition of councils of administration. De Gasperi's program, presented to Parliament in January 1946, hinted at possible legislative regularization of the status of the councils and their functions. The General Confederation of Italian Industry took a firmly adverse stand at this point and sent a letter, expressing these views, to De Gasperi, as the President of the Council of Ministers. A violent debate flared up in the press throughout the country. For the first time since Liberation, conservative voices, earlier silenced or muffled by the clamor for worker control, now began to assert themselves in opposition.[16]

Bitterness increased even more after the first free postwar national elections of June 2, 1946 when the voters favored a republic and, in choosing deputies to the Constituent Assembly, revealed the popular strength of the Christian Democratic, Socialist, and Communist Parties as well as the surprising weakness of the Action Party and the Democracy of Labor. The Constituent Assembly, with a mandate from the people to draft the constitution of the young Republic, met for the first time on June 25, 1946 and elected Giuseppe Saragat of the Socialist Party as its president. On June 28, Enrico De Nicola became the Provisional Head of the Italian Republic. De Nicola called upon De Gasperi, who had resigned, to form a new cabinet. De Gasperi announced his second government on July 13, 1946. The Action Party and the Democracy of Labor, both debilitated by the election results and internal dissension, withdrew from participation in the government along with the Liberal Party. The Republican Party, which had refused to serve prior ministries because of its opposition to the monarchy, accepted two places on the Council of Ministers. During this period of institutional change and constitutional labors to establish stable democratic government, the committees of liberation, when called upon by law to disband, refused. The C.G.I.L. redoubled its efforts and elaborated a program based upon expanding the number of councils of administration. In the city and province of Milan, the factory committees of liberation declared that they would not move aside until councils of administration appeared to take their places.[17]

The unions chose to enforce their demands for councils through a bargaining technique which they had employed six months before in dealing with the impact of mounting unemployment. As early as January 20 and February 13, 1945, the Salò Republic had blocked the dismissal of industrial workers. After Mussolini's fall, the Milan accord of May 25, 1945 continued the ban and also extended the benefits of the Cassa d'Integrazione (an employer contribution fund which supplemented wages cut by reduced operations) even to workers whose hours of labor reached zero. The terms of the accord continued on in decree 523 of August 21, 1945 and covered industrial workers north of the Gothic Line. The modified features of decree 788 of November 9, 1945 replaced decree 523. After decree 788 terminated on December 31, 1945, decree 50 of February 8, 1946 extended its provisions intact to January 31, 1946, and, with certain changes, from February 1, to April 30, 1946. Decree 50 also established norms for the gradual resumption of dismissals. On September 30, 1946, the block on dismissals officially lifted. Meanwhile, during the run of these enactments, as the end of 1945 approached, officials of four ministries pressed the C.G.I.L. and the General Confederation of Italian Industry to reach an agreement which would modify the strict provisions against dismissals. Following meetings arranged by these participants from government, labor and management concluded an agreement on January 19, 1946.

The accord of January 19, 1946 stressed the need for rehabilitating the total economy as well as individual plants which staggered under the load of surplus workers. Since both of the contracting parties and the government understood the adverse social and personal consequences of unemployment or sharply reduced hours of labor, articles 8 and 9 fixed schedules of payments in the event of reduced hours, layoffs, or dismissals, chargeable against the Cassa d'Integrazione. The accord also stressed the immediate execution of large-scale public works and described the role of grievance committees in the procedure specified for the dismissal of workers. It assured members of grievance committees against dismissal except under conditions circumscribed by safeguards.[18]

The parties of the left undoubtedly looked upon councils of administration as first-step devices to gain ultimate control of the nation's economic life. With the vast potentialities of this backdoor revolution in mind, the socialist and communist factions within the C.G.I.L. took advantage of the procedure laid down for implementing the interconfederal accord on layoffs: the mandatory application of its terms to individual industries, plant by plant. Consequently, as a condition for consenting to dismissals in particular establishments, the local unions insisted upon the creation of councils of administration. No published information has yet come to light which reveals the precise extent to which these radical advocates of a purified world of social justice exchanged the jobs of workers for councils of administration.[19]

Meanwhile, the C.G.I.L. had already indicated that it would not rest content with mere plant-by-plant victories. In November 1945, the Confederation took the first step toward the realization of its nationwide goal by spurring the creation of interplant, city-wide, provincial, and other types of coordinating committees for the councils. It also announced the formation of a National Coordinating Committee.[20] This committee invoked a National Congress of Plant Councils of Administration in Milan on October 13, 1946 where the Ministers of Industry and Commerce (Rodolfo Morandi (1902–1955), a left-wing socialist), of Post-War Assistance (Emilio Sereni (1907–   ), a communist), and of Labor and Social Insurance (Ludovico D'Aragona, a right-wing socialist and the general secretary of the C.G.L. before fascism) endorsed the councils and promised to strive for their legal obligatory creation.[21] By the summer of 1946 the number of councils had reached five hundred.[22] But the left-wing parties and the C.G.I.L. now envisaged the chief responsibility of the National Coordinating Committee as advancing beyond the systematization of council activities throughout the country to encompass the maintenance of close cooperation with the government in planning the economy of Italy.[23]

During this period of left-wing agitation, propaganda, and congresses, the De Gasperi government backed away from clarification of the council issue. When he presented the program of his second government on July 15, 1946 after the elections, the Prime Minister made no mention of legislative recognition or mandatory creation. In contrast, the third subcommittee of the constitutional committee of the Constituent Assembly, after three sessions held in October 1946, attempted to settle the controversy by verbal acrobatics. Article 46, Part I, Title III of the Constitution of the Italian Republic (approved by the Constituent Assembly on December 22, 1947 and effective on January 1, 1948) has preserved the language of the subcommittee's declaration, drawn vaguely enough to evoke different interpretations from each of the political parties:

> In order to promote the social and economic improvement of labor, and in accordance with the requirements of production, the Republic recognizes the right of workers to participate, by the methods and within the limits established by laws, in the management of enterprises.[24]

In November, D'Aragona presented a bill which called for the obligatory formation of councils of administration. A second bill, submitted shortly thereafter, represented the work of Morandi. D'Aragona then withdrew his measure in favor of the more radical, detailed, and comprehensive Morandi project.[25] Bitter controversy continued into the next year, 1947. The challenge of the D'Aragona and Morandi bills precipitated active opposition by management organizations like the Confederation of Business Executives and the General Confederation of Italian Industry. Local, provincial, and regional associations of businessmen and industrialists, in addition to organizations of specialized industries and trades, also memorialized the government. Since the Minister of Industry and Commerce, Morandi, had repeatedly stated that over 700 councils functioned, the General Confederation of Italian Industry conducted a survey of councils of administration. The resulting study claimed that 103 firms with 271 factories reported councils of administration on March 31, 1947. A large percentage of these enterprises formed part of the I.R.I. complex, a congeries of banking and industrial firms controlled, but not directly managed, by the Institute of Industrial Reconstruction through its ownership of considerable proportions of their stocks.[26]

Later, when De Gasperi presented his fourth cabinet, constituted on May 31, 1947 without communist or left-wing socialist representatives, the Prime Minister promised to study the council controversy. The question did not die with De Gasperi's word since the opposition parties now began to direct their year-long technique of cold war political strikes and demonstrations against the government in livid fury at their exclusion from ministerial office and in unquestioning subservience to Russia's opposition to the Marshall Plan. Arising before the Constituent Assembly in October, Di Vittorio demanded the immediate legal recognition of the councils. De Gasperi, in reply, pointed out that grievance committees already functioned and he did not consider the creation of councils of administration urgent. He also expressed doubts about the wisdom of attempting to wrestle with an issue of such magnitude during a period of devastating economic crisis. Had he wished to do so, he might also have employed another argument. Rodolfo Morandi had admitted publicly in 1946, after observing the councils of administration in Turin, that they merely duplicated grievance committees and did not pursue their full activities fervently enough.[27]

As the debate on the councils boiled, the cost of living soared astronomically; it explained, in large part, the economic and social tensions which found expression in utopian schemes and rhetorical gadgets. Taking 1913 as the base year, the cost of living in Italy increased from 453.9

in 1939, when Hitler's armies marched against Poland, to 10,398 in 1945 when the Allied armies liberated North Italy. By 1946, the index mounted to 12,271.6 and leaped to 19,887.5 in 1947. The index of real wages tumbled from 105.68 in 1939 to 22.3 in 1945. Under pressures of mass discontent, individual employers granted cost-of-living allowances, but they lacked uniformity in principle and operation. Since all factions within the C.G.I.L. realized that the prestige of the Italian labor movement depended upon its ability to preserve the level of real wages for all workers in all segments of the economy in all areas of the country, the C.G.I.L. pressed for interconfederal accords, the terminology used to designate agreements negotiated between the Confederation as a whole, rather than its individual constituent category federations, and nationwide employers organizations which covered the largest segments of the economy, like industry or commerce, rather than the individual constituent associations like metal-mechanical industrialists or retail merchants. Thus, between 1945 and 1947, the C.G.I.L. and the General Confederation of Italian Industry stipulated wage accords for all industrial workers employed in the enterprises affiliated with the category societies of industrialists, leagued together, in turn, by Confindustria, the short Italian designation for the General Confederation of Italian Industry. The tendency of Italian labor and management to veer toward highly centralized bargaining, already well exploited under fascism, now gained reinvigorated strength under the economic exigencies of postwar freedom, confusion, and turmoil. Very soon, open dissension and schism within the labor movement, crippled still more by the congenital weakness of the category federations at national, local, and plant levels — a partial consequence of the inevitable desire of politically oriented union confederations to control their constituent bodies from above — would insure the continuance of nationwide accords, as well as nationwide individual category agreements actually managed by the confederations, as permanent features of labor relations in Italy.

On December 6, 1945, C.G.I.L. and Confindustria agreed upon an accord for North Italy which gathered up the rank underbrush of hundreds of different types of cost-of-living bonuses into a single cost-of-living allowance (*indennità di contingenza*) and impaled the elements of the basic wage within set bounds. On May 23, 1946, the two confederations extended this accord to Central and South Italy. The terms stipulated that after specially constituted commissions determined the cost of living for each province, workers would receive allowances proportionate to the cost-of-living index guide set at 100 lire a day and determined by averaging the cost of living in two high-cost provinces and two low-cost provinces. The accord set maximum and minimum payments, awarded male workers twice the percentage increase granted to women, and made mandatory the monthly recalculation of provincial costs of living. Two years later, on November 28, 1947, the two confederations drew up principles to govern downward movements in the cost of living. Motivated by grave awareness of the low level of real wages in Italy, Confindustria consented to the following formula: no reduction in allowances for the first 8% decrease in the cost of living, a 1.2% reduction for the next 4% decline, and a 4% cut for the following 8% fall.

The accords of December 6, 1945 and May 23, 1946 also clarified the terms of piecework payments. They held that "the minimum income of all workers within a given department working on piecework, must not be less than 10% more than the minimum wages established by agreement." They also required that a piecework employee who did "not succeed in earning the minimum established by collective contract, because of reasons independent of his will and his ability . . ." was "entitled to the above stated contractual minimum." The unions took additional advantage of article 2101 of the Civil Code of 1942 to insist that management could establish minimum piecework rates only after a trial period. Industrial employers, furthermore, made other concessions to ease the economic hardships of their work force. Article 17 of the interconfederal accord of October 27, 1946 granted Christmas bonuses equivalent to one month's salary for white-collar employees and 200 hours of labor for factory workers. Family allowances continued simultaneously with these gains, and the government installed a bread bonus (*indennità caropane*) on May 6, 1947 after it freed the price of bread to assume market levels. The wage clauses of the interconfederal accords of May 30 and June 23, 1947 favored common laborers, who formed the main mass of Italian workers, and reflected the pressure and policy of the left-wing parties. They also helped to intensify already narrowing wage differentials brought on by earlier cost-of-living benefits. This wide range of improvements — cost-of-living concessions, piecework payments, Christmas allowances, family grants, and bread bonuses — raised the index of real wages from 22.3 in 1945 to 57.1 in 1946 to 98.58 in 1947.[28]

The most centralized bargaining — whether between confederations exercising jurisdiction over broad segments of the economy or between national category federations of workers and associations of employers in one industry or several related groups of industries — must ultimately depend upon recognized representatives of workers within the factory itself to aid in the constructive administration of contractual arrangements. To this end, C.G.I.L. and Confindustria concluded their second accord dealing with grievance committees on August 7, 1947 since the accord of September 2, 1943 limited its own life to three years. The new document endowed grievance committees with responsibilities better defined than the general functions set forth in the earlier agreement. This tightening of understanding, predicated upon more than three years of experience under trying circumstances and accomplished through an accord of considerable length, pleased the unions because they felt certain that increased precision would enhance their powers. At the same time it also pleased the industrialists because they hoped that more specific language would erect acknowledged barriers against the proclivity of grievance committees to press for ever larger spheres of influence under phraseology as general as the wording of the 1943 accord.

The communists and socialists within the C.G.I.L. had hardly allowed their signatures upon this contract to dry when they inaugurated a chain reaction of demonstrations and strikes to establish the incapacity of De Gasperi to govern without them. On November 23, 1947, as a link in their cold war tactics, they summoned the Second National Congress of Councils of Administration to Milan. Some 6,000 representatives of plant councils and grievance committees participated in the proceedings while 3,000 partisans of the communist Garibaldi brigades bivouacked near the sports stadium. The congress closed, after shouting down government spokesmen, with a parade of the partisans. Pressed by these political manifestations, the Italian government proposed the creation of an investigatory commission made up of nine members of Confindustria, nine members of C.G.I.L., and five specialists named by the government. The C.G.I.L. challenged the principle of equal representation for Confindustria and demanded that the government allow the unions to select the technicians.

The election of April 18, 1948 offered a rich array of choices to voters as they approached their polling stations to select the first members of the Chamber of Deputies freely designated by the people since the advent of fascism and to name the first senators ever elected by popular vote in Italy. They found a varied assortment of right-wing parties on the ballot: the Italian Social Movement (Movimento Sociale Italiano — M.S.I.) which espoused doctrines reminiscent of fascism; the National Monarchist Party; the Common Man's Front (Fronte dell'Uomo Qualunque) which propounded hazy and delicately fascist ideas; the Nationalist Movement for Social Democracy, a dissident group of the Common Man's Front, which presented a platform scented with monarchist tendencies; and the Liberal Party. The Common Man's Front and the Liberal Party, backed by Francesco Saverio Nitti and other independents, united into the National Bloc. In the center of the political line-up stood the Christian Democrats, while the Democracy of Labor, always more an expression of Ivanoe Bonomi's prestige than a political party, surrendered its franchise. Despite its radical past, the Republican Party lost its chief reason for existence with the departure of the monarchy and survived, as a tiny minority, to represent unexciting decency in public life. On the left, the Action Party faded away and passed on its faithful adherents to the republicans, the socialists, and the communists. The Communist and Socialist Parties banded together as the Popular Democratic Front. The Italian Workers Socialist Party (P.S.L.I.) presented itself as the most novel feature on the radical political slate. In exile, the right and left wings of the Socialist Party had managed to flap together. But as early as the convocation of the Constituent Assembly, the leaders of the right wing, headed by Giuseppe Saragat, grew anxious about the unfolding consequences of the unity-of-action pact between the socialists and the communists. Under Pietro Nenni, the Socialist Party did not act like the second strongest political force in the country. Instead, it engaged in oratorical splendors and maximalist demagoguery and surrendered initiative to the communists. In the fall of 1946, Nenni drew the Socialist Party even closer to the Communist Party. When the P.S.I. met at Rome University on January 9, 1947, discord between the right-wing and Nenni socialists hung so heavily upon them that the Saragat group withdrew to the Palazzo Barberini and there inaugurated the P.S.L.I. Ludovico D'Aragona, among the staunchest opponents of the unity-of-action pact with the communists, stood with the founding fathers of the P.S.L.I. Afterward, Ivan Matteo Lombardo, Ignazio Silone (1900–   ), and other important members of the P.S.I. also withdrew and eventually formed the Socialist Union. The two right-wing Socialist Parties joined in alliance for the 1948 elections. The fear that the Popular Democratic Front of communists and left-wing socialists might win a majority of the votes filled the Catholic clergy, Church officials, anticommunists, and representatives of the United States in Italy with a cooperative sense of urgency. American supporters of Italian democracy urged everyone with friends and relatives in Italy to appeal to them by letter to vote against the Popular Democratic Front.

The greatest miracle of postwar European parliamentarism surprised the world when the results of the Italian elections appeared. The Christian Democrats obtained 307 seats in the Chamber of Deputies, an absolute majority. The communists elected 135 deputies and the left-wing socialists sent 51 members to Montecitorio. The strongest of the minor alliances, the right-wing socialists, won 33 seats. The Christian Democrats also secured a majority of the members of the Senate. On May 11, the joint session of the Chamber and the Senate elected Luigi Einaudi, the illustrious economist, professor, minister, and statesman as President of the Republic. The people's judgment at the polls braced the government's stability since De Gasperi could now depend upon his own party to see legislation through Parliament. It also reanimated the spirit of the propertied classes and the industrialists who had supported the Christian Democrats. But they enjoyed only short-lived satisfaction. On July 14, 1948, a fanatically anticommunist student attempted to assassinate Togliatti as he emerged from Montecitorio and wounded him severely. Bitter with disappointment at the election returns, the social-communists had been spoiling for retaliation. With the C.G.I.L. under their control, they proclaimed a nationwide general strike, in reality the climactic second installment of the offensive waged by them against the De Gasperi government during the preceding year.

Following the Socialist Party split in January 1947, De Gasperi re-shuffled his cabinet and strengthened the position of his own party by selecting Mario Scelba (1901–   ) to serve as Minister of the Interior. From this post of control over the entire system of Italian local govern-ment, Scelba moved with the firmest determination to loosen the hold of the communists over remote rural areas and to restore respect for law and order. Togliatti, nothing daunted and too shrewd to suspect De Gasperi of superior finesse, kept preaching the importance of preserving the coalition of the three mass parties. As evidence of his good faith and behavior, he ordered his followers in the Constituent Assembly to sup-port the Christian Democratic move to include the terms of Mussolini's Concordat with the Vatican in the constitution under discussion. But at the very moment that De Gasperi accepted Togliatti's unsolicited sup-port, the Prime Minister had already perfected bold plans to maneuver the social-communists into political isolation. During a trip to Washing-ton early in the year, American officials had assured him of economic aid and of even more enthusiastic patronage were he to rid the Italian gov-ernment of its communist ministers. When De Gasperi announced his fourth cabinet on May 31, 1947, he excluded the communists and left-wing socialists from the government. A month later, the President of the Council, free from Togliatti's threat of "either a perpetual crisis or a communist program," enrolled Italy among the Marshall Plan nations on June 28 when Italy received $601,000,000 for economic rehabilitation. The Republic entered the Organization for European Economic Cooperation in March 1948.

Between the summer of 1947 and the General Elections of April 1948, an interval of bitterly mounting conflict between East and West, the so-cial-communists used their undesired ministerial exile to exploit the C.G.I.L. for political ends. From July 1947 to the close of the year, they perpetrated general strikes in one community after another, all carefully planned to arouse utmost alarm and publicity while avoiding major casualties in order to stave off severe police retaliation. By June 1947, the communists controlled 80% of all chambers of labor. Left-wing workers, led by the heads of these chambers, marched on city halls, prefectures, and hostile newspaper offices to protest against purported evils in neighboring towns. In August, the peasant day laborers of the Po Valley struck in a body. On September 21, the communist officers of the Federation of Land Workers (Federterra) sent instructions to their zonal activists to prepare for a simultaneous mass invasion of unoccupied or badly cultivated lands by peasants throughout the province of Rome. The communication advised the enrollment of women and children to lend the demonstrations festive air, the unfurling of the tricolor of Italy at the head of the columns, the presence of a priest to bless the marchers and the flag, and the active participation of the mayors and councilmen in the proceedings. On September 26, 10,000 families took possession of 30,000 hectares of land in 56 communes of the province.

On November 23, the Second National Congress of Councils of Administration met, as already noted, in Milan, flanked by 3,000 partisan fighters to remind the authorities of communist prowess. Shortly thereafter, the chamber of labor at Milan declared a general strike of protest against the presumptive transfer of the prefect elsewhere. Between November 27 and 28, the communists arranged for a so-called citizens committee to assume the powers of the prefect, partisans occupied the prefecture where they dismissed its functionaries, and demonstrators also threatened to send the mayor of Milan packing. Although Rome alerted the head of the Legnano Division, he did not have to take military command of the city. Yet the insurrection raised perturbing thoughts: the chamber of labor of Milan revolted against governmental authority with the approval of the executive committee of the C.G.I.L. for purposes wholly extraneous to the legitimate demands of the labor movement. The example of Milan subsequently stirred Ancona, Leghorn, Lecco, Catanzaro, and Messina to labor action. But the most serious general strike occurred in Rome on December 11. Declaring that the government had neglected the unemployed, the executive committee of the Rome chamber of labor ordered its members out on the streets although discussions at the Ministry of Labor had not yet ended and although the social-communists knew that the government had budgeted 10,648,000,000 lire for public works projects of immediate execution and another 3,000,000,000 lire for future construction. The Christian Democratic current within the Rome chamber of labor had opposed the strike and then had publicly urged workers in the city not to lend themselves to political exploitation. The strike collapsed when the demonstrators discovered that the police reacted in dead earnest and when the government's emergency transportation system began to function.

The social-communists fostered this concatenated turmoil because they wished to demonstrate to the entire nation that De Gasperi could not rule without them. Shortly after the general strike of Rome, Giuseppe Romita (1887–1958) told the Constituent Assembly that the disturbances which rocked the nation rolled out of the chasm which "separated the Country and the Government as a result of the formation of a monochromatic Ministry." Nenni on December 13 and Togliatti on December 18 drove home the message when they threatened worsening internal strife and ascribed its past and future origin to the absence of the representatives of the working class from the cabinet. But De Gasperi stood out firmly against blackmail by public disorder during 1947 and kept the social-communists outside. If the social-communists too often that year indulged in the crassest political deception and kept the country in continual civic chaos to destroy De Gasperi, and all to no avail, they did not always strain the truth. They came rather close to the mark when they castigated the government for its failure to suppress the patently fascist Italian Social Movement and to implement the award of an arbitration tribunal which De Gasperi himself had headed and which had favored the sharecroppers of Central Italy against the landowners by upsetting the traditional 50–50 system and approving a 60–40 arrangement.

The general strike of July 14 to 16, 1948, like the 1947 disorders just described, aimed for De Gasperi's ouster at best, or, at worst, for the re-entry of the social-communists into a De Gasperi coalition cabinet. Again, the Prime Minister mastered events as the strike approached insurrection in Genoa and elsewhere in the North and as communist bands, armed with weapons they had hidden away in caches three years back, erected barricades and commanded the streets without opposition. After a day and a half of indulging these gestures of revolution, the government halted the threat to the State by firm military action. Stern police measures by Scelba against fresh political strikes called that autumn by the C.G.I.L. against the European Recovery Program stemmed the third assault of the social-communists within two years. Their triple repulsion helped to consolidate government authority. Following the inception of the Marshall Plan, increased production and relatively stable prices, induced by the coherent economic and fiscal program devised by Professor Einaudi as Vice-Premier and Minister of the Budget, sealed the fate of the social-communists as potent threats to the established order in Italy.[29]

As early as 1945, Christian Democratic leaders within the C.G.I.L., including Achille Grandi who had earnestly advocated labor unity, grew apprehensive and then alarmed at the constantly spreading control by the social-communists over the administrative machinery of the Confederation. Internal dissension among members of the executive agencies sharpened. Left-wing unionists attacked Catholic Action for organizing the Christian Associations of Italian Workers (Associazioni Cristiane dei Lavoratori Italiani — A.C.L.I.) and protested against A.C.L.I.'s interference in labor affairs as inimical to labor unity. They accused the Catholic current of duplicity in maintaining close ties with A.C.L.I. The Christian Democrats declared their independence of Catholic Action. With regard to A.C.L.I., they retorted that those groups represented the preunion phase of educational and welfare endeavors in behalf of Catholic workers, thereby supplementing rather than subverting the role of C.G.I.L. Had they surrendered on this issue, they would have left similar programs of the Communist and Socialist Parties in full monopolistic control.

The Christian Democrats, in turn, objected to the frequency of labor disturbances fostered for political ends by the social-communists. Indeed, when the directive committee of the C.G.I.L. deliberated the proclamation of a national general strike for May 3, 1947 — the first since 1922 — in protest against the slaying of Sicilian labor organizers on May 1 at Portella delle Ginestre, the Christian Democrats refused to vote with the majority for a venture solely calculated to embarrass the De Gasperi government. The social-communists charged them with disloyalty to the working class. Later, at the Florence Congress of the C.G.I.L. from June 1 to 7, 1947, the Christian Democrats, who could claim only 13% of the 5,775,000 asserted members of the Confederation, heard Catholic speakers hissed whenever they cited a religious authority and suffered the indignity of shouts, whistling, catcalls, and uncontrolled uproar when a Christian Democrat referred to Jesus of Nazareth as the First Worker. But they also listened to a barrage of declarations, resolutions, motions, and protestations of dedication to labor unity without receiving definite guarantees that the C.G.I.L. would limit its future activities to the tasks of labor relations.

The following winter, after the Christian Democrats spoke out publicly against the general strike of Rome in December 1947, bitterness among the currents deepened still more. Renato Bitossi (1899–   ),

473

a communist member of the directive committee, proposed to censure the Catholic unionists for violation of discipline at the meeting of December 29, 1947. Giulio Pastore (1902–   ) took the offensive in refuting Bitossi. (After the death of Achille Grandi on September 20, 1946, Giuseppe Rapelli (1905–   ) became the head of the Christian Democratic current in the C.G.I.L. When he soon suffered a nervous breakdown, Pastore, the national secretary of A.C.L.I. and president of its social services branch, assumed leadership.) He pointed out that between August 1944 and May 1947, a period of 33 months, the C.G.I.L. engaged in 47 political strikes. By contrast, he demonstrated that between May 1947 and December of the same year, an interval of only 7 months dating from the time of the expulsion of the social-communists from the cabinet, the left-wing activists stirred up 84 political strikes. Pastore demanded greater freedom of action for C.G.I.L.'s minority wings and a referendum vote among the workers concerned before the Confederation or its constituent bodies could sanction strikes. The social-communists rejected the referendum proposal, but Di Vittorio offered a *modus vivendi* concerning more independence for the minorities. At the directive committee meeting of February 24 and 25, 1948, the social-communists approved the *modus vivendi* overwhelmingly. They acted despite the serious reservations expressed by the Christian Democrats in their reply to Di Vittorio published in the January 21 issue of *Il Popolo* (*The People*) and even after Renato Cappugi (1901–   ) warned them that the policies of the *modus vivendi* revised the substance of both the Pact of Rome and the constitution and therefore required the ratification of the confederal congress.

During this same session, Pastore urged the necessity of C.G.I.L. representation at an international labor conference which the British Trade Union Congress had called in London for March 9 and 10 to study the Marshall Plan. Against the opposition of the social-communists who argued that the presence of C.G.I.L. delegates would violate the spirit of discipline required by the World Federation of Trade Unions, Giulio Pastore of the Christian Democratic Party, Giovanni Canini (1894–   ) of the P.S.L.I., and Enrico Parri of the Republican Party prepared to leave for London. Late second thoughts finally induced Di Vittorio of the Communist Party and Fernando Santi (1902–   ) of the Socialist Party to fly to England on the last day of the conference in the naïve hope of persuading James Carey of the C.I.O. to their views. They met with disillusion, for Carey, an experienced victim of communist intrigue in the United States, contradicted their reassuring statements to the press by revealing that he had told them that the Marshall Plan tolerated no middle way: either they accepted it as a whole, or repudiated it entirely.

This challenge slapped hard against Italy's brittle labor unity, already fractured almost beyond repair. The decisive Christian Democratic victory in the General Elections a month later allowed daylight to pass through the widening cracks. Finally, the general strike of July 1948, officially resisted by the Catholic labor leaders, insured the inevitable major break after Pastore appealed to his followers to resume their jobs. The social-communists denounced him and his associates as traitors. The national council of A.C.L.I. hurriedly assembled in Rome from July 20 to 22 and supported the position taken by the Christian Democratic members of the directive committee of C.G.I.L. It also urged a new regrouping of labor: autonomous, democratic, and free of all political influences. The specially summoned National Congress of A.C.L.I. met in extraordinary session at the Great Hall of the Lateran Athenaeum in Rome from September 15 to 18. At the conclusion of debate, the delegates cast 580,000 votes in favor of creating a free, autonomous, and democratic union, completely independent of party directives and government pressures, while the motion supporting a confessional labor movement received only 40,000 votes. On October 16, delegates to the constituent assembly of the proposed organization met in Rome and on the following day acclaimed the birth of the Free General Italian Confederation of Labor (Libera Confederazione Generale Italiana del Lavoro — L.C.G.I.L.). So ended labor unity in the C.G.I.L. Even from its beginnings in 1944, skillful equivocation on all sides necessarily outbalanced sincere efforts to eschew every form of extraneous political stratagem since the organization rested squarely upon the federative principle of recognized party allegiance.[30]

Unionists of divergent political faiths, troubled by the persistence of conflict within the C.G.I.L. and the grave obstacles encountered in launching the L.C.G.I.L., sought to establish a constituent labor conference (costituente sindacale) as a central clearing house for advancing the development of a democratic labor movement independent of parties. After this catch-as-catch-can group's initial meeting on January 16, 1949, the conference gathered under more formal circumstances on April 10 to explore the thoughts of participants like Giovanni Gronchi, Giuseppe Rapelli (now recovered from his nervous breakdown and openly resentful of Pastore for not transferring the mantle of L.C.G.I.L.'s leadership to him), and Leopoldo Rubinacci (1903–   ), Christian Democrats; Ludovico D'Aragona, Alberto Simonini (1896–   ), and Corrado Bonfantini (1909–   ), right-wing socialists; and Enrico Parri, the republican. The organizers of the conference had not invited the leaders of

L.C.G.I.L. to participate in its deliberations, a curious but not surprising maneuver by Italian politicians publicly dedicated to democratic labor unity. Meanwhile, Saragat's social democrats of the P.S.L.I. and the republicans had remained within the C.G.I.L. Then, in May, they also severed their partnership with the social-communists. However, they founded their own union at Rome on June 4, the Italian Federation of Labor (Federazione Italiana del Lavoro — F.I.L.), since they could not bring themselves to associate with the L.C.G.I.L. which they somehow regarded as clerical in impulse. After the Socialist International expelled its Italian affiliate, the P.S.I., in May 1949 for continued collaboration with the communists, the P.S.L.I., Ignazio Silone and his followers, and the most recent refugees from Nenni's party, headed by Giuseppe Romita, attempted to join forces in politics through the P.S.L.I. and in the labor movement through F.I.L. This endeavor failed because of personal rivalries and ambitions. It also stumbled over the inability of these leaders to agree upon the proper stance to assume toward the government, one of cooperation or one of opposition. Consequently, the Romita and Silone sects formed the Unitarian Socialist Party (Partito Socialista Unitario — P.S.U.).

On August 6, 1949, delegations from L.C.G.I.L. and F.I.L. signed an agreement to foster unity of action through an exchange of views and a joint discussion of policies; they also committed themselves to strive for the eventual merger of the democratic labor forces of the country by designating the two delegations as a permanent unification committee. Anticlerical groups within F.I.L., the P.S.L.I., the P.S.U., and the Republican Party opposed this move. Nonetheless, the unification committee took gladly to its assignment under the amicable pressure of anticommunist labor leaders in the United States, officials of the United States in Rome (led by Colonel Thomas Lane, the noted labor attaché at the American Embassy on the Via Veneto, who had rendered valiant service in the reconstruction of the Italian union movement during World War II and therefore possessed intimate knowledge of its inner life), and Italian politicians anxious to hold the nation within the orbit of the West. On December 15, 1949, the committee published two important documents. The first report elucidated the formative principles and guides to action which would control the new confederation; the second report contained governing rules and regulations for enactment in the event of unification. The national congress of F.I.L., held at Naples on February 5 and 6, 1950, approved the merger of all free unions into a nonconfessional confederation divorced from government and parties. On February 16, the L.C.G.I.L. supported Pastore's motion to seek unification with F.I.L. and other democratic unaffiliated unions. The F.I.L. resolution, as subsequent developments seemed to indicate, expressed more the influence of American and Italian well-wishers from the side-lines and less the overwhelming desire of the membership. It soon became clear that many chambers of labor in F.I.L. did not accept the Naples decision, especially those dominated by Romita's P.S.U., and tended to favor the establishment of a third confederation. Acting upon socialist principles of the most recondite refinement, they sought out the leaders of the Italian Confederation of Independent Unions (Confederazione Italiana Sindacati Indipendenti — C.I.S.I.), former corporative labor officials who had grouped themselves around Luigi Fontanelli's *Rassegna del Lavoro* (*Labor Review*), a periodical still impressed with Sorel's doctrines. The positive results of these encounters led to the constituent assembly of March 5, 1950 when 3,000 delegates claiming to represent 250,000 to 300,000 members of republican, socialist, and ex-fascist political persuasions founded the Italian Union of Labor (Unione Italiana del Lavoro — U.I.L.). On March 24, 1950, Naples witnessed the rise of the Italian Confederation of National Workers Unions (Confederazione Italiana Sindacati Nazionali Lavoratori — C.I.S.N.A.L.). Out of Italy's shattered labor movement, it gathered up unaffiliated unions, veterans groups, and workers organizations with monarchist leanings. Although C.I.S.N.A.L denied fascist inspiration, it espoused corporative ideas. At the Theater Adriano in Rome a month later on April 30, 1950, the long-negotiated merger took place between L.C.G.I.L. and those members of F.I.L. who followed the leadership of Enrico Parri and A. Claudio Rocchi (1915–   ), subsequently expelled by the Republican Party, and the right-wing socialist leadership of Giovanni Canini. A third element, the Union of Autonomous Italian Workers Federations (Unione Federazioni Autonome Italiane Lavoratori), also joined forces with L.C.G.I.L. and F.I.L. to create the Italian Confederation of Workers Unions (Confederazione Italiana Sindacati Lavoratori — C.I.S.L.).[31]

These four competing confederations of labor — C.G.I.L., U.I.L., C.I.S.N.A.L., and C. I. S. L. — confronted the General Confederation of Italian Industry (Confindustria), the General Confederation of Agriculture (Confederazione Generale dell'Agricoltura), the General Confederation of Commerce (Confederazione Generale del Commercio), and the General Confederation of Handicrafts (Confederazione Generale dell'Artigianato). Midway between the unions of workers and the associations of employers stood the National Confederation of Independent Farmers (Confederazione Nazionale Coltivatori Diretti), organized in 1944 to represent the interests of peasant farmers, leaseholders, and beneficiaries of grants under the land reform programs. The Confederation, headed by Paolo Bonomi (1910–   ), while confining most of its activities to working farmers who cultivated their own lands, also organized substantial numbers of landless sharecroppers claimed by the agricultural labor federations.

The Far Side of Labor Paradise: 1950 to 1960

By 1950, Italy's labor confederations, sporting distinctive political emblems, including the banner of autonomy, once more resumed their natural and preferred wanderings in party Edens of their own, despite their avowed attachment to the central Marxist heaven of proletarian unity. Interunion rivalry, fattened by politics and prodigal of men, talent, time, and money, perforce concentrated administrative power at the confederal level and neglected the national category federations, their local branches, and the factory institutions so necessary to the life of large-scale industrial unionism. Even the C.G.I.L. abandoned the councils of administration, while all confederations began to use grievance committees, stripped more and more of effective power by them and the employers, as scoreboards of their influence among workers.

During the political struggles which tore the labor movement apart, the social-communists wrote off the councils of administration as devices for the control of industry and exploited them openly as political instruments. In October 1948, the National Coordinating Committee urged a united front between councils and unions to force the government to recast its economic policy, particularly with regard to the European Recovery Program. That fall, major industrial disputes centered in those firms with councils of administration. In the absence of councils, grievance committees took over the tasks of provoking disorder. In Parliament, social-communist deputies went through the motions of demanding the revision of article 46 of the Constitution to require the mandatory creation of councils of administration. But after 1948, interest in them waned. Workers and unions, exhausted by internecine strife, and even the parties of the left, demonstrated less and less enthusiasm for them. They disappeared, like liquid air, from the factories of Italy, even from Fiat, Montecatini, Breda, and other important companies where they had enjoyed troublesome reigns during the years between 1945 and 1950.[32]

The failure of the council movement, so reminiscent of 1919 and 1920, traces back directly to world-wide communist policy during Liberation and immediately after the close of the war in Europe. In Italy, the Communist Party and its socialist allies followed the dictates of Moscow and favored cooperation with all democratic forces, however conservative. Even as early as 1944, Togliatti had shocked hard-shelled Marxists by forcing upon them close collaboration with the King and Badoglio. This pragmatic approach continued to prevail during the early phases of the council movement. Under such restraint, the parties of the left forsook violence. But those were the very months when the hatred of fascism and the memory of the role of the partisans in saving the factories of the North surged strongest. That irrecoverable moment of history represented the time, in Leninist terms, to strike hard, with extralegal means if necessary, for only during that brief interval did the sense of guilt of the propertied classes paralyze them and open up the mastery of events to insurgent social forces.

The labor movement set up a majority of the councils during the summer of 1945, largely in metal and engineering shops, again duplicating the pattern of 1919 and 1920. For the most part, they took hold in establishments where commissioners had replaced the heads of concerns tainted with fascism or nazi collaboration. Too, some councils found life for a price: the disbanding of otherwise recalcitrant committees of liberation after the June 1946 elections. Another group sprang out of bargains which replaced emergency commissioners by restoration of normal operations. Certainly, the parties of the left, no less captivated by the euphoria of the early postwar months than their companions to the right, fumbled the main chance for acquiring industrial control of Italy in 1945 and early 1946. By 1947 and 1948, despite raucous propaganda, furor, demonstrations, plant violence, and political strikes, they lost the gamble. The National Elections of 1948 then sealed the fate of this radical twice-lost cause. The costly controversy succeeded only in weakening the real functions of grievance committees either through neglect or perversion.

While the national debate on councils of administration raged, the less publicized grievance committees encountered grave difficulties, not unrelated to the broader controversy. As already indicated, economic dislocations forced employers to seek relief from the burden of overmanned factories by insisting upon consent to modification of the block on dismissals, dating from August 21, 1945. The agreement of January 19, 1946 achieved this end. Notwithstanding its provisions, the industrialists could carry out collective dismissals only by overcoming the most serious and dangerous obstacles. The unions, naturally enough, resisted ferociously. The grievance committees, despite the article in the 1943 agreement calling for cooperation, found it impossible, given the bitter economic and political situation which had developed, to consent to such proposals. They resisted. Inevitably, the new agreement of August 7, 1947 detailed not only the creation, election, and duties of grievance committees, but also spelled out a definite procedure for dismissing workers, both collectively and individually. Although the law blocking dismissals no longer operated, the employers realized that the spectre of unemployment still dominated the minds of workers and that some system for making limited dismissals possible would need their consent. Because employers sensed their moral, social, and economic obligations, especially because they respected the capacity of the unions for violence, grievance committees received important functions in the dismissal process under article 3.

The agreement of 1947 did not function well under the industrial and political circumstances then prevalent in Italy. The plight of most industrial firms grew worse, especially in relation to foreign trade, where their products could not compete in the international market because of the excess number of workers in their plants. The 1947 agreement expired on December 31, 1948. The agreement provided for automatic renewal unless the parties announced their intention of not renewing the agreement two months before the date of expiration. The General Elections of April 1948 had undoubtedly infused industrialists with psychological fortitude. As a result, Confindustria, in the person of Dr. Angelo Costa (1901–   ), its president, communicated with the C.G.I.L. on October 26, 1948, stating that Confindustria could not continue the 1947 agreement unless the unions rigorously followed the procedures concerning dismissals. The letter also alluded to the lack of cooperation on the part of the unions, implying that employers would no longer tolerate acts of violence and frequent, disruptive strikes called for political ends and not for economic and union purposes. President Costa went on to conclude that Confindustria might continue the agreement, as an experiment, for three months to see if the unions would actually mend their ways and follow the procedures of article 3.[33]

On January 31, 1949, President Costa sent a second communication to the C.G.I.L. In that letter, he called attention to the absence of a reply to his letter of October 26, 1948; he also stated that employers had not yet noted any change in the attitude of the unions toward observing procedures under article 3 of the 1947 agreement. On the contrary, Dr. Costa went on, local violence had repeatedly occurred during the three-month experimental period. He then declared that Confindustria had no objection to grievance committees and would therefore willingly return to the provisions of the 1943 agreement. (He well knew that its clauses described their functions in more general terms than those of the 1947 agreement.) However, since the agreement of 1947 contained specific provisions for the number of members on grievance committees and for their selection, President Costa indicated the readiness of Confindustria to recognize the pertinent articles of the 1947 agreement.[34] The unions protested this action by Confindustria, but had to accept the situation. From that time for almost five years, no formal accord existed on the establishment, composition, election, duties, and functions of grievance committees. Between the end of 1948 and May 1953, labor and management handled all of these matters informally; they followed by custom certain regulations of the 1943 and 1947 agreements.

The resistance of the unions to both individual and collective dismissals prompted the refusal of Confindustria to renew the terms of the 1947 agreement without tightening pertinent provisions and without receiving assurances from the unions that they would cooperate in establishing an orderly procedure for layoffs. For two years, until 1950, Italian labor and industrial management had to operate as best they could, without a contract, in the explosive realm of dismissals. On April 21, 1950, they finally reached agreement on mass dismissals; on October 18, 1950, they signed an accord regarding individual layoffs. These accords still continued as valid in 1960.

If labor and Confindustria reached agreement in 1950 on dismissals, it would appear logical to regard the time as also auspicious for formalizing, once again, the arrangements on the election and functions of grievance committees. However, the union movement, now split and politically competitive, could not concur on election procedures. The employers merely shrugged their shoulders and indicated that the unions had to resolve the issue since it affected the industrialists only indirectly. Confindustria suggested that when the unions attained a meeting of minds, they could then come back to the employers who would undoubtedly favor a reasonable proposal.[35] Finally, C.G.I.L., C.I.S.L., and U.I.L. reconciled their differences long enough to achieve the interconfederal accord on grievance committees of May 8, 1953. This accord still remained in force at the end of 1960.

The 1950 agreements revealed the rift which had spread between the unions and grievance committees. By then, both right- and left-wing unions wished to clip the wings of the committees. Under the terms of the accords, the unions enlarged their own roles in the dismissal procedure at the expense of the grievance committees. Even before the liberation of the industrial North, labor leaders in areas already freed began to realize that grievance committees were assuming the initiative in handling problems theoretically within the province of the unions. However, the unions lacked power to insist upon their rights since they functioned, for the most part, only from the top. They could not have asserted their competence locally, even had the grievance committees invited them to do so by patiently awaiting union action on urgent matters.

The future power of councils of administration, rather than the pacific ministrations of grievance committees, occupied C.G.I.L.'s thoughts at the plant level almost exclusively during 1945 and 1946. This policy perverted grievance committees into factory centers of agitation, or surrogate councils, wherever real councils did not function. In addition, when questions of dismissals arose, C.G.I.L.'s social-communists encouraged grievance committees to resist at any cost, including slow-downs, strikes, and violence. Such behavior irresistibly created suspicion in the minds of employers that grievance committees had failed, in fact, as the agencies of cooperation envisioned by the 1943 agreement. Nor did the unions, in spite of their forced reliance upon the committees for plant-level execution of policy, relish the emerging prestige of the committees. When the 1943 agreement came to an end and the 1947 accord replaced it, the concern of the unions about their prerogatives rose to the surface. One general provision directed the committees to submit to their unions all those matters which involved "the collective regulation of labor relations and pertinent controversies."

Both the 1943 and 1947 agreements assigned to grievance committees key positions of power over individual and collective layoffs. Since unemployment preoccupied the workers of the entire nation, their allegiance turned, understandably, not to distant bureaucracies, but to that close and ever-present factory institution which alone might save their jobs. But the unions, also understandably, began to fear and resent this loyalty toward a plant group which represented, theoretically, all workers in the factory, union as well as nonunion. They reasoned that popular grievance committee members might easily take it into their heads some day to act independently of the unions and that Italian workers, who never paid union dues with enthusiasm, might follow their lead. So, by 1948, grievance committees had lost the respect of employers, due to the pressure of events and left-wing confederal policy, but, at the same time, had not won the real affection of the unions.

The metamorphosis achieved by the committees discomforted all union leaders, but these creatures of the labor movement troubled the communists most; instead of acting like lambs, submitting to their bidding, the committees betrayed the possibilities of raging like lions. Perhaps the social-communists, sensing their impending failure in the struggle for councils of administration, finally also realized the political danger of nurturing a workers group at the factory level too imbued with self-importance and independence. They even complained that the committees often comported themselves irresponsibly against employers — at a time, no doubt, when communist tactics called for conciliatory maneuvers.

But events soon intervened to shape an answer. After the attempt on Togliatti's life and the ensuing general strike of July 1948, many employers refused admittance of union representatives to their factories. This development forced the unions to rely heavily upon grievance committees and unwillingly to confer upon them even more prestige and power. In addition, union representatives found that they lacked familiarity with specific factory problems — hours of work, incentive pay, demotion or promotion, the quality and price of meals in the cafeteria — and had to turn to the committees for knowledge as well.

The secessions from C.G.I.L. between 1948 and 1950 deprived grievance committees of their former pretensions as "unitary forces," to borrow a phrase from the communists. While a large majority of committee members still belonged to C.G.I.L., the minority members of the committees began to assert themselves. Henceforth, unless C.G.I.L.'s adherents on the committees understood official policy clearly, they might easily vote along with their fellow workers outside the dotted line. Of even greater danger, they might not understand the wider political implications of seemingly simple decisions. Consequently, union organizations replaced the committees in the procedures established in 1950 for the handling of the most important industrial issue in Italy: individual and mass discharges. From then on, whenever these procedures saved a worker's job or spared a group of workers from mass layoff, gratitude would flow directly to the particular union of the workers and not to the grievance committee where they would have to render triple thanks to the C.G.I.L., U.I.L., and C.I.S.L.

The final step in the emasculation of the committees followed when C.G.I.L. created new factory institutions. To maintain access to necessary plant information, to buttress its impaired power since the split, and to insure a direct channel of communications, it created the factory union committee made up of the most active and intelligent members of C.G.I.L. in each plant. Union leaders selected the members. These committees supplied a basic need in the administrative structure of the Italian labor movement: direct union representation at the shop level. C.G.I.L. went even further to consolidate its position and to weaken the grievance committee in each establishment. It began to use the factory union dues collector as an agent of propaganda and as a channel of information about the problems of individual workers.

Not until after 1953 did C.I.S.L. and U.I.L. acquire the strength to attempt to duplicate fully C.G.I.L.'s protective measure. Moreover, a crisis within the Christian Democratic Party blighted the prestige which C.I.S.L. had acquired as a result of its yeoman services in combating communist propaganda and policy within industrial plants. In January 1952, Guido Gonella (1905–   ), the right-wing secretary of the Party, declared in Turin that the Christian Democrats should build a Catholic labor movement of their own. Giulio Pastore, the secretary general of C.I.S.L., and himself a leader within the Christian Democratic Party, disagreed with Gonella whose utterances placed the union in delicate and embarrassing straits. On January 11, 1952, the secretariat of C.I.S.L. met and reaffirmed its faith in a nonpolitical and nonconfessional labor movement. Nonetheless, the Christian Democrats began to organize Catholic workers in each factory into plant and trade groups (*gruppi d'azienda e di categoria della Democrazia Cristiana*) to combat the work of C.G.I.L.'s factory union committees.

From 1953 until 1960, as each of the confederal contestants for the loyalty of industrial workers endeavored to fix its own organization within each factory, C.G.I.L., C.I.S.L., and U.I.L. proceeded to illustrate, in the supposedly down-to-earth conduct of labor affairs, the unique Italian talent for floodlighting the façade of events with dramatic intensity while consigning inner reality to obscurity. They elevated the elections of grievance committee members to events of strident national concern — less gripping, perhaps, than the adored *calcio* (football) matches, but laden, nonetheless, with the fascination and immediacy of the partisan struggle between the social-communists and the democratic unions, between East and West. Preoccupation with the outcome of these plant-by-plant frenetic trials of strength extended to the Embassy of the United States of America as well as to the American press.

The unions, in the heat of battle, with their eyes averted from strict accuracy, hailed the grievance committees (*commissioni interne*, C.I. in abbreviation) as the special guardians of all employees, as the vigilant protectors of the contractual interests of workers, and as the champions of labor welfare in the daily give-and-take of factory life. Accepting the alleged importance of these pivotal institutions, each confederation, naturally enough, proclaimed its own adherents as alone worthy of directing the affairs of the C.I. The 3,000 to 4,000 annual elections, conducted according to procedures set forth with specific clarity in the interconfederal accord of May 8, 1953, have furnished campaigns replete with the full panoply of speakers, pamphlets, posters, sound-trucks, and the host of other modern devices adopted in political elections to influence the judgment of the electorate. Prior to the campaigns, the three major confederations of labor, and the lesser organizations as well, concentrated their efforts to prepare shops and plants for the battle of votes. Union activists received intensive instruction in the rules and regulations concerning the proper conduct of elections; the techniques best suited to mold favorable public opinion, including the careful composition of slogans, posters, and pamphlets; the importance of well-planned house-to-house visits, with the aid, at times, of members of friendly political parties and organizations; and, finally, the steps necessary to insure that all qualified voters, including the sick and ailing, would actually arrive at the polls and mark their ballots correctly, both from a technical and union point of view. If vast expenditure of human energy and financial resources could endow an institution with power and importance, then certainly the C.I. would have ranked among the most vital institutions of all Italy during the decade from 1950 to 1960.

Indeed, the national press came to accept this judgment at face value. It accorded reading space to the results of C.I. electoral campaigns usually reserved for political engagements of national interest. Depending upon the coloration of the winning ticket and the political proclivities of the newspaper reporting the story, the accounts triumphantly acclaimed the outcome as major victories for C.G.I.L., C.I.S.L., or U.I.L. Often, they either minimized or entirely ignored returns unfavorable to preferred confederations. In such exultation, publicity, and juggling of figures lodged the implicit belief that the union loyalty of workers, as expressed on their C.I. election ballots, necessarily reflected their voting propensities at political elections. Italian newspapers, finally aware after 1953 that the position of unions in the life of the nation merited more than neglect, hostility, or passing comment, nevertheless confused, in the case of C.I. elections, appearances with reality — a lapse they shared in common with the unions themselves and with most other Italians and foreigners supposedly well informed about the labor movement.

When laborious investigation of C.I. election returns replaced fanfare and when objective appraisal of grievance committees in the pursuit of their duties supplanted wishful thinking, two inescapable conclusions emerged. First, any judgment concerning the relative strength of the confederations in C.I. elections had to contain strong reservations since the principal statistical evidence derived not from one official unimpeachable source, but from the central headquarters of C.G.I.L., C.I.S.L., and U.I.L. A fourth collection of data combined information assembled by *24 Ore*, the newspaper closely associated with Confindustria, and other publications. The diverse statistical universe of each source for all years rendered comparisons of election results not only difficult, but also hazardous. Conclusions based upon these four compilations had to assume the most tentative form. Nor could even the bare numerical results of C.I. elections escape suspicion when careful investigation of their journey from remote shop to the adding machines in Rome tempered partisan enthusiasm. If, for these reasons, the meaning of available evidence lacked clarity, it could hardly follow that C.I. election returns recorded, with useful degrees of accuracy, the political convictions of workers. Moreover, in the unlikely event that the three confederations reported the C.I. voting records for the same plants in a community with miraculous uniformity, the lack of information concerning the behavior of labor in political elections, locality by locality, would thwart meaningful inferences. Secondly, in those industrial plants where C.I. managed to survive, they failed, for the most part, to function as successful guardians of the contractural rights of workers. Dispassionate assessment of their performance has reinforced the surmise that the unions, the newspapers, and the public permitted the elections to assume far more prominence than the effectiveness of the C.I. in the workaday life of the factories in the nation would warrant. Employers either controlled or sabotaged the C.I., when they allowed them to exist at all, while the three principal confederations, each protesting its freedom from political ties, lent themselves to the continued exploitation of grievance committees for political ends.[36]

Despite the manifold shortcomings of the data at hand, the statistics presented in Table 42 of Appendix A, *Results of Grievance Committee Elections for Italy as a Whole, 1953–1958, according to Reports by C.G.I.L., C.I.S.L., U.I.L., and "24 Ore,"* lend themselves to the identification of very general trends since three of the sources agreed within broad limits. (U.I.L. restricted its candidates for election to those factories where it enjoyed greatest strength and reported only the percentage distribution of seats, omitting the proportionate allotment of votes. That obvious distortion in U.I.L. data excluded their use in the analysis of trends.)

1. Comparison of the three sources of data for 1957 shows that C.G.I.L.'s vote control did not dip below 47%, or rise above 54%. These limits failed to change beyond one point in 1958. Clearly, C.G.I.L. has remained the dominant confederation in the Italian labor movement. In 1957, C.I.S.L. stood in second place and commanded between 34% and 39% of the fac-

tory vote. According to C.I.S.L.'s own returns for 1958, it gathered up 36% of the votes. However, C.G.I.L. ascribed only 30% of the votes to C.I.S.L. that year. C.G.I.L.'s chief rival, then, could justly claim approximately one-third of the electorate. U.I.L. appealed to about 8% of factory workers in 1957 and its percentage of votes for 1958, according to C.G.I.L. and C.I.S.L., continued within the same range.

2. C.G.I.L.'s own figures have conceded a decline in votes of slightly below 17 percentage points between 1953 and 1958. The majority confederation also admitted a loss of seats amounting to 7 percentage points between 1955 and 1958. C.G.I.L., C.I.S.L., and *24 Ore* agreed that C.G.I.L.'s control over the voters fell 15–17 percentage points between 1954 and 1957, the four years when all three sources provided information. Between 1955 and 1957, the three years when they furnished data on seats, C.G.I.L.'s proportion of members elected to grievance committees fell 5.5–8.5 percentage points. C.I.S.L., like C.G.I.L. itself, reported slight gains in the percentage of votes and seats obtained by C.G.I.L. for 1957 to 1958.

3. All three sources showed C.I.S.L. gains in votes of 10–12 percentage points from 1954 to 1957. C.I.S.L.'s control over seats grew within a range of 2–5.5 percentage points between 1955 and 1957. C.I.S.L.'s own tabulations disclosed slight losses in the percentage of votes and seats won by C.I.S.L. in 1958 as compared with 1957.

4. All three sources concurred in ascribing a rise of 4–5 percentage points in the number of votes which U.I.L. attracted between 1954 and 1957. They also agreed upon a percentage increase ranging a few points below and above 2 percentage points in the number of seats gained by U.I.L. from 1955 to 1957. Both C.G.I.L. and C.I.S.L. conceded slight improvements for U.I.L. in the ratio of votes and seats captured between 1957 and 1958.

Unfortunately, neither the conclusions presented here, nor detailed analysis of two additional statistical series — gathered, for the first time since C.I. elections began, to cover not only the country as a whole, but also its 39 most important industrial provinces and the metal-mechanical, textile, and chemical industries during the years from 1953 through 1957 — succeed in clarifying the exact strength of the three principal competing confederations of labor. This lack of precision about the results of the flamboyant C.I. electoral campaigns waged in over 3,500 plants throughout the length and breadth of Italy combines all the elements of tragicomedy. The entire procedure, from beginning to end, unfolds as though thousands of games of football were played each year before millions of spectators behind a cloud of fog which does not obscure vision completely, but just enough to make it impossible for anyone in the nation to know precisely what has happened. To add to the confusion, the competing teams themselves keep score without benefit of impartial referees. Although the situation abounds in plainly ludicrous overtones, its ridiculous quality has not affected the shouting and enthusiasm of the players and the spectators, nor has it influenced the zeal for placing bets upon the unknowable results. But most oddly dire, no one has raised the question publicly: Is the game really worth playing?

Members of the C.I. appraised their influence and contributions in the second half of the 1950's as negligible. At a time when both unions and management preached the gospel of increased productivity throughout Italy, the C.I. pressed without success for clear, satisfactory, and timely answers to important and complicated questions of piecework. Management seemed to fear that decisions on workloads, timing, incentives, and systems of compensation might involve the setting of precedents. This fear resulted in a policy of delay which persistently poisoned the relationship between management and the labor force. Moreover, it stamped the C.I. as powerless and useless. It also bred the not unnatural suspicion that employers were bent upon weakening the C.I. in every possible way. Press and convention declarations by industrialists about human relations, however nobly phrased, could not counteract these doubts. The workers needed concrete daily evidence that employers wished to cooperate with the C.I. in resolving not only grievances on wages, but also complaints about hiring procedures, hours of work, job classification, promotions, social welfare assistance, and facilities for meals. In the view of C.I. members, satisfactory answers to these grievances met the fate of those dealing with piece rates.

Since interviews with hundreds of C.I. members and scores of union officials established their own deeply felt conviction that management had adopted a policy of not permitting the C.I. to fulfill the duties assigned to them by the accord of 1953, three questions pressed for answer: (1) Have the accomplishments of the C.I. justified the high excitement, time, energy, and money expended upon the elections of their members? (2) Have the C.I. exerted sufficient industrial importance to charge an official agency with the task of collecting and publishing the results of the elections? (3) What specific forces have weakened the C.I.?[37]

All those who believed that a democratic state could not develop in Italy without the creation of a strong, noncommunist labor movement, answered the first question in the affirmative. They freely admitted that the C.I. did not function well, but insisted that the highly publicized elections served a useful purpose despite the imprecise statistical results. The returns aided C.I.S.L. and U.I.L. by demonstrating that C.G.I.L. no longer held a monopoly on the loyalty of Italian workers and did not have the sole right, as it pretended, to speak in their name. The elections also upset the notion of C.G.I.L.'s invincibility since C.G.I.L.'s own statistics revealed a decline in its majority of 16.7 percentage points between 1953 and 1958. Those who supported the worth of C.I. elections believed, too, that continuing progress by the noncommunist unions in winning support among workers would eventually redeem the C.I. by achieving true labor-management cooperation in those plants where C.I.S.L. and U.I.L. obtained majority control. They cited the constructive relationship in the Fiat plants between noncommunist members of the C.I. and management as a beneficent portent of the future. Fiat's position as the single largest industrial complex in all Italy lent prestige to the innovations it encouraged and incited workers in other companies to press their employers to follow Fiat's exemplary lead.

This hope proved too sanguine. The C.I. elections at Fiat in early 1958 exposed doubts, expressed earlier only by experts who knew Turin intimately, about Fiat's motives in cooperating with C.I.S.L. and U.I.L. The 1958 elections witnessed the second split since 1953 in C.I.S.L.'s ranks at Fiat. The results weakened C.I.S.L., left U.I.L.'s 1957 position intact, strengthened C.G.I.L., which had lost ground steadily after 1954, and, because of Fiat's exalted stature among Italian industries, threatened the sustained progress of the free labor movement. Those disturbing returns, when read along with the chronicle of labor events in Turin since 1948, tended to support the surmise that Dr. Vittorio Valletta (1883–   ), Fiat's directing force, consistently encouraged union developments within his plants which best insured his control over them. He directed his energies, quite understandably, not toward the patronage of democratic unionism, but toward the welfare, as he saw it, of the vast organization he headed.

On July 6, 1953, a few months after Clare Boothe Luce became Ambassador to Italy, but before she had instituted her policy of withholding off-shore procurement contracts from Italian employers who did not show enough zeal in fighting their communist employees, *Time* reported:

> Though this still large membership in the Communist union worries U.S. military men, it does not worry Valletta. The big C.G.I.L. membership, he points out, does not mean that all are Communists, but merely that workers have chosen the largest, oldest and strongest union in Italy. Says Valletta: "If I were a worker, it's the one I would belong to myself."[38]

That year, when C.G.I.L. still controlled 65% of the votes at Fiat, C.I.S.L. took the national lead in forcing Confindustria to frame an accord which would abandon a wage structure built upon absurdly low base rates, laminated by ever-proliferating fringe benefits of infinite variety, in favor of a consolidated, rational factory payroll (*conglobamento*). The conclusion of the accord on June 12, 1954 strategically enhanced the reputation of C.I.S.L. C.G.I.L., which obstructed the entire *conglobamento* campaign, had to stand aside while Confindustria signed the agreement with C.I.S.L., U.I.L., and C.I.S.N.A.L. Later, it lost face even more by accepting the same terms negotiated by its rivals. But C.I.S.L. paid heavily for the benefits it wrested from employers for all Italian workers by hazarding civil war within its ranks at Fiat. During C.I.S.L.'s campaign in 1953 for establishing an integrated wage structure, the recalcitrance of Confindustria forced C.I.S.L. to send out a strike call to back up its demands. Despite orders from Rome, Edoardo Arrighi (1922–   ), the head of C.I.S.L.'s members at Fiat, refused to cooperate. The rumor ran that Dr. Valletta had pressed him and his associates not to strike. After their expulsion from C.I.S.L., Arrighi and the other ousted leaders took offices in the Piazza Statuto, directed C.I. affairs from there, and continued to publish the plant newspaper, *Il Lavoratore Fiat* (*The Fiat Worker*). Again, informed opinion agreed that Dr. Valletta probably financed the insurgent group then and continued to do so as late as 1960. Indeed, subsequent events tended to bring into focus the likelihood of substantial employer influence over the inner life of labor unions at Fiat.

During the C.I. elections in 1954, C.G.I.L. won 63.3% of the total vote. This ratio represented only a slight decline from 1953, but a telling fall from its record of 75.7% in 1948. C.I.S.L., on the other hand, obtained only 10.5% as compared with 23.3% in the preceding year. U.I.L.'s proportion remained fixed at 11.3%, but Arrighi's Free Independent Workers (Lavoratori Liberi Indipendenti — L.L.I.) received 14.7% of the vote. In 1955, after Dr. Valletta grasped fully the portent of Ambassador Luce's pronouncements on off-shore procurement contracts, C.G.I.L.'s share of the vote plummetted to 36.7%. C.I.S.L. and L.L.I., amicably persuaded by American and Italian well-wishers, through no-more-of-this-nonsense pressure, to run a joint slate of candidates, scored 40.5%. U.I.L. doubled its proportion by gathering in 22.5% of the votes. During 1956 and 1957, C.I.S.L. presented single lists of C.I. candidates unaccompanied by the L.L.I. attached label. With the two factions united and with the now strongly anticommunist attitude of management comprehended by all sensible Fiat workers, the Confederation's list swept up 50% of the votes and 55.6% of the seats in 1957. C.G.I.L. managed to garner only 21.1% of the votes and 16.6% of the seats and moved into third place since U.I.L. ranked second with 28.5% of the votes and 27.8% of the seats. Skeptical observers took to wondering about Dr. Valletta's next move. In view of C.I.S.L.'s clear majority of seats and Pastore's penchant for independent action, Fiat's uneasy management needed forthright, plausible, and divisive union action. It soon occurred. *Il Lavoratore Fiat* staged a meeting of C.I.S.L.'s grievance committee members in the entire Fiat complex at the Gobetti Theater in Turin from June 23 to 25, 1957 after C.I.S.L.'s confederal leadership had already sponsored a Turin provincial conference of C.I. members in May. The funds for Arrighi's June conference obviously did not come from the central coffers of C.I.S.L. in Rome. The assembly not only listened to talk about a new autonomous category federation of automobile workers, but also afforded an honored place in its proceedings to Giuseppe Rapelli, Pastore's open and bitter adversary in the Christian union movement. Rapelli pleaded for labor unity and deplored Fiat's exclusion of C.G.I.L. representatives from bargaining sessions between management and the C.I. members of C.I.S.L. and U.I.L., a policy strongly supported by C.I.S.L.'s leadership and other democratic forces in the country.

By 1958, Arrighi and Rapelli had fathered a new confederation, the Italian Union of Free Democratic Workers (Sindacato Italiano Lavoratori Liberi Democratici — S.I.L.L.D.). Immediately after its birth, they met in Paris with leaders of the International Federation of Christian Trade Unions (I.F.C.T.U.); later, they held a press conference in Rome attended by a representative of the I.F.C.T.U. The 1958 C.I. elections at Fiat registered slight percentage gains in votes and seats for C.G.I.L. over the preceding year: 25.3% and 17.6%. The new split reduced C.I.S.L.'s majority strength in the preceding year to 12.9% of the votes and 7.4% of the seats. U.I.L.'s score remained stationary with 28.4% of the votes and 28.4% of the seats. Not unexpectedly, the Arrighi group secured 31.1% of the votes and 46.1% of the seats. The danger for Dr. Valletta had passed. C.I.S.L.'s clear majority of seats in 1957 — 55.6% — vanished overnight and exposed the dependence of C.I.S.L.'s electoral power upon *Il Lavoratore Fiat* support and, by ultimate implication, upon the whims of management. The Arrighi-Rapelli move successfully converted each of the four principal labor currents at Fiat into minorities. The two leading national confederations, C.G.I.L. and C.I.S.L., dropped into third and fourth place, while the weakest or most easily controlled of the union groups, the new S.I.L.L.D. and U.I.L., pushed into first and second place.

491

The following table, which lists the percentage distribution of votes and seats among the union groups at Fiat for 1958, 1959, and 1960, shows that Arrighi's organization has maintained the lead it gained in the year of its triumph:

Organizations	1958		1959		1960	
	Votes	Seats	Votes	Seats	Votes	Seats
C.G.I.L.	25.3	17.6	21.1	15.0	21.8	15.0
C.I.S.L.	12.9	7.4	16.7	15.5	16.1	16.4
U.I.L.	28.4	28.4	26.6	27.5	27.5	29.0
Arrighi	31.1	46.1	33.4	41.0	32.7	39.1
C.I.S.N.A.L.						
and others	2.3	0.5	2.2	1.0	1.9	0.5

The bitterly contested C.I. elections at Fiat — that Piedmontese cynosure of enlightened cooperation between management and its democratic workers — have thus ended up by placing the company's grievance committees more completely in Dr. Valletta's hands than ever before. Since most observers agreed that the operation of grievance committees at Fiat between 1955 and 1958 represented their peak performance in all Italy, Dr. Valletta's manipulation of union rivalries, political hatreds, and personal ambitions in his own favor could hardly warrant an affirmative answer to the first question: Have the accomplishments of the C.I. justified the high excitement, time, energy, and money expended upon the elections of their members?[39]

Those who answered affirmatively the second question which called for clarification — Have the C.I. exerted sufficient industrial importance to charge an official agency with the task of collecting and publishing the results of the elections? — cited the absence of authoritative figures concerning union membership as the leading handicap in the legislative effectuation of article 39 of the Constitution. Article 39 states: "Registered unions, represented as integral units with representation proportionate to their membership, may stipulate collective labor contracts which will be binding on all persons belonging to the categories to which the contract refers." But these advocates of a government census believed that the number of votes obtained in C.I. elections by unions, rather than the number of union members, measured their true strength. They contended that this reasoning more nearly met the spirit, if not the letter, of article 39. In line with this principle, discussion chiefly centered upon four proposals for determining union power. Giuseppe Di Vittorio put forth the suggestion that a commission, with equal membership from each of the three major confederations, undertake the task of gathering and publishing periodically the results of all C.I. elections. A second recommendation, also emanating from the left, assigned to the Ministry of Labor the responsibility of publishing a monthly bulletin containing these statistics. A third proposal, again from the left, supported the device "of assuming that the members of the various social security institutes constitute a true union electoral body and of proceeding to elect representatives of the workers enrolled in these agencies by means of secret and direct vote, using the same system as is employed for local and national political elections." Italo Viglianesi (1916–   ), the head of U.I.L., fathered the fourth proposal: the creation of union census bureaus, located at provincial offices of the Ministry of Labor, to determine, on an elective basis, the representational strength of the unions. These proposals, obviously, cared little about the state of health of the C.I., but wished to use C.I. elections to implement article 39 of the Constitution.

Interviews with hundreds of grievance committee members provided dismal answers to the third query: What forces have weakened the C.I.? The spectre of unemployment has doomed most workers to live in daily fear of losing their jobs. Intimidated by anxiety, they refused to court the disfavor of employers by bringing grievances to the C.I. Thus, the very men and women in greatest need of assistance assured the progressive debilitation of the C.I. The stubborn character of unemployment in Italy has precluded hope for the early removal of this impediment to the effective operations of the C.I. Nor has the concomitant of chronic unemployment — the practice of hiring and rehiring workers on contract for limited periods of time (*contratti a termine di breve scadenza*) — shown any lively disposition to disappear despite legal admonitions against abuse. These technically temporary employees have sought so earnestly to insure their retention that they set exaggerated work-paces for themselves, thus arousing the resentment of other workers, dividing the labor force into factions which despise each other, and creating almost insoluble problems for the C.I. to handle. Beyond unemployment, the disunity of the labor movement, the ambivalent attitude of the unions themselves toward the C.I., and the recalcitrant attitude of many employers toward the simple existence of C.I. in their factories have also severely handicapped grievance committees in discharging their obligations. In 1960, they seemed doomed to impotence.[40]

The failure of grievance committees reflected in miniature the deep frustration of the larger labor movement. During the expansive decade from 1950 to 1960, when Italy accomplished prodigies of social melioration and economic growth, the unions failed to satisfy even the modest demands of their members. This debility, ironic in the wake of unprecedented prosperity, issued from two principal points of focal infection: persistent unemployment, already mentioned, and the overemphasis placed by Italian labor upon interconfederal accords and industry-wide collective agreements — bargaining procedures which the Republic inherited, ready made, from the fascist era. Before describing the highly centralized structural and administrative arrangements imposed by this national system of contractual relations, and before analyzing their organizational and economic consequences, the full measure of the country's postwar prosperity should be gauged.

Between 1943 and 1952, Italy received $3,544,000,000 in net foreign aid, consisting of large official and private donations, primarily American in origin, and smaller amounts of dollar credits. During the war years, these funds fed the population and slowly pumped life into the economy. Then, from 1946 onward, the munificent gifts of precious dollars helped to restore the railroad system, reconstruct and modernize the iron and steel industry, relieve the critical housing shortage, augment the power supply, inaugurate a vast program of public works including irrigation and flood control, and redeem the South and the Islands through an integrated scheme of development under the aegis of the Fund for the South (Cassa per il Mezzogiorno).[41] As early as 1949, industrial production reached 110 as compared with the 1938 base of 100. Agricultural output rose to 103. Economists generally regard this recovery, only three years after the cessation of hostilities, as remarkable in view of the conclusion by the Central Institute of Statistics that the real net national product for 1938 matched the record of 1929 and exceeded comfortably the achievements of all intervening years.[42]

By 1951, when the index of industrial production had soared 43 points above the 1938 base, the population census of 1951 classified 6,289,733 persons as goods-producing industrial workers. This represented an increase in the industrial work force of 22% over 1936 when the population census for that year enumerated 5,154,324 persons as goods-producing industrial workers. As Table 20 of Appendix A indicates, the long-term trend in the proportion of workers engaged in industries using agricultural, hunting, and fishing products continued downward although the actual number of people in this category increased between 1936 and 1951. The actual number of persons employed in the clothing and allied trades decreased in 1951, as compared to 1936, while the proportion of workers fell from 19.2% to 12.2%. The long-term trend with regard to textile employment reversed itself modestly by 1951, both in numbers and percentage. The proportion of all industrial labor engaged in the mineral working, metal, and mechanical industries; the extractive industries; and the construction trades increased creditably between 1936 and 1951. The construction trades recorded the most noteworthy proportional gains: from 19% in 1936 to 23.4% in 1951. In the three broad classifications mentioned, the actual number of workers also grew.[43]

The industrial censuses of 1937–1939 and 1951 corroborated, in the main, the pattern of industrial activity derived from the population censuses of 1936 and 1951. Yet, in contrast with the population censuses which recorded an increase of 22% in the size of the industrial work force between 1936 and 1951, the industrial censuses indicated a standstill in actual numbers between 1937–1939 and 1951. With regard to the proportional distribution of workers among the various branches of industry, the two types of censuses differed substantially for only two important industry groups. Although the population censuses showed an increase in the ratio of workers in the construction trades between 1936 and 1951, the industrial censuses registered a drop of 2.2 percentage points between 1937–1939 and 1951. According to the industrial censuses, the percentage of workers in the chemical industry moved slightly upward between 1937–1939 and 1951 in contrast to the decrease of 0.9 percentage points reflected by the population censuses.[44]

Italy's industrial economy in 1951 still remained predominantly oriented toward the consumer goods industries although the long-term trend toward gains in the producer goods industries continued. Both the population and the industrial censuses agreed, rather broadly, that the consumer goods, printing, and construction industries claimed well over half of all industrial workers: 55.5% according to the industrial census as against 63.1% according to the population census (see Appendix A, Table 15).

According to the industrial census counts, the imbalance of industrial employment between North, Central, and South Italy had not lightened by 1951, but had actually become heavier. Of the 4,166,254 industrial workers enumerated, 67.5%, or 2,814,209, found employment in the North; 15.4%, or 642,257, in Central Italy; and 17.1%, or 709,788, in South Italy and the Islands. In North Italy, both the actual number and proportion of industrial workers had increased above their 1937–1939 magnitudes of 2,651,975 and 65.3%. Between enumerations, Central Italy lost both in actual numbers and percentage-wise. The 1951 size and proportion of the industrial population in South Italy and the Islands also declined from their 1937–1939 total of 746,048 and 18.6%.[45]

The steady progress registered for industrial employment between

1936 and 1951 (at least according to the population censuses), although unevenly matched between the North and the South, continued the course so clearly established during earlier decades by the proportional distribution of the active population among economic activities: agriculture, fishing, forestry, and hunting; goods-producing industries; and services. The percentage of the active population engaged in agriculture dropped from 48.2% in 1936 to 41.1% in 1951, a decline of 7.1 percentage points from the prewar to the postwar era. The ratio engaged in industrial pursuits increased by 4.4 percentage points during the same time span, while services also moved upward slightly from 23.7% to 26.4%.[46]

A comparison of the distribution of the labor force in Italy, India, Japan, France, Germany, Great Britain, and the United States revealed that by 1951 Italy had acquired a pattern characteristic of industrialized countries. Although Italy could not yet match the proportional designs achieved by Germany, Great Britain, or the United States by 1951, the allocation of its labor force among the principal segments of economic activity more nearly resembled Japan's than in previous decades. As compared with Japan, a substantially higher proportion of Italy's workers still engaged in agriculture: 41.1% as against 32.6%. For Italy, those employed by goods-producing industries in 1951 amounted to 32.5% of the labor force, while the comparable percentage for Japan stood at 34.6%. The gap opened wider in the service industries: Italy, 26.4% and Japan, 32.8%. Despite Italy's undeniable progress, the proportion of its 1951 active population engaged in industry and the services – 32.5% and 26.4% – compared with the labor force ratios for other countries of the West, indicated the magnitude of Italy's continued economic lag: France, 41.4% and 38.4%; Germany, 49% and 39.1%; Great Britain, 49.7% and 46.1%; and the United States, 37.4% and 50.8%. Withal, by May 8, 1957, the ratio of the employed population in Italy recorded as industrial exceeded the proportion in agriculture for the first time in history. Of 18,508,000 employed persons, 6,718,000, or 36.3%, were engaged in industry; 6,260,000, or 33.8%, in agriculture; and 5,530,000, or 29.9%, in other activities.[47]

Changes in the proportional distribution of Italy's gross internal product among the chief divisions of the private sector of the economy illustrate, even more than the statistics just cited, the overriding importance of industrialization to that country's progressive welfare. Between 1936 and 1951, the percentage of the active Italian population occupied with industrial pursuits in the private sector of the economy rose by 4.9 percentage points; yet the contribution of industry to the gross internal product increased by 11.6 percentage points between 1936–1940 and 1951–1955. The percentage of the gross internal product ascribed to the service trades dropped 9.3 percentage points during this same time interval, although the proportion of the working population engaged in the services had increased by 2.3 percentage points. In comparison with a decrease of 7.2 percentage points in the number of agricultural workers, the gross internal product dropped only 2.3 percentage points. By 1956, the contribution of the service trades to the gross internal product of the private sector of the economy had increased by 2 percentage points to a total of 28.9%; industry's proportion rose 1 percentage point; agriculture's ratio fell 3 percentage points.[48]

Social advance kept pace with economic growth. Of the 42,300,635 persons considered in 1958, the Central Institute of Statistics classified 5,456,005, or 12.9%, of the population over six years of age, as illiterate. This figure contrasted sharply with the total of 27% recorded for 1921 and the count of 21% published for 1931. Moreover, as late as 1901, 48.5% of all Italians over six years of age could neither read nor write.[49]

By 1957, all means of communications had expanded widely to join the distant parts of the elongated Italian peninsula into a more and more integrated unit. The national highway system covered 24,986 kilometers as compared with 20,803 in 1938. In 1957, 47,304 kilometers of provincial roads and 108,728 kilometers of communal roads supplemented the national arterial network. The total highway kilometrage for Italy as a whole amounted to 181,018 in 1957 as compared with 173,296 in 1938.[50] Prodigious increases in the number of licensed motor vehicles accompanied the expansion of highways. The authorities registered 601,959 vehicles during the war years from 1941 to 1950, as compared with 454,369 listed for the previous decade. But the revolution in the Italian way of life did not explode until the period between 1951 and 1955 when the number of registered vehicles quadrupled and soared to 2,801,507. The magnitude of correspondence handled by Italian post offices also increased, but at a more even rate. During 1931–1940, post offices expedited 2,546 million pieces of mail. This total rose by 350 million pieces in the 1941–1950 decade and then reached 3,205 million pieces during 1951–1955. From the decade, 1931–1940, to 1951–1955, the number of private telephones almost quadrupled, increasing from 395,886 to 1,287,059.[51]

The state of the nation's health improved miraculously even from 1941 to 1950, despite five years of war and enfeebling deprivations. The number of deaths from all causes dropped to 1,265.1 per 100,000 of population from the average of 1,394.2 during the previous decade. Then, between 1951 and 1955 alone, the figure sank to 968.3. The reduction of deaths from infectious and parasitical diseases, as well as deaths from respiratory ailments, illustrated the dramatic conquest of disease. During 1941–1950, deaths caused by infectious and parasitical diseases per 100,000 inhabitants fell to 135.2 from the level of 177.3 during the previous decade. But during the five years from 1951 to 1955, the incidence of death had diminished to 44.2. Deaths from respiratory diseases declined about 80 points in each of the decades between 1931 and 1951. Then, from 1951 to 1955, the figure dropped to 91.1 from 171.7 recorded for 1941–1950. Not unexpectedly, the rate of typhoid and paratyphoid cases amounted to 100.7 per 100,000 population during the 1941–1950 war decade, an increase of 22.6 points over the previous ten-year period. However, during the half decade from 1951 to 1955, the rate dropped to 57.6. In contrast with the occurrence of 330.05 malaria cases per 100,000 inhabitants during 1931–1940 and 92.3 per 100,000 population in the next decade, the health authorities reported an average of only 17 cases of malaria per 100,000 persons during the 1951–1955 period — so small an incidence that the statistical summary did not calculate the rate.[52]

By 1958, the nation's complex and proliferous system of social insurances offered workers (at high administrative cost) aid against most of the hazards of life. The National Institute of Social Security supervised six programs: (1) invalidity, old-age, and survivors insurance which paid pensions to over 3,500,000 persons in 1957; (2) tuberculosis insurance which assumed the expense of institutionalizing 107,000 patients during the same year; (3) unemployment insurance which extended benefits to some 500,000 farm laborers and almost 830,000 nonagricultural workers; (4) family allowances; (5) the Cassa Integrazione Guadagni Operai Industria, a fund financed by industrial employers to supplement unemployment insurance payments; and (6) a mixed array of other types of insurance.

In 1957, the Istituto Nazionale Assicurazione contro gli Infortuni sul Lavoro processed 1,220,000 workmen's compensation claims for both agricultural and industrial workers and approved 915,000 applications. The Istituto Nazionale Assicurazione contro le Malattie provided sickness insurance to more than 11,550,000 persons and indemnified 3,315,000 cases. The Federazione Nazionale Casse Mutue Malattie Coltivatori Diretti offered the same type of protection to almost 6,400,000 independent farmers. Two other sickness insurance funds covered the provinces of Bolzano and Trento, while a third federation furnished health benefits to handicraft workers. The Casse Marittime per gli Infortuni sul Lavoro e le Malattie administered workmen's compensation and sickness insurance for three groups of maritime workers. Employees of the national government received social insurance and assistance through five funds; four funds supplied similar services to workers in local government agencies; another fund aided employees of organizations vested with the public interest; and nineteen additional funds protected workers in other categories.[53]

Substantial gains in Italy's real per capita national income and total consumption accompanied the economic and social advances which have just passed in summary review: burgeoning industrial production, the recent achievement of greater proportionate employment in industry than in agriculture, the increasing ratio of industry's contribution to the gross national product, the decline in illiteracy, the modernization and growth of all means of communication, the dramatic improvements in public health, and the expansion of social security. During 1946–1950, real per capita national income amounted to 2,940 lire, as measured in 1938 prices, and contrasted with 2,428 lire for the 1941–1945 time span. Then, the figure shot up to 3,758 lire during 1951–1955, but did not linger there. Instead, the per capita national income reached 4,242 lire in 1956. With 1938 still serving as the base year, the index of per capita total consumption in Italy climbed steadily from 78 in 1947 to 137 in 1954.[54]

Economic expansion and social progress after World War II not only witnessed gains in real per capita income and total consumption, but also saw modest rises in real wages for the nation's laboring classes. The index of real nominal wages for agricultural laborers, exclusive of family allowances, increased from 136 in 1948 to 145 in 1958 (1938= 100). During this period, when the index of the cost of living exploded skyward by 1,860 points, the index of real nominal wages for industrial workers climbed from 108 to 121. Workers in land transportation fared less well; the index for them read 93 in 1948 and reached only 103 in 1958. For workers in commerce, as distinguished from their clerical colleagues, the index ran from 101 to 115 during this same time span.

Unfortunately, large and populous areas of the country failed to share fully in the improved tenor of economic and social life. Toward the end of April 1960, the Committee of Ministers for Southern Development saw fit to lift the press ban from its report to Parliament on the accomplishments of the Cassa per il Mezzogiorno since 1950. Despite the attractive financial incentives proffered to industry by the Cassa, despite its huge program of public works, and despite annual industrial investments of $170,000,000 from private sources outside the South and $85,-000,000 from state funds, the per capita income of the South, as compared with North and Central Italy, diminished between 1952 and 1959.

In 1952, it stood at 51.5% of the average for North and Central Italy. By 1959, this proportion had fallen to 45.5% as a result of the unprecedented economic prosperity of North Italy.

The report of the Cassa revealed that during the decade from 1950 to 1960, only limited types of industries entered the South in restricted locations. Chemical and mining operations accounted for 40% of all industrial investments there, while the building materials industry absorbed 17% and the food industry 16% of these funds. The metal-mechanical and textile industries remained rooted in the North, except for the isolated southern ventures of Olivetti, Valletta, Remington Rand, Marzotto, and Rivetti. Sicily received 42% of total industrial investments in the South, due largely to its potash, sulphur, and petroleum deposits. The province of Syracuse claimed more than half of the Sicilian share. Naples drew 17% of industrial investments and attracted the few metal-mechanical industries which chose to move into the South. The rest of the Campania region, apart from Naples, received 6% of industrial investments, while Sardinia received 10% and Latium 7%. Thus, four regions obtained 82% of these funds, while the remaining 18% dribbled out into the most destitute areas of the impoverished South: Abruzzo, Molise, Lucania, and Calabria.

The heroic ten-year program of the Cassa failed to create enough new jobs to absorb into industry and public projects the standing army of unemployed workers in the South. Consequently, in this anciently depressed and forgotten land, the migration of agricultural laborers from their homes far exceeded in magnitude the population shifts which tore apart customary habits of life in all parts of Italy during the postwar period. These farmhands abandoned their villages either to establish themselves in northern industrial centers, or to replace northern peasants who had forsaken the poverty of their own rural life, or to seek jobs in the new industrial hubs of the South itself. Meanwhile, Central Italy, untouched by the bounties lavished upon the South, sank into depression as war-stimulated lignite mines closed down and important industries curtailed production or padlocked their plants. The crisis in agriculture, which normally engaged between 50% and 60% of the active population, forced thousands of peasants in this classic home of sharecropping to leave their farmsteads in the mountains and hill country.[55]

The pervasive prosperity of the industrial North and the fear by its established workers of competition from migrant newcomers tempered extreme manifestations of labor unrest in the nation from 1950 to 1960 despite the widespread social ferment which agitated Central and South Italy. Although the beginning and end of the decade witnessed vigorous strike action, the middle years marked a decline in union militancy. In 1950, over 3,100,000 persons in the goods-producing industries and the services took part in 1,060 strikes, while nearly 420,000 agricultural workers engaged in 190 strikes. The number of strikers fell considerably during 1951 and 1952, only to ascend again in 1953 when more than 4,346,000 goods-producing and service workers, joined by 325,000 agricultural laborers, participated in almost 1,400 strikes. However, by 1957, only 1,117,000 goods-producing and service workers left their jobs. The number of strikers in agriculture fell to 110,000. During the early part of 1959, the labor movement still suffered the effects of 1958's economic recession which brought widespread industrial layoffs in its wake. Most workers faced unemployment with resignation and did not imitate the employees of the Galileo works at Florence, renowned for its optical products and precision instruments. There, when presented with dismissal notices, union members protested by seizing the plant and refusing to leave. This action, although exceptional, served as a portent. Later in 1959, the tide of labor peace turned as the deadline drew near for the renewal of 38 national category collective bargaining contracts. In contrast to 1958, the number of hours lost in strikes during 1959 tripled. Some 5,500,000 workers left their jobs in 31 different industries and trades.[56]

Under the benign influence of industrial expansion and prosperity, however restricted in character and geographical range, the Italian labor movement, despite chronic unemployment and internal political division, should have experienced some limited measure of positive growth in membership, funds, and power. Such modest development would have satisfied the normal expectation that unions thrive best during periods of economic well-being. Instead, the Italian labor movement of the late 1950's continued to live, as in the past, from hand to mouth and from crisis to crisis. The majority of Italian workers remained unorganized; others grouped themselves into unions independent of the major confederations. Consequently, C.G.I.L., C.I.S.L., and U.I.L. experienced increasingly grave financial difficulties. Certainly, the Medusa of political strife had her share in freezing union progress. Certainly, persistent unemployment involving from 1,500,000 to 2,000,000 human beings, along with underemployment of equal dimensions, gave further edge to crisis. Nor should honest analysis underestimate the retrogressive influence of many employers who, like their predecessors of the early twentieth century, remained recalcitrant toward progress in the attitudes of industrial relations generally accepted by management in advanced societies of the West.

Although these forces alone might well have insured the failure of the labor movement, another evil, and perhaps the central defect of unionism in Italy, must take its place alongside the other malevolent influences: the proclivity of Italian labor to organize itself from the top downward under predominantly horizontal rather than vertical leadership. This inclination condemned union members after 1945 to a corporative system of centralized interconfederal accords and industry-wide collective bargaining. But in postwar Italy, the parties contracted freely, unaided by fascist legislative fiat and administrative surveillance. Economic strength determined the outcome. Since left-wing unionism had placed all its hopes and energies upon councils of administration, thereby weakening the grievance committees beyond redemption while losing the councils entirely, the unions soon found themselves helpless to enforce the terms of either the grandiose interconfederal accords or the industry-wide contracts. They lacked the essential tools of constraint: effective organization at the plant and local levels.

By February 1953, C.I.S.L. began to question officially the wisdom of interconfederal accords and industry-wide collective bargaining as the sole approach to wage formulation. It admitted publicly that industry-wide contracts, far from insuring adequate wages, hours, and working conditions, served merely to set basic standard rates which satisfied the needs of the least efficient, marginal firms. This type of bargaining made inevitable, at the same time, disproportionately high profits for well-organized and technically progressive companies. C.I.S.L. drew from this realistic appraisal the fundamental doctrine of its wage policy. It would no longer accept the interpretation of employers that the contracts established maximum rates and conditions. Thereafter, improvements would be sought not only at the national seat of bargaining, where failure had occurred, but also at the plant level.

But plant bargaining required formal union bodies in each factory. Unfortunately, none existed. To remedy this lack, C.I.S.L. began a campaign within its own organization to create factory unions. The effort elicited the immediate opposition of C.G.I.L. to individual plant bargaining. That confederation continued its counterpropaganda, based on the Marxist concept of the solidarity of all workers, for three years. In early 1956, however, C.G.I.L. reversed itself after mounting stresses within its own ranks indicated all too clearly that it had failed to improve the lot of its members under conventional bargaining dispensations. It not only approved factory unions, but amended the confederal constitution as well to confer official status upon them — a statutory recognition of change never accorded to factory unions by C.I.S.L. At the same time that C.G.I.L. moved toward plant bargaining as a possible method of recovering prestige among Italian workers, Confindustria began to express openly its opposition to this reversal of traditional collective bargaining policy.

It would be impossible to appreciate fully C.I.S.L.'s courage in advocating so radical a departure from cherished bargaining procedures inherited from the fascist era without understanding in detail the structure and government of the Italian labor movement during the 1950's. The designations, "territorial" or "horizontal," will cover those organizations which included all union groups within an indicated geographical range: the top confederations with their country-wide jurisdictions, the provincial chambers of labor, and the communal chambers of labor. They resembled the national A.F.L.-C.I.O. and the city, county, and state central bodies in the United States. The terms, "category" or "vertical," will refer to those organizations which gathered together workers in particular segments of industry, the crafts, commerce, and agriculture: the *sindacati di categoria*. They resembled American national and international unions. For all territorial as well as category units within an Italian confederation, a common pattern of institutions has evolved: congresses, councils, committees, secretariats, "colleges," service institutes, and training units. The nature and functions of these universal institutions will be described first. Afterward, the various levels of the confederal hierarchy — each utilizing the institutions just sketched — will be defined and their effectiveness appraised. Chart 1 of Appendix B particularizes the composition, number, elective powers, duties, and responsibilities of these institutions in all units from the national headquarters of the three principal confederations down to the factory unions.[57]

The following institutions have created the common pattern:

1. The *assembly, congress,* or *convention* legislated policy, approved estimated and final budgets, and elected members of specified committees and councils.

2. The *general council* served as the chief deliberative body. The directive committee (described below) and a wide representation of pertinent territorial and category organizations constituted its membership.

3. The *directive committee* interpreted the policy decisions and directives of the assembly or congress and had the ultimate responsibility of seeing that they were carried out.

4. The *executive committee* aided the secretariat (described below) in carrying out the decisions of the directive committee and the congress.

5. The *secretariat,* which formed part of the body which elected it, was headed by a secretary-general, responsible secretary, or secretary.

It carried out, from day to day, the policies set by the congress and the decisions taken by the directive committee.

The *secretary-general* accomplished his coordinating tasks with the aid of a varying number of secretaries and vice-secretaries in the larger territorial and category bodies. These secretaries assumed responsibility for specific functions. The full range of these activities, present only at the confederal level, three or four national category union headquarters, and the important provincial chambers of labor, were as follows: organizing activities, union controversies and technical aspects of collective bargaining, research, education, social insurance and assistance, press and propaganda, youth programs, special services for women workers, and internal administration — purchase, supply, and financial control.

6. The *college of honest men (probiviri)* settled controversies between individual union members and between constituent organizations. It also acted in cases of a disciplinary nature. The *college of auditors* was responsible for insuring financial regularity and efficiency. The quasi-independent *institutes of social welfare and insurance* helped union members to process claims for various types of social insurance and assistance. These institutes were financially supported by government subvention based upon the number of cases handled. The quasi-independent *institutes of vocational training* were also subsidized through government funds which were granted in proportion to the number of union workers trained in the classes organized by the institutes.

All of the institutions described had regularly established times of meetings, as well as special meetings which could be called under constitutionally provided circumstances and methods. The pattern of institutions in the different organizational units varied in degree of completion; it became fuller as the hierarchical level rose from factory union up to national confederation.

Factory unions were called *sezioni sindacali di fabbrica* in C.G.I.L., *sezioni aziendali sindacali* in C.I.S.L., and, when they existed at all in U.I.L., *nuclei di fabbrica*. With time, patience, skill, money, and more good fortune than could be foreseen in the late 1950's, the basic building block in the Italian labor movement might become the factory union. But at the verge of 1960, the prospects of success were less than fair since two conditions still needed to be fulfilled: factory unions had to be organized and kept alive; in addition, they had to function effectively. During field interviews in 1957, local officials of the confederal offices and of the category unions admitted that most of the factory unions claimed by C.G.I.L. and C. I. S. L. (C.G.I.L., 6,600; C.I.S.L., 1,500; U.I.L., very few) were little more than paper organizations, yet in an embryonic stage of development.

But presupposing that they actually functioned, under what circumstances might they have been effective? Given the chief premise of C.I.S.L.'s new wage policy, successful bargaining at the plant level could have taken place only in those companies where the profit margin was large enough to warrant concessions above the rates established in the national contract. In Italy, this would have limited considerably the number of factories where C.I.S.L. could pursue its policy. Of even more importance was the fact that in most plants C.I.S.L. could not hope to press its case alone. Its factory unions would have needed the aid of C.G.I.L.'s or U.I.L.'s factory unions. Yet such cooperation would have assured success to C.G.I.L.'s propagandistic efforts for unity of action among all workers and would have proved very embarrassing indeed to the top leadership of C.I.S.L. and U.I.L. Therefore, C.I.S.L. had to limit the achievement of favorable plant contracts to those firms where the employers were sufficiently anticommunist and sufficiently friendly to C.I.S.L. to present the prestige of a contractual victory to a minority union group in their plants. On May 22, 1956, the management of the huge Fiat complex at Turin signed a history-making local agreement reducing the hours of work for its employees, without loss of pay, to the lowest level in Italian factories. Ironically enough, Fiat's management concluded this pioneering agreement not with C.I.S.L.'s and U.I.L.'s factory unions, which do not exist in the Fiat plants, nor, in the absence of factory unions, with C.I.S.L.'s and U.I.L.'s provincial category unions. Rather, it treated with the representatives of C.I.S.L. and U.I.L. on the grievance committees where these two confederations then controlled a majority of the seats, thus isolating C.G.I.L. Although there was some question whether, under the terms of the interconfederal accord creating grievance committees, the committees had the right to negotiate contracts, in contrast to the clear right to supervise the administration of contracts, both C.I.S.L. and U.I.L. hailed the Fiat contract on reduction of hours as a landmark victory for the democratic unions. No doubt, the victory was a resounding one, but not for the concept of factory unions and of local supplementary agreements signed by those unions. The 1958 split in C.I.S.L.'s ranks at Fiat and the re-emergence of Arrighi's independent group have confirmed the suspicion that Dr. Valletta would never willingly treat with factory unions allied with national category federations, or even suffer their formation within his plants. The most important agreement, actually embodying the principle of collective bargaining at the factory level, was signed on January 19, 1957 at Perugia by C.I.S.L.'s local representatives and the "Luisa Spagnoli" firm, large producers of women's clothing.

Since union officials did not even pretend that factory unions existed in most plants, and since they still had to be formed, the question naturally arose: Where could factory workers look for guidance in the creation and sustaining of factory unions? The answer seemed to lie in the direction of the communal category unions or the communal chambers of labor. There are over 7,900 communes in Italy. In each commune, whenever a sufficient number of workers in the same industry or trade had been organized, a communal category union was formed. These communal category organizations were known as unions or leagues. The latter term usually applied to communal groups of agricultural and building trades workers. At times, when not enough members of the same category existed in one commune, a district or zonal category union *(sindacato mandamentale o zonale di categoria)* was set up. Conversely, in a few very large cities, when workers were too numerous in certain categories to make communal category meetings manageable, ward category unions *(sindacati rionali di categoria)* have been created. C.G.I.L. claimed 16,000 communal category unions; C.I.S.L., 15,000; and U.I.L., an estimated 15,000. Direct observation indicated that communal category unions were either pitifully weak, manned by a lone volunteer after working hours, or nonexistent. Even in the industrial North, they were effective only in large cities like Milan, Turin, and Genoa. Clearly, help and guidance for the factory unions could not be expected from communal category unions which needed help and guidance themselves.

Nor was the prospect of aid from the communal chambers of labor much brighter. Communal chambers of labor were called *camere del lavoro comunali* in C.G.I.L., *uffici comunali* in C.I.S.L., and *camere sindacali comunali* in U.I.L. In theory, they encouraged, aided, and coordinated the local labor movement, since they united all members of all category unions in the commune. Again, except in the larger cities, they existed mostly on paper, despite C.G.I.L.'s claims of 2,250 communal, ward, and zonal chambers of labor; C.I.S.L.'s nearly 7,000 communal and 750 district chambers of labor; and U.I.L.'s estimated 3,000 communal and 600 district chambers of labor. Again, the affairs of the local chamber, miserably housed, were handled by a volunteer who appeared in the late afternoon, having already put in a full day's work at the plant or shop. These chambers were so poverty-ridden, starved for personnel, and isolated that they were largely ineffective. Factory unions had to look elsewhere for help and comfort.

The communes of Italy were grouped into ninety-two provinces. The provincial category union has been designed to coordinate and direct the activities of all local unions of a given industry, trade, or profession within the province. These union groups could easily seem to be the logical organizers and advisers of the factory unions. But the claimed number of provincial category unions (C.G.I.L., 2,500; C.I.S.L., 3,900; and U.I.L., an estimated 3,000), like the claimed number of communal category unions and communal chambers of labor, concealed grave weaknesses. Even the best of the national category unions — the metal-mechanical workers, the chemical workers, and the textile workers – were able to maintain but few provincial category unions of their own. Usually, they assigned one or two full-time officials to the provincial chambers of labor in the larger cities. All too often, the salaries of even these officials had to be supplemented by grants from the provincial chambers and the parent Confederations: C.G.I.L., C.I.S.L., and U.I.L. Since this arrangement held true for some of the larger national category unions, the state of the provincial unions of the other categories could arouse no hope of assistance to factory unions. If it were not for the monthly subsidies of the parent Confederations, both to the weaker national categories and to their provincial units, they would have been reduced to utter ineffectiveness.

As this long survey of Italian labor history has already noted, the provincial chambers of labor formed the traditional centers of the Italian labor movement away from Rome. They were called *camere del lavoro provinciali* in C.G.I.L., *unioni provinciali* in C.I.S.L., and *camere sindacali provinciali* in U.I.L. The chambers grouped all provincial category unions and all communal chambers of labor in the province within their coordinating and directive orbits. Because of the weakness or absence of the units already described, the chambers of labor assumed the duties and responsibilities better undertaken by communal and provincial category unions were they organized and equipped to do so. Officials in the average provincial chamber of labor — overworked, underpaid, perpetually short of payroll and office expense funds, beset by transportation difficulties, and torn between the demands of the national headquarters in Rome and local exigencies — had to organize and direct strikes, keep in touch with workers throughout the province, and supply technical knowledge to scores of groups ranging from those in agriculture, food processing, and the underemployed building trades to those in small metal-fabricating shops, textiles, banks, commercial establishments, and public employment. Small wonder that one provincial chamber officer, when asked what he did to bring unorganized workers into the unions, replied: "Well, you know, within the larger plants there already is a natural spirit of unionism and the workers there tend to organize themselves. We just do not get at the smaller plants."

Of the full range of services listed in the description of the secretariat, only the offices of organizing activities, union controversies and collective bargaining, and social insurance and assistance functioned in the average C.G.I.L. provincial chamber of labor. According to C.G.I.L., only one-third of its chambers provided the full range of services, but even in these larger bodies, research facilities were often either very weak or entirely absent. Since C.G.I.L. still counted as the strongest of the confederations, both numerically and financially, the proportion of fully serviced provincial chambers in C.I.S.L. fell below one-third and dipped considerably more for U.I.L. The concept of strength in the Italian labor movement must be employed with due consideration of its relative meaning. The Milan chamber of labor, C.G.I.L.'s most powerful provincial body, closed its books in 1955 with a deficit of almost $15,000 (9,285,596 lire), a large amount for Italy. This figure did not include the deficits of the various provincial category unions. The Turin provincial chamber of labor, C.G.I.L.'s second largest, closed its books in 1955 with rental debts of $11,200 (7,000,000 lire) and unpaid social insurance contributions for its employees amounting to $12,800 (8,000,000 lire).[58]

Despite their shortcomings in services rendered and revenues produced, C.G.I.L.'s provincial chambers of labor, so eminently suited by history and character for kindling among their members militant union action in the pursuit of the Confederation's political goals, exchanged their *de facto* pivotal roles within the C.G.I.L. for *de jure* recognition at the Confederation's Fifth National Congress in Milan during April 1960. With the avowed aim of increasing democratic procedures throughout C.G.I.L.'s entire structure, the Congress adopted a new constitution. This document ostensibly bestowed more freedom upon national category federations: the congresses of provincial chambers of labor would henceforth designate all delegates to the national congresses of C.G.I.L. (previously, the national category federations divided this function with the chambers), including officials of C.G.I.L. and the national category federations if they wished to serve as delegates. C.G.I.L.'s leaders thus "unhooked" the national congresses of category unions, which formerly chose their share of representatives at the national congresses of C.G.I.L., from the necessity of coordinating their assemblies with those of the Confederation. Although the national category unions retained a proportion of members on the directive council and executive committee of C.G.I.L., the new arrangements simplified and clarified the task of running the national congresses of C.G.I.L.: all delegates came from the provincial chambers of labor which the Confederation in Rome controlled directly by constitutional right.

The increased freedom granted to C.G.I.L.'s national category unions will probably serve them as effectively as the autonomy granted to their counterparts by the constitutions of C.I.S.L. and U.I.L. Like national and international unions in the United States, the national category unions grouped all members of a given trade, industry, or profession into a country-wide organization. In 1960, there were 75 national category unions in C.G.I.L., 35 in C.I.S.L., and 55 in U.I.L. Logically, they should have formed the dynamic centers of the Italian labor movement. But most of them were weak and dependent upon the parent Confederations for their very existence. In C.G.I.L., only five national category unions were sufficiently well organized to afford the full complement of secretariat services: the metal-mechanical workers, textile workers, chemical workers, agricultural day laborers, and sharecroppers. In C.I.S.L., this situation held true for only the first three categories mentioned, while in U.I.L. perhaps only the chemical workers could have claimed similar strength.

The inability of most national category federations to function effectively on their own, without financial aid, administrative help, and bargaining assistance from their parent Confederations, had not seriously convinced Italian labor leaders by the end of the 1950's to forego their heavy reliance upon industry-wide national agreements. As compared with the estimate for the United States of over 150,000 collective agreements in force, all of organized labor in Italy operated within the terms provided by a few hundred collectively bargained contracts. Although provincial agreements concerning agricultural workers, day laborers, and sharecroppers increased in importance before 1960, industry-wide agreements continued to dominate the industrial segment of the economy where they totalled nearly 100. The number of these agreements stipulated in any one year varied greatly: 1949, 63; 1952, 15; 1955, 40; 1957, 22; and 1958, 38.

In 1959, after a series of militant strikes conducted in an atmosphere of bitter intransigence, labor and management finally concluded national contracts which covered 4,000,000 workers in 38 categories. Also, more than 1,000,000 government employees won the sliding scale and other important economic gains. In addition, provincial and interprovincial contracts brought improvements to 1,000,000 agricultural laborers, 200,-000 employees in commercial establishments, and 100,000 workers in the food industry. On the average, the new contracts secured wage concessions of 8%–9%; they amounted, annually, to 200 billion lire. Other benefits concerned holidays, seniority rights, overtime, piecework minima, wage grades, and apprenticeship. Negotiations in dairy plants and the textile industry resulted in progress toward attaining equal wages for equal work among men and women, while the metallurgical workers and miners obtained regulation of piecework and revision of job classifications.

The achievements of labor in 1959 should not obscure the long and arduous struggles which strained the limited resources of even the strongest Italian category unions, the metal-mechanical federations of C.G.I.L., C.I.S.L., and U.I.L. Their key agreement, first stipulated in 1948, covered the entire range of workers in basic steel, fabricating plants, mechanical shops, automobile and aircraft factories, shipyards, and scores of allied activities. But its very scope served to conceal the confined limits of its application and the poverty of its provisions. The metal-mechanical federations had succeeded in organizing less than 40% of the workers in the numerous industries under their jurisdiction. Moreover, eight years elapsed before the unions could convince employers to bring to full conclusion the partial agreement drawn up in 1948. Too, the concessions won by the metal-mechanical workers in 1959 came hard and only after the longest and most arduous strike conducted that year. So has industry-wide collective bargaining fared in the pattern-setting category federations for the entire world of Italian labor.[59]

Toward Rome, then, led all union roads as well.

The national headquarters of the three principal Confederations exercised centralized control over most union activities which, in the United States, have been assumed by the national and international unions and their subordinate bodies. Whenever confederal control relaxed, the cause could be sought less in the absence of will than in the lack of funds and personnel. Instead of rehearsing in detail the activities of each of the offices of one of the Confederations in Rome, a simple listing of the accomplishments during a single month of one of the departments will suffice to illustrate the degree of centralization which existed.

The office of organizing activities reported to its particular secretariat that it had summoned congresses of agricultural workers in one of the important regions of the country; provided confederal speakers for more than three score May Day meetings; acted as peacemaker between provincial chambers and category unions concerning the division of confederal dues and monthly category dues; aided in the formation of a new national category union; called meetings of provincial groups of activists to encourage the creation of factory unions; continued its special programs for women workers; arranged meetings and prepared printed materials as part of the plan for unionizing agricultural workers; and, as part of a vast program for extending the influence of the Confederation in central and southern Italy, called conferences to identify the specific problems of particular provinces, arranged for courses adapted to the needs of the provinces, provided for visits of personnel from Confederation headquarters to local groups, and took action with public officials in behalf of the building trades unions to constrain contractors, working on the reform projects fostered by the Fund for the South, to pay a union scale of wages. To ensure the efficacy of the special program for central and southern Italy, the office of organizing activities assigned personnel, specially trained and paid directly by confederal headquarters, to key provincial chambers of labor in order that new zonal offices might be adequately supervised.

The daily tasks assumed by this confederal office of organizing activities demonstrated, impressively, the practice of highly centralized control. However, to uncover its most dramatic manifestations, analysis must turn to the stipulation of interconfederal accords and to an appraisal of the kinds of dues utilized by the Italian labor movement and the involved, almost incomprehensible arrangements made for their collection by the Confederations themselves.

The three chief labor Confederations, and C.I.S.N.A.L. as well, have concluded accords with employers associations which applied to all workers in total segments of the economy like industry or commerce. The principal accords stipulated between 1943 and 1949 have already been described elsewhere in this narrative. On August 5, 1949, the Confederations signed an agreement with Confindustria which set standards for readjusting the narrowing wage differentials among laborers, semi-skilled workers, skilled employees, and specialized help in all plants operated in all kinds of industries by members of Confindustria. There followed the accord of October 18, 1950 on individual dismissals of industrial workers; the accord of December 8, 1950 which dealt again with unbalanced industrial wage differentials; the agreement with Confindustria of December 20, 1950 on procedures for collective dismissals; the establishment of the sliding scale for cost-of-living wage adjustments throughout industry as a result of the accord of March 21, 1951 which the parties renewed on January 15, 1957; the provision of family allowances by agreement with Confindustria on June 14, 1952 — benefits which special legislation extended to workers beyond the reach of the accord; the May 8, 1953 agreement on the establishment and functions of grievance committees; the famous *conglobamento* (unification) accord with Confindustria on June 12, 1954 which reorganized base wage rates by merging items on the industrial payroll proliferated by war and postwar compensation practices; and the extension of the *conglobamento* principle to commercial employees through the accord of December 5, 1955, renewed by the parties on April 29, 1957. On April 18, 1956, the Confederations stipulated an accord for workers in all municipalized enterprises which provided them with a "mess indemnity." During World War II, many Italian enterprises established midday mess facilities for their employees due to food shortages and transportation difficulties which made it impossible for workers to go home for lunch, as many had previously done, during the shortened wartime noon recess. When plants discontinued this practice after 1945, employees demanded cash payments in lieu of the meals which the employers had furnished at very reasonable, but heavily subsidized, prices. Where such arrangements still continued, many workers who brought their own lunches wished their share, in cash, of the subsidy which management expended for those who did use the mess. These demands by the labor Confederations started a long controversy which drew to a close in the accord for employees of municipalized enterprises and ended in the far more important agreement on the same subject with Confindustria on April 20, 1956. Thus, the Confederations have replaced the ineffective category federations in collective bargaining areas of the most vital concern to workers by concluding accords for all associated industrial or commercial endeavors in Italy.

A careful exploration of the dues collection procedure will demonstrate that confederal headquarters and their provincial chambers of labor completely dominated the entire transaction. Chart 2 of Appendix B has been prepared as a guide through this tortuous course since it has never been described even in Italy.

The income of the Confederations in Rome depended wholly upon the sale of confederal dues cards (*tessere*). While C.I.S.L. headquarters was theoretically entitled to a share of national category union dues, it actually received none; U.I.L. headquarters made no attempt to share in the dues of the national category unions. On the other hand, C.G.I.L. attempted to collect 6% of the national category dues. However, in a large majority of instances, C.G.I.L. headquarters had to subsidize the category unions. Thus, income from the confederal dues cards was vital to the existence of the central Confederations. These cards were printed in Rome and then distributed to the various provincial chambers of labor. C.G.I.L. and C.I.S.L. effected this distribution by means of the central headquarters and provincial branches of the Banca Nazionale del Lavoro, a private institution which had no official connection with the Italian labor movement. In U.I.L., the distribution was made directly by the confederal offices in Rome to the provincial chambers. Consequently, each member of a given Confederation, regardless of the category union to which he belonged, received his dues book from the Confederation, by way of the provincial chamber, and not from his category union. Since these dues cards did not indicate the category to which a worker belonged, emblems for each category had to be printed, distributed to the provinces, and pasted on the dues cards when they were sold to individual members. In C.G.I.L. and C.I.S.L., the emblems were printed by the national category unions and then sent out to the provinces. In U.I.L., they were all printed centrally in Rome and distributed to the national category unions, which, in turn, made them available to the provincial chambers. Below the national confederal level, the constituent organizations lived on the proceeds from their share of the confederal dues (*tessere*) and from their share of the monthly category dues (*contributi*). The monthly category dues were collected through the sale of stamps (*bollini*). These stamps, in various colors and denominations, were printed by C.G.I.L. and C.I.S.L. headquarters in Rome and then distributed to the appropriate organizations. Only U.I.L. allowed the provincial chambers to print the monthly category dues stamps, thus losing one means of ensuring uniformity and control.

The Confederations knew well enough that this system of centrally printed and distributed dues books and monthly stamps rested upon cumbersome, complicated, and time-consuming procedures which huffed and puffed only to bring forth miserably inadequate collections. Under these arrangements, C.G.I.L., C.I.S.L., and U.I.L. barely managed to draw from 30% to 40% of the dues owed to them.[60] Yet they remained powerless to devise simpler methods which would also guarantee even these meager returns. The Confederations could rely neither upon the national category unions nor upon the provincial chambers, poverty-stricken as they were, to collect dues efficiently and to remit to the parent bodies their proper share of the proceeds. Quite understandably, the Confederations have refused to allow themselves to become dependent upon their dependent subsidiary adherents. So, as of old, union weakness and poverty continued to spin the plot. They bolstered centralized control by precluding the successful growth of factory unions which demanded ample resources of men, money, and strong category federations.

On July 14, 1959, the consequences of the calamitous conditions of

Italian labor throughout its history — perpetual want, the twin obstacles of unemployment and employer hostility to the unionization of workers, impotency in bargaining collectively for men and women already organized, and, as if in compensation for widespread weakness, inescapable confederal domination over the entire movement — manifested themselves in the passage of temporary law 741. Welcomed in the labor press as a boon for union as well as unorganized workers — with second-thought reservations expressed only later about the dizzying complexities of application — the terms of this enactment mirrored all too clearly the helpless predicament of the labor movement. Ever since the Constitution of the Italian Republic took effect on January 1, 1948, labor leaders and their friends in Parliament, joined by the National Council of the Economy and Labor after its creation by law 33 of January 5, 1957 (a body of 20 experts and 59 representatives of employers and labor, envisioned by the Constitution as consultative to both chambers of the legislature and the government), have debated the terms of various bills proposed to effectuate the key passage of article 39: "Registered unions, represented as integral units with representation proportionate to their membership, may stipulate collective labor contracts which will be binding on all persons belonging to the categories to which the contract refers." C.G.I.L., still blessed with majority status in the labor world, kept urging prompt approval of enabling legislation in conformity with the clear language of the Constitution. C.I.S.L., under no delusions about the reality of C.G.I.L.'s predominance, refused to entertain proposals which would have tied minority unions to the terms imposed by C.G.I.L.'s bargaining strength, or, alternatively within the realm of possibility, to C.G.I.L.'s politically motivated refusal to come to any reasonable agreement at all with employers. C.I.S.L. also objected vigorously to the clauses of article 39 which mandated the registration of all unions, once they sought to benefit from the *erga omnes* privileges that legislation would confer upon them. Since C.I.S.L. feared registration as the start of governmental interference with the freedom of unions, and since it refused to invite inferior status for itself at the bargaining table, that Confederation opposed all legislation based upon article 39. It also called for the constitutional amendment of article 39.[61]

With the three leading Confederations implacably at odds on this issue, and with employers decidedly content to leave well enough alone, the Christian Democrats and their political allies did not hasten to bestow upon the social-communists of C.G.I.L. union leadership in the collective bargaining procedures of the nation. Instead, Parliament turned away from article 39 of the Constitution, so unyielding to compromise, and sought inspiration from article 36: "The worker is entitled to a recompense proportionate to the quantity and quality of his work and in any case adequate to the needs of a free and dignified existence for himself and his family."[62] Law 741, although limited in duration, obliged the government to assure minimum standards of economic treatment to all workers in the same category. Article 1 specified that these regulations had to conform to all clauses in labor accords and collective agreements stipulated before the law went into effect in October 1959. According to article 2, the government also had to harmonize its regulations with the provisions of those accords and collective agreements which controlled the economic relationships of specified agricultural groups. Article 4 described certain types of provincial contracts which the government also had to consider. Article 3 stated that the government needed to conform in its regulations with only those authenticated agreements which one of the parties to the contract had deposited with the Minister of Labor and Social Insurance.

The long cavalcade of Italian labor's suffering and sacrifices for sporadic and niggardly gains began with the slow transformation of mutual aid societies into leagues of resistance toward the middle of the nineteenth century. After more decades of privation, exploitation, desperate revolts, and ruthless repressions, workers in local unions drew together time and again, but created a permanently organized movement only with the turn of the century. The General Confederation of Labor, never fully shielded from the winds of socialist and syndicalist doctrine, achieved unparalleled size and force shortly after the close of World War I. Under the impact of socialist paralysis of will, communist intransigence, and fascist violence, it collapsed into ever-fainter verbal protest until its final dissolution. Lifted from the dead after the fall of Mussolini, socialist, communist, and Catholic unions, federated in the C.G.I.L., rose to new heights of membership, if not of internal cohesion, only to succumb to political dissension after 1948. By 1959, the three principal Confederations — C.G.I.L. led by Agostino Novella (1905–   ) after the death of Giuseppe Di Vittorio in 1957, C.I.S.L. guided by Bruno Storti (1913–   ) since the resignation of Giulio Pastore to assume public office in 1958, and U.I.L. still headed by Italo Viglianesi — thwarted as bargaining agents and at a standstill of membership gains and influence, obligingly placed their hopes for the immediate future upon a piece of minimum wage legislation. Compared with the straightforward arrangements of similar laws elsewhere, its transitory character hardly warranted the technical and practical intricacy of its administrative devices. Beset by weakness, the social-communists of C.G.I.L. who dreamed of soviets in the countryside of Leonardo da Vinci, the social democrats of U.I.L. who yearned for the nationalization of Italy's still scant means of production, and the Christian Democrats who envisioned a world of labor-management cooperation fashioned after the principles of the papal encyclicals, accepted law 741 and the determination of minimum wages by the leisurely grinding of bureaucratic machinery. Out of sheer necessity, they invited the government of the nation to bestow relief, as they knew they could not, upon the still unorganized majority of workers in Italy and to lift from the thin shoulders of union members a burden they alone could not bear.

FOOTNOTES – CHAPTER X

[1] Decree law 668 of July 29, 1943 abolished the Special Tribunal for the Defense of the State, decree law 706 of August 2, 1943 abolished the Fascist Grand Council, decree law 705 of August 2, 1943 abolished the Chamber of Fasci and Corporations, and decree law 704 of August 7, 1943 abolished the National Fascist Party.

[2] Gradilone, cited above, III, 2, pp. 254–255, 259.

[3] The same, p. 263, footnote 11; Mario Einaudi, Jean-Marie Domenach, and Aldo Garosci, *Communism in Western Europe*, Part III (Garosci), pp. 179–180.

[4] Maurice F. Neufeld, *Labor Unions and National Politics in Italian Industrial Plants*, pp. 18–19, 108–111.

[5] Giorgio Candeloro, *Il movimento sindacale in Italia*, pp. 144–145; Gradilone, cited above, III, 2, p. 262; Italo Mario Sacco, *Storia e dottrina sindacale*, p. 150; A. Toldo, *Il sindacalismo in Italia*, p. 107.

[6] George C. S. Benson and Maurice F. Neufeld, "American Military Government in Italy," in Carl J. Friedrich and Associates, *American Experiences in Military Government in World War II*, pp. 130–133.

[7] For the text of the Pact of Rome, see C.G.I.L., *La C.G.I.L. dal patto di Roma al congresso di Genova*, Vol. I, the photographic reproduction of the original text between pages 32 and 33; Candeloro, cited above, p. 142; Gradilone, cited above, III, 2, pp. 258–262; Joseph LaPalombara, *The Italian Labor Movement: Problems and Prospects*, pp. 14–15; Salvatorelli and Mira, cited above, pp. 1045–1104; Toldo, cited above, pp. 79–80. Gradilone gives the date of the signing of the Pact of Rome as June 14 and explains that it occurred ten days after the Allied troops entered the capital. LaPalombara and Toldo prefer June 4. Candeloro states that the signing took place on June 3. The photographic reproduction of the text bears the dateline: "Roma, 3.6. 1944."

[8] C.G.I.L., cited above, Vol. I, pp. 20–26.

[9] The same, pp. 17–70 for views expressed by Schevenels, O'Brien, Lawther, Baldanzi, and Antonini, and pp. 75–90 for activities of the Russian delegation. For the *Proceedings* of the Naples Inaugural Congress from January 28 to February 1, 1945, see pp. 95–243. For the constitution adopted at Naples, see pp. 257–274. For article 9, see p. 258.

[10] C.G.I.L., cited above, Vol. I, pp. 247–254.

[11] Gradilone, cited above, III, 2, pp. 271–272.

[12] Confederazione Generale dell'Industria Italiana (Confindustria), *I consigli di gestione*, Vol. II, pp. 12–13; see also, documents 10, 11, 12, and 13, pp. 67–76.

[13] The same, documents 14 and 15, pp. 76–79.

[14] The same, document 16, pp. 80–81.

[15] Bonomi had formed his second cabinet on December 9, 1944 after the Action Party and the socialists refused to participate any longer as members of the cabinet in protest against the veto by the Allied Control Commission of the nomination of Count Carlo Sforza as Minister of Foreign Affairs. Bonomi then constituted a conservative cabinet with communist representation; it lasted until Ferruccio Parri, the Parsifal-like leader of the Action Party and the Committee of National Liberation for North Italy, became Prime Minister on June 20, 1945.

[16] Confindustria, cited above, p. 18; also, document 66, p. 190.

[17] The same, p. 20.

[18] For the text of the agreement of January 19, 1946 concerning dismissals, see Circ. N. 5, Prot. N. 2090, published by the Associazione Industriale Lombarda, dated January 29, 1946. See also, Gino Giugni, "La disciplina interconfederale dei licenziamenti nell'industria," *Rivista di Diritto del Lavoro*, Quaderno IV, 1954, pp. 8–9.

[19] Confindustria, cited above, document 54, p. 173; document 92, pp. 219–220.

[20] The same, document 98, pp. 232–233.

[21] The same, p. 23; see also, documents 101, 102, 103, 104, and 105, pp. 235–249.

[22] The same, p. 21; see also, document 99, pp. 233–234.

[23] The same, document 104, Part IV, pp. 244–245.

[24] The same, p. 21; Amos J. Peaslee, *Constitutions of Nations*, Second Edition, Vol. II, p. 488.

[25] Confindustria, cited above, pp. 23–25; see also, documents 106, 107, 108, and 109, pp. 250–274. For the texts of the D'Aragona and Morandi bills and the report accompanying the Morandi bill, see Confindustria, cited above, Vol. I, pp. 146–171.

[26] Confindustria, *Labor Management Councils in Italy*, pp. 29–31. See also, Confindustria, *I consigli di gestione*, Vol. I, pp. 26–145. For a discussion of the extent of I.R.I.'s influence over the management of individual plants, see Commissione Indagine e Studi sull'Industria Meccanica, Gruppo di Consulenza dello Stanford Research Institute, *Economic and Industrial Problems of the Italian Mechanical Industries*, pp. 303–334.

[27] Confindustria, *Labor Management Councils in Italy*, pp. 31–32; see also, Confindustria, *I consigli di gestione*, Vol. II, p. 22.

[28] John Clarke Adams, cited above, pp. 459–461; Appendix A, Table 33; Luisa Riva Sanseverino, "Collective Bargaining in Italy," in Adolf Sturmthal, Ed., *Contemporary Collective Bargaining in Seven Countries*, pp. 224, 226–230.

[29] John Clarke Adams, cited above, p. 443, footnote 61; Hilton-Young, cited above, pp. 191–205; Hughes, cited above, pp. 156–159, 163–165; Neufeld, cited above, pp. 28, 111–119; Toldo, cited above, pp. 82–92; Vinciguerra, cited above, pp. 177–187.

[30] Candeloro, cited above, pp. 158–171; Gradilone, cited above, pp. 280–304; La Palombara, cited above, pp. 17–24; Toldo, cited above, pp. 88–100.

[31] Gradilone, cited above, pp. 304–317; La Palombara, cited above, pp. 24–29; Toldo, cited above, pp. 100–113.

[32] Confindustria, *Labor Management Councils in Italy*, pp. 35–46.

[33] It was impossible to obtain a copy of this letter. However, its contents were summarized for me by Serafino Agostini, research director, Associazione Industriale Lombarda, on May 21, 1952.

[34] Associazione Industriale Lombarda, Circ. N. 5, Prot. N. 2839, dated February 14, 1949.

[35] Conversation with Serafino Agostini, research director, Associazione Industriale Lombarda, Milan, May 21, 1952.

[36] For further details concerning the sources, nature, and limitations of the first C.I. election statistics ever assembled for Italy as a whole, for its 39 most important industrial provinces, and for the metal-mechanical, textile, and chemical industries, see Maurice F. Neufeld, "Appunti sul funzionamento delle commissioni interne," *Il Diritto del Lavoro,* No. 6, November-December, 1956.

[37] The same, pp. 11-16.

[38] *Time,* "Fiat into Spain," Vol. 62, July 6, 1953, p. 81.

[39] For a recent study of the monopolistic features of Fiat, of its workers' freedom of political and union association, of C.I. elections in its various plants, and of the life stories, work experiences, and opinions of the company's workers — written with open sympathy for F.I.O.M., C.G.I.L.'s category federation within the Fiat factories — see Giovanni Carocci, "Inchiesta alla Fiat: indagine su taluni aspetti della lotta di classe nel complesso Fiat," *Nuovi Argomenti,* No. 31–32, March-June 1958. The percentage distribution of votes and seats in the Fiat grievance committee elections from 1948 through 1958 were based upon figures published in the issue of *Nuovi Argomenti* just cited, p. 240. Comparable percentages for 1959 and 1960 were based upon data supplied in *Il Lavoro Italiano,* April 12, 1960, p. 1.

[40] For the findings of the Parliamentary Commission of Investigation on the Conditions of Workers in Italy (*La Commissione Parlamentare di Inchiesta sulle Condizioni dei Lavoratori in Italia*), see *Rassegna del Lavoro,* February 1958, pp. 199–213, "Il contratto a termine," and pp. 238–251, "Le commissioni interne."

[41] George H. Hildebrand, "The Postwar Italian Economy: Achievements, Problems, and Prospects," *World Politics,* Vol. VIII, No. 1 (October 1955), pp. 57–58.

[42] The same, p. 51.

[43] For the derivation of the classifications used, see Appendix A, Table 20, footnote on sources.

[44] Appendix A, Table 21.

[45] Confindustria, *L'industria italiana alla metà del secolo xx,* p. 83. The total figure used by Confindustria in computing regional differences for 1937–1939 differed slightly from the 1937–1939 total which Confindustria employed to compute the percentages of distribution among various industrial classifications: 4,058,170 as against 4,162,500.

[46] Appendix A, Table 13.

[47] Appendix A, Table 12. For the 1957 statistics, see *Annuario statistico italiano 1958,* pp. 306–307.

[48] Appendix A, Table 14; *Indagine . . .,* cited above, p. 36, Table 3.

[49] *Italian Affairs,* May-August 1958 (VII–3-4), pp. 2195–2196.

[50] Appendix A, Table 10.

[51] *Sommario . . .,* cited above, pp. 137, 149, 151; see also, Appendix A, Table 11.

[52] *Sommario . . .,* cited above, pp. 69–75; see also, Appendix A, Table 4.

[53] *Annuario statistico italiano 1958,* pp. 323, 325, 327–329, 333.

[54] Appendix A, Table 30; George H. Hildebrand, cited above, p. 51.

[55] Appendix A, Table 33 A; "Italy a Hundred Years Later — II," *The Economist,* May 21, 1960, pp. 760–762.

[56] Appendix A, Table 38; Pier Paolo Barattini, "Bilancio dell'annata sindacale," *Il Mulino,* 93 (February 1960), pp. 90–91; Rosario Purpura, "I conflitti di lavoro in Italia," *Rassegna del Lavoro,* October 1958, p. 1688.

[57] The constitutions (*statuti*) of the three confederations and of the national category unions do not furnish specific enough details concerning their actual modes of operation. Constitutional provisions were therefore supplemented by observations in the field and by frequent interviews with officials in the three confederations. Warm thanks must be given to Dott. Bruno Trentin and Dott. Alieto Cortesi of C.G.I.L., to Dott. Giuseppe Jelmini of C.I.S.L., and to Dott. Vincenzo Berteletti of U.I.L. for information imparted with great patience.

[58] These figures were published in a series of three articles by Giancarlo Galli which appeared in *Il Giorno* on July 17, 18, and 20, 1956.

[59] Barattini, cited above, p. 92; *Politica Sindacale,* "Esperienza e contributo della CISL allo sviluppo della contrattazione collettiva," Anno II, N. 3 (June 1959), pp. 284–286; Antonio Toldo, *Il sindacalismo in Italia,* p. 161.

[60] Giancarlo Galli, cited above, in the three articles mentioned.

[61] *Politica Sindacale,* "L'opposizione della CISL alla legge sindacale," Anno II, N. 4 (August 1959), pp. 349–353. For a brief study of the various attempts between 1944 and 1958 to invest labor organizations with legal status, accompanied by the texts of the various draft laws and official parliamentary proposals, see "Organizzazione sindacale e contratti collettivi: i disegni e le proposte di legge," *Rassegna del Lavoro – Quaderno 11* (1958).

[62] For the texts of both articles 36 and 39, see Amos J. Peaslee, *Constitutions of Nations,* Second Edition, Vol. 2, p. 487.

Appendix A

Table 1.

Dates of Italian Population Censuses and Square Kilometrage of Italy at the Time of Each Census.

Dates of Population Censuses	Square Kilometrage of Italy
1861—December 31	259,320[1]
1871—December 31	286,610
1881—December 31	286,610
1901—February 10	286,610
1911—June 10	286,610
1921—December 1	310,120
1931—April 21	310,120
1936—April 21	310,120
1951—November 4	301,023

[1] Before the annexation of Veneto, the Mantuan districts, and Rome.

Table 2.

Population of Italy, 1770 to 1955.

Year	Total Population[1]	Number of Persons per Square Kilometer[2]	Year	Total Population[1]	Number of Persons per Square Kilometer[2]
1770....	16,477,000	57.5	1871....	27,578,000	93.0
1800....	18,125,000	63.2	1881....	29,278,000	99.0
1816....	18,383,000	64.1	1891....	31,421,000	106.0
1825....	19,727,000	68.8	1901....	33,513,000	113.0
1833....	21,212,000	74.0	1911....	35,905,000	123.0
1838....	21,976,000	76.7	1921....	37,452,000	126.0
1844....	22,937,000	80.0	1931....	40,814,000	137.0
1848....	23,618,000	82.4	1936....	42,503,000	141.0
1852....	24,348,000	84.9	1941....	44,357,000	148.0
1858....	24,861,000	86.7	1951....	47,223,000	158.0
1861....	25,756,000	87.0	1955....	48,185,000	163.0

[1] The *Annuario statistico italiano 1911*, p. 4, published population estimates for the years from 1770 to 1858. These calculations were based upon population figures reproduced in the *Annuario statistico italiano 1887–1888*, pp. 152–153, for the individual states which occupied the territory comprised by the eventual Kingdom of Italy prior to March 17, 1861.

For the population statistics from 1861 to 1955, see, Istituto Centrale di Statistica, *Sommario di statistiche storiche italiane*, p. 39.

The population totals for all the years from 1770 to 1955 cover the *de facto*, or so-called present population, defined as persons actually present in each commune at the time of the census, whether or not they claimed legal residence there.

The figures from 1861 to 1955 cover the population included in all areas within the *present* boundaries of Italy.

[2] The density of population from 1770 to 1858 was based upon the present population for those years, while the density of population from 1861 to 1955 was based upon the legal, or so-called resident population.

Table 3.

Italian Emigrants: Total and Those of Working Age, according to Occupation, 1869 to 1955.

Year	Total No. of Emigrants	Total No. of Emigrants of Working Age	Agricultural Occupations	Nonagricultural Occupations		No Occupation or Occupation Not Indicated
				Total	Workers & Artisans	
1869.....	134,865	—	—	—	—	—
1871.....	122,479	—	—	—	—	—
1876.....	108,771	100,993	20,970	79,680	70,223	343
1881.....	135,832	123,656	54,590	68,654	60,051	412
1891.....	293,631	241,487	122,156	117,594	101,826	1,737
1901.....	533,245	476,985	212,098	256,508	227,812	8,379
1902.....	531,509	483,348	206,346	272,841	240,623	4,161
1903.....	507,976	461,407	197,070	259,411	226,280	4,926
1904.....	471,191	420,792	136,998	267,686	235,307	16,108
1905.....	726,331	649,960	232,108	390,326	342,196	27,526
1906.....	787,977	704,392	256,720	414,038	359,471	33,634
1907.....	704,675	632,438	212,759	387,129	338,279	32,550
1908.....	486,674	438,207	138,969	278,841	246,836	20,397
1909.....	625,637	561,286	194,084	336,142	294,165	31,060
1910.....	651,475	581,977	192,953	356,366	306,267	32,658
1911.....	533,844	478,444	137,673	315,555	270,357	25,216
1912.....	711,446	638,955	194,211	411,346	352,068	33,398
1913.....	872,598	783,213	257,293	485,195	420,249	40,725
1914.....	479,152	421,371	119,137	280,185	243,784	22,049
1920.....	614,611	560,717	148,407	337,609	293,223	74,701
1921.....	201,291	169,085	54,042	72,299	60,955	42,744
1931.....	165,860	143,090	14,965	92,697	82,482	35,428
1936.....	41,710	32,550	3,000	15,898	12,128	13,652
1941.....	8,809	6,525	1,454	2,845	1,564	2,226
1951.....	293,057	261,274	55,473	148,280	137,691	57,521
1955.....	320,140	—	—	—	—	—

Source: Istituto Centrale di Statistica, *Sommario di statistiche storiche italiane,* p. 65, Table 20; p. 68, Table 24.

Table 4.

Death Rates per 100,000 Inhabitants in Italy, by Causes Shown, and Reported Incidence of Selected Diseases per 100,000 Inhabitants, 1887 to 1955.

YEAR	DEATHS			INCIDENCE		
	Total	Infectious and Parasitical Diseases	Respiratory Ailments	Typhoid and Paratyphoid	Malaria	Pellagra
1887.....	2,799.2	789.9	515.2	—	—	—
1891.....	2,611.4	547.3	551.0	178.9	—	—
1901.....	2,197.9	367.9	448.5	120.8	—	—
1911.....	2,141.9	365.4	431.9	108.1	535.6	4.6
1921.....	1,741.5	264.9	292.9	96.3	725.6	0.5
1931.....	1,480.0	220.9	261.5	70.7	491.9	0.2
1936.....	1,372.4	167.5	264.2	65.3	318.2	0.8
1941.....	1,386.9	150.4	241.9	97.5	140.7	0.8
1951.....	1,033.1	61.3	108.1	69.5	1	0.1
1955.....	912.0	35.9	79.1	49.1	1	0.1

Source: Istituto Centrale di Statistica, *Sommario di statistiche storiche italiane,* pp. 69, 70, 73, 74, 75.
[1] Only 20 cases were reported in 1951 and 6 in 1955.

Table 5.

Average Annual Amounts of Selected Available Foodstuffs per Inhabitant of Italy, in Kilograms, 1861 to 1955.

| Year | Wheat | Corn | Unpolished Rice | Fresh Vegetables | Citrus Fruits | Fresh Fruits | Meats | | | | Fish, Fresh, & Preserved | Olive Oil |
							Bovine	Swine	Sheep and Goat	Other		
1861	134.9	32.6	5.8	37.0	10.0	16.1	5.7	7.3	2.2	4.1	2.6	8.6
1871	137.2	42.6	15.9	32.0	8.6	19.0	4.0	4.0	1.7	3.8	3.1	7.5
1881	117.6	41.5	15.7	38.5	10.7	19.0	5.3	5.7	2.2	3.8	3.7	8.8
1891	123.2	30.6	8.9	36.7	9.5	29.2	6.8	5.6	2.0	3.3	4.2	8.0
1901	145.7	39.3	15.1	35.2	11.9	27.9	6.0	4.8	1.6	3.2	3.7	4.7
1911	146.7	38.5	11.1	57.9	13.7	27.5	7.2	5.1	1.5	3.5	5.0	3.2
1921	168.3	29.8	12.0	64.1	11.6	28.7	7.5	5.0	1.4	3.9	7.4	5.6
1931	164.9	36.3	10.7	65.6	12.0	28.7	9.3	6.0	1.2	4.6	5.6	3.9
1936	162.3	25.5	12.2	59.3	8.7	21.8	8.8	5.2	1.2	4.9	5.7	6.0
1941	143.0	40.3	16.1	50.4	7.4	23.5	7.5	5.4	1.3	5.3	6.6	6.9
1951	167.9	20.5	7.7	73.9	11.6	39.6	6.9	3.2	1.0	4.3	6.4	4.2
1955	166.3	24.7	11.5	72.9	12.7	45.6	9.6	3.8	0.9	5.3	7.1	6.7

Source: Istituto Centrale di Statistica, *Sommario di statistiche storiche italiane*, pp. 229–232.

<h1 align="center">Table 6.</h1>

Average Daily Available Amounts of Nutritive Substances and Calories per Inhabitant in Italy, 1861 to 1955.

YEAR	NUTRITIVE SUBSTANCES IN GRAMS						CALORIES	
	Protein		Fats		Carbohydrates			
	Total	Of Animal Origin	Total	Of Animal Origin	Total	Of Animal Origin	Total	Of Animal Origin
1861.......	82.6	16.2	72.4	29.0	370.6	3.8	2,517	346
1871.......	86.1	14.3	59.8	20.1	418.2	3.6	2,612	256
1881.......	65.4	16.7	64.1	26.9	276.8	4.3	1,987	332
1891.......	77.6	17.3	61.8	26.4	341.9	4.2	2,282	329
1901.......	92.8	16.5	54.2	24.0	436.9	4.5	2,665	305
1911.......	97.4	19.6	61.3	28.1	429.3	4.9	2,717	356
1921.......	94.8	20.0	62.9	28.0	430.8	4.4	2,727	354
1931.......	94.0	21.9	58.0	30.6	427.8	5.0	2,667	389
1936.......	89.7	21.2	57.3	27.9	403.2	4.9	2,542	361
1941.......	85.6	20.2	49.0	28.5	418.9	4.7	2,514	361
1951.......	88.8	22.3	53.4	26.3	412.2	6.4	2,540	357
1955.......	93.6	26.1	61.1	29.2	438.7	7.3	2,739	402

Source: Istituto Centrale di Statistica, *Sommario di statistiche storiche italiane*, p. 233.

<h1 align="center">Table 7.</h1>

Percentage of Illiteracy among the Italian Population Six Years of Age and above, by Regions, 1861 to 1951.

Regions	1861	1871	1881	1901	1911	1921	1931	1951
Piedmont.................	54[1]	42	32	18	11	7	4	3
Valle D'Aosta............	*	*	*	*	*	*	*	3
Liguria..................	54[1]	56	44	27	17	10	7	4
Lombardy...............	54	45	37	22	13	9	5	3
Veneto..................	*	65	54	35	25	15	11	6
Venezia Tridentina (Trentino-Alto Adige)....	*	*	*	*	*	2	2	1
Venezia Giulia and Zara....	*	*	*	*	*	15	12	*
Friuli-Venezia Giulia.......	*	*	*	*	*	*	*	5
Trieste..................	*	*	*	*	*	*	*	0
Emilia-Romagna..........	78[2]	72	64	46	33	21	15	8
Tuscany.................	74	68	62	48	37	28	18	11
The Marches (Marche).....	83	79	74	63	51	35	26	14
Umbria..................	84	80	74	60	49	37	26	14
Lazio....................	*	68	58	44	33	26	19	10
Abruzzi and Molise........	86[3]	85	81	70	58	45	34	19
Campania................	86[3]	80	75	65	54	41	35	23
Apulia (Le Puglie).........	86[3]	84	80	70	59	49	39	24
Basilicata (Lucania).......	86[3]	88	85	75	65	52	46	29
Calabria.................	86[3]	87	85	79	70	53	48	32
Sicily...................	89	85	81	71	58	49	40	25
Sardinia.................	90	86	80	68	58	49	36	22
ITALY								
Male..................	68	62	55	42	33	24	17	10
Female................	81	76	69	54	42	30	24	15
Total..................	75	69	62	48	38	27	21	13

Sources: Direzione della Statistica Generale del Regno, *Popolazione. Parte I. Censimento generale (31 Dicembre 1861)*, p. 72, for 1861 (illiterates 5 years of age and above); *Annuario statistico italiano 1905–1907*, pp. 246–248, for 1871; *Annuario statistico italiano 1938*, p. 265, for 1881, 1901, 1911, 1921, and 1931; 1936 statistics were never available in the yearbooks since the *Annuari* from 1937 through 1943 cite 1931 figures; *Annuario statistico italiano 1956*, pp. 25, 27–28, for 1951.

An asterisk, *, signifies that the regions did not form part of Italy or were not designated as regions during the years indicated.

[1] Statistics for Piedmont and Liguria were combined in the 1861 census.

[2] Statistics for three regions designated separately in the 1861 census — Parma and Piacenza; Modena, Reggio, and Massa; and Romagna — were combined to approximate the present region of Emilia-Romagna.

[3] The 1861 census combined the present regions of Abruzzi and Molise, Campania, Apulia, Basilicata (Lucania), and Calabria, designated them as the Neapolitan Provinces, and provided only one set of combined statistics for these five regions.

Table 8.

Participation in Italian National Elections, 1861 to 1953.

Election Dates	Number of Eligible Voters	% of Eligible Voters to Total Population	% of Eligible Voters Who Exercised Their Franchise
1861—January 27 and February 3.....	418,696	1.9	57.2
1865—October 22 and 29.............	504,263	2.0	53.9
1867—March 10 and 17..............	498,208	1.9	51.8
1870—November 20 and 27...........	530,018	2.0	45.5
1874—November 8 and 15............	571,939	2.1	55.7
1876—November 5 and 12............	605,007	2.2	59.2
1880—May 16 and 23................	621,896	2.2	59.4
1882—October 29 and November 5....	2,017,829	6.9	60.7
1886—May 23 and 30................	2,420,327	8.1	58.5
1890—November 23 and 30...........	2,752,658	9.0	53.7
1892—November 6 and 13............	2,934,445	9.4	55.9
1895—May 26 and June 2............	2,120,185	6.7	59.0
1897—March 21 and 28..............	2,120,909	6.6	58.5
1900—June 3 and 10................	2,248,509	6.9	58.3
1904—November 6 and 13............	2,541,327	7.5	62.7
1909—March 7 and 14...............	2,930,473	8.3	65.0
1913—October 26 and November 2....	8,443,205	23.2	60.4
1919—November 16..................	10,239,326	27.3	56.6
1921—May 15.......................	11,477,210	28.7	58.4
1924—April 6......................	11,939,452	29.0	63.8
1929—March 24.....................	9,638,859	23.4	89.9
1934—March 25.....................	10,426,259	24.3	96.5
1948—April 18 (Chamber of Deputies).	29,117,554	62.2	92.2
1953—June 7 (Chamber of Deputies)..	30,280,342	64.2	93.8
1948—April 18 (Senate).............	25,874,809	55.3	92.1
1953—June 7 (Senate)..............	27,172,871	57.6	93.8

Source: Istituto Centrale di Statistica, *Sommario di statistiche storiche italiane*, p. 105.

Table 9.

The Italian Railroad Network, 1839 to 1955.

Year	Total Number of Kilometers
1839	8
1841	20
1851	702
1861	2,773
1871	6,710
1881	9,506
1891	13,964
1901	16,451
1911	18,394
1921	20,556
1931	22,571
1936	22,890
1941	23,062
1951	21,711
1955	21,923

Source: Istituto Centrale di Statistica, *Sommario di statistiche storiche italiane*, p. 137.

Table 10.

Kilometrage of Italian Vehicular Roads, according to Type, and in Relation to Territorial Area and Population, 1875 to 1957.

Year	National	Provincial	Communal	Total	Per 100 Sq. Kilometers of Territory	Per 100,000 Population
1875.........	8,265	24,383	46,155	78,803	27.5	287
1885.........	8,446	24,953	48,078	81,477	28.4	278
1890.........	7,891	34,778	36,965	79,634	27.8	264
1904.........	6,656	43,554	87,887	138,097	48.0	417
1910.........	8,303	44,671	95,406	148,380	52.0	432
1921.........	10,336	—	—	—	—	—
1931.........	20,692	—	—	—	—	—
1936.........	20,636	—	—	—	—	—
1938.........	20,803	42,213	110,280	173,296	55.9	396
1946.........	20,987	41,639	107,965	170,591	56.7	377
1951.........	21,735	42,075	106,753	170,563	56.7	362
1956.........	24,920	44,487	107,541	176,948	58.8	357
1957.........	24,986	47,304	108,728	181,018	60.1	363

Sources: Annuario statistico italiano 1878, Part I, p. 127, for 1875; *Annuario statistico italiano 1886*, pp. 406–407, for 1885; *Annuario statistico italiano 1890*, pp. 632–633, for 1890; *Annuario statistico italiano 1911*, p. 200, for 1904; *Annuario statistico italiano 1914*, p. 282, for 1910; *Annuario statistico italiano 1919–1921*, p. 378, for 1921 (no provincial or communal highway data were available for 1921 and 1931 and the *Annuario* for 1933 indicates that the *Annuario* for 1913 was the last yearbook to present such data); *Annuario statistico italiano 1932*, p. 370, for 1931; *Annuario statistico italiano 1937*, p. 97, for 1936 (*Annuari* from 1937 through 1943 cite only national highway kilometrage); *Annuario statistico italiano 1944–1948*, p. 270, for 1938 and 1946; *Annuario statistico italiano 1955*, p. 236, for 1951; *Annuario statistico italiano 1957*, p. 248, for 1956; and *Annuario statistico italiano 1958*, p. 247, for 1957.

Table 11.

Registered Motor Vehicles, Tonnage and Operation of the Merchant Marine, and Development of Communications in Italy, 1861 to 1955.

Year	Registered Motor Vehicles	Merchant Marine				Communications			
		Tonnage under Mechanical Propulsion	Tonnage under Propulsion by Sail	Tonnage of Arriving Goods	Tonnage of Departing Goods	Correspondence (millions of pieces)	Private Telegrams (millions)	Telephone Subscribers	Public Telephones
1861	—	37,517	993,912	—	—	108	0.1		
1871	—	93,698	895,359	5,487,000	4,104,000	230	2.6		
1881	—	199,945	625,812	8,486,000	5,171,000	362	6.0	900	
1891	—	424,711	575,207	12,317,000	4,881,000	397	8.3	12,093	42
1901	—	696,994	410,991	21,998,000	7,529,000	677	9.4	18,443	143
1911	—	1,075,200	—	16,164,000	4,017,000	1,239	15.2	76,644	1,254
1921	87,939	2,043,273	120,741	25,091,000	8,411,000	1,808	20.7	116,922	3,181
1931	333,449	1,832,487	103,576	24,521,000	11,874,000	2,406	29.6	317,409	10,693
1936	429,489	2,905,724	138,767	10,705,000	9,663,000	2,557	25.1	389,802	15,770
1941	220,282	3,156,037	114,850	33,796,000	11,645,000	3,389	37.0	534,616	17,945
1951	1,730,952	4,055,085	102,604	48,008,000	17,226,000	2,797	30.2	929,641	12,722
1955	3,928,705					3,565	32.2	1,708,155	20,996

Source: Istituto Centrale di Statistica, *Sommario di statistiche storiche italiane,* pp. 137–139, 149–151.

Table 12.

Percentage Distribution of the Labor Force among the Three Major Sectors of the Economic Process, 1901, 1911, 1921, 1931, 1941, and 1951, in Italy, India, Japan, France, Germany, Great Britain, and the United States.

Country	1901	1911	1921	1931	1941	1951
Italy						
Agriculture	59.8	56.1	56.2	51.0	48.2	41.1
Goods-Producing Industries	23.8	26.9	24.3	27.2	28.1	32.5
Services	16.4	17.0	19.5	21.8	23.7	26.4
India						
Agriculture	64.2	68.2	69.7	69.5	—	69.4
Goods-Producing Industries	22.2	16.8	15.5	14.6	—	10.7
Services	13.1	15.0	14.8	15.8	—	19.9
Japan						
Agriculture	59.4	48.0	41.3	36.2	28.6	32.6
Goods-Producing Industries	18.3	24.8	28.5	27.0	34.8	34.6
Services	21.9	27.0	30.2	36.7	36.6	32.8
France						
Agriculture	33.1	30.1	28.5	24.5	24.7	20.2
Goods-Producing Industries	42.0	39.2	36.6	41.0	36.1	41.4
Services	24.9	30.8	34.9	34.5	39.2	38.4
Germany						
Agriculture	—	23.8	17.8	18.1	14.0	11.8
Goods-Producing Industries	—	50.6	48.9	46.5	47.1	49.0
Services	—	25.6	33.3	35.4	38.9	39.1
Great Britain						
Agriculture	8.7	7.8	6.7	6.1	—	4.5
Goods-Producing Industries	46.8	46.7	50.1	46.5	—	49.7
Services	43.5	45.5	42.9	47.4	—	46.1
United States						
Agriculture	38.0	32.0	27.6	22.6	18.3	11.6
Goods-Producing Industries	30.6	32.1	34.7	31.8	33.1	37.4
Services	31.3	35.9	37.7	45.4	48.6	50.8

Sources: Annuario statistico italiano 1955, p. 377, for the data on Italy; Colin Clark, *The Conditions of Economic Progress* (Third Edition), pp. 510–520, for the data concerning the other countries.

Data for all countries except Italy refer to the labor force. The Italian data refer to the active population. As defined by official Italian sources, the term, "active population," differs from the term, "labor force" — apart from other minor causes of divergence — because it does not include those seeking work for the first time.

In the data from the Colin Clark volume, the heading, "Agriculture," includes agriculture, forestry, and fishing. The heading, "Goods-Producing Industries," includes mining, construction, manufacturing, and the production of electricity and gas. The heading, "Services," includes transportation, communications, commerce, finance, professions, entertainment, the armed forces, other government services, private domestic services, and other services. These three categories for Italy's active population are defined in Table 13, *Percentage Distribution of Italy's Active Population by Economic Activity and Total Number of the Active and Inactive Population in Relation to the Entire Population, 1861 to 1951*.

The percentages based upon the Colin Clark data were tabulated from the figures exactly as they were published. Where the percentage totals do not equal or exceed 100, the discrepancies reside in the Colin Clark statistics. In several instances, the figures presented for individual countries do not pertain to the year indicated, but refer to that census or survey year closest to the year indicated, as, for example, 1936 instead of 1941 for Italy, in the absence of an Italian population census in 1941.

Table 13.

Percentage Distribution of Italy's Active Population by Economic Activity and Total Number of the Active and Inactive Population in Relation to the Entire Population, 1861 to 1951.

YEAR	% OF TOTAL ACTIVE POPULATION IN			TOTAL ACTIVE POPULATION		TOTAL INACTIVE POPULATION	
	Agr., Fishing, Forestry, Hunting	Goods-Producing Industries	Services	Number	% of Total Population	Number	% of Total Population
1861	59.2	24.1	16.7	13,017,000	59.8	8,760,000	40.2
1871	61.4	23.1	15.5	14,230,000	53.2	12,538,000	46.8
1881	56.8	27.9	15.3	15,152,000	53.2	13,308,000	46.8
1901	59.8	23.8	16.4	15,904,000	49.0	16,571,000	51.0
1911	56.1	26.9	17.0	16,357,000	47.2	18,314,000	52.8
1921	56.2	24.3	19.5	18,067,000	47.6	19,907,000	52.4
1931	51.0	27.2	21.8	18,341,000	44.5	22,836,000	55.5
1936	48.2	28.1	23.7	18,802,000	43.8	24,117,000	56.2
1951	41.1	32.5	26.4	19,659,000	41.7	27,485,000	58.3

Sources: Direzione della Statistica Generale del Regno, *Popolazione. Parte I. Censimento generale (31 Dicembre 1861),* p. 79, for 1861; *Annuario statistico italiano 1878,* p. 40, for 1871; *Annuario statistico italiano 1885–1886,* p. 96, for 1881; *Annuario statistico italiano 1955,* p. 377, for 1901, 1911, 1921, 1931, 1936, and 1951.

The active population comprised those covered by the respective population censuses who were 10 years old or more and who engaged in an occupation, trade, or craft. "Goods-Producing Industries" included the extractive, manufacturing, construction, and electrical industries. "Services" included transportation, communication, commerce, credit, insurance, and public administration, including the armed services.

Table 14.

Percentage Distribution of the Active Population and of the Gross Internal Product in the Private Sector of the Italian Economy, 1901 to 1951.

YEAR	ACTIVE POPULATION			YEARS	GROSS INTERNAL PRODUCT		
	% Agriculture	% Goods-Producing Industries	% Services		% Agriculture	% Goods-Producing Industries	% Services
1901	62.2	24.8	13.0	1901–05	49.2	21.3	29.5
1911	58.3	28.0	13.7	1911–16	44.0	25.6	30.4
1921	59.2	25.6	15.2	1921–25	40.6	31.1	28.3
1931	54.0	28.7	17.3	1931–35	30.0	30.7	39.3
1936	51.2	29.9	18.9	1936–40	29.6	34.2	36.2
1951	44.0	34.8	21.2	1951–55	27.3	45.8	26.9

Sources: Annuario statistico italiano 1955, p. 377 for data on active population; Istituto Centrale di Statistico, *Annali di statistica,* Anno 86, Serie VIII, Vol. 9, "Indagine statistica sullo sviluppo del reddito nazionale dell'Italia dal 1861 al 1956," p. 36, Table 3, for gross internal product data.

The percentage distribution of the active population among the three chief segments of the *private* sector of the economy excludes the active population in the *public* sector of the economy and therefore differs from the distribution shown in Table 13, *Percentage Distribution of Italy's Active Population by Economic Activity and Total Number of the Active and Inactive Population in Relation to the Entire Population, 1861 to 1951.* The same definitions for the three principal segments of the economy hold for both tables.

Table 15.

Proportion of Employment Represented by Italian Producer Goods Industries and Consumer Goods Industries and Construction as Shown by the Industrial Censuses for 1903, 1911, 1927, 1937–1939, and 1951, and the Population Censuses for 1901, 1911, 1921, 1931, 1936, and 1951.

	Industrial Censuses					Population Censuses					
	1903	1911	1927	1937–1939	1951	1901	1911	1921	1931	1936	1951
Consumer Goods Industries, Printing, and Construction........	61.5[1]	61.6	64.4	60.6	55.5	81.6[2]	77.2	71.3	71.5	68.4	63.1
Producer Goods Industries.................	31.8	32.0	29.4	33.7	36.4	14.7	22.1	20.8	25.4	30.1	32.7
Miscellaneous and Unclassified Industries...	6.7	6.4	6.2	5.7	8.1	3.7	0.7	7.9	3.1	1.5	4.2

Sources: Table 21, *Number and Percentage Distribution of Italian Workers Employed by Industrial Firms among the Several Branches of Industrial Activity according to the Survey of 1903 and the Industrial Censuses of 1911, 1927, 1937–1939, and 1951,* and Table 20, *Number and Percentage Distribution of Italian Workers Ten Years of Age and above in the Manufacturing, Extractive, and Construction Branches of Industry according to the Population Censuses of 1901, 1911, 1921, 1931, 1936, and 1951.*
[1] Construction workers were not included in survey for 1903.
[2] If construction workers are not included, the percentage would be 67.4.

Table 16.

Index of Italian Industrial Production, 1901 to 1950.
Base: 1896–1900 = 100.

Periods	Industrial Production Index
1901–1905	123
1906–1910	167
1911–1915	183
1916–1920	180
1921–1925	208
1926–1930	282
1931–1935	267
1936–1940	316
1947–1950	306

Source: Confederazione Generale dell'Industria Italiana, *L'industria italiana alla metà del secolo XX,* p. 8.
The indices for the period, 1901–1940, were based upon the indices of the net product of industry calculated by Silvio Golzio in his volume, *Sulla misura delle variazioni del reddito nazionale italiano* (Torino: G. Giappichelli, 1951). For the period, 1947–1950, Confindustria linked indices calculated by the Central Institute of Statistics.

Table 17.

Index of Italian Industrial Production, 1923 to 1935.
Base: 1922 = 100.

Year	Mines and Quarries	Electricity and Gas	Metal-lurgical	Chemical	Building	Textile	General Index
1923........	121	117	119	117	147	112	116
1924........	128	135	143	135	191	129	138
1925........	149	151	193	147	241	140	157
1926........	156	173	190	155	263	145	165
1927........	159	180	170	156	249	153	162
1928........	152	197	206	153	324	159	181
1929........	162	212	226	153	440	176	202
1930........	157	219	193	150	379	160	183
1931........	128	216	160	125	262	145	156
1932........	111	218	149	119	234	137	146
1933........	111	237	174	150	279	162	167
1934........	126	250	185	164	411	161	183
1935........	141	272	226	178	419	158	195

Source: Confederazione Generale dell'Industria Italiana, *L'industria italiana alla metà del secolo XX*, p. 14.

Table 18.

Index of Italian Industrial Production, 1935 to 1942.
Base: 1928 = 100.

Year	Extractive	Energy, Heat, and Illumi-nation	Metal-lurgical	Chemical	Construction	Textile	General Index
1935........	99	136	112	100	162	77	102
1936........	110	141	106	107	92	70	96
1937........	128	155	114	133	96	84	109
1938........	135	157	121	130	91	83	108
1939........	142	177	122	163	121	87	123
1940........	126	188	122	157	83	92	121
1941........	117	208	117	140	43	79	105
1942........	111	208	109	121	36	59	91

Source: Confederazione Generale dell'Industria Italiana, *L'industria italiana alla metà del secolo XX* p. 23.

Table 19.

Index of Italian Industrial Production, 1947 to 1950.
Base: 1938 = 100.

Year	Extractive	Electrical	Metal-lurgical	Chemical	Construction Materials	Textile	General Index
1947........	68	136	64	75	78	87	77
1948........	63	149	82	80	86	87	84
1949........	69	134	75	89	94	90	86
1950........	76	162	92	107	125	98	100

Source: Confederazione Generale dell'Industria Italiana, *L'industria italiana alla metà del secolo XX*, p. 47.

530

Table 20.

Number and Percentage Distribution of Italian Workers Ten Years of Age and above in the Manufacturing, Extractive, and Construction Branches of Industry according to the Population Censuses of 1901, 1911, 1921, 1931, 1936, and 1951.

INDUSTRY BRANCHES	1901		1911		1921		1931		1936		1951	
	No. Workers	% Distribution	No. Workers	% Distribution	No. Workers	% Distribution	No. Workers	% Distribution	No. Workers	% Distribution	No. Workers	% Distribution
Industries Using Agricultural, Hunting, and Fishing Products	792,606	19.9	1,261,919	28.9	1,153,904	25.3	1,261,596	24.2	908,632	17.6	1,004,617	16.0
Clothing and Allied Trades	1,113,843	27.9	714,578	16.3	774,185	17.0	642,936	12.3	990,863	19.2	764,640	12.2
Textiles	783,253	19.6	643,203	14.7	560,307	12.3	722,787	13.8	559,494	10.9	726,475	11.5
Mineral-Working, Metal, and Mechanical	329,151	8.5	750,932	17.1	769,267	16.9	1,029,494	19.7	1,159,990	22.5	1,614,662	25.7
Construction	564,798	14.2	697,560	16.1	715,991	15.7	1,028,069	19.7	979,103	19.0	1,472,749	23.4
Extractive	227,009	5.7	113,278	2.6	99,852	2.2	120,736	2.3	128,446	2.5	179,508	2.8
Chemicals	23,140	0.5	100,509	2.4	76,776	1.7	178,735	3.4	261,685	5.1	264,472	4.2
Printing	38,717	1.0	53,271	1.2	48,165	1.0	77,392	1.5	89,924	1.7		—
Miscellaneous and Unclassified	117,299	2.7	32,845	0.7	361,135	7.9	162,385	3.1	76,188	1.5	262,610	4.2
ALL INDUSTRIES	3,989,816	100.0	4,368,095	100.0	4,559,582	100.0	5,224,130	100.0	5,154,325	100.0	6,289,733	100.0

Sources: The number and the percentage distribution of the industrial population were calculated from population census data published in *Annuario statistico italiano 1905–1907*, p. 111, for 1901; *Annuario statistico italiano 1914*, pp. 31–32, for 1911; *Annuario statistico italiano 1927*, p. 27, for 1921; *Annuario statistico italiano 1934*, p. 13, for 1931; *Annuario statistico italiano 1941*, p. 20, for 1936; *Annuario statistico italiano 1956*, p. 26, for 1951.

The 1901 census classified industrially all persons nine years of age and above, while the later censuses used the cut-off date of ten years of age and above.

The totals for each industrial category were derived by combining the following numbered classifications in the 1901, 1911, 1921, 1931, 1936, and 1951 tabulations found in the *Annuari* indicated.

(*Continued*)

Table 20 (*Sources*, Continued).

Classification in Table 20	1901 Classification Numbers	1911 Classification Numbers	1921 Classification Numbers	1931 Classification Numbers	1936 Classification Numbers	1951 Classification Used
Industries Using Agricultural, Hunting, and Fishing Products	VIII, IX (a), XI, XV	3	4, 5, 6, 7, 8, 9	9, 10, 11, 12, 13, 14	5, 6, 7, 8	Alimentari, bevande, tabacco; Legno; Carta e cartotecnica
Clothing and Allied Trades	XII	6 (9), includes domestic furnishings	18	23	15	Vestiario, abbigliamento, arredamento, pelli e cuoio
Textiles	X	6 (1–11, except 9)	16, 17	21, 22	14	Tessili
Mineral-Working, Metal, and Mechanical	IV	4, 5 (1)	11, 12, 13, 14	16, 17, 18, 19	10, 11, 12	Estrattivo-manifatturiere
Construction	VI	5 (2), including road building and hydraulic installations	15	20	13	Costruzioni
Extractive	III, V	2	1, 2, 3	6, 7, 8	4	Estrattive
Chemicals	VII	7	19	24	18	Chimiche e affini; Gomma elastica
Printing	IX (b)	8 (1)	20	25	9	No separate figures indicated
Miscellaneous and Unclassified	XIII, XIV, XVI	8 (2)	10, 21, 23	15, 26, 27, 28	19, 22	Varie (under Chimiche e manifatturiere varie); Elettricità, gas, acqua

Table 21.

Number and Percentage Distribution of Italian Workers Employed by Industrial Firms among the Several Branches of Industrial Activity according to the Survey of 1903 and the Industrial Censuses of 1911, 1927, 1937–1939, and 1951.

Branch	1903		1911		1927		1937–1939		1951	
	No. of Workers	% Distribution	No. of Workers	% Distribution	No. of Workers	% Distribution	No. of Workers	% Distribution	No. of Workers	% Distribution
Food and Allied Products	234,100	18.4	305,300	13.2	343,100	10.4	529,700	12.7	476,300	11.4
Wood	75,000	5.9	209,700	9.1	286,100	8.7	283,600	6.8	284,500	6.8
Clothing, Leather, Skins	64,600	5.1	285,500	12.5	521,700	15.8	524,200	12.6	446,000	10.7
Textiles	411,100	32.1	495,200	21.5	642,900	19.4	628,600	15.1	642,700	15.4
Mechanical	108,300	8.5	257,700	11.2	478,900	14.5	823,000	19.8	859,600	20.6
Metallurgical	34,600	2.8	141,700	6.2	122,500	3.7	103,600	2.5	141,700	3.4
Non-metallic Minerals	103,400	8.1	181,800	7.9	171,900	5.2	206,800	5.0	200,500	4.8
Construction	—	—	122,000	5.3	332,600	10.1	558,500	13.4	464,800	11.2
Extractive	122,600	9.6	104,800	4.5	98,800	3.0	137,400	3.3	114,800	2.8
Chemicals	35,000	2.8	50,600	2.2	99,500	3.0	127,900	3.1	200,800	4.8
Other	86,400	6.7	150,200	6.4	204,400	6.2	239,200	5.7	334,600	8.1
Total Number of Workers	1,275,100	100.0	2,304,500	100.0	3,302,400	100.0	4,162,500	100.0	4,166,300	100.0

Source: Confederazione Generale dell'Industria Italiana, L'industria italiana alla metà del secolo XX, pp. 70–71.

Table 22.

Percentage Distribution of the Industrial Population in 1901 and 1911 among the Various Branches of Activities for Piedmont, Liguria, and Lombardy Taken as a Whole and for Lombardy Separately, Indicating, as well, the Proportion of the National Work Force for Each Category of Industry Which the Three Regions Represented as a Whole and Which Lombardy Represented Separately.

BRANCH OF INDUSTRIAL ACTIVITY	1901				1911			
	% Dist. Ind. Activity within 3 Regions as Whole	% Dist. Ind. Activity within Lombardy	3 Regions Share of Nat. Total for Each Category	Lombardy Share of Nat. Total for Each Category	% Dist. Ind. Activity within 3 Regions as Whole	% Dist. Ind. Activity within Lombardy	3 Regions Share of Nat. Total for Each Category	Lombardy Share of Nat. Total for Each Category
Industries Using Agricultural, Hunting, and Fishing Products	18.5	18.0	32.9	18.3	22.4	22.7	30.2	17.2
Clothing	25.7	23.5	32.5	17.0	15.7	13.9	37.3	18.6
Textiles	25.3	31.6	45.5	32.4	22.8	27.9	60.2	41.5
Mineral-Working, Metal, and Mechanical	9.7	8.4	41.4	20.6	19.7	17.7	44.6	22.5
Construction	12.2	10.9	30.5	15.5	13.7	12.9	33.4	17.6
Extractive	3.3	2.9	20.7	10.1	1.1	0.7	15.9	6.2
Chemicals	0.8	0.9	50.2	30.7	2.2	1.7	36.3	16.5
Printing	1.2	1.3	45.4	26.8	1.4	1.5	44.4	26.3
Miscellaneous and Unclassified	3.3	2.5	39.8	17.1	1.0	1.0	50.4	29.3
TOTAL	100.0	100.0	35.4	20.2	100.0	100.0	38.9	21.9

Sources: Annuario statistico italiano 1905–1907, p. 112; Annuario statistico italiano 1914, pp. 34, 36.

Table 23.

Percentage Distribution of Workers Surveyed in the 1927 Industrial Census among the Various Branches of Activities for Piedmont, Liguria, and Lombardy Taken as a Whole and for Lombardy Separately, Indicating, as well, the Proportion of the National Total for Each Category of Industry Which the Three Regions Represented as a Whole and Which Lombardy Represented Separately.

Branch of Industrial Activity	% Dist. Ind. Activity Within 3 Regions as Whole	% Dist. Ind. Activity within Lombardy	3 Regions Share of Nat. Total for Each Category	Lombardy Share of Nat. Total for Each Category
Industries Using Agricultural, Hunting, and Fishing Products...	17.0	16.2	35.4	20.2
Clothing..........................	12.5	12.9	41.0	25.2
Textiles..........................	30.1	33.8	75.6	50.6
Mineral-Working, Metal, and Mechanical....................	25.0	22.8	52.7	28.6
Construction......................	7.5	7.2	36.8	21.0
Extractive........................	1.1	0.8	17.2	7.9
Chemicals.........................	3.3	3.3	54.3	32.6
Printing..........................	1.6	1.6	44.5	26.2
Miscellaneous and Unclassified.....	1.9	1.4	37.7	16.6
Total............................	100.0	100.0	48.3	28.8

Source: *Annuario statistico italiano 1928*, pp. 142–143.

Table 24.

The Proportion of the Total Number of Workers in Selected Categories of Italian Industrial Activity Which Piedmont, Liguria, and Lombardy Represented as a Whole and Which Lombardy Represented Separately, according to the Industrial Census of 1951.

Branch of Industrial Activity	3 Regions-as-a-Whole % Share of the National Total for Each Category	Lombardy's % Share of the National Total for Each Category
Food & Allied Products..........	28.7	15.9
Wood-Working.................	35.4	22.6
Clothing......................	36.1	22.9
Textiles......................	73.7	48.8
Metallurgical..................	64.2	41.9
Mechanical....................	64.5	35.1
Building Construction...........	36.2	21.9
Construction Materials..........	34.4	19.4
Extractive....................	15.6	7.9
Chemicals....................	57.3	34.1

Source: Confederazione Generale dell'Industria Italiana, *L'industria italiana alla metà del secolo XX'* pp. 109–133.

Table 25.

Percentage Distribution of the World's Manufacturing Production among Selected Countries, 1870 to 1938.

	1870	1881–1885	1896–1900	1906–1910	1913	1913[2]	1926–1929	1936–1938
United States........	23.3	28.6	30.1	35.3	35.8	35.8	42.2	32.2
Germany............	13.2	13.9	16.6	15.9	15.7	14.3	11.6	10.7
United Kingdom......	31.8	26.6	19.5	14.7	14.0	14.1	9.4	9.2
France.............	10.3	8.6	7.1	6.4	6.4	7.0	6.6	4.5
Russia.............	3.7	3.4	5.0	5.0	5.5	4.4	4.3	18.5
Italy..............	*2.4*	*2.4*	*2.7*	*3.1*	*2.7*	*2.7*	*3.3*	*2.7*
Canada............	1.0	1.3	1.4	2.0	2.3	2.3	2.4	2.0
Belgium............	2.9	2.5	2.2	2.0	2.1	2.1	1.9	1.3
Sweden............	0.4	0.6	1.1	1.1	1.0	1.0	1.0	1.3
Finland............	—	0.1	0.3	0.3	0.3	0.3	0.4	0.5
Japan.............	—	—	0.6	1.0	1.2	1.2	2.5	3.5
India..............	—	—	1.1	1.2	1.1	1.1	1.2	1.4
Other Countries......	11.0[1]	12.0[1]	12.3	12.0	11.9	13.7	13.2	12.2

Source: League of Nations, Secretariat, Economic, Financial, and Transit Department, *Industrialization and Foreign Trade*, p. 13.

[1] The figures for 1870 and 1881–1885 include the proportions for Japan and India which were not separately indicated for those years.

[2] The second column for 1913 represents the distribution according to frontiers established after World War I.

Table 26.

Index of Production in Italian Manufacturing Industries, 1861 to 1956.
Base: 1938 = 100.

Periods	National Boundaries of Period Covered	Present National Boundaries
1861–1865	18	21
1866–1870	22	23
1871–1875	24	25
1876–1880	25	26
1881–1885	28	28
1886–1890	29	30
1891–1895	28	29
1896–1900	31	32
1901–1905	39	40
1906–1910	51	53
1911–1915	59	61
1916–1920	63	64
1921–1925	67	67
1926–1930	85	85
1931–1935	80	80
1936–1940	101	101
1941–1945	66	66
1946–1950	98	98
1951–1955	162	162
1956	203	203

Source: Istituto Centrale di Statistica, *Annali di statistica*, Anno 86, Serie VIII, Vol. 9, "Indagine statistica sullo sviluppo del reddito nazionale dell'Italia dal 1861 al 1956," p. 99, Table 6.

The Central Institute of Statistics defined "manufacturing industries" in the following terms: (1) *agricultural-manufacturing* (food and beverages, tobacco and tobacco products, textiles, clothing, fur and leather, wood-working and wood products); (2) *extractive-manufacturing* (metallurgical activities, mechanical industries, processing of nonmetalliferous minerals); and (3) chemicals and allied products, paper, rubber, printing and publishing, photo-phono-cinematographic products, and miscellaneous manufacturing.

Table 27.

Indices of Italian Manufacturing Production, 1870 to 1938.

Year	Index: 1913 = 100	Index: 1925–1929 = 100
1870	17.0	10.2
1881	23.9	14.3
1891	37.8	22.6
1901	62.0	37.0
1911	96.0	57.3
1921	98.4	58.8
1931	145.1	86.7
1938	195.2	116.6

Source: League of Nations, Secretariat, Economic, Financial, and Transit Department, *Industrialization and Foreign Trade*, pp. 132–134, 138–140.
Mining is included in the indices from 1870 to 1913. Indices for 1881 through 1889 and 1891 through 1897 were interpolated on the basis of data concerning Italian coal consumption.

Table 28.

Quantum Indices of Italian Trade in Manufactured Articles, 1881 to 1938.
Base: 1913 = 100.

Period	Imports	Exports
1881–1885	51.8	24.7
1891–1895	38.1	22.2
1901–1905	53.1	52.6
1911–1913	100.9	96.9
1921–1925	43.8	69.6
1931–1935	55.8	97.4
1936–1938	47.3	107.2

Source: League of Nations, Secretariat, Economic, Financial, and Transit Department, *Industrialization and Foreign Trade*, p. 162.
The indices are based upon the values of imports and exports at 1913 prices as shown in Table X, p. 160, of this same League of Nations study.

Table 29.

Real Per Capita Income Expressed in Terms of "International Units" (I.U.) for Italy and Other Countries, 1901 to 1951.[1]

Year	Italy	United States	Great Britain	Germany	France	Switzerland	Belgium	Sweden	Finland	Greece	Japan
1901	132	411[2]	490	285	231[3]	246[4]	219[5]	193	—	—	—
1906	121	467[6]	508	295	—	—	—	232	—	—	—
1911	154	508[7]	519	306	266[8]	293[8]	314[8]	256	184[8]	149[8]	146[8]
1916	157	535	490	310[8]	—	—	—	303	—	—	—
1921	146	537	434	—	348	—	176[9]	250	—	—	143
1926	196	682	502	287	391	385	262[10]	319	196	187[10]	182
1931	160	591	521	284	368	417	307[11]	336	201	177	191
1936	168	679	627	430	361	416	358	413	258	193	223
1941	167	900	—	563[12]	—	414	—	—	258	117[13]	249[14]
1946	156	1,025	598	281[15]	442[16]	575	426	534	262	103	132
1951	250	1,122	597	410[17]	509	649	521	652	393	181	210

Source: Colin Clark, *The Conditions of Economic Progress* (1957 Edition), pp. 88–200.

[1] As defined by Colin Clark, "One I.U. of real income was taken as the quantity of goods exchangeable in the U.S.A. for $1 over the average of the decade 1925–34." Colin Clark himself raises the question of the aptness of the decade chosen as a standard of comparison. For both the definition of I.U. and justification in selecting this decade, see page 18 of his volume.

[2] 1894–1903 [7] 1904–1913 [12] Included, from date of annexation, Austria, Sudetenland, and
[3] 1900 [8] 1913 Memel, but not other annexed territories. Not included were
[4] 1899 [9] 1920 tribute from occupied countries or black market incomes.
[5] 1895 [10] 1927 [13] 1942 [16] 1947
[6] 1898–1908 [11] 1932 [14] 1940 [17] Present territory of the West German
[15] 1948 Federal Republic

Table 30.

Per Capita Italian National Income in Lire (1938 Prices), 1861 to 1956.

Periods	Per Capita National Income	Periods	Per Capita National Income
1861–65	1,851	1911–15	2,478
1866–70	1,875	1916–20	2,439
1871–75	1,895	1921–25	2,741
1876–80	1,919	1926–30	2,948
1881–85	1,884	1931–35	2,902
1886–90	1,885	1936–40	3,191
1891–95	1,888	1941–45	2,428
1896–1900	1,938	1946–50	2,940
1901–05	2,169	1951–55	3,758
1906–10	2,365	1956	4,242

Source: Istituto Centrale di Statistica, *Annali di statistica*, Anno 86, Serie VIII, Vol. 9, "Indagine statistica sullo sviluppo del reddito nazionale dell'Italia dal 1861 al 1956," p. 42, Table 6, B.

Table 31.

Regional Distribution of the Net Product of Italian Industry, Commerce, Credit, and Services in 1951.

REGIONS	TOTAL NET PRODUCT		NET PRODUCT PER INHABITANT
	Thousands of Lire	%	Thousands of Lire
Piedmont	574,470,000	12.3	163
Valle d'Aosta	18,813,600	0.4	198
Lombardy	1,339,228,300	28.6	204
Trentino-Alto Adige	73,429,200	1.6	101
Veneto	356,850,000	7.6	91
Friuli-Venezia Giulia	78,904,800	1.7	85
Liguria	294,418,800	6.3	186
Emilia-Romagna	351,608,400	7.5	99
North Italy	*3,087,723,600*	*66.0*	*148*
Tuscany	321,656,400	6.9	102
Umbria	57,330,000	1.2	71
The Marches	82,555,200	1.8	61
Lazio	389,610,000	8.3	116
Central Italy	*851,151,600*	*18.2*	*98*
Abruzzi and Molise	60,325,200	1.3	36
Campania	226,231,200	4.8	52
Puglia	131,929,200	2.8	41
Basilicata	16,801,200	0.4	27
Calabria	61,682,400	1.3	30
South Italy	*496,969,200*	*10.6*	*42*
Sicily	178,214,400	3.8	40
Sardinia	65,941,200	1.4	52
The Islands	*244,155,600*	*5.2*	*43*
Italy	*4,680,000,000*	*100.0*	*99*

Source: Confederazione Generale dell'Industria Italiana, *L'industria italiana alla metà del secolo XX,* p. 108.

Table 32.

The Gross Internal Product for the Private Sectors of Italy's Economy, 1861 to 1956.

PERIODS	TOTALS IN BILLIONS OF CURRENT LIRE			PERCENTAGES		
	Agriculture[1]	Industrial Activity[2]	Tertiary Activities[3]	Agriculture	Industrial Activity	Tertiary Activities
1861–65	4.2	1.5	1.7	56.7	20.3	23.0
1866–70	4.8	1.7	1.9	57.2	20.2	22.6
1871–75	5.8	1.9	2.4	57.4	18.8	23.8
1876–80	5.6	1.9	2.6	55.5	18.8	25.7
1881–85	5.1	2.0	2.6	52.6	20.6	26.8
1886–90	5.0	2.1	3.0	49.5	20.8	29.7
1891–95	5.2	2.0	3.1	50.5	19.4	30.1
1896–1900	5.4	2.1	3.3	50.0	19.4	30.6
1901–05	6.0	2.6	3.6	49.2	21.3	29.5
1906–10	6.8	3.8	4.6	44.7	25.0	30.3
1911–15	8.4	4.9	5.8	44.0	25.6	30.4
1916–20	26.0	16.5	13.2	46.7	29.6	23.7
1921–25	44.4	34.0	30.9	40.6	31.1	28.3
1926–30	45.8	40.1	40.7	36.2	31.7	32.1
1931–35	27.9	28.5	36.5	30.0	30.7	39.3
1936–40	40.4	46.7	49.4	29.6	34.2	36.2
1941–45	281.2	117.6	116.0	54.6	22.9	22.5
1946–50	1,994.0	2,197.0	1,379.0	35.8	39.4	24.8
1951–55	2,569.0	4,308.0	2,535.0	27.3	45.8	26.9
1956	2,800.0	5,395.0	3,324.0	24.3	46.8	28.9

Source: Istituto Centrale di Statistica, *Annali di statistica,* Anno 86, Serie VIII, Vol. 9, "Indagine statistica sullo sviluppo del reddito nazionale dell'Italia dal 1861 al 1956," p. 36, Table 3.
[1] Agriculture, forestry, and fishing.
[2] Extractive, manufacturing, construction, electric, gas, and water industries.
[3] Transportation and communications, commerce and various services, credit, and insurance.

Table 33.

Average Daily Wages of Italian Industrial Workers in Lire, Index of Nominal Wages,
Index of the Cost of Living, and Index of Real Wages, 1899 to 1950.

1.	2.	3.	4.	5.
YEAR	Daily Wages in Lire	Index of Nominal Wages (1913 = 100)	Index of the Cost of Living (1913 = 100)	Index of Real Wages (Col. 3 ÷ Col. 4)
1899	2.33	65.8	86.5	76.07
1900	2.44	68.9	90.0	78.47
1901	2.48	70.1	88.3	79.39
1902	2.55	72.0	87.7	82.10
1903	2.58	72.9	90.3	80.73
1904	2.57	72.6	91.4	79.43
1905	2.54	71.8	91.5	78.47
1906	2.64	74.6	93.2	80.04
1907	2.96	83.6	97.6	85.56
1908	2.94	83.1	96.6	86.02
1909	3.33	94.1	93.9	100.21
1910	3.26	92.1	96.5	95.44
1911	3.30	93.2	98.9	94.24
1912	3.40	96.0	99.8	96.19
1913	3.54	100.0	100.0	100.00
1914	3.53	99.7	100.0	99.70
1915	3.54	100.0	107.0	93.45
1916	4.03	113.8	133.9	85.00
1917	4.90	138.4	189.4	73.07
1918	6.04	170.6	264.1	64.60
1919	8.84	249.7	268.1	93.13
1920	14.27	403.1	352.3	114.41
1921	18.74	529.4	416.8	127.01
1922	18.13	512.1	414.3	123.61
1923	16.92	478.0	411.9	116.05
1924	17.00	480.2	426.4	112.62
1925	18.96	535.6	479.0	111.81
1926	20.39	576.0	516.7	111.48
1927	20.20	570.6	472.4	120.79
1928	18.71	528.5	437.8	120.72
1929	18.26	515.8	444.8	115.96
1930	18.15	512.7	430.7	119.04
1931	16.74	472.9	389.1	121.54
1932	15.88	448.6	378.9	118.39
1933	15.25	430.8	356.5	120.84
1934	14.86	419.8	338.1	124.16
1935	14.30	404.0	342.9	117.82
1936	14.20	401.1	368.8	108.76
1937	14.83	418.9	403.7	103.76
1938	15.47	437.0	434.7	100.53
1939	16.98	479.7	453.9	105.68
1940	20.22	571.2	529.7	107.83
1941	21.75	614.4	612.9	100.24
1942	24.85	702.0	708.4	99.10
1943	28.95	817.8	1,188.0	68.80
1944	45.25	1,278.3	5,279.4	24.20
1945	81.93	2,314.4	10,398.0	22.30
1946	248.00	7,005.8	12,271.6	57.10
1947	694.00	19,604.5	19,887.5	98.58
1948	944.00	26,667.1	21,056.9	126.51
1949	988.00	27,909.0	21,366.0	130.67
1950	1,010.00	29,040.0	21,079.0	137.77

Source: Antonio Fossati, *Lavoro e produzione in Italia dalla metà del secolo XVIII alla seconda guerra mondiale,* pp. 630–634.

540

Table 33A.

Index of Nominal Wages, Exclusive of Family Allowances; Index of the Cost of Living; and Index of Real Wages for Italian Workers in Agriculture, Industry, Transportation, and Commerce, 1948-1958.

(1938 = 1).

1	2	3	4	5	6	7	8	9	10
	NOMINAL WAGES				Cost of Living	REAL NOMINAL WAGES			
YEAR	Agr.	Ind.	Transp.	Com.		Agr. (Col. 2 ÷ 6)	Ind. (Col. 3 ÷ 6)	Transp. (Col. 4 ÷ 6)	Com. (Col. 5 ÷ 6)
1948	65.69	52.53	45.21	49.21	48.44	1.36	1.08	.93	1.01
1949	68.73	53.37	46.10	52.24	49.15	1.40	1.09	.94	1.06
1950	69.42	54.86	47.72	53.89	48.49	1.43	1.13	.98	1.11
1951	71.35	59.99	52.09	57.17	53.20	1.35	1.13	.98	1.07
1952	75.11	62.44	55.20	59.69	55.46	1.35	1.13	1.00	1.08
1953	79.41	64.18	56.34	61.91	56.54	1.40	1.14	1.00	1.09
1954	82.75	66.53	57.01	63.27	58.06	1.43	1.15	.98	1.09
1955	86.46	69.70	60.16	65.18	59.69	1.45	1.17	1.01	1.09
1956	90.30	73.77	64.03	69.86	62.66	1.44	1.18	1.02	1.11
1957	93.15	77.11	66.19	73.29	63.87	1.46	1.21	1.04	1.15
1958 (Jan.-Oct.)	97.47	80.85	68.77	77.27	67.04	1.45	1.21	1.03	1.15

Sources: Annuario statistico italiano 1951, pp. 358, 374; *Annuario statistico italiano 1952*, p. 350; *Annuario statistico italiano 1953*, p. 335; *Annuario statistico italiano 1955*, pp. 300, 312; *Annuario statistico italiano 1956*, pp. 347, 359; *Annuario statistico italiano 1958*, pp. 310, 313.

Table 34.

Comparative Weekly Wage Rates in Selected European Countries, the United Kingdom, and New York and Chicago in 1878.

Occupations	Belgium	Denmark	France	Germany	Italy	Spain	United Kingdom			United States	
							England	Ireland	Scotland	New York	Chicago
Agricultural laborers:											
Men, without board or lodging	$6.00	—	$3.15	$2.87	$3.50	—	$3.60	$3.40	$1.50 to $4.25	—	—
Men, with board and lodging	5.40	$4.25	1.36	1.48	1.80	—	2.60	1.30	1.80 to 3.25	—	—
Women, without board or lodging	5.40	—	1.10	1.08	1.55	—	1.80	2.16	.60 to 1.00	—	—
Women, with board and lodging	6.00	—	—	.75	.60	—	1.15	.75	—	—	—
House-building trades:											
Bricklayers	5.40	—	4.00	3.60	3.45	$5.12	8.12	7.58	9.63	$12.00 to $15.00	$6.00 to $10.50
Carpenters and joiners	6.00	—	5.42	4.00	4.18	4.88	8.25	7.33	8.12	9.00 to 12.00	7.50 to 12.00
Gasfitters	—	4.45	—	3.65	3.95	—	7.25	7.95	8.40	10.00 to 14.00	10.00 to 12.00
Masons	—	4.15	5.00	4.30	4.60	4.80	8.16	7.58	8.28	12.00 to 18.00	12.00 to 15.00
Painters	—	—	4.90	3.92	4.35	—	7.25	7.54	8.16	10.00 to 16.00	6.00 to 12.00
Plasterers	—	—	—	3.80	3.90	7.20	8.10	7.68	10.13	10.00 to 15.00	9.00 to 15.00
Plumbers	—	—	5.50	3.60	3.90	—	7.75	8.46	7.13	12.00 to 18.00	12.00 to 20.00
Slaters	—	—	—	4.00	—	—	7.90	—	8.30	10.00 to 15.00	12.00 to 18.00
General trades:											
Bakers	4.40	4.25	5.55	3.50	3.90	5.40	6.50	—	6.60	5.00 to 8.00	8.00 to 12.00
Blacksmiths	4.40	3.90	5.45	3.55	3.94	4.65	8.12	—	7.04	10.00 to 14.00	9.00 to 12.00
Bookbinders	—	3.72	4.85	3.82	3.90	3.60	7.83	—	6.50	12.00 to 18.00	9.00 to 20.00
Brassfounders	4.50	4.20	—	3.20	5.49	—	7.40	—	6.90	10.00 to 14.00	8.00 to 15.00
Butchers	4.80	4.50	5.42	3.85	4.20	4.20	7.23	—	4.75	8.00 to 12.00	12.00 to 18.00
Cabinet-makers	—	—	6.00	3.97	4.95	4.95	7.70	—	8.48	9.00 to 13.00	7.00 to 15.00
Coopers	—	4.10	7.00	3.30	4.35	—	7.30	—	6.10	12.00 to 16.00	6.00 to 15.00
Coppersmiths	—	3.85	—	3.30	3.90	—	7.40	—	7.10	12.00 to 16.00	15.00 to 20.00
Cutlers	—	3.85	4.63	4.00	4.00	—	8.00	—	6.25	10.00 to 13.00	15.00 to 10.00
Engravers	—	—	—	4.00	3.50	—	9.72	—	8.75	15.00 to 25.00	9.00 to 30.00
Horseshoers	—	3.85	5.40	3.25	4.95	—	7.20	—	7.00	12.00 to 18.00	15.00 to 25.00
Millwrights	—	4.00	—	3.30	2.90	—	7.50	—	7.50	10.00 to 15.00	12.00 to 20.00
Printers	4.80	4.62	4.70	4.80	3.90	—	7.75	—	7.52	8.00 to 18.00	12.00 to 18.00
Saddlers and harness-makers	—	3.85	5.00	3.60	3.90	—	6.80	—	6.15	12.00 to 15.00	6.00 to 12.00
Sailmakers	—	4.85	—	3.30	4.32	3.90	7.30	—	6.33	12.00 to 18.00	12.00 to 15.00
Shoemakers	—	3.30	4.75	3.12	4.30	3.90	7.35	—	7.35	12.00 to 18.00	9.00 to 18.00
Tailors	4.80	4.10	5.10	3.58	3.60	3.90	$5.00 to 7.30	—	7.00	10.00 to 18.00	6.00 to 18.00
Tinsmiths	3.00	3.90	4.40	3.65	2.60	3.00	7.30	—	6.00	10.00 to 14.00	9.00 to 12.00
Laborers, porters, &c.	—	—	—	2.92	—	—	5.00	—	4.50	6.00 to 9.00	5.50 to 9.00
Railway employees:											
Engineers, passenger trains	—	—	11.33	8.35	9.50	—	9.12	9.00	8.70	—	—
Firemen, passenger trains	—	—	6.25	3.30	4.50	—	6.00	4.50	4.96	—	—
Brakemen, passenger trains	—	—	3.60	3.22	—	—	5.50	4.00	4.69	—	—
Signal men	—	—	5.85	3.52	4.00	—	5.60	5.00	5.12	—	—
Switchmen	—	—	5.50	3.41	4.40	—	5.60	5.00	5.19	—	—
Porters	—	—	5.00	2.60	3.40	—	4.50	4.00	4.44	—	—
Laborers	—	—	3.35	3.10	3.30	—	4.50	4.00	4.27	—	—

Source: U.S. Congress, House, Executive Document No. 5, 46th Congress, 1st Session, *State of Labor in Europe: 1878*, p. 30.

Table 35.

Comparative Retail Prices of Food and Other Necessities in Selected European Countries, the United Kingdom, and New York and Chicago, 1878.

Articles	Belgium	France	Germany	Italy	Spain	Switzerland	United Kingdom			United States	
							England	Ireland	Scotland	New York	Chicago
	Cents	*Cents*	*Cents*	*Cents*	*Cents*	*Cents*	*Cents*	*Cents*	*Cents*	*Cents*	*Cents*
Bread...........per pound.	4 to 5	3	3 to 7	6	6¼ to 7½	4	3½ to 4½	4	4	4 to 4½	4 to 4½
Flour...............do....	—	4	5½	10	—	7	3½ to 4½	4	4	3 to 4	2½ to 4½
Beef:											
Roasting.......per pound.	20	22	22	20		30	22	—	22	12 to 16	8 to 12½
Soup..............do....	16	16	14	12		18	15	—	16	6 to 8	5 to 8
Rump steak........do....	20	20	20	20	18	30	26½	—	26½	14 to 16	8 to 12½
Corned............do....	16	16	13	12		18	18	—	20	8 to 12	4 to 7
Veal:											
Fore quarter...per pound.	16	16		15		—	18	—	—	8 to 10	6 to 10
Hind quarter.......do....	18	20	14	20	25	18	22½	—	25	10 to 12	10 to 12
Cutlets............do....	20	22		22		20	27	—	30	20 to 24	12½ to 15
Mutton:											
Fore quarter...per pound.	16	16		15		—	17	—	16	9 to 10	5 to 12½
Hind quarter.......do....	20	18	14½	18	14	18	22	—	20	12 to 14	5 to 15½
Chops.............do....	20	20		18		—	25	—	24	14 to 16	10 to 15
Pork:											
Fresh..........per pound.	16	14	17	13	24	18	16	10 to 12	13 to 16	8 to 10	4 to 5
Salted.............do....	16	14	17	18	—	20	15	10 to 12	13 to 16	8 to 10	6 to 12
Bacon..............do....	18	20	20	22	—	—	12 to 16	—	—	8 to 10	7 to 12
Ham................do....	25	25	22	25	45	28	13 to 23	—	25	8 to 12	7 to 15
Shoulder...........do....	20	18	20	20	—	—	12	—	—	8 to 10	4 to 10
Sausage............do....	20	16	19	20	—	—	18	—	—	8 to 10	6 to 10
Lard................do....	20	20	21	22	21	—	15 to 18	12	—	10 to 12	6 to 10
Codfish.............do....	—	—	—	9	10	—	8	—	6	6 to 7	5 to 9
Butter..............do....	20 to 50	25	22	28	45	36	29 to 38	26½	32	25 to 32	16 to 40
Cheese..............do....	20 to 25	—	24	26	28	23	15 to 21	—	20	12 to 15	5 to 16
Potatoes.........per bushel.	56	50	50	$1.15	$1.10	60	$1.12 to $2.00	68	95	$1.40 to $1.60	60 to 80
Rice............per pound.	—	—	9	6	7	—	3½ to 8	—	5	8 to 10	5 to 10
Beans...........per quart.	—	—	10	13	12	—	9	—	—	7 to 10	5 to 9
Milk................do....	—	—	4	7	—	5	6 to 9	—	5	8 to 10	3 to 6
Eggs............per dozen.	20 to 25	18	20	18	29 to 25	20	19 to 30	14	28	25 to 30	10 to 24
Oatmeal.........per pound.	—	—	8	—	—	—	3½ to 4½	3½	4	4 to 5	4 to 5
Tea.................do....	—	—	75	—	70	50	43 to 88	80	70 to 88	50 to 60	25 to $1.00
Coffee..............do....	30 to 40	30	35	32	45	30	28 to 42	—	32 to 50	20 to 30	16 to 40
Sugar...............do....	15 to 20	—	11	8½	11	8	5½ to 9	8	10	8 to 10	7 to 10
Molasses........per gallon.	—	—	—	—	—	—	—	—	—	60 to 70	40 to 80
Soap............per pound.	—	—	10	4	10	—	5½ to 9	—	—	6 to 7	3 to 8
Starch..............do....	—	—	9	10	10	—	10 to 12	—	14	8 to 10	5 to 10
Coal...............per ton.	—	—	$4.25	$11.00	$9.00	—	$3.20 to $4.10	—	$2.65	$3.00 to $5.25	$3.00 to $6.75

Source: U.S. Congress, House, Executive Document No. 5, 46th Congress, 1st Session, *State of Labor in Europe: 1878*, p. 32.

Table 36.

Wage Rates Paid during 1878 in Selected U.S. Consular Districts of Italy for the Occupations Listed.

Occupations	Piedmont — Wages in dollars Max.	Min.	Hours per day	Genoa — Wages in dollars Max.	Min.	Hours per day	Florence — Wages in dollars Max.	Min.	Hours per day	Rome — Wages in dollars Max.	Min.	Hours per day	Messina — Wages in dollars Max.	Min.	Hours per day
Agricultural Laborers															
Not classified by sex or age															
Men	.70[2]	.24[2]	15-6[2]	.76	.16		.60	.35		.60[3]	.26[3]		.65[1]	.30[1]	30[1]
Women	½ men's wage		Same	.58	.09					.22[3]	.12[3]				
Children	$20-24 per year[4]									Same as women					
Blacksmiths															
Masters, Journeymen	1.20	.50	12	.76	.29[5]		.80			.60	.20		.70		
Apprentices					.58					.15	.05				
Bricklayers															
Masters, Journeymen	1.20	.50	12	.74	.68	10	.75			.60	.35		.80		
Apprentices					.29					.40	.35				
Boys															
Carpenters															
Masters, Journeymen	1.20	.50	12	.70		10	.85			.70	.40		.80		
Apprentices				.54						.30	.10				
Boys				.03											
Common Laborers															
Railroads & Public Works	.60[6]	.32[6]													
Men				.58		10					.05		.70	.30	
Women				.26											
Boys				.34											
Other, including manufactories															
Not classified by age or sex															
Men				.46			.40			.60	.40				
Women				.25						.30	.20				
Boys				.28											
Machinists															
Masters, Journeymen							1.00			2.00	.40		1.20		
Apprentices										.30	.10				
Shoemakers															
Masters, Journeymen				.81	.34		.70			1.00	.30		.95		
Apprentices					.38					.20	.05				
Women															
Tailors															
Masters, Journeymen				.70			.80			.90	.50		.90		
Apprentices										.30	.10				

544

Table 36. (Continued)

Occupations	Piedmont Wages in dollars Max.	Min.	Hours per day	Genoa Wages in dollars Max.	Min.	Hours per day	Florence Wages in dollars Max.	Min.	Hours per day	Rome Wages in dollars Max.	Min.	Hours per day	Messina Wages in dollars Max.	Min.	Hours per day
Tanners															
Masters, Journeymen..........							.60						.70		
Textiles															
Cotton Spinning & Weaving															
Spinners and Weavers															
Men..........						12				.60	.30				
Women..........						12				.60	.40				
Dyers..........				.70	.38					.15	.10				
Carders..........				.54	.21					.60	.20				
Bobbin Winders..........															
Weavers..........															
Silk Spinning & Weaving															
Dyers..........										.60	.50				
Spinners															
Not classified by age or sex..	.24[7]	.18[7]	13							.40	.30				
Women..........	.24	.24	12												
"Others"..........															
Weavers															
Not classified by age or sex..															
Men..........				1.95	.38					1.00	.60				
Women..........				.38	.10										
Woolen Spinning & Weaving															
Washers & Dyers..........										.60	.30				
Carders..........										.60	.40				
Spinners..........										.60	.40				
Weavers..........										1.00	.60				
Tinsmiths..........							.60						.70		

Source: Data for this table were selected from statistics contained in the official document, *State of Labor in Europe: 1878*, published in 1879 as Executive Document No. 5, 46th Congress, 1st Session, House of Representatives. See pp. 286–303. The report was based on the findings of the U.S. Consuls in the United Kingdom and eight European countries, made in response to a circular from the Department of State. The Secretary of State, William M. Evarts, submitted the report to the Speaker of the House, Samuel J. Randall. Wage rates have been converted from lire to dollars. The average value of the Italian paper lira during the course of the year, 1878, was quoted at $0.1750. Listed wage rates were those paid when board was not provided to the worker.

1 Experienced hands in summer, 45 cents, in winter 65 cents; ordinary hands in summer 30 cents, in winter 38 cents; common laborers on farm, 30 cents. It seems against normal practice that farm hands should earn more in winter than in summer, but the statistics in the report state the facts this way.
2 For 9-hour day, 24 cents per day; for 12-hour day, 40 cents per day; during 3 months of harvest season, for 15-hour day, 60 to 70 cents per day: in winter, average wage, 30 cents per day.
3 Including room but not board.
4 Boys, 14–16 years old, including board. Some field hands received $18 per year with board.
5 Described as third class.
6 Figures refer to wages of railroad laborers. Public works were let out to the lowest bidder; contractors generally paid lower wages than those cited for railroads.
7 Common lodging, wood, and light provided.

Table 37.

Amount of Worktime Required to Purchase Selected Food Items in 1925.
(All Units of Food in Kilos.)

Type of Worker	Rome	Milan	London	Berlin
Skilled (Carpenter)				
White Bread....	35 mins.	37 mins.	15 mins.	35 mins.
Potatoes........	16 mins.	18 mins.	9 mins.	5 mins.
Bacon..........	2 hrs. 57 mins.	3 hrs.	1 hr. 48 mins.	2 hrs. 44 mins.
Flour...........	38 mins.	41 mins.	17 mins.	29 mins.
Cheese.........	4 hrs. 37 mins.	4 hrs. 24 mins.	1 hr. 20 mins.	1 hr. 22 mins.
Rice...........	46 mins.	40 mins.	18 mins.	36 mins.
Unskilled				
White Bread....	48 mins.	59 mins.	20 mins.	46 mins.
Potatoes........	21 mins.	28 mins.	11 mins.	6 mins.
Bacon..........	4 hrs. 4 mins.	4 hrs. 46 mins.	2 hrs. 21 mins.	3 hrs. 34 mins.
Flour...........	53 mins.	1 hr. 5 mins.	23 mins.	37 mins.
Cheese.........	6 hrs. 19 mins.	7 hrs. 38 mins.	1 hr. 45 mins.	1 hr. 47 mins.
Rice...........	1 hr. 3 mins.	1 hr. 4 mins.	24 mins.	47 mins.

Source: International Labour Office, *Wage Changes in Various Countries 1914 to 1925*, Studies and Reports, Series D (Wages and Hours) No. 16, pp. 28–29, Table XII.

Table 38.
Total Number of Strikes and Strikers, 1881 to 1957, in Italy.

Year	Goods-Producing Industries and Services		Agriculture		Total	
	Number of Strikes	Number of Strikers	Number of Strikes	Number of Strikers	Number of Strikes	Number of Strikers
1881	44	8,272	1	100	45	8,372
1882	47	5,854	2	2,200	49	8,054
1883	73	12,900	3	262	76	13,162
1884	81	23,967	10	245	91	24,212
1885	89	34,160	62	8,857	151	43,017
1886	96	16,951	17	3,846	113	20,797
1887	69	25,027	9	2,275	78	27,302
1888	101	28,974	5	1,366	106	30,340
1889	126	23,322	4	1,087	130	24,409
1890	139	38,402	8	1,950	147	40,352
1891	132	34,733	24	7,795	156	42,528
1892	119	30,800	10	3,504	129	34,304
1893	131	32,109	18	12,390	149	44,499
1894	109	27,595	8	4,748	117	32,343
1895	126	19,307	7	1,765	133	21,072
1896	210	96,051	1	100	211	96,151
1897	217	76,570	12	24,135	229	100,705
1898	256	35,705	36	8,495	292	44,200
1899	259	43,194	9	1,895	268	45,089
1900	383	80,858	27	12,517	410	93,375
1901	1,042	196,540	629	222,985	1,671	419,525
1902	810	197,514	221	146,592	1,031	344,106
1903	549	109,327	47	22,507	596	131,834
1904	631	124,834	208	94,756	839	219,590
1905	628	110,832	87	43,695	715	154,527
1906	1,299	264,029	350	117,595	1,649	381,624
1907	1,881	321,499	377	254,131	2,258	575,630
1908	1,459	197,958	286	173,425	1,745	371,383
1909	930	140,452	132	46,569	1,062	187,021
1910	1,021	172,969	97	25,805	1,118	198,774
1911	1,107	252,853	148	132,738	1,255	385,591
1912	914	144,124	176	95,841	1,090	239,965
1913	810	384,725	97	79,842	907	464,567
1914	782	173,103	123	43,819	905	216,922
1915	539	132,136	69	47,508	608	179,644
1916	516	123,616	61	14,892	577	138,508
1917	443	168,626	27	6,191	470	174,817
1918	303	158,036	10	675	313	158,711
1919	1,663	1,049,438	208	505,128	1,871	1,554,566
1920	1,881	1,267,953	189	1,045,732	2,070	2,313,685
1921	1,045	644,564	89	79,298	1,134	723,862
1922	552	422,773	23	25,146	575	447,919
1923	200	66,103	1	110	201	66,213
1924	355	162,488	6	2,728	361	165,216
1950	1,060	3,100,642	190	419,882	1,250	3,520,524
1951	1,117	2,056,481	62	84,321	1,179	2,140,802
1952	1,426	951,844	132	503,406	1,558	1,455,250
1953	1,264	4,346,190	132	325,255	1,396	4,671,445
1954	1,805	1,512,854	174	527,099	1,979	2,039,953
1955	1,847	920,000	115	94,000	1,962	1,014,000
1956	1,781	1,240,000	123	438,000	1,904	1,678,000
1957	1,646	1,117,000	85	110,000	1,731	1,227,000

Sources: Annuario statistico italiano 1919–1921, p. 512, for years from 1881 to 1924; *Annuario statistico italiano 1953*, p. 334, for 1950, 1951, and 1952; *Annuario statistico italiano 1954*, p. 308, for 1953; *Annuario statistico italiano 1955*, p. 311, for 1954; *Annuario statistico italiano 1956*, p. 358, for 1955; *Annuario statistico italiano 1957*, p. 355, for 1956; *Annuario statistico italiano 1958*, p. 309, for 1957.

From 1926 until the fall of fascism, strikes were illegal. This fact and the difficulties of the postwar years explain the absence of statistics between 1924 and 1950.

Before 1924, "Goods-Producing Industries and Services" included the categories of hunting and fishing. In the statistics from 1950 to 1957, the categories of forestry, hunting, and fishing are combined under "Agriculture." The statistics from 1950 to 1957 refer to strikes which began and ended in the year indicated.

Table 39.

Number of Strikes and Strikers, Duration of Strikes, and Total Number of Strike Man-Days, 1878–1890, Italy.

Year	Total No. of Strikes	Known No. of Strikers		Known Duration of Strikes				Total Number Strike Man-Days	
		Strikes	Strikers	Strikes	Up to 3 days	From 3 to 10 days	More than 10	Strikes	Days
1878[1]	19	18	2,963	19	9	8	2	18	10,274
1879	32	28	4,011	32	18	12	2	28	21,896
1880	27	26	5,900	26	18	4	4	26	91,899
1881	44	39	8,272	41	24	10	7	38	95,578
1882	47	45	5,854	46	33	10	3	45	25,119
1883	73	67	12,900	70	41	22	7	65	111,697
1884	81	81	23,967	78	44	19	15	78	149,215
1885	89	86	34,160	85	47	21	17	82	244,293
1886	96	96	16,951	95	67	19	9	95	56,772
1887	69	68	25,027	66	43	12	11	66	218,612
1888	101	99	28,974	96	54	28	14	95	191,204
1889	126	125	23,322	124	80	31	13	123	215,880
1890	139	133	38,402	132	92	31	9	129	167,657
Total	943	911	230,703	910	570	227	113	888	1,600,096

Source: Annuario statistico italiano 1892, p. 500.
[1] For second half of year only.

Table 40.

Classification of Strikes according to Industries in Which They Occurred, 1878–1890, Italy.

Year	No. of Strikes	Textiles	Metallurgical, Mechanical, Mineral	Day Laborers, Bricklayers, Kiln Workers	Typographers and Lithographers	Hatters, Tanners, and Other Apparel Workers	Bakers and Other Food Processing Workers	Misc.	Carpenters, Glass Workers, Coachmen, Conductors, Boatmen, Carters, and Porters
1878[1]	19	5	3	2	1	2	—	4	2
1879.....	32	5	2	7	1	6	3	5	3
1880.....	27	9	5	2	1	2	2	5	1
1881.....	44	4	4	6	1	4	5	6	14
1882.....	47	11	4	8	2	6	1	7	8[2]
1883.....	73	15	3	26	—	9	5	7	8[2]
1884.....	81	15	6	17	1	13	10	14	5
1885.....	89	17	7[3]	32	1	7	8	8	9
1886.....	96	14	9	33	1	6	9	11	13
1887.....	69	15	4	21	2	4	4	9	10
1888.....	101	33	12	23	2	4	7	11	9
1889.....	126	38	18[4]	23	3	7	7	18	12
1890.....	139	29	28	31	9	9	12	11	10
Total ...	943	210	105	231	25	79	73	116	104

Source: Annuario statistico italiano 1892, p. 503.
[1] For second half of year only.
[2] 2 strikes in Genoa of ship crews were included.
[3] 6 strikes of railroad shop workers were included.
[4] 3 strikes of railroad shop workers were included.

Table 41.

Causes of Strikes and Their Outcome, 1878–1890, Italy.

A. To Obtain Raise in Wages

Year	No. of Strikes	Outcome Known: Favorable	Outcome Known: Partly Favorable	Outcome Known: Unfavorable	Favorable: No. of Strikes	Favorable: No. of Strikers	Favorable: No. of Man-Days	Partly Favorable: No. of Strikes	Partly Favorable: No. of Strikers	Partly Favorable: No. of Man-Days	Unfavorable: No. of Strikes	Unfavorable: No. of Strikers	Unfavorable: No. of Man-Days
1878	7	—	2	5	—	—	—	2	550	3,650	4	680	1,500
1879	14	4	3	7	2	162	498	3	297	1,861	7	1,175	6,610
1880	16	4	5	7	4	1,160	3,980	5	1,360	66,340	7	699	1,398
1881	25	2	12	11	2	43	55	7	2,362	7,858	11	1,865	16,808
1882	30	4	13	13	4	472	1,394	13	1,703	8,894	12	1,487	7,356
1883	42	9	22	11	9	1,517	18,733	20	4,102	73,232	11	1,114	6,274
1884	51	9	23	19	9	3,637	9,617	23	6,580	43,756	17	5,041	50,995
1885	49	15	17	15	14	13,500	62,605	17	7,383	27,174	15	2,087	27,649
1886	44	3	22	19	3	295	765	22	4,022	14,774	19	2,974	8,008
1887	37	4	15	17	4	3,878	17,948	15	12,344	158,424	16	4,350	20,024
1888	48	8	21	16	8	5,890	47,680	21	4,460	64,020	16	3,490	11,715
1889	60	6	33	19	5	350	350	33	10,296	164,396	19	2,823	8,720
1890	81	16	34	26	15	10,632	53,117	34	9,307	49,099	24	3,137	11,331
Total	504	84	222	185	79	41,536	216,742	215	64,766	683,478	178	30,922	178,388

B. To Obtain Reduction in Hours of Work

Year	No. of Strikes	Outcome Known: Favorable	Outcome Known: Partly Favorable	Outcome Known: Unfavorable	Favorable: No. of Strikes	Favorable: No. of Strikers	Favorable: No. of Man-Days	Partly Favorable: No. of Strikes	Partly Favorable: No. of Strikers	Partly Favorable: No. of Man-Days	Unfavorable: No. of Strikes	Unfavorable: No. of Strikers	Unfavorable: No. of Man-Days
1878	2	—	2	—	—	—	—	2	180	420	—	—	—
1879	1	—	1	—	—	—	—	1	120	240	—	—	—
1880	2	1	1	1	—	—	—	1	180	900	1	85	85
1881	5	—	1	3	—	—	—	1	85	425	3	328	939
1882	1	—	—	1	—	—	—	—	—	—	1	7	14
1883	2	—	—	2	—	—	—	—	—	—	2	221	2,421
1884	3	1	3	—	—	—	—	3	228	390	—	—	—
1885	3	1	1	1	1	80	160	1	43	516	1	110	110
1886	8	3	2	3	3	346	5,892	2	245	245	3	370	4,430
1887	5	—	4	1	—	—	—	4	425	1,255	1	40	40
1888	8	5	2	1	5	1,898	11,598	2	110	250	1	80	80
1889	6	3	1	2	3	488	1,794	1	140	140	2	145	145
1890	11	2	4	5	2	800	1,400	4	440	1,660	5	1,380	3,650
Total	57	15	22	20	14	3,612	20,844	22	2,196	6,421	20	2,766	11,914

549

Table 41. (Continued)

C. To Resist Reduction in Wages

Year	No. of Strikes	Strikes for which the Outcome is Known			Favorable			Partly Favorable			Unfavorable		
		Favorable	Partly Favorable	Unfavorable	No. of Strikes	No. of Strikers	No. of Man-Days	No. of Strikes	No. of Strikers	No. of Man-Days	No. of Strikes	No. of Strikers	No. of Man-Days
1878	4	—	2	2	—	—	—	2	140	900	2	75	470
1879	4	—	3	1	—	—	—	2	160	400	1	25	75
1880	2	1	1	—	1	90	180	1	280	560	—	—	—
1881	4	—	2	1	—	—	—	1	26	372	1	400	1,200
1882	4	—	—	4	—	—	—	—	—	—	4	720	3,180
1883	7	1	5	1	1	200	1,000	4	3,304	4,700	1	25	75
1884	7	2	3	2	1	300	600	3	690	960	2	225	625
1885	7	4	3	—	4	610	3,890	3	382	1,824	—	—	—
1886	9	—	4	5	—	—	—	4	1,050	1,050	4	709	904
1887	7	—	5	1	—	—	—	5	450	3,386	1	70	70
1888	13	4	5	4	4	890	1,600	5	2,435	10,835	4	590	5,140
1889	13	—	7	6	—	—	—	7	1,360	10,750	6	456	2,050
1890	14	2	3	7	2	490	3,290	3	490	9,050	8	2,002	9,976
Total	95	14	43	34	13	2,580	10,560	40	10,767	44,787	34	5,297	23,765

D. To Resist Increase in Hours of Work

Year	No. of Strikes	Strikes for which the Outcome is Known			Favorable			Partly Favorable			Unfavorable		
		Favorable	Partly Favorable	Unfavorable	No. of Strikes	No. of Strikers	No. of Man-Days	No. of Strikes	No. of Strikers	No. of Man-Days	No. of Strikes	No. of Strikers	No. of Man-Days
1878	—	—	—	—	—	—	—	—	—	—	—	—	—
1879	—	—	—	—	—	—	—	—	—	—	—	—	—
1880	1	1	—	—	1	40	200	—	—	—	—	—	—
1881	—	—	—	—	—	—	—	—	—	—	—	—	—
1882	—	—	—	—	—	—	—	—	—	—	—	—	—
1883	—	—	—	—	—	—	—	—	—	—	—	—	—
1884	5	2	1	2	2	1,320	1,400	1	150	650	2	51	271
1885	2	—	1	1	—	—	—	1	200	1,000	1	250	750
1886	1	—	1	—	—	—	—	1	800	800	—	—	—
1887	3	1	2	—	1	85	170	2	920	3,300	—	—	—
1888	2	—	2	—	—	—	—	2	480	960	—	—	—
1889	2	1	1	—	1	50	50	1	200	1,800	—	—	—
1890	1	1	—	—	1	45	90	—	—	—	—	—	—
Total	17	6	8	3	6	1,540	1,910	8	2,750	8,510	3	301	1,021

Table 41. (Continued)

		STRIKES FOR WHICH THE OUTCOME IS KNOWN			FAVORABLE			PARTLY FAVORABLE			UNFAVORABLE		
YEAR	NO. OF STRIKES	Favorable	Partly Favorable	Unfavorable	No. of Strikes	No. of Strikers	No. of Man-Days	No. of Strikes	No. of Strikers	No. of Man-Days	No. of Strikes	No. of Strikers	No. of Man-Days
E. Causes Other Than Those Listed Above													
1878[1]	6	1	2	3	1	70	770	2	390	1,560	3	878	1,000
1879	13	—	6	7	—	—	—	4	940	16,990	7	972	3,222
1880	8	—	3	5	—	—	—	2	800	14,900	5	1,436	3,736
1881	9	1	2	7	1	150	150	2	1,980	10,280	7	923	3,261
1882	12	2	3	8	1	53	106	3	500	1,100	7	815	3,031
1883	23	4	7	14	4	767	1,567	5	633	1,633	12	1,403	4,323
1884	17	6	6	6	6	1,370	3,650	5	2,774	27,220	6	1,144	10,214
1885	29	4	11	9	4	195	555	10	3,749	100,969	8	2,499	15,925
1886	30	4	10	15	4	322	7,422	10	1,325	4,585	15	4,912	13,040
1887	18	5	4	10	5	1,346	3,162	4	507	2,537	10	906	7,556
1888	30	3	10	14	3	550	550	10	3,556	14,792	12	2,382	17,232
1889	43	4	21	17	3	360	4,080	20	2,917	9,495	16	2,362	12,600
1890	31	—	16	11	—	—	—	16	5,030	16,410	10	947	2,504
TOTAL	269	34	101	126	32	5,183	22,012	93	25,101	222,471	118	21,579	97,644
F. All Causes													
1878[1]	19	1	8	10	1	70	770	8	1,260	6,530	9	1,633	2,970
1879	32	4	13	15	2	162	498	10	1,517	19,491	15	2,172	9,907
1880	27	4	10	13	4	1,160	3,980	9	2,620	82,700	13	2,220	5,219
1881	44	5	17	22	4	173	435	11	4,453	18,935	22	3,516	22,208
1882	47	5	16	26	5	622	1,544	16	2,203	9,994	24	3,029	13,581
1883	73	11	34	28	10	1,570	18,839	29	8,039	79,565	26	2,763	13,093
1884	81	16	35	29	16	5,924	13,584	34	10,272	72,326	27	6,461	62,105
1885	89	24	33	26	22	15,250	67,015	32	11,707	131,133	25	4,946	44,434
1886	96	14	39	42	14	1,446	11,102	39	6,842	21,654	41	8,965	26,382
1887	69	9	29	29	9	4,285	25,540	29	14,526	166,382	28	5,366	27,690
1888	101	22	40	35	10	10,024	64,040	40	11,481	93,197	33	6,542	34,167
1889	126[2]	13	64	44	12	1,438	2,744	63	15,193	185,741	43	5,786	23,515
1890	139	25	58	49	19	12,327	61,977	58	15,467	78,019	47	7,466	27,461
TOTAL	942	153	396	368	128	54,451	272,068	378	105,580	965,667	353	60,865	312,732

Source: Annuario statistico italiano 1892, pp. 501–502.
[1] Second six months of year only.
[2] Includes one strike for which the cause was not known.

Table 42.

Results of Grievance Committee Elections for Italy as a Whole, 1953–1958, according to Reports by C.G.I.L., C.I.S.L., U.I.L., and 24 ORE.[1]

	C.G.I.L.						C.I.S.L.					
	1953	1954	1955	1956[2]	1957	1958	1953	1954	1955	1956	1957	1958
No. of Plants	3,780	3,462	3,810	1,332	3,605	2,653	—	3,021	3,968	3,699	3,479	3,081
No. of Valid Votes	904,233	950,002	1,008,054	429,263	1,009,740	808,466	—	958,457	1,090,637	1,042,514	996,631	905,295
No. of Seats	—	—	14,880	—	14,508	10,802	—	13,282	15,846	15,108	14,310	12,673
C.G.I.L.												
% Votes	71.3	68.3	61.4	57.2	53.5	54.6	—	64.7	56.2	51.7	47.8	48.5
% Seats	—	—	65.8	—	57.4	58.9	—	60.2	51.7	47.2	43.6	44.0
C.I.S.L.												
% Votes	22.5	23.9	29.5	32.9	33.9	29.9	—	27.1	33.9	37.0	38.8	35.9
% Seats	—	—	26.1	—	31.5	28.9	—	31.9	38.5	41.4	44.0	42.7
U.I.L.												
% Votes	3.3	3.5	5.5	7.2	7.8	8.6	—	3.8	5.6	6.8	8.1	8.1
% Seats	—	—	3.1	—	4.9	5.6	—	2.5	3.6	4.6	5.3	5.3
Others												
% Votes	2.8	4.2	3.6	2.7	4.8	6.9	—	4.4	4.3	4.5	5.3	7.5
% Seats	—	—	4.9	—	6.2	6.6	—	5.4	6.2	6.8	7.1	8.0

Appendix C

Outline of the Three Main Italian Confederations of Labor, C.I.S.N.A.L., and the Principal Independent Unions, 1960.

C.G.I.L.

C.G.I.L. (Confederazione Generale Italiana del Lavoro) was still the largest union confederation in Italy at the end of the 1950's. Membership estimates have run from more than 4,000,000 claimed by C.G.I.L. itself and accepted by *L'Unità*, the official newspaper of the Italian Communist Party, to less than 2,500,000.

In order to support its claim of being the most representative organization as well as the most numerous, it recognized at least eight political currents within its ranks:

1. Communists, the largest single political group and the controlling one.
2. Nenni socialists, the second largest group.
3. Social Democrats, a small group, since the largest number of Social Democrats were in U.I.L., with a sprinkling in C.I.S.L.
4. Unitary Christians, who were alleged to be members of the Christian Associations of Italian Workers (A.C.L.I.) as well. Most Catholic workers, however, were affiliated with C.I.S.L.
5. Anarchists who have allegedly joined in order to defend labor unions.
6. Independents and some Liberal Party and Radical Party members.
7. The Popular Unity current, adherents of the former tiny party of Ferruccio Parri, leader of the resistance and postwar Premier of Italy.
8. Republicans, especially those who remained faithful to the "true" principles of Mazzini. Most Republican Party workers were in U.I.L., with a sprinkling in C.I.S.L.

In June 1960, U.I.L., the right-wing socialist foe of C.G.I.L., published the results of its survey of the political affiliation of C.G.I.L.'s leaders. The sample covered the responsible secretaries of 53 national category unions, 542 provincial federations of eight categories (building trades, agriculture, metal-mechanical, chemical, textile, mining, railroads, and postal and telegraph), and 90 provincial chambers of labor (Udine, Viterbo, and Trieste were not included). The study classified political affiliation as communist, Nenni socialist, or independent. Of the 699 leaders covered: 547, or 78.3%, were communists; 140, or 20%, were Nenni socialists; and 12, or 1.7%, were independents. The communists claimed the allegiance of 74% of national category union leaders and 82% of provincial chamber of labor officers. In the provincial category federations, communist adherents ranged from 90% among the textile and agricultural workers to 53% among the postal and telegraph workers. The Nenni socialists accounted for only 22.6% of the national category union secretaries and 18% of the provincial chamber of labor leaders. Their strength in the eight provincial category federations varied from a maximum of 39.4% among the postal and telegraph workers to a low of 8.9% among agricultural workers.

C.I.S.L.

C.I.S.L. (Confederazione Italiana Sindacati Lavoratori) took its present name in 1950. In October 1948, the Christian Democratic labor leaders in C.G.I.L. withdrew and formed the Free General Italian Confederation of Labor (L.C.G.I.L.). In June 1949, labor leaders of right-wing Socialist and Republican Party persuasions left

555

C.G.I.L. to form the Italian Federation of Labor (F.I.L.). On April 30, 1950, under the amicable pressure from anti-Communist labor leaders in the United States, some leaders of F.I.L. were convinced that they should join with L.C.G.I.L. Upon the adherence of a third group, the Union of Autonomous Italian Workers Federations, the name of the united organization was changed to C.I.S.L. Membership estimates have run from less than 1,000,000 to 2,500,000.

U.I.L.

U.I.L. (Unione Italiana del Lavoro) was constituted on March 5, 1950. To form U.I.L., labor leaders faithful to the third Socialist Party in existence at that moment, the Unitary Socialist Party, who had also left C.G.I.L. during the summer of 1949, joined forces with those elements in F.I.L. who refused to consent to a merger with L.C.G.I.L., an organization they considered Catholic-dominated. Into this alliance also entered leaders of the Italian Confederation of Independent Unions who had served as labor officials under the corporative system. Membership estimates have run from 125,000 to more than 750,000.

C.I.S.N.A.L.

The Italian Confederation of National Workers Unions (Confederazione Italiana dei Sindacati Nazionali dei Lavoratori—C.I.S.N.A.L.) is generally regarded as the labor wing of the neo-fascist Italian Social Movement (M.S.I.), and is thought to espouse corporative ideology. C.I.S.N.A.L. has set its own gross membership figure at more than 900,000. However, C.I.S.N.A.L. included in this figure, in addition to actual members, so-called adherents: those assisted by C.I.S.N.A.L.'s welfare institute, E.N.A.S.; workers who voted for C.I.S.N.A.L. in grievance committee elections; and workers who participated in strikes called by C.I.S.N.A.L. C.I.S.N.A.L. itself evaluated its actual membership at about one-third of the figure cited. Independent observers believed that actual membership did not exceed 50,000.

C.I.S.N.A.L.'s strength is limited to those areas where the political influence of the extreme Right is most pronounced: Rome, Naples, Salerno, Bari, Foggia, Palermo, Catania, and Cagliari. In these areas, C.I.S.N.A.L. has achieved its greatest organizational success among governmental employees in national, local, and parastatal offices.

Of the 87 provincial chambers of labor claimed by C.I.S.N.A.L., 10 had their offices at M.S.I. headquarters and another 10 had offices at the headquarters of other organizations. C.I.S.N.A.L. claimed to have organized 69 national category unions. Since it is known that C.I.S.N.A.L. recruited a large part of its membership from public employees in Rome and Southern Italy, it can be assumed that many of these category unions were largely paper organizations.

The administrative structure of C.I.S.N.A.L. follows, in all important aspects, that of the three principal confederations of labor. C.I.S.N.A.L. dates from March 24, 1950.

Principal Independent Unions

1. Italian Confederation of Company Executives (Confederazione Italiana Dirigenti di Azienda—C.I.D.A.) is made up of five union federations which cover establishments in industry, commerce, credit and finance, insurance, and agriculture.

2. General Confederation of Executives in Public Employment (Confederazione Dirigenti Statali—D.I.R.S.T.A.T.), which joins together four federations with jurisdiction over national administrative offices, the state-owned railroads, communal and provincial secretaries, and heads of state institutions.

3. The National Federation of Autonomous Unions (Unione Nazionale Sindacati Autonomi—U.N.S.A.) of which the National Autonomous Union of Elementary School Teachers, listed below, forms the principal part.

4. The Community Movement was limited to certain plants in Piedmont and Lombardy. It was organized in the 1940's and was directed by the highly esteemed, imaginative, socialistic, and somewhat erratic head of the efficient, prosperous, and humane Olivetti enterprises. In addition to its labor program, it proclaimed a political philosophy which sought to "conciliate socialism and freedom." In January 1958, Adriano Olivetti announced that the Community Movement would present candidates for the parliamentary elections in the spring of 1958 in most or all constituencies.

Although Olivetti gained a seat in the Chamber of Deputies, *Comunità* went down to heavy defeat. Olivetti himself resigned from Parliament in October 1959 before his untimely death in February 1960, but after members of his family in control of the Olivetti enterprises had acted to strip their latter-day Robert Owen of power and leadership—a move which did not prove wholly feasible.

5. Of the large number of independent railway workers unions, the following four are the most important:

   (a) Union of Locomotive Engineers, Assistant Engineers, and Heads of Repair Depots (Sindacato Macchinisti, Aiuto-Macchinisti, e Capideposito—S.M.A.C.).

   (b) Union of Administrative and Technical Employees of the State Railways, Group B (Sindacato Funzionari Amministrativi e Tecnici delle FF.SS., Gruppo B—S.I.F.A.T.).

   (c) National Union of Railroad Workers, Group C (Sindacato Nazionale Ferrovieri, Gruppo C—S.N.F.G.C.).

   (d) Union of State Railway Technician Heads and Workers (Sindacato Capi Tecnici, Operai delle Ferrovie dello Stato—S.C.O.F.S.).

6. Of the large group of independent school and university teachers unions, the following five are considered most important:

   (a) National Union of High School Teachers (Sindacato Nazionale Scuola Media—S.N.S.M.).

   (b) National Autonomous Union of High School Teachers (Sindacato Autonomo Scuola Media Italiana—S.A.S.M.I.), a group which broke away from S.N.S.M.

   (c) National Autonomous Union of Elementary School Teachers (Sindacato Nazionale Autonomo Scuola Elementare—S.N.A.S.E.).

   (d) National Union of Art Teachers (Sindacato Nazionale Istruzione Artistica—S.N.I.A.).

   (e) Union of Tenure Professors and Department Heads (Sindacato Presidi e Professori di Ruolo—S.P.P.R.).

7. A multitude of unions in the banking and insurance field.

8. The National Confederation of Independent Farmers (Confederazione Nazionale Coltivatori Diretti), while confining most of its activities to the organization of working farmers who own their own land, has also taken into its fold a substantial number of sharecroppers, thus arousing the ire of the sharecroppers unions of the three labor confederations, C.G.I.L., C.I.S.L., and U.I.L.

For further details concerning some of the independent organizations listed, as well as others, see "La indipendenza delle organizzazioni sindacali," *Rassegna del Lavoro*, November 1955, pp. 1633–1666. The standard directory for the names and addresses of organizations of all kinds, including labor unions and management associations, is *Guida Monici*.

557

Appendix D

English–Italian Guide to Labor Relations Terminology

Compiled by Maurice F. Neufeld and Dr. Federico Mancini, University of Bologna

Absentee landlord	Latifondista non residente nelle sue terre
Absenteeism	Assenteismo
Administrative organization	Struttura organizzativa
Advancement	Avanzamento
Age limit	Limite di età
Allowance	Assegno, gratifica, indennità
Application blank	Modulo per assunzione; domanda d'impiego
Apprentice	Apprendista, tirocinante
Apprenticeship	Apprendistato, tirocinio
Arbitration	Arbitrato
Arbitration award	Lodo arbitrale
Arbitration board	Commissione arbitrale
Arbitrator	Arbitro
Assembly line	Catena di montaggio
Belonging	Spirito di corpo, senso di appartenenza
Black list	Elenco dei lavoratori sindacali considerati indesiderabili dai datori di lavoro ostili ai sindacati
Bonus	Indennità, gratifica, premio
Boss	Padrone, capo, datore di lavoro
Boycott	Boicottaggio
Building trade	Edilizia
Business	Affare; *also*, impresa or azienda (when referring to a firm)
Businessman	Uomo d'affari
Case	Causa, lite
Case study	Analisi di situazione o di istituzione particolare
Casual worker	Lavoratore avventizio
Checkoff	Trattenuta sulla retribuzione per i contributi sindacali
Childbirth	Parto
Child labor	Lavoro dei fanciulli
Civil servant	Impiegato pubblico
Civil service	Pubblico impiego
Clerical	Impiegatizio
Clerk	Impiegato
Collective agreement	Contratto collettivo
Collective bargaining	Contrattazione collettiva
College of auditors	Collegio dei sindaci
College of honest men	Collegio dei probiviri
Company	Società, ditta, impresa, azienda
Company union	Sindacato dipendente dall'impresa
Conciliation	Conciliazione
Conference	Discussione

558

Convention	Riunione, congresso
Cooling-off period	Periodo di preavviso precedente lo sciopero
Corporation	Società commerciale, società per azioni
Counselor	Consulente, assistente
Craft	Mestiere
Craft union	Sindacato di mestiere
Day laborer (in agriculture)	Bracciante
Dead time	Percentuale di tempo fissata nel computo del cottimo per eventuali ritardi
Demotion	Declassamento, retrocessione
Directive council or committee	Consiglio direttivo, comitato direttivo
Discharge	Licenziamento
Domestic worker	Domestico, domestica (feminine)
Double-time pay	Doppia retribuzione
Draft	Chiamata, o richiamo, alle armi
Dues	Contributo totale sindacale comprendente il pagamento della tessera confederale
Dues collection	Esazione dei contributi sindacali
Eight-hour day	Giornata di otto ore
Employee	Prestatore di lavoro, dipendente, impiegato
Employment contract	Contratto individuale di lavoro
Employer	Datore di lavoro, imprenditore
Engineer	Tecnico, ingegnere
Entrepreneur	Imprenditore
Executive	Dirigente
Executive committee	Comitato esecutivo
Factory	Fabbrica, officine, stabilimento
Family allowances	Assegni familiari
Foreman	Caposquadra
General council	Consiglio generale
Grading	Attribuzione della qualifica e delle mansioni
Graveyard shift	Turno di notte
Grievance	Reclamo, lagnanza, controversia individuale, vertenza, grana (dialect)
Grievance committee	Commissione interna di fabbrica
Guaranteed employment	Impiego garantito
Guaranteed wages	Salario garantito
Handicraft	Artigianato
Handicraftsman	Artigiano
Hire (to)	Assumere
Hiring	Assunzione
Hiring card	Lettera d'assunzione
Holiday	Festività
Holiday pay	Retribuzione per il lavoro festivo
Holiday work	Lavoro festivo
Housewife	Casalinga
Human relations	Relazioni umane
Incentive	Incentivo
Income	Reddito
Independent union	Sindacato non aderente ad alcuna confederazione
Industrial accidents or injuries	Infortuni sul lavoro
Industrial disease	Malattia professionale, tecnopatia
Industrial relations	Rapporti di lavoro nell'industria
Industrial union	Sindacato organizzato verticalmente
Job	Lavoro, occupazione, posto di lavoro
Job analysis or description	Descrizione delle caratteristiche principali del lavoro

Job classification	Classificazione dei lavori secondo le loro qualifiche
Job evaluation	Valutazione delle mansioni del lavoro per la determinazione della retribuzione
Job instruction	Addestramento sul lavoro
Job methods	Metodi ed istruzioni per migliorare il lavoro
Job safety	Sicurezza sul lavoro, anti-infortunistica
Job tenure	Stabilità nell'impiego
Joint-stock corporation	Società per azioni
Judicial decision	Sentenza
Labor	Mondo del lavoro, forze del lavoro, manodopera, maestranze, laburista, laburismo (when referring to British politics)
Labor court	Magistratura del lavoro (under fascist régime, *also* now existing in Germany and Australia)
Labor dispute	Controversia collettiva di lavoro
Labor force	Forze di lavoro
Labor leader	Dirigente sindacale
Labor relations	Rapporti di lavoro
Labor spy	Agente provocatore padronale, spia del padrone
Labor turnover	Avvicendamento della manodopera
Labor union	Sindacato
Land lease (in agriculture)	Affitto di fondo rustico
Layoff	Sospensione dal lavoro, licenziamento temporaneo
Lay off (to)	Sospendere
Leadership	Capacità di comando
Lessee (in agriculture)	Affittuario di fondo rustico
Line (as distinguished from "Staff")	Personale dirigente con funzioni esecutive
Lockout	Serrata
Management	Direzione dell'impresa
Manpower	Manodopera
Manual worker	Manovale, operaio comune, lavoratore manuale
Mediation	Mediazione
Meeting	Assemblea, riunione, comizio (when called in a public square)
Membership card	Tessera
Merit rating	Criteri di valutazione del personale
Ministry of Labor and Social Security	Ministero del Lavoro e della Previdenza Sociale
Naval yard	Cantiere navale
Night work	Lavoro notturno
Notice of discharge	Preavviso di licenziamento
Old-age insurance	Assicurazione per la vecchiaia
Organizing committee	Comitato organizzativo
Overtime	Lavoro straordinario
Overtime pay	Retribuzione maggiorata per lavoro straordinario
Ownership	Proprietà
Pace setter	Operaio scelto per determinare il tempo del cottimo
Participation in management	Congestione
Partnership	Società di persone
Pay	Retribuzione, paga, salario (said of worker), stipendio (said of clerk)
Pension	Pensione
Per capita tax	Tesseramento confederale
Performance	Adempimento della prestazione di lavoro
Personnel management	Direzione del personale

Picketing	Picchetto, piantonamento
Piecework	Lavoro a cottimo, or simply, cottimo
Plant	Fabbrica, stabilimento, officina
Pregnancy	Gravidanza
Probationary period	Periodo di prova
Probationary worker	Lavoratore in prova
Procedure	Procedura
Proceedings	Verbale di riunione
Production	Produzione, rendimento (when referring to an individual worker)
Production process	Processo produttivo
Promotion	Promozione
Protection of women workers	Tutela delle lavoratrici
Public relations	Rapporti col pubblico
Quickie strike	Sciopero a singhiozzo
Rank and file	Base (said of a party or trade union)
Rate cutting	Riduzione delle medie nel cottimo
Reactionary	Reazionario, retrogrado
Reformist	Riformista
Retirement	Cessazione del lavoro per limiti d'età; congedo (in the public and semipublic service)
Revolutionary	Rivoluzionario
Right to strike	Diritto di sciopero
Rules	Regolamenti, norme
Sabotage	Sabotaggio
Safety	Sicurezza, prevenzione contro gli infortuni
Salary	Stipendio
Scab	Crumiro
Scientific Management	Organizzazione scientifica del lavoro
Seasonal unemployment	Disoccupazione stagionale
Secretariat	Segreteria
Semiskilled worker	Operaio di media qualifica
Seniority	Anzianità
Severance pay	Indennità di licenziamento
Sharecropper	Compartecipante, colono parziario, mezzadro
Sharecropping	Compartecipazione, colonia parziaria, mezzadria
Shift	Turno
Shop	Stabilimento, fabbrica, officina, impresa
Sit-down strike	Sciopero bianco
Skilled worker	Operaio specializzato
Sliding scale	Scala mobile
Slowdown	Non collaborazione
Social insurance	Assicurazioni sociali
Social security	Previdenza sociale
Social service	Servizio sociale
Speed-up	Accelerazione del lavoro senza adeguato compenso
Staff	Personale direttivo e impiegatizio, personale direttivo con funzioni deliberative (in technical administrative sense)
Standard of living	Tenore di vita
Steward	Membro di commissione interna
Straight time	Orario normale di lavoro
Strike	Sciopero
Strike-breaker	Crumiro
Subforeman	Capogruppo
Suggestion box	Cassetta per i suggerimenti
Sunday work	Lavoro domenicale
Supervisor	Caporeparto
Sympathetic strike	Sciopero di simpatia

Team work	Lavoro a squadra, lavoro di gruppo
Technological change	Riorganizzazione del lavoro, introduzione di nuovi ritrovati tecnici
Technological unemployment	Disoccupazione tecnologica
Tenure	Stabilità nell'impiego
Test	Prova, reattivo
Textile workers	Lavoratori tessili
Time and motion study	Studio dei tempi e dei movimenti
Timework	Lavoro a tempo, lavoro in economia
Trade	Commercio, mestiere (in sense of "craft")
Trade union	Sindacato
Training	Addestramento, formazione
Transfer	Trasferimento
Transmission chain	Cinghia di trasmissione (said of unions in communist terminology)
Umpire (impartial)	Arbitro
Unemployment	Disoccupazione
Unemployment insurance	Assicurazione contro la disoccupazione
Union representation	Rappresentanza sindacale di tutti i lavoratori
Unmarried mothers	Ragazze madri
Unskilled worker	Manovale, operaio a bassa qualifica
Upgrading	Promozione
Vacation	Ferie
Vacation with pay	Ferie retribuite
Vocational guidance	Orientamento professionale
Vocational selection	Selezione professionale
Vocational training	Formazione professionale
Wage earner	Salariato
Wages	Salario, paga, retribuzione
Welfare	Benessere
Welfare state	Stato di tipo laburista o scandinavo
White-collar worker	Impiegato
Wildcat strike	Sciopero spontaneo, sciopero non proclamato dal sindacato
Work premises	Locali di lavoro
Work simplification	Semplificazione del lavoro
Work stoppage	Arresto del lavoro
Worker	Operaio, lavoratore, maestranza
Working conditions	Condizioni di lavoro
Workmen's compensation	Indennità per infortunio sul lavoro
Yellow-dog contract	Contratto di lavoro con clausola anti-sindacale

Appendix E

Italian Industrial Development, by Regions, before 1860

The Kingdom of the Two Sicilies

Textile production and trade were much less important in the Kingdom of the Two Sicilies than in either Piedmont or Lombardy. Despite climatic advantages, silk production in the Kingdom was less than one-sixth that of Lombardy in 1830, just reaching one-quarter as late as 1855. No undertaking, whether in silk spinning or weaving, took on an industrial character; the industry remained essentially handicraft in nature. Silk weaving, especially, had enjoyed a rich tradition, but every attempt to reinvigorate it failed. Technicians were imported from Lyons, Piedmont, and Tuscany; prizes were offered; new looms were purchased abroad. Nothing helped. Not even the famous plant at San Leucio, employing 700 or 800 looms, could find ways to maintain an economical existence, despite its European reputation.

In the Kingdom of the Two Sicilies, which raised half the sheep of Italy, the ancient woolen art had enjoyed considerable importance during its handicraft stage. The mild climate, however, established the supremacy of vegetable cloths and the consumption of woolen cloth therefore never attained the proportions reached in the North. Spinning was almost wholly confined to cottage production during the entire period under consideration. After 1835, there is evidence of weaving on a small manufacturing scale in 117 workshops producing carpets, shawls, hats, and caps. The first mechanical spinning mill was not installed until 1852. By 1867, it was estimated that the Neapolitan provinces possessed 25% of the spinning and weaving installations of the country.

The production of hemp was neglected during the period before 1860, and the making of linen was confined to peasants who spun and wove for their own use.

In the field of textiles, cotton production alone created units of manufacture approaching modern concepts. The blockade of the Napoleonic wars and the cutting off of American supplies during the Civil War had encouraged the cultivation of cotton in the Kingdom and had prolonged the illusion that the tired soil of the Italian South could compete with virgin lands. This fantasy was to prove costly to the economy of the South. Sicilian raw cotton supplied household needs and the limited demands of the few workshops of record on the island. On the mainland, the spinning of cotton also remained, for the most part, a cottage industry. However, the establishment of five sizeable spinning plants, chiefly in the environs of Salerno, after 1830, the enumeration of 30,000 spindles and 2,650 workers in 1840, and the sixfold increase in the import of cotton from 1840 to 1860 would indicate the beginnings of true factory production. The foreign names linked with these pioneering spinning mills reveal plainly the origin of initiative, capital, technical supervision, and management: Egg, Mayer, Marstaller, Zoblin, Vonwiller, Schlaepfer, Wenner, Escher, Glarner, and Meyer. In contrast to spinning, the weaving of cotton attracted no foreign interest and was rarely industrialized. Cloth remained primitive and coarse, made by peasants to satisfy peasant needs. Of 13 million meters of cotton cloth produced in 1840, only one-sixth had been woven on mechanical looms.

The handicraft state of the metal-mechanical trades amply satisfied the narrow market: simple agricultural tools, a few home implements, and fittings for small fishing boats. The State ordered rifles, cannon, projectiles, and munitions, but its needs, like those of demand generally, were stationary. Expansion came briefly, toward 1840, in response to the erection of bridges, the temporary spurt of railroad construction, and the building of a few new industries which required machine parts. Even so, at mid-century, only four blast furnaces and a few foundries existed in the entire Kingdom. At the time of unification, therefore, many small handicraft shops still dominated the scene, with the exception of the government plant at Pietrarsa, founded in 1840. It employed, from the start, 600 workers and 200 soldiers and became one of the principal mechanical establishments in the new Kingdom of Italy.

With the negligible exception of the few small workshops which turned out textiles, hats, candles, glass, leather, and furniture in Palermo, Catania, and Messina, the only substantial resource of Sicily was sulphur. Between 1833 and 1836, 134 sulphur mines were recorded as active. Some 5,400 persons were employed in them, of whom 3,200 were children. The government itself shared in the shameful mistreatment of these children, for the State enjoyed monopoly rights over the sulphur mines and granted concessions for their exploitation. The terms of the agreements aroused the cupidity of the State as well as the companies. Despite periodic, ambitious projects for the improvement of performance, both parties remained more interested in profits than in advancing skills and bettering the miserable lot of the harassed miners and their families. The methods of extraction remained so primitive that a third of the usable materials were lost through technical incapacity. Over and over again, complaints arose because of the total absence of machinery in the mines and of any rational criteria for working the deposits. The only other industry in Sicily which merits even passing mention was naval construction. However, as in Naples, except for a few unusual shipyards, operations had not passed beyond the handicraft stage.[1]

The Duchies of Parma and Piacenza, of Reggio and Modena, and of Lucca

In addition to agricultural products and hemp, the Duchy of Parma possessed 96 silk spinning mills in the later 1840's, two factories which wove woolen cloth, the same number of glass works, a few iron-processing shops, and tiny paper plants. Silk raising and reeling were dominant in Modena, while the neighboring regions of Massa-Carrara, famous for their marble, employed, respectively, 210 persons in 37 quarries and 2,260 persons in 70 quarries. Lucca was credited with 700–800 silk looms, 900 weavers of woolen goods, a few hat shops, small paper mills, and scattered iron works.[2]

Tuscany

In 1855, Tuscan silkworm production constituted merely 1/25 of Italy's total output. As for the weaving of silk, the local workshops, descendants of the famous botteghe of the Middle Ages and the Renaissance, employed little more than 4,000 looms in 1860. Nor were cotton spinning and weaving important occupations. The tariff policy of Tuscany permitted large importation of cotton goods: in 1860, cotton and cotton products amounted to one-third of the total value of all imports. Yet, as early as 1826, modern looms had been introduced and formed the nucleus of the Dini and Pontecorvo firms. In 1850, 24 mechanical looms were in operation, with steam engines as motive power. Nonetheless, manual household looms predominated in the number of 46,000, while 5,620 looms for the hand weaving of flax were enumerated.

The art of making woolen cloth had been traditional in the northern valleys of the Arno, in the Arezzo region, and in Florence. But it was the city of Prato which modernized its handicraft production by introducing modern machinery as early as 1820. The plants of Prato specialized in the manufacture of reprocessed woolen cloth, probably because of the concentration of the rag trade in Leghorn and the importance of rags in the packing of marble in the nearby Apuan mountains. Although, in time, Prato would become one of Italy's most important woolen centers, as late as 1868 the city was reported to have only 64 spinning machines, 530 industrial looms, and 9,000 employees in the woolen trade.

Other occupations, noteworthy enough to mention, were still handicraft in nature, with the exception of about 100 paper mills which boasted production in 1860 equal to that of Piedmont. But the mechanical trades were limited to small blacksmith shops offering for sale the simplest agricultural tools. The furniture craft, widely distributed, emphasized finely inlaid woods and pieces of artistic value. Also characteristically Tuscan and partaking of no industrial character was the output of marble, alabaster, and leather works of art, and the famous straw shops, 56 all told in 1855, of which 14 were located in Florence.[3]

Lombardy

Silk reeling or winding (the drawing of the filament from the cocoon) tarried as a cottage industry in Lombardy until 1815. Afterward, the appearance of reeling mills bestowed a more industrial character upon the process. In 1809, a total of 33,000 persons were recorded as tending 14,000 boilers, so vital in the reeling process. By 1856, the number of boilers had increased to 39,000, but were watched over by only 18,000 persons, half of whom were young girls. Obviously, productivity had increased. However, even as late as 1856, methods were still shockingly antiquated. Only 144 reeling mills, constituting less than 5% of all plants but housing 25% of all boilers, used steam for heating the boilers. There is evidence that 75% of all boilers were heated by the application of direct flame. There are no data on the total number of establishments in 1809, but it is known that in 1856 there were 3,088 silk reeling plants with an average of 25 workers for each mill.[4]

In contrast to silk reeling, the spinning of silk was not so closely linked to agriculture as were the growing of cocoons and the reeling of silk, both tied down to the seasonality of the cocoon harvesting period. However, since the more modern spinning mills sought the countryside where they could be close to the sources of water power, rather than the cities, most of the labor force also worked in the fields to supplement their earnings. Beyond doubt, by 1856, water power had come to be the prime motor force, although both men and horses were still being used in some spinning mills. In that year, only 19,000 spindles, out of a total of 530,000 in Lombardy, were installed in 93 establishments in Milan, whereas 492,000 spindles were in plants scattered throughout the provinces of Bergamo and Como, away from the larger urban areas. With regard to the actual number of spinning mills, it is known that they increased from 219 in the decade 1830–1840 to 383 in the decade 1850–1860. Although it is possible to calculate that the average mill in 1830 employed about 19 workers, no comparable figure can be cited for 1860 due to the lack of data.[5]

Available evidence suggests that weaving, the third branch of the silk industry, had not advanced as far in Lombardy as silk spinning. Greenfield presents two sets of figures for 1844, from which the stage of development in the weaving industry can be determined. According to the first set of statistics, there were 8,000 looms in the two provinces of Milan and Como; according to the second source, there were only 4,431 looms in all of the provinces of Lombardy. Greenfield deduces from this discrepancy that the smaller figure probably included only those looms installed in factories. Thus, silk weaving was presumably equally divided, as yet, between true factory production and the "command center"-cottage industry type of operation. It is difficult to obtain a firm impression concerning the size of weaving operations because of the dearth of data. One source mentions 140 weaving plants employing 7,000 workers in 1840, or an average of 50 workers to each establishment. Very rarely did the number of looms in each plant exceed 100; normally they ranged between 30 and 40. A considerable proportion of the total number of looms was scattered among peasant homes.[6]

The cotton industry was new to Lombardy. In the time of Napoleon, the local manufacture of cotton goods had barely started, although northern Italians had already learned to use cotton fabrics imported from England, Switzerland, Saxony, and France. So notably did this industry expand that by 1860 it ranked second only to silk in the incipient industrial hierarchy of Lombardy. Cotton spinning mills in the decade 1831–1840 numbered 17, employing 2,295 persons, or an average of 135 workers for each mill. Comparable data for 1841–1850 were: 28 mills, 3,186 workers, and an average force of 113–114. In the following decade, increases in the number of plants and employees took place, but the average number of workers in each mill remained about the same: 33 mills, 3,810 workers, and an average force of 115–116. The average size of undertaking revealed by these figures undoubtedly points to an industrial environment approaching the modern factory. The cotton spinning branch of textiles started free of any hostages to local agricultural habits or prejudices, since raw cotton had to be imported. Moreover, it was abetted by high fashion in England and Western Europe which had decreed cotton in vogue. It was also assured of a ready market by a widespread endowment of hand looms and eager users of them at peasant and artisan homes. In brief, the organization of cotton spinning represented the first attempt in Lombardy, and therefore in Italy, to found and operate an industry according to modern criteria and methods. By way of marked contrast, the weaving of cotton yarn remained a household industry which produced cloth of coarse quality. Nonetheless, cotton weaving apparently expanded, despite a tariff which favored cotton spinning at its expense by rendering prohibitive the importation of fine cotton yarns, not made in Italy, but necessary for profitable weaving operations. The documented progress of weaving is marvellously confused. One set of statistics states that in 1839, 52,000 cotton looms were in operation in Lombardy, mostly in peasant homes during the winter season. The number of persons engaged in cotton weaving the next year was placed at 50,000. Yet another source stated that in 1845, 14,560 cotton looms were centered in Milan province, representing 91% of the total number for Lombardy. Since another collection of data for the same year estimated that 99,000 men, women, and children were employed in Milan province alone at 71,000 looms, it is comforting to assume that cottage looms were included in the larger figure. Still a fourth series gave a very different result for the very same year. Then, ten years later, the number of looms in Lombardy stood at 17,000, according to a different group of data, while 34,000 persons worked them. Thus the ratio of looms to operators presumably decreased from slightly more than 1 to 1 in 1839 to $\frac{1}{2}$ to 1 in 1855![7]

Both spinning and weaving of linen were spread throughout the countryside of Lombardy where an excellent quality of flax grew. The chief form of export was thread. But the manufacture of linen suffered from the easy competition of cotton. By 1839, when cotton spinning plants had grown relatively large, the linen industry remained predominantly in the hands of peasants and continued there throughout the period under discussion. However, in 1841 two modern mechanical linen spinning mills were established, one equipped with 4,000 and the other with 6,000 spindles. A third plant with more than 1,000 spindles appeared on the scene later. In 1854, all three employed only 872 persons, one-third of whom were boys. Notwithstanding low salaries, these firms lived from hand to mouth, contending with an inexperienced labor force, public prejudice against machine-made linen thread, and competition of foreign producers.[8]

The spinning and weaving of wool was an older art in Lombardy and North Italy than the fashioning of silk and cotton. The industry declined as an exporter of choice woolen cloths before the invasion of Napoleon and never recovered from the loss of its supply of fine wools from Spain during the wars of 1808–1809. After being forced into the home market to produce coarse fabrics, the industry hardly survived the competition of cheap cloth from Austria after the restoration. As late as 1854, the 27 weaving mills in Bergamo province, which were unique enough to be noted, possessed only 400 looms for cloth and 50 looms for carpets and blankets. If eight Bergamascan spinning mills with 3,700 spindles and two Milanese spinning mills built between 1837 and 1841 are excepted, the entire production of woolen thread in Lombardy was dependent on the handiwork of the peasants.[9]

The mining and metallurgical industries languished in Lombardy. Of 200 mines enumerated for Lombardy at the beginning of the century, only 79 survived in 1846 at Bergamo, Como, Brescia, and Sondria. In 1825, the only year for which figures are available, the average number of persons working the iron mines of Brescia was only 11 for each mine.[10] Iron production fared no better than iron mining. In the Napoleonic period, the smelting furnaces of Lombardy yielded 9,300 metric tons. By 1846, this total had only reached 10,000 metric tons, including a small quantity of pig iron. During 1856–1858, 12,800 metric tons were produced, including 1,500 metric tons of pig iron. (In 1855, the United Kingdom produced 3,218,000 tons of pig iron; this figure rose to 3,826,000 in 1860.) The remainder of the tonnage was in merchant iron and steel. Clearly, the industry was of small importance and gave employment in 1854 to only 1,200 workers. At the close of the era under review, no plants producing steel of fine quality had as yet taken hold.[11]

The metal-fabricating industry still manufactured small customary products. Even the skilled arms industry of Brescia faltered. These famous shops could not cope with Austria's refusal to purchase their products or to permit their exportation. In 1825, there were 76 shops employing 776 craftsmen. In 1846, not more than 400 craftsmen were employed at the production of arms in all of Lombardy. By midcentury, a scattering of specialized plants sprang up in Milan and Pavia which fabricated cutlery and springs from English steel, but they were unique. At Bellano, another mill inaugurated the manufacture of sheet iron.

Like the fabrication of metal products, the machinery industry also froze at the handicraft-artisan stage of small and medium-sized operations. The workshops were limited to putting together simple agricultural machinery like mills, presses, threshers, ploughs, and utensils; rude looms; and other tools for silk reeling and domestic textile chores. Gradually, toward 1845, slow and undramatic industrial improvements here and there generated new needs. Since the few modern machines in operation within the region had been imported, replacement and repair parts as well as auxiliary equipment were needed on the spot. The increase in water-driven machinery necessitated wheels and contrivances for the transmission of motor energy. The growth of communications and vehicles also required mechanical parts, although, to be sure, wood was still very much in use and shops still employed carpenters and woodworkers for this purpose.

The decade from 1845 to 1855 saw the establishment of metal-mechanical workshops of greater size than had been normal for Lombardy: Grondona & C., the first nucleus of Miani-Silvestri; Bouffier & C., now Breda; Schlegel & C.; Edoardo Suffert; and Balleydier. These names betray the foreign origin of the leading industrial organizers in Lombardy at this time. Tremelloni observes: "In Lombardy, in addition to names like Kramer, Krumm, Preyssel, Mueller, Coizet, Delacroix, Balleydier, Roux, Fritsch, Dufour, Bouffier, Schlegel, Suffert, Izar, Zuppinger, Mieville, Hoesly, and Schoch, we find names which last on . . . in Italian industry." [12]

Although no figures on employment in these new establishments are available, it is clear from the kinds of machinery manufactured that industry in Lombardy was undergoing organic development. "In 1855 there were seventeen establishments engaged in manufacturing machinery . . . : hydraulic motors and their spare parts, sugar and tobacco machines, steam engines, spinning and winding mills, boilers, pumps, paper machines, oil and flour mills, hydraulic presses, threshers, railway mechanisms, looms and factory equipment. The local manufacture was criticized as still deficient, in failing to produce large machines for sugar refineries, centrifugal pumps, 'continuous machines' for paper mills, spinning jennies, locomotives and rails. . . ." [13] Growth there was, and, of more significance, change in the very structure of these pioneering ventures. Yet a warning signal against exaggerated notions of progress must be raised. According to Antonio Fossati, at midcentury there were only three limited-liability joint stock companies operating in the metal-mechanical trades in all of Italy. Combined, they commanded 2,000,000 lire of capital, or the rough equivalent of $2,000,000 today. In 1860, there were still only five limited-liability joint stock companies manufacturing metal-mechanical products. They were capitalized at 3,000,000 lire. [14]

Of the remaining industries in Lombardy, only three distinguished that region from the other states. The wholesale production of felt hats and furniture for popular consumption at reasonable prices had timidly begun. Around 1850, 3,000 craftsmen, scattered among many small workshops, especially in Brianza, were turning out this type of furniture. In addition, Lombardy enjoyed a European reputation for the high quality of the carriages it manufactured. In Milan alone, 2,500 persons worked at this trade in 40 factories. The skills imparted prepared workers to shift to the production of railroad carriages, while, at the end of the century, this regional experience proved invaluable in the new automobile industry. [15]

Piedmont

The industrial life of Piedmont between 1800 and 1850 dragged on in limited, but not entirely hopeless, fashion. Piedmont's silk production in 1783 had accounted for 78.7% of its total exports. At that time, its quality was without peer for Italy and Piedmont's silk workers journeyed south to teach spinning methods to less advanced craftsmen. [16] With the turn of the eighteenth century, 17,000 workers were recorded as engaged in raising cocoons and reeling filament. Almost a half century later, according to estimates made by Antonio Fossati for 1848, the Kingdom's silk industry employed 56,000 workers: 39,000 reelers in 844 mills, 11,000 spinners connected with 156 shops, and 6,000 weavers employed by 38 establishments, most of whom worked at home. In 1855, the number of silk workers was given as 57,000. That same year the Kingdom produced one-fifth of the cocoons in Italy. [17]

Cotton spinning was encouraged by the tariff policy of the State. In 1844, 60 to 70 spinning plants operated with 100,000 spindles and 4,500 workers. Lombardy utilized the same number of spindles, but they were distributed among only 38 mills, tended by little more than two-thirds the number of workers. Obviously, the average size of plant in Piedmont was small: three mills possessed more than 10,000 spindles; 10 others had more than 2,000 but less than 10,000; the rest had fewer than 2,000. Cotton weaving, too, was less advanced in Piedmont than in Lombardy as of 1844. Some 250 plants were recorded as working 14,500 looms, mostly by hand; of these establishments, 213 had a maximum of 10 looms, and only 6 had from 41 to 80 looms. Fossati's estimates for 1848 weave the same total image of Piedmont's cotton textile industry: 26,000 workers employed by 320 firms of which only some 30 were of substantial size.

As compared with Lombardy, where it was contracting, the woolen industry took on new, if not robust, life in Piedmont. The art of producing wool was ancient in this region, especially in the area of Biella, where records of drapers' guilds date from the sixteenth century. As early as 1817, Pietro Sella had introduced Belgian rotating engines for carding and spinning of wool. Although the factories of this era were small indeed, they seemed like monsters to the workers who called them "machines." They resented the idea of reporting to duty at the sound of a bell. They also disliked the inability to set their own pace, as they did when they worked at home.[18] The years between 1817 and 1844 were noteworthy not because of rapid technical changes in the woolen industry in Piedmont but because of increases in the number of plants. The spinning branch, utilizing carded wool, centered in only four or five establishments with a total of 24,000 spindles. Not until a decade later did spinning with combed wool commence. Weaving, on the other hand, gave employment in 1844 to 11,300 workers in 249 plants utilizing 1,755 looms, or an average of seven looms and little more than 45 workers to a shop. This average was higher for Biella since half of all weavers worked there in only 79 shops with 816 looms, or almost half the total number. As yet, 50% of the weavers in Piedmont were adult men, showing that the use of women and children was not as widespread in the industry as it would later become. Fossati's estimates for 1848 corroborate the impression of a lively but still primitive industry: 63 firms operated 220 workshops, employing 3,484 spinners and 13,000 weavers. Of the 63 firms, about 50 operated at the handicraft stage.

Mining and quarrying data for 1848 assign 3,900 laborers to 40 workings. Metallurgy claimed fewer hands still: only 700 operatives in all the Kingdom of Sardinia in 1844 engaged in producing iron at 130 smithies or forges. Constantly lamented were the laughable quality of available coal and the limited supply of wood. Crude and diminutive as iron production, the metal-fabricating and machinery industries, just visible as the simplest of artisan fabrications, supplied simple wants like hydraulic wheels and agricultural instruments. Not until 1843 did Taylor and Prandi establish a small repair plant at Sampierdarena. After ten years, it failed. Then, in 1858, Cavour stimulated its metamorphosis into Ansaldo, now famous. In 1846, the Westermann shop was founded at Sesti Ponente. These pioneering ventures, and others like them, located almost always on the Ligurian coast because of lower ocean freight charges, the possibility of serving the nearby railroad lines, and proximity to military and naval installations. Ship construction was about to emerge from the rule of the small carpenter and to enter upon industrial beginnings. Fossati's combined statistics for the metal-mechanical trades in 1848 show 9,100 craftsmen employed by 66 firms and 342 workshops. Fossati makes a bold-face distinction between firms and workshops in his tabulation and also clearly states that the industrial data for 1848 include handicraft operations.

Piedmont's other industries offered employment to relatively few hands: 1,380 workers in 334 leather and skin operations; 348 employees in Turin's 72 famous confectionery shops; 1,290 laborers in 23 chemical plants; 3,000 operatives in 106 paper mills; and 800 craftsmen in 16 glassworks. Figures are empty of employees for 70 recorded soap factories, while the manufacture of knit goods and woolen hats was noteworthy, but simply in this bare fashion.

APPENDIX E – FOOTNOTES

1. Roberto Tremelloni, *Storia dell'industria italiana contemporanea dalla fine del settecento all'unità italiana*, pp. 228–245.

2. The same, pp. 253–254.

3. The same, pp. 245–250.

4. The same, pp. 185–186; Kent Roberts Greenfield, *Economics and Liberalism in the Risorgimento*, p. 99, footnote 13.

5. Tremelloni, cited above, p. 186.

6. Greenfield, cited above, p. 101, footnotes 18 and 19; Tremelloni, cited above, p. 188, footnote 1.

7. Greenfield, cited above, pp. 101–104; Tremelloni, cited above, pp. 188–193.

8. Greenfield, cited above, pp. 104–105; Tremelloni, cited above, pp. 194–195.

9. Tremelloni, cited above, pp. 196–197.

10. The same, p. 197; Greenfield, cited above, p. 113.
11. Tremelloni, cited above, p. 198; Witt Bowden, Michael Karpovich, and Abbott Payson Usher, *An Economic History of Europe since 1750*, p. 386.
12. Tremelloni, cited above, p. 137, footnote 2; pp. 198–200.
13. Greenfield, cited above, p. 137.
14. Antonio Fossati, *Lavoro e produzione in Italia*, p. 663, Table: "Sviluppo delle Società per Azioni metal-meccaniche."
15. Tremelloni, cited above, pp. 200–206.
16. The same, p. 39.
17. For statistics mentioned for the silk industry and about to be enumerated for other industries in Piedmont, see the same, pp. 210–220; Fossati, cited above, pp. 675–676. All of Fossati's data refer to 1848.
18. Rinaldo Rigola, *Storia del movimento operaio italiano*, pp. 26–27.

Selected Bibliography

Adams, John Clarke. "Italy," Chapter 6, *Comparative Labor Movements*, Walter Galenson, ed. New York: Prentice-Hall, 1952.

Albrecht-Carrié, René. *Italy from Napoleon to Mussolini*. New York: Columbia University Press, 1950.

Annali di statistica. Serie IV, No. 75. "Elenco delle pubblicazioni fatte dal 1861 al 1894." Roma: Ministero di Agricoltura, Industria e Commercio, Direzione Generale della Statistica, 1894.

————. Anno 86, Serie VIII, Vol. 9. "Indagine statistica sullo sviluppo del reddito nazionale dell'Italia dal 1861 al 1956." Roma: Istituto Centrale di Statistica, 1957.

————. Anno 87, Serie VIII, Vol. 7. "Le rilevazioni statistiche in Italia dal 1861 al 1956." Roma: Istituto Centrale di Statistica, 1958.

Annuario statistico italiano. Prima Serie: 1878 (Parts I and II), 1881, 1884, 1886, 1887–1888, 1888–1890, 1892, 1895, 1897, 1898, 1900, 1904, 1905–1907 (2 vols. in 1, fasc. I–II). 13 vols. Roma: Ministero di Agricoltura, Industria e Commercio, Direzione Generale della Statistica.

————. Seconda Serie: 1911, 1912, 1913, 1914, 1915, 1916, 1917–1918, 1919–1921, 1922–1925. 9 vols. Roma: Ministero di Agricoltura, Industria e Commercio, Direzione Generale della Statistica e del Lavoro; Ministero dell'Economia Nazionale; Direzione Generale della Statistica.

————. Terza Serie: 1927, 1928, 1929, 1930, 1931, 1932, 1933. 7 vols. Roma: Istituto Centrale di Statistica.

————. Quarta Serie: 1934, 1935, 1936, 1937, 1938, 1939, 1940, 1941, 1942, 1943. 10 vols. Roma: Istituto Centrale di Statistica.

————. Quinta Serie: 1944–1948, 1949–1950, 1951, 1952, 1953, 1954, 1955, 1956, 1957, 1958. 10 vols. Roma: Istituto Centrale di Statistica.

Archivio Economico dell'Unificazione Italiana. Vols. 1–9 (1956–1959). Roma: Archivio Economico . . . (Industria Libraria Tipografica Editrice, Torino).

Azzoni, Ugo. "Fascismo e antifascismo." *Il Mulino*: IX, No. 1, February 1960, pp. 7–28.

Babbage, Charles. *On the Economy of Machinery and Manufactures*. London: Charles Knight, 1832.

Beals, Carleton. *Rome or Death: the Story of Fascism*. New York and London: The Century Co., 1923.

Benson, George C. S., and Maurice F. Neufeld. "American Military Government in Italy," Chapter VI, *American Experiences in Military Government in World War II*. New York: Rinehard and Co., 1948.

Bloch, Marc. *The Historian's Craft*. New York: Alfred A. Knopf, 1953.

Borgese, Giuseppe Antonio. *Goliath: the March of Fascism*. New York: Viking Press, 1937.

Bowring, Sir John. "Report on the Statistics of Tuscany, Lucca, the Pontifical and the Lombardo-Venetian States, with a Special Reference to Their Commercial Relations." *Commons Papers*, Vol. XVI (Cd. 165). London: Great Britain, House of Commons, 1839.

Bulferetti, Luigi. *Le ideologie socialistiche in Italia nell'età del positivismo evoluzionistico (1870–1892)*. Firenze: Felice Le Monnier, 1951.

Cameron, Rondo E. "French Finance and Italian Unity: The Cavourian Decade." *American Historical Review*, Vol. LXII, No. 3, April 1957, pp. 552–569.

Cammett, John McKay. "Antonio Gramsci and the 'Ordine Nuovo' Movement: A Study in the Rise of Italian Communism." Ph.D. Dissertation, Columbia University, 1959.

Candeloro, Giorgio. *Il movimento sindacale in Italia*. Roma: Edizioni di Cultura Sociale, 1950.

Carocci, Giovanni. "Inchiesta alla Fiat: indagine su taluni aspetti della lotta di classe nel complesso Fiat." *Nuovi Argomenti*: Nos. 31–32, March–June 1958.

Catholic Encyclopedia. New York: Robert Appleton, 1910.

Chiurco, G. A. *Storia della rivoluzione fascista,* Vols. IV and V. Firenze: Vallecchi, 1929.

Cipolla, C. M. "List of Books and Articles on Italian Economic History Published in Italy, 1939–49." *The Economic History Review,* Second Series, Vol. IV, No. 2, 1951, pp. 271–280.

Clark, Colin. *The Conditions of Economic Progress.* London: Macmillan and Company Limited—New York: St. Martin's Press, 1957.

Clough, Shepard B., and Carlo Livi. "Economic Growth in Italy: an Analysis of the Uneven Development of North and South." *The Journal of Economic History,* Vol. XVI, No. 3, September 1956, pp. 334–349.

Colajanni, Napoleone. *Gli avvenimenti di Sicilia e le loro cause.* Palermo: Sandron, 1895.

———. *Il socialismo.* Palermo: Sandron, 1884.

———. *L'Italia nel 1898: tumulti e reazioni.* Milano: Soc. Edit. Lombarda, 1899.

Colombi, Arturo. *Pagine di storia del movimento operaio.* Roma: Edizioni di Cultura Sociale, 1951.

Commissione Indagine e Studi sull'Industria Meccanica, Gruppo di Consulenza dello Stanford Research Institute. *Economic and Industrial Problems of the Italian Mechanical Industries.* Tivoli: The Commission, 1952.

Confederazione Fascista dei Lavoratori dell'Industria. *Organizzazione sindacale e ordinamento corporativo,* Serie B, No. 1. Roma: La Confederazione, 1934.

Confederazione Generale dell'Industria Italiana. *Labor Management Councils in Italy.* Rome: The Confederation, 1951.

———. *I consigli di gestione.* 2 vols. Roma: La Confederazione, 1947.

———. *L'industria italiana alla metà del secolo XX.* Roma: La Confederazione, 1953.

Confederazione Generale Fascista Industria Italiana. *Lo sviluppo dell'industria italiana nel I° decennio dell'era fascista.* Milano: La Confederazione, 1932.

Copeland, Melvin Thomas. *The Cotton Manufacturing Industry of the United States.* Cambridge, Mass.: Harvard University Press, 1923.

Costanzo, Giulio. "The Principal Types of Co-operative Society in Italy." *International Review of Agricultural Economics,* New Series, Vol. 1, 1923, pp. 50–80.

Croce, Benedetto. *A History of Italy 1871–1915.* Oxford: At the Clarendon Press, 1929.

Dal Pane, Luigi. "Storia del lavoro in Italia dagli inizi del secolo XVIII al 1815," Vol. IV, *Storia del lavoro in Italia.* Milano: A. Giuffrè, 1944.

D'Annunzio, Gabriele. 'Orazione per la sagra dei Mille, V Maggio MDCCCLX— V Maggio MCMXV' in "Per la più grande Italia," Vol. 42, *Tutte le opera.* Verona: Istituto Nazionale per la Edizione di Tutte le Opere di Gabriele D'Annunzio, 1927.

Direzione della Statistica Generale del Regno. *Censimento generale 31 dicembre 1861: popolazione di diritto.* Firenze: Tipografia Letteraria e degli Ingegneri, 1865.

———. *Popolazione: parte I: censimento generale (31 dicembre 1861).* Firenze: Tipografia di G. Barbèra, 1867.

Dizionario Enciclopedico Italiano. Roma: Istituto della Enciclopedia Italiana, 1956.

Einaudi, Luigi. *Le lotte del lavoro.* Torino: Piero Gobetti, 1924.

Einzig, Paul. *The Economic Foundations of Fascism.* London: Macmillan and Company, 1934.

Ellena, Vittorio. "La statistica di alcune industrie italiane," *Annali di statistica,* Serie 2ª, Vol. 13. Roma: Ministero di Agricoltura, Industria e Commercio, Direzione di Statistica, 1880.

Enciclopedia Cattolica. Città del Vaticano: Ente per l'Enciclopedia Cattolica e per il Libro Cattolico, 1952.

Enciclopedia Italiana. Roma: Istituto della Enciclopedia Italiana, 1934.

Encyclopaedia Britannica. "Italy," Vol. 12. Chicago, London, Toronto: Encyclopaedia Britannica, Inc., 1957.

Fenicia, Salvatore. *La cooperazione in Piemonte.* Torino: Fratelli Bocca, 1901.

Ferrero, Guglielmo. *Four Years of Fascism.* London: P. S. King & Son, Ltd., 1924.

Field, G. Lowell. *The Syndical and Corporative Institutions of Italian Fascism.* New York: Columbia University Press, 1938.

Finer, Herman. *Mussolini's Italy.* New York: Henry Holt and Co., 1935.

Fossati, Antonio. *Lavoro e produzione in Italia dalla metà del secolo XVIII alla seconda guerra mondiale.* Torino: G. Giappichelli, 1951.

Fremantle, Anne. *The Papal Encyclicals in Their Historical Context.* New York: New American Library of World Literature, 1956.

Garibaldi, Giuseppe. *Autobiography of Giuseppe Garibaldi.* 3 vols. (Translation from Italian by A. Werner with a Supplement by Jessie White Mario.) London: Walter Smith and Innes (late Mozley), 1889.

Gentile, Panfilo. *Cinquanta anni di socialismo in Italia.* Milano: Longanesi & C., 1947.

Germino, Dante L. *The Italian Fascist Party in Power: A Study in Totalitarian Rule.* Minneapolis: University of Minnesota Press, 1959.

Gerschenkron, Alexander. *Description of an Index of Italian Industrial Output, 1881–1913.* Cambridge, Mass.: Russian Research Center, Harvard University, 1955. Mimeo.

———. "Notes on the Rate of Industrial Growth in Italy, 1881–1913." *The Journal of Economic History,* Vol. XV, No. 4, December 1955, pp. 360–375.

———. "Rosario Romeo e l'accumulazione primitiva del capitale." *Rivista Storica Italiana,* LXXI, No. 4, 1959, pp. 557–586.

Giolitti, Giovanni. *Memoirs of My Life.* London & Sydney: Chapman & Dodd, Ltd., 1923.

Giunta per la Inchiesta Agraria e sulle Condizioni della Classe Agricola. *Atti della Giunta....* 15 volumes in 24 parts. (Final Report, Vol. XV, Fascicolo I, "Relazione finale sui risultati dell'inchiesta redatta per incarico della Giunta dal Presidente, Conte Stefano Jacini.") Roma: Forzani, 1881–1886.

Golzio, Silvio. *Sulla misura delle variazioni del reddito nazionale italiano.* Torino: G. Giappichelli, 1951.

Gradilone, Alfredo. "Italia," Vol. III, Parts 1 and 2, *Storia del sindacalismo.* Milano: A. Giuffrè, 1959.

Greenfield, Kent Roberts. *Economics and Liberalism in the Risorgimento. A Study of Nationalism in Lombardy: 1814–1848.* Baltimore: Johns Hopkins Press, 1934.

Gualerni, Gualberto. *La politica industriale fascista.* Vol. 1 (1922–1935). Milano: Istituto Sociale Ambrosiano, 1956.

Gualtieri, Humbert L. *The Labor Movement in Italy.* New York: S. F. Vanni, 1946.

Guarneri, Felice. *Battaglie economiche tra le due grandi guerre.* 2 vols. Milano: Aldo Garzanti, 1953.

Hassall, W. O. *A Select Bibliography of Italy, 1000 Books.* Washington: Association of Special Library and Information Bureau, May 1946.

Hildebrand, George H. "The Italian Parliamentary Survey of Unemployment." *American Economic Review,* Vol. XLV, No. 5, December 1955, pp. 884–899.

———. "The Postwar Italian Economy: Achievements, Problems, and Prospects." *World Politics,* Vol. VIII, No. 1, October 1955, pp. 46–70.

Hilton-Young, W. *The Italian Left: A Short History of Political Socialism in Italy.* London, New York, Toronto: Longmans, Green and Co., 1949.

Hostetter, Richard. *The Italian Socialist Movement—I: Origins (1860–1882).* Princeton: D. Van Nostrand, 1958.

Hughes, H. Stuart. *The United States and Italy.* Cambridge, Mass.: Harvard University Press, 1953.

International Labour Office. *Conciliation and Arbitration in Industrial Disputes.* Studies and Reports, Series A (Industrial Relations), No. 34. Geneva: ILO, 1933.

———. *Hours of Labour in Industry—Italy.* Studies and Reports, Series D (Wages and Hours), No. 8. Geneva: ILO, 1923.

———. *Wage Changes in Various Countries 1914 to 1925.* Studies and Reports, Series D (Wages and Hours), No. 16. Geneva: ILO, 1926.

Istituto Centrale di Statistica. *Sommario di statistiche storiche italiane 1861–1955.* Roma: ISTAT, 1958.

Jacini, Stefano. *See* Giunta per la Inchiesta Agraria e sulle Condizioni della Classe Agricola.

Jemolo, Arturo Carlo. *Chiesa e stato in Italia negli ultimi cento anni.* Torino: Giulio Einaudi, 1948.

Joll, James. *The Second International 1889–1914.* New York: Praeger, 1956.

Jones, H. Stuart, and Hugh Last. 'The Early Republic,' Chapter XIV, "The Hellinistic Monarchies and the Rise of Rome," Vol. VII, *The Cambridge Ancient History.* Cambridge, England: At the University Press, 1928.

King, Bolton, and Thomas Okey. *Italy To-Day.* London: James Nisbet and Co., 1901.

Laboulaye, Charles. *Économie des machines et des manufactures* (*d'après l'ouvrage anglais de Ch. Babbage*). Paris: Librairie du Dictionnaire des Arts et Manufactures, 1880.

LaPalombara, Joseph. *The Italian Labor Movement: Problems and Prospects.* Ithaca, New York: Cornell University Press, 1957.

League of Nations Secretariat. Economic, Financial and Transit Department. *Industrialization and Foreign Trade.* [Geneva]: League of Nations, 1945.

Leonetti, Alfonso. *Mouvements ouvriers et socialistes* (*chronologie et bibliographie*): *l'Italie* (*des origines à 1922*). Collection Dirigée par E. Dolléans et M. Crozier. Paris: Les Editions Ouvrières, 1952.

Leonetti, pp. 161–195, supplies an excellent bibliography divided into the following categories:

Bibliographies
XI–XVI Centuries
XVII–XVIII Centuries
XIX Century—Babeuf and Saint-Simon, Their Doctrines and Followers
Carbonari and Other Secret Societies
The Risorgimento
The Social Question during the Risorgimento
1848–1849
Giuseppe Mazzini
Mazzini and the Workers Societies
Mazzini and the Socialists
Mazzini and Bakunin
The First Internationale in Italy
Socialists and Socialism—Histories and General Studies
The Workers Party, 1882–1892
The Italian Socialist Party, 1892–1898
The Events of 1898
1899–1909
1910–1915
Italian Socialists during the First World War
Post-War, 1919–1920

1921–1922
Communists and Communism
The Russian Revolution, Bolshevism and Anti-Bolshevism
Anarchism and Anarchists
Syndicalism
Catholics and Christian Democracy
Other Parties
The Labor Movement and Labor Problems
Cooperation and Municipal Ownership
Emigration
Insurance and Social Legislation
Socialist Doctrine, Historical Materialism and Marxist Economics
Translations of Socialist Works
The Land Problem
The Problem of the South
Sicily and Socialism
Memoirs and Monographs
Women
Reviews and Periodicals
Histories of Italy
Finance and Economics
Fascism

Lloyd, E. A. *The Cooperative Movement in Italy.* New York: International Publishers, 1926.

Mack Smith, Denis. *Italy: A Modern History.* Ann Arbor: The University of Michigan Press, 1959.

Magri, Francesco. *Controllo operaio e consigli d'azienda in Italia e all'estero:* (*1916–1947*). 2nd ed. Milano: Academia, 1947.

————. *Dal movimento sindacale cristiano al sindacalismo democratico.* Milano: La Fiaccola, 1957.

Manacorda, Gastone. *Il movimento operaio italiano attraverso i suoi congressi dalle origini alla formazione del partito socialista* (*1853–1892*). Roma: Edizioni Rinascita, 1953.

Michels, Roberto. *Le prolétariat et la bourgeoisie dans le mouvement socialiste italien particulièrement des origines à 1906.* Paris: M. Giard et Cie, 1921.

————. *Storia critica del movimento socialista italiano dagli inizi fino al 1911.* Firenze: Società An. Editrice "La Voce," 1926.

Milone, Ferdinando. *L'Italia nell'economia delle sue regioni.* Torino: Edizioni Scientifiche Einaudi, 1955.

Ministero di Agricoltura, Industria e Commercio, Direzione Generale della Statistica. *Banche popolari anno 1893.* Roma: Tip. Nazionale di G. Bertero, 1895.

————. *Introduzione alla statistica delle banche popolari italiane* (*1881–1883*). Roma: Il Ministero, 1885.

————. *L'Italia economica nel 1873.* Roma: Tipografia Barbèra, 1873.

————. *L'Italie économique en 1867, avec un aperçu des industries italiennes à l'exposition universelle de Paris.* Florence: Impr. de G. Barbèra, 1867.

————. *Movimento dei prezzi di alcuni generi alimentari dal 1862 al 1885.* Roma: Tipografia Eredi Botta, 1886.
————. *Statistica delle banche popolari.* Roma: Il Ministero, 1882.
————. *Statistica industriale: riassunto delle notizie sulle condizioni industriali del regno.* 3 parts. Roma: Tipografia Nazionale di G. Bertero, 1905–1906.
Mira, Giuseppe. "Storia del lavoro nel medio evo e nell'età moderna (sec. XIII–XVIII)," Vol. I, *Storia del movimento operaio.* Roma: Edizioni dell'Ateneo, 1949.
————. "Dalla fine del settecento alla vigilia della seconda guerra mondiale," Vol. II, *Storia del movimento operaio.* Roma: Edizioni dell'Ateneo, 1949.
Mussolini, Benito. *Opera omnia di Benito Mussolini.* Edoardo and Duilio Susmel, eds. 27 vols. Vol. XIX, "Dalla marcia di Roma al viaggio negli Abruzzi (31 Ottobre 1922—22 Agosto 1923)." Firenze: La Fenice, 1951–1959.
Neufeld, Maurice F. "Appunti sul funzionamento delle commissioni interne." *Il Diritto del Lavoro,* 1956, No. 6.
————. "Il movimento sindacale italiano: panorama di una crisi." *Il Mulino,* No. 66, April 1957, pp. 243–258.
————. *Labor Unions and National Politics in Italian Industrial Plants.* Ithaca, N.Y.: Institute of International Industrial and Labor Relations, Cornell University, 1954.
Odon, Por. *Guilds and Co-operatives in Italy.* London: The Labour Publishing Co., Ltd., 1923.
Parravicini, Giannino. *La politica fiscale e le entrate effettive del Regno d'Italia, 1860–1890.* Torino: Industria Libraria Tipografica Editrice (Archivio Economico dell'Unificazione Italiana, Serie 2, Vol. 1), 1958.
Peaslee, Amos J. *Constitutions of Nations.* 3 vols. 2nd ed. The Hague: Martinus Nijhoff, 1956.
Pentad. *The Remaking of Italy.* Harmondsworth, Middlesex: Penguin Books, 1941.
Rabbeno, Ugo. *La cooperazione in Italia.* Milano: Fratelli Dumolard, 1886.
Rigola, Rinaldo. *Storia del movimento operaio italiano.* Milano: Editoriale Domus, 1947.
Romano, Salvatore Francesco. *Storia dei fasci siciliani.* Bari: Laterza, 1959.
Roselli, Enrico. *Cento anni di legislazione sociale 1848–1950.* 2 vols. Milano: Editrice Bernabò, 1951.
Rosenstock-Franck, L. *L'économie corporative fasciste en doctrine et en fait: ses origines historiques et son évolution.* Paris: Librairie Universitaire J. Gamber, 1934.
Rosselli, Nello. *Inghilterra e regno di Sardegna dal 1815 al 1847.* Torino: Giulio Einaudi, 1954.
————. *Mazzini e Bakounine: 12 anni di movimento operaio in Italia (1860–1872).* Torino: Fratelli Bocca, 1927.
Rossi, A. (Angelo Tasca). *The Rise of Italian Fascism, 1918–1922.* London: Methuen, 1938.
Ruini, Meuccio. "The Italian Co-operative Movement." *International Labour Review,* Vol. V, No. 1, January 1922, pp. 13–33.
Sacco, Italo Mario. *Storia del sindacalismo: il "risorgimento" del lavoro.* Milano: Istituto per gli Studi di Politica Internazionale, 1942.
Salomone, Arcangelo William. *Italian Democracy in the Making: The Political Scene in the Giolittian Era 1900–1914.* Philadelphia: University of Pennsylvania, 1945.
Salvatorelli, Luigi, and Giovanni Mira. *Storia d'Italia nel periodo fascista.* Torino: Giulio Einaudi, 1957.
Sanseverino, Luisa Riva. "Collective Bargaining in Italy," Chapter VI, *Contemporary Collective Bargaining in Seven Countries,* Adolf Sturmthal, ed. Ithaca, N.Y.: Institute of International Industrial and Labor Relations, Cornell University, 1957.
————. *Il movimento sindacale cristiano dal 1850.* Roma: Zuffi, 1950.
Schneider, Herbert W. *The Fascist Government of Italy.* New York: D. Van Nostrand Co., 1936.
————. *Making the Fascist State.* New York: Oxford University Press, 1928.
Spadolini, Giovanni. *Giolitti e i cattolici (1901–1914).* Firenze: Felice Le Monnier, 1960.
Spinelli, Oscar. *La mutualità in Italia e all'estero.* Roma: "La Rivista della Cooperazione," 1955.
Sprigge, Cecil J. S. *The Development of Modern Italy.* London: Duckworth, 1943.
Stekloff, G. M. *History of the First International.* London: Martin Lawrence Ltd., 1928.
Sturzo, Luigi. *Italy and Fascismo.* London: Faber and Gwyer, 1926.

574

Toldo, Antonio. *Il sindacalismo in Italia.* 2nd ed. Milano: Centro Studi Sociali, 1953.

———. *Il sindacalismo: natura e missione.* 2nd ed. Milano: Centro Studi Sociali, 1953.

Tremelloni, Roberto. *L'industria tessile italiana.* Torino: Giulio Einaudi, 1937.

———. *Storia dell'industria italiana contemporanea dalla fine del settecento all'unità italiana.* Torino: Giulio Einaudi, 1947.

———. *Storia recente dell'industria italiana.* Milano: Aldo Garzanti, 1956.

United Nations Educational, Scientific and Cultural Organization. "World Illiteracy at Mid-Century." *Monographs on Fundamental Education—XI.* Paris: UNESCO, 1957.

U.S. Bureau of the Census. *Historical Statistics of the United States 1789–1945.* Washington: The Bureau, 1949.

U.S. Congress. House. *State of Labor in Europe: 1878.* Executive Document No. 5, 46th Congress, 1st Session. Washington: Government Printing Office, 1879.

Welk, William G. *Fascist Economic Policy: An Analysis of Italy's Economic Experiment.* Cambridge, Mass.: Harvard University Press, 1938.

Wiskemann, Elizabeth. *Italy.* London, New York, Toronto: Oxford University Press, 1947.

World Health Organization. *United Nations Epidemological and Vital Statistics Report*, Vol. 7, No. 9. Geneva: World Health Organization, 1954.

Index

576

Chamber of Deputies, 14, 406, 425, 439, 468–470 *passim*
Chamber of Fasci and Corporations, 439–440, 446
Chamberlain, Houston Stewart, 238
Chambers of commerce, *see* Employers, organizations
Chambers of labor, *see* Unions, chambers of labor
Chambers of Labor, Italian Federation of, 321, 322, 330–331, 335
Chambers of Labor of North Italy, First Congress of, 458
Charles Albert, 11–12, 34, 50
Charter of Labor, Fascist, 387, 388, 403, 425, 432
Chekiang adventure, 223
Chemicals, *see* Industry, chemicals
Chiantore, Gustavo, 116
Chigi Palace, labor-management agreement, 385
Child labor, 141, 142, 159, 213, 243, 296–297
Chile, labor movement, 334–335
China, Chekiang Bay occupation by Italy, 223; economic and social development, 123
Christian Associations of Italian Workers (A.C.-L.I.), 473–475 *passim*
Christian Democracy and Christian Democrats, 220, 232, 233, 238, 241, 333, 334, 356–357, 445, 448, 451, 452, 454, 455, 457, 459–462 *passim*, 469–475 *passim*, 514, 516
Christian Democratic Party, 462, 484
Christian social movement, *see* Catholic social movement
Christian Trade Unions, International Federation of, 491
Christmas bonuses, 467
Church-State relations, *see* Catholic Church
Churchill, Winston, 453, 454
C.I.L., *see* Italian Confederation of (Catholic) Workers
Cipriani, Amilcare, 117, 214
C.I.S.I., *see* Italian Confederation of Independent Unions
C.I.S.L., *see* Italian Confederation of Workers Unions
C.I.S.N.A.L., *see* Italian Confederation of National Workers Unions
Cities, development, 131
Civil liberties, *see* Political liberties
Civil rights, *see* Political liberties
Civil War, American, 134
Clark, Colin, 310
Class hatred, 119, 124, 129, 197, 385
Clemenceau, Georges, 254
Clerical Workers of Italy, National Union of, 386
Clothing, *see* Industry, clothing
Clough, Shepard B., 148
Colajanni, Napoleone, 89, 210, 212
Collective accords, interconfederal, 440–441, 449–450, 458, 463, 466–468, 479–480, 490, 494, 502, 511–512, 515
Collective agreements, category-wide, 440–441, 458, 466, 492, 494, 501, 502, 509–510, 515
Collective bargaining, agriculture, 213, 430, 438, 440, 472, 509; *erga omnes*, 423, 447; general, 319, 323, 341–342, 359, 386–387, 423, 424, 428, 430, 432–434 *passim*, 447, 494; industry, 186, 342–344, 370, 372, 378, 381, 391–393 footnote 64, 430, 434, 439–441, 449–451 *passim*, 509, 510; services, 430–431, 440, 509, 512
Collective contracts, plant-level, 502; provincial, 509, 515
Collegi tecnici, *see* Piecework joint technical committees
Colombino, Emilio, 372, 388
Colonization, 417–418
Comintern, *see* International, Third
Commerce, domestic, 21, 27–30 *passim*, 79–80; foreign, 35, 79–80, 83–84, 134, 300, 405, 406, 408, 410–411, 415–416, 480, Appendix A, Table 28; General Confederation of, 477
Commission of Eighteen, 386, 419
Commission of Fifteen, 386
Commissioni interne, *see* Grievance committees
Committees of National Liberation, 445–446, 452, 454, 455, 459–463 *passim*
Common Man's Front (Uomo Qualunque), 468
Communes, 127

Communications, 20, 23, 125, 130, 208, 293, 398, 497, Appendix A, Table 11; influence on social altitudes, 208–209; inter-country comparisons, 23
Communism and communists, 6, 163, 267–269, 278, 279, 281, 286, 372, 373, 379–381, 400, 421, 445, 448, 451–465 *passim*, 468–476 *passim*, 482, 483
Communist Manifesto, 116, 211
Communist Party, 262, 268, 275, 373, 449, 461, 462, 469, 478
Como, 146
Compagnonnages, 62
Comte, Auguste, 117
Conciliation and mediation, *see* Arbitration and mediation
Concordat, Church-State, 398, 470
Conditions of work, *see* Working conditions
Confédération Générale du Travail, 286, 350, 388
Confederation of Industrial Workers, 434, 437, 448, 449
Confederations, labor, *see* names of specific confederations. *See also* Appendix B, Chart 1; Appendix C
Confindustria, 377, 379–381 *passim*, 385, 386, 406, 409, 421, 422, 434, 449, 462, 463, 465–468 *passim*, 477, 480, 481, 490, 511–512
Confino, 189
Conglobamento, 490, 511–512
Connubio, 201
Conseils des prud'hommes, 323
Conservatism and conservatives, 223, 224, 226, 236, 241, 269, 270, 272, 275, 277, 311
Consigli di fabbrica, *see* Factory councils
Consigli di gestione, *see* Councils of administration
Consorteria, 201
Consortia, 407, 409, 410
Constituent Assembly, 1946–1947, 462, 464, 465, 469, 470, 472
Constituent Assembly, post-World War I idea, 256–258 *passim*, 367
Constitution, Italian Republic, *see* Republic of Italy, Constitution
Consumer cooperatives, *see* Cooperatives, consumer
Cooperation, National Credit Institute for, 369
Cooperation, National Fascist Institute of, 387
Cooperative Alliance, Turin, 64
Cooperative Confederation, Italian (Catholic), 369, 387
Cooperatives, 63–65, 110, 151, 174, 176–182, 190, 193, 196, 243, 273, 335, 336, 360–361, 369, 376, 381; Catholic, 333, 335, 356, 357–358, 366, 369; consumer, 64, 180–181, 193, 335, 336, 361, 387; credit, 178, 357, 387; Federation of Agricultural (Catholic), 357; Federation of Italian, 181, 361; housing, 361; insurance, 361; Italian Union of (fascist), 385, 387; labor, 179–180, 193, 270, 335, 336, 387; National League of, 333, 335, 340, 361, 369, 387; producer, agricultural, 179, 270, 335, 336, 357, 361, 376–377, 387; producer, industrial, 63–64, 178–179, 361, 380, 385
Corazzin, Giuseppe, 365
Corporations, *see* Joint stock companies
Corporations, fascist, 420–431, 436, 446
Corporative employers associations, *see* Employers, organizations, fascist
Corporative ideas, 256–257, 260, 367, 381, 384, 386, 402, 419–420, 423–426, 439–440
Corporative State, 386–388 *passim*, 395–396, 419–431, 434, 439–440, 446, 450, 456
Corporative unions, *see* Unions, fascist
Corradini, Enrico, 237, 238, 384
Corridoni, Filippo, 245, 247, 249, 366
Corrispondenti di reparto, *see* Shop stewards
Costa, Andrea, 95, 98, 99, 100, 101, 103, 107–110 *passim*, 115–117 *passim*, 222, 223, 233
Costa, Dr. Angelo, 480–481
Cost of living, 43–44, 160–166 *passim*, 371, 406, 440, 458, 465–467, 499, 511, Appendix A, Tables 33, 33A, 37
Cottage industries, *see* Handicraft production
Councils of administration (*consigli di gestione*), 451–452, 459–468 *passim*, 471, 478–479, 482, 483, 502
Court of Cassation, 224
Covelli, Emilio, 104

578

Credit cooperatives, *see* Cooperatives, credit
Credito Italiano, 459
Crimean War, 13, 134
Crispi, Francesco, 81, 82, 85–88, 112, 166, 197, 201, 204, 208, 209, 214–217 *passim*, 221, 223, 227, 228, 230, 322
Croce, Benedetto, 76, 87, 88, 117, 126, 215, 222, 238, 249–250, 264, 276, 281, 285, 386, 453, 454
Croce, Giuseppe, 109, 113, 116, 117, 205, 206
Cusumano, Vito, 107

Dal Pane, Luigi, 17
D'Annunzio, Gabriele, 224–225, 237, 249, 250, 259–261, 263, 264, 266, 274, 362, 382, 396, 419
Dante, Alighieri, 8, 254, 382
D'Aragona, Ludovico, 366, 382, 387, 388, 464–465, 469, 475
Darwin, Charles, 117
Das Kapital, 113
D'Azeglio, Massimo, 57, 119
De Ambris, Alceste, 246, 247, 347, 364, 366
De Amicis, Edmondo, 207
De Andreis, Luigi, 220, 222
De Angeli (company), 221
De Bono, General Emilio, 276, 280
De Brouckére, Louis, 207
De Felice, Giuseppe Giuffrida, 209, 211, 214–215, 223, 240
Defense, 128
De Gasperi, Alcide, 462, 464, 465, 468, 470, 472
Dell'Avalle, Carlo, 206
Demand, uniform, and mechanization, 37–38
Democracy of Labor, 445, 452, 455, 462, 469
Demonstrations, *see* Revolts, demonstrations, uprisings
De Nicola, Enrico, 270, 279, 453, 462
Denmark, cooperatives, 179; wages, 162
Depression, 1930's, 407–411
Depretis, Agostino, 81–85, 101, 109, 114, 197, 201, 202, 227
De Ruggiero, Guido, 448
De Stefani, Alberto, 404–405
De Vecchi, Count Cesare, 275, 276
Dialects, 16–17
Diaz, General Armando, 252, 253, 275
Di Menza, Giuseppe, 105
Direct Action (syndicalist labor group), 353
Di Rudinì, Marquis Antonio Starrabba, 204, 217–218, 221, 222, 224, 228
Dismissals, workers, 463–464, 479–483 *passim*, 511
Disputes settlement, collective, 436; individual, 437–438
Disraeli, Benjamin, 400
Di Vittorio, Giuseppe, 448, 454–457 *passim*, 465, 474, 492, 515
Dogali, defeat at, 1887, 237
Domicilio coatto (enforced residence), 216, 217
Don Rodrigo, 210
Dopolavoro, Opera Nazionale, *see* Leisure Time, National Service for
Dreyfus Affair, 222
Duce, *see* Mussolini

Earthquake, Messina and Calabria, 1908, 243
Economic activity, attitude toward, *see* Feudalism, economic
Economic aid, receipt by Italy, 470, 494
Economic and social reform, 56–57, 61–63, 173–174, 180, 181, 243, 417
Economic and social thought, 48–57 *passim*, 61–63, 92, 101, 104–105, 107, 110, 111, 113–114, 117, 125–126, 133, 135, 137, 146–147, 169, 174–175, 256–259, 419; Catholic, 182–185, 255–256, 355–358, 381, 384
Economic Unions, Italian Confederation of (fascist), 384
Eden, Anthony, 400
Education, agriculture, 136–137; Church relation to, 86, 87, 241, 278, 398; elementary, 15, 18, 75, 84, 125, 127–129, 208, 235, 243, 294, 397; elementary, relation to labor movement, 18, 128; elementary, United States, 18; fascist, 278; government expenditures, 290, 294, 399; higher, 294, 397; middle schools, 294, 397
Edward VII, 247

Egypt, illiteracy, 15, 126
Einaudi, Luigi, 302, 470, 473
Elba, iron mining, 149
Elections, Church attitude toward, 86; dates: 1861, 14; 1874, 80; 1876, 82; 1880, 84; 1882, 84, 111; 1886, 114–115, 191; 1895, 216; 1897, 217; 1900, 225; 1904, 232, 334; 1909, 241; 1913, 241; 1919, 260–263 *passim*; 1921, 268–270; 1924, 278–279; 1929, 396; 1946, 462, 479; 1948, 468–470, 479, 480; Appendix A, Table 8; participation in, *see* Suffrage
Ellena, Vittorio, 140–141
Emigrants, occupations, 132–133, 290–291, 418; postal savings, 290, 418; remittances, 290, 418
Emigration, 132–133, 148, 243, 289–290, 354, 417, 418, Appendix A, Table 3
Emilia, cooperatives, 178–181 *passim*, 360; economic conditions, 147, 148; housing, workers, 360; industry, goods-producing, 148; labor movement, 189, 322, 353, 378, 384; mutual aid sociities, 62, 175; politics, 203; revolts, 170–172, 219; social conditions, 130, 132
Employers, attitudes toward workers, 41; organizations, 341, 347, 354, 372, 377, 422–423, 450, 465, 477–478; organizations, Catholic, 358; organizations, fascist, 409, 421–424 *passim*, 428–429; resistance to unions, 318, 334, 341, 347, 354, 381–382, 493
Employment, *see* Agriculture, Industry (various branches), and Services
Employment services, public, 368, 410, 433, 450
Engels, Friedrich, 92, 105, 107
England, agricultural revolution, 21; cooperatives, 177; *Das Kapital*, appraisals of, 107; diplomatic relations with Italy, 237, 401, 405; economic and political relations with Piedmont, 13, 35, 146; economic relations with Lombardy, 33; hours of labor, 27, 40; income, real per capita national, 310–311, Appendix A, Table 29; industrialization, 1, 30, 37, Appendix A, Table 25; labor attitudes, 41; labor force distribution, 25, 298–299, 414, 496, Appendix A, Table 12; labor movement, 188, 456, 459, 474; mutual aid societies, 60, 66; natural resources, 133, 137; railroads, 22; revolutionary activities, 51, 168; textile production, 142–143; wages, 162
Enti nazionali, 408–410 *passim*
Entrepreneurial attitudes, 151–152, 301, 302
Erga omnes, *see* Collective bargaining, *erga omnes*
Establishments, industrial, *see* Industry, manufacturing establishments, *and* Industry, specific branch, establishments
Estrema (Extreme Left), political grouping, 80, 202, 217, 223–225, 230, 345
Ethiopa and Eritrea, 83, 87, 237, 399–401
Ethiopian War, *see* Abyssinian War
Europe, economic and social development, 2; mutual aid societies, 60, 66; wages, 162
European Recovery Program, 472, 478
Evarts, William M., 162
Expenditures, governmental, *see* Government, expenditures
Exports, *see* Commerce, foreign
Extreme Left, *see* Estrema

Facta, Luigi, 272, 274, 276, 277, 282–283
Factory control movement, 1945–1946, 459–468 *passim*, 471, 478–479
Factory councils (*consigli di fabbrica*), 374, 381
Factory occupation movement, 1919–1920, 264–265, 368, 373–374, 377–381, 384
Falck (company), 146, 459
Falck, Enrico, 459–460
Family allowances, 417, 434, 440, 467, 498, 511
Fano, Enrico, 180, 181
Faraglia, N. F., 44
Farinacci, Roberto, 270, 282–284 *passim*, 444
Farmers, National Confederation of Independent, 477–478
Farmers Brotherhood (fascist), 384
Fasci di Azione Rivoluzionaria, *see* Fasci Italiani di Combattimento
Fasci Italiani di Combattimento, 247, 258, 263, 266, 270, 370
Fasci operai, *see* Unions, *fasci operai*

579

139, 301, Appendix A, Table 25; labor attitudes, 41; labor force distribution, 299, 414, 496, Appendix A, Table 12; labor movement, 188, 337, 459; national income, 37; natural resources, 133; railroads, 22; revolutionary activities, 168; textile production, 142; wages, 162
Gerschenkron, Alexander, 138, 139, 149–153 *passim*, 300–303, 305
Gewerkschaften, 188
Ghana, nationhood, 3, 119
Giannelli, Andrea, 167
Gioberti, Vincenzo, 10–11, 76
Gioja, Melchiorre, 21
Giolitti, Giovanni, 6, 82, 200–203, 204, 212, 216, 217, 223, 225–236 *passim*, 239–242 *passim*, 245, 247–253 *passim*, 260–272 *passim*, 275–279 *passim*, 281, 286, 289, 295, 299, 302, 303, 312–313, 334, 338, 345, 369, 380, 404, 432
Giustizia, 113, 194, 283
Gladstone, William, 131
Glossary, English-Italian, labor relations, Appendix D
Gnocchi-Viani, Osvaldo, 105–107 *passim*, 109, 115, 116, 194–195, 320
Gobetti, Piero, 286
Gompers, Samuel, 188, 341
Gonella, Guido, 484
Government, centralization, *see* Government, national; communal, 76, 128, 131, 152, 218, 278; expenditures, 127–131 *passim*, 150, 152, 264, 290, 293, 294, 399, 404, 410, 415, 430, 471–472; fiscal policy, 35, 75, 77–79, 82, 263, 264, 401, 405–406, 411, 432; intervention in economic and social affairs, 403–411, 415–419; monopolies, 404; national, 74–77 *passim*, 127–131 *passim*, 152, 218–219, 247, 447; prefectural (provincial), 14, 76, 128, 131, 152, 218, 250, 273, 278–281 *passim*, 283–285 *passim*, 327; role in industrialization, 143, 149–154, 301–302
Governments and Prime Ministers, 1860–1960, 70–71
Gramsci, Antonio, 268, 285, 286, 373, 379
Grandi, Achille, 358, 365, 366, 448, 451, 454, 455, 457, 461, 473, 474
Grandi, Count Dino, 270, 276, 384, 444
Great Britain, *see* England
Greece, income, real per capita national, 310, Appendix A, Table 29
Green, William, 341
Greenfield, Kent Roberts, 24–25, 29, 32, 63
Grey, Viscount Edward of Fallodon, 244
Grieco, Ruggiero, 286
Grievance committees (*commissioni interne*), 343, 371–374, 381, 423, 438–439, 449–450, 460, 463, 465, 467–468, 478–493, 502, 511; adverse influences on, 493–494; confederation attitude toward, 481–484, 493; elections, 484–488, 492–493, Appendix A, Table 42; elections, Fiat, 489–492; influence and contribution, 488–489, 492–493
Grievance procedures, 437–439
Gronchi, Giovanni, 365, 451, 461, 475
Grondona (company), 221
Gross internal product, 138–139, 299, 414–415, 496–497, Appendix A, Tables 14, 32
Gualtieri, Humbert, 89, 93
Guarantees, law of, 81–82
Guesde, Jules, 106
Guilds, 20, 27, 30, 54, 58–59
Guillotine, parliamentary, 223

Hamilton, Alexander, 75
Handicrafts, *ente nazionale*, 409; General Confederation of, 477; production, 24, 31–33, 80, 140–142
Health insurance, *see* Social insurances
Herzen, Alexander, 52, 92
Heusch, General, 215
Highways, *see* Roads
Hiring, limited contracts, 493
Hitler, Adolf, 227, 401, 402, 447
Holland, economic and political relations with Piedmont, 35; local government, influence on Italy, 76; wages, 162
Holy Alliance, 8

Hours of labor, 27, 40, 158, 348–349, 370, 382, 385, 391–393 footnote 64, 406, 410, 432; inter-country comparisons, 27
Housing, workers, 56, 110, 243, 310, 323, 345, 360, 375, 417; workers, regional distribution, 360
Hugo, Victor, 211
Humbert I, 87, 103, 221, 225, 227
Humbert II, 453, 454, 458
Hungary, diplomatic relations with Italy, 401; industrialization, 19

Illiteracy, inter-country comparisons, 15, 126, 294–295; national, 15, 125, 126, 242, 293–294, 317, 396–397, 497, Appendix A, Table 7; regional, 15, 126, 148, 293, 317, Appendix A, Table 7
Ilva (company), 375, 378, 403
Imbriani, Matteo, 223
Imperialism, Italian, 83, 87, 216–217, 223, 237, 239, 240, 245, 254, 278, 399–401
Imponibile di mano d'opera, 377
Imports, *see* Commerce, foreign
Income, real per capita national, 37, 125, 138, 310, 431, 499, Appendix A, Tables 29, 30; real per capita national, inter-country comparisons, 37, 310–311, Appendix A, Table 29
Indennità di contingenza, see Cost of living
India, economic and social development, 123; illiteracy, 15, 126; industrialization, 137, 140, 300, Appendix A, Table 25; intellectual proletariat, 129; labor force distribution, 25, 298, 414, Appendix A, Table 12; nationhood, 3; trade with Europe via Italy, 150
Indonesia, economic and social development, 123; illiteracy, 15, 126; nationhood, 3, 119; rebel activities, 75
Industrial "big push," 300–303
Industrial censuses, *see* Censuses, industrial
Industrial revolution, excesses, 137
Industrial triangle of the North, illiteracy, 126; industry, development, 145; industry, employment, 307–309; labor movement, 322, 350–351; labor movement, Catholic, 356
Industrialists and financiers, influence on government, 226, 263, 265, 275, 278, 470
Industrialization, 4, 19, 21–25, 28, 29, 30–36, 79–80, 125, 138, 140–141, 145, 151, 153–154, 300–310, Appendix A, Tables 13–28, 32, Appendix E; inter-country comparisons, 1–2, 19, 149, 151, 295, 298, 300–301, Appendix A, Tables 12, 25; and union development, 24
Industry, agriculture-hunting-fishing products, employment, 305, 306, 411–412, 494; chemicals, development, 144; chemicals, employment, 144, 305, 306, 412, 413, 495; chemicals, production, 139, 300–301, 305, 404, 407, 408, 411; clothing, employment, 144, 305, 306, 412, 494; communications, I.R.I. holdings, 404; construction, employment, 144, 307, 412, 495; construction, production, 404, 407, 408, 411; consumer goods, development, 143–144; consumer goods, employment, 306, 307, 413, 495, Appendix A, Table 15; electric power and gas, production, 407, 408, 410, 411; engineering products, *see* Industry, metal-mechanical; food-processing, employment, 144; food-processing, production, 139, 300–301, 305, 306; General Confederation of Italian, *see* Confindustria; goods-producing, employment, 144, 306, 411–412, 494–495, Appendix A, Tables 20, 21; goods-producing, employment, regional, 308–309, 495; goods-producing, gross internal product, 139, 299, 414–415, 496–497, Appendix A, Tables 14, 32; goods-producing, production, 300–301, 411, 494, Appendix A, Table 16; machinery, *see* Industry, metal-mechanical; manufacturing, employment, 141; manufacturing, establishments, size, 141; manufacturing, production, 139–140, 300, 404, 407, 413, Appendix A, Tables 26, 27; manufacturing, production, inter-country comparisons, 139–140, 300, 404, 407, 413, Appendix A, Table 25; metal-mechanical, collective bargaining, 510; metal-mechanical, development, 33, 36, 37, 144–146 *passim*, 149, 153–154, 263, Appendix E; metal-mechanical, disputes settlement, 436; metal-mechanical, employment, 144, 145, 305,

Mazzini, Giuseppe, 4, 9–10, 12, 47, 50, 53, 57, 73, 76, 77, 89–98 *passim*, 167, 173, 177, 211, 222, 248, 286
Mazzini, Giuseppe (Buozzi-Mazzini accord, 1943), 449–450
Mazzinianism and Mazzinians, 83, 98, 117, 187, 197, 202–203, 209, 256
Mazzonis (company), 378–379
Mechanical and Metallurgical Employers Association, Milan, 372
Mechanization, 22, 25, 31, 37–38, Appendix E
Meda, Filippo, 357
Mediation and conciliation, *see* Arbitration and mediation
Menelik, 87, 216, 400
Merchant marine, expenditures, *see* Military expenditures
Merlino, Francesco Saverio, 89
Merry del Val, Rafael, 232
Mess indemnity, 512
Messina, wages, 165–166
Metal-mechanical industries, *see* Industry, metal-mechanical
Metal-mechanical unions, *see* Unions, metal-mechanical
Metal-Mechanical Workers, Italian Federation of (F.I.O.M.), 339, 342–344, 348–349, 351, 370–372 *passim*, 377–379, 391–392 footnote 64, 430
Mezzadria, *see* Sharecropping
Mezzogiorno, *see* South Italy
Miani and Silvestri (company), 346, 378–379
Michelangelo, Buonarroti, 131
Michelin (company), 449
Michels, Roberto, 91, 109, 116, 130, 206, 331
Middle classes, role in labor movement, *see* Labor movement, dependence on educated classes; role in political and social stability, 225–227, 231, 253, 376, 383; role in socialist movement, *see* Socialism and socialists, role of middle classes
Middle East, nationalism, 49
Migration, internal, *see* Internal migration
Milan, agricultural study, 136; economic development, 146; economic role in Middle Ages and Renaissance, 147; "Five Days," 11, 19, 46, 220; industrial plants, 220–221; labor movement, 186–187 *passim*, 231, 333–334, 379, 462–463, 508; May Events, 219–222, 225; politics, 11, 19, 219–220, 224, 274; revolts, 219–222, 225, 365; social conditions, 219–220; Socialist League, 116, 117, 204–206 *passim*; Sons of Labor, 111–113 *passim*, 115, 195, 206; strikes, 186–187 *passim*, 231, 333–334, 346–347, 449, 471
Military expenditures, 128, 294, 399
Milling tax, 1868, 166–174 *passim*
Minghetti, Marco, 76, 79, 80, 151
Ministeriali, 202
Ministry of Corporations, 409, 424, 425, 427–430 *passim*, 436, 446
Ministry of Labor and Social Insurance, 458, 463
Mobility, labor, *see* Labor, mobility
Mocchi, Walter, 231
Modena, political events, 9, 14
Modigliani, Giuseppe, 239, 240, 275, 286
Modigliani, Vera, 286
Monarchist Party, National, 468
Monarchists, 477
Monastery of Monforte, Capuchin, 221
Money, 20, 24
Montalto, Giacomo, 211
Montecatini (company), 405, 478
Monti frumentari, 177
Morandi, Rodolfo, 464–465
Morocco, French occupation, 237; illiteracy, 15, 126
Morra di Lavriano, General, 214, 215
Mortality rates, *see* Public health
Mosca, Gaetano, 219, 238
Motor power, 141–143 *passim*, 148
Motor vehicles, 293, 398, 497, Appendix A, Table 11
M.S.I., *see* Social Movement, Italian
Murri, Don Romolo, 255, 357
Mussi, Muzio, 220

Mussolini, Benito, 6, 201, 203, 225, 226, 235, 238, 240, 241, 245–247 *passim*, 249, 253, 258–264 *passim*, 266, 269–285 *passim*, 318, 366, 375, 383, 386–388 *passim*, 395–396, 398–402 *passim*, 404, 405, 407, 411, 413, 415–419 *passim*, 426, 427, 430–432 *passim*, 439–440, 444, 445, 447, 448, 451–454 *passim*, 458, 459, 470, 515
Mutual aid societies, 57, 60–63, 84, 113, 114, 174–176, 186, 188–196 *passim*, 210, 335, 358–359, 434; Catholic, 182–185 *passim*, 335, 355–356, 357, 366; Federation of (Catholic), 357; inter-country comparisons, 60, 176; Italian Federation of, 333, 340, 359, 361; regional distribution, 62, 175, 359
Mutual Aid Society of Italian Railroad Engineers and Firemen, 188
Mutuality and Social Insurances, Federation of (Catholic), 369

Naldi, Filippo, 246
Naples, communications, 23; economic conditions, 26, 147; industry, investment in, 500; labor movement, 185–187 *passim*, 451; politics, 8, 9, 11, 13, 14, 147, 209; region, *see* Campania; social conditions, 131; strikes, 185–187 *passim*, 231, 375
Napoleon Bonaparte, 8, 20, 49, 246
Napoleon III, 13, 73
Napoletano, Salvatore Ingegneros, 106
National Association of Italian People's Banks, 181, 333
National Bloc, 469
National Brothers, 100
National Confederation of Fascist Syndical Unions, *see* Fascist Syndical Unions, National Confederation of
National Confederation of Independent Farmers, *see* Farmers, National Confederation of Independent
National Council of Corporations, 425–427 *passim*, 429, 431, 446
National Council of the Economy and Labor, 333, 514
National Labor Office, 322, 332, 334, 351
National Labor Union, 321
National League of Italian Cooperatives, *see* Co-operatives, National League of Italian
National Service for Leisure Time, 435
National Trades' Union, 321
National Union (opposition to fascism), 282
National Workers Insurance Fund for Invalidity and Old Age, 218
Nationalism and nationalists, 237–239, 250, 259–261, 266, 269, 272, 275, 277, 279, 384
Nationalist Movement for Social Democracy, 468
Nationhood, 119, 124, 128–129, 225–227
Navigation, 23, 27, 35, 149, 293, Appendix A, Table 11
Navy, expenditures, *see* Military expenditures
Nazism and nazis, 234, 401, 402, 447, 448, 450, 452, 454, 458–461 *passim*
Near East, *see* Middle East
Nenni, Pietro, 240, 286, 469, 472, 476
Neo-Guelphs, 11
Net Product, economic sectors, Appendix A, Table 31
Nicotera, Giovanni, 83
Nitti, Francesco Saverio, 78, 208, 252, 258, 260, 263, 264, 275, 286, 468
Non expedit, 86, 87, 232–233
North Italy, cooperatives, 179–181, 360–361; economic conditions, 125, 135, 136, 138, 145–149 *passim*; government policy toward, 147; industry, 307–309, 409, 413, 452, 495; labor movement, Catholic, 358; mutual aid societies, 61–63, 175; politics, 226, 270; public works, 23, 147; railroads, 151; social conditions, 16, 125, 126–127, 128, 147
North Italy–South Italy, disequilibrium between, 145–149, 307–309, 413, 495, 499–500, *see also* North Italy *and* South Italy
Norway, economic and political relations with Piedmont, 35; wages, 162
Novella, Agostino, 515
N.R.A., 409

585

Sea, Federation of Workers of the, 382
Second International, see International, Second
Secret police, fascist, see O.V.R.A.
Sella, Quintino, 79
Senate, 14, 425, 470
Sensales, 212
Sereni, Emilio, 464
Serrati, Giacinto, 275
Services, gross internal product, 139, 299, 414–415, 497
Settembrini, Luigi, 50
Seven-and-One-Half Days, Palermo, 92
Sforza, Count Carlo, 264, 282, 286, 453, 454
Sharecropping, 125, 472
Shop stewards, 439
Sicilian Events, 1898, 213–216
Sicilian Vespers, 210
Sicily, agriculture, 210; commerce, 210; communications, 23; cooperatives, 178; economic conditions, 133, 136, 148, 190, 210, 376; *fasci*, 209–214 *passim*; government, 217; illiteracy, 216; industry, goods-producing, employment, 308–309; industry, investments in, 500; labor movement, 209–214 *passim*, 217, 328, 375, 473; mutual aid societies, 62, 175, 211; peasants, poverty, 190, 210; politics, 11, 13, 14, 209, 212; railroads, 150, 209, 398; revolts, 211, 212, 213–216, 219, 225; roads, 209; social conditions, 126, 128, 132, 210, 213; strikes, 212, 213; taxation, 210, 211, 217; wages, agricultural, 212
Sila, peasants, poverty, 190
Siliprandi, Francesco, 192
Silone, Ignazio, 469, 476
Silvestri (company), 221
Simonini, Alberto, 475
Skills, managerial, 31; technical, 31; vocational, 31
Skorzeny, Captain Otto, 445
Smith, Adam, 49
Snia Viscosa (company), 405
Social attitudes, influence of army and navy on, 208–209; influence of communications on, 208–209; influence of economic development on, 36, 37–38, 126, 208–209
Social insurances, 55–57 *passim*, 84–85, 218, 235, 243, 296–297, 358–359, 368, 408, 410, 432–435, 450, 451, 493, 498–499
Social Insurances, National Fund for, 368, 433
Social legislation, see Legislation, social
Social mobility, 15–16
Social Movement, Italian (M.S.I.), 468, 472
Social reform, see Economic and social reform
Social security, see Social insurances
Social Security, National Institute of, 498
Social Security, National Fascist Institute of, 433–434
Social stability, role of middle classes, 225–227
Social thought, see Economic and social thought
Social welfare and insurance, institutes of, 504
Social-communists (Nenni socialists and communists), 470–476 *passim*, 478, 482, 483, 514, 515
Socialism, inter-country comparisons, 115, 203, 229–230, 235, 245; left-wing, 204, 207, 208, 228–236 *passim*, 240–244 *passim*, 246, 252–254 *passim*, 258, 259, 262, 264, 265, 267–268, 271, 274, 279, 282, 286, 331, 333–335, 336, 338, 339, 345, 347, 362, 372, 377, 464, 465, 468–470 *passim*, 478; parliamentary, see Socialism, right-wing; reform, see Socialism, right-wing; revolutionary, see Socialism, left-wing; right-wing, 105–107 *passim*, 108–112 *passim*, 114–115, 117, 204, 209, 217, 223, 228–231 *passim*, 233–236 *passim*, 240, 242, 251, 253–255 *passim*, 260–262 *passim*, 271, 275, 277, 279, 331, 334–335, 336, 339, 347, 361, 372, 464, 469, 475, 477, 516; role of middle classes and intellectuals, 111, 130, 229, 234
Socialism and socialists, 4, 48, 52, 53–54, 72–73, 88–119 *passim*, 124, 126, 128–130 *passim*, 135, 173, 193–194, 200, 209, 213, 215–220 *passim*, 224–239 *passim*, 242, 243, 245, 247, 250, 257, 261, 263, 265–274 *passim*, 278, 331–333, 345, 348, 357, 361, 363, 375, 382–383 *passim*, 388, 398, 419, 445, 448, 451, 452, 454, 455, 459–464 *passim*, 469, 515
Socialist League of Milan, 116, 117, 204–206 *passim*

Socialist Party, 5, 49, 104, 109, 117, 203–208, 216, 220, 228–236 *passim*, 239–242 *passim*, 245, 246, 249, 252–254 *passim*, 256–275 *passim*, 330, 334, 345, 347, 348, 350, 352, 362, 364–367 *passim*, 375, 380–383 *passim*, 461, 462, 469, 470, 474, 475; congresses: Milan, 1891, 205; Genoa, 1892, 205–206; Reggio Emilia, 1893, 206–208; Parma, 1895, 228; Florence, 1896; 228; Rome, 1900, 228–229; Imola, 1902, 230; Bologna, 1904, 231; Rome, 1906, 233–234; Florence, 1908, 234–235, 345, 349; Milan, 1910, 235; Modena, 1911, 236, 239; Reggio Emilia, 1912, 240–241; Ancona, 1914, 241–242; Bologna, 1919, 261–262; Leghorn 1921, 267–268; Milan, 1921, 271; Rome, 1922, 275
Socialist Party, Italian Workers (P.S.L.I.), 469, 474, 476
Socialist Party, Reformist, 241, 247, 251
Socialist Party, Unitarian (post-World War II), 476, 477
Socialist Party, Unitarian (pre-fascist), 279, 283
Socialist Party of Italian Workers (1893–1895), 206
Socialist Party of Italian Workers (1922), 275, 279
Socialist Union, 469
Socialists, participation in elections, see Socialism, right-wing
Società anonime, see Joint stock companies
Societies, secret, 50, 100; see also Carbonari
Societies of resistance, congresses: Parma, 1893, 321; Milan, 1900, 322; Reggio Emilia, 1901, 330, 332, 335; Milan, 1902, 331; Genoa, 1905, 336–337; Modena, 1908, 349
Society of Italian Catholic Youth, 182
Sonnino, Baron Sidney, 125, 190, 202, 210, 218–219, 223, 225, 235, 242, 244, 245, 247, 251, 254
Sons of Labor, Milan, 111–113 *passim*, 115, 195, 206
Sorel, Georges, 334, 336–337, 347, 348, 477
Soult, Nicolas, 168
South Italy, economic conditions, 14, 78–80, 125, 136, 145–149 *passim*, 152, 208, 219, 376; government policy toward, 14, 78–79, 81, 145, 152; industry, 307–309, 409, 495; labor movement, 235; politics, 13, 81, 226, 234–235, 452; social conditions, 125, 126, 128, 147, 148; railroads, 150; revolts, 171, 173, 209, 213–216; taxation, 148–149
S.P.A. (Società Piemontese Automobili, company), 449
Spadaccini (company), 378
Spain, civil war, 400–401, 457; constitution, 9; wages, 162
Spaventa, Silvio, 150–151
Special Tribunal for the Defense of the State, 286, 435, 446
Spencer, Herbert, 117
Sprigge, Cecil, 9, 75
Squadristi d'azione, 267, 269, 270, 272–278 *passim*
Staccanella, Valentino, 111
Stalin, Joseph, 227
Standard of living, workers, 43–44, 160–166 *passim*, 190, 311–312, 431
Statuto, Piedmont, 11, 12, 14, 18, 60, 65, 74
Steel, see Industry, metal-mechanical
Stefani news agency, 276, 388
Steffenone, Vincenzo, 65
Stigler (company), 220
Storti, Bruno, 515
Strasser, Adolph, 188
Streetcar Workers Union, 382
Strike, right to, 217, 222, 227–228, 235, 435
Strike Commission (Bonasi), 1878, 189–190, 227
Strikers, number, 195, 363, 370, 379, 383, 435, 501, Appendix A, Table 39
Strikes, 45–48 *passim*, 84, 112, 168–169, 186–190 *passim*, 195–196, 212, 263, 264–265, 302, 323, 345–349, 354, 358, 363, 370, 374–375, 378, 379, 383, 386–387, 435–436, 449, 452, 459, 462, 465, 468, 474, Appendix A, Tables 38–41; agricultural, 190–194 *passim*, 213, 234, 346–348, 363, 370, 375, 379, 383, 471, 501; causes, 189; duration, 195, Appendix A, Table 39; general, 4–5, 168, 231, 232, 234, 239, 242–244, 258, 265, 272, 274, 326–328, 333–335, 336, 345–349 *passim*, 350, 352, 353, 365, 371, 375, 377, 380, 383, 452, 470–

272, 325, 337–338, 347, 351, 358, 375, 382, 384, 422; recognition, *see* Right of association; stone, clay, and glass, 351, 393 footnote 64; streetcar, 328, 375, 382; technical, 368; textile, 186, 188, 328, 334, 351, 358, 370, 375, 378–379, 388, 392 footnote 64, 406, 448; women, 65, 186; wood-workers, 328, 351, 378, 392–393 footnote 64; World War I, 363

Unitarian Socialist Party, *see* Socialist Party, Unitarian

United States, diplomatic relations with Italy, 405, 469; education, elementary, 18; income, real per capita national, 310–311, Appendix A, Table 29; industrialization, Appendix A, Table 25; labor force distribution, 299, 414, 496, Appendix A, Table 12; labor movement, 114, 175, 188, 348, 456–457, 474–475; labor movement, independence from educated middle classes, 18; mutual aid societies, 60, 66; strikes, 162–164 *passim*, 348; suffrage, 18; textile production, 142–143

Uomo Qualunque, Fronte dell', *see* Common Man's Front

Uprisings, *see* Revolts, demonstrations, uprisings

Urban development, *see* Cities, development

U.S.I., *see* Syndical Union, Italian

Utopianism, 48

Vago (company), 221
Valente, Giovanni Battista, 365, 369
Valera, Paolo, 221
Valletta, Dr. Vittorio, 489–492 *passim*, 500, 504
Vallombrosa, 137
Vandervelde, Emile, 207
Vatican, *see* Catholic Church
Venetia, *see* Veneto
Veneto, communications, 23; cooperatives, 178–181 *passim*, 360; economic conditions, 146, 148; housing, workers, 360; industry, goods-producing, 148; labor movement, 187, 188; labor movement, Catholic, 356; mutual aid societies, 62, 175, 359; politics, 8, 73, 77, 203; railroads, 22; revolts, 170–171, 187; social conditions, 131, 132
Venezia Giulia, "unredeemed" territory, 245
Venezia Tridentina, *see* Trentino-Alto Adige
Venice, economic role in Middle Ages and Renaissance, 147; guilds, 59; political events, 11; rule by Austria, 14; strikes, 231
Verri, Pietro, 49
Verro, Bernardino, 211, 214
Veterans Associations, 375, 377, 387
Victor Emmanuel II, 12, 13, 72, 75, 82, 87, 103, 202
Victor Emmanuel III, 225, 227, 240, 247, 249, 263, 269, 270, 274–277 *passim*, 281, 400, 444–448 *passim*, 452, 453, 479
Victoria, 400
Vidoni Palace, labor-management agreement, 386, 419, 421
Vietnam, illiteracy, 15, 126
Viganò, Francesco, 180, 181
Viglianesi, Italo, 493, 515
Villar Perosa (R.I.V., company at), 449
Villari, Pasquale, 126

Vinsani, Professor, 193
Virgil, 134
Vital statistics, *see* Public health
Vittorio Veneto, 253
Volpi di Misurata, Count Giuseppe, 405, 406
Voluntary Militia for National Security, 278–280 *passim*

Wage surveys, Appendix A, Tables 24, 36; National Workmen's Compensation Fund, 311–312; *State of Labor in Europe: 1878*, 162–166
Wages, 431–432, 435; agricultural, 41–44 *passim*, 164–166 *passim*, 170, 190–193 *passim*, 212, 406, 435, 499, Appendix A, Tables 33A, 36; industrial, 41–44 *passim*, 159–166 *passim*, 193, 311, 348–349, 382, 406, 435, 451, 466–467, 490, 499, 510, 511, Appendix A, Tables 33, 33A, 36; inter-country comparisons, 42, 142–143, 163–164, 312–313, Appendix A, Tables 34, 37; minimum (law 741, 1959), 513–516; real, 42–44 *passim*, 160–162 *passim*, 166, 311–312, 317–318, 345, 363, 368, 432, 466, 467, 499, Appendix A, Tables 33, 33A; regional, 163–166 *passim*, 312, 440, Appendix A, Table 36; services, 431, 499, Appendix A, Table 33A
War of Independence, 11–14
Wealth, 138
William II, 204
Wilson, Woodrow, 254
Witte, Count Sergyey, 149
Wollemborg, Leone, 178
Women in industry, 141, 142, 144, 159, 243, 297, 363, 433, 467
Wood-working, *see* Industry, wood-working
Workers bands, *see* Unions, *fasci operai*
Workers consulates, Milan and Como, 113, 114
Workers Invalidity and Old-Age Insurance, Fund for, 368
Workers Party, 109–117 *passim*, 204–206 *passim*
Working class, role, *Risorgimento*, 17–18
Working conditions, 39–41, 432–433
Workingmen's societies, congresses, 118, 187
Workingmen's Society of Naples, 185
Workmen's circles, 109–110, 435; Catholic, 184
Workmen's compensation, *see* Social insurances
Worktime required, food purchases, inter-country comparisons, *see* Prices, retail, inter-country comparisons
World Federation of Trade Unions, 474
World War I, 244–255; union cooperation, 363
World War II, 401–402, 444–461; Italian armistice, 447

Young Europe, 10
Young Italy, 10, 50, 57

Zamboni, Anteo, 285, 387
Zanardelli, Giuseppe, 83, 202, 208,' 223, 225, 227–228, 332
Zanardelli Code, 227
Zaniboni, Tito, 270, 283
Zola, Émile, 222

The text of this book was set on the Linotype in Caledonia.

 3

Statute Miles
Kilometers
25 0 25 50 75 100

8°   10°   12°   14°   16°

SARDINIA (IT.)

Santa Teresa Gallura
Bonifacio
Strait of Bonifacio
La Maddalena
ASINARA I.
ASINARA PT.
C. CAPRERA
Santa Teresa Gallura
Porto Torres
Fertilia
Stintino
ASINARA I.
Sassari
Bonorva
Alghero
Bosa
Ozieri
Tempio
Pausania
Olbia
Nuoro
Siniscola
Cuglieri
Dorgali
Macomer
C. COMINO
Oristano
Arborea
Gulf of Oristano
Bauneì
Lanusei
PUNTA LA MARMORA 6,017 FT.
C. DI MONTE SANTU
Villacidro
Villaputzu
Muravera
S. ANTIOCO
Carloforte
S. PIETRO
Iglesias
Portoscuso
Carbonia
Teulada
Quartu
Sant'Elena
Pula
Cagliari
Gulf of Cagliari
C. CARBONARA
C. SPARTIVENTO
Tirso
Mannu
Flumendosa

TUNISIA (FR.)
ALGERIA (FR.)
MONTS DE LA MEDJERDA
La Calle
Le Tarf
Tabarka
Souk-el-Bejaa
ZEBLA 2,349 FT.
Thibar
Mateur
Ferryville
1,371 FT.
Djedeida
Bizerte
C. BLANC
Medjez-el-Bab
Tunis
CARTHAGE
Gulf of Tunis
ZEMBRA
Grombalia
Soliman
ZAGHOUAN 2,608 FT.
Zaghouan
Korba
MAMOURA
Nabeul
Kelibia
C. MOSTEFA
C. BON
Galite Channel
LA GALITE

PANTELLERIA (ITALY)
2,743 FT.
Scauri (ITALY)

Longitude East of Greenwich

Mediterranean Sea

Tyrrhenian Sea

USTICA

SICILY
Trapani
Erice
EGADI IS.
Marsala
Mazara del Vallo
Castelvetrano
SELINUS (RUINS)
SEGESTA (RUINS)
Alcamo
Salemi
Castellammare
Monreale
Palermo
Bagheria
Termini Imerese
Cefalù
Carini
Prizzi
Corleone
Sciacca
Ribera
Menfi
Belice
Agrigento
Favara
Canicattì
San Cataldo
Caltanissetta
Nicosia
Mistretta
Mazzarino
Piazza Armerina
Enna
Leonforte
Adrano
Paternò
Taormina
MT. ETNA (VOL.) 10,868 FT.
Acireale
Catania
Gulf of Catania
Augusta
Licata
Gela
Vittoria
Comiso
Caltagirone
Grammichele
Palazzolo Acreide
Vizzini
Palagonia
C. SANTA CROCE
Siracusa
Ragusa
Modica
Noto
Avola
Gulf of Noto
Pozzallo
C. PASSERO
C. SPARTIVENTO

LIPARI IS. (VOL.)
STROMBOLI (VOL.)
PANAREA
SALINA
LIPARI
FILICUDI
ALICUDI
VULCANO
Milazzo
Messina
Strait of Messina
Reggio di Calabria
MT. ALTO 6,417 FT.

CALABRIA
Bagnara
Palmi
Nicotera
Tropea
Vibo Valentia
C. VATICANO
Sant'Eufemia
Gulf of Sant'Eufemia
Pizzo
Catanzaro
Gulf of Squillace
Soverato
Squillace
Lamezia
Nicastro
Pellaro
Gioiosa Ionica
Laurianova
Siderno Marina
San Giovanni in Fiore
Cosenza
Paola
Amantea
Belvedere Marittimo
Cetraro
Cariati
Rossano
Corigliano
Castrovillari
Amendolara
Crotone
C. COLONNE
Isola Capo Rizzuto
C. RIZZUTO
Policastro
Gulf of Taranto

BASILICATA
Potenza
Melfi
Rionero in Vulture
Lavello
Venosa
Gravina
Altamura
Matera
Pisticci
Metaponto
Policoro
Scanzano
Sala Consilina
Sapri
Maratea
Lauria
Moliterno
Rotondella
Policastro
Gulf of Policastro
Belvedere Marittimo
C. LICOSA
Agropoli
Vallo della Lucania
Pisciotta
Palinuro
C. PALINURO

CAMPANIA
Napoli (Naples)
Gulf of Naples
ISCHIA
PROCIDA
CAPRI
Gulf of Salerno
Salerno
Sorrento
Torre Annunziata
Torre del Greco
VESUVIUS (VOL.) 3,842 FT.
Pompei
Nola
Avellino
Benevento
Caserta
Santa Maria
Capua
Aversa
Gaeta
Gulf of Gaeta
Formia
PONZA
PONTINE IS.
Terracina
Fondi
Minturno
Sabaudia
Latina
Anzio

PUGLIA (APULIA)
San Bartolomeo
Cerignola
Ariano Irpino
Canosa
Andria
Corato
Ruvo
Bari
Bitonto
Molfetta
Trani
Barletta
Mola
Monopoli
Murge
Gioia del Colle
Gravina
Altamura
Martina
Ceglie Messapico
Fasano
Ostuni
Brindisi
Mesagne
Francavilla Fontana
Grottaglie
Taranto
Gulf of Taranto
PT. DELL'ALICE
Manduria
Nardò
Otranto
Maglie
Lecce
Casarano
Gallipoli
C. SANTA MARIA DI LEUCA
Gagliano del Capo